READINGS IN THANATOLOGY

John D. Morgan, Ph.D.
*King's College of
the University of Western Ontario
London, Canada*

Death, Value and Meaning Series
Series Editor: John D. Morgan

Baywood Publishing Company, Inc.
AMITYVILLE, NEW YORK

Copyright © 1997 by the Baywood Publishing Company, Inc., Amityville, New York.
All rights reserved. Printed in the United States of America on acid-free recycled paper.

Library of Congress Catalog Number: 96-36868
ISBN: 0-89503-149-3 (Cloth)

Library of Congress Cataloging-in-Publication Data

Readings in thanatology / [edited by] John D. Morgan.
    p. cm. - - (Death, value, and meaning series)
  Includes bibliographical references and index.
  ISBN 0-89503-149-3 (cloth)
  1. Death- -Study and teaching. I. Morgan, John D., 1933- .
II. Series.
BD443.8.R43 1997
306.9- -dc21   96-36868
                                                                             CIP

Table of Contents

CHAPTER 1 1
Death Education in the Context of General Education
John D. Morgan

PART I: INTRODUCTION:
          NORTH AMERICAN DEATH ATTITUDES 7

CHAPTER 2 11
Living Our Dying and Our Grieving: Historical and Cultural Attitudes
John D. Morgan

CHAPTER 3 33
Prologue to a Study of Death in Film
John Orange

CHAPTER 4 45
An Approach to Death in Adult and Children's Literature
Gary H. Paterson

CHAPTER 5 61
Some Notes in Aid of Thinking about Music and Death
Rev. Ronald Trojcak

CHAPTER 6 67
Patterns of Bereavement in Indian and English Society
Pittu Laungani

CHAPTER 7 77
The Economics of Death
Lawrence Fric

CHAPTER 8 109
Economics and Death: Private Good/Public Good
P. Albert Koop

CHAPTER 9 117
Death Walks the Wards: Dying in the Hospital
Joseph W. Lella

CHAPTER 10 141
Get it Under Cover: AIDS, Death, and Censorship
James Miller

PART II: INTRODUCTION:
THE CARE OF THE TERMINALLY ILL 163

CHAPTER 11 167
Structure and Stresses: When a Family Member is Dying
Michael A. Bull

CHAPTER 12 181
Caring for the Dying
Ira R. Byock

CHAPTER 13 197
Nursing Care of the Dying
Reena McDermott

CHAPTER 14 203
The Role of Social Work in Palliative Care
Andrew M. Feron

CHAPTER 15 213
Home Care
John Hinton

PART III: INTRODUCTION: BEREAVEMENT 237

CHAPTER 16 241
Bereavement: What Most People Should Know
C. Murray Parkes

CHAPTER 17 255
Funerals and Funeral Directors: Rituals and Resources for
Grief Management
Richard J. Paul

CHAPTER 18 275
Disenfranchised Grief: An Exposition and Update
Kenneth J. Doka

CHAPTER 19 285
Using Counseling Techniques to Help Bereaved and Dying People
Rose Marie Jaco

CHAPTER 20 309
Complicated Bereavement
Jo Ann Silcox

CHAPTER 21 327
Working with Widows in Groups
Peggy M. L. Anderson

CHAPTER 22 339
Men and Grief
Tom Golden

CHAPTER 23 347
Middle-Aged Children's Bereavement After the Death of an Elderly Parent
Miriam S. Moss and Sidney Z. Moss

PART IV: INTRODUCTION: CHILDREN AND DEATH 357

CHAPTER 24 359
The Pattern of Grief in Children and Adolescents
Eleanor J. Deveau

CHAPTER 25 391
Adolescent Grief
Barbara L. Anschuetz

CHAPTER 26 403
Bereaved Black Children
Ronald K. Barrett

PART V: INTRODUCTION: QUESTIONS OF VALUES 421

CHAPTER 27 423
Autonomy and the Person in the Dying Patient
Jim Kow

CHAPTER 28 439
Assisting Suicide: An Analysis of the Legal (i.e., Moral) Arguments in Judgments of the Supreme Court of Canada in the Sue Rodriguez Case
Gilbert E. Brodie

CHAPTER 29 475
Immortality
John D. Morgan

CHAPTER 30 485
Resurrection
Rev. Ronald Trojcak

CHAPTER 31 495
The Problem of Death and Dying in Major Eastern Traditions
Jaroslav Havelka

PART VI: INTRODUCTION: SUICIDE **511**

CHAPTER 32 513
Suicide Theories
Bruce Connell

CHAPTER 33 525
Suicide Intervention
Ralph L. V. Rickgarn

CHAPTER 34 539
"All the King's Horses and All the King's Men . . ."
Picking Up the Pieces in the Aftermath of Youth Suicide
Robert G. Stevenson

CHAPTER 35 551
Suicide Among the Elderly: Understanding with Mind and Heart
Judith M. Stillion

Contributors 569

Index 575

CHAPTER 1

Death Education in the Context of General Education

John D. Morgan

Education, the process by which one develops one's potential for one's own sake as well as for that of society, has included education about death and bereavement since prehistoric times. Different cultures have introduced their young to the realities of ultimate loss as a part of tribal or religious custom and more recently through formal teaching.

The term "death education" has many meanings, but three seem basic. In analogy to many specific forms of education such as medical education, death education has the sense of "preparation for death." The *I Ching, The Tibetan Book of the Dead,* the *Ars Moriendi* literature, and the Hebrew-Christian Bible have, to a greater or lesser degree, the purpose of preparing the person for death and death-related issues such as immortality, funeral rites, and bereavement behaviors. Since each of the major religions—Hinduism, Buddhism, Judaism, Christianity, and Islam—teaches that the person in this life is in a transition to another life, one can argue that one of the purposes of all religion has been the preparation for death.

The second meaning of death education is education for those decisions affected by actual or possible death. The practice of medicine and nursing; law; religious ministry; counseling; military, police, and fire-fighting provision; and funeral direction are all affected by the possibility of preventing or causing death, and by the consequences of a death. The training of practitioners in these careers would be incomplete if it did not include serious discussion of the definitions of death and of the personal, moral, legal, and economic issues involved in the death-related decisions made by these professionals.

The third meaning of death education, and the one that is the primary focus of this book, refers to a course or part of a course focusing on the meaning of death, attitudes toward death, and ways of coping with death. These courses often have as their purpose the realization that (1) death is a part of the natural life cycle, (2) dying persons are still fully alive and have unique needs in the terminal stage of their illnesses, (3) the bereaved have normal reactions and needs, (4) the needs of the dying and bereaved can be satisfied by a supportive community, and (5) children have the right to know about the fullness of the life cycle, including death and bereavement. Death education differs as it is taught in elementary, high school, and university programs, but the above five elements are common enough to be considered a general orientation.

The aim of this book is the integration of education about death, dying, and bereavement within the context of a basic education in the humanities and the social sciences. We show how the principles of liberal arts education can be useful for education about death, dying, and bereavement for the non-specialist as well as for the education of those who will deal with the dying and bereaved on a professional basis.

Each reader brings their own agenda to any book but especially to one such as this which touches basic human questions so fundamentally. It is for this reason that education about death, dying, and bereavement can make a contribution to general education. Death education deals not with what the reader might see as disembodied dull abstract questions but with the fundamental problems of human life in their harshness, their beauty, their complexity, and their interrelatedness.

True education consists of analyses of human problems in a sufficiently abstract and rigorous way that disciplined habits of mind occur. These habits of mind develop logical skills which act as a tool both for learning and for the articulation of learning. Death education as the authors have developed it in this book effects such goals.

THE NEED FOR FORMAL DEATH EDUCATION

In earlier centuries, one did not have to live too many years before being exposed to the death of a sibling, a parent, a grandparent, or a neighbor. Today, due to longer life as well as the professionalization of death-related activities such as medical care and funeral direction, death is less frequently experienced immediately. It is common in the developed world to grow into one's twenties or even thirties without having experienced the death of a significant other. In a questionnaire which this author distributed to over 3000 Canadian students between 1975 and 1996, whose ages ranged from seventeen to seventy, the answer to the question "What was your first experience of death?" was rarely a family member or friend. Vanderlyn Pine notes that "for American [university] students, death courses, formal instruction, seminars, projects, mini-courses, and so forth, provide an opportunity for the acquisition of experiential knowledge regarding dying and death. Given the other institutional structures existing today, such educational socialization seems essential" [1, p. 77]. Since it is less known, death is less accepted as an integral part of a human life.

Contemporary formal education about death and bereavement is primarily a North American phenomenon. In a 1993 survey this author found that education about death and bereavement occurs in Europe, Africa, and Australia as part of religious education, professional ethics, and, to a lesser extent the training of the health-care professional, however, education about death and bereavement for the average elementary, high school, or college student has seemingly developed only in Australia and North America. One possible reason for this is that with the exception of Quebec, the hospice movement began as an English-speaking movement and remained so until fairly recently. The hospice movement—the establishment of programs to provide only supportive care for persons with advanced progressive disease—started in England with the work of Dr. Cicely Saunders and was brought to Canada and the United States in the 1970s. Only since 1985 have there been hospices in Europe, South America, or Asia.

Death education as we know it today began in universities and colleges, and later filtered into elementary and high schools. For the most part, death education at the university level seems to be limited to one or two courses in departments of sociology, psychology, religion, or philosophy. Even in medicine, nursing, or social work, few formal courses exist, and what training there is in the psychosocial aspects of death and bereavement, occurs at the discretion of the instructor.

Few formal courses devoted to death education exist in elementary and high schools. What are found are modules, or units within courses, that deal with loss and grief. There are three basic orientations to education about death and bereavement below the university level. The first and most common form of death education, at least at the level of secondary schooling, is suicide prevention. Staffs in schools are deemed by the courts to be responsible if they do not act in "a reasonably prudent manner" in reporting possibly suicidal behavior [2, p. xiii], so school boards across North America have emphasized the importance of education as a form of suicide prevention. The second most common form of death education is an immediate response to a tragic event, such as the death of a child, a teacher, or a parent. Literature dealing with the support of the bereaved child in the classroom is now well developed. Since a curriculum is a statement of priorities, the third form of death education, proactive learning prior to a loss, would be the most important. It is, however, the least developed form of death education.

THE CONTENT OF DEATH EDUCATION

A study of the literature dealing with death and bereavement in the thirty years since the publication of Dr. Herman Feifel's ground-breaking book *The Meaning of Death* indicates seven basic themes in death education [3] These themes are: the interrelationship between North American social structures and death attitudes; the care of the terminally ill as a philosophy; bereavement as a normal human reaction to loss; persons of all ages, including children, have death concerns; values about life are to be articulated; the influence of death in arts, literature, and social structures themselves; and the question of suicide. This book examines these issues. The first part deals with the social and psychological roots of death and bereavement attitudes and ideas; the second with the care of the dying; the third with bereavement. The interrelationship between children and death is examined in the fourth part. Any discussion of death evokes our fundamental beliefs about values and meaning. The values questions, philosophical and religious ideas about death and with death, are examined in part five. Finally, suicide is covered in part six.

The essayist Alexander Pope said that the "proper study of man is man himself." A renewed awareness of this is the greatest contribution which death education can make to education as a whole. For academic purposes, we may consider economics, political science, history, biology, religious studies, law, and child development as several distinct areas. Researchers must think "departmentarily" if the store of human knowledge is to increase. But we must never lose sight of the fact that there is only one human reality. The person whom we consider in ethics is the same whom we consider in biology of law. Education about death, dying, and bereavement makes a great contribution to education as a whole because this commitment to learner-centered education and to the person-as-integrated has been a part of the death awareness movement since its rebirth in the 1960s.

THE AIMS OF DEATH EDUCATION

Judith Stillion has pointed out that "rarely has a course been called upon to meet such variety of expectations: to teach people to live peacefully with each other, to appreciate life, and to give service to others as they seek meaning in living and dying. All this plus teaching a body of knowledge and research are the tasks of the death educators" [4, p. 158]. Since death education involves coming to understand one's place in the world, and the reality of ultimately limited resources, such knowledge should contribute to general education as a basic for personal development.

Many goals have been established for death education. The list below represents what occurs in the literature from 1977 to the present, however, one must not assume that every course, much less every module, effects these goals. The goals cited are: (1) to remove the taboo aspect of death language; (2) to promote comfortable and intelligent interactions with the dying; (3) to educate children about death so they develop a minimum of death-related anxieties; (4) to understand the dynamics of grief; (5) to understand and be able to interact with a suicidal person; (6) to understand the social structure of dying (the "death system"); and (7) to recognize the variations involved in aspects of death both within and among cultures [5, p. 44]. In reality, most courses effect no more than an understanding of the definitions of death, the meaning and necessity of palliative care, funerals, the dynamics of grief, and children's awareness of death [6, p. 17].

THE CURRICULUM

The death education curriculum has a cognitive aspect that includes the development of a body of knowledge and an affective aspect that includes changes in attitudes and values. The International Work Group on Death, Dying and Bereavement has recommended the following criteria for education about death and bereavement: (1) that it be based on the current state of knowledge from a variety of disciplines; (2) that it integrate theory and practice; (3) that it promote sensitivity, awareness, and skills development through role modeling and supervised practice; and (4) that it provide emotional support and foster confidence [7, p. 236].

THE NEED FOR EVALUATION

Death education has not been universally accepted. From a practical standpoint, it is one more thing to be added to the already overcrowded general or professional curriculum. While there is some resistance to formal death education programs, death in literature, family life, or health has found more acceptance. There have been abuses in death education courses—for example, the practice of taking students to funeral homes and without adequate preparation encouraging them to lie in a coffin. Only since 1989 has the Association for Death Education and Counseling had a code of ethics.

The code of ethics of the Association for Death Education and Counseling demands that members maintain competence in the field and act responsibly toward their clients, their employers, and society as a whole since death-related anxieties and guilt have a ripple effect which affects many. In addition, death educators are enjoined to make sure that assistance is available to students when exercises used in the course may evoke memories or other reactions that are threatening. Educators are reminded to be honest in the claims that their courses make about content, to be responsible for the accuracy of the content taught, and to be attentive to the development of appropriate skills for those students who may be preparing to do sensitive work with the young, the dying, or the bereaved. Finally, death educators are expected to be aware of their own limitations and to refer students to appropriate professionals when necessary [8, p. 24].

THE FUTURE OF DEATH EDUCATION

If education about death and bereavement is to fulfill its possibilities, those engaged in it must examine more clearly the goals they wish to accomplish. It is impossible for a single course or unit of study to accomplish all that is expected from death education, from transmitting a body of research to improving the lot of the dying and the bereaved, to reducing violence in the world. More attention must be paid in teacher education programs to the importance of education about death and bereavement, so that the discussion of such matters is not left to the discretion of young teachers, often inexperienced in death-related issues. There must be greater concern for the effectiveness of death education. The few studies that have been done are inconclusive. Persons who take death education courses are more comfortable with the reality of death in life, but it is not known if this acceptance of death is an effect or a cause of taking death education courses. Finally, there must be more stress on the discussion of ethical issues in all death-related courses or units, not just those formally called such with the hope that the more focused ethical discussion will bring greater depth to the public debate on such important topics as grief, suicide, and euthanasia.

REFERENCES

1. V. Pine, A Socio-Historical Portrait of Death Education, *Death Studies, 1*(1), pp. 57-84, 1977.
2. A. A. Leenaars and S. Wenckstern, *Suicide Prevention in the Schools,* Hemisphere, Washington, D.C., 1991.
3. H. Feifel, *The Meaning of Death,* McGraw Hill, New York, 1956.
4. J. M. Stillion, Discovering the Taxonomies: A Structural Framework for Death Education Courses, *Death Education, 3*(2), pp. 157-164, 1979.
5. D. Leviton, The Scope of Death Education, *Death Studies, 1*(1), pp. 41-56, 1977.
6. J. Morgan, *Death Education in Canada,* King's College, London, Ontario, 1990.
7. C. A. Corr, J. D. Morgan, and H. Wass, *International Work Group on Death, Dying, and Bereavement: Statements on Death, Dying, and Bereavement,* King's College, London, Ontario, 1994.
8. Association for Death Education and Counseling, "Code of Ethics," *Directory of Members,* Association for Death Education and Counseling, Hartford, 1993-94.

PART I

Introduction: North American Death Attitudes

Death, the cessation of biological functions, is a fact. While age-specific death rates have changed over the centuries, the most elementary datum has not. Death is still one per customer, and one for every customer. Although death is a fact, something that happens to all, dying and grieving are activities in which one engages according to the attitudes one holds about them. An attitude about death, dying, and bereavement, a more or less enduring readiness to behave in a characteristic way, does not differ from other attitudes. One is socialized into it by a culture, which the Spanish philosopher Jose Ortega y Gasset has defined as the "ideas by which we live." In this section of the book, we examine the way we are taught to think, feel, believe, and behave in regard to dying and grieving.

In John Morgan's chapter we examine the North American death system at the end of the twentieth century in light of what we know about other death orientations. Morgan believes that death orientations differ as does the experience of dying and grieving. We experience dying and grieving by our exposure to it, by our life expectancy, and in light of the predominant philosophies of our control over nature and our beliefs about the importance of the unique individual.

In other cultures, and in our own prior to the middle of the twentieth century, there were many teachers of beliefs and values—the church, the school, and the family. Today the mass media have replaced the influence that more natural social structures once had. John Orange examines the influences that film has in teaching us about death and bereavement. The topic of death turns up in films the way it turns up in all of the arts. Death, of course, is *the* unfathomable mystery of existence; it is natural that the arts will be obsessed with it. Films have treated topics such as homicide, suicide, euthanasia, grief, burials, genocide, and the afterlife from every angle. The content of films does not differ widely from other arts when it comes to death and all its attendant forms and consequences. There are thousands of films that have at least some aspect of death in them. Some of these films are useful tools in grief therapy, or in the understanding of psychological reactions to death in families or the various reactions to the news that one has only a short time left to live. If, then, the theme of death is present in films just as it is in the other arts, what is distinctive in the ways film treats the topic? Some of the answers to this question are obvious and others are more subtle. Orange's treatment of death in film presents a kind of aerial photograph—that is an exploration of the topic at a fairly high level of generalization—in the hope of stimulating more detailed discourse on the topic by interested viewers. For purposes of organization, the topic can be divided into the properties of film that encourage certain kinds of death, and alternative portrayals of death in films made outside of the Hollywood standard.

After film, the second strongest teacher in North America is literature. Dr. Gary Paterson examines the lessons that literature, especially poetry, convey. They include intense emotion as well as subtle nuances of feeling through sound patterns, rhythm, imagery, and symbolism. These techniques provide a far greater sensory impact upon the reader than merely by stating realistic fact. This chapter will show how various aspects of genre, tone, language, and symbolism can express some of the most profound statements about death and, ironically, life itself. The first half is concerned with the theme of death in literature primarily for adults; the second half in children's literature. Paterson notes that death figures in literary works in three ways: (1) the expression of grief and mourning over the loss of a loved one; (2) actual descriptions of the dying and the dead; (3) expression of attitudes toward one's own death or of death in general.

While much have been written about music as therapy, I believe that this is the first chapter written about music as a teacher of death ideas and values. Rev. Dr. Ronald Trojcak states that "One of the great teachers in the Western World, certainly today, and perhaps throughout history, has been music." The role of music has been to entertain, to provide solace, to titillate, to worship, to encourage prayer, and meditation. By providing these other functions, music has also taught us what to believe and what to value. In his chapter on music and death, Dr. Ronald Trojcak distinguishes between service music and music that is existential, that is, music that serves some ulterior purpose such as a background for worship for Christmas sales, and music that expresses something significant about the human situation.

While Dr. Pittu Laungani's title indicates a comparison of British and Indian views of death, his "conceptual model of cultural differences" is a useful tool to examine any culture. Laungani uses four factors to understand patterns of bereavement. The factors are: individuals vs. communalism; cognitivism vs. emotionalism; free-will vs. determinism; and materialism vs. spiritualism. These concepts are to be understood as extending along a continuum, starting Individualism at one end, and extending into Communalism at the other.

In the Western world today, economic realities are major influences on values. Dr. Lawrence Fric examines the traditional role of economics, namely, the science of choices made about scarce resources, and applies that definition to questions about care of the dying and disposal of the remains. Dr. Fric reminds us that while sometimes economics influences our values, as often as not, our values influence our economics. This is particularly evident in questions of disposal.

Dr. P. Albert Koop's article flows from Dr. Fric's. Koop holds that there is a general social interest in the decisions that are made about the transfer of wealth at the time of death. He considers how individual needs, both of the dying and of survivors, are met by various inheritance practices. The economist, however, focuses on the social interest, social justice. Second, economists are careful to distinguish between two terms—income and wealth—which are often used interchangeably in daily conversation. Income is a measure of an individual's claim on the flow of society's output over a particular period of time, usually over a year. Wealth is a measure of an individual's ownership of assets at a moment in time. Koop believes this distinction is necessary in examining certain social issues.

We live in a highly medicalized culture. One need only reflect on the popularity of certain television shows to realize that we have given to the medical profession the hopes and ideals that the church once had. The doctor is today's priest, that is, one who by specialized language, knowledge, and activity has the key to happiness. Dr. Joseph Lella, a medical sociologist, examines the history of medicine to show how the culture of the hospital has lead to a bureaucratic treatment of disease rather than of patient. Lella is particularly interested in the role that the medical school has played in this development. He then shows the effect of these ideas on patients in hospitals.

Dr. James Miller is a Professor of Literature who has become an AIDS activist. He collects and shows safer sex posters as a symbol of the culture's attitudes to death, sexuality, and sexual orientation. Since the arts are basic modes of expression and communication, the arts have responded to AIDS. The art world has been badly hurt by the death of creative young artists and performers. Miller compares the present orientation to AIDS with the medieval presentation of the black death, the infection that killed one-third of the population of Europe in a decade. While the AIDS posters have meant to teach safer sexual activity, there has been a great deal of repression of the explicit, usually homoerotic, nature of these posters,

An examination of the chapters in this section will give a good analysis of the North American, indeed Western-world, death culture. We feel, think, believe, and act as we are taught. However, the reader is advised to return to the final pages of Morgan's chapter to take the opportunity to critique our culture. Does our culture serve us, especially in the crises which death entails?

CHAPTER 2
Living Our Dying and Our Grieving: Historical and Cultural Attitudes

John D. Morgan

Death, the cessation of biological functions, is a fact. While age-specific death rates have changed over the centuries, the most elementary datum has not. Death is still one per customer, and one for every customer. Although death is a fact, something that happens to all, dying and grieving are activities in which one engages according to the attitudes one holds about them. An attitude about death, dying, and bereavement, a more or less enduring readiness to behave in a characteristic way [1, p. 289], does not differ from other attitudes. One is socialized into it by a culture, which the Spanish philosopher Jose Ortega y Gasset has defined as the "ideas by which we live" [2, p. 70].

The purpose of this chapter is to examine and to critique the death culture in North America at the end of the twentieth century. This living of dying and grieving has been called a death system [3, p. 193]. I will show that there are other ways of looking at death, dying, and bereavement than the ways that we have learned. These other ways are found in some modest way in our own culture, but they are no longer dominant here; but still are dominant in other settings. I will show that death cultures differ because of four major factors—life expectancy, exposure to death, perceived control over the forces of nature, and understanding of what it is to be an individual human person. Death cultures are not static. Our death culture has changed since our grandparents' time, changed after the Second World War, and changed again after the 1960s as a result of books and courses such as the one in which this chapter is included [4, p. 73].

A DEATH SYSTEM

The term "death system" was coined by Dr. Robert Kastenbaum to describe the manner in which we live our dying [3, p. 193]. A death system is cognitive, affective, and behavioral [5, p. 9], that is, it teaches us what to think about death, how to feel about it, and what do with reference to it. *The death system is the sum total of the persons, places, ideas, traditions, acts, omissions, emotions, and statements that we think or make about death.* In other words, it is the total picture of death, dying, and bereavement we have at any given time. The expectation that we will live to our mid- or late-seventies is part of the death system. The hesitation we have in discussing death with children is a component of the death system. This awkwardness we feel in going to a funeral visitation because we do not know what to say is part of the death system. The death system is "the total range of thought, feeling, and behaviour that is directly or indirectly related to death" [3, pp. 191-192].

Attitudes toward death are multilayered rather than single responses. They contain feelings about dependency, pain, indignity, isolation, separation, possible rejection, leaving loved ones, afterlife, finality of death, facing the unknown, and the fate of the body [6]. The difficulty of categorizing such diverse attitudes with any exactness is compounded by the fact that one may be very open about death and bereavement on a verbal level but quite anxious below the level of consciousness or at the fantasy level [7]. Persons, places, and things that represent death or bereavement to us are part of the death system. While some places are more or less consistently identified with death (such as a cemetery or funeral home), there are other places such as the emergency room in a hospital, the neonatal intensive care unit, or some churches, that may have a death purpose for only a few moments, but might retain a death relatedness in one's consciousness for a long time. The same is true of persons. Persons such as funeral directors are almost always associated with death, but others are associated by our experience. A nurse, physician, or clergyperson spends little of his/her time doing death related work, but to the members of the bereft family, that person will be associated with death for a long time. This *halo-effect* that we use to identity a person or place as death related, may also apply to inanimate things. A car, for example, is not necessarily related to death. But for the family of a traffic victim, the car will forever have death overtones.

The traditions from which we think and act about death are important parts of the death system. We often speak of someone "passing away," or "going to God," or "having expired." This inability to speak of death without circumlocutions is part of the death system. It is estimated that children see tens of thousands of deaths on television, from the realistic deaths on news broadcasts to the absurdly fictional deaths and resurrections on cartoons. While many nursery rhymes have a death content, it is rare that parents will take a child to visit a terminally ill patient or to a funeral. This "protection" of children from death is a part of the death system. We hospitalize our dying persons for many reasons, ranging from the fact that there are fewer and fewer adults at home today to care for the dying, to the fact that most of us would not be able to provide the complicated care sometimes needed. The effect of such hospitalization is that the dying are cared for by professionals rather than by the family. Once a person has died, we allow other service providers to prepare the body, arrange visitation and funeral services, and make the final disposition of the body. This "professionalization" of death [8, p. 1] is a part of our death system. The sending of flowers, religious remembrances, and memorial gifts such as those to charitable organizations are traditions that shape our consciousness of death, as does the publishing of obituaries in the newspaper.

Roles also play an important part in the death system. Physicians who must sign death certificates, nurses who wash the body and take it to the hospital morgue, funeral directors who prepare the final service and disposition of the body, clergypersons who give the eulogy or offer prayers have particular roles with respect to death. In some cultures the dying person and the bereaved themselves have had well defined roles. They knew what they were supposed to do because they saw it practiced by the parents and grandparents. This is significantly less true in our death system.

Whatever the contemporary attitudes toward death, there are other ways of looking at death, dying, and bereavement than the ones prominent in the West. Though these are found in the West today to a modest degree, they are not dominant, but they have been dominant at other times, and are still dominant in other settings. Death attitudes in most cultures have changed since the beginning of the twentieth century. They changed after World War II, and again after the 1960s as a result of hospices and what has been called the death awareness movement. This chapter will discuss the historical development of Western attitudes toward death, examine the effects of the death attitude system by showing the interaction between the North American death system and those most affected by it (the dying, the bereaved, and health-care professionals) and propose suggestions for an appropriate death attitude system.

Key Factors

Since death systems are cultural, they change as key factors of the culture change. Specifically a death system is shaped by two types of elements, one factual and one theoretical [3, p. 193]. The factual elements are our exposure to death and life expectancy. The theoretical element is composed of our perceived control over the forces of nature, and our sense of the individual person.

Exposure of death and bereavement is the first element in our understanding of death. If we have little experience of the loss of significant others, our death attitudes will be limited by our inexperience. Attitudes toward funerals provide a good example. Very many persons will speak of funerals as a waste of money or a rip-off. Usually this critique is made by one who as yet has little personal experience of death. However, after one has received the support that comes from a tastefully planned and executed funeral, the attitude changes. Thus the person's experience now allows a fuller participation in the death system. Our inexperience of death is not universal, even in North America. The child of a funeral director or emergency room physician grows up with a greater exposure to death than does the average American or Canadian. A hospice volunteer is much more conscious of the fragility of life than is a butcher, baker, or candlestick maker.

Exposure to death is related to *life expectancy*. A baby born in North America can be expected to live to his/her mid- or late-seventies. One of the consequences of longevity is that since his/her relatives will probably also have a similar life span, the probability is that a child will have little, or perhaps even no personal exposure to the death of a significant other until his/her twenties or thirties. There are many places in the world, even today, where this is not the case. In the many war-, starvation-, and violence-torn places on the globe, a child grows up with the realization that persons die, and often die young. Our "innocence of death" was unheard of even fifty years ago. Our grandparents had a different understanding of the fragility of life. The vast majority of our ancestors where acquainted with death intimately. At the time of Plato (5th century B.C.E.) average life expectancy was twenty years; thirty-three for St. Aquinas and St. Anselm (12th century C.E.). At the time of William James, the beginning of this century, average life expectancy was no more than forty years [9, pp. 7-8]. The above figures do not imply that people did not live to advanced years in prior ages. We know that Socrates, Plato's teacher, was seventy when he died, for example. What is implied is that so many children died in the first two years of life, and so many women died in childbirth, that the *average* age at death, thus the average life expectancy was quite low.

On the theoretical level, our attitudes to death are shaped by our philosophy, our view of the world and our place in it. Our *understanding of the physical universe* is important in our death attitudes. If we believe that we are impotently subject to the laws of nature then our death attitudes will differ from those whose view is that we have significant control over the forces of nature. In North America, the dominant attitude is that nature is there for us to use and control. Other cultures do not share that view. Even in North America, the aboriginal peoples believe that they are an integral part of nature and that the prime mandate is to respect nature rather than to use it. Those who live in the flood plain of Bangladesh or shadow of Mount Pinatubo have a different perception of their control over nature than do those of us who move about or reside in climate controlled cars, offices, and homes. If we believe that we can be protected from nature, then we will have less respect for the power of nature over life.

The second theoretical element is *our perception of what it is to be a human person*. In a culture such as ours that puts its emphasis on the uniqueness of the individual, and individual rights, persons will have a different orientation toward death than does a culture which perceives each individual as having meaning primarily as a part of the whole, whether that whole is religious [10] or political [11, p. 155], or perhaps not having any meaning at all. While the distinction between an individual (1 member of the species) and a person (a individual substance of a rational nature) is as old as the sixth-century Roman philosopher Boethius [12, p. 102], the full implications of that distinction have been realized only in the twentieth century. It would be a mistake to assume that everyone places the same value on individual uniqueness as do we.

WESTERN ATTITUDES IN HISTORY

The French historian Philippe Ariès postulated that attitudes to death over the centuries are indications of the person's awareness of himself or herself, and of his or her degree of individuality [13]. In other words, attitudes about death and bereavement differ because of differing conceptions of what it is to be a person and the relationship of the person to his or her community, to the world, and to God. Ariès groups these attitudes historically around four basic orientations that he calls "tamed death," "the death of the self," "the death of the other," and "death denied" [3, p. 602].

Tamed Death

> All living beings become old like a garment, for the decree form of old is, "you must surely die!" Like flourishing leaves on a spreading tree which sheds some and puts forth others, so are the generations of flesh and blood: one dies and another is born. Every product decays and ceases to exist, and the man who made it will pass away with it [14, VII, 1-8].

Ariès characterizes as "the unchronicled death throughout the long ages of the most ancient history" the orientation he calls tamed death, which dominated until the Middle Ages [13, p. 5]. Since life was, as Thomas Hobbes wrote, "solitary, poor, nasty, brutish and short" [15, p. 95], one was constantly exposed to, and therefore familiar with, death as "a knife at our throat or a scourge at our child's bedside" [13, p. 206]. The effects of this "uncontrolled mortality" was that since child and maternal deaths were common, one did not spend much time in preparation for adulthood: courtships were short, relationships were understood to be limited, education was minimal. The very fact that one survived into one's thirties or forties indicated wisdom and as a result one was treated as a sage [9, p. 8]. Living in a yet untamed world, violence, evidenced by skulls marked with blows, was the usual cause of death [9, p. 7]. Death was a familiar, even if not always welcome, neighbor.

There were both positive and negative effects of this nearness to death. An affective consciousness of death makes life more precious [16, p. 286], but due to ignorance of most of its causes, death appeared mysterious, and mostly affected the young and other vulnerable segments of the population [5, p. 12]. Since death was seemingly ever-present, one did not extend childhood irresponsibility, given the prospect that the adult years would be so limited [13, p. 192]. Kinship groups were important in view of their relatively long endurance; families were large because fertility was a protection of the society against the ravages of death; early marriages were necessary as there was not time for courtship; reduced emotional ties between parents and offspring as a consequence of the high mortality rates of children were common; the presence of a large proportion of orphans and young widows, and an orientation toward religious, or other-worldly explanation of death were frequent and public features of daily life [5, p. 13].

The view of the person was that found in the *Epic of Gilgamesh* written approximately 2000 years before the present era. Death is the lot of the human race.

> For when the Gods created man, They let Death be his share, and life Withheld in their own hands. Gilgamesh, fill your belly—Day and night make merry, Dance and make music day and night . . . Look at the child that is holding your hand, And let your wife delight in your embraces. These things alone are the concern of men [17, p. 105].

By examining the philosophical and religious traditions of the ancient and medieval world, we can capture a picture of the perception of death common to the average person. The basic theme was found in Ecclesiastes: "There is a time to be born and a time to die" [14, III, 1]. Both the Hebrew Bible and Christian revelation stressed not only that the individual is mortal but indeed, "all existence must be perceived as futile, as death-directed" [18, p. 245]. The sixteenth-century essayist, Michel Montaigne says that "we may die at any moment of the slightest cause; rather than be surprised, we should expect death everywhere. If we can conquer our fear of death, we can face all the tribulations of life with equanimity" [19, p. 34]. This stoicism in the face of death has been the predominant theme of philosophy in the West from Heroditus [20, p. 236], through Epicurus and Seneca [p. 238], to Spinoza [p. 240]. Stated in terms of Erickson's psychology, a stoic philosophy provided persons with more ego integrity and thus lessened death fear [21, p. 193].

Such familiarity with death seemingly effected a more conscious dying than many persons experience today. Death was not viewed as some remote possibility, but as a dominant fact of life. Having seen relatives and friends die, the dying person knew the role and prepared for it, saying goodbyes, commending himself or herself to God, even lying in bed with arms crossed. Such role enactment continued at least until the Civil War in the United States, when soldiers prepared themselves in a like manner [22]. Death was public; family members would be present, as were neighbors who came to accompany the dying person in this last stage of life's journey. Care for the dying and funeral arrangements were the tasks of the family, not of professionals outside the family. Family members had as their role models the relatives and neighbors they had seen confront loss by death. Death was a familiar, if not always welcome, neighbor.

Sudden death which did not give one the opportunity to put one's physical and spiritual affairs in order, was considered a curse. A sudden death in a life already short, was considered vile, ugly, and frightening; a "thing that nobody dared talk about" [13, p. 11]. The "litany of the saints," a prayer said often throughout the church year, had an invocation "to preserve us from a sudden death." This prayer seems less attractive to us in the light of the chronic debilitative diseases of the closing days of the twentieth century but to those of the tenth to fourteenth centuries, whose life span was already short, the prospect of a sudden death was more terrifying.

Ariès believes that death was perceived to be not a purely isolated act. Death is celebrated by a solemn ceremony whose purpose is to express the solidarity with family and community [13, p. 603]. A death was not only a personal drama but an obligation of the community, which was responsible for maintaining the continuity of the race [5, p. 12]. The community, weakened by the loss of one of its members, had to recover its strength. Rituals had the effect of bring the community together for reestablishment [13, p. 603]. The facility with which this happened was a test of the community [23, p. 195].

Community integrity was stretched almost beyond the possibility of reintegration during the fourteenth century in Europe. The Black Plague killed one-third of the population [24, p. 94]. In Avignon 400 died daily, Pisa 400, Vienna 600. One gets a sense of the calamity by considering that Paris had 800 deaths a day out of a population of only 100,000 [24, p. 95]. Even in our society with hospitals, funeral directors and cemeteries, none of our cities of 100,000 could handle 800 deaths a day [25, p. 100]. Persons died without either religious (the last rites), or legal formalities (a will). Burials were haphazard, further contributing to the spread of the disease.

> one man shunned another . . . Kinsfolk held aloof, brother was forsaken by brother, oftentimes husband by wife; nay what is more, and scarcely to be believed, fathers and mothers were found to abandon their children to their fate, untended, unvisited as if they had been strangers [23, p. 97].

This is the period which Goldscheider called "uncontrolled mortality" [25]. The disruption of the social order persisted for nearly a century. Land titles were meaningless as was government. One can readily see why the church chose the idea "requiem" (rest) as the dominant prayer for the dead. This understanding of life after death as a state of repose or peaceful sleep became the most tenacious attitude toward death [13, p. 605], found in the Pythagoreans [20, p. 236], Plato [p. 237], the early writings of Aristotle [p. 237].

In sum, this attitude of *Tamed Death* represents an orientation in which mortality is calmly accepted as part of what it is to be human. Attention is focused almost entirely upon this world and its activities: responsible life in a community called to serve God.

The Death of the Self

> Perchance he for whom this bell tolls may be so ill as that he knows not it tolls for him; and perchance I may think myself so much better than I am, as that they who are about me and see my state may have caused it to toll for me, and I know not that . . . No man is an island, entire of itself; every man is a piece of the continent, a part of the main . . . Any man's death diminishes me because I am involved in mankind, and therefore never send to know for whom the bell tolls; it tolls for thee [26, p. 440]. (Original was written in the sixteenth century.)

In the second historical period, which Ariès dates from approximately the twelfth to the fifteenth century, the individual became aware of himself or herself as distinct from the community. Whereas the earlier period emphasized familiarity with death, the second orientation, called "my death," emphasized the termination of one's own life, one's personal death. Death was the last act of a personal drama. This is the period of the *Ars moriendi* genre, manuals on dying that were meant to guide the reader's behavior as he or she faced the end of life. Elaborate tombs memorializing the life became common, as did placing these tombs in churches of various sizes. One of the consequences of the awareness of personal death was concern about the judgment of the soul. Each moment of life would be weighed before all the powers of heaven and hell: the just would be rewarded, and the wicked would be condemned. The Latin hymn from the liturgy for the dead, *Dies irae*, which solicits mercy for the dead, dates from this period. Both the individual and his or her family prayed for conversions, even at the point of death. Wills, especially those that arranged for prayers by the living for the deceased as he or she met God, were common.

Eleventh-hour conversions were prayed for both by the individual and his/her family. [St. Augustine, Bishop of Hippo in the fourth century of the Christian period and known for his classics *Confessions* (written in 397 C.E.) and *The City of God* (written in 426 C.E.) is quoted as saying "Lord, give me chastity—but not yet." This idea is consistent with the period of which Ariès' speaks [27, p. 42]. Dostoevsky's citing of an eleventh-hour conversation of a thief is consistent with this orientation [28, p. 133]. Wills regained predominance, especially wills which arranged for prayers for the deceased as s/he met God [13, p. 180]. One believed that such arrangements brought merit before God which would guarantee salvation. Consciousness of one's own sinfulness had the twofold effect of fear of hell.

Being aware of his/her uniqueness, the strong individual of the later Middle Ages could not be satisfied with the peaceful but passive conception of eternal rest, s/he would survive as a full person even if s/he had to split his/her self into two parts: a body and an immortal soul that was released by death [13, p. 606]. The concept of immortality of the soul was an important aspect of this period. The person, as we perceive it to be, is rendered apart at death to a fate known only by faith.

Death was perceived as the last act of a private, unique drama. It was the duty of the dying person to be master over one's own death and to create an appropriate scene. Cyrano de Bergerac's farewell to Roxanne is an example of a death in which the central character has "staged" his/her death to be consistent with life style and his/her values [29]. Elaborate tombs, often depicting praying figures, became common even the placing of these tombs in cathedrals [13, p. 266].

In this second of Ariès' orientations—*Death of the Self*—we see that death is no longer quite the welcomed friend as it was in the earlier period. Death was the end of the individual person as s/he is known—but with a hope for continuity. However, the fear of hell, and the sense of one's unworthiness made death a fearsome reality.

The Death of the Other

In the nineteenth century, the ideas of "death as a neighbour" and "death as the personal end" declined in favor of a third orientation, "death of the other." Life was viewed as having meaning primarily through relationships, thus death was perceived of as the loss of that relationship. Death was no longer as public, since privacy had become necessary for these relationships to develop. Dying was not mourned as the loss of community, as the end of life, or as judgment, but as physical separation from the beloved. The image of the beyond in the earlier periods, which had ranged from eternal sleep to a glorious heaven or damned hell, become in the nineteenth century the scene of the reunion of those whom death had separated. The death of the other is a dominant theme in opera. Perhaps the best example is the death of Mimi in *La Boheme*. The fourth act is dominated not by Mimi's slipping away but by Rudolfo's grief at her death [30].

Interestingly few wills were written at the time as though it would be a breach of trust to have a will when one had loved ones to carry out one's wishes. In the eighteenth century family affection was considered more solid than the last will and testament [31, p. 56].

This *Death of the Other* orientation anticipates much of what we today know about bereavement. The person is composed of a unique history of relationships, illustrated in contemporary bereavement literature. Lindemann's classic study of bereavement indicates five common elements of grief. They are: bodily distress, psychological preoccupation with the deceased person, feelings of guilt, loss of the ability to feel anything emotionally, and disorientation [32, p. 222]. If life is relationship, then the bereaved person has *literally* lost a part of oneself. Persons are composed not only of body parts, but also of history and relationships. The bereaved person is wounded as truly as if blood were dripping from torn flesh. This loss of the other was first reflected in the nineteenth century.

CONTEMPORARY WESTERN DEATH ATTITUDES

At least the remnants of the above three orientations to death are sufficiently familiar in the twentieth century that death is sometimes viewed as a familiar guest, as the last act of a personal drama, or as the ending of an important relationship. However, the present Western death culture differs significantly from those that preceded it. Ariès names the twentieth century the period of "death denied." To understand this designation, one must look at the parameters of contemporary death attitudes. They differ among cultures because of four major factors: exposure to death, life expectancy, perceived control over the forces of nature, and the understanding of what it is to be a human being.

Precisely because exposure to death has changed, as has life expectancy, one's view of his/her place in nature, and one's self-definition, death systems are not static. The North American death system changed from calm acceptance in the pre-war years to denial in the post-war years and has changed again since then. The death system not only changes attitudes but is itself changed by attitudes. For example, until fairly recently, although cigarette smoking was known as a cause of poor health, including heart disease and cancer, the prevalent attitude has been one of *laissez faire*. These acceptances of death as a result of cigarettes were a part of the North American death system after the second world war. As a result of the death awareness movement, as well as increased knowledge of the dangers, the attitudes have changed and we no longer tolerate smoking in public places without complaint. Our present trend toward disposal without a funeral, or funerals without visitation, and the increasing use of cremation as a form of disposal will reshape our death system in the next few years. We must now examine how these same elements create our own death system and indicate the adequacy of our culture's view of death.

Life Expectancy

Almost two-thirds of the two million persons who will die in the United States in a given year will be sixty-five years of age or older, even though they represent only 9 percent of the total population. Children under the age of fifteen account for 29 percent of the total United States population, but only 5.5 percent of the total deaths. This is radically different from the situation in 1900, when children under the age of fifteen accounted for 34 percent of the population but for 53 percent of the deaths [33, p. 91].

Earthquakes in Mexico, volcanic eruptions in the Philippines, and Central America; and chemical and nuclear disasters in India and Russia indicate that even our age is subject to uncontrolled mortality. However, these events create headlines precisely because they are unusual. Ours is a period of increased longevity and predictable age-specific death rates due to better sanitation and food supplies as well as improved medical care. The discoveries that contagious diseases could be prevented, sometimes eliminated, through inoculation [34, p. 39] neutralized the diseases which killed most of the population in earlier times. Consequently, it is today reasonable to assume that mothers will not die from infections in childbirth and that the child will live to maturity.

In the 1900s, there were approximately seventeen deaths per one thousand live population, whereas today there are fewer than eight deaths per one thousand live population. Because the rate has decreased from seventeen per one thousand, death is less common. It also means that although we have more deaths numerically we have proportionately less death occurring in our everyday experience [35, p. 44]. The very old constitute the fastest growing segment of the population. Four-fifths of those over sixty-five years of age have one or more living children, about half have great-grandchildren, and one-in-ten has a child who is already over sixty-five [36, p. 188].

Women outlive men as they have always. The age adjusted mortality rate, which fell 26 percent for elderly males between 1940 and 1980, dropped 48 percent for elderly females at the same time [36, p. 197]. In cases of persons with relatively similar life styles, such as a monastery of men and a convent of women, both leading lives of quiet prayer, the women still outlive men [25, p. 101]. However, today the gap is closing. This seems to be because of the increased number of women holding jobs which previously were held only by men. These range from the dangers involved in construction work to military activity and the stress related deaths of the executive.

Although death rates improved in the population as a whole, the benefits were not shared equally. In North America, race, poverty, and poor education are predictors of early death. The mortality rate from heart disease in 1986 for blacks was 1.3 times higher than for whites [37, p. 436]. From 1983 to 1988 the percentage of individuals with an annual income over $60,000 who had limited activity due to a chronic condition declined, while for those with incomes less than $10,000 it increased [37, p. 436]. Poor or poorly educated persons have higher death rates than wealthier or better educated persons, and these differences increased from 1960 to 1986 [37, p. 105]. This is as true of Canada with its socialized medicine as it is in the United States with entrepreneurial medicine. No doubt the causes are related to the sense of possibilities open to the poor. In better neighborhoods persons accept the fact that they will see physicians, are aware of nutritional needs and can afford to purchase vegetables, fruits, and protein substances. Finally, the incidence of alcoholism among the native people of North America is a high source of mortality. In general, the poor experience high mortality rates at young ages and from communicable diseases while the middle class, especially males, experience high mortality rates in the older ages, from degenerative diseases. The blue-collar working class, appears to experience the lowest mortality rates. "Longevity progressed until our own century when it peaked in the United States in 1915 at 54.5 years. The great Flu epidemic was a setback, but longevity returned and increased to 69.6 years in 1967" [9, p. 9].

Since the birth rate has slowed, we will increasingly see more deaths. The percentage of the population over sixty-five will increase and with it the more likelihood of death. For example, in recent years the incidence of Alzheimer's disease has increased. It is estimated that 90 percent of the population will have it if they do not succumb to other diseases first.

Today's elderly are increasingly retired and live physically and psychologically removed from their children and grandchildren. Medical technology not only makes possible the prolongation of life, it is also the basis for repeated and often extended separations of the chronically ill or dying persons from the family. The disengagement of the aged from their families prior to their death means that their death may have little effect on the day-to-day life of the family [33, p. 92], depriving the elderly of traditional family assistance [38, p. x]. For example, Fulton and Fulton report, that a disproportionate number of deaths occur among elderly patients soon after commitment to an institution [33, p. 97]. Frequently professional care givers experience grief at the loss of a patient and react as bereaved survivors themselves. Attending care givers often find themselves participating in the emotional support of patients under their care [39, p. 243].

The effect of increased life span is a lessened consciousness of death and lessened respect for death. The community no longer thinks it necessary to defend itself against a nature that has been domesticated once and for all by the advance of technology. Because it no longer has a developed sense of community, it has abandoned responsibility for the organization of life [13, pp. 612-613]. The community in the traditional sense of the word, persons coming together with common interests to live their lives in common, has been replaced by atomized individuals. Long life has become the goal rather than personal salvation. Fulton has said that for two millennia, sacred texts—the *I Ching*, *Tibetan Book of the Dead*, *Egyptian Book of the Dead*, and the *Ars Moriendi* literature of the West— served as guidebooks for the passage of the soul. Today, however, our focus is on the need to comfort the dying person and to offer assistance to the grieving survivors [40, p. xii].

Exposure to Death

As Fulton said previously, the very appearance of death has changed. We now do not admit that a death has occurred until we have technological "proof." "Death has moved from the moral order to the technological order" [41, p. 121]. The increased life span and the changes from diseases of childhood to diseases of longevity have had the effect of increasing the number of deaths which have occurred in hospitals. Hospitals have become increasingly more important as medicine has become more specialized. In earlier days the physician's primary role was to be with the sick and to encourage life's own recuperative powers to regenerate the body, and as Ramsey stated, "to (only) care for the dying" [42]. As medicine has specialized, it has become increasingly more difficult for one physician to do everything. As specialization occurred the place of medicine changed. Medicine was no longer practiced in the doctor's office or in the patient's home but more and more in hospitals. Today at least 75 percent of persons die in hospitals. The consequence of this is that dying is today seen by fewer people than it was previously. We do not have the mass deaths which once were viewed on streets, nor do we have persons dying at home.

Since formal education about death and bereavement is not a common part of the school curriculum, and since the churches no longer have the educational influence they once did, the entertainment media have been the main teachers of death attitudes. According to recent studies, television has taught three messages about death and bereavement. The first is that death is entertainment: cartoon characters systematically annihilate one another, only to reappear unscathed in the next episode. The second lesson is that life is brutal and lethal: young males kill or are killed through the malevolence of others with little grief entailed. The third is that death, when it actually occurs, occurs elsewhere and mostly to foreigners, to people alien in appearance, language, and national ideology [43]. North Americans have become uncomfortable with functions that forebears viewed as natural and manageable. There is an ideology of personal happiness which holds that life consists of a series of snares to be avoided and problems to be solved [44].

Today at least 75 percent of persons die in hospitals; actual death is seen by few persons. Fewer persons die at home, much less in public, as they might have during the Black Plague. The very appearance of death has changed. At one time one could "put one's finger" on death through a pulse. Death has an increasingly technology-defined dimension, making it more isolating than in the past. One is now aware of "cardiac death" and "brain death," and only doctors can certify that the various types of death have occurred. In earlier days the physician's primary role was to be with the sick and to encourage the body's recuperative powers. Today, doctors deal as much with drugs and machines as with people. In prolonging life, medical technology separated the chronically ill and the dying from their families. This medicalization of death has affected the entire Western culture's view of death.

A 1991 Gallup poll indicated that most Americans do not think about death. "Miracle" drugs and organ transplantation have become sufficiently common that the expectation is that an illness is always correctable. Thus personal experience and the bias that cure is readily available [45] teach that accidents, disease, and death happen to others. When one finally has personal exposure to death, often as late as the third decade of life, it appears as unusual and thus cruel. This innocence of death is compounded by what has been called an oxymoronic view: the four leading causes of death across all age groups in the West are heart disease, cancer, stroke, and accidents, causes that are partly of human origin [45]. Vast resources are spent to save lives at the same time that even greater resources are spent on weapons of mass destruction or on polluting the planet.

The medicalization of death has had the effect of the entire culture accepting the medical profession's view of death. The medical profession has defined its roles as curing, researching, and teaching. Persons who become physicians are bright, hard-working, self-starters. The death of a patient may be the first time in the young physician's life when s/he meets a problem which will not respond to his/her enterprise. Death becomes viewed as defeat [46, p. 30]. Doctors, when questioned, state that their goals are to accompany the patient in his/her illness, yet the reality is that they view such "mere" accompanying as failure [47, p. 129]. Feifel et al. confirms that the fear of death was a consideration in the choice of a medical career [8, p. 202]. Physicians were more afraid of death than the physically sick or healthy normal groups, despite the finding that 63 percent of the physicians stated that "they were *now* less fearful of death than heretofore" [8, p. 201].

Sense of the Self

The most important element in the development of attitudes toward death is the perception of what it is to be a person. Most people in the West today believe that the person is unique, what Ernest Becker refers to as "the ache of cosmic specialness" [48, p. 4]. In a culture that emphasizes the individual and individual rights, persons will have a different orientation toward death than will members of a culture that perceives each individual as having meaning primarily as a part of the whole, whether religious or political, or perhaps as not having any meaning at all. Those who believe that each life is unique will perceive the end of that life as a different order of loss than those who perceive that a life has meaning only within a whole.

The Person a Unique Subject

Never before in the history of the universe did this person exist, never again will s/he do so. Several years ago, when the World's Fair was held in New York City, the Vatican gave permission for Michelangelo's masterpiece "the Pieta" to be brought for exhibit. There was general concern for the safety of the statue since boats and planes do have accidents. Luckily, no disasters occurred. However, Michelangelo made several copies of the statue. The statue is, in that sense, replaceable. More fundamentally, the statue is a piece of marble that is replaceable fundamentally although the accidental characteristics that the artist gave to it could only be replaced with difficulty. But the death of any individual person is a greater loss. There is no fundamental or accidental way of replacing the person. Each person is a once-in-the-lifetime-of-the-universe-event. This uniqueness of the person—the realization that never before in the history of the human race has this person existed and never again will s/he exist—is what Becker refers to as "the ache of cosmic specialness" [48, p. 4].

William James wrote that the word "good" fundamentally means "destined to survive" [49, p. 13]. When an individual says that something is good, he or she implicitly affirms that the thing ought to exist. The effect of this self-awareness is the following enigma: "I am. I am good. Yet I shall die." This awareness is, in the words of William James, "the worm at the core of our pretensions to happiness" [48, p. 15]. Death ultimately is the proof that no matter what powers humans have or develop, they still are not God [46]. If James is right that good means "destined to survive," then death is nature's way of saying that humans are not absolutely good. Perhaps the human situation is best summarized in the lines that Becker quotes from Andre Malraux: "it takes sixty years of incredible suffering and effort to make such an individual, then he is good only for dying" [48, p. 269].

Ours is a society that speaks about the sanctity of life and death with dignity. However, the sanctity of life does not exist outside of the religious context of North American culture. In spite of lessened church attendance, ours remains a religious culture. By religion is meant the sense that the individual is part of a larger whole and has a responsibility to that whole. The religious attitude also entails a sense that we belong to a history that makes our individual lives more meaningful. If one believes that the universe came from the hand of a loving creator—as do all the great religious traditions—then one must ask "why is the world the way it is?" "Why do pain and evil exist?" or in the words of Rabbi Kutscher "Why do bad things happen to good people?" [50]. One answer is that the "gift" of life must be acknowledged and developed. Life is precisely the gift by which the creative will of God is to be carried out. It is a gift from God which places on the individual the obligation to use for the good of the human community and, in accepting the reality of human limitation, the obligation to surrender the gift of life by the acceptance of death [46, p. 5].

The idea of life as a gift is important to our discussion. Obviously life is a gift in the sense that no one ever earned it. There is however a deeper meaning. Life is a gift in the sense in which we identify "gift" and "talent." We speak of one having a gift for languages or for music. The meaning here is that there is a talent which is being developed and which amplifies this person and all around. There is a sense of responsibility to acknowledge the gift, to develop it, and be thankful for it. The religious view is that life is a gift in this sense, the person has a special status in creation.

Death ultimately is the proof that no matter what powers we as humans have or develop, we still are not God [46, p. 7]. If James is right that good means "destined to survive" [49, p. 13], then death is nature's way of telling us that we are not absolutely good. Death gives meaning to our lives because it is the act by which we complete the task for which we were born [49, p. 16].

Control over Nature

Attitudes toward death are particularly shaped by one's view of the world and one's place in, and perceived control of it. One who believes that persons are entirely subject to the "laws" of nature will have a death attitude different from one whose view is that he or she has significant control over the forces of nature. In the West the dominant attitude is that nature exists to be used and controlled. Other cultures do not share that view. Those who live on the floodplain of Bangladesh or in the shadow of Mount Pinatubo in the Philippines have a different perception of their relationship to nature than do those who move about in climate-controlled cars and reside in air-conditioned and insulated offices and homes. Persons who believe they can be "protected" from nature have less respect for the power of nature over life.

There is no aspect of our lives that has not been touched by the engineering progress of North America. We transmit words and pictures instantaneously via radio, telegraph, television, and now facsimile. Closed circuit television has allowed greater surveillance of both persons and property. Computer linkups have created enormous databases that allow us to access information in a way never before imagined. At a push of a button we can be aware of books, monographs, articles, and other references on almost any topic. We can check fingerprints and records. As a result primarily of labor contracts, the average worker today has health and other insurance programs that guarantee a standard of living undreamed of before. Dental care, prescriptions, hospital care are taken today to be rights rather than privileges. The same is true of education and care of the aged. Old Age pensions such as social security provide a basic if not always adequate guarantee of a retirement period that is relatively free of care for the basic necessities. Few cultures are as "progress" oriented as is ours.

After two centuries of conquering problems, we became convinced that we could conquer all problems. One of the biggest obstacles to the "green" movement is our implicit belief that given enough time we can solve all problems. We do not need to conserve or recycle. Our belief is that the universe is raw material for our dreams. Few would openly espouse the position that we will eradicate death, but it is a hope in the back of the minds of many [25, p. 2]. Today death is viewed as something that does not have to happen when it does happen and "the idea is being entertained that it is remotely conceivable that for a very significant minority, that death eventually won't need to happen at all" [40, p. 11].

Death Denied

Ariès referred to contemporary death attitudes as "death denied." This denial of death is not cognitive. Living in the shadow of the Holocaust and possible nuclear destruction, people in the twentieth century have seen more real and threatened deaths than any people in the previous history of the human race. No one doubts the validity of the syllogism "All persons are mortal, I am a person, therefore I am mortal." Indeed, the evidence is that college students think about death more often than did their grandparents [51]. Rather, death is denied in the psychological sense.

Contemporary Western culture does not seem to take seriously the fact that death is the end of possibilities, the collapse of personal space and time, the end of all relationships. As death is removed from daily consciousness, it appears to be less appropriate and thus contributes to more cases of complicated mourning [52].

The community seemingly no longer thinks it necessary to defend itself against a nature that has been domesticated by the advance of technology. Even community in the traditional sense of the word, persons with common interests coming together to live their lives in common, has been replaced by atomized individuals. Death is a slap in the face of the great North American dream that time and money can remove all obstacles to human enjoyment. As Feifel put it:

> We witnessed a shift from spiritual mastery over self to physical conquest of nature. A major consequence was that we became impoverished in possessing religious or philosophic conceptual creeds, except nominally, with which to transcend death. Death became a "wall" rather than a "doorway." A taboo of considerable measure was placed on death and bereaved persons. Death and its concomitants were sundered off, isolated, and permitted into society only after being properly decontaminated. In this context, further circumstances making the area uncomfortable to deal with were (a) an expanding industrial, impersonal technology that steadily increased fragmentation of the family and dismantled root neighbourhoods and kinship groups with more or less homogeneous values . . . thus depriving us of emotional and social supports with which to cushion the impact of death when it intruded into our lives; (b) a spreading deritualization of grief, related to criticism of funery practices as being overly expansive, baroque, and exploitive of the mourner's emotions; (c) a gradual expulsion of death from everyday common experience; death has developed into a mystery for many people, increasingly representing a fear of the unknown, and has become the province of the "professional," whose mastery, unfortunately, is more technical than human these days; and (d) in a modern society that has emphasized achievement, productivity, and the future, the prospect of no future at all, and loss of identity, has become an abomination. Hence, death and mourning have invited our hostility and repudiation [7, p. 537].

One indication of the death denial of contemporary North Americans can be found in the media coverage of the Gulf War (Operation Desert Storm). The public has a stake in denying that death occurs in a war. The words "death," "die," and "kill" rarely appeared in media reports, euphemisms for death were used instead [53]. The contemporary view of death in the West is that every death is contingent, a matter of chance, and that, in principle, there is no reason why any particular injury or disease cannot be overcome [22].

The AIDS epidemic is cornerstone to our death system. In AIDS we have persons dying who are usually significantly younger than the anticipated date for their age cohort. They have contracted AIDS, for the most part, because they engaged in practices which they believed were consistent with their own personal needs and views of reality. For the most part, these young persons are bright and well educated who believe that AIDS is a form of genocide for their community [54, p. 65]. Thus the AIDS epidemic calls into question our presuppositions about the reasonableness of the universe in which we live, creating greater death anxiety and depression [55, p. 333]. Death for many people today is a barrier to life's meaning rather than a transformation [56, p. 305].

How Effective is Our Death System?

When one considers the persons, places, objects, and roles related to death, one becomes aware of the breadth of influence that death attitudes have on everyone in the culture. It is virtually impossible to read a newspaper or watch a television set without being aware of death, euthanasia, suicide, funerals, or questions of ultimate value. While everyone is affected by, and in turn affects, the death system, it is instructive to focus on the effects that death attitudes have on those most immediately involved: the dying, the bereaved, and health-care workers.

There is substantial evidence that the violence that grows daily, addiction, and poverty are results of the refusal to take seriously the human reality of death [57]. Not taking death seriously allows one to risk the lives of unknown others, loved ones, and oneself. Violence exists in spite of the fact that for millennia the great religions have taught responsibility for each other and that the Creator can be seen in the least of one's neighbors. Apart from religion, philosophical systems have agreed with Immanuel Kant that one ought never to use another person as a means. Violence, according to Becker, is "a symbolic solution of a biological limitation" [48, p. 99]. It is easy to believe that one is master of his or her own life when one holds someone else's fate in one's hands.

Effects on the Dying

Although the culture as a whole denies the importance or reality of death, the dying and the bereaved cannot do so. The effect of this situation is to alienate the dying and the bereaved from the support they have a right to expect. Most dying patients do not expect "miracles" to reverse their biological condition. What is essential is care and concern. The hospice movement has shown that when the physical and emotional needs of dying patients are attended to, there is less depression, blaming, and guilt for the patient and for the family, and death is the death of a person rather than an illness [58, p. 6]. Most persons arrive at some sense of acceptance: a realization that time is limited, that one's work is complete, and that one's life has been good.

The most important element of the Western view of life and death is that life and death are profoundly different and completely unrelated states; that once one is born, one maintains a constant state of life until the moment of death, and that once one is dead, one maintains a constant state of being dead; and that the event of death is an instantaneous leap from one state to the other (there is no transitional state, no grey or ambiguous area) [59]. Those who tend to infuse death with a sense of purpose or meaning, who see it as an event that leads to some form of continued existence, find more meaning [60]. The major question to be faced by the dying is whether death is to be understood as within or outside of human life [22]. There is a major difference between seeing death as a wall and seeing death as a door. For those who see death as a wall, death entails self-annihilation, loss of self-fulfillment, and loss of identity [61]. For those who see death as a door, death is a transformation of life's meanings [56].

Effects on the Bereaved

Although bereavement is one of life's greatest stressors, most of the bereaved have found that within one year of the death, the death of a loved one has been an opportunity for growth. The main goal of the bereaved is to seek a meaning in the death [62]. The discovery of the meaning of the death, as well as the sense of purpose in their own lives, is the major factor that brings a satisfactory adjustment.

Effects on Health-Care Professionals

Medicine and religion have much in common. Both address the fears of humanity and the meaning of events surrounding life and death. Religion has responded to these needs by constructing theologies; medicine, by providing a scientific theory of health and sickness [44]. Labeling a biological state as a disease is akin to declaring that there is an evil that ought to be eliminated. The rescue fantasy, that one can "snatch the patient away from the jaws of death" [44, p. 139], is an important part of medical culture and the popular folklore about physicians. As Becker has pointed out, all power is ultimately viewed as power over death; thus the conceptions of the physician's powers flow from the view that medicine is a priesthood with power over evil [48]. Cardiopulmonary resuscitation is an example of the rescue fantasy becoming a reality. Cardiopulmonary resuscitation was developed for a select group of patients with temporary cardiac arrhythmias who would die without resuscitation. The procedure became standard practice and now the presumption is that no one should be allowed to die in a hospital without an attempt at resuscitation even though less than 20 percent survive [44].

Medical and nursing cultures attach value to life saving activity. The inability to prevent or slow a patient's death represents loss of power and ability of control to the physician. This is especially true when the death is of a "significant patient" [63], one in whom the practitioner has invested a great deal of time or clinical effort. In addition, care givers not only have to deal with critically ill and dying people, but also have to face several people dying at one time [64]. As a protection from loss of professional control, nurses and doctors may become "impermeable." This reaction of building a wall between oneself and the patient is caused by the heavy workload, the emotional demands of frequent contact with dying patients, dealing with the adjustment problems of the patients and their families, and their own anxieties and uncertainties. The role that has been historically assigned to medical doctors is that of suprahuman mediator between life and death [48].

If the purpose of life is to live well, then the patient has a right to a medical relationship that ensures that he or she will be treated with respect and that medical knowledge will be used to further his or her life plans and values [44]. The ongoing personal relationship with each patient is the corresponding tool of the trade for the primary-care physician.

TOWARD AN APPROPRIATE DEATH ATTITUDE SYSTEM

Death becomes acceptable, according to Daniel Callahan, when it comes at the point in a life when (1) further efforts to deter dying are likely to deform the process of dying, or (2) there is a good fit between the biological inevitability of death in general and the particular timing and circumstances of that death in the life of an individual [22]. The achievement of such an peaceful death should be the goal of life, and therefore of medicine. The process of dying is deformed when it is extended unduly by medical interventions or when there is an extended period of loss of consciousness well before one is actually dead.

An integrated death system would enable individuals to achieve such an acceptable death by thinking, feeling, and behaving with respect to death in ways that they might consider effective and appropriate. Avery Weisman outlined what he considered the parameters of an appropriate death. They include (1) relative freedom from pain, (2) control of social and emotional impoverishment, (3) resolution of residual conflicts, (4) satisfaction of those ego ideals consistent with the dying person's present condition, (5) the yielding of control to others, and (6) maintaining or severing key relationships [65]. In judging the helpfulness of attitudes to death, one should ask if this death attitude system promotes the type of death that Weisman describes.

Because there can be no guarantee that an acceptable or peaceful death will be available, some store of courage must be available [22].

REFERENCES

1. R. A. Kalish, Attitudes Toward Death, in *Encyclopedia of Bioethics*, Vol. 1, W. T. Reich (ed.), Free Press, New York, 1978.
2. J. Ortega y Gasset, *Mission of the University*, Norton, New York, 1944.
3. R. Kastenbaum and R. Aisenberg, *The Psychology of Death*, Springer, New York, 1972.
4. H. J. Irwin and E. B. Melbin-Helberg, Enhancement of Death Acceptance by a Grief Counselling Course, *Omega*, 25(1), 1993.
5. C. A. Corr, Reconstructing the Face of Death, in *Dying: Facing the Facts*, H. Wass (ed.), 1979.
6. M. R. Leming, Religion and Death: A Test of Homans' Thesis, *Omega*, 10(4), pp. 347-364, 1979-80.
7. H. Feifel, Psychology and Death: Meaningful Rediscover, *American Psychologist, 45*(4), pp. 437-543, 1990.
8. H. Feifel, S. Hanson, R. Jones, and L. Edwards, Physicians Consider Death, *Proceedings: 75th Annual Convention, APA,* American Psychological Association, Washington, D.C., 1967.
9. M. Lerner, When, Why and Where People Die, in *The Dying Patient,* O. G. Brim, H. E. Freeman, S. Levine, and N. A. Scotch (eds.), Russell Sage, New York, 1970.
10. M. B. Kapp, Living and Dying in the Jewish Way: Secular Rites and Religious Duties, *Death Studies, 17*, pp. 267-276, 1993.

11. K. Marx and F. Engels, The German Ideology, in *The Study of Human Nature,* L. Stevenson (ed.), Oxford, New York, 1980. (Original work published 1845.)
12. Boethius, Contra Eutychen, in *A History of Philosophy: Volume II—Medieval Philosophy, Augustine to Scotus,* F. J. Coplestone (ed.), Newman, Westminster, 1978.
13. P. Ariès, *The Hour of our Death,* Knopf, New York, 1981.
14. Ecclesiastes, *New Jerusalem Bible,* Doubleday, New York, 1982.
15. T. Hobbes, The Leviathan, in *The Great Books of the Western World,* Encyclopedia Britannica, Vol. 23, Chicago, 1952. (Original work published 1651.)
16. H. Feifel and A. B. Branscomb, Who's Afraid of Death? *Journal of Abnormal Psychology, 81*(3), 1973.
17. *Epic of Gilgamesh,* N. K. Sanders (Intro.), Penguin, Baltimore, 1964.
18. L. Bailey, Death in Western Thought: 1. Death in Biblical Thought, in *Encyclopedia of Bioethics,* Vol. 1, W. T. Reich (ed.), Free Press, New York, 1978.
19. M. Montaigne, *Essays,* in *Great Books of the Western World,* Encyclopedia Britannica, Vol. 23, Chicago, 1952. (Original work published 1588.)
20. J. Gutmann, Death: III Western Philosophical Thought, in *Encyclopedia of Bioethics,* Vol. 1, W. T. Reich (ed.), Free Press, New York, 1978.
21. B. L. Goebel and B. E. Boeck, Ego Integrity and Fear of Death: A Comparison of Institutionalized Dependency and Independently Living Older Adults, *Death Studies, 11,* pp. 193-204, 1987.
22. D. Callahan, *The Troubled Dream of Life: Living with Mortality,* Simon and Schuster, New York, 1993.
23. B. W. Tuchman, *A Distant Mirror: The Calamitous 14th Century,* Knopf, New York, 1984.
24. R. Hertz, Death and the Right Hand, cited in *The Psychology of Death,* R. Kastenbaum and R. Aisenberg (eds.), Springer, New York, 1976.
25. C. Goldscheider, *Population, Modernization and Social Structure,* Little, Brown, Boston, 1971.
26. J. Donne, *The Complete English Poems of John Donne,* Meditation, XVII.C., A. Phtrides (ed.), Dent, London, 1985.
27. Augustine, *Confessions,* in *The Great Books of the Western World,* Encyclopedia Britannica, Chicago, 1952. (Original work published 397.)
28. F. Dostoevsky, Rebellion, in *The Brothers Karamazov,* in *Great Books of the Western World,* Encyclopedia Britannica, Part II, Book V, Chicago, 1952.
29. E. Rostand, *Cyrano de Bergerac,* E. Sasquelle, Paris, 1930.
30. J. Puccini, La Boheme, in *Complete Stories of the Great Operas,* M. Cross (ed.), Doubleday, Garden City, 1958.
31. P. Ariès, The Reversal of Death, in *Death and Dying: Challenge and Change,* R. Fulton, E. Markusen, G. Owen, and J. L. Scheiber, (eds.), Addison-Wesley, Reading, 1978.
32. E. Lindemann, Symptomology and Management of Acute Grief, in *Death and Dying: Challenge and Change,* R. Fulton, E. Markusen, G. Owen, and J. L. Scheiber, (eds.), Addison-Wesley, Reading, 1978.
33. R. Fulton and J. Fulton, A Psychosocial Aspect of Terminal Care: Anticipatory Grief, *Omega, 2,* 1971.
34. L. Thomas, *The Medusa and the Snail,* Bantam, Toronto, 1979.
35. V. R. Pine, An Agenda for Adaptive Anticipation of Bereavement, in *Loss and Anticipatory Grief,* D. C. Heath, Lexington, 1986.
36. N. C. Kowalski, Anticipating the Death of an Elderly Parent, in *Loss and Anticipatory Grief,* D. C. Heath, Lexington, 1986.

37. G. Pappas, S. Queen, W. Hadden, and G. Fisher, The Increasing Disparity in Mortality Between Socioeconomic Groups in the United States, 1960-1986, *New England Journal of Medicine, 329*(2), 1993.
38. R. Fulton, Forward in *Loss and Anticipatory Grief,* D. C. Heath, Lexington, 1986.
39. R. Fulton, Anticipatory Grief, Stress and the Surrogate Griever, in *Death and Dying: Challenge and Change,* R. L. Fulton (ed.), Addison-Wesley, Reading, 1978.
40. R. Fulton, E. Markusen, G. Owen, and J. L. Scheiber (eds.), *Death and Dying: Challenge and Change,* Addison-Wesley, Reading, 1978.
41. E. J. Cassell, Dying in a Technological Society, in *Death and Dying: Challenge and Change,* R. L. Fulton (ed.), Addison-Wesley, Reading, 1978.
42. P. Ramsey, *The Patient as Person,* Yale, New Haven, 1970.
43. R. Fulton and G. Owen, Death in Contemporary American Society, in *Death and Identity* (3rd Edition), R. Fulton and R. Bendikson (eds.), Charles, Philadelphia, pp. 12-27, 1994.
44. H. Brody, *The Healer's Power,* Yale University Press, New Haven, 1992.
45. K. H. Beck, Human Response to Threat, in *Horrendous Death, Health and Well-Being,* D. Leviton (ed.), Hemisphere, New York, pp. 31-47, 1991.
46. T. Parsons, R. C. Fox, and V. M. Lidz, The "Gift of Life" and its Reciprocation, in *Death in American Experience,* A. Mack (ed.), Schocken, New York, 1973.
47. G. Family, Projected Image and Observed Behaviours of Physicians in Terminal Cancer Care, *Omega: Journal of Death and Dying, 26*(2), pp. 129-136, 1992-93.
48. E. Becker, *The Denial of Death,* The Free Press, New York, 1973.
49. W. James, Sentiment of Rationality in *Essays in Pragmatism by William James,* A. Castell (ed.), Hafner, New York, 1959. (Original work published 1879.)
50. H. Kushner, *Why Do Bad Things Happen to Good People?* Avon, New York, 1983.
51. D. Lester and D. M. Becker, College Students' Attitudes Toward Death as Compared to the 1930's, *Omega: Journal of Death and Dying, 26*(3), pp. 219-222, 1993.
52. T. Rando, The Increasing Prevalence of Complicated Mourning: The Onslaught is Just Beginning, *Omega: Journal of Death and Dying, 26*(1), 1993.
53. D. Umbertson and K. Henderson, The Social Construct of Death in the Gulf War, *Omega: Journal of Death and Dying, 25*(1), pp. 1-16, 1992.
54. J. J. Lévy and A. Nouss, Death and its Rituals in Novels on AIDS, *Omega: Journal of Death and Dying, 27*(1), pp. 67-74, 1993.
55. J. Hintze, D. I. Templer, G. G. Cappelletty, and W. Frederick, Death Depression and Death Anxiety in HIV Infected Males, *Death Studies, 17,* pp. 333-341, 1993.
56. L. M. Ross and H. R. Pollio, Metaphors of Death: A Thematic Analysis of Personal Meanings, *Omega: Journal of Death and Dying, 23*(4), pp. 291-307, 1991.
57. D. Leviton, *Horrendous Death. Health and Well-Being,* Hemisphere, New York, 1991.
58. W. M. Lamers, Hospice: Enhancing the Quality of Life, *Oncology,* May 1990.
59. P. Ramsdem, Alice in the Afterlife: A Glimpse in the Mirror, in *Coping with the Final Tragedy: Cultural Variation in Dying and Grieving,* D. R. Counts and D. A. Counts (eds.), Baywood Publishing, Amityville, New York, pp. 27-41, 1991.
60. L. E. Holcomb, R. A. Neimeyer, and M. K. Moore, Personal Meanings of Death: A Content Analysis of Free-Response Narratives, *Death Studies, 17*(4), pp. 299-318, 1993.
61. V. Florian and M. Mikulincer, The Impact of Death-Risk Experiences and Religiosity on the Fear of Personal Death: The Case of Israeli Soldiers in Lebanon, *Omega: Journal of Death and Dying, 26*(2), pp. 101-110, 1989.
62. D. Gallagher, S. Levett, P. Hanely-Dunn, and L. W. Thompson, Use of Select Coping Strategies During Late-Life Spousal Bereavement, in *Older Bereaved Spouses,* D. A. Lund (ed.), Hemisphere, New York, pp. 111-121, 1989.

63. J. Q. Benoliel, *Occupational Stress in the Care of the Critically Ill, the Dying and the Bereaved,* Hemisphere, New York, 1987.
64. S. M. Aronson, A Physician's Acquaintance with Grief, in *Loss and Anticipatory Grief,* T. Rando (ed.), Lexington, Lexington, Massachusetts, 1986.
65. A. Weisman, An Appropriate Death, in *Death and Dying: Challenge and Change,* R. Fulton, E. Markusen, G. Owen, and J. L. Scheiber (eds.), Addison-Wesley, Reading, 1978.

CHAPTER 3
Prologue to a Study of Death in Film

John Orange

The topic of death turns up in films the way it turns up in all of the arts. Death, of course, is *the* unfathomable mystery of existence; it is natural that the arts will be obsessed with it. Films have treated topics such as homicide, suicide, euthanasia, grief, burials, genocide, and the afterlife from every angle. The *content* of films does not differ widely from other arts when it comes to death and all its attendant forms and consequences. There are thousands of films that have at least some aspect of death in them. Some of these films are useful tools in grief therapy, or in the understanding of psychological reactions to death in families or the various reactions to the news that one has only a short time left to live. The following titles (to mention only a few) *Ordinary People* (1980), *Sophie's Choice* (1982), *Love Story* (1970), *Dead Poets Society* (1989), *'Nite Mother* (1986), *Terms of Endearment* (1983), *Beaches* (1988), *Accidental Tourist* (1988), *Steel Magnolias* (1989), *Whose Life Is It Anyway* (1981), are some the more popular Hollywood treatments of the topic. Foreign films such as the films of Sweden's Ingmar Bergman, the British *Truly, Madly, Deeply,* (1991) the French *Forbidden Games* (1951), or the Italian *Three Brothers* (1980)[1] are good examples of how other countries whose film styles and attitudes have evolved along lines different from Hollywood have a more mature tradition of depicting killing and death—that is, when they are not imitating the Hollywood formulas. If, then, the theme of death is present in films just as it is in the other arts, what is distinctive in the ways film treats the topic?

Some of the answers to this question are obvious and others are more subtle. This brief treatment of death in film attempts to present a kind of aerial photograph—that is an exploration of the topic at a fairly high level of generalization—in the hope of

---

[1] I will not attempt to give references for all the films listed in this chapter. There are many good reference lists for film and video available which give all the information on these titles. They are generally organized by title so that finding information on any of the films mentioned here is very simple. To avoid the clutter of too much information, I omit the usual references.

stimulating more detailed discourse on the topic by interested viewers. For purposes of organization, the topic can be divided into the properties of film that encourage certain kinds of death to be depicted, the possible sociocultural effects (emotional, moral, psychological, aesthetic) of film's depiction of death, and alternative portrayals of death in films made outside of the Hollywood standard. I have purposely limited my remarks to the most popular American films and genres because these films (one can easily intuit) have the most impact on the general population, which means in large part they seem to cut across age, gender, and economic demographics.

THE PHENOMENON OF KILLING: THE ACTION-ADVENTURE

If measured by sheer volume, death is portrayed most often and most explicitly in the related film genres of action-adventures, gangster, westerns, thrillers and, of course, horror films. In the early decades of filmmaking the scenes of killing and dying owed a great deal to the stage, especially nineteenth-century melodramas which in turn can be traced back to the scattered bodies of the dead in the last scenes of Renaissance tragedies. In films even up to the end of the 1930s, characters died as they did on stage—after lengthy speeches, exaggerated gestures, tremulous music, and much weeping from attendants. The silent film demanded an exaggerated acting style to compensate for the lack of sound, so the dramatic stage versions of death made sense technically. As on stage, even violent deaths were relatively bloodless. Gradually, however, good directors realized that the properties of film allowed for different versions of killing and dying than those depicted in stage plays and novels, one that expanded the uses of time, space, and especially motion—expansions that only film can accomplish. Hence westerns, gangster, horror films, and eventually thrillers, evolved into the slaughterfests we have today. As film technology advanced, bullet wounds made with squibs, bloody stabbings, explosions, and now morphing techniques that destroy and reconstruct bodies in seconds, became a kind of techno-competition to see who could push the envelope of shock and gore. This has resulted in a kind of celebration of dying, best exemplified by the famous slow-motion ballet of death in the seminal Sam Peckinpah film *The Wild Bunch* (1969).

Anyone who has seen many films in theaters or on television knows intuitively that popular genre films specialize not so much in death as in killing. In the last twenty-five years or so, some of these films have been so popular that they have cloned themselves a surprising number of times, and each time the killing and the explicit display of gore has been increased a notch or so. The first Clint Eastwood *Dirty Harry* film came out in 1971 and was followed by almost two decades of sequels. The *Death Wish* (1974) series starring an aging Charles Bronson was up to number eight in 1994, and such series as *Lethal Weapon* (1987), *Die Hard* (1988), the James Bond Films, *Under Siege* (1991), not to mention the horror series such as *Halloween* (1978), *Nightmare on Elm Street* (1984), and all the Stallone (*Cobra*, *Rambo*) and Schwarzenegger films of the past fifteen years show no sign of dying themselves. These kinds of films are immensely popular and the profits they make can be gauged by the number of sequels they generate. The killing quotient in these kinds of films, including the very popular ninja type action adventures, has been as high as a killing every few seconds. In this respect they parallel the computer games that children (mostly boys) now grow up with.

Why are these kinds of films so popular? We run across all sorts of statistics on the subject of killing in popular entertainment. By the age of sixteen, one study concluded, the typical North American child has witnessed an estimated 200,000 acts of violence including 33,000 murders.[2] There have been reports of "gross-out parties" where twelve- to fifteen-year-olds show four or five slasher movies at one sitting. Studies of children who watch violence on the screen suggest that they are more aggressive for a time after exposure to such material. There is a good deal of anxiety expressed in the press and in legislatures that the social fallout from all of this can only be destructive. In a few recent murder trials the defense has been that the pervasiveness of killing in films and videos has led to murderous tendencies in the accused. So far this defense has not had the credibility of related deterministic and dangerous arguments such as the so-called Repressed Memory Syndrome, PMS, or the Abused Wife Syndrome, but its day is no doubt coming.

The logical argument *against* the destructive social effects of depicting all this killing is that the vast majority of the people who see these movies and videos do not go out and kill people. If there were a strong correlation between seeing these slaughters and imitating the behavior, or even as some would suggest the desensitization of the general population, then one would expect that violent crime statistics of the past thirty years would reflect a dramatic increase in murders and attempted murders. In fact, official government statistics (as opposed to those the police associations put out) show a *decline* in these kinds of crimes in the last twenty years or so, even though the violence on the screen has been intensified exponentially.

These two sides of the argument can be assigned to two models of behavior: the *mimetic model* and the *cathartic model*. The theory behind the mimetic model is that people learn behavior from works of art as well as from everywhere else, and that film in particular is such an intrinsically and intensely visual medium that movies influence, to a greater degree than the other arts, the behavior of viewers. Some people will be so influenced or impressed with the "reality" of what they see that they will go out and mimic or imitate it in their lives. If impressionable children watch heroes solving problems with violence including killing, they will model their behavior on those solutions to problems, or variations of those solutions. If rogue cops or cowboys do not feel the need to follow the laws of the land, then children will learn to ignore those laws and rules as well. The answer seems to be censorship legislated by government and enforced by special branches of the law. Some filmmakers themselves believe in this theory of the relationship of art and life, at least to some extent. Clint Eastwood is reported to have said that his film *Unforgiven*

---

[2] See, for example, *Time*, June 12, 1989. There have been many reports in the popular magazines of numbers such as these. No one can know how valid they are without knowing the criteria used to arrive at them. For our purposes, it doesn't matter too much. The point is that the numbers are very large.

should say something to the rioters in Los Angeles. Some people have argued that attitudes to such issues as divorce and abortion have been influenced in the direction of acceptance by the incessant biased pounding of Hollywood movies on these topics since the early 1950s. Others have answered that art only *reflects* the changing attitudes in society and does not *lead* to the changes.

The second model of behavior is the cathartic model that suggests that some forms of art, especially the visual arts, act as a purge of emotions such as desire, anger, even lust and hate. This theory, to put it rather too simply, holds that every person learns to bottle up unsocial and anti-social responses such as rage against perceived injustices, taboo sexual desires, frustration at the failure to reach goals, hate or jealousy for someone else more powerful, etc. In other words, by finding ways to express these bottled up emotions, art can act as a kind of social release valve, or vent, for the need we all have to express our anxieties, desires, or resentments against the social order that represses us. The externalizing or "projecting" of deep seated emotions has been called the "carnivalesque" in some literary circles. The ideal is that most cultures, at significant times during the year, put on festivals which are designed to suspend the normal social rules and allow the general population to "blow off steam" so that they can go back to living inside the rule of law for the rest of the year. In this view, films depicting pornographic sex, violence, killing, swearing, and the like perform indirectly a useful social service. The vicarious "acting out" of the central characters releases pent-up psychopathologic tendencies in the viewers without doing any social harm. Of course, there are any number of studies to back up this theoretical position. The gangster film, for example, is seen as a product of the Great Depression since viewers were inclined to admire anti-heros who fought against an oppressive system even though civilized order demanded that they had to be destroyed eventually. There was a cathartic effect just in seeing the individual battle against a social system that was felt to be keeping everyone down.

The answers may include elements of both theories, or may even fall outside of them. Many of the other elements in these films are ignored by polemicists. For one thing, the violence in most Hollywood films is ostensibly meant to show how good eventually overcomes evil. Also implicit in the formula of these genres' treatments of the victory of the "good" is the celebration of American individualism. The collective forces of the law or any other authority (state, parents, church, education system) are inadequate to meet evil. Only an individual who can operate freely outside of these apparently repressive, repressed, or weakened forces can find the resources needed to overcome the mayhem of evil. Genre films are successful insofar as they tap into current cultural mythology, and since the late 1960s there has been an increasing cynicism in North American society about the "establishment." Social institutions and politicians are portrayed in the media as bloated by bureaucracy, self-justifying, and often filled with internal corruption. Hence these genres have tapped into popular attitudes. Because the male hero acts outside of the rules, he prevails. All the killing is necessary in order for "good" to triumph, and the question of means justifying the end is usually a moot one from the beginning.

Does this mean, then, that a great many people who frequent these films have a strong cruel streak in them; that millions of people hunger as least to *see* a lot of killing, if not to kill someone themselves? It would take a very pessimistic view of human nature to affirm this premise. It is more likely that these genres tap into very basic anxieties and frustrations that are part of everyday life in a world of rapidly growing communication networks where bad news is the norm. Moreover, vengeance is the emotion underneath the pleasures of these kinds of films. To this end, the rapid editing techniques, the pounding and/or sinister music, the special effects, the impressive stunt work, all give these films the air of a circus and a car accident combined. At the deepest psychological level, perhaps, is the pattern in all of them of the hunt. These films are all rooted in hunting: stalking, spying, tracking, chasing, and killing. The final chase is the set piece of these films. The chase on horseback of the old westerns has been replaced by cars and trucks, boats, planes, and even rockets. Final shoot-outs have become auto wrecks and fires and huge explosions in which the evil characters are vaporized. The alienated hero, exiled from the system, prevails and is then taken back into the community as its savior, very often gaining the love of the woman whom he has been annoying all through the film. The prize of the hunt is not only the kill but the desired woman. In the horror genre, the prize is often more ambiguous. If tapping into trapped anger, vengeance, frustration, or taboo desires is what "escapist" means, then one cannot underestimate the escapist excitement in these genres. The killing may be part of its escapist appeal.

There is also the issue of the curiosity of viewers to see what the latest in film technology can do. The earliest films were very discreet about showing blood. Only in the late 1960s, when the studios were weakening, did American films display a new and confident freedom from censorship codes which allowed them to show blood spurting, exit holes in bodies, and eventually the displays of dismembered and decaying bodies so common in films nowadays. Explosions have graduated from small to massive, from climax scenes to scenes all through the films, from one at a time to sequences of pyrotechnical displays. Paradoxically, as these results of film technology have become more and more impressive, we have learned to take them less and less seriously. This exuberance for technological showing off, combined with the notion of killing as escapist anticipates the next line of argument.

If individualism, righteousness, love, the validating of social myth, the release of anxiety and revenge, and curiosity about "magic" effects are the driving forces behind the success of these kinds of films, how does the killing, and the notion of death built into them, function for the viewers? Is there a social price tag that comes with this indulgence? Possible answers may be found in the way death is portrayed in the film form. By studying a few representative sequences, we may be able to glimpse how the killing works psychologically. This can lead in turn to another possible model of the social consequences of these genres.

A short sequence from *Dirty Harry* will serve to establish some typical elements in the portrayal of death in these kinds of films. In a much quoted sequence Detective Harry Callaghan enters his favorite coffee shop and orders a hot dog. He notices that across the street there is a bank robbery in progress. After instructing the owner to call the police, he settles into eating. Just after Harry takes the first bite, however, the robbers exit the bank and he has to go after them, all the while chewing on the piece of hot dog in his mouth. He even orders the robbers to halt through a mouthful of hot dog. The robber shoots a shotgun blast at Harry who is standing fully exposed in the middle of the street; nevertheless he misses him, and Harry kills him with one shot. Others follow, firing at Harry but also missing and dying for their lack of marksmanship. What follows is a sequence of about twenty rapidly edited shots in which Harry shoots and presumably kills five escaping men, all the while chewing on his hot dog. In a final medium close up, we see him lower his gun and take the final chews. If that hot dog was some sort of phallic joke at the beginning of the sequence, its function has expanded by the end.

There are some conventions embedded in this scene that we find in all of these kinds of films. First, the hero is invulnerable to the guns of the evil men no matter how many there are, how exposed he is, how often they shoot, or even how far away they are. Second, the dead men simply tumble out of the edges of the frame and are not seen again, as if their deaths are inconsequential. Most interestingly, the hot dog prop in *Dirty Harry* functions in a variety of ways. It establishes how little time it takes for Harry to finish off five men; it shows how tough he is in that killing is as casual an act as eating junk; it associates his killing of the men with the chewing up of junk meat; and, most importantly, all of these stylistic elements combined give the scene an edge of humor. The use of the prop signals that none of this—the deaths, the mayhem of shooting, explosions, and destruction of property—needs to be taken at face value. The scene, much like the famous "Go ahead, make my day" scene in the next film in the series, never fails to get a laugh in the theaters.

In the film's concluding sequence, Harry chases and corners the murderer who now uses a small boy as a shield in the final confrontation. Harry shoots the man anyway and wounds him. Finally, he taunts him to pick up his gun, repeating a motif from an earlier part of the film having to do with how many bullets he has fired from his .44 magnum which is powerful enough to "blow your head off." The criminal, of course, goes for his pistol and Harry shoots him dead. The final closeups of Harry's face reveal a ruthless hatred alternating with shots of the badly mangled body of the "punk" floating in the river. The convention being followed here is that the hero, presented as an ambiguous individualist, is potentially, if not actually, becoming increasingly like the people he is hunting. What is implied is that this kind of life turns one into a criminal, and only the steeliest of men can avoid being compromised completely. Also implied is that by operating on the margins of the law, the hero can accomplish far more in terms of justice (vengeance, revenge, efficiency) than the by-the-book bureaucratic superiors who, more often than not, are also sources of corruption. Those who are killed in these films are usually dismissed as ciphers who deserve whatever they get. Their deaths are treated so casually that death's reality is all but ignored.

All of these issues are relevant to the attitudes toward death that are gradually built up in these films. Another exemplary sequence of the treatment of killing and death in the action adventure or thriller genre can be found in the popular *Death Wish* (1974). Charles Bronson plays an architect whose wife and daughter are raped and killed by thugs. The police seem unable to do anything to bring the criminals to justice. Eventually the bereaved husband becomes a vigilante, hunting for muggers in the park and killing them. He gets his idea from a visit to a California movie set where he watches stunt men perform a shootout in a western, thus linking this movie to its parent genre. As cowboys shoot each other, and stunt men fall and fake death, close-ups of Bronson indicate he is getting the idea. Crowds of tourists stand around clapping as each outlaw falls, anticipating how the population of New York will react later to the vigilante killer. Those crowds are surrogates for the movie audience who has also come to see some violence and applaud some killing. (The most ingenious example of this "through-the-looking-glass" technique can be found in the opening sequence of *Stunt Man*, an American film that explores, among other things, the use of this kind of violence in film.) Bronson's character is shown killing a number of attackers, but as he becomes more vicious (shooting fleeing muggers in the back, for example), he seems to be transforming himself into the kind of person he has set out to eradicate. This kind of ambiguity usually creeps into these films thus providing the audience with a sense of occupying higher moral ground, while at the same time allowing the producers to imply their denunciation of the use of violence because of its personal consequences, if such a defense becomes necessary in the face of public outcries against the film.

The killings in *Death Wish* are the same as in most of the films in these genres. The tension in the scenes, the fast-paced editing, the displays of gore, all increase in intensity and quantity right up to the crisis in the plot. The dead seem to disappear outside the frame and are quickly forgotten. The Vigilante is shot at continuously, is often caught in a hail of bullets, but he is rarely injured or even rattled by his exposed position. The criminals, on the other hand, are killed in quick succession, usually with one shot from the "hero." Audiences seem happy to accept the convention of the criminals as terrible marksmen without complaint. It is simply something that goes with the genre.

The Film *Cobra* (1986) quickly becomes an orgy of violence. In chase sequences, bodies fly in all directions until dozens of nameless men are simply dispatched off the edges of the screen, and there are no repercussions at all in the rest of the narrative regarding their corpses, families, or burials. There is also a scene in which Cobra and his sidekick get cynical instructions from their police superiors. When the superiors leave, the sidekick says he would like to make a hole in the officer's chest. Stallone says that the trouble with his partner is "You're too violent." This comment is akin to the scene in *Death Wish* that attaches the violence to old westerns, and to the scenes in *Dirty Harry* which call attention to the artificiality of the killings.

If one were to attempt to trace this set of conventions back in film history, it is fair to say that it has always been present in one form or another. In Howard Hawkes' *Scarface* (1932), to take a conspicuously important but by no means unique example, the machine guns rattle and bodies fly or crumple, but the deaths of the mobsters are not treated as complex or even significant events, no matter how important they may be to the plot; or, to put it another way, they are important *only* to the plot. Comic interludes which dilute the violence serve the same purpose as the flippant dialogue in *Dirty Harry* or *Cobra*. There is a scene in *Scarface* in which a comical sidekick of Tony Camonte tries to take a phone message while bullets buzz all around him, making holes in the hot water urn behind him. (He jumps aside only when he realizes that he might get wet.) He is unhurt and mostly unaware of the danger. This comic turn in the film (one of many in this film) serves to turn the film's horror around on itself and invite the viewers to relax with the reminder that this is only a movie.

These kinds of self-reflective moments in the film genres that depict killings and deaths in quantity work to undermine the seriousness or significance of death itself. They serve to remind viewers constantly that this is only a movie, an exciting story, perhaps something of a game that filmmaker and viewer are playing together. By calling attention to the film's constructedness, and to the implicit rules of the genre itself—rules that the director and the viewer have contracted to follow—the makers of these kinds of films evoke almost consciously an attitude that takes us back to childhood games when we played cowboys, or space invaders, or funeral; when we pretended to die when it was our turn, and we popped up again when the "rules" said it was now our turn to be the righteous sheriff, the strongest pirate, or the heroic pilot. Some of the most violent films of the last few years, *Natural Born Killers* (1993), *True Lies* (1993), and *Pulp Fiction* (1994) all depend on taking this kind of self-reflexivity as far as it can be taken without completely destroying the illusion of reality. The result is a combination of edginess and humor inside the treatments of the killing and deaths—a treatment that serves to undermine the seriousness of the deaths and violence and turn them into a sort of tacit game between film and viewer—one of those contracts between filmmaker and viewer that genres make to follow certain conventions while at the same time allowing for playful modifications.

When killing is treated with this cavalier attitude, it is difficult to argue *either* of the two theoretical models, mimetic and cathartic, that most people espouse. What these models ignore is that the films have built-in failsafe techniques of narration and style that reinforce the "as-if" or "just pretend" experience of watching a film. Even children at a fairly young age understand the notion of pretending.

Perhaps, in fact, a third theoretical model can explain how killing in films is experienced by people with normal healthy minds. Children do not perceive death the way adults do. They do not know or believe that it is permanent or irreversible. They see it as a sleep, at most, from which they can awake. In fact, we know that the actors in films do not permanently "die" because they show up in subsequent films. Most viewers nowadays simple want to see how realistically the stunt can be performed or the gore can be faked. Death is not believed to happen to "real" people, only to characters in a story.

Add to this that children generally do not know or believe that death can happen to them. They believe that it happens to someone or something else. Thus the heros in films of the action genre are invulnerable no matter how exposed or vulnerable (wounded or incapacitated) they are; no matter how many shots are fired at them. The implicit text here is that the righteous, or the forces of good, are not subject to death the way the evil characters are. In a child's version of the world, death is not part of nature: by wishing it, it can happen to someone else. The convention of the hero hitting his target with one shot (or punch) functions as an extension of this same concept—wishing it makes it happen. In action thrillers and especially in slasher-horror films, characters who are dismembered, filled with holes, even at times buried, rise up at the last minute and attack again. If they are the heros, they conquer death itself.

In other words, the parallels between the way children perceive death and the ways killing and subsequent deaths are presented in the action-thriller genres suggest that these films are popular not because of some deep and dangerous bloodlust in people, but because they evoke a childish nostalgia in adults for the way killing and death were perceived by us in more innocent days. It is just part of imaginative play, part of a world less foreboding and dark. In a paradoxical way, the movies that show killings may hold deep emotional echoes of the excitement and comfort of childhood—that death does not exist at all; it isn't real.[3] Adults witness "killings" and are invited to respond like children—to feel relief in the face of terrible human destruction. Most of us have been to these kinds of films and shrugged or laughed them off, especially after the initial shock or scare has worn away. However, when we see actual killings and death in television news stories, we are aghast and disgusted for weeks or months. We intuitively feel the difference. There is a difference.

This may be a new version of the cathartic model, or a third possible model to mull over. If this notion has any merit, then it would not be surprising that the millions of patrons of these films do *not* go out and imitate what they see. Rather than being desensitized (in the usual understanding of that term), perhaps viewers are in fact resensitized to death's reality by way of contrast to the childish portrayal of death in these movies. We remember how naive we were and recall emotionally and psychologically the rather charmed attitudes we used to have. At the most superficial level, these films offer an escape back to childhood's imagination. Thus, it may be too simple to suggest that these films are *only* desensitizing or *only* cathartic. They may be offering the viewer the consoling myth that death is only for the bad guys; that it is not random; is not arbitrary or permanent; nor is it complete, so that things stay alive; and that it does not hurt—it is just an illusion.

THE OBJECTIFICATION OF DEATH

If these genre films have found ways to make killing and death comfortable concepts by evoking childish escapes, how successful are other ways of presenting death that are especially attractive to filmmakers? There have been, of course, other conventions established in cinema for the presentation of death and dying that are more than the simple dramatic presentations of death one would expect to find on the stage. Film benefits from more options than the stage, and filmmakers have learned how to "image" death in symbolical and metaphorical terms—something like using imagery in poetry.

---

[3] The obvious parallel is with cartoons. In cartoons we see characters cut into pieces, whipped to a pulp, fall into oblivion, succumb to every form of carnage, and simply reform themselves and shake off the trauma as though it is just another of life's little inconveniences. Children see death as just this kind of temporary setback. There is not much conceptual difference between the ways death is depicted in the genres under study here and the way it is treated in cartoons.

An expected extension of the stage technique is the use of an *allegorical figure*. In Ingmar Bergman's *The Seventh Seal* (1957), to use a famous and much parodied example (see *The Dove* or *Monty Python's The Meaning of Life*), we meet Death as a rather pale and portly man dressed in black tights and a cape. He plays chess with a medieval knight on the beach and promises he will eventually win the game of life. There have been other examples of allegorical figures—even in the guise of rather ordinary looking figures in business suits. The difficulty with allegorical figures in cinema is that they seem to lose force in the relative intimacy of the photographic medium. On stage, the possibility of their "reality" is more immediate because of the intimacy of the real actor playing there, while on screen they are at least once removed and have the same force as a prop or a shadow regardless, it seems, of how powerful their dialogue may be. They remain objects. In *The Adventures of Baron von Munch[h]ausen* (Gilliam, 1989), death is a very impressive gargoyle that breaks free of its stone prison and comes to life to fly around terrorizing the hero and the children. Too soon, however, the figure seems more comic than terrifying—a neat effect, but little more.

In fact, filmmakers have avoided allegorical figures in favor of another objectifying technique that takes us closer to symbols and metaphors. Very often at the precise moment a character dies, the cinematographer, in an unmotivated camera movement, discreetly focuses on an object nearby that will signal the death of the character. There have been innumerable variations of this convention depending often on whether the director wishes to signal the end of a life, or the release of a soul. Objects such as the extinguishing of candle flames, the slow rotation of wheels to a stop, the fall of china which breaks to pieces, fallen leaves, the clouds covering a moon turning the landscape dark, or as in Fellini's *Amarcord* (1974), incense that hangs in the air where the coffin used to be in the cathedral, signal the end of life. In the famous shower scene in *Psycho* (1960), the ebbing of life is imaged in the pulling away of the shower curtain from the shower rod and the slow swirl of blood down a drain. In *Scarface,* one man's death is constructed as bowling pins falling and spinning to a stop.

Sometimes the image is used to suggest the release of the soul. Most often birds suddenly fly into the air as in the startling scene of burial in David Lean's *Doctor Zhivago* (1965) when blackbirds rise into a cloudy sky. Directors have imaged death as sparks flying up into the dark, curtains softly and gently wafting outwards through an open window, or waves receding into the sea. These kinds of images indicate attempts to make the notion of death dynamic to suit the needs of the medium. The choice of image suggests whether the director wants the viewer to see death as final or as some sort of transition to another condition. In some ways, however, this is another technique to avoid depicting death as it is. "Real" death just will not sell tickets. By turning the camera eye to an object in the mise-en-ecene, the filmmaker indicates that neither catharsis nor mimesis interests him: the viewer is allowed to experience death as an abstraction and to take comfort in the visual appeal or witty conceit of the symbol itself. Death is reduced to its idea.

DEPICTING DEATH AS REAL

There are producers and directors who have decided not to worry about profits. Sometimes directors and producers decide to make a film for a smaller market of viewers who want to see something different in films—something more artistic and adult than the usual Hollywood product. Foreign films found their way into North America increasingly in the late 1960s, and these imports generally were more sophisticated in their treatments of death. In art films such as Ingmar Bergman's *Cries and Whispers,* the camera gazes on death as though it is transfixed. The opening sequence of this film is uncompromising in its depiction of the slow and painful process of dying. Dark and fog surround a house at four o'clock in the morning. A woman cannot sleep. The camera checks all the clocks. Time and silence become the preoccupations of a woman in obvious pain who knows she is dying. The face of suffering and death becomes unavoidable, very powerful, and very painfully real. In a more recent American film that evidently does not worry about box-office, *The River's Edge,* the camera lingers over the dead body of a strangled high school cheerleader on a number of occasions so that the viewers see the corpse begin to decompose. The student friends of the victim do not seem to see the reality of the death that confronts them because they have only known death as depicted in Hollywood films and television movies. The film plays off the ironies in this set-up by depicting death as "real" in order to make the point that films traditionally have not done so, and consequently this has warped our notions of death. Other examples of films showing death in realistic terms are *Manon of the Spring* (1986) and the television version of *Brideshead Revisited* in which Sir Laurence Olivier portrays with absolute conviction a dying man.

As long as films need to make profits, it is probably safe to say that death will be sanitized, avoided, falsified, or romanticized in one way or another. In this respect, it may be that our anxiety about the social consequences of "all this killing and dying in the media" is misplaced or exaggerated. However, the potential in film for dealing with death has been barely tapped. That it is possible to treat death in mature and sophisticated ways has been demonstrated by the more poetic strategies in adult films. Film can be a surprisingly intimate art form. Masters of film art have demonstrated the power of that intimacy. When film matches its ability to portray death intimately, it exposes its most fundamental powers.

This prologue has touched on a number of social, psychological, and aesthetic issues in the depicting of killing and death in films. Anxieties about the social consequences of graphic depictions of death in the quantities and with the casualness that contemporary films offer have been discussed with reference to three possible models of responses to art. The tentative conclusion here is that Hollywood genre films tend to appeal to childhood perceptions of death as a vehicle of entertainment and escape. More mature treatments of death still try to evade its reality, and so far only a handful of directors have met death head on. A good deal of study has to be done before we leap for mechanisms to control these images. Like any other art form, film is capable of almost infinite variation. It has only begun to find ways of dealing with death and killing.

CHAPTER 4

An Approach to Death in Adult and Children's Literature

Gary H. Paterson

DEATH IN ADULT LITERATURE

Death is a subject of universal concern. No matter how much one tries to escape from it, suppress it, or even make fun of it, death remains an omnipresent mystery that must be confronted in some way by every living individual. From the earliest recordings of ancient civilizations, attitudes toward death have been reflected in various forms of art including dance, caveman hieroglyphics and, in the last three or so thousand years, language.

Literature, especially poetry, is capable of conveying intense emotion as well as subtle nuances of feeling through certain devices such as sound patterns, rhythm, imagery, and symbolism. These techniques provide a far greater sensory impact upon the reader than merely by stating realistic fact. This chapter will attempt to show how various aspects of genre, tone, language, and symbolism can express some of the most profound statements about death and, ironically, life itself. The first half will be concerned with the theme of death in literature primarily for adults; the second half will comprise an approach to death in children's literature.

For purposes of simplification, one can notice that death figures in literary works in three ways: (1) the expression of grief and mourning over the loss of a loved one; (2) actual descriptions of the dying and the dead; (3) expression of attitudes toward one's own death or of death in general. It will be helpful to survey these in turn.

The Expression of Mourning for a Dead Person

This is probably the most common and best known treatment of death in literature. The particular poetic genre of this expression is called the *elegy* and, significantly, it is one of the oldest modes of literature, dating back as it does to ancient Roman, Greek, and Hebrew times. Generally speaking, the mood of the elegy moves from profound sorrow in which all nature grieves for the lost one, through a statement of regret at the transience of being, to an attempt to find some permanence either in the concept of immortality or in the hope for something lasting in life to be found in the memory and relics of the deceased.

Ancient elegies often took on a pastoral tone (the tradition began with the Sicilian poets, Theocritus, Bion, and Moschus and was continued by Vergil) with the poet assuming the role of shepherd and the coffin being strewn with flowers by the procession of rustic mourners. The pastoral influence can also be found in such modern elegies as Milton's *Lycidas* (1637) [1], Shelley's *Adonais* (1821) [2], and Arnold's *Thyrsis* (1866) [3].

In Shelley's poem, written on the death of fellow-poet, John Keats, we have a fine example of the classical elegy suited to Shelley's particular style and philosophy. After the lengthy description of the formal mourning on the part of Shelley and other poets and, indeed, all of Nature, we have the statement of consolation, found in Shelley's Platonism:

> Dust to the dust: but the pure spirit shall flow
> Back to the burning fountain whence it came,
> A portion of the Eternal, which must glow
> Through time and change, unquenchably the same... [2, p. 727]

While many elegies look for permanence in aspects of art, human memory, or the Platonic world of spirit, the Christian elegy seeks consolation in the doctrine of Immortality and the reunion of the living and the dead in heaven. Tennyson's elegy, *In Memoriam* (1850) [4], dedicated to his close friend, Arthur Hallam, traces the experience of bereavement comprehensively, from the agonizing first moments of shock on hearing of his friend's death, through the pain of celebrating the joys of Christmas in the midst of sorrow, the expression, as well, of the realities of loneliness, difficulties in accepting orthodox Christian faith in the face of recent geological and astronomical discoveries, to triumphant recognition of faith in the immortality of the soul. This lengthy poem presents a kaleidoscopic spectrum of human emotions.

In studying the elegy, we are interested in the sense of distance or objectivity in the tone of the speaker. Arnold's *Thyrsis* [3] does not ultimately seem to present any great emotional bond between Arnold and the dead poet, Clough; on the other hand, the opening sections of Tennyson's *In Memoriam* [4] evoke a passionate sense of loss for Arthur Hallam, which is saved from sinking into maudlin sentimentality by the use of certain images (such as the yew tree, the dark house, and the grasping of hands) which tend to distill the emotion away from the poet into the poem.

Observe how emotion can be distracted from the poet in the commonplace details of the opening stanza of Auden's elegy, *In Memory of W. B. Yeats*:

> He disappeared in the dead of winter;
> The brooks were frozen, the airports almost deserted,
> And snow disfigured the public statues:

The mercury sank in the month of the dying day.
O all the instruments agree
The day of his death was a dark cold day [5, p. 2267].

The time of winter, appropriate for death, is shown in natural and human terms: ultimately, the machines collaborate to signify what is really not of significance to the dead, but rather to the living survivors: darkness and coldness. Even the idea of immortality—here the permanence of the great poet's verse—is given an uncertain, ironical statement in two lines dealing with the problem of varying interpretation of poetic meaning: "The words of a dead man / Are modified in the guts of the living" [5, p. 2268].

There are many contemporary elegies which are not as highly stylized or traditionally patterned. This poetry will probably appeal more to the modern reader; yet, interestingly enough, it will ultimately ask many of the same questions as the older reflections had. Consider the following example by Canadian poet, Al Purdy:

Elegy for a Grandfather

Well, he died I guess. They said he did.
His wide whalebone hips will make a prehistoric barrow
men of the future may find and perhaps may not:
where this man's relatives ducked their heads
in real and pretended sorrow
for the dearly beloved gone thank Christ to God,
after a bad century: a tough big-bellied Pharaoh,
with a deck of cards in his pocket and a Presbyterian
grin—

Maybe he did die, but the boy didn't understand it,
the man knows now and the scandal never grows old
of a happy lumberjack who lived on rotten whisky,
and died of sin and Quaker oats age 90 or so.
But all he was too much for any man to be,
a life so full he couldn't include one more thing,
nor tell the same story twice if he'd wanted to,
and didn't and didn't—

Just the same he's dead. A sticky religious voice
folded his century sideways to get it out of sight,
and lowered him into the ground like someone still
alive who made other people uncomfortable:
barn raiser and backwoods farmer,
become an old man in a one-room apartment
over a drygood store—
And earth takes him as it takes more beautiful things:
populations of whole countries,
museums and works of art,

> and women with such a glow
> it makes their background vanish
> > they vanish too,
> and Lesbia's singer in her sunny islands
> stopped when the sun went down—
> No, my grandfather was decidedly unbeautiful,
> 250 pounds of scarred slag.
> And I've somehow become his memory,
> taking on flesh and blood again
> the way he imagined me,
> floating among the pictures in his mind
> where his dead body is,
> laid deep in the earth—
> and such a relayed picture perhaps
> outlives any work of art,
> survives among its alternatives [6, pp.14-15].

In spite of the somewhat offhand, flippant opening, there is the (albeit qualified) praise of the dead man, the statement of sorrow, even the grandfather's being in harmony with Nature, and the final sense of the future possibilities of immortality: "And I've somehow become his memory / taking on flesh and blood again . . ."

The *dirge* is also a poem expressing sorrow upon a death; it is usually short, rather informal and it is meant to be sung. A good example is "Fear No More the Heat of the Sun" from Shakespeare's play, *Cymbeline*. Here is the opening stanza:

> Fear no more the heat o' the sun,
> > Nor the furious winter's rages;
> Thou the wordly task hast done,
> > Home art gone, and ta'en thy wages:
> Golden lads and girls all must,
> As chimney-sweepers, come to dust [7, p. 257].

There is no outcry of grief here. Death is depicted flatly as an inevitable conclusion to every life on the social scale. Much the same sentiment is expressed in another dirge, this one by James Shirley (1596-1666). Again, the opening stanza:

> The glories of our blood and state
> > Are shadows, not substantial things;
> There is no armour against fate;
> > Death lays his icy hand on kings:
> > > Scepter and crown
> > > Must tumble down,
> And in the dust be equal made
> With the poor crooked scythe and spade [8, p. 106].

Here rhythm and sound patterns emphasize the certainty of our final end. The uneven and shortened lines (5-6), in which the pace quickens, are followed by the long, slow paced vowel sounds and the cacophony of "poor crooked scythe and spade" (l. 8).

Descriptions of the Dying and the Dead

This aspect of death in literature will obviously appear most frequently in the sensational news-stand blockbuster and we are treated to its counterparts in TV and cinema violence. In good literature, however, the description of a dying person must be approached with definite artistic purpose.

Ancient epics such as *The Iliad*, *The Odyssey,* and *The Aeneid* treated death in the proud heroic manner. Actual descriptions of death, although often grisly, were surrounded with intense emotions such as ambition, loyalty, terror, and revenge.

Following is the description of the last moment of Emma in Flaubert's novel, *Madame Bovary* (1857) [9]. The realistic touches are all too obvious; yet, notice in the sentimental picture of Charles, the cloddish yet loving husband holding the hands of his once beautiful, often unfaithful wife and the refrain of the blind beggar's song, which harkens back to Emma's days of splendor as mistress of the handsome Leon, we have a statement of the futility of human pretensions and the grim reminder that death awaits all—the beautiful and witty as well as the ugly and stupid:

> And just then she looked all round her, slowly, as one waking from a dream. In a clear voice she asked for her mirror, and remained bowed over it for some time, until big tears began to trickle out of her eyes. Then she threw up her head with a sigh and fell back on the pillow.
> At once her lungs began to heave rapidly, the whole of her tongue protruded from her mouth, her rolling eyes turned pale like the globes of two guttering lamps; she might have been dead already but for the frightful oscillation of her ribs, that shook with furious gusts as though her soul were leaping to get free. Felicite knelt before the crucifix; even the chemist bent his knees a little; Monsieur Canivet stared vaguely out into the square. Bournisien had started praying again, his face bowed over the edge of the bed, his long black cassock trailing across the floor behind him. Charles knelt opposite, his arms stretched out towards Emma. He had taken her hands and was pressing them in his, shuddering at every beat of her heart as at the reverberation of a falling ruin. As the death rattle grew louder, the priest hastened his orisons; they mingled with Bovary's stifled sobs, and sometimes everything seemed to be drowned in the dull murmur of the Latin syllables, that sounded like the tolling of a knell.
> Suddenly there was a clumping of sabots on the pavement outside, the scraping of a stick, and a voice came up, a hoarse voice singing:
> "When the sun shines warm above,
> It turns a maiden's thoughts to love."
> Emma sat up like a corpse galvanized, her hair dishevelled, her eyes fixed, gaping.
> "All across the furrows brown
> See Nanette go bending down
> Gathering up with careful hand
> The golden harvest from the land."

"The blind man!" she cried.

And Emma started laughing, a ghastly, frantic, desperate laugh, fancying she could see the hideous face of the beggar rising up like a nightmare amid the eternal darkness.

"The wind it blew so hard one day,
Her little petticoat flew away!"

A convulsion flung her down upon the mattress. They moved nearer. She was no more [9, pp. 336-337].

Leo Tolstoy's novella, *The Death of Ivan Ilych* (1886) is of particular interest in its treatment of death, because we have descriptions not only from the point of view of outsiders, but also, as will be shown later, of the dying man himself [10]. Early in the work, a group of business associates, attending the wake, observe the corpse of Ivan Ilych:

The dead man lay, as dead men always lie, in a specially heavy way, his rigid limbs sunk in the soft cushions of the coffin, with the head forever bowed on the pillow. His yellow waxen brow with bald patches over his sunken temples was thrust up in the way peculiar to the dead, the protruding nose seeming to press on the upper lip. . . . The expression on the face said that what was necessary had been accomplished, and accomplished rightly. Besides this there was in that expression a reproach and a warning to the living. This warning seemed to Peter Ivanovich out of place, or at least not applicable to him. He felt certain discomfort and so her hurriedly crossed himself once more and turned and went out of the door—too hurriedly and too regardless of propriety, as he himself was aware [10, p. 488].

There is the subtle implication of satire in this part of the story: each person sees Ivan as *someone other than himself.* His surviving colleagues are happily alive, enjoying their careers, their social status, their game of bridge at the club; everything, in fact, that Ivan had enjoyed until only a few months previously. The emphasis in this passage and other closely related sections of the novella, is really upon life rather than death: the meretricious lives of smug upper-middle class Russian society of the nineteenth century. There is no thought for an afterlife; the attitude toward life and death is definitely *carpe diem.*

Opposed to this materialistic philosophy is the recognition of the dead body, but also endurance of an immortal soul after death, a concept that is rarely expressed in literature. One such passage occurs in Antoine de Saint Exupery's sensitive story which appeals to adults and children alike (and therefore included here), *The Little Prince* (1943) [11]. Close to the end, when the little prince is consoling the aviator by telling him always to look up at the stars where the little prince will be laughing at him, there is a reference to the dead body:

"Tonight—you know . . . Do not come . . ."
"I shall look as if I were suffering. I shall look a little as if I were dying. It is like that. Do not come to see that. It is not worth the trouble . . ." [11, p. 105].

And a little later:

> There was nothing there but a flash of yellow close to his ankle. He remained motionless for an instant. He did not cry out. He fell as gently as a tree falls. There was not even any sound, because of the sand [11, p. 108].

Notice that, in a reading of this section of the novel, the emphasis is clearly away from the dead body toward the stars, traditional symbols of permanence, where the little prince promises he will be laughing in an eternal private joke.

Another aspect of description of death and dying in literature is a kind of physical death-in-life, usually associated with old age. Matthew Arnold's poem, *Growing Old*, ends with the following bleak stanzas:

> It is not to spend long days
> And not once to feel that we were ever young
> It is not to add, immured
> In the hot prison of the present, month
> To month with weary pain.
>
> It is to suffer this
> And feel but half, and feebly, what we feel.
> Deep in our hidden heart
> Festers the dull remembrance of a change,
> But no emotion—none.
>
> It is—last stage of all—
> When we are frozen up within, and quite
> The phantom of ourselves,
> To hear the world applaud the hollow ghost
> Which blamed the living man [12, pp. 1378-1379].

Here the physical decay is matched with an agonizing loss of spirituality and will to live. Death is ultimately a release from the rigours of existence—but not a very welcome one.

Expressions of Attitudes Toward One's Own Death or of Death in General

The gamut of emotional and intellectual attitudes toward death expressed in literature varies from fear, panic, and horror, to anger, outrage, reconciliation, and even triumph. Only a few examples can be given here; it is the immense *variety* that should become obvious immediately.

Consider the following chilling lines from Shakespeare's *Measure for Measure*:

> Ay, but to die, and go we know not where;
> To lie in cold obstruction, and to rot;

> This sensible warm motion to become
> A kneaded clod; and the delighted spirit
> To bathe in fiery floods, or to reside
> In thrilling region of the thick-ribbed ice;
> To be imprison'd in the viewless winds
> And blown with restless violence round about
> The pendent world: or to be worse than worst
> Of those that lawless and incertain though
> Imagine howling—'tis too horrible.
> The weariest and most loathed worldly life
> That age, ache, penury and imprisonment
> Can lay on nature, is a paradise
> To what we fear of death [13, pp. 65-66].

It is not necessary even to know the context of this speech in the play to experience the horrors of death and the unknown beyond so often depicted in Medieval and Renaissance art—right down to the gruesome details of the fire-and-brimstone sermon in James Joyce's *A Portrait of the Artist as a Young Man*, Chapter 3 (1916) [14].

In the final section of Tolstoy's *Death of Ivan Ilych* [10]. Ivan in flashback recounts his dying moments, seen in terms of being thrust into a dark sack. When he has gained full insight, however, the darkness changes to light and he can see life—and eternity—in its proper perspective:

> "So that's what it is!" he suddenly exclaimed aloud. "What joy!"
>
> To him all this happened in a single instant, and the meaning of that instant did not change. For those present his agony continued for another two hours . . .
>
> "It is finished!" said someone near him.
>
> He heard these words and repeated them in his soul.
>
> "Death is finished," he said to himself. "It is no more."
>
> He drew in a breath, stopped in the midst of a sigh, stretched out, and died [10, p. 525].

In spite of the detailed realism of the dying man, there is a statement of reconciliation and a strong hint of immortality here. The tragedy of *The Death of Ivan Ilych* is that he did not learn to live life fully and meaningfully until the moment he died [10].

Defying death as an intellectual argument is the theme of John Donne's *Holy Sonnet No. 10* [15, p. 1116]. As an emotional expression, defiance is perhaps most explicitly conceived in Dylan Thomas' famous poem cast in the demanding French form called a *villanelle*, which Margaret Laurence chose as the epigraph for her fine novel of death and dying, *The Stone Angel* [16]:

> Do not go gentle into that good night,
> Old age should burn and rave at close of day;
> Rage, rage against the dying of the light.

Though wise men at their end know dark is right,
Because their words had forked no lightning they
Do not go gentle into that good night.

Good men, the last wave by, crying how bright
Their frail deeds might have danced in a green bay,
Rage, rage against the dying of the light.

Wild men who caught and sang the sun in flight,
And learn, too late, they grieved it on its way,
Do not go gentle into that good night.

Grave men, near death, who see with blinding sight
Blind eyes could blaze like meteors and be gay,
Rage, rage against the dying of the light.

And you, my father, there on the sad height,
Curse, bless me now with your fierce tears, I pray.
Do not go gentle into that good night.
Rage, rage against the dying of the light [17, p. 2286].

And now, a note of triumph: here is the death speech of Cleopatra when she realizes that Antony awaits her in the afterlife and that the life she is leaving behind is peopled with the pettiness of the Caesars of this world:

Give me my robe, put on my crown, I have
Immortal longings in me. Now no more
The juice of Egypt's grape shall moist this lip.
Yare, yare, good Iras; quick: methinks I hear
Antony call. I see him rouse himself
To praise my noble act. I hear him mock
The luck of Caesar, which the gods give men
To excuse their after wrath. Husband, I come:
Now to that name, my courage prove my title!
I give to baser life [18, p. 334].

Notice that attitudes toward death need not be directed at actual instances of death and dying, but rather a mood or a sense of death-in-life as seen in the cyclical progression of decay and renewal in the seasons, for example, which we have all experienced. Study this beautifully elegiac moment of vision of a child realizing the stern laws of transience in the world by the nineteenth-century Jesuit, Gerard Manley Hopkins:

SPRING AND FALL
TO A YOUNG CHILD

Margaret, are you grieving
Over Goldengrove unleaving?
Leaves, like the things of man, you
With your fresh thoughts care for, can you?

> Ah! as the heart grows older
> It will come to such sights colder
> By and by, nor spare a sigh
> Though worlds of wanwood leafmeal lie,
> And yet you will weep and know why.
> Now no matter, child, the name:
> Sorrow's springs are the same.
> Nor mouth had, no not mind, expressed
> What heart heard of, ghost guessed:
> It is the blight man was born for,
> It is Margaret you mourn for [19, p. 155].

In assessing a literary work dealing with the theme of death, it is important, first of all, to understand the writer's stance, his involvement or detachment in relation to his materials. Is he so thoroughly emotionally a part of his work that it becomes an amorphous spilling-out of random sentiment? What techniques, such as structurally rigorous forms (such as the sonnet) or imagery and symbolism divert the reader away from the writer's emotion to the aesthetics of the poem itself? Next, consider the *direction* of the literary treatment of death. Does it tend to concentrate graphically on the emotional and physical traumas of death and dying, or downplay the material and tend toward at least an intimation of immortality through the careful use of symbolism. Finally, feel free to be your own critical spokesperson. How *you* react to the depiction of death in literature is ultimately the most meaningful criterion.

DEATH IN CHILDREN'S LITERATURE

Historically, an important thing to remember about children's literature is that in the beginning, there was no strict division between adult and child. From an early age, children would have been exposed to the epics, sagas, and tales of heroism and romance that also fascinated adults in bygone civilizations with their stories of courage, loyalty, and cunning.

As time passed, folklore came to include popular tales of a humbler and homelier tone and what still remains popular today, the fairy tale. In the fairy tale, death is generally portrayed in two ways. There is, on the one hand, a grisly punishment, often graphically described, for the villain—ogre, giant, witch, or evil magician. As well, there often occurs a kind of death-in-life in the form of enchantment or a death-like sleep from which the hero(ine) awakes and proceeds to live "happily ever after" in a quasi-paradise on earth; "Sleeping Beauty" comes to mind here.

Nineteenth-century children's literature often viewed death as a form of black humor. We have, for example, Lewis Carroll's monomaniacal Queen of Hearts, who solves every problem with the exclamation, "Off with his head! . . . Off with his head!" [20, p. 65], or the limerick of Edward Lear which mentions "an old man of New York, / Who murdered himself with a fork" [21, p. 35]. This tradition was continued into the twentieth century in Barrie's *Peter Pan* [22]. As well, there are detailed descriptions of violent death in both *Huckleberry Finn* [23] and *Treasure Island* [24].

In the twentieth century, with the dark realities of two World Wars, the return to domesticity in the 1950s and the sometimes erratic search for peace and tranquility in the 1960s, it is not surprising that death becomes a "forbidden" topic in a world that was trying, over the decades, to survive a depression, to escape the terrors of war, or simply to put together the pieces of a frightening and fragmented universe. The emphasis in children's literature of this period was upon secure familial relations, "harmless" adventure stories, and variations on the American Dream. *The Wind in the Willows*, for example, with all its cosiness and camaraderie, contains only one oblique reference to death [25].

In the past three decades an abrupt reversal in the attitude toward death in children's books has taken place. The year 1952, with the publication of *Charlotte's Web* by E. B. White, is a landmark in this departure [26]. Here the peaceful, yet solitary death of Charlotte, the spider, depicted as the natural conclusion to a meaningful life, is contrasted with the horrible panic experienced by Wilbur, the pig, when he is informed of his impending slaughter. Although death is faced directly here, it still deals with animals so that children might find some kind of detachment or emotional distancing. In the 1970s and 1980s, however, while books for very young children dealt with the death of a pet, the trauma of a grandparent's death, then a parent, then the death of a sibling brought the subject much closer to home for the child reader. In fact, the theme of death can be placed in the company of other hitherto "taboo" themes such as divorce, alcoholism, and sexuality that form the so-called "dark realism" of contemporary children's literature.

The range of approaches to death in children's books is apparently endless, but I think they can be usefully categorized as (1) factual questions including intellectual scientific information, (2) emotional problems, and (3) spiritual concerns.

1. Factual Scientific Information

A child's curiosity is a constant source of delight. We know that even the very youngest children have had some conscious or unconscious contact with death, whether of a human, animal, or plant. The transience of time is everywhere in the cycle of the seasons, the movement of water, or the growth of a flower. A little boy on a current television commercial asks his father how long their pet dog will live. Passing a cemetery or funeral procession can evoke questions about what happens to dead people.

The specifically factual material about dying (When is a person really dead? What happens at a funeral parlor? Won't the person be cold in the cemetery during winter?) has been excellently handled in the book, *Talking About Death: A Dialogue between Parent and Child*, presents separate texts for child and adult [27]. The explanation is based largely on seeing life—and death—in two ways just as we experience both the light and darkness of reality. *About Dying*, by Sara Bonnett Stein, also with child's and adult's texts, uses the death of a bird and then of a grandfather as springboards for discussion of death appropriate for children three to eight years [28].

These texts, providing children with answers to their questions are excellent educational tools best used before the brush with death is experienced at close range. The didactic element is not camouflaged and, for that reason, they do not pretend to qualify as "literature" in the strict sense.

In children's fiction dealing with death, there is also an opportunity to explore the scientific facts of death. In a finely written, unsentimental novel by Virginia Lee, *The Magic Moth*, a ten-year-old girl, Maryanne Foss, dies of complications of a heart defect [29]. Early on, the question of what happens to a dead body occurs to her young brother. It is explained that it becomes part of the ground. Mark-O remembers his dead guinea pig and wants to dig him up. His mother urges him that the buried body "is the least important part" [29, p. 26].

The concept of dead people going on a journey from which they will return, a common belief in children three to five years, is addressed in a variety of ways. Close to the beginning of *The Magic Moth*, a ball bounces out of sight and young Mark-O thinks it will drop to China and return, just as his dying sister will. There are references to the myth of Proserpine returning from Hades every six months. These images fade, however, when Mark-O slowly realizes that his sister will, indeed, not come back. The harsh reality comes upon him as irrevocably as Charlotte's bleak statement in E. B. White's classic: "I shall not be coming back to the barn" [26, p. 173].

It is, however, the second and third categories—emotional and spiritual concerns—that I should like to examine in some detail. Virginia Lee's book, just mentioned, and a novel by a Canadian, Jean Little, *Mama's Going to Buy You a Mocking Bird*, provide excellent studies of both [30].

2. Emotional Problems

Emotional reactions to death and dying are, admittedly, extremely difficult to portray in any literature and most especially in books written for children. The gamut of emotions from denial and hostile reaction toward the dying loved one to a complete abandonment of grief is certainly all part of life and coping, but the aesthetic distance, the degree of sentimentality or reserve with which these emotions are presented in literature makes artistic creation a difficult business, indeed.

Jean Little's novel, *Mama's Going to Buy You a Mocking Bird*, deals with sensitive emotional states from the opening pages [30]. Sibling rivalry for parental affection, feelings of insecurity, fear, hostility, loneliness, and guilt: each is carefully presented in a leisurely exposition as brother and sister try to cope with the impending death of their father. At the funeral, the change in mother-son roles is addressed briefly:

> On their way into the funeral home, Mum was walking between them and holding Sarah's hand. She had not held his hand in public for a long time. Yet right then he wanted her to and suddenly it came to him that he was old enough now to take her hand, not because he needed to cling to her but because he knew she needed him to be close. When she felt his fingers curl around hers, Mum

glanced down at him and, as quickly looked away. She kept her head high and her shoulders straight. But their fingers stayed locked from that instant [30, p. 118].

All the facade is stripped away, however, in one brief but rhythmically poignant paragraph:

The calm he had been building up so carefully shattered. His breath came in ragged gasps. His hands tightened into fists. He was alone and his father was gone. Alone. Gone [30, p. 115].

Such deep emotional expression could so easily have been overdone. Jean Little is able to bring the wrenching scene to reality, suspend it momentarily, and then proceed immediately to consideration of other somewhat less painful matters.

What is being shown here is the absolute necessity, at some point, of giving into an inevitable outburst of emotion. The child reader must accept this as believable behavior and acceptance will depend upon the credible delineation of character, carefully built up from the beginning of the story: the reader must be able to sympathize with the *angst* of the protagonist.

How is emotional consolation satisfactorily expressed to the bereaved in children's literature? Writers for children seem to be overwhelmingly unanimous on this point.

First, there is the intensified bonding of family. In *The Magic Moth*, what the children learn from the untimely death of Maryanne is stated quite directly: "Mostly, I guess, how much we appreciate our family" [29, p. 56]. New role playing is stressed in *Mama's Going to Buy You a Mocking Bird* when Jeremy begins to assume a paternal protectiveness toward his mother and sister:

"You sounded like Daddy."
"I did not," he retorted automatically. He hadn't meant to. The words and the tone in which they were spoken had just come to him. Had he heard his father say them? He guessed he had [30, p. 165].

After family, it is friends and the meaning of friendship which supply the emotional sense of security in children's books. Friendship and the loss of a friend is a central theme in both St. Exupery's *The Little Prince* [11] and White's *Charlotte's Web* [26]. In *Mama's Going To Buy You a Mocking Bird* [30], Jeremy meets Tess, awkwardly tall and tomboyish; yet, gradually the two become close friends as each begins to understand the other's losses in life [30].

3. Spiritual Concerns

Part of the bereavement process involves finding consolation and ultimately new attitudes and new life. These may be described as "spiritual" concerns but in art, they are almost always expressed in concrete terms. Certain images—or symbols— become a part of the fabric of the novel, but also are an integral part of the reader's response and, ultimately, the experience in learning about death.

In Virginia Lee's novel, *The Magic Moth* [29], I mentioned earlier how there had been repeated reference to *things coming back:* a ball from China, a Prosperine returning from Hades for the summer months. As Mark-O's vision of reality extends and matures in his acceptance of the death of his sister, so the images in the novel begin to change. Instead of a ball bouncing back from China—remaining essentially the same ball in the process—there is the insistence on the miracle of a moth emerging from a cocoon. Grapefruit seeds planted spring up in a different form. It is not coincidental that, at the funeral, the minister's message is summed up in the sentence: "Life never ends—it just changes" [29, p. 45].

In examining a variety of children's books dealing with death, the most significant theme of reconciliation that emerges might be summarized as the need to accept change and to search for permanence in a world of shattered ideals. In Jean Little's novel, a game of Monopoly supplies some of this:

> Jeremy fetched the box from the pile of games. Mum won as usual. Although he said it wasn't fair, Jeremy found that he was secretly more glad than sorry. It was reassuring to know that some things didn't change [30, p. 133].

It is, however, through the recurrence of certain symbols, that the memory of the deceased persists more vividly. In *The Magic Moth*, it is the moth itself, which bursts from its cocoon and flies out of the window the moment Maryanne dies [29]. The moth becomes an obvious, but appropriate symbol of her soul emerging in glory from the dead cocoon body and, for that reason, it is dubbed the "magic moth." In *Mama's Going to Buy You a Mocking Bird* [30], the symbols are a carved stone owl (a present to Jeremy from his dying father), a foundling kitten, and a novel by Kipling, *Kim*. The owl is a remembrance of a special, shared experience between father and son when they encountered a live owl together, so that even before the death, the stone owl is taking on symbolic significance. When Jeremy's father goes to the hospital for the final time, the carved owl goes with him—on loan. After Mr. Talbot's death, the owl returns and Jeremy places it "behind his dictionary at the back of his desk . . . so that he wouldn't have to see it every time he looked up" [30, p. 178]. By the end of the novel, however, when the owl reappears, after having been mislaid, he is overjoyed to see it, acknowledges how much he has missed it, and sets it "where he would be sure to see it every time he looked up from his homework" [30, p. 201]. The owl becomes an index of Jeremy's heightened awareness and ability to cope as well as a symbol of permanence.

Other forms of consolation are to be found in the affirmation of life and living things. E. B. White's *Charlotte's Web* [26] spends the better part of a chapter describing in minute detail the emergence of new life in the spring; in *The Magic Moth*, the grapefruit seeds sprout into new growth; in *Mama's Going to Buy You a Mocking Bird* [30], the life-symbol is "Blue," the foundling cat, who was close to Jeremy's dead father and who brings new joy into the bereaved household.

The concept of death as part of the cycle of life is well used by White in *Charlotte's Web* [26], but does little to explain the untimely death of a child since the part of the novel dealing with Wilbur's slaughter never becomes a reality. Virginia

Lee addresses the problem in an interesting and, I believe, successful manner in *The Magic Moth* when she suggests a kind of determinism as a way of looking at death in another perspective:

> Mark-O had the strange feeling that everything that was happening was part of a Big Law that had to be obeyed. You could see all these unpleasant things getting ready to happen, but you couldn't keep them from happening. Even if you could, he guessed you wouldn't because you would have to stay behind while the rest of the family went on and that would be worse [29, p. 51].

This concrete application of a difficult philosophical problem also serves as a crucial aesthetic device to distance the emotional experience. It is a statement that is made many times in *King Lear* [31]; it is also a concern of many writers including such important novelists as George Eliot and Thomas Hardy.

In every level of artistic experience—intellectual, emotional, or spiritual—the success of literature will have primarily to do with the identification of the child reader with the protagonist. How the child relates to the difficult emotions and ideas expressed in the literature depends, in turn, on the excellence of the literature as art. The examples I have chosen, with their use of image and symbol, rhythmic prose, sensitive portrayal of emotion, and psychologically believable characterization are ample indication that such excellence is possible and, in the process, a handsome amount of education is provided as well. This is a long way from the brutal "Off with his head . . . Off with her head" of the Queen of Hearts in Lewis Carroll's *Alice in Wonderland* [20].

REFERENCES

1. J. Milton, *Lycidas*, in *The Norton Anthology of English Literature*, Vol. 1 (6th Edition), M. H. Abrams (ed.), Norton, New York, pp. 1450-1456, 1993.
2. P. B. Shelley, Adonis, in *The Norton Anthology of English Literature*, Vol. 2 (6th Edition), M. H. Abrams (ed.), Norton, New York, pp. 718-731, 1993.
3. M. Arnold, Thyrsis, in *The Norton Anthology of English Literature*, Vol. 2 (6th Edition), M. H. Abrams (ed.), Norton, New York, p. 1373, 1993.
4. Alfred, Lord Tennyson, In Memoriam, in *The Norton Anthology of English Literature*, Vol. 2 (6th Edition), M. H. Abrams (ed.), Norton, New York, pp. 1085-1132, 1993.
5. W. H. Auden, In Memory of W. B. Yeats, in *The Norton Anthology of English Literature*, Vol. 2 (6th Edition), M. H. Abrams (ed.), Norton, New York, 1993.
6. A. Purdy, Elegy for a Grandfather, in *Poets of Contemporary Canada*, E. Mandel (ed.), McClelland and Stewart, Toronto, Canada, 1982.
7. W. Shakespeare, *Cymbeline*, D. Bevington (ed.), Bantam, Toronto, 1982.
8. J. Shirley, The Glories of our Blood and State, in *Poetry*, E. Drew (ed.), Dell, New York, 1959.
9. G. Flaubert, *Madame Bovary*, A. Russell (trans.), Penguin, Harmondsworth, England.
10. L. Tolstoy, The Death of Ivan Ilych, in *The Experience of Literature*, L. Trilling (ed.), Holt, Rinehart, New York, 1967.
11. A. de Saint Exupery, *The Little Prince*, Harcourt Brace, New York, 1943.

12. M. Arnold, Growing Old, in *The Norton Anthology of English Literature,* Vol. 2 (6th Edition), M. H. Abrams (ed.), Norton, New York, 1993.
13. W. Shakespeare, *Measure for Measure,* D. Bevington (ed.), Bantam, Toronto, 1980.
14. J. Joyce, *A Portrait of the Artist as a Young Man,* Viking Press, New York, 1960.
15. J. Donne, Holy Sonnet No. 10, in *The Norton Anthology of English Literature,* Vol. 1 (6th Edition), M. H. Abrams (ed.), Norton, New York, 1993.
16. M. Laurence, *The Stone Angel,* McClelland and Stewart, Toronto, 1970.
17. D. Thomas, Do Not Go Gentle into that Good Night, in *The Norton Anthology of English Literature,* Vol. 2 (6th Edition), M. H. Abrams (ed.), Norton, New York, 1993.
18. W. Shakespeare, *Antony and Cleopatra,* M. Spevack (ed.), Modern Language Association of America, New York, 1990.
19. G. Manley Hopkins, Spring and Fall: To a Young Child, in *The Norton Anthology of English Literature,* Vol. 2 (6th Edition), M. H. Abrams (ed.), Norton, New York, 1993.
20. L. Carroll, *The Adventures of Alice In Wonderland,* Norton, New York, 1991.
21. E. Lear, *A Book of Bosh,* Puffin, Harmondsworth, England, 1975.
22. Sir James Barrie, *Peter Pan,* Grosset and Dunlop, New York, 1965.
23. M. Twain, *Huckleberry Finn,* Norton, New York, 1962.
24. R. L. Stevenson, *Treasure Island,* Ryerson, Toronto, 1962.
25. K. Grahame, *The Wind in the Willows,* Signet, New York, 1969.
26. E. B. White, *Charlotte's Web,* Dell, New York, 1952.
27. E. Grollman, *Talking About Death: A Dialogue Between Parent and Child* (2nd Edition), Beacon Press, Boston, 1976.
28. S. Bonnett Stein, *About Dying: An Open Family Book for Parents and Children Together,* Walker, New York, 1974.
29. V. Lee, *The Magic Moth,* Sexbury Press, New York, 1992.
30. J. Little, *Mama's Going to Buy you a Mocking Bird,* Penguin, Markham, Ontario, 1984.
31. W. Shakespeare, *King Lear.*

CHAPTER 5
Some Notes in Aid of Thinking about Music and Death

Rev. Ronald Trojcak

> How to write about music? Find words and grammar to communicate the musical fact? Can language ever tell us what music means—where the notion of "meaning" is itself a kind of helpless analogy? At least ninety percent of what is written about music is impressionistic twaddle [1].
>
> George Steiner

In support of Steiner's contention, let me suggest the following experience. I read a review of a recording or a performance of a piece of music. And then I *hear* the piece itself. The language of review and the experience of hearing the music are widely disproportionate if not altogether disconnected. I think this experience is not only common, but is the normal one. So in the first part of this chapter I want to try to explain why this disproportion or disconnection appears, and what significance this has for a discussion of music and death.

It is probably simplest to begin by comparing the "musical experience" with experience of all other arts: painting, sculpture, dance, drama, and all diverse forms of literature. Several things seem clear. There is certainly a gap between reading about a piece of sculpture and the sensuous experience of feeling its contours and texture. And this is true, to a greater or lesser extent in the case of all arts. Nevertheless, I can meaningfully speak of death as either an item within, or the centerpiece of, any of these art forms. A corpse can be painted or modeled in wood or stone; mortality can be the subject of a dramatic dialogue; the poet can lament the loss of a parent or lover. And even in the gestural language of dance, grief can be imaged, and death can even be literally mimicked. In a word, in all these instances there can be clear if polyvalent connections with, by the way of reference to, death. This is possible despite the enormous variety of the shapes of those references. And there is an equally rich variety of responses to artistic expressions of death. Who has not enjoyed even a bit of "gallow's humour," or been moved to tears at the death of a heroine, or to satisfaction at the death of a villain?

And this is true even if, as is necessary, large allowances are made for those artistic expressions which are self-consciously produced and proclaimed as abstract. In these cases, seemingly any reference to a reality beyond that of the artwork itself is discounted. Here, the shapes or colors are self-referential. Such aesthetic quality as these works have, derive from the inner-relationships of the work, or they refer only to earlier instances of shape or color in the history of a given art. (In the case of any of the verbal arts, I suspect that such pure abstraction from objects outside the work itself is much more difficult, although some poets might disagree.)

But the case is massively different when one tries talking about music. I think this is the point of Steiner's sagacious comment. It seems that of its very nature, music, the basic elements of which are only pitch and rhythm, is non-referential. Or at the very least music is not referential in anything like the conventional sense. That is, music is not so either in the same way or to the same degree that any of the other arts are. Verbal language used to speak about music, more often than not, misleads and so fails because it too quickly attempts to make music refer to anything *in a way* that is non-musical. This is why music critics can so often be justifiably accused of selling snake-oil, or of simple self-promotion. Even the verbal language which seeks to describe the technical qualities of a musical performance, e.g., that would speak of it as "crisp" or "slovenly," is obviously highly analogical, and at its most effective, is merely suggestive.

One can, of course, speak of a piece of music as imitative of, or otherwise influenced by another piece or style of music. When a writer speaks of the melodies of Andrew Lloyd Weber's work as "derivative" form Puccini and Strauss, I understand what the writer is saying. And many great composers write in reference to another, usually greater composer's work. Heitor Villa Lobos' "Bachianas Brasileiras" are a clear and conscious act of homage to the music of J. S. Bach. And most amateur pianists have attempted to play, say, a popular song "in the style" of Mozart or Beethoven. In all these cases we know what is going on. But the crucial point is this: the referents in all these cases are purely musical ones.

The problem of music's referential capability is even sharper when the reference becomes more specific. And this is exactly our problem. How can we speak of music as referring to death? (Just for the moment we will ignore musical settings of texts.) To address the most likely instances of music referring to something outside itself, we need to look at the case of so-called "program" music. This is music explicitly written to "describe" some non-musical reality. The instances here are numerous. Some famous ones: Mussorgsky's *Pictures at an Exhibition*; Richard Strauss' tone poems, e.g., *Don Juan,* or a *Hero's Life;* Smetana's *the Molddau;* Beethoven's Sixth Symphony, the *Pastorale;* many of Debussy's piano pieces. (I suppose the most famous attempt to use music to point to extra-musical realities, is the Disney film, *Fantasia.*) However, I suggest that one's enjoyment of any of this music is neither increased nor decreased by knowing the program. It may even be true that such knowledge interferes with really hearing the music well at all.

But the problem of the relationship between music and death might seem to be "solved" or at least simplified, when we look at vocal music: music which accompanies a text. (In fact I hope to develop a possibility which emerges from this consideration, for making certain modest proposals later on about the relationship between music and death.) The amount of musical material bearing texts touching on death is enormous. Probably in Western music, the prime instance of such music is the Requiem Mass. This is a musical setting of the texts of the funeral service of the Roman Church. (The word "requiem" is simply the first word sung in this service.) I think it is safe to assume that the people who wrote music to carry texts having to do with death, or with anything else for that matter, make their musical choices "under the influence" of these texts, and so, of their referential power. But we need to keep in mind that that "power" is largely dependent upon the quality of the texts.

In the case of music bearing texts about death we can attempt an assessment of the adequacy of the music as a vehicle for the text. How well does the music accommodate the text? This is a question that seems to me to be legitimately askable. If nothing else, the occurrence of a singularly inept mating of text and tune itself raises the question. (For example, I have always been put off by Handel's jolly choral declaration, in his "Messiah," that "we like sheep have gone astray.") There would appear to be a number of applicable criteria: e.g., the matching of word rhythms with the music's own rhythmic movement; the placing of emphasis, by the way of pitch or volume, on one word or another; the pace (tempo) at which the words are sung; the correlation of accented syllables with the shape of melody. Those songs which we consider classic, such as *April in Paris,* or *September Song,* or Anton Bruckner's setting of the *Te Deum,* are regarded as classic because most people feel the texts and tunes are well-matched. The point I wish to make here is this: the power and impact of a text can be amplified, intensified, deepened by its successful musical setting. Conversely, that power can also be diminished or destroyed by an ill-suited tune.

This fact, in turn, illumines another element which I see as critical to any discussion of the relationship of death and music which would be more than "impressionistic twaddle." This element has to do with the very nature of music. I repeat here what I suggested earlier: to understand music as pictorial, as being somehow able to refer to an extra-musical reality in some literal fashion, is to miss the very musicality of music. Indeed, if music were pictorial, we could reasonably ask, why bother with music at all? It would seem to be also true that a picture is worth more than a thousand notes of music. Furthermore, even if it were pictorial, music would be merely a curiosity, like a model of the Eifel tower made of tooth-picks, and not the soul-shattering reality we sometimes experience music to be.[1] But I must return to this business of the nature of music. To speak of the aptness of a musical setting of a text, or of the further empowering of a text by music, suggests that music *is* referential, but in a uniquely musical way. (Thus, music is not just a matter of pitches and rhythms playing with themselves.) Instead, I propose that music arises, however

---

[1] Even those art forms which seem to represent reality, e.g., photography, or the magical realist school of painting, do not do so literally. Precisely as art, these media are also transformations of the realities to which they refer.

mysteriously and however remotely, as a response to reality. Music is thus somehow rooted in one's experience, one's interaction with the world. *The transformative process whereby experience comes to be musically expressed, so far as I know, remains inexplicable.* But it should be clear that, just because we cannot explain something, our incapacity does not mean that that "something" does not exist. Now the "usual" form of human response to the world is expressed in words, in language. What I would like to suggest is this: to understand music as language is the most fruitful basis for understanding and/or theorizing about music. But for our present purpose, such a way of understanding music opens the possibility of a "post-twaddle" way of thinking and speaking about music.

Let me summarize what I hope we have accomplished so far. Music is not ersatz literature, or photography. Nor is music a purely self-referential undertaking (it is "about" more than just sonic frequencies and rhythms interacting). Therefore, music does in some way "refer" to something outside itself. It is an expressive response to extra-musical reality and it is so whether this expression is conscious or unconscious, intentional or unintentional. (It is useful to remember that one's hopes and fantasies are also real.) So, in some way, music can "refer" to death.

Although the case of text-bearing music is the easiest and most obvious instance, I suggest that "pure," i.e., non-verbal music, can also "deal" with death.[2]

At this point I would like to introduce a final set of categories for trying to think about, and judge the aptitude of, one piece of music over another, as a response to death. That this is actually the case is undeniable: we do in fact choose one piece of music over another. An example: I doubt that anyone who heard it, would have denied the impact of Leonard Bernstein and the strings of the New York Philharmonic playing the *Adagietto* of Mahler's *Fifth Symphony* at the funeral of Robert Kennedy. I also doubt that anyone would have not been altogether upset if "Chopsticks," or even *the Funeral March of a Marionette*[3] had been played instead. But our question is: why? Why a different response? More pointedly: what is the difference in the music? I hope we can sharpen the question by making another suggestion. Bernstein could have played any number of movements from Mahler symphonies. They were all in his repertory. The First Symphony and the Second both contain funeral marches, music which on Mahler's own testimony, are conscious responses to death. But if one were to listen to these three pieces, the aptness of the *Adagietto* becomes evident. So the question again is: why this aptness? What is present in this music that is not present, or present to a different degree or kind, in the other music? Finally, here is my reading of the difference. The response to reality in the *Adagietto* comes from a far greater existential depth than do the other two

---

[2] Here I want only to advert to the fact of vastly different cultural forms, which is to say that all artistic references are the expressions of the peculiar way of experiencing reality that is the essence of a given culture.

[3] This piece, by Charles Gounod, is likely unfamiliar by its title, but equally likely familiar as the theme music for Alfred Hitchcock's television series.

movements. One might well suspect that in suggesting this we have indeed fully entered the realm of twaddle-dom. But let me try to explain.

It is normal for us to use the metaphor of depth in speaking of things human, just as we also readily use the metaphor shallowness in the same regard. By depth or shallowness I think we are referring to what is closest to or most remote from what most people understand or intuit as essential to our humanity. There is a core to *the human* and we can live closer to or farther from that core. We can respond from the center of our humanity, or from some surface (superficial) point, and from all the intervening points as well. The process of maturing, for example, is best understood as the growth and development of that core.[4] We judge the quality of our own and others' lives by the extent to which we live from and consistent with our depths.

If all this is true, however vague it may appear, and difficult to articulate, this means that, at least in principle, we should be able to distinguish between musical responses which come from greater or lesser depths as well. We should, again at least in principle, be able to distinguish between pieces of music which "respond to," are somehow expressive of more important human realities.[5] Certainly our awareness of death lies at the heart of our humanity, and may even be the chief characteristic of what it is to be human,[6] just as the capacity to create the language of music is one of the hallmarks of humanity as well.[7]

In conclusion: what have all these words about music yielded? I hoped to have established the following: a hermeneutic of suspicion is altogether appropriate regarding any discussion of the relationship between death and music. The relationship is too subtle and too complex for any straightforward or facile reading of it. Nevertheless, such a relationship does exist, and post-twaddle discourse on it is possible. But such discourse must be self-consciously discourse "about" a phenomenon which is ultimately beyond verbalization. In this sense, such discourse is analogous to that discourse on God we call theology. Next, the category of "existential depth" is a useful one in framing that discourse. And finally, that category can be employed, by the right hands and with the requisite caution to

---

[4] Here I am assuming the existence of human universals. The experience of death; love; loss; hope; fear; the creation of meaning; all artistic creation: it is the universality of these phenomena and the highly diverse cultural forms they take which give the grounds for the categories of depth and shallowness.

[5] Here is another group of factors which must also be considered in thinking about this matter. Clearly the musical skill of a composer is of critical importance. So in her/his human maturity as well as their own age. It is no surprise that Richard Strauss wrote his tone poem, "Till Eulenspiegel" with its mocking, detached reference to death when Strauss was very young. This same composer's "Four Last Songs," were written a year before he died at the age of eighty-five.

[6] In speaking of "awareness of death," it should be clear that this awareness can be quite diffuse (e.g., a sensitivity to the ephemeral quality of all things in life) or quite specific (e.g., awareness occasioned by the death of a parent, spouse, child, lover.) In other words there is an enormous spectrum of such "awareness." And the range of the forms of death is also enormous. We are, for example, just beginning to recover music written by prisoners in Hitler's death camps, and there is a growing body of music explicitly written in response to deaths caused by AIDS.

[7] Olivier Messiaen and Francois Couperin (among many) have used the "songs" of birds in their compositions. But no birds have used Messiaen or Couperin to expand their, i.e., the birds' repertoire.

distinguish the quality of musical responses to death. All this is little enough, but it is something.

REFERENCE

1. G. Steiner, Food of Love, *New Yorker*, p. 85, July 24, 1995.

CHAPTER 6

Patterns of Bereavement in Indian and English Society

Pittu Laungani

INTRODUCTION

Let us start with a truism.

Children are the inheritors and the custodians of the future. Whether the child is one of the many unfortunate ones from the appalling slums of Dharavi in Bombay, or one of the few privileged ones from Buckingham Palace, makes not the slightest difference. For when they die, the future dies with them and gets into the past. In that sense therefore, the death of a child is the most traumatic event in any parent's life. The resultant grief, sorrow, pain, and suffering experienced by the bereaved at the death of their loved ones—children or adults—are universal affective states. As far as one knows, no society, no culture is exempt from such emotional feelings and experiences [1]. What is different, however, is the process and pattern of bereavement and the way in which it is manifested. This of course varies from culture to culture and from group to group. Even within a single culture, one observes variations in the patterns and processes of bereavement. This chapter serves a twofold aim. First, we shall look at the familial and socio-situational factors related to patterns of bereavement in India. Second, in order to explain the salient values and behaviors which underlie mourning and bereavement practices in India and in England we shall present a conceptual model. This will enable us to examine the similarities and differences in the process of bereavement between English and Indian societies.

FAMILIAL AND SOCIO-SITUATIONAL FACTORS

How the parents react to the death of their child, how long the period of mourning lasts, is related to several factors, of which the following two merit a brief discussion:

1. Sex of the child
2. Age and ordinal position of the child

1. Sex of the Child

The sex of the child plays an extremely important part in understanding the extent and severity of mourning. In India the death of a male child is taken far more seriously than the death of a female child, for a variety of reasons. Male children are potentially dowry earners. Given the continuation of the extended family system, most Indian parents see boys as future economic assets. There is a strong cultural expectation that when parents become old and infirm they shall be taken care of and looked after by their sons. There is a religious element too which needs to be considered. In accordance with Hindu scriptures only sons can and are expected to light the funeral pyre and perform the last funeral rites of their parents in order to ensure the repose of the souls of their departed parents [2]. Finally, as is common to most societies all over the world, it is only through the sons that the family lineage gets perpetuated.

In the event of the death of a female child, the situation changes significantly. Although female children are seen as pledges of honor, and it is the sacred duty, or "dharma" of parents to discharge the pledge by having their daughters handsomely married, the death of female child, may, in certain instances, be perceived as a relief. The iniquitous dowry system, although banned by an Act of Parliament, is a custom, more honored in the breach than the observance. Dowries can very seriously cripple a family of even more than humble means. Several studies have shown that the dissatisfaction with the dowry received can lead to very tragic consequences for the bride—leading in some cases to her death—and her family.

2. Age and Ordinal Position of the Child

Perinatal death and deaths within the first one or two years of the infant's life seldom arouse the same depth of sorrow as when older children die. However, the factor of age by itself tells us very little. It needs to be examined in relation to the ordinal position of the child that dies. One needs to determine if it is the first child, the only child, or the sixth or seventh, or eighth child in the family. If it is one of many, the parents soon come to accept the loss of their child as an inevitable fact of life. The extremely high under-five infant mortality rates (U5MR 154 per 1000 births) creates in Indian parents a belief that not all their children will survive. Death, as was stated earlier, is a commonplace occurrence. This belief is further reinforced by the fact that 40 percent of the urban population and 51 percent of the rural population live below the absolute poverty level [3]. It is only natural that some children will die of malnutrition and other infectious diseases. Safety therefore lies in numbers, in having more children, in the hope that the sturdy or the lucky ones will survive.

It is hardly surprising therefore that pregnancies in India are seldom carefully planned. It is in fact the marriages which are carefully planned and arranged by the parents in India. Not the pregnancies. Pregnancies occur soon after marriage—

almost as an inevitable consequence. And they occur at a very early age too. This is because children in India are married early—and in many cases even *before* they reach their recognized legal age of eighteen years. Instances of child marriages too are not as uncommon as might seem at first sight. Thus if a child were to die when the mother was in her teens, it would not be seen as a great calamity, for within another eighteen months, or even less, the mother could have another baby.

CONCEPTUAL MODEL OF CULTURAL DIFFERENCES

To understand the differential patterns of bereavement in Western (English) and Eastern (Indian) societies, four factors from which hypotheses have been deduced and tested by Sachdev [4] and Sookhoo [5], have been postulated. The factors are:

Individualism—Communalism
Cognitivism—Emotionalism
Free Will—Determinism
Materialism—Spiritualism

It should be noted that the two concepts underlying each factor are *not* dichotomous; they are to be understood as extending along a *continuum*, starting at, say, Individualism at one end, and extending into Communalism at the other. It is suggested that the salient attitudes, values and behaviors of groups of people may be more Individualism-oriented and less Communalism-oriented; and vice-versa. In fact, the salient values, and behaviors can be represented at any point along the continuum, and may, over time, change in either direction.

Before discussing each factor, it needs to be pointed out that the concepts to the *left* of each factor are applicable more to the English and those on the *right* to the Indians. Let us now examine each concept briefly.

Let us now turn to Individualism—Communalism. One of the distinguishing features of Western society is its increasing emphasis on Individualism. The English family structure, particularly from the postwar period onward has undergone a dramatic change. The nuclear family structure has come to be recognized as the norm. With the gradual increase in one-parent families, at present around 14 percent (as a caveat, it should be pointed out that as a result of the diverse and often incompatible procedures of gathering social statistics, these figures are not as clear-cut as is sometimes made out to be) combined with the fact that just under 25 percent of the population live alone—the present nuclear family structure, over the ensuing years, is likely to change even more dramatically.

The concept of individualism has been the subject of considerable debate among Western thinkers such as Bellah [6], Lukes [7], Waterman [8]. It has been argued by some of the writers mentioned above that the notions of individualism are incompatible, even antithetical with communal interests. Self-realization which is the basis of individualism, conflicts with communal interests [9].

How does the notion of Individualism affect our understanding of bereavement?

1. Individualism tends to create conditions which *do not permit an easy sharing of one's problems and worries with others*. As Albert Camus pointed out several years ago, individualism creates in people an existential loneliness, compounded by a sense of the absurd [10]. The emphasis on self-reliance, the expectation of being able to cope with one's problems, imposes severe stress on the individual. The bereaved family is not only expected to overcome its grief and loss by itself, but it is likely to be left alone.
2. One of the dominant features of Individualism is its recognition of and respect for an individuals "physical and psychological space." People do not normally touch one another, for that is seen as an encroachment of one's physically defined boundaries. Even eye-to-eye contacts are normally avoided. Several studies have shown that the effects of violating another person's physical space lead to severe stress and in extreme cases, to neurosis.

"Psychological space" is concerned with defining boundaries which separate the psychological self from others. It is an idea of immense value in the West, respected in all social situations. It comes into play in all social encounters, from the most casual to the most intimate. One hears of people feeling "threatened," "upset," "angry," "awkward," "confused," etc., when they feel that their subjectively defined space is invaded. The bereavement in the family is perceived as primarily an individual problem, of sole concern to the affected family. One does not intrude, for fear of invading the other person's "psychological" space. As has been pointed out elsewhere, the notion of physical and psychological space is closely related to the concept of privacy [11]. Privacy implies a recognition of and respect for another person's individuality. Several studies have demonstrated that the invasion of privacy leads to severe stress [12].

Indian society on the other hand has been and continues to be community-oriented (Kakar [2], Lannoy [13], Laungani [14, 15, 16], Mandelbaum [17], Sinari [18]). Most Indians—both Hindus and Muslims—grow up and live in an *extended family* network. Indian society cannot be seen in other than familial and communal terms. It is and has been for centuries a family-oriented and community-based society. Consequently when a problem affects an individual it affects the entire family, and if the problem is acute or important enough it affects the community of which the family is an integral part. The problem becomes one of concern for the whole family. Seldom does one see personalized "private" problems.

It may be of passing interest to note that Indians, in their day-to-day speech often use the collective pronoun "we." The use of the term we or "hum" in Hindi and Urdu signifies the suppression of one's personal ego into the collective ego of one's family and community. One speaks with the collective voice of others, and in so doing gains their approval [19].

However, it needs to be pointed out that for an individual to stay part of the family and of the community, it is expected that the individual will submit to communal norms, and will not deviate to an extent where it becomes necessary for the deviant to be ostracized. The pressure to conform to family norms and expectations can of course have adverse effects on individual members in the family, leading, in some instances, to psychotic disorders and hysteria [20, 21]. As we saw earlier the extended family network provide the bereaved inbuilt safety measures.

The next factor Cognitivism—Emotionalism, is concerned with the way in which the British and the Indians construe their private and social worlds. In broad terms it has been suggested by Pande [22] that Indian society is *relationship-centred*, and British society, *work-and-activity-centred*. These different constructions of their private and social worlds are not accidental cultural developments. They stem from their inheritance of their different philosophical legacies.

In a work-and-activity-centered society, people are more likely to operate on a *cognitive* mode, where the emphasis is on rationality, logic, and control. Public expression of feelings and emotions—particularly among the middle classes—is often frowned upon. It causes embarrassment, and in certain social classes, is even seen as being vulgar. In such a society, relationships are formed on the basis of shared commonalities. One is expected to work at a relationship—in a marriage, in a family situation, with one's colleagues at work, and even with friends at a social level. Even at dinner parties, one is expected—to use an Americanism—to "sing for one's dinner," and one's performance at the table determines whether one shall "be written," kept on ice, or reinvited. Obviously in a work-and-activity-centered society, a need arises for the creation of professional and semi-professional settings which permit the legitimate expression of specific feelings and emotions, and their handling by experts trained in the specific area. Thus one sees in Western society the growth of specialist counselors, including bereavement counselors, cancer counselors, AIDS counselors, marriage guidance counselors, family therapists, rational-emotive therapists, and last but not least, the psychotherapists and psychoanalysts of different theoretical persuasions.

A relationship-centered society, on the other hand, is more likely to operate on an *emotional* mode. In such a society, feelings and emotions are *not* repressed, and their expression in general is not frowned upon. Crying, dependence on others—both in females and males—excessive emotionality are not in any way considered as signs of weakness.

Above all, in a relationship-centered society, no agenda of shared commonalities is necessary for the cultivation of a relationship. Since feelings and emotions—both positive and negative—are expressed easily, there is little danger of treading incautiously on others' sensibilities or vulnerabilities. Given the extended-family structure of relationships, emotional outbursts are, as it were, "taken on board" by the family members. Often the emotional outbursts are symbolic, even ritualistic. To appreciate fully the ritualistic component of emotional outbursts among Indians, be they Hindus or Muslims, one must visualize it against the backdrop of the living conditions in India. In the urban areas—for those who are fortunate enough to live in a "puka" house—it is not uncommon for a family of eight to ten persons to be living together in one small room. Given the extreme closeness of life, the paucity of amenities, the total lack of privacy, the inertia evoked by the overpowering heat and dust, the awesome feeling of claustrophobia, it is not at all surprising that families do quarrel, fight, and swear at one another (and from time to time assault one another too). But their quarrels and outbursts are often of a symbolic nature, for otherwise, such quarrels would lead to a permanent rift, the consequences of which would be far more traumatic than of those living together. There is in such emotional outbursts a surrealistic quality; for at one level, they appear stark and real, the words and abuses hurled at one another are often vicious, callous, and hurtful, yet at another level, bewilderingly unreal. Emotional outbursts, to a large measure, serve no function other than the cathartic relief which such outbursts bring.

Let us now examine the factor Free Will—Determinism. There does not appear to be a satisfactory end in sight to the philosophical and scientific wrangles concerning the nature of free will, predestination, determinism, and indeterminism. The Aristotelean legacy, although it has undergone several transformations, has remained with us for over two thousand years [23]. Prior to Newton's spectacular achievements, determinism was enmeshed in its theistic and metaphysical connotations. After the publication of Newton's *Principia* in 1687, the concept of determinism was partially freed from its theistic connotations and a non-theistic and mechanistic view of determinism in science, and indeed in the universe, gained prominence. A scientific notion of determinism, with its emphasis on causality, or conversely, its denial of non-casual events, found favor among the rationalist philosophers who embraced it with great fervor [24]. However, it was not until the emergence of quantum mechanics in the early twentieth century that determinism in science, if not in human affairs, once again came to be seriously questioned. In keeping with his own views on the subject, Popper avoids the term determinism and free will altogether [25]. He proposes instead, the term indeterminism, which he argues is not the opposite of determinism nor is it the same as free will.

Notwithstanding the unresolved debates in philosophy on the subject, *there is a peculiar dualism in Western thinking concerning free will and determinism* [26]. Scientific research in medicine, psychiatry, biology, and other related disciplines, including psychology, is still based on the acceptance of a deterministic framework—hence the concern with seeking casual explanations and with predictability in accordance with rational scientific procedures of prediction. Yet, at a social commonsense level there is a strong belief in the notion of free will.

Free will might be defined as a *non-casual, voluntary action*. However, at a commonsense level it suggests responsibility for one's actions, or control over one's actions. Thus free will allows an individual to do what he/she wills, and in so doing, take "credit" for his/her successes, and accept blame for his/her failures and mishaps. This feature of Western society by which a person is held responsible for his/her own actions, entraps a person into his or her own existential predicament. There does not appear to be an easy way out.

Indians, by virtue of subscribing to a deterministic view of life, in a teleological sense at least, are prevented from taking final responsibility for their own actions. The notion of determinism plays an extremely crucial role in Indian thinking. *The law of karma* which involves determinism and fatalism has shaped the Indian view of life over centuries [18, 27, 28]. In its simplest form, the *law of karma* states that happiness or sorrow—there is no equivalent word for depression in Hindi or in Sanskrit—is the predetermined effect of actions committed by individuals sometimes either in their present life or in one of their numerous past lives. Things do not happen because *we* make them happen. Things happen because they were destined to happen. If one's present life is determined by one's actions in one's previous life, it follows that the untimely death of a child in a family, was *destined* to happen. "God willed it" is the most commonly accepted form of rationalization among Indians.

A belief in determinism and the *law of karma* also takes the venom out of the sting of suffering. It also engenders in the Indian psyche, a spirit of passive, if not resigned, acceptance. This prevents a person from plunging into an abyss of despair—a state from which the English, because of their fundamental belief in the doctrine of free-will, cannot be protected. The main disadvantage of determinism—and there are many—lies in the fact that it may occasionally lead to a state of existential, and in certain instances, moral resignation, compounded by a profound sense of *inertia*. One takes no proactive measures; one merely accepts the vicissitudes of life without qualm, if not with equanimity. It is clear that there is in the Indian psyche an unquestioning acceptance of life and all its vicissitudes, including illness, misfortunes, natural disasters, calamities, and death.

Let us turn to the last factor: Materialism—Spiritualism refers to a belief in the existence of a material world, or a world composed of matter. What constitutes matter is itself debatable, and the assumed solidity of matter is in itself a myth [29]. Such debates, however, are confined to scientific journals and journals of philosophy, while the popular myth that all explanations of phenomenon ranging from lunar cycles to lunacy, from cot-death to cancer, need to be sought within the materialist framework, gets perpetuated within the medical profession. Non-material explanations are treated at best with scepticism, and at worst with scorn. Interestingly enough, the belief in a materialist philosophy often undergoes a dramatic transformation when examined within the context of death and bereavement. It is not at all unusual to see that under such circumstances one's rationally acquired beliefs in a materialist philosophy are jettisoned, and emotional beliefs concerning spiritualism—e.g., the survival of the spirit after the dissolution of the body, the permanence of the spirit, the resting of the soul, etc.—are salvaged. While spiritualism is firmly kept out of the front door, it gains a surreptitious entry through the back door. Indian thinking on the other hand remains unperturbed by such dilemmas.

The notion of *materialism,* so vital in the *West,* is a relatively unimportant concept in Indian thinking. Indian beliefs and values revolve round the notion *Spiritualism.* The ultimate purpose of human existence is to transcend one's illusory physical existence, renounce the world of material aspirations, and attain a heightened state of spiritual awareness. Any activity which is likely to promote such a state is to be encouraged. For it is through transcendence—inward-seeking consciousness—that one is able to attain salvation or *moksha.*

The external world to Indians is not composed of matter. The external world is seen as being *illusory.* It is *maya.* Unfettered by materialistic boundaries, the

Indian mind resorts to explanations where material and spiritual, physical and metaphysical, natural and supernatural explanations of phenomenon coexist with one another. What to a Western mind might seem an irreconcilable contradiction, leaves an Indian mind relatively unperturbed. As Sinari says, "For the lacuna between the superstitious and the critical, the naive and the reflective, the mythological and the scientific, is almost nonexistent in Indian consciousness" [18, pp. 6-7]. To a Westerner if A is A, A cannot then be not-A. If the death of a child is caused by unknown, unexplained viruses, it cannot be caused by the influence of the "evil-eye." The two are logically and empirically incompatible. But the Indians do not shy away from such contradictions. A is not only A, but under certain conditions, A may be not-A. Ambiguity, as Sinari points out, is an inseparable accompaniment of the inward-seeking consciousness [18].

For instance, a woman living in India may accept a firmly established system of folk "theories" as to what constitutes illness and its causes. The belief system which she takes for granted is the one which is culturally accepted in her country. To her, the death of her child might seem to be the definite influence of the "evil eye," and although it might have been diagnosed as due to bacteria by an Indian doctor trained in Western medicine, her view would be unlikely to be subjected to ridicule. The two views—the natural and the supernatural—would reside side by side. Over time, the woman in question may come around to believing that her child's death was caused by armies of unknown, unseen "germs." Thus the bacteriological view might ultimately come to prevail. But whether she does or does not come around to accepting the bacteriological view, her own views concerning the causes of her child's death are the ones which find ready acceptance among her own people and within her own community. In England however, the same Indian woman would find herself out of step and out of sympathy were she to persist in supernatural explanations of her child's death.

In keeping with the notion of spiritualism, the causes of illness, disease, and even death in India are also explained in the terms sorcery, bewitchment, and evil spirits [30]. The belief in magical explanations is widespread, and persons specially qualified to remove spells, exorcise evil-spirits such as *bhoots, balas,* and *shaitans* are summoned by the family members of the afflicted persons to come to terms with their loss [30]. Faith-healers, mystics, shamans, pirs, bhagats, gurus, yogis, practitioners of ayrvedic, and homeopathic medicine, are accorded the same respect and veneration as the doctors trained in Western medicine.

CONCLUSION

Clearly, no culture or no society has all the answers concerning the ideal way of mourning and recovering speedily and positively from the death of ones loved ones—if there is an ideal way to recover. It is only when cultures meet—on equal terms and as equal partners—and express a genuine willingness to learn from each other, that one might find tentative answers to the questions which concern us all. But for the West to assume that there is little or nothing which they might profitably learn from Eastern cultures, many of which have sustained and perpetuated themselves for over four thousand years, is precisely the kind of attitude which is inimical to a genuine cross-cultural understanding.

"There are," as Hamlet exclaimed, "more things in heaven and earth, than are dreamt of in your philosophy."

REFERENCES

1. P. C. Rosenblatt, Grief in Small-Scale Societies, in *Death and Bereavement Across Cultures,* C. M. Parkes, P. Laungani, and B. Young (eds.), Routledge, London, 1996 (in press).
2. S. Kakar, *The Inner World—A Psychoanalytic Study of Children and Society in India,* Oxford University Press, Delhi, 1981.
3. P. Gupte, *The Challenge for Change,* Methuen, London, 1989.
4. D. Sachdev, *Effects of Psychocultural Factors on the Socialisation of British Born Indian Children and Indigenous British Children Living in England,* unpublished doctoral dissertation, South Bank University, London, 1992.
5. D. Sookhoo, *A Comparative Study of the Health Beliefs and Health Practices of British Whites and Asian Adults with and without Myocardial Infarction,* paper read at the 53rd Annual Convention of the International Council of Psychologists, Taipei, Taiwan, August 1995.
6. R. N. Bellah, *Habits of the Heart: Individuation and Commitment in American Life,* University of California Press, Berkeley, 1985.
7. S. Lukes, *Individualism,* Basil Blackwell, Oxford, 1973.
8. A. A. Waterman, Individualism and Interdependence, *American Psychologist, 36,* pp. 762-773, 1981.
9. D. Archard, The Marxist Ethic of Self-Realization: Individuality and Community, in *Moral Philosophy and Contemporary Problems,* J. D. G. Evans (ed.), Cambridge University Press, Cambridge, 1987.
10. A. Camus, *The Myth of Sisyphus,* Hamish Hamilton, London, 1955.
11. P. Laungani, Stress in Eastern and Western Cultures, in *Stress and Emotion, Vol. 15,* J. Brebner, E. Greenglass, P. Laungani, and A. O'Roark (eds.), Taylor and Francis, Washington, D.C., pp. 265-280, 1995.
12. C. Spielberger, *Understanding Stress and Anxiety,* Harper and Row, London, 1979.
13. R. Lannoy, *The Speaking Tree,* Oxford University Press, Oxford, 1976.
14. P. Laungani, Accidents in Children—An Asian Perspective, *Public Health, 103,* pp. 171-176, 1989.
15. P. Laungani, Cultural Differences in Stress: Indian and England, *Counselling Psychology Review, 9*(4), pp. 25-37, 1994.
16. P. Laungani, Patterns of Bereavement in Indian and English Societies, *Bereavement Care, 14*(1), pp. 5-7, 1995.
17. D. G. Mandelbaum, *Society in India, Vol. 2,* University of California Press, California, 1972.
18. R. A. Sinari, *The Structure of Indian Thought,* Oxford University Press, Delhi, 1984.
19. P. Laungani, Cultural Variations in the Understanding and Treatment of Psychiatric Disorders: India and England, *Counselling and Clinical Psychology Quarterly, 5*(3), pp. 231-244, 1992.

20. S. M. Channabasavanna and R. S. Bhatti, A Study on Interactional Patterns and Family Typologies in Families of Mental Patients, in *Readings in Transcultural Psychiatry*, A. Kiev and V. Rao (eds.), Higginsbothams, Madras, pp. 149-161, 1982.
21. B. B. Sethi and R. Manchanda, Family Structure and Psychiatric Disorders, *Indian Journal of Psychiatry, 20,* pp. 238-288, 1978.
22. S. Pande, The Mystique of "Western" Psychotherapy: An Eastern Interpretation, *The Journal of Nervous and Mental Disease, 146,* pp. 425-432, June 1968.
23. A. Flew, *An Introduction to Western Philosophy,* Thames and Hudson, German Democratic Republic, 1989.
24. K. Popper, *Objective Knowledge: An Evolutionary Approach,* The Clarendon Press, Oxford, 1972.
25. K. Popper, *The Open University: An Argument for Indeterminism,* Hutchinson, London, 1988.
26. P. Laungani, Death and Bereavement in India and England: A Comparative Analysis, *Mortality, 1*(2): pp. 191-212, 1996.
27. W. D. O'Flaherty, *The Origins of Evil in Hindu Mythology,* University of California Press, California, 1976.
28. M. Weber, *The Sociology of Religion* (4th Edition), Allen and Unwin, London, 1963.
29. W. Heisenberg, *The Physical Principles of Quantum Theory,* University of California Press, California, 1930.
30. S. Kakar, *Shamans, Mystics and Doctors,* Mandala Books, Unwin Paperbacks, London, 1982.

BIBLIOGRAPHY

Laungani, P., Death in a Hindu Family, in *Death and Bereavement Across Cultures,* C. M. Parkes, P. Laungani, and B. Young (eds.), Routledge, London, 1996.

CHAPTER 7
The Economics of Death

Lawrence Fric

The basic question which this chapter addresses is how economic analysis helps to gain some insights into the variety of personal relationships and social issues surrounding death in our society. This chapter is divided into three major parts. After defining economics and its relationship to death, Part I deals with the quantitative description of death in society; Part II with the issues that emerge given the choices that individuals and society make as they both obtain and provide the necessary services; Part III focuses on two particular concerns: (1) the structure and role of the funeral services industry, and (2) cemetery land, a disappearing resource. The basic data utilized in this chapter are contained in the Statistical Appendix at the end of this chapter.

The term "economics" or "economic analysis" can be defined in a variety of different ways. The various definitions emerge from the kinds of things that economists try to do. The first task of economics is to *describe* events. In this sense economists are said to be social scientists with quantitative imaginations. This statement provides the simplest definition of economics: Economics is a science which quantifies events.

A more complex definition follows from an examination of how society goes about meeting its perceived needs in a world in which human wants are believed to be unlimited. Moreover, in a modern industrialized society the economist does not find it very useful to distinguish between needs and wants. The economist is left with trying to *analyze* or to *explain* how humans go about the business of organizing their consumption, production, and accumulation of wealth activities in the context of limited means to achieve individual and social objectives. This leads to a definition of economics as the study of how people or society *choose* (with or without the use of money) to use scarce or limited productive resources (natural resources, labor, capital, technical knowledge) to produce various commodities and to distribute them to the various members of society in the effort to satisfy unlimited human wants [1]. This second definition embodies what turns out to be the central problem for economics. That is, if the collective and individual objective of society and the people in it is to maximize the social and individual well-being, then given the scarcity of productive resources, *choices will have to be made.*

The problem now before us is to focus these definitions and concepts of economics on the reality of death both to increase our understanding and our well-being.

I. THE QUANTITATIVE ASPECTS OF DEATH

The basic problem in quantifying death is answering the question, "How much death is there?" We can go further and characterize death by its causes, by its demographic and geographic aspects, by the trends and variations in all the data. From an economic point of view we could also ask, "How many productive resources do we commit to the handling of death in our society?" It turns out that the statistics on death are among the oldest kinds of statistics collected in society. Statistics Canada collects and reports such in a wide variety of sources.[1] In brief, the number of deaths has been rising annually in Canada; from an annual average of 126,666 in 1951-55 to 163,585 in 1971-75, to 171,029 deaths in the year 1981, to 195,568 in 1991 and to 201,020 in 1993. On the other hand, the death rate (expressed as deaths per thousand of population), which had been steadily declining over the years, has recently shown a increase. The numbers have gone from an annual average of 8.5 in 1951-55 to an average of 7.3 in 1971-75, to 7.2 in the year 1980, to 6.8 in 1984 (which seems to have been the low point) then either 7.0, 6.9, or 7.1 for every year since until 1993. (An alternative estimate for the year 1993 suggested it may have again reached 7.2 per thousand).[2]

Interestingly, death rates in Canada are low compared to those in other countries. In 1991, the lowest estimated death rate is that of Mexico (5.52), followed by Japan (6.91), and then Australia (6.73). Countries with death rates higher than Canada include New Zealand (7.68) and the United States (8.53). All of the European countries are generally higher than Canada: United Kingdom (11.1), France (9.2), Germany (11.2), Denmark (12.4), Belgium (12.58) (see Table 1). Data from other countries for various recent years prior to 1991 include Sweden (11.0), Switzerland (9.3), Poland (9.8), USSR (10.4), and Hungary (13.6). Some statistics in Canada are also reported for urban areas. For example, in the year 1977 there were 1,662 deaths

---

[1] Unless otherwise noted, all data in the following paragraphs were obtained from a wide variety of readily available Statistics Canada documents, a number of which are specifically cited in the "Bibliography" at the end of this chapter. Further, specific references to various Statistics Canada documents are shown in the particular tables in the Statistical Appendix also at the end of this chapter.

[2] It has been argued that the historical decline in death rates can be shown to be related to improvements in public health (personal cleanliness, sanitation facilities, running water, etc.) at least until the middle of this century. More recently the decline has been attributed to improvements in modern medicine. The recent increases that we seem to be experiencing (or at least the end of the era of declining death rates) seems to be related to Canada's aging population.

in the city of London, Ontario while for the year 1992 the number of deaths reached 2,299 [interview with the Middlesex-London Health Unit].

Given this large amount of data it is possible to analyze it and to note trends. For example, one might look at Table 2a and decide to move to the Northwest Territories as it is the area with the lowest death rates in Canada. However, if you want to find a safe place to give birth to a baby, avoid the north and move to British Columbia or Quebec. Other data show death rates are closely related to gender and to age. Note that less than 1.0 rates for females under thirty and males under fifteen in all provinces. While females have lower death rates for all age groups; it is only after age sixty that they and after age fifty-five that men reach death rates that exceed the Canadian average. Ranking provinces by death rates, readily reveals that a large part of the geographical differences in death rates are explained by the ages of the populations in the regions; the low death rates in the Northwest Territories seem related to the low median age of the people who live there [see Table 2]. But, age is not the only factor as on that basis the death rates of Prince Edward Island, Nova Scotia, New Brunswick, and Saskatchewan are too high while those of Quebec, Ontario, British Columbia are too low. Perhaps average income is also a factor? One might also wonder why the death rates are higher for males than for females in every age group.

The data reveal other intriguing factors. For example in Table 3 which shows the decreases in death rates by age and gender, the rates for females have generally declined more than the rates for males. Indeed, the same was true in the ten years 1966-76 but then the only group for whom death rates increased was males aged fifteen to nineteen (Canada Year Book 1980-81, p. 146). Perhaps more significantly *in the sixteen years 1976 to 1992* there are decreases in the death rate for females in every age group [Table 3]. The same is true for males under seventy but in the recent years the over seventy males have seen larger decreases than the females. Has there been more improvement in medical treatment for "old males" and less for everybody else or did modern medicine just have more room for improvement in prolonging life for "old males" than for anybody else? Given the general decline in medicine's ability to reduce death rates across all age groups except the "old males" has medicine reached some biological limit where scope for further reductions in the death rate is either too limited or too costly? Age and gender death rate differences also show substantial variation if one were to investigate the different causes of death. Perhaps somewhat more intriguing are the seasonal variations in death rates [Table 4]. Why is it that the annual pattern of deaths seems to always show more people die in the month of December than any other month of the year and proportionately fewer people die in the summer months? Clearly this tendency of Canadians to die in the winter months surely deserves some further research.

It is not only possible to observe the numbers, trends, and relationships of the past but from these statistics to draw inferences and make choices about the future. For example, Statistics Canada tells us that the sixty-five and over age group were 9.5 percent of the population in 1981. This percentage will increase to 12.1 percent by the year 2001 and to 19.1 percent in 2026. As this age group has a death rate of at least twenty per thousand of population higher (that is 2% higher) than the younger age groups, one can project a *rising* average death rate in the future. Proportionately then, death will be a more frequent occurrence and presumably of more concern to our society. Clearly all of these types of inferences lead first to research into the accuracy of our "conclusions" (hypotheses?) and then to policy choices about what, if anything, to do about the perceived trends. That is, society must make choices about whether or not it wishes to allocate some resources to solve the problem. For example, would it be better to spend money on health care facilities or on education programs to keep young men from suicide, or dying in car accidents and older men from killing themselves in stressful jobs or gun related events? With this number of deaths, a quantitative economist might next examine the question of the resources used to handle death in society. As a brief example of this approach let us examine the data for London, Ontario. The 1996 telephone directory lists ten funeral homes (up from 9 in 1983).[3] These homes deal with approximately 2275 deaths on about 255 working days. This works out to 8.9 (6.7 in 1983) deaths per working day in the city or about .89 (.74 in 1983) deaths per home per day. Of course not all the homes are the same size, the smaller ones handling just over 100 deaths per year, while the two largest are estimated to deal with over 300 and over 500 respectively. Each of these homes requires a large building containing preparation facilities, a viewing area, a chapel, an area for the display of inventory (caskets) and offices. Each also has a hearse and perhaps other automobiles. The smaller funeral homes have one or two permanent employees while the larger ones may well have ten or more. For the city as a whole it seems likely that there are at least thirty-seven and no more than forty-five permanent employees. Another way of describing the resources utilized is simply to look at the total monetary value of this industry to the city. As the 1992 average cost of a funeral in Ontario was $4,412.35 [Funeral Pricing Survey, February, 1993],[4] (up from $2,400 in 1983) then, given the 2,299 deaths, the value of the industry in the City of London alone was $10,143,992 in 1992 (up from $4,080,000 in 1983). The nature of the rapidly growing "Death Industry" including the problem of the cost of funerals together with the problem of the land used for cemeteries will be dealt with in the third and fourth parts of this chapter.

II. DEATH AND ECONOMICS AS THE SCIENCE OF CHOICE

Focusing on a definition of economics as the science of choice leads me to an explicit statement of the economic problem caused by the occurrence of death. When death occurs what "needs" arise? How are they being met? Could they be met more efficiently? The basic needs are easily identified. First, we must dispose of the body. Second, the responsibilities and the functions of the deceased in many ways

---

[3] A telephone call to the Middlesex-London Health Unit elicited the response that there were eleven but that one had just been opened. Therefore for our purposes of statistical estimates the number ten was used throughout.

[4] The same document showed the 1995 average cost was $4,775, but death data for 1995 was not yet available.

continue and somehow society must find ways of absorbing or handling these. Each of these needs has both a "private" and a "social" character. Satisfying them requires the use of private and social resources and gives rise to many questions (issues) regarding the appropriateness of their use.

Consider the function of disposing of the body. In the private sense there is not only the physical problem but also the psychological and religious needs of the survivors. For the latter we have evolved such things as the funeral, the reading and perhaps publication of the will, and commemorative markers, services, and public announcements in various media. Of all of these the funeral seems to be the most contentious.

Funerals are essentially a private matter in the sense that they have their primary impact on the individuals or immediate family. Of course, the more prominent the individual the larger the group concerned. One could consider great state occasions such as the Churchill, DeGaulle, or Kennedy funerals or the criminal tragedies such as the killing of all the children at the Dunblane Primary School, Scotland (March 13, 1996), but even in these kinds of events there were very strong private or personal elements. Moreover, for the large majority of individuals, society has little or no interest in the conduct of their funerals. Reasons for having funerals include such things as expressing love for or honoring the dead, celebrating their lives, placating the gods, providing for some sort of afterlife for the body and the soul, and "preserving" the body. The word funeral itself seems to derive from an East Indian word meaning "smoke" and is clearly related to the traditional method for disposing of the body in that society—cremation. Some of the customs surrounding funerals in society, such as wearing black and a funeral procession behind the corpse (walking from church to grave is still practiced in parts of Europe) appear to have originated in Roman times. Others seem to derive from Christianity, for example the throwing of a bit of earth onto the coffin. Whatever one does in a funeral service would not, in general, appear to be an area into which the state (society as a whole) has a right or responsibility to intervene. Specifically, we can conclude that the state should not regulate how much private individuals spend on funeral services for their loved ones. Nonetheless, to the extent that the funeral impinges on others in society, such as the funeral processions interference with traffic, the public health concerns that arise if a corpse is handled in a way that might endanger public safety, the disappearance of scarce resources used for the funeral that might in a social sense be better used elsewhere; then the state clearly has a role to play in the conduct of funerals.

As to the physical disposal of the body, a number of concerns seem to emerge. First, there is the concern that the remains of a human being should be treated with dignity and respect. Second, there is the rate at which the corpse will decay. Third, the cause of death may be a factor in that it is necessary to prevent the spread of communicable disease. Fourth, there is the problem already noted that the method of disposal may require scarce resources that society might better use for some other purpose. Fifth, there is the possibility that the body itself may be a socially useful resource. All of these factors involve both private and social aspects.

There seems little that needs to be said about the private desire to treat the corpse of a loved one with respect. However, most societies have found it necessary to develop laws and regulations defining acceptable practices. It is generally recognized that everyone has the right to be buried but different legal jurisdictions have different rules. In England it seems to be "common law" which determines that all (except executed felons) have the right to be buried in the burial ground of the parish in which they die. The person under whose roof the death occurs must arrange to transport the decently covered body to the grave. The executors or legal representatives of the deceased are bound to bury the body. The body itself is not "owned" by anyone but comes under the jurisdiction of the courts. Turning to the United States we find that every person has an inherent right of burial. But, those who are executed by the state, those whose bodies are not claimed by relatives or friends, those who meet death by violence and whose bodies cannot be identified, and those who will their bodies to science do not receive a "Christian" burial. Such bodies find their way to either a "potters field" at the expense of the city or town in which they die or to the dissecting tables. A noteworthy distinction in the United States is that a body itself "belongs" to the surviving relations—first to the spouse of the deceased, then the children, then in order of "blood succession." The expenses of burial are a first charge against the estate and those who are financially not able are not obligated to bury their relatives but may call upon civic authorities to assume the expense. In Canada, we tend to follow closely English common law. Jurisdiction in matters respecting bodies and funerals rests with the provincial governments (usually administered by the Departments of Health) hence there are the usual inter-provincial differences. Common features of the legislation are that the executors or legal representatives *must* bury or dispose of a body. In Canada a body is not "owned" by anyone, (not even the person who inhabited a body when alive can dispose of it after death) and the courts have jurisdiction over it. Burial expenses take precedence over all other obligations including debts. Everyone is entitled to a Christian or other religious burial except those who are legally executed, those whose bodies are not claimed, and those who will their bodies to science [Canadian Encyclopedia Digest, p. 22.9].[5] Also, it should be noted that it is an offence under the Criminal Code of Canada to subject human remains to any "indignity".[6]

There are of course exceptions to all of these rules. We have all heard of "burials at sea" where a ship's captain is obliged to deal with any who have died. Another exception notes that the rights of coroners take precedence over those of families when it is deemed that an inquest is necessary. Also, there are special regulations dealing with the disposition of the bodies of those dying from specific causes even to the prohibition or restriction of funerals for those who die of some communicable diseases.

---

[5] Further, legislation in Ontario on this subject is not found in any one specific piece of legislation. The 1990 revisions of the two pieces of legislation governing funeral establishments and cemeteries together with the 1980 legislation are cited in the attached Bibliography.

[6] The specific offence is found as s.178 under the section titled "Nuisances" in the general category "Sexual Offences, Public Morals, and Disorderly Conduct."

While everyone is entitled to be "buried" just what that means seems open to different legal interpretation in different jurisdictions. In Ontario for example, the term "burial" is no longer used in a specific legal sense. Instead, the Cemeteries Act uses the term "inter" which means "the burial of human remains and includes the placing of human remains in a lot." Human remains means "a dead human body and includes a cremated human body." "Lot" means "an area of land in a cemetery containing, or set aside to contain, human remains and includes a tomb, crypt, or compartment in a mausoleum and a niche or compartment in a columbarium." [Ontario Cemeteries Act, R.S.O. 1990, pp. 2-3]. Clearly one can infer from all these definitions that in Ontario to be "buried" now can easily mean that the "human remains" could be cremated and then placed in a "niche" in a "columbarium."

The general public confusion and the misinformation about what "burials" require seem to result from what people believe to be required by tradition, custom, religion, as well as law. Law itself has undergone substantial change as can be shown by comparing the present legislation [Cemeteries Act, R.S.O. 1990] with the previous version [The Cemeteries Act, R.S.O. 1977]. It is quickly apparent that much of the detail of the older law is now not a matter of law but rather relegated to the "regulations." Two results follow from this kind of legal change. One, detail in the regulations is often vague and or ambiguous, is more easily changed to fit more modern circumstances or technology and the like. Two, public confusion about what is required grows. For example, if under the old Act, interment (then not including cremation) in sealed crypts or compartments in a mausoleum was chosen, the corpse had to be interred in a vault that would prevent the escape of "noxious or unhealthful gases." If a corpse was to be cremated then that could not normally take place within forty-eight hours after death (exceptions can be made if communicable disease is involved). If a dead body (note the change from "human remains") was to be buried in the ground than it had to be contained in a "coffin or other receptacle" and covered by at least three feet of earth. Every grave of a deceased person over the age of sixteen had to be eight feet in length and three feet in width. No grave could be within fifteen feet of any building.

Returning to the consideration of current law some issues have been made more explicit. One such issue involves where a burial must take place. "No person shall inter human remains except in a cemetery that has been consented to by the Registrar and is owned by an owner licensed under this Act" [Cemeteries Act, R.S.O. s.47]. (Obviously, the law in Ontario requires cremated human remains be interred in a cemetery.) Sections of the Act dealing with "cremation" have increased: no person may cremate human remains except in a crematorium established in a cemetery; prior to cremation a "coroners certificate" must be obtained; containers must be made of flammable material; "pacemakers" or prescribed devices cannot be with the remains. The legislation also defines "burial sites" (i.e., land containing human remains that is not an approved cemetery) and if such sites are discovered how such human remains are to be handled. It is also notable that there are now explicit prohibitions against persons committing damage, disturbance or a nuisance in or to a cemetery. Explicit penalties for offences under the Act are also stated (for each offence by an individual a fine of not more than $20,000 or imprisonment for not more than 1 year). More generally, any person, corporation, church, or group of people can "own" a cemetery but its creation must be approved by a special by-law of the municipality in which it is located and it must be licensed by the Province. The remainder of the Act deals with applying for a license, closing of cemeteries, disinterment of human remains, trust fund for prepayment of cemetery services, definition of such services, restrictions on advertising the availability of or soliciting customers for cemetery lots and services, and more. The foregoing are basically the only rules, regulations, restrictions, on burials contained in the Cemeteries Act. Other legislation imposes other requirements. The Vital Statistics Act requires that a "Death Certificate" be obtained by the person conveying the corpse to the cemetery. The Anatomy Act allows a dead body to be claimed by "relatives or any other person" willing to give a "bona fide" undertaking "to dispose of the body." It is noteworthy that there are no requirements anywhere about the "laying out" of the corpse, embalming of a body if it is simply to be buried, nature of the container, nor restrictions on the number of corpses buried in a particular grave. *Perhaps most significantly the law does not say that a "funeral service" is required.*

The legislation governing funerals in Ontario [Funeral Directors and Establishments Act, R.S.O. 1990] was also extensively revised in 1990. Most notably there is now a distinction between "funeral services" and "transfer services." A firm can be licensed as a transfer service but it is not necessarily a "funeral establishment" licensed to perform "funeral services." "Transfer services" are defined as "a service to the public with respect to the disposition of dead human bodies, including the transportation of dead human bodies and the filling out of the necessary documentation with respect to the disposition of dead human bodies" [Funeral Directors Act, 1990, s.1, p. 3]. Thus, such a service can pick up a body at the place of death, convey it (locally or at some significant distance) to a cemetery in a container, in which the cemetery will proceed with the interment. Hence the new legally undefined term "direct disposition" has appeared. In areas in which local funeral homes are not available transfer services have even been allowed to set up "visitation centers" (another new and not legally defined term) in which mourners can be with the corpse in its container. Conversely "funeral services" are defined to be "the care and preparation of dead human bodies and the co-ordination of rites and ceremonies with respect to dead human bodies . . ." [Funeral Directors Act, 1990, R.S.O. s.1, p. 2]. Such services must be performed by licensed "funeral directors." Only they can perform such services as embalming. Funeral establishments which "care for and prepare" dead human bodies must maintain specialized rooms and sterile equipment and conditions to carry out their work at the address were they are licensed. The law provides for inspection and regulation of their services. Traditionally they also have "visitation rooms" as part of the establishment. They are also allowed to provide the transfer service but they could hire an independent "transfer service" provider. Probably the largest part of the Funeral Directors and Establishments Act deals not with the funerals themselves but rather with the rules and regulations required to license and inspect these entities, and to protect consumers (those charged with the responsibility of disposing of the body) from being "oversold" services at a vulnerable point in their lives.

Clearly the legal requirements regarding cemeteries and funeral homes are rapidly evolving and those relating to the disposal of the body are relatively minor. The elaborate funeral services, the ever more complex handling of the corpse, which since the middle of the nineteenth century have become more and more usual, appear to stem from a concern to "protect society" (relating both to public health and consumer protection issues) as well as from the private psychological or religious need to deal with death.

These two concerns lead to somewhat contradictory practices. Much of our law dealing with the disposal of bodies has emerged precisely because of a fear of communicable diseases (the particular diseases are specified in the legislation's regulations). When disease is present, the thrust of the legislation is to get rid of the corpse as quickly and as privately as possible. Hence, in such cases, cremation *can* be permitted immediately after death. If a burial in the earth is intended, the body must be contained in a hermetically sealed coffin, viewing of the remains and transporting them on public transportation is not permitted, the funeral service itself must be "private," etc. In all such cases the funeral director is required to take special precautions such as insuring all materials coming into contact with the corpse are buried with it. From a more historical perspective, one can readily conclude our modern legislation regarding cemeteries had its origins in the overcrowded churchyards of the nineteenth century[7] and the fact that people feared becoming ill by visiting them. More recently, death from communicable disease appeared to be rare prior to the 1980s [interview at Middlesex-London Health Unit, 1983]. Unfortunately, this problem is again on the increase. AIDS related deaths totaled 165 in London in the period 1990 to 1995 inclusive. An additional twenty-three deaths were reported as related to various types of hepatitis. Further it was believed these 188 deaths reflect a very high rate of under-reporting of the approximately 10,000 total deaths in the period [interview with the Middlesex-London Health Unit, 1996]. This view was supported by an admittedly cautious local funeral-director who estimated a low of 5 percent to a high of 7 percent of all his funerals now required "sealed" caskets or containers.

If the "public" or societal concern with disposing of the body focuses on speed and protection, the "private" or "personal" issues involved seem concerned with emotions like love, honor, and "holding on." A desire to stop or at least slow down the decay process has real and physical causes as well as psychological and even "religious" overtones. The rate and onset of putrefaction of the corpse is extremely variable. On the one hand, there are examples in the literature of dead bodies being found in very good condition even after hundreds of years.[8] Also, funeral directors

---

[7] On a visit to Sienna, Italy, it was brought to my attention that dead bodies infected with medieval plagues were even used as weapons of war. When the Florentine army surrounded Sienna the infected dead were used as catapult projectiles. When they were not sufficient, animal bodies were used giving us the expression "It's raining cats and dogs."

[8] Media stories in this regard are fairly common. In May 1996, a number appeared regarding the discovery of a 500-year-old well-preserved body of a thirteen-year Inca female—apparently the result of ritual sacrifice. A year earlier, the discovery of a tens of thousands of year old body of a tribal hunter appeared in the glaciers of the Italian Alps.

can often cite cases where they have handled bodies that have been found weeks after death in which little decay is obvious. Other cases have been cited by both funeral directors and medical personnel in which very rapid and extreme decomposition of the body occurs within hours of death. The physical health of the individual at death, the kinds of illnesses or treatments involved prior to death, deliberate efforts made to preserve the body or the natural conditions (i.e., ice, muskeg bogs) surrounding the remains all seem to be factors affecting the time involved. In general, the decay process is considered to be rapid causing "noxious odours and unhealthful gases" in a matter of a few days. Given society's growing tendency to transport corpses great distances from the place of death to the place of burial (a month can easily be involved in making all the necessary arrangements); the large number of deaths caused by accidents in which disfigurement of the body is common; the practice of viewing the body (still done in over 60 percent of funeral services); and the practice of delaying the funeral for at least three days after death (is this to allow relatives to gather or to provide the pschological certainty the individual is really dead?);[9] some sort of preservation and cosmetic handling of the remains seem desirable if not strictly necessary.

Accepting the need for some level of handling the body leaves unanswered the concern about the amount of resources society might deem acceptable for such purposes. As has already been noted, governments in Canada have chosen not to set any limits. If our society were generally to follow the extremes of the ancient Egyptians, or in more modern examples the handling of Lenin's and Mao's remains, or the most recent development, "cyrogenics"[10] one might anticipate a rising public concern. These extreme cases demonstrate a misuse of scarce resources in a social sense.

Another major resource utilized by this industry is the labor force employed. Current data seemed difficult to obtain. Nonetheless, as it can be shown that the number of funerals per worker per year has not changed significantly, the available 1981 data do provide some insight. In that year Canada had 3,205 *full-time* workers employed as Embalmers, Funeral Directors, and Related Occupations [see Table 5 in the Appendix]. This number includes 1,410 in Ontario. Given the number of deaths [see Appendix Table 6], these data suggest the average number of cases per full-time employee is 54.5 for Canada and 45.6 for Ontario in 1981. With no more than 255 working days per year, each death required at least five full days of work just to

---

[9] The time period involved can depend on a variety of criteria such as the Jewish religious requirement that the dead be interred in twenty-four hours or a Coroner's need to delay interment in cases of suspicious death.

[10] A 1983 court case in California is of interest here. A cryogenically preserved couple (one since 1974; the other since 1978) may now be thawed and disposed of as the heirs of their son, who had paid the annual fees to this point, refused to pay the annual fee of $2,900. The president of the company providing the service filed suit asking the courts to compel payments [*American Funeral Director, 106,* 1983, p. 48]. Unfortunately, the court decision does not seem to have been reported.

handle the corpse.[11] Such a number is arrived at without counting the part-time workers, the hairdressers, the make-up specialists, the car drivers, the grave-diggers, the cemetery grounds staff, or others. If all of these were to be counted it seems as if 10.86 funerals per worker per year in 1995 would not be an unreasonable estimate [Loewen Group, 1995 p. 4]. One cannot but wonder if all this effort is really necessary, and more importantly, could the industry not be organized to provide the *same level* of service somewhat more efficiently? These questions are dealt with in more detail in the sections of this chapter that follow.

The final consideration in this review of the issues that emerge from the way in which society as a whole and the individuals in it physically dispose of dead bodies are the choices involving the use of the body itself as a resource. In the most obvious application, there appear to be no records of the number of corpses either currently used or required as teaching or research tools. Clearly, not all bodies are suitable nor could all of them be used in such a manner. Moreover, the problem of what to do with the remains after science has run its course still must be dealt with.[12] A second application, in this day of organ transplants, would be to use the dead body as a "spare parts bank." The introduction of the Anatomy Act in Ontario in the 1980s and since that time the public encouragement of people to choose to dispose of their own bodies by allowing "donation" of their organs at death, shows a greater social acceptance of this option. The still common communications media articles commenting on organ shortages suggest too many people are still saying "not me" or "not my son or daughter." A third option we might consider is to utilize bodies for food. The volume of literature on the acceptability of cannibalism in primitive tribes or in times of emergency serves to emphasize the fact that we do make such a choice. If the body could be used for food, why not a fourth option, for fertilizer, or a fifth,

---

[11] In the last paragraph of Part I of this chapter (p. 80 above) it was noted that in 1992 London Ontario recorded 2299 deaths while between thirty-seven to forty-five full-time workers were employed in city funeral homes. These numbers imply between a high of 62.1 to a low of 51.1 deaths per worker or again in the range of five worker days required for each death.

[12] In this regard there seems to be considerable variation in the practices at various hospitals and teaching hospitals. At the University General Hospital in London, when *organs only* are donated, then at death, the remains are immediately taken to a normal surgery where the donated remains are removed if possible while the heart is still beating. (That is necessary to maintain the viability of the donated organs.) The remainder of the physical remains are then delivered to a funeral director in the normal fashion of any death occurring in the hospital. The next-of-kin retain the moral and legal obligation to properly dispose of them. If they do not wish to make such arrangements, then University Hospital will do so for them (i.e., dispose of the remains in the University plot at a local cemetery), but the next-of-kin are expected to pay for such expenses in such cases (these seem to be quite rare).

When human remains are donated *in their entirety* to a teaching hospital, then at the University of Western Ontario, the body is donated to the Department of Anatomy. It is the responsibility of the next-of-kin to arrange delivery of the remains in an unembalmed state within forty-eight hours of the death. The remains are utilized for scientific purposes for approximately one to one and one-half years (depending on the time in the academic year when the remains are received). The remains are then *always* cremated. The next-of-kin can then claim the remains for disposition as they wish. Alternatively the remains are buried under a common marker in a University plot at Woodlands Cemetery.

for fuel. All of these resources are known to be scarce in our ever more crowded world. Simply to let the body decay seems extremely wasteful. A contrary view could also be expressed. In this environmentally conscious world, this space ship earth, would it not be more efficient to let our bodies decay as rapidly as possible so that the elements of which they are created can return to some natural cycle of reuse (rebirth?).[13]

Consider now the question of how society absorbs or handles the responsibilities of the deceased person. In this chapter it is not the intention to deal fully with this complex problem but only to introduce the kinds of issues involved. When individuals who have accumulated considerable private wealth die, there are all the usual issues involving inheritance. As the population as a whole continues to get older, more and more attention seems to being paid to the "correct" timing of the "intergenerational" transfer of wealth at both a private and a social level. Another issue involves both older people who are "retired" and young people have few responsibilities in the sense that little material contribution or support is expected of them by others such as their family, their employers, or their friends. The same cannot be said of those in their middle years. When such people die, both private and social losses are incurred. In a private sense how will the family income or living standards be maintained? As individuals are ultimately the only way in which wealth is "owned" (our entire concept of private property is involved) some system for the transfer of wealth is required. Through the years we have developed different institutions such as the "friendly society," the Fraternal association or club,[14] life insurance companies, survivor's pensions, and inheritance or estate legislation in order to cope with the problems that arise. In a social sense the problem is qualitatively different. The state must not only devise all the legislation, rules, and regulations to supervise the institutions created but it must also act when private individuals have not provided for themselves. The classic "poor widows and orphans" problem needs to be solved.[15] One final note, while it is always possible to transfer individual responsibility or wealth to some groups or to transfer those of small groups to a larger group, there is a real loss (a cost which ultimately must be paid somewhere) to both individuals and the state whenever a productive, creative person dies.

---

[13]One public health official interviewed for this study suggested that perhaps our forefathers were wiser in this respect. Corpses covered with simple shrouds could decay more quickly. Furthermore, they did not use a vast array of building materials (wood, metal, cement, etc.) for an ultimately futile purpose.

[14]Clubs such as the Oddfellows, the Foresters, the Elks, and the Moose are obvious examples.

[15]The widows and orphans benefits under the Canada Pension Plan are indicative of the modest arrangements society now makes.

III. THE STRUCTURE AND THE ROLE OF THE FUNERAL SERVICES INDUSTRY

It is difficult to obtain an accurate description of the funeral services industry. The available data are either incomplete, dated, or gathered with inconsistent definitions. Moreover, the distinction between it and the "cemetery" industry is not all that well maintained. Also, the need to make comparisons and to try to distinguish when one is concerned with one industry or the other makes a total separation of the topics difficult. Nonetheless, in this part of this chapter the emphasis and issues dealt with will relate primarily to "funeral services." Also, the following data are somewhat impressionistic rather than wholly accurate.

In terms of the numbers of locations, owners, and employees the data have not changed in any significant way over the last few decades. In 1971, Canada had 1,446 funeral home locations with 468 of them in Ontario. These firms had 745 owners and 4,008 employees in Canada and 262 owners and 1,579 employees in Ontario [Statistics Canada, 1971 Census, Vol. IX(9-2), Table 1]. These data imply an average of 3.29 workers per location in Canada and 3.93 in Ontario. The similarity of the average number of workers employed in London, Ontario funeral homes in 1983 (page 80 above) and in 1996 [interview with local funeral home director, 1996] should be noted. As the number of funeral homes licensed to do business in Ontario has changed little in that time period—520 in November, 1983 and 517 in February 1993 [Funeral Pricing Survey, 1993]—and the average number of employees is in the same range, it seems unlikely that the total numbers employed have changed significantly. Note, however, that during the time that the small decline in the number of funeral homes in Ontario did occur, there was an increase in London from nine to eleven. There is other evidence of some rural/urban shift; examples include the occasional media stories of the lack of funeral homes in smaller centers and in northern Ontario, and the change in legislation that provided "visiting centres" noted earlier in this article.

Trying to determine an accurate estimate of the dollars spent in buying the services of the death industry is difficult to establish. Statistics Canada reported the "average cost" of a funeral service as $1,611 in 1980 while funeral directors and their association suggested $2,400 would be more accurate in 1982.[16] (The latter includes the cost of the cemetery fees while the former is for funeral services alone. Adding these fees to the former would make the numbers comparable.) The comparable numbers in 1995 are $4,775.36 [Funeral Pricing Survey, p. 2] for the funeral service in Ontario plus a low of $800 to a more usual $1,300 for the cemetery fees [interview with Mr. John O'Neil of Hinnegan and O'Neil Funeral Directors, May,

---

[16]Reported in interviews with various funeral directors in Ontario in 1983 and supported by the $2,500 average in the United States [*American Funeral Director, 105*(10), (1982), p. 50].

1996].[17] Using the 1992 averages of $4,412.35 and $1,051.08[18] [Funeral Pricing Survey, pp. 6 and 8] together with the numbers of deaths (Table 6) produce calculated results as follows:

1992 Revenues of Ontario Funeral Services Establishments[19]

	Total Revenue	Firm Average
Full Service Funeral Services	$563,695,361	$1,090,320
Direct Dispositions	72,304,844	139,855
Total Funeral Services	$636,000,205	$1,230,175
Cemetery Revenues		
Casket and Corpse Interments	$191,631,000	
Cremations and Interments	90,804,082	
Total Cemetery Revenues	$282,435,082	

The crude estimates suggest that the "body disposal" industry in Ontario alone was at least $918,435,287 in 1992 and easily over one billion dollars in 1995. Interestingly, Statistics Canada reported $109.6 million spent on funeral services plus $9.5 million spent at cemeteries and crematoria or a total of $119.1 million in 1971. Adjusting this number by increasing it 265 percent to reflect the rate of inflation for 1971-1992, plus an additional 20 percent for the increase in the annual rate of deaths in the same period yields $521,658,000. The one billion total for 1995 would seem to be excessive were it not for the fact that, in the period 1982 to 1991 alone, society can be shown to be spending approximately 60 percent more (after inflation) dollars on each funeral service.[20] Adding this additional 60 percent real increase brings the new total to $834,652,800 which is almost exactly within 10

---

[17]The particular assistance of Mr. John O'Neil of Hinnegan and O'Neil Funeral Directors of London Ontario is most gratefully acknowledged. Mr. O'Neil gave generously of his time in interviews, provided data and direction to those individuals who provided other or confirming data, and helped to explain the meanings of technical terms and the like. His assistance throughout this entire chapter was invaluable.

[18]Note that the "averages" reported in the Funeral Pricing Survey are: for 1995 the actual purchases made by consumers in each funeral services establishment for the ten consecutive calls immediately prior to April 30, 1995; for 1992, the ten consecutive calls prior to December 31, 1992.

[19]There are not data on the market share of transfer services compared to full service funeral homes. Consequently, it was necessary to estimate that share using the number 65/35 ratio of earth burials to direct dispositions reported in the Funeral Pricing Survey which covered *all* funeral service establishments in Ontario. However, despite the responses by 482 of the possible 517 firms we do not know how many of the thirty-five non-reporting establishments were the independent transfer services. To the extent that the latter systematically under-reported the reported revenues will be too high.

[20]It has been recorded above that annual funeral service averages in 1982 was $2,400; in 1995 they were $4,775, an increase of 199 percent. In the same period general price inflation was only 139 percent. Hence average funeral prices increased by 60 percent more than other things.

percent of the estimate above.[21] Clearly the rising revenues in the period have been influenced by three factors: the rising numbers of deaths, price inflation in general, and a tendency to buy more *"funeral services"* per death.

What services does a consumer get for the money paid? This question is best answered by considering the manner in which funeral services are priced. There are two basic pricing methods used in the industry. One is the "Package Price" method. The consumer is shown a series of caskets of varying quality each with an associated price. The price of the casket includes a variable package of services that goes along with it. This pricing method is preferred by many customers as 89 percent [Funeral Pricing Survey, p. 2] of funeral services are bought immediately after the death of a loved one when the customers are emotionally uninterested in discussing numerous seemingly petty financial details. The alternative pricing method is the "Functional Price" approach. Here, each detail is independently priced and the client must make separate choices. A list of services and the associated prices for a funeral are shown below [Funeral Pricing Survey, pp. 6 and 8].

AVERAGE PRICES FUNERAL AND CEMETERY SERVICES—1992

Part 1 — Full Service Funeral Establishments	Average Paid
1. Professional Services including: a) Removal of the remains to the funeral home b) Preparation of the body (with "cosmetic" preparation)	$849.85
2. Embalming	237.40
3. Facilities (i.e., visitation rooms)	603.06
4. Shelter (storage of the body)	148.28
5. Transfer (i.e., from hospital and to cemetery)	128.88
6. Funeral Coach	184.08
7. Clergy/Lead Car	95.50
8. Family Car	133.32
9. Pallbearer Car	102.82
10. Other Cars	106.09
11. Documentation—obtaining legal papers such as death certificate, permission to cremate, transportation documentation, etc.	130.10
12. Stationery (cards, etc.)	87.32
TOTAL AVERAGE SERVICE CHARGE PAID	$2,500.99

(Note: The total is an average of reported amounts—not an addition of the reported averages in the column)

13. Average Casket purchased	1,990.63
TOTAL AVERAGE FUNERAL SERVICE PURCHASED	$4,412.36

---

[21] It is also of some interest to note that calculating the proportion of cemetery to funeral services revenues from the data in this paragraph yields 7.97 percent in 1971 and 44.41 percent in 1995. These proportions reflect very closely the rapid increase in the number of cremations in Ontario in the same period and the consequent shift in revenues from the full service establishments to the transfer and direct disposition firms and cemeteries.

Part 2 — Transfer Services

1. Professional Services (body preparation)	$343.29
2. Transfers	128.90
3. Shelter	152.67
4. Service Vehicle	106.09
5. Documentation	129.41
TOTAL SERVICE CHARGE PAID	$836.86
6. Casket/Container	265.00
TOTAL AVERAGE TRANSFER SERVICE CHARGE PAID	$1,051.08
TOTAL ALTERNATIVE "PACKAGE" PRICE FOR ABOVE	$841.49
7. Memorial Service (List price only as few prices paid reported)	$481.72

If a customer were to select a minimal cost but traditional service from Part 1 of the average price list the necessary items would be numbers 1, 2, 3, 4, 5, 6, and 11 for a total of about $2,050. In addition a simple gray cloth covered casket with a simple lining is available for an average cost of $750 to $800 for a total of $2,850 (the container would be made of a low cost wood or particle board). *The customer would still have to cover additional costs such as the services of a priest or minister, an organist, a soloist, use of a church. The funeral directors will recommend about $200 or $250 should be paid for each of such item utilized.* In London, in 1996 "package prices" for such funerals (very limited visitation, a memorial service, and not a church service) are available for approximately $2,900 [interviews with local Funeral Directors, April, May 1996]. *In addition, the customer would be required to cover the cemetery and if desired, the cremation costs as shown in the table below* [data obtained in interviews with local Cemetery and Crematoria operators]. Of course, one could choose the "Transfer Service" option in Part 2. The "service charge" for that simple alternative service (note the Toronto company of a similar name that heavily advertises such an option) whether provided by an independent "Transfer Service" establishment or as one of the options provided by a "Full Service Funeral Home," already totals $1,051.08. *Again, cemetery and cremation costs would be additional.*

CEMETERY AND CREMATION COSTS — LONDON, ONTARIO — 1996

Cemetery Costs	Local Averages
Cost of the cemetery plot (minimum)	$750
Opening and closing of the grave	450
Simple marker	250
TOTAL CEMETERY COSTS FOR SIMPLEST EARTH BURIAL	$1,450
Optional concrete vault (minimum type)	500

Cremation Costs

Cremation of the remains	$300
Coroners certificate	32
Simplest container/urn	75
Interment of remains in common ground or on an already owned grave plot	<u>160</u>
TOTAL MINIMAL COST OF CREMATION WITH INTERMENT	$567
Cost of cemetery plot (minimum and optional)	750
Cost of 12" x 12" niche in Columbarium (optional)	800

Considering even the possible number of options of minimum cost it is not surprising the "at need" customer is bewildered. Given the data in the above two tables, three basic alternatives are the following. One, a *minimal* traditional funeral service together with a minimal but traditional earth burial (interment in a grave)— funeral home service charge $2,900 plus cemetery cost $1,450 totaling $4,350. Two, traditional funeral service at $2,900 with cremation and interment of remains at $1,317 or $1,367. Three, transfer service only at $1,051.08 or at the "package price" 841.49 with cremation at $407 and disposition of the remains left to the funeral director and through that person to the customer thus the lowest total is $1,248.49. Clearly, the disposition of the human remains costs are highly variable. A large part of the variation comes from the choice of container/casket. The lowest cost container may well be an undecorated, unlined, sealed (with "waxes" or other sealants) heavy "cardboard."[22] The more elaborate the interior finishing of the casket, the "better" quality of woods used together with a variety of possible exterior finishes and "hardware" (handles and such), can easily raise the cost of the casket to $3,000. Should the customer wish a metal (i.e., lead) lining, or an entirely metal casket (copper and aluminum are common) prices are even higher. Finally, "hermetically" sealed caskets are sometimes requested and these can easily be $10,000 plus. Urns for cremated remains are also highly variable in price—from the lowest, a plastic one at about $75.00, to intricately carved marble at $3,000. Other optional items are often wanted such as flowers, extended visitation times, reconstruction of accident victims' remains, newspaper notices, etc. Cemetery plots also vary in price depending on factors like size and even location within a particular cemetery. Of course, the town, city, or area a cemetery is located in, the "desirability" of a cemetery, available space within it, are all other factors involved in setting "plot" prices. Yet at $1,929.91 for a "single" or $4,825.23 (plus GST) in historic Mount Pleasant in central Toronto, [Toronto Star, September 3, 1995, p. D5] cemetery plot costs are not nearly as consequential as those for the variety of caskets. However, a lot of cemeteries are now "requiring" installation of the in-ground

---

[22]One local funeral director provides a locally made "plywood" or low grade but "solid pine" box at a similar price.

concrete vaults. Should the customer wish an external "mausoleum" then of course even higher costs result.[23]

The list of services and their cost shows that the cost of funeral services is what it is because of the quality and volume of the services purchased. If one examines the lists for excessive costs, given any reasonable comparisons that can be made, it would be difficult to argue that excesses exist. For example, if one added up the cost of an ambulance trip, the rental cost of three "cadillac" type cars for one-half day, the wages of three drivers, the rental of a hotel room (or a small hall), the cost of lumber to make the equivalent of a large box or piece of fine furniture, together with any type of professionals hourly wage rate multiplied by even minimal body preparation time, then the funeral directors total service fees certainly seem reasonable.[24]

Nevertheless, people do feel that the cost of services is high. Questions are asked such as: do we really require so much service or is there not another way in which the industry could be organized so the same level and quality of service could be provided at less cost? There seems to be little question that the services being provided are growing; that is, there is a trend to ever more elaborate funerals in general despite the growth of "direct dispositions." There are a number of examples of growth in "services" requested. Historically, even every corpse requiring its own casket is a relatively new phenomenon. There is evidence that for funerals in the early nineteenth century in England individual churches "owned" the coffin in which the corpse was placed for the church service only. The shrouded body was removed for burial and the coffin used another day.[25] The practice of embalming the corpse is a good example of the long-term increase in funeral services. Just over a century ago only the remains of leaders of governments and the extremely wealthy were so handled, whereas a 1983, 99 percent of dead bodies were embalmed. (This despite the fact that the 1977 Ontario legislation required that a body be embalmed only when it was going to be transported via "public" transportation (i.e., airlines).)[26] As noted above (page 86) with more immigration, more travel in society, more deaths away from "home," more time needed between the death and the interment, more embalming is performed. One local funeral director also commented that the very recent trend to more advanced age at death, together with much more medical

---

[23]A London cemetery operator stated that the highest cemetery billing in London in recent years exceeded $45,000.

[24]Despite the already noted 60 percent increase in "real" costs in the last decade, in the longer run real costs of funerals do not appear to have risen. A poor man's coffin (if he had one) in 1838 in England cost 14 shillings which was about three quarters of a week's wages for a laborer at that time [*Toronto Star*, March 28, 1983, p. C2]. That appears comparable to the cost of the minimum casket today at a price of about $250. Of course, the other, more optional costs might well be behaving differently.

[25]Although no London funeral establishment is yet engaging in the practice, anecdotal comment suggests that in some larger centers "full service" establishments can now be found that will "rent" elaborate caskets for visitation and church purposes when cremation in a plainer casket is intended. Of course, the interior "liners" of the rented casket would have to be replaced with the "used materials" cremated with the human remains.

[26]In the current laws if such detail is still there it has been relegated to the "regulations."

treatment prolonging life, the corpse is regularly received by the funeral director in much "poorer condition" than in the recent past. While the 1983, 99 percent had by 1996 declined to "at least 90%" of the traditional funerals conducted in that funeral home (which still utilizes "open" caskets in the services) embalming with much stronger concentrations of the necessary chemicals is now required just to make the remains "acceptable" to the mourners.[27] Still another "services" enhancement is the now more common and sometimes required (usually by the by-laws of the particular cemetery) concrete vault.[28]

Of course, there are some obvious declines in the use of some items in funeral services. A frequently heard comment notes a rapid decline in the use and the amount of flowers at funerals. Cremation, rather than "earth burial," as a percentage of all funerals, is more commonly practiced today (see data on cremation Table 8, page 107 below). In London, Ontario in 1983, one funeral director estimated the proportion of cremations as 5 to 6 percent of funerals for those of "European" (Catholic) background and 10 to 12 percent for those of "WASP" origins. Considerable regional as well as religious variation in rates of cremation are evident in what little data are readily available. The cremation rate in 1980 in one Ottawa establishment was 30.5 percent. Again in 1983, the average in the United States was 10.96 percent up from 3.62 percent in 1961. The rates varied from lows of from 1.29 percent in some east and southern states (Alabama, Mississippi, Kentucky) to highs of 31.09 percent in the Pacific states (Alaska, California, Washington, Hawaii) [AFD, 105(9) 1982, p. 54]. In urban England rates as high as 60 percent were reported [AFD 105(8) 1982, Letters].

Current cremation rates for either Canada or even Ontario are not available. However, the 1995 rate for Toronto was 47 percent [Toronto Star, October 16, 1995]. The two crematoria in London performed almost 1600 cremations in 1995 or almost as many as 70 percent of all deaths in the city [interviews with managers of both local establishments]. But, many of these are from much of south-western Ontario as the only other crematoria between Toronto and Windsor are in Kitchener/Waterloo and Chatham. One of the London firms was able to tell us that 65 percent of their volume came from City of London funeral directors. On that basis one can infer that 44.5 percent of funerals in London involve cremation. (This percentage tends to be confirmed by the "best guesses" of local funeral directors many of whom felt that in excess of 40% of customers chose cremation.) Importantly, in only 25 percent of the cremations were the "human remains" (i.e., ashes) returned to the funeral directors to

---

[27]However, a very large Ottawa funeral home is on record that "closed caskets" in their establishment increased from only 1 percent of funerals in 1940 to 39 percent in 1980 [*Canadian Funeral Director*, 1983, p. 21]. Factors such as different or changing religious beliefs of the large part of the particular clientele of a particular establishment might go a long way toward explaining such contradictory trends.

[28]This practice is sometimes a legal requirement especially if the cemetery is in a low lying area and the water table is high. Even so, the value of such a practice is dubious. It was reported by a public health officer that hermetically sealed concrete vaults have been known to rise from the ground due to the water pressure. As a consequence, if the vaults are not built with holes in them, cemetery maintenance personnel have been known to "crack" the vaults to insure trouble-free interments.

deal with in ways requested by the clients. The remaining 75 percent of cremations were "interred" either in cemetery plots or in columbaria.

From all of the foregoing numbers, it is not clear that the total quantity of services per death has decreased. If a decrease does exist it has occurred only in the last one or two decades after over a century of rapid increase in the resources used for funerals and cemeteries. What seems to be much more likely, despite the increase in things like "direct dispositions," is that even more resources (dollars per death) are being used. There are substitutions going on (columbaria for grave plots; cremations—together with the required energy resources—rather than ever more elaborate caskets, vaults and mausoleums; some people are spending less while others are spending even more) and the costs of funerals continues to rise.

The funeral services industry has been criticized on the grounds that, to the extent that services are becoming more elaborate, the marketing techniques of the industry are blamed for this growth of demand. It is argued that the elaborate showrooms with elegant coffins prominently displayed (with cheaper models deliberately placed in dark corners or simply "out of stock") coupled with unit pricing tends to "persuade" the client caught at a weak moment, to spend more than might be rational.[29] Advertising and sales promotion are not seen as appropriate activities for this industry—admittedly each firm is a private, profit-oriented business but this is a business that is "different."

A second type of criticism stems from what economists call "vertical integration." Given the type of service provided, (everybody will have to "buy" sooner or later and the basic service, the death and the disposal of the body, is essentially the same for everyone), theory and business experience both suggest that the industry should be characterized by "economies-of-scale." That is, the bigger the firm is, the more efficient it could be. This occurs because all the resources employed by the firm can be used more intensively. For example, the hearse and the preparation rooms and equipment would be more efficiently used if they were busy every day instead of the current average of only once a week. If "bigger is better" (i.e., lower cost), then why not link firms into "chains" and share common facilities? Moreover, why not unite all the related services provided under common ownership from the making of the coffins, burial vaults, grave markers, together with the funeral homes and cemeteries? There is even good historical precedent for that kind of organization in that the funeral homes, as we now know them, often originated as offshoots of local furniture or cabinet making businesses.

Such chains do exist. In Canada, Arbor Memorial Services, a funeral industry company, has a subsidiary Memorial Gardens (Ontario) Ltd., which owned twenty-three crematoria and forty-four cemeteries [Toronto Star, Sept. 3, 1995, p. D6]. Memorial Gardens (Canada) Ltd. originated the concept of selling the "in grave" concrete vaults which are now sold by the funeral directors. The parent company

---

[29]Regulations under the legislation currently require transfer services to show to the customers the least expensive containers available. Funerals directors are generally required to show eight different types of containers/caskets in all price ranges including one in the lowest cost range.

also owns or has financial ties to funeral homes in the United States and its subsidiary acknowledged a one-third interest in five funeral homes in Hamilton, Ontario. The association between the two services is growing despite the fact that Ontario legislation prohibits funeral homes from owning cemeteries and vice-versa [Funeral Directors Act, 1990, s. 39 and Cemeteries Act, 1990, s. 45]. The largest company in Canada is The Loewen Group Inc. of Burnaby B.C. which operates in seven Canadian provinces and thirty-eight American states (the largest company in this industry in North America is Service Corp. International of Houston, Texas; the Loewen Group is in a distant second place). In 1994, the Loewen Group had total revenues of US$417,479,000; US$353,904,000 from providing 94,000 funerals (implicit average price US$3,765); and US$63,575,000 from 17,000 interments (implicit average US$3,740).[30] This Canadian company, which started in small town Fort Frances, Ontario in 1969 with two funeral homes, had a total of forty-five by 1986, 641 in 1994, and continues to grow rapidly. In 1994 alone it purchased 110 funeral homes, forty-six cemeteries and a 26 percent interest in Arbor Memorial Services Inc. [Loewen Group].[31]

The "over-selling" of services and the "vertical integration" criticisms noted would require growing monopoly control of the industry in order to create the control of the marketplace necessary to charge prices well in excess of the cost of the services provided. Despite the rapid growth in the large size of the firms in this industry, there is little evidence that such market control exists. On the contrary, the evidence suggests a high degree of competition at two different levels.

The firms in the industry are relatively small, many having revenues in the million dollar range or less in 1995. Also each has only three or four permanent employees and most serve less than 300 clients per year.[32] Eighty-seven percent of the more than 22,500 funeral homes in the United States are still in "family" hands [Globe and Mail, Toronto, Dec. 16, 1995, p. B4]. In Ontario, almost one-half of the licensed funeral directors do not seem to be working in the industry which suggests an apparent oversupply of trained professionals. Second, there are a number of factors which make the development of large scale, profit-motivated enterprise difficult. One of these is the already noted legislative restriction on ownership of the different kinds of firms. (Though some indirect linkages between owners of cemeteries and funeral homes in Ontario are believed to exist—such as the Loewen Group's indirect interest in Memorial Gardens (Canada) Ltd. through its Arbor Memorial Services interest, the Loewen Group does not directly own any Ontario

---

[30]Note that the average U.S. dollar funeral price in North America converted to Canadian dollars at a 1.35 exchange rate yields CDN$5,083 or only slightly higher than the reported Ontario average of $4,775.

[31]This company seems a veritable "growth stock." In 1994 the Annual report said its share price (at a high near $37.00) was now thirteen times its 1991 issue price. In 1996 the shares reached $56.00, then fell to $22.00 after a small Mississippi funeral home company successfully sued for $500 million U.S. in a breach of contract/restraint of trade case. The Loewen Group has settled for U.S.$165 million and the share price is now back in the $38.00 range.

[32]Local funeral directors suggested homes with more than 500 clients per year were very few while the very largest serve 1,000 to 1,200 clients.

cemeteries.) These facts imply that the industry is "competitive" in nature. Economic theory suggests that in such circumstances the industry is operating in a most efficient manner in terms of allocating resources and providing the desired services at minimum cost.

Perhaps the major factor insuring competition and realistic prices for the services provided is rising large scale and effective "consumerism." The consumerism trend, which is associated with the rejection of involved handling of the corpse and elaborate funerals, is also causing changes in the structure of the funeral services industry (i.e., the emergence of the "transfer service" and "direct dispositions"). Memorial Societies have been organized in many of the major cities of North America. For a small annual fee, (often less than $50.00), these societies provide their membership with the necessary information for the disposal of dead bodies in simple, inexpensive fashion (the "do-it-yourself" funeral). The smaller societies are usually able to provide lists of names of cooperative funeral directors who are willing to provide such services while the larger societies may actually employ one. Still something of a novelty in the Eastern half of the continent these organizations are quite large in the West. (Of course, there are potentially more economies-of-scale in simple, standardized procedures.) First Memorial Services Ltd. has operated in Vancouver for three decades and in 1983 served approximately 4,000 clients which then represented one-quarter of the available market. (Perhaps it is not so surprising that normally high cost British Columbia records near the lowest average cost of funerals of all the Provinces.[33]) In California, the "Neptune Society," which serves more than 8,000 clients per year, has purchased cemeteries so that it could offer to its members low cost earth burial [AFD 105(9), 1982, p. 30]. The push for simplicity and low cost has led to novel procedures. The Memorial Society of Maine, in a pilot project, engaged the services of a registered nurse to pick up the corpse, store it in a body bag for the required forty-eight hours, obtain the legal documentation, engage a trucker to deliver the remains to a crematorium, all for a fee one-tenth the usual costs [AFD 105(10) 1982, p. 50]. Other kinds of changes are also observable in the structure of the funeral services industry. Cooperatives owned twenty-four funeral homes which conducted 2,652 funerals in Canada in 1980 [AFD 106(1), 1983, p. 76]. But the average funeral cost and firm size seem no different from the privately owned industry. In the United States a private firm "United Dignity Inc." attempted to establish a chain of twenty-five franchised "discount" funeral homes with the objective of providing "simple and inexpensive funerals with the emphasis on dignity and respect" [AFD 105(10) 1982, p. 50]. (Is this a MacDonald's syndrome?) In Vancouver, Canada's first "retail" casket store opened in the belief that it could deliver to consumers far lower priced caskets, and that independent funeral

---

[33]The *American Funeral Director*, *106*(1), (1983), p. 70 attribute the following information to Statistics Canada. Average cost of a funeral in Canada in 1980 was $1,611. By province it was: Nfld. $1,484; P.E.I. $1,517; N.S. $1,501; N.B. $1,594; P.Q. $1,196; Ont. $1,693; Man. $1,396; Sask. $1,593; Alta. $1,593; B.C. $1,304. If cremations were included the average dropped to $1,155.

directors would accept both the dead body *and the casket* from clients [AFD 106(1) 1983, p. 89].

The common thread through all of these different ways to own and organize firms is the observed tendency toward ever increasing firm size. If economies-of-scale persist, then, in the ultimate, economic theory suggests that a monopoly would be the most efficient type of organization. That is, a single firm would be the method of production of the desired services that could achieve the lowest costs in terms of resources required. (Transportation costs would define the extent of the geographic area that each firm would serve—perhaps we would have a single firm in every city or town of certain size.) As everyone must use the service the appropriate type of firm is a "public utility." Public utilities can be government owned and operated "crown corporations" (the Bank of Canada, Ontario Hydro) or privately owned (Bell Telephone, Union Gas, Canadian Pacific). These types of industrial organizations require substantial government regulation to insure low prices and equitable access to some standard level of service. While low cost funeral services could be produced in this way (perhaps some country in the world currently operates such a system) there does not seem to be any move on the part of the industry, government, or the public at large to even consider such a change. It seems that as private individuals we prefer (choose?) the great variety of quality and cost of service offered to us.[34]

We can summarize all these remarks regarding the structure and role of the funeral services industry as follows. This relatively small industry in terms of both total sales and employment is undergoing considerable change. On the one hand, there exists a traditional sector. It processes as much as 80 percent of all deaths. The funeral services provided are extensive and the handling of the dead body could be said to reflect the growing real incomes and materials consumption characteristic of our Western society. In this sense, the trend that began early in nineteenth century, *and still continues* toward ever more lavish and complex funerals is not surprising. Neither is it surprising that this sector of the industry *and the private individuals who choose* such services exhibit a reluctance to change. On the other hand, the smaller segment of the industry which tends to provide simple, low-cost funerals, serving clients motivated by such things as environment, conservation, and consumerism concerns, has been rapidly growing especially in the last two decades. Both sectors exhibit a trend to even larger firm size. Nonetheless, considerable competitive pressure is evident. Consequently, the criticisms of the industry appear exaggerated if not unwarranted. It seems unlikely that the identical services could be provided at less real cost by any alternative arrangements to produce those services.

---

[34] A suggestion made by a funeral director was that the average price of the funeral was not as significant in the choice of the funeral home as the socio-economic group served. Funeral homes tend to *specialize* on class and religious lines! Each large city will have its "establishment," "Protestant middle class," "Roman Catholic," "Ethnic" funeral home in which a particular kind or "customary" funeral will be expected.

IV. CEMETERY LAND: A DISAPPEARING RESOURCE

Perhaps the most significant issue for the "cemeteries" industry is the limited supply of land available for its use.

Articles on the subject appear regularly in both trade journals and the popular press. One, with the same title of this part of this chapter appeared in 1983 [CFD S9, 1983, pp. 21-22]. Another "No Room at the Graveyard," in 1988 [Toronto Star, July 28, 1988, pp. H1-H2]. A recent one, "Grave Shortage of Land" appeared in 1995 [Toronto Star, September 3, 1995 pp. D5 and 6]. In this most recent one cemetery administrators predict Metro Toronto has space for burials for about one decade more. The city's three major cemeteries, Necropolis, Mount Pleasant, and Prospect are expected to be full by 2001. Scarborough's major cemetery may be full by 2000 and North York's by 2008. In London, Ontario its Mount Pleasant Cemetery is also expected to be full by 2001; its older Oakland Cemetery was recently redeveloped to make more effective use of empty space thus extending its life for another decade (interview with Cemetery Manager). The economic consequence of the predictable shortage of grave spaces is that they have become more expensive; in Toronto about eighteen times more expensive than in the 1960s (which represents a price increase 3 times faster than the rate of inflation). This kind of price increase was not only predicable given market conditions but with the fixed, or at least inelastic supply of land coupled with the increasing numbers of deaths due to population size, such price increases can be expected to continue.

In attempting to assess just how scare cemetery land really is, the first problem is to determine just how many cemeteries exist. Again current data was difficult to obtain. However, the numbers have shown only little change in the last decade. Hence, the 1983 data shown in Table 7 are indicative. Ontario reported 4,818 cemeteries of which 2,016 were "closed" (no longer accepting dead bodies for burial) while 2,802 are still "active." Of these active cemeteries only forty are "for profit" private businesses. It would be more helpful to know how much active or closed area existed so that one could estimate the available capacity. While the available land area in cemeteries is known to the government ministry responsible for licensing them, such data are not published. Nevertheless, the present situation in London, Ontario can be developed as a suggestive example. London has eleven cemeteries: six small ones are closed. The five active cemeteries covered 420 acres of land (after the large annexation of area by London on Jan. 1, 1993 this represents about .402% of the City's land). As an acre of land provides places for 700 to 1,200 dead and as most of the land is used, it is very likely the dead outnumber the living even in this relatively young city.

While the City may now have additional land available, municipalities are not likely to be favorably disposed to its development as cemeteries for a number of reasons. The Ontario Cemeteries Act states municipal by-laws must be passed to approve new cemeteries and that municipalities can prohibit cemetery development. Also, assets of cemeteries that are abandoned by their owners become the property of the municipality in which they are located but that municipality must also assume the obligations for its care and maintenance. While it is true that cemeteries are obligated to maintain "Care & Maintenance Trust Funds" into which they must currently place about one-quarter of the sale price of new plots, and the investment income from these funds provides the maintenance budget, the adequacy of such income to meet the maintenance expense is not at all certain (especially for "full" or "closed" cemeteries).[35] Moreover, the numbers of cemeteries data in Table 7 show that 1,877 of the 2,016 closed cemeteries were abandoned and now being maintained at municipal expense. Second, of the 2,802 active cemeteries, 1,637 were run by churches and 634 by other non-profit (hence non-taxable) organizations. Four hundred and ninety-two were operated by the municipalities themselves and only forty (1.5%) were run by profit oriented business. This lack of potential revenue is exacerbated by the increase in vandalism since the 1950s (hence, more maintenance costs), and increasing financial pressures on municipal politicians. On the other hand the private, "for profit" cemeteries can generate substantial revenues. At prices for nearby rural land at $20,000 per acre plus $60,000 per acre for the necessary expense of preparing grave sites, the $80,000 per acre cost [Toronto Star, Sept. 3, 1995, p. D6] would appear to be readily offset by the gross revenues of over one-half million dollars (700 graves per acre times three-quarters of even the $750 minimum plot cost is $421,875). However, even in the case of these private cemeteries, the problem of their long run ownership remains. New cemetery land may be scarcely less desirable and just as difficult for a municipality to justify as new "sanitary land fill" sites.

Another aspect of the problem of the supply of cemetery land is the length of time for which such land is alienated. When land is sold to a private property owner for most purposes that land can be recovered by the state. Buildings do get old, torn down, and the property redeveloped. If all else fails, expropriation is always a possibility. Even land used for public purposes, (roads, parks) can be put to alternative uses. Cemeteries are intended to be "perpetual." The Cemeteries Act of Ontario does provide for both the closing of, and the expropriation from their owners, of cemeteries. However, the closing of a cemetery does not mean that the land can be re-used. If the latter is intended, the bodies must be disinterred, removed, and reinterred in some cemetery in the same or adjacent municipality. Such an eventuality can only occur after all plot owners have been given notice. Considerable care must be used for disinterment (prior to the 1990 legislative revisions "hand tools" had to be used). During the actual removal of the remains a representative of the local medical officer of health must be in attendance. Moreover, "When a cemetery must be moved, it is essential that the area be thoroughly searched to eliminate the distressing possibility of missed graves" [Middlesex-London Health Unit]. In past

---

[35] Japan's recent experience in this regard is of some interest. Expressing the Japanese yen values in Canadian dollar equivalents shows that the $13,500 to $27,000 cost of the funeral including interment, the Japanese family must pay about $13,500 for a cremation plot space of 30 × 60 centimeters and then must pay annual maintenance fees of $270! Those families unwilling to pay the annual fees can sell the sites back to the cemetery for 70 percent of its current market value [The Economist, Nov. 5, 1994, p. 69].

such cases, the Health Unit required that diagonal trenches (about 2′ 6″ wide on 4′ to 5′ centers), to burial depth (6 ft.) be dug across the property. This trenching and searching technique in one case recovered 102 additional burials not previously known or suspected. One official of the Health Unit charged with the regulatory supervision of disinterments commented that the Health Unit had to serve as the "conscience of the community" in such "closing of cemetery" cases.[36] Despite these somewhat onerous conditions cemeteries have been moved; the best known example is perhaps the one which occurred during the construction of the St. Lawrence Seaway. Another large move occurred in Grimsby, Ontario in 1958/59. As to the actual length of time "perpetual" means, it is interesting that some of the larger private cemetery companies make their business plans in terms of 100 years.

If the available land is not likely to be increased, could it be used more intensively? Some such steps are already being taken. The practice of interring two bodies per grave (one above the other) is now quite common. In the plots provided for the indigent in London, three are now being buried. One wonders why it should not be possible to reuse a grave after a number of years. The City of Calgary in the 1980s turned down a serious proposal made by civic staff that the city's grave sites should only be "leased" and reused after 50 to 100 years. The "precious little remains" at that time could be transferred to mass graves [CFD 59(2), 1983, pp. 7-8]. The practice does seem to be common elsewhere in the world. The Greek Islands are reputed to re-use their graves after five years moving the remaining bones to a "charnel house." In Hong Kong, the dead "rest" in the cemetery for six years. After that, the remains are cremated. Alternatively, for a rental fee of about $7.00 per month, they are placed in a niche in an above ground "coffin home" where relatives are accorded "visiting" privileges [D. Murray, CBC. The National, Jan. 4, 1983]. While Canadians (at least Calgarians) may not yet be ready for such an alternative, unless one is found, the conclusion that the supply of cemetery land is fixed (or inelastic) is inescapable.

Other issues regarding the cemeteries industry, such as pre-need purchasing of grave sites, increased advertising by the industry, and the problems caused by the differences in legislation in different jurisdictions, have not yet been specifically dealt with. Also, very little has been said about the structure and organization of the cemeteries business and its impact on both client demand and supply. From the sketchy data obtained to this point little can be concluded. Let it suffice to say that there are significant differences between the cemeteries industry and the funeral services industry. The former is made up largely of public non-profit owners and the innovations in the industry are being initiated by the relatively new, rapidly growing, private, profit-motivated firms. These new firms are relatively large as firms but they still account for but a small share of the total market. The situation is precisely reversed in the funeral services industry in almost every respect. In both industries

---

[36]Note that single grave disinterments occur frequently—on average about one grave every two weeks! In these days of broken and divided homes the survivors worry about who the dead are with and some poor souls are moved two or three times.

growing firm size is a factor and both cause public concern when they consider "marketing" or "advertising" strategies. For example, what is the impact on services sold the public; or, should the cemeteries firms be allowed to continue to pay their salespeople on commission basis? There is also the public concern with the potential for fraud with respect to both the funds paid for both prepaid funerals and those provided for the "perpetual care" of grave sites. The large parts of both the Ontario Cemeteries and Funeral Services Acts and their recent revisions are evidence of this concern. And yet, the number of known incidents of fraud have been few, and the sums involved small, relative to the size of the industries.

To conclude, considerably more research needs to be done in both of these industries. The need for more knowledge seems greater in the cemeteries area if only because the ultimate needs (personal choices) create a somewhat more difficult economic problem.

STATISTICAL APPENDIX

Table 1. Deaths and Death Rates, Selected Countries, 1991

Belgium	105.2	12.58
Denmark	59.5	12.49
Germany	900.8	11.24
Greece	93.5	9.12
Spain	338.2	8.65
France	526.0	9.19
Ireland	31.5	8.92
Italy	546.8	9.46
Luxembourg	3.7	9.49
Netherlands	129.9	8.58
Portugal	104.4	10.60
United Kingdom	643.1	11.16
Canada	196.1	7.19
United States	2,165.0	8.53
Mexico	481.5	5.52
Australia	118.9	6.73
New Zealand	26.5	7.68
Japan	829.5	6.91

Derived from Statistics Canada, *Canada Year Book,* 1994, Table 3.1.

Table 2a. Number of Deaths, Death Rates,[a] and Average Ages, Canada, Provinces, and the Territories, 1981 and 1991

Region	Number of Deaths[b]		Death Rate[b]		Average Ages[c]	
	1981	1991	1981	1991	1981	1991
Canada	171,029	195,568	7.0	7.2	33.1	35.3
Newfoundland	3,230	3,798	5.7	6.6	29.5	33.2
Prince Edward Island	992	1,188	8.1	9.1	33.3	35.3
Nova Scotia	6,958	7,255	8.2	8.1	33.3	35.6
New Brunswick	5,139	5,469	7.4	7.5	32.3	35.1
Quebec	42,684	49,121	6.6	7.2	32.9	35.7
Ontario	62,838	72,917	7.3	7.4	33.7	35.4
Manitoba	8,648	8,943	8.4	8.2	34.0	35.4
Saskatchewan	7,523	8,098	7.8	8.1	33.5	35.3
Alberta	12,823	14,451	5.7	5.7	30.5	32.9
British Columbia	19,857	23,977	7.2	7.5	34.0	36.2
Yukon	141	114	6.1	4.2	28.0	30.5
Northwest Territories	196	237	4.3	4.3	24.9	25.2

[a]Number of deaths per 1,000 population.
[b]Statistics Canada Cat. 82-003, Health Reports 1993, Vol. 5, No. 2.
[c]Statistics Canada Cat. 91-537, Occasional: Revised Intercensal Population and Family Estimates.

Table 2b. Rank Order Death Rates and Median Ages, by Provinces, 1981 and 1991[a]

Region	Death Rates[b]		Median Ages[c]	
	1981	1991	1981	1991
Newfoundland	2	4	3	4
Prince Edward Island	10	12	7	6
Nova Scotia	11	9	7	10
New Brunswick	8	7	5	5
Quebec	5	5	6	11
Ontario	7	6	10	8
Manitoba	12	11	11	8
Saskatchewan	9	9	9	6
Alberta	2	3	4	3
British Columbia	6	7	11	12
Yukon	4	1	2	2
Northwest Territories	1	2	1	1

[a]Calculated from Table 2a.
[b]Rank order lowest to highest.
[c]Rank order youngest to oldest.

Table 3. Death Rates, Males and Females, 1976 and 1992

Age Group	Males		Females	
	1976	1992	1976	1992
0 years	15.0	7.0	11.9	5.9
1-4	0.8	0.4	0.6	0.3
5-9	0.4	0.2	0.3	0.2
10-14	0.4	0.3	0.2	0.2
15-19	1.4	0.9	0.5	0.4
20-24	1.8	1.2	0.5	0.4
25-29	1.5	1.2	0.7	0.5
30-34	1.5	1.3	0.8	0.5
35-39	2.0	1.5	1.2	0.8
40-44	3.2	2.1	1.7	1.3
45-49	5.6	3.2	3.0	1.9
50-54	8.9	5.3	4.3	3.1
55-59	14.3	9.4	6.7	5.3
60-64	22.1	15.5	10.4	8.2
65-69	33.3	25.1	16.4	13.3
70-74	51.4	37.1	26.3	19.9
75-79	77.3	62.2	44.7	34.8
80-84	118.3	94.5	76.8	57.2
85-89		148.5		98.5
85+	195.5		154.7	
90+		226.1		192.4
All Ages	8.4	7.5	6.1	6.3

1976 data from Statistics Canada, *Canada Year Book 1980-81,* p. 146, 1992 see Table II.

Table 4. Death Rates, Canada, By Month, 1992

January	17,545
February	15,494
March	17,137
April	16,122
May	16,496
June	15,445
July	15,715
August	15,581
September	15,265
October	16,614
November	16,495
December	18,636
Total Deaths	196,54

Statistics Canada, *Annual Demographic Statistics 1993,* Cat. CS 91-213.

Table 5. Number of Funeral Directors[a] by Province—1989[b]

	Male	Female	Total
Newfoundland	55	0	55
Prince Edward Island	15	0	20
Nova Scotia	160	20	175
New Brunswick	140	10	150
Quebec	575	70	645
Ontario	1,275	135	1,410
Manitoba	75	0	75
Saskatchewan	130	10	145
Alberta	255	20	285
British Columbia	220	30	255
Yukon	0	0	0
Northwest Territories	0	0	0
CANADA	2,910	300	3,205

[a]Occupational Group No. 6141—Funeral Directors, Embalmers, and Related Occupations.
[b]Statistics Canada, *1981 Census, Population, Labour Force,* Cat. No. 92-917, Vol. I, Table I.
Note: Columns do not necessarily add due to estimating procedures used.

Table 6. Number of Deaths and Death Rates
Canada and Ontario

	Canada			Ontario		
Year	Deaths	Rate 1	Rate 2	Deaths	Rate 1	Rate 2
1982	174,413	7.1		63,696	7.3	
1983	174,484	7.0		64,507	7.3	
1984	175,727	7.0	6.8	64,703	7.2	7.0
1985	181,323	7.2	7.0	66,747	7.4	7.2
1986	184,224	7.2	7.0	67,865		7.2
1987	184,953	7.2	7.0	68,119		7.0
1988	190,011	7.3	7.1	70,679	7.5	7.2
1989	190,965	7.3	7.0	70,907	7.3	7.0
1990	191,973	7.3	6.9	70,818	7.4	6.8
1991	195,568	7.2	7.0	72,917		7.0
1992	196,545		6.9	73,206		6.9
1993	201,020		7.0	73,600		6.9

All data are from various Statistics Canada sources. Rate 1 is primarily from Canada Year Books and Rate 2 is Annual Demographic Statistics 1993.

Table 7. Ownership of Cemeteries and Crematoria in Ontario—
November 1983[a]

Type of Owner		
A. Active (open)		2,802
Churches	1,637	
Anglican	290	
Roman Catholic	428	
United	376	
Presbyterian	91	
Mennonite	72	
Baptist	38	
Lutheran	83	
Jewish	176	
Other Religions	81	
Plot Owners (co-op)	634	
Municipal	492	
Profit Type Business	40	
B. Closed		2,016
Abandoned (Maintained by Municipality)	1,877	
Closed (Maintained by a Church or Charity)	139	
TOTAL		4,818

[a]Data provided by Ontario, Ministry of Consumer and Corporate Relations, Cemeteries Branch, Toronto.

Table 8. Cremations in Ontario[a]

1975	6,798
1976	7,798
1977	8,310
1978	9,128
1979	9,562
1980	10,554
1981	11,806
1982	12,488
1983	13,562
1984	14,608
1985	15,680
1993	33,120

[a]1975-85 data from London Free Press, Jan. 19, 1987. 1993 data are an estimate based on current 45 percent cremation rate.

REFERENCE

1. P. A. Samuelson, W. B. Norohaus, and J. McCallum, *Economics* (6th Canadian Edition), p. 3.

BIBLIOGRAPHY

American Funeral Director, esp. Vols. 105 and 106, 1983 and 1984.
Board of Funeral Services (415 Yonge St., Toronto) *Survey of Funeral Pricing Conducted In Ontario, December, 1992, Summary Report* and *Funeral Establishment 1995 Survey Quick Facts.*
Canadian Funeral Director, esp. Vols. 59 and 60, 1983 and 1984.
D. Flynn, *The Truth About Funerals* (self published, 1995).
The Globe and Mail (Toronto) *The Dying Game,* Dec. 16, 1995 pp. B6-B4.
The Loewen Group Inc. (Burnaby, British Columbia), *Annual Report 1992, Annual Report 1994* and *Annual Report 1995.*
Middlesex-London District Health Unit (London, Ontatio) Circular Program #001, Activity #004, *Disinterment and Reburial.*
Queens Printer for Ontario (Toronto),
 The Cemeteries Act, (Rev.), RSO 1990, Chap. C.4 (1992);
 The Cemeteries Act, RSO 1980, Chap. 59;
 The Cemeteries Act, RSO 1977, Chap. 37;
 Funeral Directors and Establishments Act, RSO 1990, Chap. F.36 (April, 1993);
 Funeral Services Act, RSO 1977, Chap. 1977.
Statistics Canada, (Ottawa),
 Canada Year Book 1991 and *Canada Year Book 1980-81;*
 Causes of Death, 1981 Cat. 84-203;
 1981 Census of Canada, Population, Cat. 92-901;
 1981 Census of Canada, Population, Labour Force, Cat. 12-917;
 Health Reports, Vol. 5, No. 2, Cat. 12-003 (1993);
 Statistiques Démographiques Annuelles 1993, Cat. 91-213 Annual
 Vital Statistics, Vol I, Births and Deaths, 1981 Cat. 84-204.
The Toronto Star, *Grave Shortage of Land,* Sept. 3, 1995, pp. D5 and 6; *No Room at the Graveyard,* July 28, 1988, pp. H1 and 2.

CHAPTER 8
Economics and Death: Private Good/Public Good

P. Albert Koop

> Economics is the study of the use of scarce resources to satisfy unlimited human wants [1].

> Economics is the study of how men (sic) and society end up choosing, with or without the use of money, to employ scarce productive resources, which could have alternative uses, to produce various commodities. It studies how the commodities are distributed for consumption, now and in the future, among various people and groups in society. It analyzes the costs and benefits of improving patterns of resource allocation [2].

Why a section written by an economist in a book entitled *Readings in Thanatology?* Do economists have anything useful to say here? Many are skeptical. Needless to say, I am not. Even a cursory reflection on industries such as funeral services or health care demonstrates the value of analysis from an economic perspective for both service providers and users. There is a general social interest as well. The definitions given above point out that economics is a social science. What interest does society have in these issues? This question will provide the focus for most of this chapter.

INTRODUCTORY COMMENTS

First of all, what do I mean when I say that there is a general social interest? It may be helpful to look at a specific issue. Later on in this chapter I will talk about inheritance. Quite properly, I will consider how individual needs, both of the dying and of survivors, are met by various inheritance practices. The economist, however, focuses on the social interest. How are society's needs met? What social goals are fostered by these various practices? Is social justice achieved?

Second, economists are careful to distinguish between two terms—income and wealth—which are often used interchangeably in daily conversation. Income is a measure of an individual's claim on the flow of society's output over a particular period of time, usually over a year. The claim may be exercised immediately in current consumption or it may be saved for the future. Wealth is a stock, not a flow. It is a measure of an individual's ownership of assets at a moment in time. Keeping these concepts, and especially the distinction between them, in mind helps to avoid confusion when discussing the issues dealt with here. Of course, emphasizing the distinction between them does not mean that they are unrelated. Asset ownership may well be the source of income flows. This is especially the case for high income individuals.

PRIVATE GOOD

As indicated above, a brief digression to consider the issue of individual need and well-being is appropriate, even though the economist's main concern is with social welfare. The death of an individual is the occasion for the transfer of wealth and income. The amounts may at times be substantial. Very few of us attain what some might consider the ideal of leaving this world as we entered, that is, with nothing. We are concerned about the well-being of loved ones, especially, but not necessarily exclusively, family members. There are moral and legal obligations we have toward dependents which may well not disappear on our death. These are best addressed through a well prepared will and an appropriate life insurance program. If you do not tackle these very real questions of inter-generational claims and obligations on an individual basis, the state will intervene and do it for you.

Appropriate terms for your will, and which life insurance policies you should buy, are individual decisions. These are the vehicles available for you to actualize your concern for the well-being of others in the eventuality of your untimely death. The ability to transfer the risk through these instruments is the source of their utility. It may bring peace of mind for the dying person and may ease the grieving process for survivors. One should, however, be careful not to use the will or the life insurance policies as a means of control over others. To delay transfer of assets until one's death may well be inappropriate.

SOCIAL GOOD

What is the social interest as far as these issues of wealth and income are concerned? What do we perceive as social justice here? This is a complex issue and these few pages will not resolve everything for you. It is appropriate, however, to start by identifying three basic principles which seem to find general support in our society. First of all, an individual's claim to income must be perceived as legitimate. Second, individuals should be free to use income based on a legitimate claim as they see fit. Finally, the resulting distribution of income should be socially acceptable, generally taken to mean an avoidance of extreme disparities. At the very least, the last point is taken to mean that differences in incomes among people should be based on some reasonable notion of differences in the contributions individuals have made to the production of the product of society. When these principles are in conflict, when to live up to one means to violate the other, then the choice of appropriate social policy is far from obvious. Much of the more acrimonious political debate that we observe revolves around different interpretations of these three basic principles.

Before considering specific issues regarding the redistribution of income and wealth on an individual's death, we need to consider the question of what constitutes a legitimate income claim. When analyzing personal income we identify three sources. First there is labor income. This is income received because of an individual's participation with time and effort in the production of output. Then there is property income. This is income received because of ownership of assets which are used in the production of output. Finally there is transfer income. This is income transferred to an individual for reasons other than participation in productive processes. The transfer may be made because of the specific personal characteristics of the individual, age or disability are examples, or it may be a relationship to another person as in parent to child, or it may be totally gratuitous as in charity.

Are all three sources of income equally legitimate? Is there anything approaching a social consensus here? On some aspects the answer seems to be yes, on others no. There is widespread support for the idea that labor income is legitimate income. Some years ago the Catholic Church could speak of "the primacy of labour" without too much opposition [3]. We do not, however, generally accept the idea that labor is the only legitimate source of income. Critics challenged the bishops on the grounds that their document implied that property income is not legitimate. This clearly was not acceptable to many Canadians, including many Catholics.[1] Transfer income is generally received with a considerable degree of scepticism. Not all transfers are considered illegitimate, however, the burden of proof seems to have shifted. Just as labor income is assumed to be legitimate unless demonstrated otherwise, so transfer income is suspect unless demonstrable need or other acceptable characteristic legitimates the transfer.

With these principles in mind we are ready to examine certain institutions, laws, policies, and practices which affect the redistributions of wealth and income which occur on the death of an individual person. We will look at the life insurance industry[2] and at inheritance laws and practices. Let it be clearly understood that this discussion is far from definitive, merely giving a sample of the problems and a feel for the nature of the appropriate analysis.

The typical life insurance policy involves the transfer of wealth or income to a beneficiary on the death of the insured.[3] Is this transfer socially acceptable? Does society have an interest in it? The right to this transfer was created during the lifetime of the insured who gave up income to pay the premium. The principle of

---

[1] The slogan "property is theft" has been attributed to Marcel Prudhon, a nineteenth-century French socialist.

[2] Borch [5] provides the best, if somewhat technical, discussion of the life insurance industry from an economic perspective.

[3] Life insurance companies also sell annuities which involve payments starting at a specific point in time during the lifetime of an individual and terminating at death. Aspects of life insurance are introduced when so-called "joint and survivor" options are introduced.

free use of legitimate income suggests that it is none of society's business. The case is not so clear, however, when it is recognized that it represents transfer income to the beneficiary and social norms questioning the legitimacy of transfer income are commonplace.

The life insurance industry's approach to this problem is through the development of the concept of an "insurable interest." To use our terminology, we would say that an "insurable interest" exists if the beneficiary has a legitimate claim on the income of the insured. In turn, this legitimacy is determined by the nature of the relationship between them. It is recognized that a business relationship may be the basis for such a claim. The income earning capacity of a group, say partners or members of a firm, may well be bigger than the sum of individual earning capacities. Thus, partners have an insurable interest in each others lives. Of greater interest are the claims within the family. In our society, the rights within the nuclear family are well established. One spouse has a legitimate claim on the income of the other. Children have a claim on the income of parents. Most commonly, the spouse is the named beneficiary. At times it may be a child. Often, even though the spouse is named, the indirect beneficiaries may be children. It used to be the case that parents' rights to the income of their children were just as well recognized. This, however, is no longer the case. Old age security has become the province of state social security systems, pension entitlements acquired through employment or personal savings during ones income earning years.

To say that the legitimacy of a claim on transfer income is based on relationship is only part of the story. A claim cannot be excessive and it must be timely. In practice this means that the beneficiary should be able to maintain the accustomed life style for a reasonable length of time after the death of the insured. Of course, this leaves the term "reasonable" to be defined. In general, the objective seems to be a transition period sufficiently long, keeping the needs of children in mind, to enable the beneficiary to enter (or re-enter) the labor force.

Two examples of products developed by the life insurance industry illustrate my point. One is the guaranteed family income benefit frequently sold as a rider attached to a basic life insurance policy. This guarantees an income to the beneficiary commencing on the death of the insured and terminating at a specified date in the future. This may well be a child's twenty-first birthday. Whatever the date, the transitionary period is long enough to allow the child to enter the labor force. The commonly used group life insurance policy, usually a fringe benefit of employment, is another example. The amount of insurance protection is usually stated in terms of years of salary, frequently three years. Here it is implied that three years is a reasonable length of time for the beneficiary to make alternate income arrangements.

When discussing inheritance law and custom we could repeat many of these same points.[4] The focus has been on the first two of the three principles of social justice

---

[4] Posner [6], a U.S. lawyer and judge who has a long-standing interest in the use of economic analyses of legal issues, presents an extensive discussion of these issues. See especially chapter 5 on family law and chapter 18 on the transmission of wealth at death.

listed earlier, namely that income claims be legitimate and that legitimate income be freely disposable. It is when considering the third principle, namely that the overall income distribution be equitable, that the special characteristics of property income become particularly relevant. Remember that many people consider property income in the same light as transfer income. They see it as unearned, and consequently suspect. The basic social policy issue is to what extent, if any, should wealth and/or wealth transfers be taxed. Of course, inheritances represent a significant proportion of wealth transfers and gifts while the donor is alive may well be made with the intent of avoiding inheritance tax where such a tax is levied.

A comprehensive discussion of inheritance taxation is beyond the scope of this brief chapter. A consideration of just two questions, the effect of inheritances on the overall distribution of income and the effect of inheritance taxation on incentives, is enough to give a feel for the issues under discussion.

An examination of Canada's income distribution with a view toward understanding why present disparities exist shows that property income plays a key role in creating and sustaining them. This does not mean that eliminating property income would create an equitable income distribution. Labor income differentials may result from differences in skills or from membership in professional associations. As such, they may be acceptable if they are tied to productivity differentials. Even if they are not, they do not explain the extremes. The incomes of the very rich, those at the extreme upper end of the income distribution, are for the most part property incomes. These incomes may be more acceptable if the property has been acquired by the past effort and sacrifice of the current owner, however, where the property is inherited this justification does not apply.[5] Inheritance is a very important means of acquiring property in Canada [4].

How can we explain these wealth concentrations? Why do they persist? Inheritance practices clearly exacerbate the situation. Consider primogeniture and endogamy. Primogeniture is the practice of passing the whole estate, or at least the bulk of it, to the oldest son.[6] Endogamy is the practice of marrying within ones own social class. The two practices together make for ever greater wealth concentration over the generations. It is probably too strong a statement to make to say that primogeniture and endogamy are Canadian social norms. There are, however, tendencies in this direction to be of concern.[7] The case for heavy, perhaps even confiscatory, inheritance taxes rests on these considerations, assuming the acceptance of the egalitarian value system implied by the third principle of social justice mentioned earlier.

---

[5] I will spare you my usual lecture on the social damage done to our society by our reliance on lotteries and other forms of gambling to raise funds for public projects.

[6] The important point as far as the concentration of wealth is concerned is that the estate is passed on intact from one generation to the next. Some Eastern European societies practice ultimogeniture where the youngest son inherits.

[7] Differences in these practices go a long way toward explaining why wealth is more concentrated in the United Kingdom than it is in either Canada or the United States.

Every social policy issue seems to have two sides. That certainly is the case here. Consideration of arguments against inheritance taxation leads directly to a consideration of the issue of incentives. All taxes affect incentives and thus affect individual behavior. Inheritance taxation affects the portfolio choices of individuals, that is, it affects the kind of assets people choose to hold. Assets may be held in financial, physical, or human capital form. Financial assets are the obligations expressed in monetary terms that others have toward you. They are usually documented by pieces of paper (the term "paper assets" may be used) such as bonds, mortgages, share certificates, and the like. Physical assets, as the name implies, are real, but non-human, factors of production such as land, buildings, and machines which are used to generate output and, from the point of view of an individual, to generate income. Human capital is at best a nebulous concept. It involves expenditures made by, or on behalf of, an individual in order to make that person more productive. Educational and training expenditures come immediately to mind. Healthy people are also more productive, so expenditures on health and nutrition also involve human capital formation. As well, people may be more productive in an urban factory than on a subsistence farm, so rural to urban migration may also qualify as human capital investment.

Different forms of investment have clear social implications. Adding to a society's stock of physical and human capital adds to its capacity to produce goods and services for its citizens. It creates the possibility for everyone to be better off. Financial assets are not themselves directly productive.[8] It is important that the tax system, and in this case inheritance taxation, does not bias asset ownership in an undesirable direction. In this regard it is important to note that an inheritance tax is levied on financial and physical assets and it is collected in money terms (tax collectors usually will not take a tractor or a painting, they want cash). First of all, if an individual wants to assure the heirs of a good income with as little as possible diverted in taxes, there is an incentive to avoid both financial and physical capital and to concentrate on human capital formation. Stated in non-technical terms, inheritance taxation encourages parents to provide their children with education and training, with good nutrition, rather than with other forms of property. On the other hand, the tax collectors need for cash biases the holdings away from physical assets toward financial assets. These are more easily converted into cash and are generally divisible into appropriate monetary units.

Again we see that social policy presents interesting dilemmas. In this Information Age, the time of a Knowledge Revolution, inheritance taxation seems to be fairly good social policy in that it encourages human capital formation. But what about the family farm? All we need do is to think of the problem of maintaining family businesses intact over succeeding generations in order to see the pernicious effects that inheritance taxation may have.

---

[8] This does not mean that they are useless. A well-developed market for financial assets is necessary in that it facilitates the accumulation of other forms of capital. The basic point, however, remains.

This brief discussion of the incentive effects of inheritance taxation is far from comprehensive. This chapter has focused primarily on the issue of social justice. It must be remembered that society is concerned both with social justice and with productive capacity.[9]

In summary, a death is the occasion for substantial transfers of wealth and income. The interest of the heirs directly involved is obvious, however, society has a stake here as well. Inheritance practices and related tax policies may well affect the productive capacity of society and directly affects society's ability to achieve social justice.

REFERENCES

1. R. G. Lipsey, P. N. Courant, and D. D. Purvis, *Economics* (8th Canadian Edition), Harper Collins, New York, 1994.
2. P. A. Samuelson and A. Scott, *Economics* (5th Canadian Edition), McGraw-Hill Ryerson, Toronto, 1980.
3. Canadian Conference of Catholic Bishops, Episcopal Commission of Social Affairs, *Ethical Reflections on the Economic Crisis,* 1983.
4. L. Osberg, *Economic Inequality in Canada,* Butterworths, Toronto, 1981.
5. K. H. Borch, *Economics of Insurance,* Elsevier Science Publishers, Amsterdam, 1990.
6. R. A. Posner, *Economic Analysis of Law* (2nd Edition), Little, Brown and Company, Boston, 1977.
7. J. A. Schumpeter, *The Theory of Economic Development,* Harvard University Press, 1934.

---

[9] Schumpeter's thoughts on these issues, although written some sixty years ago, are still worth reading [7].

CHAPTER 9
Death Walks the Wards: Dying in the Hospital

Joseph W. Lella

INTRODUCTION

Death and dying in hospital, what it is like, why it is that way and what can be done to improve it are not easy issues to address with great certainty. We have no firm knowledge of: how many people die in the hospital; what are the circumstances of their deaths; and, what causes the human problems associated with them. There is still less known with certainty about what is being done about problems and for whom. There is much, however, that we do know. We have a rough idea of the proportions of those who die in hospitals and other "medical" institutions and it is large.[1] Novels, short stories, movies, autobiographies, and other reminiscences are filled with descriptions of how people die; personal descriptions of what it feels like, and what the circumstances have been. We also have numerous data-based analyses of the history, ideology, and social organization of the modern health care system. We know how that system has evolved, what its dominant beliefs, values, and justifications have been—its ideology. We know much about the patterns of relationships of the social organization that make it up. From all of this, it is possible to derive relatively sound ideas about our topic, and even if those ideas are only relatively sound, it is important to put them forth since we all shall die, and most of us, I suspect, would like to die as comfortably and as peacefully as possible—with our God, and/or ourselves, and our loved ones. Whether and how we are allowed to do this is one crucial test of the humanity of our society. We need to work at understanding our topic.

---

[1] "Mortality statistics for 1980 in the United States show 60.5 percent of deaths occurring in hospitals or medical centers, 13.5 percent in other institutions, 8.4 percent classified as dead-on-arrival, 17.5 percent occurring in other places, and 0.1 percent unknown. These results suggest that the final period of living for the majority of those who die takes place in hospitals, but the length of time involved and the setting for dying is not completely clear" [1, p. 166].

DEATH IN THE FIRST PERSON

I am a student nurse. I am dying. I write this to you who are, and will become, nurses in the hope that by sharing my feelings with you, you may someday be better able to help those who share my experience . . .

Nursing must be advancing, but I wish it would hurry. We're taught not to be overly cheery, to omit the "Everything's fine" routine, and we have done pretty well. But now one is left in a lonely silent void. With the protective "fine, fine" gone, the staff is left with only their own vulnerability and fear.

You slip in and out of my room, give me medications and check my blood pressure. Is it because I am a student nurse, myself, or just a human being, that I sense your fright? And your fear enhances mine. Why are you afraid? I am the only one who is dying.

I know, you feel insecure, don't know what to say, don't know what to do. But please believe me, if you care, you can't go wrong. Just admit that you care . . . Don't run away . . . wait . . . all I want to know is that there will be someone to hold my hand when I need it. I am afraid. Death may get to be a routine to you, but it is new to me. You may not see me as unique, but I've never died before. To me, once is pretty unique!

You whisper about my youth, but when one is dying, is he really so young any more? I have lots I wish we could talk about. It really would not take much more of your time because you are in here quite a bit anyway.

If only we could be honest, both admit of our fears, touch one another. If you really care, would you lose so much of your valuable professionalism if you even cried with me? Just person to person? Then, it might not be so hard to die . . . in a hospital . . . with friends close by.

Anonymous [2, p. 25]

WHO DIES IN THE HOSPITAL AND WHY?

Like this young woman, most people today die in a hospital. This seems to be the result of a number of interacting factors. First, people are living longer lives:

> In *1931* the average life expectancy at birth was 62.1 years for females. For males it was 60.0 years.
>
> By *1983-1985* life expectancy for females had continually increased over those five decades to 79.8 years; while for males the figure was 72.9 years [3, p. 60].

Second, mortality rates have shifted upwards:

> The percentage of all deaths occurring during a given year declined, in the under one year old's, from 11.7 percent in 1951, to 2.1 percent in 1981; while the same figure increased for those sixty-five years old and over from 53.6 percent in 1951 to 67 percent in 1981 [4].

People are also tending to die of accidents (largely younger people), and degenerative diseases (heart disease, cancer, and stroke) which tend to occur among the elderly [4]. These conditions, especially in their terminal phases, may leave the person who suffers from them at least partially disabled and difficult to care for at home given the organization of modern life. With more divorced people in our society needing to support multiple households; with more and more of both adults in cohabiting couples working to support their households, and with many of these subject to the shifting demands of the economy—often relocating in order to maintain employment—it becomes difficult for many to care for the seriously and terminally ill at home. Thus, they go to the hospital.[2]

This tendency has been reinforced over the past several centuries by an evolution in the ideology[3] and social organization[4] of modern life. We tend to define and deal with serious illness and death, less as the unavoidable and inevitable accompaniments of life, more as experiences which we have the right and duty to minimize, avoid and indeed to conquer [10]. To paraphrase a distinguished anthropologist, we have come to believe that we are nature's masters rather than her children, that we have the right to control rather than the duty to submit or at least to respect her. We define success as "doing" rather than "being" and see our futures in the near, short term. We see ourselves as discrete individuals rather than inevitably social beings [11, 12] and have tended to organize our families residentially as small and nuclear (focused on mother, father, and children) rather than as large, multi-generational and multi-linear or extended. We have done all this to fit in with demands of an economy of production and profit (domination and control of nature for the short-term benefit). We need to be mobile and flexible, individually or in small-family groups, to go where the work and profits are. Thus, illness and death are to be avoided and ignored or minimized when they occur because they just don't fit in [10].

But these experiences are unavoidable. They do occur however much we try to put them off or deny their existence. And so, in order to *make* them fit in we give them over to "experts" so that these may conquer them or at least get them out of the way [10, 13, 14].

And thus, more and more of us are living out the end of our lives and dying in hospitals and other medical institutions, the places where these experts work. If we are not to hide our heads in the sand we must try to answer the following question.

---

[2] This is a complex argument made in too sketchy a fashion. For those who are interested, an introduction to its many issues can be found in Blieszner and Bedford [5, 6].

[3] A system of "relatively well-organized ideas and judgements used to describe, explain, interpret, and/or justify a group's situation." Ideologies appeal, to a certain extent, to values (definitions of the good to be sought, the evil to be avoided). They propose definite directions for action for groups and their members [7, 8].

[4] A relatively stable, patterned, set of reciprocal relationships (social roles and norms) that creates the possibility of predictable behavior [79].

WHAT IS HOSPITAL DYING LIKE?

Impersonal Professionalism

It is difficult, if not impossible, to know with any degree of certainty what the quality of experience is for those who die in the vast range contemporary hospital situations. The anonymous nursing student quoted above, however, has given us a personal introduction.

> We're taught not to be overly cheery now, to omit the "Everything's fine" routine.... But now one is left in a lonely silent void. With the protective "fine, fine" gone, the staff is left with only their own vulnerability and fear....
>
> But for me, fear is today and dying is now. You slip in and out of my room, give me medications and check my blood pressure... I know, you feel insecure, don't know what to say, don't know what to do. But please believe me, if you care, you can't go wrong. *Just admit that you care....* We may ask for why's and wherefores, but we don't really expect answers. Don't run away... wait... *all I want to know is that there will be someone to hold my hand when I need it. I am afraid. Death may get to be a routine to you, but it is new to me.*
>
> You may not see me as unique, but I've never died before. To me, once is pretty unique!... *If you really care, would you lose so much of your valuable professionalism if you even cried with me? Just person to person? Then, it might not be so hard to die... in a hospital... with friends close by.*

There are a number of similar descriptions of ordinary people left on a ward to die subjected to irrelevant professional practices and cold bureaucratic routines [15-17]. They are made more comprehensible based upon broader analyses of hospital life and work.

The following are two fictional incidents based on cases from my experience as a social process-ethics consultant to families and staff trying to cope with terminal patients. The incidents highlight additional dimensions of dying in a hospital and provide further reference points for our analysis of its sources, or "why's." I can assure you that if they are not factual, they are "real" in their characteristics.

Poor Communication with the Family of a Comatose Patient

> Mr. Montour was a seventy-five-year-old French Canadian male from the Ottawa Valley. An active dairy farmer all his working life, he had retired at the age of sixty because of a farm injury to his right leg which had been ignored and became gangrenous leading to an amputation above the knee. He later developed kidney disease which rapidly progressed to end stage associated with heart disease. Because of the latter he had numerous hospital admissions for chest pain and fluid in the lungs. For a while, Mr. Montour was given renal dialysis on an outpatient basis for his kidney disease. He managed reasonably well at home. However, Mr. Montour gradually became more and more mentally confused with increasingly frequent episodes of dangerously unreliable behavior. He was diagnosed as suffering from Alzheimer's disease. He subsequently developed a serious peritoneal infection, became even more confused, and was ultimately

admitted to the hospital. His infection was successfully treated and he was sent home. However, his behavior continued to deteriorate and the infection returned. Upon readmission to the medical intensive care unit (ICU), he lay motionless in bed and cried out loudly when he was asked to be washed or when bed linens needed to be changed. He regularly refused to eat and interfered vigorously with attempts to feed him. Over two months, he became unable to recognize family or staff. After a series of weekly reviews, staff reluctantly decided that dialysis should be stopped. A meeting with family, however, did not produce an agreement to this effect. Staff reluctantly continued treatment and arranged for feeding through a series of largely unsatisfactory alternatives. Mr. Montour then suffered a stroke and became comatose. The family was consulted again concerning termination of treatment. They again refused. It was at this point that an ethics consultation was sought. A brief note to us read: "Staff wish to discontinue therapy which would lead to the patient's death. Family (the patient's wife, and three sons) express unreasonable desires to continue. What to do?"

The clinical ethics consultation team in this situation included a physician and a sociologist-ethicist. The hospital had established a service, run by a multidisciplinary committee, which in addition to supplying ad hoc consultations, held four- to eight-week series of ethics rounds on a number of hospital services e.g., medical intensive care, surgical intensive care, geriatrics, psychiatry. The rounds entailed discussions among consultants and attending physicians, residents, interns, medical students, nurses, attendants, social workers, etc., of cases that they found difficult to deal with—cases with ethical and often social-emotional dimensions. The Clinical Ethics Service also did more formal teaching presentations, set up research ethics committees, consulted on ethical issues at administrative levels, and pursued research projects on ethically related matters.

In our initial meeting with ward staff, the above picture was graphically portrayed. Staff was concerned that "nothing more could be done for the patient," and, that keeping him alive was doing him a disservice since he was unconscious and seemed to be in great distress if not actual physical pain. They felt that they were prolonging his suffering, and even inflicting more upon him through their medical procedures. Finally, he was seen to be using a bed which could have been used to greater benefit for another patient.

They were aware that physicians had the right to terminate treatment in such situations but were concerned with the family's lack of agreement. They felt that family (especially the sons) may have been acting "selfishly" upon guilt feelings over prior treatment of their father during his illness. Staff also feared legal action. Consultants were sympathetic with the ICU's position but felt that we should speak with the family before making any recommendations.

Members of the family were anxious to speak with ethical consultants. A meeting was quickly arranged. Their view of matters was consistent with staff's interpretation but differed in subtle but important ways. They had gradually come to accept the inevitability of Mr. Montour's death, and appreciated the competent and sensitive care which he had been given. They even realized that he was in discomfort, but had come to resent what they defined as the hospital's desire to "get rid of him," the current treatment of him as a "vegetable . . . and us as selfish." "We know we are going to have to let him go, but is a bit more time too much to ask? My mother needs to sit here and hold his hand for awhile while he is still breathing." With tears in her eyes, Mrs. Montour said, "We know he feels us there . . . we all need time to say goodbye."

The consultants expressed their appreciation of these views and indicated that they would discuss the matter further with staff. Staff were surprised to hear what the consultants reported. They felt a bit abashed at their own views and agreed to continue treatment "until the family feel that they're ready." Consultants assured them that it would be little longer than a week. A follow-up conference with the family was arranged, and they agreed that a week was reasonable. Indeed, they seemed relieved to set a time limit on their "goodbyes." They arranged with staff and the hospital chaplain to have their father receive the last rites of the church in their presence and for life support services to be withdrawn in a dignified way.

Lack of Communication with an Elderly Patient in a Case of Non-Elective Surgery

>Ms. Harcourt was eighty-seven years of age. She had worked for many years as a cleaning woman in a downtown office building. Now living meagerly on a small pension and social insurance, she was admitted to surgery complaining of severe pain. She was discovered to be suffering from pancreatitis which had been associated with gallstones. Ms. Harcourt had never been married, was living alone, and had become quite frail in recent years. A very close friend and her husband, residents in the same low rental housing complex, looked in on her daily since "she is often out of breath and has chest pains but refuses to go to the doctor." Ms. Harcourt came under the care of Dr. James, an attending surgeon, who debated a cholecystectomy, i.e., removing her gall bladder. He decided not to do so indicating in the patient's chart that she was too frail to undergo the operation, especially at such an advanced age. He discussed the options neither with her nor her friend, not wishing to alarm them unnecessarily, especially since the pain from her pancreatitis had begun to subside. She was discharged after an admission of two weeks duration.
>
>Several months later, Ms. Harcourt suffered another, and more serious, life threatening attack. This time, Dr. James had no choice but to operate. Ms. Harcourt was saved, but respiratory function had become compromised by the two attacks and the operation. She was now completely bed-ridden and on a ventilator. After a period of recuperation, she was discharged to a chronic nursing facility with little hope of returning home.

Dr. James was troubled by this case. After a grand rounds seminar on informed consent, he approached the sociologist-ethicist to discuss it at lunch time in the hospital cafeteria. He had been running the case over and over again in his mind wondering whether he had made a mistake in not operating right away. An earlier operation would have had a better chance of correcting the problem— when Ms. Harcourt was in better health. Our discussion revealed that not only had he been worried about Ms. Harcourt's frailty at the time of the earlier admission, but that he had been unwilling to discuss the options and potential outcomes with her, especially the possibility of her dying from the operation. He thought that she could not or would not like to face this; and, that she was too old, or "poorly educated to consider the options objectively." When asked how he knew this, he said, "After years of practice, you can tell these things." The sociologist-ethicist responded, "Are you sure you didn't operate because *you* didn't feel like discussing her possible death with her?" He replied, honestly, "No, I'm not sure of that."

DISCUSSION

Each of these situations portrays heath-care professionals dealing with rather common situations related to the death and dying of modern men and women, situations not too far removed from those in which many of us, sooner or later, will find ourselves. In each of these situations, we see professionals who are competent in dealing with the technical dimensions of care. They know how to take temperatures and administer other diagnostic procedures—our nursing student recognized that. They know how to recognize disease process in the body, and how to institute ways of minimizing their effects—Mr. Montour's physician correctly instituted a regime of renal dialysis which gave him additional years of life; they dealt with the complications of that procedure, and cured his peritoneal infection for a time. Dr. James did save his patient's life by taking out her gall bladder. And yet when it came to dealing with the most important aspects of their patients' lives, helping them (and their families) cope with the possibility of, and circumstances surrounding their impending death, our health-care professionals were ham-handed.

It is clear to me, from my personal experience with relatives and friends, from my reading of the literature, and my professional experience that such cases are not uncommon [18, 19]. It seems clear too, that despite all the death education taking place in medical, nursing, and other heath professional schools over the past thirty years, despite the proliferation of palliative-care programs and institutions, despite the writings of Herman Feifel, Robert Fulton, Elisabeth Kübler-Ross, Robert J. Lifton, Balfour Mount, C. Murray Parkes, Cicely Saunders, and so many others, and despite the many conferences and training institutes run by such persons and organizations as Professor John D. Morgan and the King's College Centre for Education about Death and Bereavement,[5] we still have a health care system a network of hospitals and other in-patient heath-care institutions—where most of us will die—where death is more difficult than it should be, more of a sudden and messy intruder than the inevitable, unavoidable, and natural companion to the end of our lives, that it could be.

Because this is so, we are obliged to consider our next "Why?"

---

[5] See [13] and [14] for further reading and bibliography on these issues and by these authors.

THE WHY OF THE HOSPITAL'S WAY OF DEATH

Ideology

Why is death in a hospital so often impersonal and bureaucratic, with less consideration for social (familial) and individual (subjective) points of view than there could be? A quick response would assert that it is that way because the ideology and social organization modern health care are still largely defined by bio-medicine. As noted above, "we have come to believe that we are nature's masters rather than her children, that we have the right to control rather than the duty to submit or at least to respect her. We define success as 'doing' and see our futures in the near short term. We are more individualistic than society oriented." In ideas which are closely linked to these, the "bio-medical approach" which has been evolving for centuries tends to include the following definitions:

a) A human being is primarily his/her body. Thoughts about, feelings about the meanings which persons attach to themselves and their bodies are independent of and have little or no influence of what goes on there.
b) Health is primarily a balance in bodily, physical function, which is to be understood in terms of the increasingly smaller parts which make it up.
c) Disease is a visible disturbance in the relations among parts of the body.
d) Diagnosis is coming to know (to see) what that disturbance is.
e) Therapy is rearranging it (prevention is arranging the condition of parts to avoid disturbance of them).
f) The mind, the soul, the feelings, the self-definitions of the observer, scientist, physician, have little to do with (aside from his "objective" observational abilities) with the process of diagnosis, and therapy [20].

We are nature's *masters;* we *dominate* and *control* her first, by objective knowledge (statements a, b, c, and d) and then by using that knowledge (*doing*) (statement e).

The development of this point of view regarding the study of human anatomy and the use of cadavers is summarized in Lella and Pawluch [21]. It can be illustrated with regard to "the feelings and meanings" attached by medical science to the human body. Consider the statements of Claude Bernard, the eminent French physiologist (in 1865), and Abraham Flexner, the architect of modern medical education (1912). Bernard notes:

> A physiologist is not a man of fashion, he is a man of science, absorbed by the scientific idea which he pursues; he no longer hears the cry of animals, he no longer sees the blood that flows, he sees only his idea and perceives only the organisms concealing problems which he intends to solve. Similarly, no surgeon is stopped by the most moving cries and sobs, because he sees only his idea and the purpose of his operation. Similarly again, no anatomist feels himself in a horrible slaughterhouse; under the influence of a scientific idea he delightedly follows a nervous filament through stinking livid flesh, which to any other man would be the object of disgust and horror [22, p. 103].

Flexner states:

> ... modern medicine strives to be honestly and modestly inductive, consulting the situation for relevant facts and cautiously drawing provisional conclusions, subject to revision whenever the issue of experience suggests modification ...
> (Since the 18th century) ... the scientific viewpoint (has) made its way by slow stages ... in consequence the human body is now viewed as an item in the universe of matter and life, without recourse to essences and principles [23, pp. 5-6].

Flexner also has praised the "laboratory" for the medical student as ". . . a wholesome discipline (since) it banishes from the mind metaphysical principles such as vital force, depression, etc., ... His actual contact with the acts put him squarely on his feet and cures him once and for all of mystical vagaries" [23, pp. 5-6].

Table 1. Selected Major Innovations in Medical Science

Date	Innovator	Event
1628	William Harvey	Description of circulation of the blood
1670	Peter Chamberlen	Invention of obstetrical forceps
1673	Anton Leewenhoek	Invention of microscope
1694	William Cowper	Description of muscular system
1761	Giovanni Morgagni	Description of pneumonia, cancer
1769	Percival Pott	Description of fractures
1776	Matthew Dobson	Description of sugar diabetes
1797	Edward Jenner	Discovery of smallpox vaccine
1809	Ephraim McDowell	First ovariotomy performed
1816	Rene Laennec	Invention of the stethoscope
1842	Crawford Long	First surgery with ether (U.S.)
1846	Robert Liston	First surgery with ether (Britain)
1846	William Morton	Perfection of ether as an anesthetic
1849	Claude Bernard	Discovery of glycogen
1851	Herman Helmholtz	Invention of ophthalmoscope
1855	Manuel Garcia	Invention of laryngoscope
1858	Rudolf Virchow	Description of cellular pathology
1866	Gregor Mendel	Discovery of genetic transmission
1866	Joseph Lister	First use of antiseptic methods in surgery
1872	Jean Charcot	Description of nervous system
1876	Robert Koch	Discovery of anthrax bacillus
1877	Robert Koch	First microphotographs
1882	Robert Koch	Discovery of tubercle bacillus
1883	Robert Koch	Discovery of cholera bacillus
1892	William Welch	Discovery of staphylococcus
1895	Wilhelm Roentgen	Discovery of x-ray

Note: Adapted from [74].

These ideas become more and more sharply focused and embodied in a broad range of scientific discoveries and their outcomes over the last few centuries (see Table 1). In short, as Lella and Pawluch note:

> Diseases . . . [came to be] seen . . . not so much of states of being, or essences to be grasped verbally or conceptually, more as visible lesions or disturbances in tissue and cells and their relations [24, 25]. This was helped both by increased precision in the techniques of physical examination [discovered in the earlier 19th Century] (e.g., percussion and auscultation using the stethoscope), and by advances in post-mortem pathological investigation. . . .
> Later in the 19th century, the discovery of anaesthesia and the development of aseptic operating techniques allowed surgeons more time to see, to saw and to sew, lessening the pain and iatrogenic consequences of their work. Some of the causes of disease could be observed and verifiably eliminated in dramatic fashion. On the level of public health, the discovery and the use of small-pox vaccine seemed to have an important and positive impact on mortality rates [21, p. 137].

In short, why spend time worrying about patients' feelings, even when dying, about relations with families, about patients' views concerning the circumstances of death, if the more important job is seeing and doing, i.e., curing disease and or avoiding death?

Social Organization

But ideas would have had little effect had they not become embodied in institutions, in the day-to-day practices, behaviors, and inter-relationships of those physicians and other health professionals who care for people dying in hospitals. For this to happen, they also had to be embodied in the relations of power which surround and make up the hospital—in the social organization of health care.

The Profession of Medicine and its Monopoly

Through identifying itself with the achievements noted above, it was the profession of medicine that staked the most powerful claim to "mastery" to "doing" to the advancement of prevention and cure of disease, warding off dying. Its claim was related to and fit neatly into the evolving ideology of modern industrialized society noted above. And thus, medicine found a broader clientele, (especially the emerging, industrially-based elites) more willing to trust its ministrations. It also found the modern state (certainly in tune with these elites) more willing and able to grant it a monopoly and autonomy: (1) in controlling licensing for practice in health care; (2) in determining ethical and other standards for practice; and (3) in determining the standards for entry and curriculum in medical education. Under the impetus of state supervisory bodies, medical training gradually abandoned the more loosely organized methods of individual apprenticeship, university study, hospital training, or various combinations of these and adopted more tightly defined training in universities, and university related hospitals staffed by clinician-scientists [21, 26-29].

In short, curricula were now orientated toward producing physicians who could be seen as justifying the state's trust, who could be seen as able to practice scientifically legitimate medicine, medicine which could make a difference. (Whether and to what extent it really did make a difference, is, of course another story) [21, 30].

Specialization and the Paramedicals

Governed by the above ideology of care, medicine evolved in its scientific-professional development toward knowing more and more about smaller and smaller segments of the body, more and more minutely differentiated ways of looking at and treating it. Those who practiced based upon this knowledge organized themselves to pursue the same sort of monopoly, and autonomy over licensing, education, standards, etc., and this led to the development of medical specialties and sub-specialties. Along, and sometimes associated with these, came the para-medical practitioners to some of whom were left less desirable tasks, often the "dirty work" associated with particular specialties and technical developments. These then followed medicine's suit and sought and often achieved "professional" autonomy and monopoly dominance in their areas.

Thus, for example, Table 2 notes those specialties which in 1948 were included as specialties certifying medical practitioners through American Specialty Boards [31]: The range of paramedical professions, some of which have specialties and sub-specialties of their own includes: dietitians, physio and occupational therapists, speech therapists, medical physicists, x-ray technicians, medical social workers, a range of nurses and sub-nursing specialists including medical, surgical, intensive care, psychiatric, obstetric (including peri-natal) and geriatric, infection control, palliative care, public health, etc. [31-34].

The Modern Hospital and Its Organization

All of this had a powerful impact on the modern hospital (see Figure 1) [35], setting the stage for the kinds of "death" care that we have talked about.

In order to accommodate all of the technical-medical-heath-care functions, (which tended to be inserted according to specialists' requirements (in order to achieve accreditation for residency training, linked to hospital quality ratings), hospitals set up a range of separately organized, specialty services (e.g., internal medicine, surgery, obstetrics-gynecology, etc.). They also needed to include services oriented around special techniques and the medical paramedical staff expert in their use (e.g., nursing, anaesthesia, dietary, social work, etc.) These, along with the "hotel" functions: housekeeping, food service, laundry, heating, and billing (necessary for "putting up" people); along with the fiscal fiduciary functions made the hospital an extremely complex organization. It now includes a plethora of departments, at several levels of organizational functioning, often with overlapping or even conflicting tasks, each of which at its base sees to a different dimension of the patient and his/her care. But all of these are experienced by the patient who, after all, is one

Table 2. Approved American Specialty Boards

	Year of Incorporation	Certificates Awarded until June 6, 1969
1. Ophthalmology	1917	7,117
2. Otolaryngology	1924	6,564
3. Obstetrics and Gynecology	1930	10,901
4. Dermatology	1932	2,896
5. Pediatrics	1933	13,045
6. Radiology	1934	10,606
7. Psychiatry and Neurology	1934	10,103
8. Orthopedic Surgery	1934	6,093
9. Colon and Rectal Surgery	1934	397
10. Urology	1935	3,907
11. Pathology	1936	9,241
12. Internal Medicine	1936	20,212
13. Anaesthesiology	1937	4,735
14. Plastic Surgery	1937	907
15. Surgery	1937	17,496
16. Neurological Surgery	1940	1,472
17. Physical Medicine and Rehabilitation	1947	771
18. Thoracic Surgery	1948	2,258
19. Preventive Medicine	1948	2,797
20. Family Practice	1969	

Note: Adapted from [31].

subjective individual. All of these are experienced, too, in different (and sometimes uncoordinated and conflicting ways) by the patient's family [36].

The Ward and Physicians

For the purposes of our discussion let us limit our analysis to the ward level. Here, attending physicians have ultimate responsibility for medical decisions. However, they have responsibilities and contacts throughout the hospital, often in various wards, and not just for individual patients, but for medical education, research, various dimensions of hospital accreditation, and other aspects of administration. They often delegate their medical decision-making power to the interns, residents, medical students whose education they supervise "down the line," i.e., attending physicians supervise residents who supervise interns, who supervise medical students. The physicians in training have various responsibilities too, not just limited to the patient on the ward. They rotate for limited periods through the various services and thus will care for some patients only for a short period of time.

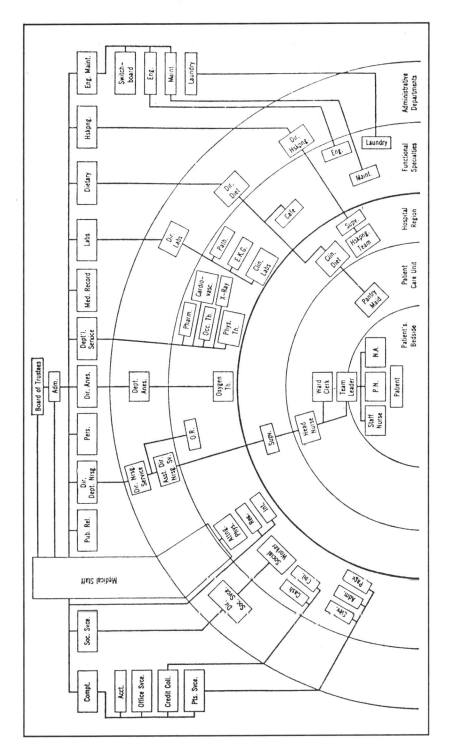

Figure 1. The functional and territorial organization of a hospital.

Nurses

Nurses are generally on the ward for eight hours a day, and see the patient for his/her length of stay. However, even they don't get the whole picture: there are day nurses, night nurses, and in between shift nurses, and there is much coordination to be done among these. Further, doctors and nurses must coordinate a range of technical information, e.g., lab test results, as well as various para-medical services, for the patient. And nurses must make sure that housekeeping, dietary, and medical records, plus contacts with the family are all smoothly arranged.

Communication on the Ward

Each of the professional and paraprofessional groups have their own level of technical training and expertise, career perspectives and prospects, and view their work in the hospital in slightly different ways. It is no wonder that the perspective of the patient often gets lost in the shuffle [34-37].

As one can see in Table 3, in a study of conversations on a medical ward between members of various occupational groups, these professionals and others communicated primarily with members of the same occupational groups, an indication of the lack of coordination [37]. This, of course, is an oversimplification, but if the doctors had spent more time on the wards, and spoken to the nurses, the social workers and the patient and the patient's family, perhaps they could have uncovered e.g., the real concerns of Mr. Montour's family, or given Ms. Harcourt a chance to say, "Yes, I'll have that operation—I'll risk it." And, if the nurses had not been burdened with attempting to coordinate the myriad of technical, housekeeping, and specialized medical services, perhaps they could have come to know our Anonymous Nursing Student who was dying. Perhaps they would have had the emotional energy to offer themselves to her more fully—to cry, or at least be, with her.

Table 3. Distribution of Conversations between Members of Various Occupational Groups on Two Wards

Group with which Interaction was Observed	Doctors $(N = 228)^d$	Nurses $(N = 562)$	Others $(N = 441)$
Within own group	74.12%	61.57%	61.68%
With remaining groups of relatively HIGHER status	23.24[a]	9.43[c]	1.36[c]
With remaining groups of relatively LOWER status	2.64[b]	29.00[b]	36.96[a]

[a]Nurses
[b]Others
[c]Doctors
[d]N's refer to total number of conversations observed involving members of each group.
Source: Adapted from [37].

Medical Education

But this, too, is an over simplification. Physicians have the most authority over health-care decisions in the hospital—whether and when to admit and discharge, what medications and other treatments to prescribe, whether or not to operate, etc. Until very recently they have been systematically taught the medical model described above. In short, they have been taught that: knowledge of the biological symptoms and manifestations of disease, it's "physical diagnosis," its technical (biomedical) treatment is the most important element of health care. While there have been a number of attempts at reform which we discuss below the medical education that most physicians have received has been primarily bio-medical discipline and specialty oriented [38-42].

To take the example of a curriculum within which I taught for a number of years (see Table 4)—in the first year of what was then called Phase One (the first year and one-half of medical school), students spent the large bulk of their time being taught by scientists, or clinical scientists-specialists in the range of what were known as the basic science disciplines. Gross Anatomy, the larger structures, organs and organ systems (viewed as static) of the human body, was taught in classroom and laboratory. In the lab, students were divided into groups of four and, throughout the course of the year, dissected a human cadaver in order to observe the human body in all its parts and in their relationships. Physiology dealt with the functioning of those parts in relation to one another. Central Nervous System dealt with the structure and functioning of the brain and the rest of the nervous system. Histology considered the microscopic dimensions of the tissues that made up the body down to the cellular level; Genetics considered the structure and functioning of inheritance of bodily characteristics; and Bio-chemistry examined the chemical composition and transformations which occur within the body.

There were a number of courses included in this eighteen months that were oriented toward bringing the curriculum an holistic approach to the living patient. Behavioral science dealt with the social and psychological development of the human being along with a number of social and psychological problems observed in clinical medicine [43]. Students were introduced to a range of clinical settings and assigned a patient, living in the community, to get to know over the course of the year. Emergency medicine and reproductive medicine were further introductions to clinical medicine. Students were allowed to choose a range of basic sciences and clinically relevant options (short courses) as well.

In the beginning of second year (the final portion of Phase One), more clinical disciplines were introduced: Pathology (the study of the source and course of important diseases); Microbiology (the study of micro-organisms and their role in various diseases and disease processes); Pharmacology (the study of drugs and their use in treatment); Growth and Development (the biological development of the human organism over the life cycle); and, Social Medicine (important social issues in the development and functioning of the health-care system). Finally, in Introduction to Clinical Sciences, students were given their first clinical contacts with patients. They were taught medical interviewing and the use of the basic tools of physical

Table 4. A Medical Curriculum

A. Basic Sciences (1-1/2 years, from September of first year to January of second year medicine) PHASE ONE.
 1. Anatomy
 2. Physiology
 3. Central Nervous System
 4. Histology
 5. Genetics
 6. Biochemistry   YEAR I
 7. Behavioral Science
 8. Emergency Medicine
 9. Reproductive Medicine
 10. Options
 11. Free Time

 12. Pathology
 13. Growth and Development
 14. Microbiology
 15. Pharmacology   1/2 YEAR II
 16. Social Medicine
 17. Introduction to Clinical Sciences
 18. Free Time

B. Introduction to clinical sciences (1 Year, beginning January of second year medicine to January of third year, PHASE TWO).
 1. Continuation of Introduction to Clinical Sciences (full-time for several weeks).
 2. Clinical Rotations (a number of weeks apiece).
    a. Medicine
    b. Obstetrics-Gynecology
    c. Surgery
    d. Electives
 3. Biology of Disease (Pathological Physiology) continuous throughout the year.

C. Clinical Clerkships (1-1/2 Years, beginning January of third year through May of fourth year). Clerkships are more advanced clinical rotations. PHASE THREE.
 1. Psychiatry
 2. Pediatrics
 3. Medicine
 4. Surgery
 5. Obstetrics-Gynecology
 6. Elective or Clerkship Option (Usually a more specialized rotation)
 7. Basic Science Option (Back to disciplines of Phase One having seen "clinical material")
 8. Medical Ethics and Law
 9. Elective

examination, e.g., use of stethoscope, examination of the eyes, ears, nose, and throat, using appropriate instruments, etc.

It was clear to me, as a teacher in such a curriculum over a twenty-two-year period, that the bulk of the students' learning right from the start was bio-medical, focused on understanding the body, its functions and dysfunctions, in biological terms; that, both in time devoted to it, and in the amount of emphasis in evaluation of the students, grades assigned, etc., the system was focused on bio-medicine. To re-formulate what was noted above: the human being was defined primarily (in terms of bulk of material assigned, and importance assigned to that material for learning) as his/her body. The patient's thoughts about feelings, about meanings attached to the body were viewed as independent and having little or no influence upon what goes on there. Effectively, consideration of these latter issues was segregated off into a course (behavioral science) that had relatively little priority assigned to it by students because of its lack of bulk in evaluation and time. Health was seen primarily as a balance in bodily, physical function, which was to be understood in terms of the increasingly smaller parts which made it up. Disease was a visible disturbance in the relations among the parts of the body. Diagnosis was coming to know (to see) what that disturbance was, and therapy was eliminating or minimizing it. Prevention was arranging the condition of bodily parts to avoid their disturbance.

The rest of the curriculum continued this pattern, but largely on the wards. Students were rotated through different clinical settings in which the emphases noted above were largely continued now in responsibilities on the ward in relation to specialties of medical practice. There were minor occasions for broader social, psychological, and clinical perspectives to be introduced in some of the clinical disciplines, especially in psychiatry and in electives, options and the course Medical Ethics and Law, but, again, the weight of emphasis in hospital practice and teaching was "bio-medical."

Thus, most students, who later within the hospital system became interns, then residents, then, physicians, still learned to see the patient as a bundle of symptoms, which needed to be addressed in the body [44].

Within the framework of the hospital, then, it is no wonder that the problems noted above—of distanced and distancing professionalism, of lack of recognition of important social and psychological realities—took place.

CHANGE?

The Heath-Care System

The above paints a rather pessimistic picture. Fortunately, it is only a sketch of the system's main features. There are, however, forces for change currently at work which could change things significantly.

Because of its tendency to stress biomedical specialism and high technology, the system which I have described has become increasingly costly, consuming greater and greater proportions of the Gross National (or Domestic) Product. More machines, more highly educated and higher paid personnel to serve them, more hospitalizations for bio-medical dysfunctions for more people cost more money. From the years 1960 to 1983 in Canada, the proportion of the GDP consumed by health care increased from 5.6 percent to 8.8 percent. From 1960-1982 in the United States, the figures were 5.2 percent to 10.2 percent [45]. Significant proportions of these costs have been borne by governments which have gone into greater and greater debt to bear them along with other rising public expenses.

There have been attempts to curb these costs in health care, notable among which has been the trend toward community-based care. Even for serious bio-medical conditions, limits have been placed on lengths of stay in hospitals; in Canada the number of hospital beds has been reduced; financial "premiums" have been awarded (and or disincentives instituted) for keeping patients out of the expensive, specialized facilities which hospitals have become [46, 47]. "Cheaper" alternatives have been developed. For example, hospitals have formed networks with community clinics so that the basic care may be provided there—care which is oriented toward keeping patients out of hospitals. For the elderly, just to give one example, home-care networks with home helpers of various sorts, have come to supplement if not totally replace chronic hospitalization for many. Palliative-care networks are being developed to help families keep their dying at home. Counseling along bio-medical, psycho-social and even spiritual levels is available in such networks. Other supports such as medical consultation for the alleviation of unnecessary pain through medication, and help with housekeeping have been made available.

Perhaps, through a range of such measures, we are learning how to deal with death and illness as a natural accompaniment to life, rather than something which must be conquered. There is some question, however, concerning how broadly based and truly patient-oriented such services are. There has been some suggestion, for example, that they can be costly dumping grounds because they are often privately financed and primarily for-profit [47].

The Professions, Specialties, and Medical Education

In clinical medical practice, there has been a steep rise in awareness of the social and psychological factors in patient care. Lella and Pawluch have summarized this quite well [21]. (The following discussion is largely theirs.)

Armstrong has observed that since the late 1930s a change in the content of medical reasoning has gradually become evident in clinical textbooks and other work, through the influence of modern psychiatry and cognate disciplines in the social and psychological sciences. Mental "health" is seen to be important, and disease is now perceived as involving not only the patient's "body" but also his or her psychology and social relationships, ". . . it has become necessary once again to pay close attention to the patient's account of the problem" [48, p. 59].

The disciplines of medical sociology and social epidemiology have known enormous growth and "with them techniques through which elicit: patients' views; social psychological influences upon them; and, their influence, in turn, on the emergence of disease and illness. Thus, the concept of multi-level-causality has come into its own. It is no longer unchallenged medical orthodoxy to see disease merely in the tangible body [21, 49-51].

Within the specialties themselves and their curricula, increasing attention has been paid to social psychology and ethics. The "speciality" of family medicine is coming into its own (an indication of the importance of community care); and, family medicine is coming to see itself as the embodiment of holistic medicine [38], utilizing a bio-psycho-social model rather than a bio-medical one [52-56]. With the emphasis on cost control, prevention rather than cure has received increased emphasis in the health-care system [56-58].

Thus, the physician as recording instrument has come back into focus not only in his five senses and cognition, but also in his emotions and values. If the patient's account of the disease is crucial, it is now important for the physician to be able to understand and control his interactions with the patient in order to be able to elicit an uninhibited account; to interact in ways which influence behavior, to work toward mutually agreed upon versions of health to maximize the benefit of these for the patient [59-61]. The physician can no longer treat the patient's body, out there, as a mere object of the scientific recording mind, in here. The physician and his emotions, his philosophy, insofar as these influence his relations with patients, are just as much a part of his doctoring as are his cognitive skills, his knowledge, and his ability to be objective [21, 62, 63].

Basic Values and Patient Advocacy Groups

Finally, the basic values behind . . . (biomedical) care and cure are also being questioned. Patients' Rights movements and their legal philosophical allies in medical law and ethics have succeeded in redefining the goals of medicine. These now include not only measurable cure, or length of life, but also helping the patient achieve his own goals which may be different from these. Current insistence upon informed consent as the backbone of medical ethics and law reflects this concern [21, 64].

Various patient self-help and advocacy movements involving such groups as patients and relatives of patients with "ostomies," amputees, the mentally ill, etc., have assisted this process.

Medical Education

In response to all this, medical students are being taught awareness of how their feelings, thoughts, and values effect patients and their treatment. A range of disciplines and clinical specialties including behaviorial science, psychiatry, humanities, and ethics are teaching and indeed examining students on such matters both within medical schools, and in licensing and board qualifying examinations [21, 65-67].

In society at large, there has been a strong reaction against the repressions of feelings on death and dying and the scholarly community has called our attention to how personally destructive this can be [5, 7]. We are now urged to acknowledge and come to terms with our feelings and beliefs about death and dying. In response, many medical and other health professional schools are now attempting to teach their students how to promote "good deaths within and even outside of special hospices for the dying. Professionals are being taught to acknowledge and develop their own emotional and intellectual stances toward death so that they can recognize its influence on their work with others" [21, 70, 71].

In the long history of medicine and other health professions, however, these developments and insights must be seen as rather recent developments and by no means fully digested into their often rigidly structured training institutions. One can say that the bio-medical model is still dominant, but it is no longer unchallenged [21, 45].

Other Changes

But perhaps the most important change occurring in the system, is in the hearts and minds of young medical, nursing, and other health-care students—in increasing awareness of their own subjectivity, their own feelings and those of their patients.

My own experience in medical education and in the education of young undergraduates in medical sociology (some aspiring to health-care careers) bears ample testimony to this. Their actions within their own educational process and while walking the wards are increasingly and unabashedly sensitive [21, 72]. Many are no longer hesitant to express their empathy with dying patients and their families. Many are taking advantage of electives and optional courses in the humanities of medicine and in palliative care to cultivate these feelings, develop their clinical skills and use them to help real patients. Perhaps the most important example I can give of this occurred during a non-denominational memorial service organized by medical students and their teachers to express gratitude to the families of individuals whose bodies had been donated for dissection in the first year anatomy course.

> Family members of the dead, faculty, and students attended. The university chaplain, then the chairman of the anatomy department read brief expressions of gratitude for these gifts to science and medical education. Students then read the names of those whose bodies had been used. The names would then be inscribed in a leather bound volume. Interspersed with the reading of names (which was accompanied by organ music), different students read compositions of their own, or selections which they had chosen from poetry and literature. One student played a ... selection on the dulcimer. Readings were on various interpretations of the meaning of human life. Coffee was served after the service. Expressions of satisfaction with the beauty and fitting character of the event were common features of conversation [73].

CONCLUSION

Toward the beginning of this chapter I wrote:

> ... we have come to believe that we are nature's masters rather than her children, that we have the right to control rather than the duty to submit to or at least to

respect her. We define success as "doing" rather than "being" and see our futures in the near short term. We see ourselves as discrete individuals rather than as inevitably social beings and have tended to organize our families as small, and nuclear (focused on mother, father, and children) rather than as large, multi-linear or extended—all this to fit in with the demands of an economy of production and profit (domination and control of nature for short term benefit); to be mobile and flexible, individually (or in small family groups), to go where the work and the profits are. Thus, illness and death are to be avoided and ignored or minimized when they occur because they just don't fit in.

The movements for change that I have described are struggling against these broad tendencies and are by no means assured of victory. Our belief that we must dominate nature, that we must do rather than be, that we are essentially individuals rather than social beings—all these are woven into the biomedical model which in turn is part of the fabric of the modern society. But this fabric can be changed and indeed is changing. Whether it will be totally rewoven to ensure respect for individual life both in its living and dying, in body and soul, and in the personal and social subjectivity of its possessor, is by no means guaranteed. We can only dedicate ourselves long term to the weaving.

REFERENCES

1. J. Q. Benoliel, Institutional Dying: A Convergence of Cultural Values, Technology, and Social Organization, in *Dying: Facing the Facts* (2nd Edition), H. Wass, F. M. Berardo, and R. A. Neimeyer (eds.), Hemisphere Publishing Corporation, Washington, pp. 159-184, 1988.
2. Anonymous, Death in the First Person, in *Death: The Final Stage of Growth,* E. Kübler-Ross, Prentice-Hall, Englewood Cliffs, New Jersey, 1975.
3. J. N. Clarke, *Health, Illness and Medicine in Canada,* McClelland and Stewart, Toronto, 1990.
4. D. A. Hay, Mortality and Health Status Trends in Canada, in *Sociology of Health Care in Canada,* B. S. Bolaria and H. D. Dickinson (eds.), Harcourt, Brace, Jovanovich, Toronto, pp. 18-28, 1988.
5. T. K. Hareven, Historical Perspectives on the Family and Aging, in *Handbook of Aging and the Family,* R. Blieszner and V. H. Bedford (eds.), Greenwood Press, Westport, Connecticut, pp. 13-31, 1995.
6. K. Kinsella, Aging and the Family: Present and Future Issues, in *Handbook of Aging and the Family,* R. Blieszner and V. H. Bedford (eds.), Greenwood Press, Westport, Connecticut, pp. 32-56, 1995.
7. G. Rocher, *Introduction a la Sociologie Generale. I. L' Action Sociale,* Editions HMH, Paris, p. 27, 1968.
8. J. Lella, *The Perils of Patient Government,* Wilfrid Laurier University Press, Waterloo, Ontario, p. 182, 1986.
9. J. J. Teevan and W. E. Hewitt, *Introduction to Sociology: A Canadian Focus,* Prentice-Hall, Scarborough, Ontario, p. 527, 1995.
10. L. Lofland, *The Craft of Dying: The Modern Face of Death,* Sage Publications, Beverley Hills, California, pp. 18-36, 1978.

11. J. R. Seeley, R. A. Sim, and E. W. Loosley, *Crestwood Heights: A Study of the Culture of Suburban Life,* University of Toronto Press, Toronto, pp. 1-5, 1956.
12. C. Kluckhohn, Universal Categories of Culture in *Anthropology Today: An Encyclopedic Inventory,* University of Chicago Press, Chicago, pp. 507-523, 1953.
13. H. Wass, F. M. Berardo, and R. A. Neimeyer (eds.), *Dying: Facing the Facts* (2nd Edition), Hemisphere Publishing Corporation, Washington, 1988.
14. E. S. Schneidman (ed.), *Death: Current Perspectives* (3rd Edition), Mayfield, Palo Alto, California, 1984.
15. D. Sudnow, *Passing On: The Social Organization of Dying,* Prentice-Hall, Englewood Cliffs, New Jersey, 1967.
16. A. Strauss and B. G. Glaser, *Awareness of Dying,* Aldine, Chicago, 1965.
17. R. W. Buckingham, III, S. A. Lack, and B. M. Mount et al., Living with the Dying: Use of the Technique of Participant Observation, *Canadian Medical Association Journal, 115,* p. 1211, 1976.
18. M. Kaye and J. W. Lella, Discontinuation of Dialysis Therapy in the Demented Patient, *American Journal of Nephrology, 6,* pp. 75-79, 1986.
19. J. W. Lella and M. Kaye, Surgical Care of the Elderly, in *Ethical Issues in Surgical Care of the Elderly,* J. Meakins, and J. MacLaren (eds.), Yearbook Medical Publishers, Chicago, pp. 50-59, 1988.
20. D. R. Gordon, Tenacious Assumptions in Western Medicine, in *Biomedicine Examined,* M. Lock and D. Gordon (eds.), Kluwer, Dordrecht, Netherlands, pp. 19-56, 1988.
21. J. Lella and D. Pawluch, Medical Students and the Cadaver in Social and Cultural Context, in *Biomedicine Examined,* M. Lock and D. Gordon (eds.), Kluwer, Dordrecht, Netherlands, pp. 125-154, 1988.
22. C. Bernard, *An Introduction to the Study of Experimental Medicine,* (trans. by H. C. Green, from the French published in 1865), Henry Schuman, New York, 1949.
23. A. Flexner, *Medical Education in Europe, Bulletin No. 6,* The Carnegie Foundation for the Advancement of Teaching, New York, 1912.
24. M. Foucault, *The Birth of the Clinic: An Archeology of Medical Perception,* Tavistock Publications, London, 1963.
25. D. Armstrong, The Patient's View, *Social Science and Medicine, 18,* pp. 737-744, 1984.
26. T. A. Puschmann, *A History of Medical Education* (Facsimile of 1891 ed.), Hafner, New York, 1966.
27. T. Billroth, *The Medical Sciences in the German Universities: A Study in the History of Civilisation,* The Macmillan Company, New York, 1924.
28. C. D. O'Malley (ed.), *The History of Medical Education,* UCLA Forum in Medical Sciences, No. 12, University of California Press, Berkeley, 1970.
29. H. S. Berliner, *A System of Scientific Medicine: Philanthropic Foundations in the Flexner Era,* Tavistock Publications, New York, 1985.
30. T. McKeown, *The Role of Medicine: Dream, Mirage, or Nemesis,* Basil Blackwell, Oxford, 1979.
31. R. Stevens, *American Medicine and the Public Interest,* Yale University Press, New Haven, pp. 532-543, 1971.
32. M. G. Taylor, The Canadian Health Care System: After Medicare, in *Health and Canadian Society: Sociological Perspectives* (2nd Edition), D. Coburn, C. D'Arcy, G. M. Torrance, and P. New (eds.), Fitzhenry and Whiteside, Markham, Ontario, p. 83, 1987.
33. P. Starr, *The Social Transformation of American Medicine,* Basic Books, New York, 1982.

34. N. Aries and L. Kennedy, The Health Labor Force: The Effects of Change, in *The Sociology of Health and Illness: Critical Perspectives* (2nd Edition), P. Conrad and R. Kern (eds.), St. Martin's Press, New York, pp. 196-207, 1986.
35. H. O. Mauksch, The Nurse: Coordinator of Patient Care, in *Social Interaction and Patient Care*, J. K. Skipper and R. C. Leonard (eds.), J. Lippincott Co., Philadelphia, pp. 252-265, 1965.
36. G. L. Kreps and B. C. Thornton, *Health Communication*, Longman, New York, 1984.
37. A. Wessen, Hospital Ideology and Communication Between Ward Personnel, in *Patients, Physicians and Illness* (2nd Edition), E. G. Jaco (ed.), The Free Press, New York, pp. 325-342, 1972.
38. J. W. Lella and L. Filion-LaPorte, Family Medicine and the New Medical Identity, *Annals of Behavioral Science and Medical Education*, 1(2), pp. 103-110, 1994.
39. G. L. Engel, The Need for a New Medical Model: A Challenge for Biomedicine, *Science*, 96, pp. 129-136, 1977.
40. G. L. Engel, The Clinical Application of the Biopsychosocial Model, *Journal of Medical Philosophy*, 6, p. 101, 1981.
41. L. J. Kirmayer, Mind and Body as Metaphors: Hidden Values in Biomedicine, in *Biomedicine Examined*, M. Lock and D. Gordon (eds.), Kluwer Academic Publishers, Dordrecht, p. 59, 1988.
42. *Physicians for the Twenty-First Century: Report of the Panel on the General Professional Education of the Physician and College Preparation for Medicine*, Association of American Medical College, Washington, D.C., p. 16, 1984.
43. J. W. Lella, D. Gill, and T. McGlynn, *Basic Curriculum Content for the Behavioral Sciences in Pre-Clinical Medical Education*, Association for the Behavioral Sciences and Medical Education, McLean, Virginia, 1985.
44. K. M. Margo and G. M. Margo, Tailoring the Balint Group Seminar for First-Year Family Medicine Residents, *Annals of Behavioral Science and Medical Education*, 1, p. 39, 1994.
45. R. W. Sutherland and M. J. Fulton, *Health Care in Canada: A Description and Analysis of Canadian Health Services*, The Health Group, Ottawa, p. 86, 1988.
46. C. L. Estes and P. R. Lee, Health Problems and Policy Issues of Old Age, in *Applications of Social Science to Clinical Medicine and Health Policy*, L. H. Aiken and D. Mechanic (eds.), Rutgers University Press, New Brunswick, New Jersey, pp. 346-347, 1986.
47. H. D. Dickenson and D. A. Hay, The Structure and Cost of Health Care in Canada, in *Sociology of Health Care in Canada*, B. S. Bolaria and H. D. Dickinson (eds.), Harcourt Brace, Jovanovich, Toronto, pp. 59-60, 1988.
48. D. Armstrong, The Patient's View, *Social Science and Medicine*, 18, pp. 737-744, 1984.
49. L. F. Berkman, Physical Health and the Social Environment: A Social Epidemiological Perspective, in *The Relevance of Social Science for Medicine*, L. Eisenberg and A. Kleinman (eds.), D. Reidel Publishing Co., Boston, pp. 51-75, 1980.
50. G. L. Engel, The Clinical Application of the Biopsychosocial Model, *American Journal of Psychiatry*, 137, pp. 535-544, 1980.
51. M. Becker (ed.), The Health Belief Model and Personal Health Behavior, *Health Education Monographs*, 2, pp. 324-473, 1970.
52. R. E. Rakel, *Textbook of Family Practice* (4th Edition), W.B. Saunders Co., Philadelphia, 1990.
53. I. R. McWhinney, *A Textbook of Family Medicine*, Oxford University Press, New York, 1989.
54. P. D. Sloane, L. M. Slatt, and R. M. Baker (eds.), *Essentials of Family Medicine*, Williams and Wilkins, Baltimore, 1988.

55. S. McDaniel, T. L. Campbell, and D. B. Seaburn, *Family-Oriented Primary Care: A Manual for Medical Providers*, Springer-Verlag, New York, 1990.
56. C. Boelen, Medical Education Reforms: The Need for Global Action, *Academic Medicine, 11*(62), 1992.
57. A. Crichton and D. Hsu, *Canada's Health Care System: Its Funding and Organization*, Canadian Hospital Association Press, Ottawa, pp. 230-232, 1990.
58. R. C. R. Taylor, The Politics of Prevention, *The Sociology of Health and Illness: Critical Perspectives*, P. Conrad and R. Kern (eds.), St. Martin's Press, New York, pp. 471-484, 1986.
59. R. C. Smith, Teaching Interviewing Skills to Medical Students: The Issue of Countertransference, *Journal of Medical Education, 59*, pp. 582-588, 1984.
60. C. P. Rosenberg, A 10 Year Freshman Support Group Program: Leader Review, *Research in Medical Education, Proceedings of the 23rd Annual Conference*, American Association of Medical Colleges, Washington, D.C., 1984.
61. R. Gorlin and H. D. Zucker, Physicians' Reactions to Patients: A Key to Teaching Humanistic Medicine, *New England Journal of Medicine, 308*, pp. 1059-1063, 1983.
62. C. Helman, Communication and Primary Care: The Role of Patient and Practitioner Explanatory Models, *Social Science and Medicine, 20*, pp. 923-931, 1985.
63. B. J. Good and M. G. Good, The Meaning of Symptoms: A Cultural Hermeneutic Model for Clinical Practice, in *The Relevance of Social Science for Medicine*, L. Eisenberg and A. Kleinman (eds.), D. Reidel Publishing Co., Boston, pp. 165-196, 1980.
64. A. R. Jonsen, M. Seigler, and W. J. Winslade, *Clinical Ethics*, Collier-Macmillan, Toronto, 1982.
65. M. Menken and C. G. Sheps, Undergraduate Education in the Medical Specialties: The Case of Neurology, *New England Journal of Medicine, 311*, pp. 1045-1048, 1984.
66. American Board of Internal Medicine, Competence in Internal Medicine, *Annals of Internal Medicine, 90*, pp. 402-411, 1979.
67. Council on Medical Education of the American Medical Association, Future Directions for Medical Education, *Journal of American Medical Association, 248*, p. 3225, 1982.
68. E. Becker, *The Denial of Death*, The Free Press, New York, 1983.
69. J. D. Morgan (ed.), *Personal Care in an Impersonal World: A Multidimensional Look at Bereavement*, Baywood Publishing, Amityville, New York, 1993.
70. G. E. Dickinson, Death Education in US Medical Schools: 1975-1980, *Journal of Medical Education, 56*, pp. 111-114, 1981.
71. D. Field, Formal Instruction in the United Kingdom Schools about Death and Dying, *Medical Education, 18*, pp. 429-434, 1984.
72. J. C. Penney, Reactions of Medical Students to Dissection, *Journal of Medical Education, 60*, pp. 58-60, 1985.
73. J. W. Lella and D. Pawluch, Medical Students and the Cadaver in Cultural Context, in *Thanatology: A Liberal Arts Approach*, J. D. Morgan (ed.), King's College, London, Ontario, p. 38, 1987.
74. R. H. Major, *A History of Medicine*, Charles C. Thomas, Springfield, Illinois, 1970.

CHAPTER 10
Get it Under Cover: AIDS, Death, and Censorship

James Miller

How much is missing from the standard medical definitions of AIDS? How much is unstated, occluded, suppressed in the official narrative of the epidemic as a "crisis"? If a crisis is what the mass media typically constructs for the anxious public—namely, a manageable (if cataclysmic) disturbance in human affairs requiring massive funding to institutions of research and militant interventions by powerful professionals—then why does the promised end of the "War on AIDS" never come? Why does the "AIDS tragedy" fail to reach closure? These are difficult questions to which the arts have given considerable attention and often controversial expression since the epidemic began in 1981.[1]

Few artists would utterly reject or dispute the diagnostic definition of Acquired Immune Deficiency Syndrome (AIDS) as an "apparently" fatal suppression of the human immune system triggered in some mysterious way by the Human Immunodeficiency Virus (HIV) and manifested by an unpredictable assortment of opportunistic infections and cancers such as Kaposi's Sarcoma (KS) and Pneumocystis Carinii Pneumonia (PCP). Nor would they be likely to dismiss the solid epidemiological evidence that HIV is mainly transmitted from an infected to an uninfected person through an exchange of semen or blood during "high-risk" activities such as unprotected anal intercourse or the sharing of hypodermic needles.

The statistical picture of AIDS as a borderless global epidemic is no less appalling to artists than it is to epidemiologists. When the bad news came down from the World Health Organization that reported cases of AIDS in the United States alone were reaching 500,000 toward the end of 1995, it did not fall on deaf ears in the artworld. Artists with activist leanings were also anxious to hear what the latest totals

---

[1] On the critical response of artists and authors to the AIDS crisis, see [1-3].

had soared to in Zaire (26,131), and Thailand (13,246), and Canada (11,192).[2] What the arts have consistently refused to allow or accept, however, is that any of these seemingly objective definitions or statistical overviews covers the whole story of the epidemic, or captures the complete picture of its devastations, or even comes close to tallying up the total score of casualties on the militantly subjective human side of the "War on AIDS." The inevitable deadliness of the syndrome, for instance, has been repeatedly challenged by artists to whom medicine has handed down a death sentence along with an AIDS diagnosis.[3]

For their aggressively personal and political interpretations of the ever-expanding facts on AIDS, artists have suffered both the threat and the enforcement of censorship in various forms—police harassment, seizure of artworks, legal proceedings, funding cuts, gallery closings—which are all efforts to impose some kind of intelligible limit on the menacing indefiniteness of the plague-world that lies outside the strict borders of techno-medical control. Their exploration of the underlying connections between AIDS, death, and censorship will be the focus of my ensuing analysis of the epidemic in the West as a limit-pushing cultural calamity rather than a strictly defined medical crisis.

1. AESTHETIC NEGATION

On December 1, 1989, a handful of New York galleries marked World AIDS Day by draping artworks in black or by removing them temporarily from public view. That the annual "Day Without Art" (as it has since come to be known) was originally conceived and organized by an Irish-American curator, Patrick O'Connell, is perhaps no coincidence. It is an elegiac protest oddly reminiscent of the Irish funeral custom of shrouding mirrors for a period of moral reflection on death as the inevitable effacement of all things vain and worldly.

Unlike the old custom of mirror-draping, however, this new ritual of aesthetic negation fervently asserts the value rather than the vanity of art as a mirror of mortality. It is thus no mere "AIDS Awareness" event in a typical public health sense any more than it is an AIDS vigil or *viaticum* in a traditional religious sense. The primary purpose of the Day Without Art is not to dispense safer sex pamphlets or lubricated condoms to bewildered gallery-goers. Nor is it to drive home to a heedless public the bitter lessons about the routes of viral transmission or the clinical manifestations of the syndrome. In fact, most curators who participate in the Day Without

---

[2] The data for the United States (where the rate of AIDS cases per million has reached 1,542.3) dates from September, 1994; for Canada (393.7 cases per million), from March, 1995; for Thailand (230.0 per million) from October, 1994; and for Zaire (615.3 per million), from July, 1994). These statistics have been compiled from [4, 5].

[3] A rediscovery of the Dantean "high fantasy" of reconciliation and rebirth often accompanies artistic challenges to the fatalism as well as the fatality of AIDS. In a fantasy sequence at the end of Norman René's film, *Longtime Companion* (1990), for instance, the AIDS dead rise from their graves to throw a beach party for the survivors of the plague on Fire Island. No less religious in its implications is the theatrical "resurrection" of Miss Jesus, gay performance artist Tom Shaheen, in [6].

Art refrain from turning their galleries into temporary extensions of the medical world.[4]

If the Day Without Art adds anything to the standard diagnostic definition of AIDS, it is a warning about the limits of the immunological construction of disease. How microscopic is its frame of reference, how demoralizing its impact on the diagnosed! Hardly relevant to the Day Without Art is the daily drone of epidemiological facts about AIDS reported in the media: transmission rates increasing in this "risk-group" or diminishing in that "age-group," and so on. Contrary to the pessimistic view of the crisis provided by the global forecasts of the World Health Organization, the ascetic withdrawal of art on World AIDS Day serves to sustain a vaguely religious hope that eventually the world will rejoice in a Day without AIDS—or even, God willing, a Day Without Death.

O'Connell and his followers seek to draw public attention to the loss not only of artists to AIDS but also of "great art" that might have been produced if the epidemic had not taken such a devastating toll on the artworld at the *fin-de-millennium*. Gallery-goers are therefore invited each December to mourn the uncreated as well as the dead, the direly deprived as well as the dearly departed. By commemorating past presences in the community, the relatively small public to whom art means anything must also confront future absences in surrogate forms—blank walls, darkened rooms, closed doors, missing pages, silent instruments, shrouded statues, canceled museum tours—that reflect the spiritual and material consequences of AIDS as a cultural crisis. Yet as an aesthetic protest, a symbolic revelation of gaps and disappearances, the Day Without Art ironically affirms what it seems to deny: the function of art as a vital service during catastrophic times. Take away the pleasures of art, that precious life-support for the Human Spirit, even for a day, and society will soon learn how much it depends on aesthetic fantasies of joy and harmony and rebirth for paradisal consolations in the midst of purgatorial pain and infernal despair.

Though the Day Without Art is now marked in many different ways in a multitude of large and small galleries throughout the world, it remains a collective act of voluntary censorship that occurs, ironically, within the traditionally privileged and (in America) constitutionally protected domain of free expression. As such, it evokes and sustains a complex analogy between death and censorship which presupposes their apocalyptic opposition to life and art. Death arrests, silences, erases life. Censorship arrests, silences, erases art.

Whenever the first term in these twinned binaries is imagined as an implacable moral persecutor, its figurative embodiment (for instance, the Grim Reaper) serves to annihilate the creative processes associated with the second term. The allegorical fusion of death and censorship has been complicated by the addition of AIDS as a third term, at once popularly equated with death in media accounts of the epidemic and polemically opposed to it in activist representations of "People With AIDS" (PWAs) as valiant allies of Life. So identified with the life force have some PWAs become that they rename themselves "People Living With AIDS" in defiance of the

---

[4] For a more detailed description and analysis of the Day Without Art, see [7].

fatalistic AIDS=Death closure to their lives. In exploring the symbolic relations between AIDS, death, and censorship in this analysis of recent cultural responses to the epidemic, we must always bear in mind the instability and insufficiency of medical definitions of AIDS which may appear (and certainly try to appear) quite untouched by the censoring regimes simultaneously mirrored and defied on the Day Without Art.

2. DEATH THE CENSOR

The allegory of Death the Censor is hardly new in Western culture. Pre-AIDS versions of it can be traced back to the plague-haunted tradition of the macabre in late medieval and Renaissance iconography. Crusading corpses who look like they haven't had much fun in a long time march vengefully into the lower foreground of Pieter Brueghel's "The Triumph of Death" (painted in 1562) to put a stop to all life-affirming activities in which the arts play a key role.[5] Cheerful luteplayers are coldly hushed, and ardent love-poets choke on their sugared words as their sweethearts succumb to "rigor mortis" in the morally rigorous as well as mortally rigid sense. Their artistic participation in the life of pleasure is censured—judged to be fatally wrong from an apocalyptic viewpoint—through the censoring of their seemingly harmless activities in the Here and Now.

As Hell's executioner, an agent of Heaven's censorious regime, Death is represented as the implacable silencer of the arts in Thomas Nashe's "Litany in Time of Plague" (composed in 1600). Not that the arts don't complain bitterly about their powerlessness in the face of such a foe. They do. But Death, in his official capacity as Pleasure's Censor,

> Hath no ears for to hear
> What vain art can reply[6]

to the charges of vanity and wantonness brought against witty worldlings by the Divine Judge who has sent the plague to punish them for their sins. Too late does the poet lament the devotion of his energies to aesthetic pursuits when time for devotion in a religious sense has already run out. He is sick. He must die. His pious *cri-de-coeur* ("Lord, have mercy on us!") brings the litany to a dead halt, as if he were announcing not only the termination of his plague-racked life, but also the shutdown of the arts under Death's triumphant sway.

Though the Renaissance envisioned the Triumph of Death primarily as a military onslaught, an attack of the legions of the dead on the society of the living, it originally appeared in medieval art as a dance: the grimly satanic *chorea macabrea* or *saltatus mortis*.[7] The Dance of Death was the only artistic activity permitted to

---

[5] On a trip to Italy some years before painting "The Triumph of Death," Brueghel probably saw the medieval frescoes of the Grim Reaper and his cadaverous cohorts triumphing in the Camposanto at Pisa and in the Palazzo Sclafani in Palermo. On the iconographic relation between these paintings, see [8].

[6] For a complete text of the litany, which first appeared as a song in the play, *Summers Last Will and Testament*, see [9].

[7] On the iconography of the dance macabre, see [10-12].

continue after the final censoring of the arts on the Last Day. It was the inescapable movement to which everyone was "invited" by Death or by one of his skeleton staff, whose approach was inevitably a reproach. His invitation, in fact, was never issued without a moralizing verse on the particular sin associated with the rank or profession of the recipient: pride for the emperor, sloth for the abbot, lust for the whore, and so on, in a fatal concatenation figured as a crack-the-whip chain of doomed souls wrenched along behind their hellbent leader. The dancers, representing every rank of society, were typically portrayed—caught off guard—at the shocking moment when Death offered himself as a partner or percussionist in the dance. As a vision of their final participation in the Church's moral order, the *saltatus mortis* must have seemed intensely ironic to Christians familiar with the centuries-old ecclesiastical censure of the dance as the most carnal, and therefore the most immoral, of the arts.

Revivals of these Black Death allegories for the "Age of AIDS" are all too predictable in the wake of Reverend Jerry Falwell's media-trumpeted jeremiads on "the gay plague" as a divine punishment. We do not have to dig through academic arcana to exhume the skeletons from the old *saltatus mortis*: a cartoon bearing that very title (in Latin, no less) was drawn by Harry S. Robins in 1988 and included in a popular collection of satiric images published that year under the 'zine-like title *Strip AIDS U.S.A.* as a fundraiser for San Francisco's Shanti Project.[8] Skeletons triumph over HIV-infected mortals here with the cynical éclat of pop-art prophets. In a macabre tribute to the memory of the defunct American Left, the High and Mighty are the first to go—the Senator and the Financier falling into line at the head of the dance as ignominious carriers of the plague rather than "innocent victims" like the Wife and the Child.

The bony hand of Death the Censor is clearly visible in the section labeled "The Star" (see Figure 1). As the macho Star, surrounded by voluptuous starlets, flashes his million-dollar smile on a television screen, the hand is already poised on the "off" button. Not only will his smile disappear when he is offed by AIDS, but so too will his artfully crafted image as a heterosexual role model when he is "outed" as a closet case (à la Rock Hudson and Robert Reed) by the jeering verse beneath his panel:

> His face & voice
> the whole world knows,
> His secret tastes,
> a favored few.
> But, now his exit
> will expose
> The part he played
> which no one knew.

Now everyone will know the part he played in secret because he must exit this life as a person with AIDS, the syndrome being here morally equated with a medically

---

[8] The complete text and graphics for Harry S. Robin's *Totentanz* can be found in [13]. The pages are unnumbered. Robin's contribution is midway through the book.

Figure 1.

exposed homosexuality. His ruin is the prophesied end for all modern sodomites under the dispensation of the televangelists, who paradoxically demand both the concealment and the exposure of homosexuals. The heterosexist regime of censorship currently identified as the "epistemology of the closet" must now be expanded, via this apocalyptic strip, into an eschatology of the closet.[9]

Needless to say, the vain art of television cannot reply to the moral diagnosis of its fallen paragon without implicating itself in the heavily moralized spectacle of AIDS. Its voice is silenced and its picture erased by Death in the same act that silences and erases the Star. Ironically, even as the network controlling his public image hid the truth about his "secret tastes," so it must be censored in the end by the off-screen agent of Divine Truth whose skeletal face significantly does not appear in the Star's panel. As a metonymic symbol for the image-machine of American celebrity culture, the small screen falls under the same moral censure as the lute and the poet's scroll in the original versions of the allegory. It is a contributing cause as well as a symptom of the vainglory of the Age of AIDS.

Nowhere today is the Triumph of Death evoked more persistently for the sake of AIDS Awareness, or more ironically for the sake of moral security, than in the scary poster campaigns designed to convey self-defense tips for the wayward public. "Will you love all his partners?" is the morally loaded question fired at a sexually inclined but indecisive woman staring at an attractive male in the foreground of an AIDS poster from the Virgin Islands (see Figure 2). A quick glance at the background

---

[9] On the relation between homophobia and censorship, see [14].

Figure 2.

reveals her potential partner's former conquests: three women, one man (yikes) . . . and two grinning skeletons! So Mr. Right is a bisexual and these are the skeletons in his closet, both formerly gay men no doubt, whom the woman must see as secret plague-carriers and therefore as wholly unlovable as partners in the heterosexual dance of life. Only a necrophiliac with a taste for group sex, one supposes, would be inclined to answer "yes" to the question posed by the poster under these supernaturally revealed conditions.

A doctrinal precondition for answering "no" here, the only morally sanctioned response, is an acceptance of the allegorical equations between AIDS and Death, and between Death and Sex, demanded by an all-out apocalyptic reading of the epidemic. If the woman is surprised by her ghostly vision of Mr. Wrong's normally occluded sexual history, it can be no surprise to a medievalist familiar with the old icon of Death and the Maiden: she is simply experiencing the macabre equivalent of *déjà vu*, a sudden flashback to the prototypical scene in the *saltatus mortis* where the Lady (or the Whore) is drawn to the dance—and to her doom—by dem bones, dem bones, dem dry bones.

Death the Censor may be dry and even deaf, but he is never dumb. His bones have a voice, if not a mouth and a tongue, and woe betide anyone among the living who fails to hear it above the din of the World or behind the beat of the Flesh. Since Death's traditional function in the Triumph was to gloss the significance of its allegorizations, to deliver pithy verse homilies on the hidden links between mortality and concupiscence, we should not be surprised to find him making his comeback in the world of AIDS advertising as the mordant messenger, the clever caption-maker, the deliverer of sick punchlines.

"AIDS . . . It's a hop in the sack!" he chortles like a demented adman using sex to sell of all things—death—in a billboard that appeared on the ring-road outside Stratford, Connecticut, in 1988 (see Figure 3). Any lustful commuter who hopped into THAT sack after cruising through town for a one-night stand would have found

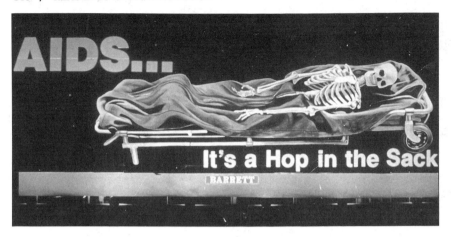

Figure 3.

himself sharing a hospital gurney with a skeleton wrapped in a winding-sheet. An eternity in the grave for him! Wheel him out! Lovingly handpainted by the civic-minded son of the owner of the local Barrett Sign Company, this Grand Guignol parody of a "Welcome to Town" sign must have served as an apotropaic talisman for the townspeople. Its religio-magic function, as an omen of moral judgment, was to ward off the Virus by scaring away its evil carriers from the honorable bourgeois beds where healthy husbands and wives are to this day monogamously preserving America from social ruin.

"AIDS Virus . . . A Deadly Saturday Night Special," proclaims another skeletal pitchman in a grotesquely reactionary poster from Los Angeles (see Figure 4). Social ruin comes in many forms, violent as well as viral, and the four Angelino street kids whom the skeleton is embracing like one of the gang don't seem to see how their group portrait is being maliciously used to set up a correspondence between gang violence as a symptom of urban decay and the epidemic as a sign of moral decay. Death, here identified with the Virus, fits right into their ethnic milieu by looking like a reveller in a Mexican folk-costume from the street parades on the Day of the Dead.[10] He even speaks their idiom: a "Saturday Night Special" is street-slang a

---

[10] A large crowd of AIDS ghosts perform a prophetic dance of death for actor Richard Gere in the 1993 HBO television adaptation of *And the Band Played On,* Randy Shilts's chronicle history of the first five years of the epidemic (St. Martins, New York, 1987). Cast in the closeted cameo-role of a legendary Broadway choreographer à la Michael Bennet, who died of AIDS in 1987, Gere pays a secretive visit to an epidemiologist in San Francisco to report his ominous symptoms. Gloomily stationing himself at a window, as "AIDS Victims" routinely do in media photography, he assumes his new role as a doomed but repentant representative of the Beautiful People crashing headlong into AIDS on the fast lane of depravity. Now he must watch Life passing him by. Life is allegorically represented by a lively parade of drag queens, leathermen, prancing clowns, and other insouciant revellers celebrating Hallowe'en on the street below. Suddenly, from Gere's morally chastened perspective, the parade is transformed into a danse macabre with cadavers and skeletons led by the ghoulish figure of Death himself, recruited (as his Mexican folk-mask suggests) from a Day of the Dead procession.

Figure 4.

sawed-off shotgun used in gang wars and robberies, though here the phrase must also take on a direly erotic meaning (a gang-bang on Saturday night, with everyone high on injection drugs?) because the poster recontextualizes it as "deadly" in relation to HIV-transmission. So infectious death once more equals "unprotected" sex in the moral calculations of the Censor. Those nasty boys are packing penises as well as guns in their jeans, and don't suppose they won't fire them at the "innocent" maidens drawn into their violent embrace by the hellish insecurity of life in the "hood."

Despite the non-judgmental tone of the self-defense advice presented on the poster—"Protect yourself! Use condoms. Clean your works. Get the facts"—the facts are plain to see from the iconography of moral judgment imposed on the documentary-style photograph of the gang, a publicity shot for the coming Triumph. They deserve to die because of their wicked ways, urges Death the Censor as he absorbs their slang and uses it for yet another macabre joke. Before they blow each other away, however, their image may at least serve as a negative advertisement for the violence of the World and the vanity of the Flesh.

These are but a few examples of the already extensive refiguration of the AIDS crisis as a spectacle of moralized morbidity, the producers of which are hardly to be distinguished from the institutional upholders of the regimes of censorship that keep the mass media as well as the artworld in check from one Day Without Art to the next. As the crisis deepens and its closure vanishes into the horizon of the new millennium, the fantasy of universal death as the promised end to all our woe will no doubt increase in popularity and sustain itself through endless variations of the skeleton-meets-sinner theme. Death the Censor is nothing if not repetitious in his warnings. Death=Sex. Sex=AIDS. AIDS=Death. We can expect no let-up in the visual and verbal "proofs" of the commutative property of allegorical equations. Just as the Middle Ages and the Renaissance developed an *ars moriendi* tradition to teach

150 / READINGS IN THANATOLOGY

the pious how to die respectably, so the Age of AIDS is producing an art of dying to silence all objections to the argument that a hop in the sack with HIV on a deadly Saturday night is the very worst way to go.

3. THE LATEX FIGLEAF

In 1988, the Metro Area Committee on AIDS, based in Halifax, published a safer sex poster that celebrated the aesthetic pleasures of voyeurism, conveyed a homo-erotically charged message, and featured full-frontal male nudity (see Figure 5). Though it would certainly have been considered "hot" by Maritime standards, its sly producers were never charged with obscenity. In fact, no right-minded vice squad would ever have dreamed of censoring it. How did the Committee pull this off? Simple: they enlisted Michelangelo's David as their poster-boy.

As any school kid knows after a quick glance at Sir Kenneth Clark's eye-popping history of the nude, the Human Body glorified by Art in the distant past is mysteriously exempt from the modern censor's black dots and x-ratings.[11] By cropping

Figure 5.

---

[11] At the risk of losing your soul, check out the illustrations in [15].

David off at the neck and knees, the Committee presented his pumped-up body as an oddly anonymous object of desire in a blowup worthy of the cover of *Torso* magazine. Perfect abs, powerful upper thighs, glamorous genitalia: pure machismo coming at you. No escaping it. As if this brash appropriation of Catholic art were not sacrilege enough, a cheeky caption ("GET IT UNDER COVER") ensured that pious eyes not inclined to dart directly to David's penis—still condomless by papal decree—would be helplessly drawn by pronominal reference to the taboo zone of patriarchal power.

Who issued this urgent cover-up order, and why? Since the menace of AIDS is not mentioned in the main caption of the poster, the implications of the image are momentarily puzzling. An art historian might suppose that some modesty-loving cardinal has ordered Michelangelo to cover up the naughty bits of his sculpture with a portable figleaf as a typological symbol of Adam's original shame. Get that *membrum virile* under cover quick lest it provoke lust-of-the-eyes, for didn't Death come into the world through Sex when Adam lost his innocence along with his nakedness? Perhaps the statue itself (rather than the spectator's soul) is in danger and needs protection from zealous curators. Iconoclasm is the ultimate form of vigilante censorship. If a deranged iconoclast could smash David's toe with a hammer not so many years ago in the Accademia, who knows what will be hit next? Is a castration in the offing?

Of course not, the anxious spectator is reassured by the tiny commandments at the bottom of the poster: "Play It Safe—Use Condoms." The cover under which IT is to be got—get it?—has to be a safe, if David is to play it safe while his admirers are playing safely with IT. Phew! The joke here, the sudden lightening of tension, can only work within the deadly serious context of moralized AIDS, a frame of reference that normally creates tense feelings about private parts by threatening to expose them to the leering public eye (and poised sword) of Death the Censor. Here the cover-up order has been issued with serious playfulness by a group sympathetically attuned to the gay aesthetic fantasy of bringing male nude statues to life, Pygmalion-style, for erotic pleasure. Threatening that fantasy is the historical reality of art censorship, the puritanical cover-up of the "obscene," which draws attention to the vanity of the image as an inanimate and worthless object *sub specie aeternitatis*. As censorship is to the art-object, a killing-off of its magic potential to arouse desire, so AIDS is to the gay male aesthete. Only with AIDS, the aesthete is killed off along with his desire.

Since David (as a statue) is likely to remain unmoved by safer sex advice, the warning on the poster will necessarily fall on deaf ears unless it hits its mark on the spectator's side of the Art-Life divide. The antecedent of "IT" must be transferred from the immortal art-image to its mortal prototype for the joke to work, and its work is to drive away the macabre shadows, to dispel the eleventh-hour gloom, from the site of erotic pleasure for the living. The dead are nowhere near this site. The bones, for once, are silent. The Censor has been censored.

Because "GET IT UNDER COVER" wittily endorses sex as a life-affirming resistance to the morbid cynicism about the Flesh typically preached by conservative health authorities, the military implications of the poster are also funny in a radically serious way. If the order to get "under cover" were issued in the trenches, say, or in a Wild West showdown, we would be inclined to duck out of sight as buzzbombs or zinging bullets flew over our heads. But in the erotic battlefield of AIDS the missiles are invisible viruses from which we cannot hide in a conventional way. Our defenses therefore must be always up when we enter the hot zones—our shields always on—if our standard-issue equipment is to be saved for future engagements in the sack.

Amusingly the poster plays tricks with the old allegorical opposition between Death and Life by setting up an ironic analogy between censorship and condom use. Both involve covering something up, to be sure, but for opposing ends: while the one deadens art, the other saves lives. So Art and Life cannot be equated here (as their creative forces typically were by the allegorization of Death) in opposition to the concealing forces of morality and mortality. What works as an expression of invincible beauty in Michelangelo's sculpture, the defiantly erotic baring of David's penis, will not work for Tom, Dick, and Harry at the baths or in the bedrooms where their bodies are on the line and their lives at stake because of the epidemic. The defiant aesthete who wouldn't dream of covering up the best part of the David must now learn to cover himself up with a condom when he in turn becomes the object of erotic attention. With subversive irony the poster seems to cancel the old equations Death=Censorship and Life=Art (as the liberation of artistic creativity). Life as a sexually active man under the oppressive regime of AIDS now means "censoring" your privates with a latex figleaf, while Art can still be bared without danger to its beauty or integrity since it belongs both to the "dead" world of inanimate objects and to the fantasy world of erotic metamorphoses.

Two more ironies, neither macabre, attend the unveiling of "GET IT UNDER COVER." The latex figleaf, once it's securely in place, hardly serves to conceal the penis it covers. Most condoms are transparent, and even the opaque models (especially if they're brightly colored) tend to focus rather than forbid erotic attention on the taboo zone. Moreover, because the David is no longer shielded even from the modest eyes of Catholic schoolgirls, it can be revealed in all its glory on an AIDS poster—a sign destined for display in the morally imperilled realm of the General Public—without risk of upset to the delicate sensibilities of the police.

But just try unveiling before the Public Eye an AIDS poster that actually shows a condom *in situ*, doing its modest best to save lives, its receptacle tip appropriately pinched, its cylindrical glove awaiting a proper application of water-based lubricant. No glove, no love. All there for prospective lovers to observe, not metaphorically mediated but photographically revealed.

What happens when condoms herald the Triumph of Life?

4. MODESTY FORBIDS

I found out the hard way a while ago when my "AIDS and Censorship" class at the University of Western Ontario helped me mount two poster displays featuring "graphic" works in the perilous sense. What "GET IT UNDER COVER" merely preached, photo-posters like the AIDS Committee of Toronto's "TAKE IT OFF—PUT IT ON," the San Francisco AIDS Foundation's "DRESS FOR THE OCCASION," and the Boston AIDS Action Committee's "HOT SAFE ALWAYS" triumphantly showed being put into practice by latex-loving hunks (see Figures 6-8). The first two images were part of an exhibition on diverse cultural responses to AIDS installed in the foyer of the Weldon Library during the spring examination period in 1992, while the third was pinned up in a glassed-in bulletin board in the University Community Centre near the end of the fall term in 1993. The official reaction to our assault on heterosexist propriety dated from around 1893, as if the Victorian

Figure 6.

Figure 7.

Figure 8.

heritage of London, Ontario were reasserting itself in a final gasp of *fin-de-siècle* panic.

Two weeks after installing the library exhibition, which included children's books on AIDS and activist graphics as well as safer sex campaign materials, I was ordered by the head of the London, Ontario Vice Squad to remove the entire offensive "thing" from public view because it was only fit for viewing "in private." Perhaps he meant in my University College office or in a peep-show booth downtown—it wasn't clear. After protesting about the urgent need for prevention efforts on the educational front during a major public health crisis, I managed to persuade him to dispatch some officers to the Heart of Darkness to inspect the contents of the exhibition for themselves. Apparently the Squad had been tipped off by a "concerned" member of a campus Christian organization who didn't want "innocent children and little old ladies" exposed to the soul-quaking images of sodomitical abandon on display in the sacred shrine of academic freedom. As society's first line of defense against moral corruption, what could the officers do?

They came. They saw. They censored. Though I somehow succeeded in convincing them that books like *Leaving Uncle Tim*, and pamphlets like the Canadian Public Health Association's *Join the Attack on AIDS*, were not likely to cast many souls to perdition, they showed signs of pious embarrassment or demonic temptation—fidgeting, stammering, squinting, snorting—in front of "TAKE IT OFF" and "DRESS FOR THE OCCASION" as well as two other all-male posters.[12] These were promptly removed from the display cases while a German brothel poster

---

[12] In [16] a gay-coded antique dealer dies of AIDS and then is promptly revived as a ghostly moral tutor for his nephew. Judith Friedman's illustration of Uncle Tim's saintly head appearing in a mystical glow on little Daniel's window pane at the end of the book is likely to give Pat Robertson and his followers nightmares about the depraved soul of America.

featuring a large blowup of a nude female prostitute was permitted to remain on view as a lure to innocent children and the odd little old lesbian with a taste for floozies.

The Library Administration did nothing to prevent this violation of academic freedom. In fact, the librarian in charge of the exhibition space docilely handed the keys of the display cases over to the cops and scuttled back to the safety of his office.

In vain did I plead with the Vice Squad about the life-saving mission of my class or the peer-outreach strategy behind their project. In vain did I point out that, apart from the censored posters, there was not one specifically gay-targeted advertisement for safer sex provided anywhere on campus for the hundreds of young gay men furtively seeking dates amid the beer-ad jollity of the student body. The cops' response was simply to quote the Criminal Code at me—as if a recitation of dominant cultural discourse was enough to shut me up for good by reducing me to the futile position of the arts in Nashe's litany. It almost was.

Though the display was a manifestly educational effort exerted in a manifestly educational space, the officers insisted on characterizing it (or at least the homo-erotic part of it) as "pornographic" and "obscene" according to Community Standards—which appeared to mean their personal standards of sexual conduct, physical attractiveness, and decorum in the choice of intimate apparel. Did they not see the homophobic slant of their unarticulated selection criterion? Of course not: to have articulated it would have been to admit just that little measure of critical self-awareness that is antithetical to the bullying institutional character of censorship as a symbolic act of ritual shaming.[13] After they piled the shameful images into my arms and headed back to the panoptical security of their campus outpost, I was left to meditate on the absolute discretionary powers of the individual censoring agent at the crucial moment when the obscenity clauses in the Criminal Code are translated into oppressive action.

As for "HOT SAFE ALWAYS," which my class rightly predicted would leave the Campus Christian Crusade cold and fuming if not hot and bothered, it did not last more than two hours behind protective glass before the police confiscated it. Getting it under cover, in this case, was not playing it safe. I suppose if the poster had been obscene in a morbid sense—if it had shown a lust-crazed homo embracing a skeleton from whose jaws issued a scroll with the Stephen-King-style teaser "CHILLING! DANGEROUS! NEVER AGAIN!" in creepy Gothic lettering—it would never have been kakked. After all, skeletons do not have penises to expose in living color: bones without boners are perfectly safe. Show them on a couple of gay guys, as on the Boston AIDS Action poster, and all hell breaks loose around it. Needless to say, I never got it back. According to a student journalist who investigated its fate for the *Gazette*, the intrepid Vice Squad had it rolled up and covered in, of all things, plastic wrap, to preserve it as "evidence."

Evidence of what? The erotic use of condoms as an aesthetic turn-on for gay Bostonians? The moral decline of Boston, a city once famed for its puritanical

---

[13]On the cultural implications of censorship of my exhibit in the Weldon Library, see [17].

scruples? The artistic folly of resisting the fatalistic moralization of the AIDS crisis? The criminal irresponsibility of a gay professor who had set himself up as the Miss Jean Brodie of AIDS education by encouraging innocent students to fight for their lives in the war between Sex and Death?

The Vice-Provost of the University sternly urged me to have my lawyer standing by because a charge was "almost certainly" going to be laid against me for once again violating community standards of decency. Was I going to feel the heat for what was "hot" in Boston—and clearly unsafe for students in a chilly climate? For two months I dwelt in suspense, the mere threat of legal action having the McCarthyite intimidation effect desired by the University Administration. The charge was never laid.

5. DEATH AND THE MAVEN

Something more powerful, more psychologically compelling, than a mere political concern to preserve and stabilize the notoriously unsteady border between the Public and the Private seems to underlie these awkward efforts to censor AIDS-related images. Could it be a collective death-fear, which might appear quite reasonable in plague-times, or a thoroughly unreasonable but irrepressible death-wish springing from centuries of homophobia?

Cultural theorists have for some time now been teaching us to perceive homophobia as a "discourse," a force-field of terminologies and distinctions sustained by the institutionalized heterosexism of dominant culture. With Foucauldian hearing aids on, we can pick up the bad vibes of homophobic discourse all over the airwaves: it rattles on in casual conversation, resonates in medical shoptalk, drones away in religious broadcasting, cranks up the volume in political propaganda. So acute has academic sensitivity to its hateful reverberations become that we can now detect it even in "the speech acts of a silencing" and other paradoxical articulations of the censorious regime of the closet.[14] Little wonder, then, with the Academy's hyperverbal attention fixated on the subtleties of discursive oppression, we have trouble SEEING homophobia as a cultural vision—a popular religious world-view—even when the sinister iconography of that world-view is staring us in the face.

Check out the photo spreads in the tabloids next time you're shopping for a bit of old time religion at the grocery store. I once challenged the Mephistophilean editor-in-chief of *The National Inquirer*, who was visiting my university as a high-paid guest of our journalism department, to justify his paper's intensely homophobic depiction of the AIDS-stricken Nureyev as a leering zombie from Sodom-on-the-Seine (see Figure 9). The tabloid czar's answer: "It depends on what you mean by 'homophobic': I don't see how the term applies to this picture!"

Clearly he'd been reading his poststructuralist volumes on the freeplay of power-ignorance. A thousand libel cases had taught him the strategic value of

---

[14]For theoretical discussion of the definition of the closet, see [14, especially pp. 42-43].

Figure 9.

the deconstructive turn: press him and you'd get deconstructive pirouettes along the semantic range of any sensitive term. To him it meant nothing more than money in the bank that his pictorial department had viciously transformed Nureyev, turbaned head held high for one last night of glory at the Paris Opera, into a ghoulish icon of gay depravity. But what did Nureyev's AIDS-metamorphosis look like, what did it mean, to the tabloid's target readers? Surely the icon was meant to promote or even to "prove" with undeniable visual evidence their markedly prejudicial (and probably market-researched) identification of homosexuality with decadence and disease.

Though a unified field theory of prejudice has yet to be formulated, synergistic connections between weak and strong forces in the universe constructed and moralized for us by the mass media have long been observed. For instance, AIDS-phobia is commonly paired with homophobia as if there were an obvious epidemiological link or fateful historical interplay between them. The one is said to have sprung from the other: AIDS terrifies the faithful readers of the tabloids not simply because it is misrepresented as contagious and satanic but also because to "catch it" from a so-called "AIDS carrier" inevitably means dying to the straight world and being reborn as a gay vampire with an intriguing but unwholesome life style. Perhaps homophobia is the strong force operating across vast stretches of tabloid time and space, while AIDS-phobia is its weak counterpart straining nerves in hospital waiting rooms and stretching lines at grocery store checkouts. While AIDS-phobia has surely revived a morbid fear of mass destruction, the psychological fallout of the Cold War, homophobia seems to mask a malicious desire FOR mass destruction—

the gay genocide prophesied in the "Silence=Death" camps of the now virtually defunct AIDS activist movement.

Malicious desires, I suspect, are stronger forces than morbid fears in the psychological and socio-political spheres where *The National Inquirer* speaks with biblical authority on the subject of AIDS. Most of the time a malicious desire to exterminate homosexuals literally goes without saying in our culture: it just isn't socially acceptable to express it outright. A morbid fear that "everyone is vulnerable to AIDS," on the other hand, is not a shameful thing to confess these days: talk show hosts even encourage us to get it off our chests like a nasty bout of PCP so that the social healing can begin. Hallelujah.

But what if the very expression of AIDS-phobia (even for educational or critical purposes) stimulates and intensifies homophobic malice? In the interplay of these twinned prejudices the stronger may need the weaker to prepare the ground for eruption. Dreadful as it is to contemplate, AIDS-phobia may well be providing homophobia with a seemingly reasonable excuse to go public with its divine plan for the Final Solution.

In 1992, for example, an anonymous iconoclast armed with the sword of righteousness and a can of black spraypaint launched a graffiti attack on a showing of my international poster exhibition "Visual AIDS" in the library of the University of Southern Maine. He—or she—ruined over a hundred images, including the small billboard "AIDS IS A VIRUS—SEX IS NATURAL" produced in 1990 for the New York activist collective Art on the Road (see Figure 10). Across the middle of the billboard, in large wonky capitals, the ominous word "SODOM" was sprayed as a warning to all gays and their doomed supporters that God was preparing his weapons once again for a holy nuking of the City of the Plain—relocated, by typological magic, to the State of Maine. The citizens of Portland had better wake up and smell the brimstone.

Figure 10.

The iconoclast's fear of AIDS, whipped up no doubt by the Falwellian prophecy that God was literally bent on plaguing all who violated the law of compulsory heterosexuality, prompted more than a blacking out of the signs of activist resistance to the Triumph of Death. If the censorious graffiti had read "Condoms break" or "Abstinence makes the heart grow fonder," the act of vandalism could have been interpreted simply as a panicky critique of the Gospel of Safer Sex. But its aggressiveness betrayed an underlying desire for vengeance against the homosexual enemies of the Almighty, who, the show must have suggested, were triumphing over the heralds of the apocalyptic truth about AIDS in the seething hotbed of liberal education. The censorship, therefore, took the form of a violent superscription of the apocalyptic truth onto the secular texts and images that were occluding or ignoring it.

Religious passions no less violent or censorious were aroused on an international scale by the exhibition of the work of New York photographer, Robert Mapplethorpe, at the Cincinnati Contemporary Arts Center in 1990. Though efforts on the part of the Goliath-slaying Reverend David Wildmon to close the show through the courts failed miserably after a brief but sensational censorship trial, the mass media could not resist the chance to pronounce judgment on the art and the artist in a stream of malicious reviews that accelerated minor particles of plague-anxiety into wild vortices of homophobic hyperbole. You didn't have to pick up a windy rag like *The National Inquirer* to get a full blast of this in the face. Upstanding mainstream newspapers were quick to join forces with Wildmon in translating the notorious show into an allegorical battleground where Life and Death fought it out for possession of the public soul. "Robert Mapplethorpe's career," observed *The Globe and Mail*'s Ruskinesque art maven John Bentley Mays with moral relief,

> was not long—only 15 years or so from the time he became the classiest photographer of New York's art-scene stars and gay demi-monde, to the time of his death, of AIDS-related causes, early last year. But from the beginning of his chilling work to its end, there is no trace of solidarity with life, humanity or art, but only the opposite: a breathtaking malice toward life itself.

The "AIDS-related causes" of his death are not spelled out, but shame on anyone who fails to see the morally obvious connection between a racy life in the gay demi-monde and a wretched death in the infectious diseases ward! Though none of the 175 images in the show focused on AIDS either literally or figuratively, Mays allegorizes the whole lot of them in the fraught context of the epidemic so that they become a phobic image of the artist's diseased soul and its corrupting influence. Why else would his otherwise irrelevant death from AIDS—irrelevant, that is, to his gorgeous productivity as an artist—loom so large in the reviewer's reflections on the show? AIDS poisoned Mapplethorpe, Mays maliciously suggests, even as (or because) Mapplethorpe poisoned Art. That is why, to Mays, the photographer of decadence becomes utterly indistinguishable from the decadent disease: his "breathtaking malice towards life itself" is simply the viral demon within him expressing itself through his "chilling work." So, if Mapplethorpe=AIDS, then his chilling work=Death.

Chilling! Unsafe! Never Again!

Reducing itself to absurdity, this argument finally demands the exercise of censorship for the protection not simply of Art but of Life itself. One glance at a Mapplethorpe photo, and it's all over for you if your soul is easily poisoned (as whose is not?) by the World, the Flesh, and the Virus. "Even if one does not believe the Mapplethorpe pictures are a grave insult to our common humanity," Mays concludes,

> the fact remains that there will always be images which cannot and must not be shown by a public art museum, if it is to maintain its commitment to civilization, and to the cultivation of the mind and the responding heart. Indeed, that commitment is embodied most strongly (but invisibly, from the public's standpoint) in the act of refusing to host exhibitions which poison the fields of intelligence and cultivated imagination that museums are pledged to tend.

So intense is the iconophobia in this statement, so absurdly vengeful the heterosexual anxiety over the moral consequences of viewing the forbidden spectacle of gay aestheticism, that you'd think Mays was reviewing the portrait of Dorian Gray in Cincinnati rather than the glamour shots of Paloma Picasso and Louise Nevelson.

Finally, even the macabre title of the review ("Strong Poison") drives home the boneheaded moral lesson that AIDS is killing certain artists for a good reason: their work is a public health menace. Though Mays' defense of censorship seems to spring from a high-minded liberal respect for art as the cultivation of humanity, it actually stems from a lowbrow conservative dread of homosexuality as antithetical to the very project of civilization. It thereby confirms the dire point made on an activist poster countering the Republican attacks on gay-themed art and gay artists around the opening of the 1990 San Francisco international AIDS conference: "AIDS IS KILLING ARTISTS/NOW HOMOPHOBIA IS KILLING ART" (see Figure 11).

If a death-fear underlies much censorship in the Age of AIDS, a touch of *memento mori* is all it takes for the baleful Triumph of Death to come marching back into public consciousness behind the banner of civilization and the cultivated imagination. At the heart of that old moral pageant lies a death-wish on a grand scale—a wrathful God's scale—to purify the human race of its sinful desires, or better yet, of its sexual outlaws whose desires supposedly brought death into the world. The ultimate irony of the macabre is that any civilization that puts the reality of death under cover as thoroughly as ours does, by casting its corporeal processes and spiritual progresses literally out of sight, condemns itself to endless visions and revisions of Death's socially annihilating dance in the theatre of allegorical fantasy.

Figure 11.

REFERENCES

1. D. Crimp (ed.), *AIDS: Cultural Analysis/Cultural Activism*, MIT Press, Cambridge, Massachusetts, 1988.
2. J. Miller (ed.), *Fluid Exchanges: Artists and Critics in the AIDS Crisis*, University of Toronto Press, Toronto, 1992.
3. T. Murphy and S. Poirier (eds.), *Writing AIDS: Gay Literature, Language and Analysis*, Columbia University Press, 1993.
4. *The Quarterly Surveillance Update: AIDS in Canada; The Weekly Epidemiological Record*, World Health Organization, Geneva, June 5, 1995.
5. Centers for Disease Control AIDS Statistics, telephone line (404) 332-4570.
6. P. Monette, *Halfway Home*, Crown, New York, 1991.
7. J. Miller, Raising Spirits: The Arts Transfigure the AIDS Crisis, *Medical and Health Annual, 1995*, Encyclopaedia Britannica, Chicago, pp. 124-149, 1994.
8. A. Wied, *Brueghel*, A. Lloyd (trans.), Studio Vista, London, pp. 70, 117, 1980.
9. R. B. McKerrow (ed.), *The Works of Thomas Nashe*, Vol. III, Basil Blackwell, Oxford, pp. 282-284, 1958.
10. J. M. Clark, *The Dance of Death in the Middle Ages and the Renaissance*, Jackson, Glasgow, 1950, reprinted in *Death and the Visual Arts*, Arno, New York, 1977.
11. M. Collins, *The Dance of Death in Book Illustration*, Ellis Library, University of Missouri, Columbia, 1978.
12. S. Cosacchi, *Makabertanz: der Totentanz in Kunst, Poesie, und Brauchtum des Mittelalters*, A. Hain, Meisenheim am Glan, 1965.
13. T. Robbins, B. Sienkiewicz, and R. Triptow (eds.), Strip AIDS USA: A Collection of Cartoon Art to Benefit People with AIDS, in *Last Gasp*, Ron Turner Publications, San Francisco, 1988.
14. E. Kosofsky Sedgwick, *Epistemology of the Closet*, University of California Press, Berkeley, 1990.
15. Sir K. Clark, *The Nude: A Study in Ideal Form*, Doubleday, New York, 1956.

16. M. K. Jordan, *Losing Uncle Tim*, Albert Whitman, Niles, Illinois, 1989.
17. J. Miller, Aparth-AIDS: Racism, Rushton and Ritual Censorship, *Descant*, 23(2), pp. 37-46, Spring/Summer 1992.

PART II

Introduction: The Care of the Terminally Ill

No matter how much money we spend on medical care, people still die. Death is the fate which waits for all. The question that we must ask is whether we are providing adequate care for those persons in the terminal phases of their lives. What constitutes adequate care, and do we have the moral and political will to provide it are the focus of this section. Patients often receive uncoordinated care from professionals who are not communicating with each other and who are confused concerning their professional role and responsibility particularly in the community. We educate our health-care professionals expecting to work within a particular system, then we wonder why they can not function in the community where the system does not exist.

The fragmentation and the lack of coordination of care is aggravated by inappropriate financing. There is a maldistribution of resources to some services and incentives created by the methods of financing professional, institutional, and community care. We have in North America, by both government policies and public attitude, perpetuated an institutionally-based acute interventionist medical model of care. This has been perpetuated by the way we pay health across the continent. This is a reflection of the failure to recognize that health care is not medical care. Health is dependant on a person's total environment, be it physical, financial, social, or spiritual.

It has been said that it is the philosophy of care, not the place that makes the hospice unique. Palliative care is universal in its application, it applies to all age groups. Patients, families, and friends are considered to be the unit of care in palliative care or hospice care. Community hospices provide care and support in the home and become a surrogate family. They cooperate with the existing home-care professionals and with the family physicians in the community. Effective pain and symptom control is the hallmark of good palliative care. Counseling, particularly psychosocial counseling, is another important component of palliative care, although it has unique characteristics for each age group.

Over the centuries, the attitude to death has changed. As Aries points out, in the beginning death was accepted without fear as part of the natural progression of life. We now live in a culture in which most deaths occur in aging populations and in institutions. It is not surprising that society is ambivalent in its reaction to death. The philosophy of palliative care brings to the care of the terminally ill a reinforcement of the belief that life is of value, that treatment, which prolongs pain and suffering is unacceptable, and that the physician has a duty to relieve suffering and to maintain respect for human dignity. Hospice also brings to the competent and informed patient the right of choice, and the enhancement of personal control over their dying.

Mr. Michael Bull reminds us of the basic principle of hospice, namely that we care for families. Bull states that the family of the dying person has always been included within the total care provided in hospice and palliative care. Consequently it is important to understand how families function and cope with the stresses of terminal illness. The family is a system, that is, a whole composed of interrelated and interdependent parts. Since the family constantly tries to effect balance, it will readjust roles and responsibilities. The ease with which this is done depends on how the family system has organized its rules and the ease with which it communicates.

Dr. Ira Byock states that care for persons who are dying is at once simple and complex. It is complex because it is multidimensional requiring a coordinated interdisciplinary team. Byock discusses the processes, qualities, and concepts of care. His five basic principles provide the superstructure of palliative care while his discussions of the nature of suffering, the social context of care, and the therapeutic stance of the clinician fill in the necessary information for implementing the principles. Dr. Byock insists that palliative care is intensive care.

Ms. Reena McDermott reminds us that each individual brings to his/her illness unique life-long coping strategies. It is very important that nurses recognize what those strategies are. It is not the nurses' responsibility to take control and "fix" everything. A healthy therapeutic relationship between nurse and patient is one in which each respects the other. The nurse as care provider encourages the patient to take control and is there to assist, guide, and support, rather than take over. Nursing care focuses on the impact of the disease and treatments on the patient and family.

Mr. Andrew Feron discusses the unique role that the social worker plays in terminal care. Although palliative care initially focuses on a patients' specific physical symptoms, it is not complete without also addressing emotional and psychological issues. These issues are most often psychosocial, systems related, or instrumental and apply equally to both patient and family. Psychosocial issues involve depression, denial, anger, fear, anxiety, sadness, blame, and issues of loss. Systems issues include the lack of coordination of the care plan, dissatisfaction with care, lack of social support, placement issues, and the need for education or information. Practical or instrumental issues include: legal and financial concerns, as well as community referrals.

Dr. John Hinton, one of the pioneer researchers in terminal care, discusses the unique contribution which home-care services provide for the terminally ill. All too easily, patients in hospitals lose their individual status, with their personal preferences ignored and their unhappiness only partly relieved by hospital visits which can be awkward and limited. In contrast, dying at home can meet personal needs and the disease is not the central focus. People belong in their own home, they can have privacy and pleasures, can enjoy the company of their family or friends with their familiar surroundings, objects and pets, be independent or show affection and sleep with their partner.

CHAPTER 11

Structure and Stresses: When a Family Member is Dying

Michael A. Bull

"Most significant losses occur within the context of a family unit . . ." [1, p. 97]. This observation by noted psychologist and grief therapist William Worden emphasizes that, as part of any examination of palliative care, it is vital to consider the family context within which a person's dying takes place. Indeed, since its inception as a specialized area of health care, palliative care has always defined the patient's family as a major focus for support, care, and service. Dr. Cicely Saunders, a pioneer in the development of hospice care, identified "concern for the patient and family as a unit of care" as a basic principle of palliative care [2, p. 523]. Attention to families has been considered part of the "total care" provided:

> Palliative care is total care in three respects: attention to the physical, emotional and spiritual needs of the patient; care in an appropriate environment, supported by auxiliary services such as social work; and supportive understanding of the needs of the patient's family [2, p. 523].

This emphasis on families within palliative care highlights the need to understand the organization and functioning of families, and to consider the experiences and stresses which can occur when a member of the family is dying. However, several writers note that limited attention has been paid to the family unit in the literature on dying, death, and grief [3-5]. This chapter examines the nature of family structures, with particular attention to how a person's dying affects interactions among family members. It will be argued that by viewing the family as a system, a more comprehensive and helpful understanding of families' needs, feelings, and actions when a member is dying can be developed. The ideas of various family-oriented writers will be used to develop the discussion, as will the author's own social work practice with families of children with cancer and other life-threatening illnesses. Finally, some implications for those who want to respond more sensitively and effectively to families with a dying member will be considered.

THE FAMILY AS A SYSTEM

Perhaps one of the most useful advances in the understanding of families over the past thirty years has been the increasing awareness that a family is more than a collection of individuals. The qualities and needs of individual family members, such as the person who is dying or the partner of a terminally-ill patient, are of course important. However, the complex dynamics and interactions within families have been more clearly recognized by viewing the family as a *system*.

In considering families from a systems perspective, one is required to make a shift from looking at the experiences of individual members to looking at the social interactions among family members. "Systems thinking" emphasizes interconnectedness—"The common-sense definition of a system is that of a whole that is composed of interrelated and interdependent parts" [6, p. 62]. The value of seeing a family as a system is that one looks beyond what is happening to individual family members, recognizing that those individual experiences affect and are affected by the experiences of other family members:

> A family . . . is a group of interconnected individuals forming a complex whole, also referred to as a family system . . . The individual is considered within the context of his or her family (or family-like) system, not as a person uninfluenced by his or her family relationships [7, p. 364].

As a system, a family has characteristics which are important to consider in terms of the interactions within the family [8]:

(a) Whatever affects an individual family member affects the whole family, and whatever affects the family as a whole affects individual members. For example, the relapse of a life-threatening illness will affect the individual patient but will also influence that person's partner, children, parents, siblings, etc. If the sick person dies, the entire family is affected while each member will also experience their own personal reactions, feelings, and thoughts.

(b) A family system constantly seeks to maintain a state of balance, commonly described as equilibrium or homeostasis. One way of understanding this concept of balance is to imagine the family as a suspended mobile with each piece of the mobile representing a family member. The family mobile is held in balance by a complex interaction of forces transmitted through the strings and crosspieces connecting the members. These forces might be viewed as the relationships which exist among family members. If any part of the mobile moves, then all parts are affected and those parts in turn affect the original part, and so on. Ultimately, a new but different balance is achieved. One major implication of this characteristic of family systems is that all actions and behaviors within the family are purposeful, i.e., to help the family maintain or regain its balance. This awareness about families in which a member is dying can be very important in understanding the purposeful nature of such seemingly unhelpful family behaviors as avoidance, overprotectiveness, or actions which suggest "denial."

(c) Each family system will have a quality which reflects the combined contributions of and interactions among the various family members. Within systems literature, this quality has been described as the whole being more than the sum of its parts [6, 8, 9].

Therese Rando summarizes some factors which contribute to a family's character:

> Each family has its own distinct characteristics, such as specific roles, rules, communication patterns, expectations, and patterns of behaviour that reflect their beliefs, experiences, coping strategies, system alliances and coalitions [8, p. 97].

In essence, families develop strong histories, established ways of interacting, and relied-upon approaches to problems which they will utilize when a family member is dying. For those working with such families, it is important to take into consideration and understand these dynamics. Therefore, it is worth examining further some of the family system characteristics outlined above.

Relationships

The quality of family relationships will very much influence the family's response to a life-threatening illness. Vachon notes that "illness can strengthen these relationships and/or cause their frailties to surface in unexpected ways" [10, p. 66]. Close relationships, characterized by openness, trust, and shared feelings, can greatly assist a family in dealing with the feelings, stresses, changes, and losses resulting from a terminal illness. However, many family relationships involve differences, past hurts and negative feelings which can be activated and become part of the response to a family member's death. Worden has identified ambivalent relationships as particularly challenged by the stress of impending or actual loss [1]. Ambivalent relationships are often seen in families in which separation and divorce have occurred, or when some other significant family problem, such as domestic violence or childhood sexual abuse, has taken place. The tension created between continuing connections and negative feelings can result in feelings of anger and guilt which may complicate the family's coping. Relationships also can be influenced by cultural beliefs, and expectations for family involvement can be determined accordingly. Some aboriginal groups, for example, strongly emphasize the importance of extended family ties and expect that all family members will attend the funeral of a relative who has died. Regardless of the quality of family relationships, it has been argued that the essence of grief is the loss of relationships [7]. In this sense, all family relationships are important and the anticipated loss of the relationship with the dying person will have a major influence on family members.

Roles

The organization of roles within the family will also affect its response to a member's dying. Clearly the family will be influenced by the threatened or actual changes in roles fulfilled by the dying person. Worden maintains that the functional position or role of the dying or deceased person is one of three major areas to consider in assessing a family system [1]. Similarly, Goldberg states that "the single most important factor in the reorganization of a family as a continuing social system . . . is the role the decedent has been assigned, and which he [sic] assumed within the family system" [11, p. 402]. The illness and death of a parent who is breadwinner, financial organizer, handyperson, and disciplinarian will have a major effect on family functioning. A dying child may play a less instrumental role in the family's day-to-day functioning, but may fulfill a central emotional role as a comedian, hug-giver, argument-defuser, or scapegoat. It is important to try to understand not only the functional nature of these roles but also the meaning that these roles carry for various family members.

In addition to the roles of the dying person, the way in which roles are organized among other family members is also significant. Of particular importance is the flexibility of role functioning within the family [3]. The ability of family members to appropriately and effectively redistribute role responsibility will assist them in sustaining the family's functioning when the dying person can do less or after that person's death. Raphael notes that children are most affected by role allocations and absences, along with other changes in the family structure [3]. This vulnerability of children suggests that the impact of family changes on children should be carefully monitored and that children should not be assigned responsibilities inappropriate to their age or their special needs when a family member is dying.

Rules

Hartman and Laird write that "coherence, stability and synchrony are maintained in the family through a series of rules which direct the family's life" [6, p. 297]. Family rules are used to help families organize themselves in many areas, such as roles, structural arrangements, communication, and influence. These rules may be explicit or implicit and may be evident in the rituals, ceremonies and family practices which hold special meaning for the family and express their beliefs and values. Scherz comments on the function of family rules:

> Each family develops conscious and unconscious rules to encompass the growth needs of its members and to regulate patterns of interaction for the purpose of providing avenues for solution of growth conflicts, for buttressing of crucial defenses against anxiety, for social direction of its members, and for stable maintenance of the family [9, p. 224].

The "buttressing of crucial defenses against anxiety" seems to be a particularly important function of family rules when a member is dying. For example, a rule apparent in some families of dying children is that the sick child and the siblings should be told very little, if anything, about the illness and specifically the possibility of death. Yet literature in this area clearly indicates that children as young as pre-school age can understand and handle a considerable amount of age-appropriate information about death, and that dying children invariably know of their diagnosis and imminent death whether or not they are told directly [12, 13]. The rule often reflects the anxiety which the parents are experiencing and their need to maintain some defenses until this anxiety is worked through. The rule serves to maintain a level of interaction and communication which is "safe" and purposeful in the midst of uncertainty, threat, and change. Often, once parents have worked on their own feelings and are given information on ways to include and inform their children, they are able to review this rule and develop approaches that may be more helpful to the children. Alternatively, families may develop new rituals which help them to deal with the dying of a family member. Patterns of visiting, allocation of responsibilities to certain family members, and routines for interacting with palliative-care staff can provide structure and security that maintain the family's functioning. Family innovation and creativity in the development of these practices should generally be encouraged and supported as a way for them to maintain some control within an often uncontrollable situation.

Communication

Much has been written about the nature of communication among family members; overall, it has been identified as a very significant and powerful dynamic within families. Communication involves the expression of both information and feelings, and can be direct or indirect, verbal or non-verbal. Communication is important not only for its content but also for the way in which communication takes place. Many family system observers would argue that it is the process of communication (how something is said) that is more important than the content (what is said). Family communication processes are often repeated and predictable and can reflect patterns of issues, feelings, relationships, power, conflict, and interactions within the family.

The importance of open communication within families is well known—". . . there is strong evidence from research on well-functioning families that clear, direct communication facilitates family adaptation and strengthens the family as a supportive network for its members" [5, p. 9]. However, those who work with families need to recognize that such communication is not always easy to achieve. When a family member is dying, communication patterns are stressed due to the importance of the content and the intensity of the feelings involved. The prospect of a family member's death intensifies the demand for communication of information, feelings, questions, and needs. This communication must take place not only within the family but also with various other systems, such as hospital staff, relatives, employers, schools, etc. Furthermore, illness, dying, death, and grief in many ways remain taboo topics about which the family may have talked very little. In light of these pressures on a family in which a member is dying, communication patterns which are "less open" may serve a specific purpose within a family, i.e., to protect a family member perceived to be too frail or vulnerable. In their study of families dealing with terminal illness, Davies et al. comment on the nature of communication within the family and with health-care providers:

> To a great extent, assessing family functioning depends upon communication with the family. Practitioners must recognize that members of some families may be reluctant to share differing view points in the presence of one another. Practitioners need to obtain information from more than one family member and

gather data over time as some families may reveal critical information only when they have developed trust... Also, practitioners cannot assume that information shared with one family member will be openly and accurately shared with other family members [4, pp. 87-88].

Clearly, communication is one expression of the quality of relationships within the family and between family and carers, and it can provide some useful indications about the nature of the family's structure and functioning.

Boundaries

One final aspect of family system structure for consideration is that of boundaries. Family boundaries serve to organize and differentiate the family in relation to the outer world. A family is part of, and must interact with, larger systems such as extended family, community, health care, etc. A family's "invisible but important" external boundary [6, p. 270] will determine the nature of interactions between the family and its social environment. Family systems are generally thought to be more effective and functional if they have open and flexible boundaries which allow information, people, resources, and support to move into and out of the family, and which can adapt when a family's needs change. Within a palliative-care context, the nature of a family's boundaries might be evidenced by which and how many family members have contact with staff members, how readily the family seeks out or accepts information, and how responsive they are to the service and support offered by the palliative-care team

Family boundaries will also be reflected in who is included within the core family social network. Hartman and Laird describe how families may organize themselves differently:

> In some families, members rely heavily on nuclear family members alone to meet their needs for family connectedness and support. Other families include grandparents or members of the larger extended family. This issue has relevance... since, in those situations where nuclear family is very small, the resources in terms of sheer numbers are limited. In a relatively closed system, however, it makes considerable difference if that system includes not only a father, mother, and children, but also an extended family of some thirty or forty members [6, p. 271].

It is important then to understand the nature of a family's boundaries to determine who the "key players" are within the family, what internal resources the family has, and how the family is likely to interact with helping persons. However, it also can be expected that the openness of the family boundaries may change under the threat of a member's death. Some families which have been relatively independent and self-sufficient may become more receptive to outside help and support as their needs increase and their internal structure changes due to the illness. On the other hand, some families may become more closed in an attempt to feel less vulnerable, more secure and more in control.

FAMILY STRESSES

The family, then, is a complex system of connections and interactions which organizes itself and functions in purposeful ways to meet its needs and to achieve some form of stability. When a member of the family is dying, this system experiences a variety of changes as the illness affects the dying person and the family as a whole. In addition, other external stressors may affect the family or its individual members. The following are some of these "forces" which can act on the family, testing its functional balance and "pressing" the family to adapt.

Intense Feelings

The emotional equilibrium within a family can be significantly disrupted by the many strong feelings stimulated by the anticipated death of a family member. Feelings such as fear, anger, guilt, sadness, grief, and helplessness may never have been experienced so intensely within the family. Stress for family members is experienced not only due to their individual feelings but also through exposure to, and perhaps the felt need to respond to, the feelings of other family members. The adult daughter of a dying father may experience her own complex feelings while feeling obligated to help her mother deal with her feelings. That stress may "ripple" through to the daughter's own partner and children, who in turn have their own feelings about the anticipated death.

Anticipatory Mourning

When death is expected, a family may begin to grieve for the anticipated loss. Indeed, anticipatory mourning has been identified as a primary task of the family before death [14]. However, anticipatory mourning involves "contradictory demands" [8, p. 97] in which efforts to begin moving away from the dying person can be in conflict with the wish to remain attached to that person. Although anticipatory grieving is to be expected, some family members may feel that the grieving is premature or that to grieve before the death is being "disloyal." Davies et al. described this as "struggling with paradox" and found that it was an issue particularly for adult children of a dying person [4].

Uncertainty

Some parents of children with cancer have reported that the most difficult thing for them is not knowing whether their child will survive or die. This issue seems increasingly significant as medical treatments improve and treatment options increase. The possibility of "one further treatment," regardless of its low success rate, may complicate the coping of the family which must struggle with the dilemma of wanting to maintain hope while needing to prepare for possible death. For some, the decision to end acute treatment and to provide palliative care may actually decrease their anxiety by providing more certainty about the prospects for their loved one.

Physical Changes

The physical deterioration, treatment side effects and loss of functioning in the dying person can be very distressing to the family. It may feel that the patient is "no longer the person I knew," that the person is already "lost." The physical frailty of the patient may also impede usual interactions with family members. One mother of a child with cancer experienced intense upset when she no longer could remember what her dying daughter looked like before she was sick, and had to look at photographs to recall the healthy image of her child.

Concurrent Family Stressors

Despite the significant role of the terminal illness in the family system, family members remain involved with and have responsibilities in other parts of their lives. The illness of another family member, business and financial pressures, a car accident, school problems—these can add to the overall stress experienced by the family. Some concurrent stresses may be related to the life-cycle stage of the family [5]. The dying of a young parent will interact with issues related to care of the children; the terminal illness of an older adult may be complicated by changes resulting from retirement. Some concurrent changes actually may be triggered by the effects of the illness. The impact of the illness may lead to job termination or separation/divorce. Weenolsen has effectively articulated how primary losses can lead to, or be associated with, losses or stresses at various other levels (e.g., secondary concrete losses, losses related to self-esteem, losses of meaning) which often will occur concurrently [15].

Realignment of Family Responsibilities

The demands of a terminal illness will frequently require considerable reorganization within the family. As discussed above, role changes must occur as the dying person is able to do less in the family. Other family members will have to take on responsibilities, such as bill paying or household management, for which they may feel unprepared and which may bring them into contact with organizations and systems which seem strange and intimidating, e.g., the supermarket or auto repair center. At the same time, the illness itself requires the family to take on new responsibilities. The demands of visiting the hospital, assisting in the patient's care, making medical appointments, or organizing home help are major and take on added significance when they are activities central to the patient's living or dying. Adult daughters are particularly vulnerable to taking on major additional responsibilities when a parent is seriously ill or dying. However, all family members may experience some sense of "burden," either of being a burden (felt by the dying person) or of being burdened (felt by other family members) [4]. It is not unusual for this process of reorganization to lead to a sense of family fragmentation, in which family members find themselves going "in all different directions" with secure routines and schedules having to be abandoned.

Practical Issues

The family in which a member is dying will often experience significant practical pressures as well as emotional and social ones. In addition to the practicalities involved in reorganizing family roles and responsibilities, there will be significant issues associated specifically with the illness and anticipated death. Within some health-care systems, the costs to the family can be considerable and severely tax the financial stability of the family. Even when health costs are subsidized, there can be major economic stress for the family due to loss of wages, travel costs, accommodation while visiting, meal expenses, telephone bills, and medications. Other specific practical issues require the family's attention—matters regarding wills, estates, funeral planning and costs, and plans for anticipated changes after the death, e.g., moving, keeping/not keeping belongings. These decisions and changes can intensify contact within the family and may have heightened urgency and meaning due to their importance for the ongoing survival and organization of the family.

Triggering of Previous Family Issues

A family's history of complex interactions may include issues and reactions which are reactivated by the experience of a family member's dying. It is clear that a current crisis can remind people of previous crises they have had, and that the feelings, thoughts, and behaviors associated with those previous crises can be evidenced in the immediate situation. Bowen has described these reactions as "emotional shock waves" from serious life events in the family [16]. These "aftershocks" can occur anywhere in the extended family system, including across generations, and arise most often after the death or threatened death of a family member. The link between previous crises and responses to the anticipated death may not be readily recognized or acknowledged by the family or health carers. Indeed, the palliative-care team may purposefully choose not to directly address these previous issues so that more immediate family needs are attended to. However, awareness of these possible links within the family can assist in understanding the nature of family responses and in determining what help might be useful.

Dilemmas of Coping

In their study of families of children with leukaemia, Futterman and Hoffman identified several dilemmas in which parents found themselves:

- to acknowledge the ultimate loss, yet maintain hope
- to attend to immediate needs, yet plan for the future
- to care for the patient, yet detach
- to maintain daily functioning, yet express intense feelings
- to trust the health-care providers, yet recognize their limitations [14].

These dilemmas apply as well to other families coping with life-threatening illness and illustrate effectively the ongoing "dual realities" with which such families are trying to cope, further highlighting the level of stress experienced.

Disenfranchisement

Doka has developed the concept of disenfranchised grief in reference to grief that is experienced when one's loss is not or cannot be openly acknowledged, publicly mourned, or socially supported [17]. This disenfranchisement results in additional problems for grief but in a context which, by its very nature, offers fewer or no supports. For families in which someone is dying, the stress of disenfranchisement can be experienced. Some health-care systems, through their rules, regulations and practices, can fail to recognize the role of family members in such areas as visiting, assisting with patient care, decision making, or staying with the body after death occurs. Specific family members, such as grandchildren, grandparents, or extended family, may be excluded because their relationship with the dying person is not acknowledged. Some families may be disenfranchised when their cultural or religious beliefs and practices are not considered acceptable within the "normal" health-care context.

Families themselves can engage in a process of disenfranchisement. Members who are perceived as "black sheep," i.e., those who are cut off or scapegoated by the family, may not be recognized as having a legitimate role in relation to the dying and thus have their participation and grief disenfranchised. Families may decide that some members are too young (e.g., pre-school children), too old (e.g., aged parents), or too limited (e.g., those affected by intellectual disabilities, mental illness, or dementia) and that they should not be included in what is happening. Also, some relationships within the family may be viewed as less entitled to involvement with the illness and anticipated death. Ex-spouses, in-laws, step-parents and step-children, and de facto partners may be disenfranchised in this way. Overall, disenfranchisement can result in heightened tension within the family, particular needs for disenfranchised members, and reduced social support within the family.

This examination of family stresses has focussed primarily on issues related to the systemic nature of family structure and organization. The areas discussed are certainly not exhaustive, and other perspectives would identify additional stressors faced by families of a dying person. For example, the extensive study by Davies et al. of families dealing with terminal illness identified several components in the process of "fading away" which accompanies the illness and dying of a family member [4]. These components each suggest associated challenges and stresses for individual family members and for the family as a whole:

> *redefining*—a shift in how family members perceive the dying person, themselves in relation to that person, and the family unit
> *burdening*—how patients can see themselves as a burden and family members can experience being burdened
> *struggling with paradox*—feeling pulled in two directions around issues of living and dying
> *contending with change*—dealing with the major changes resulting from the terminal illness
> *searching for meaning*—seeking answers that help the family to understand and make sense of their situation

living day-to-day—dealing with the uncertainty of how long the dying person will live and making the most of remaining time

preparing for death—the practical, cognitive, and emotional preparation for the anticipated death

Overall, it is clear that families in which a member is dying face a great number of potential stressors. The level of stress will vary from family to family, but the impact of these stresses cannot be measured in quantity only. While the author has certainly known families which experienced virtually all the stresses discussed above, the real impact of these issues arguably comes out of their meaning for the family—that they occur within the context of the shortening life and anticipated death of their ill family member.

SOME IMPLICATIONS FOR COPING AND CARING

When a family system, with its complex dynamics and interactions, experiences the stresses associated with the dying of a family member, that family's coping abilities will be challenged. For professionals, carers, or friends involved with such families, it is important to develop an informed understanding of family functioning and a respectful appreciation of families' efforts to cope with their changes and losses. Some issues related to family coping are outlined below, including some implications for those seeking to respond sensitively and effectively.

From the earlier discussion of systems, it can be concluded that how families attempt to cope with a member's anticipated death relates to:

- the ongoing interconnectedness and interaction among family members
- the family's purposeful effort to maintain some balance in the system
- the nature and meaning of family relationships, roles, rules, and communication
- the adjustment of family boundaries in relation to internal changes and external demands and resources

Within the context of these influences, the efforts of families to cope are usually well intentioned but not without potential difficulties. Some families will experience real crises in coping due to the stark reality of the anticipated death and their limited prior experience with illness and death [11]. Usual coping and problem-solving resources are unable to deal with the threat of the family member's death, and the crisis will significantly disrupt the family's sense of stability and feeling in control. They can feel powerless and helpless [18] while the maintenance of confidence and mastery is a major task for families with a dying member [14].

However, the family's crisis can provide real opportunities for those who seek to help. Families or individuals in crisis are more open to assistance as their usual coping abilities don't work and they recognize their need for help from elsewhere. In this sense, the family boundaries become more open so resources (people, information, support) can be utilized. From crisis theory, we also know that families after a limited time will begin to reorganize and start to again use their own strengths.

During their period of upset, assistance from carers need not be intensive or highly sophisticated but rather concrete, immediate responses to the practical and emotional needs of the family. Assistance through information, meals, getting in touch with relatives or friends, and listening attentively are the kinds of intervention which help most in a crisis situation.

Families will also cope better if they maintain their feeling of control and competence in the midst of a situation which, in many ways, is uncontrollable—the loss of the dying person. Family members' sense of control will be sustained if they are able to continue to do things for the patient and for themselves and other family members. Wijnberg and Schwartz have identified ways in which these two areas of control can be maintained. Family members can assist the dying person through:

Their physical presence—Regular contact with the dying person reduces their social and psychological isolation and facilitates ongoing communication among family members. Physical interaction with the dying person, e.g., holding their hand, can provide both comfort and reassurance in unfamiliar health-care settings.

Sustaining the patient's role activity—Helping the dying person to continue to feel useful, even in small ways, can help deal with some issues related to the family's role adjustments, and also sustain the patient's sense of competence for as long as possible.

Advocating for the patient—Family members can act as advocates at the interface between the family and the health-care system, protecting the interests of the dying person and seeking the best care.

Helping the patient with "unfinished business" before death—While this may not always be possible, family members can watch for and take advantage of opportunities to review issues which might be important for the dying person.

Family members can also help themselves and sustain their sense of control by:

Utilizing supportive relationships—Within the various systems connected to the family, e.g., extended family, neighbors, friends, church and school, practical, and social support are often available. Using these external systems can help balance the heightened demands within the family.

Delegating responsibilities and tasks—Sharing the load of day-to-day functioning can assist family members to focus on the specific needs of the dying person.

Maintaining roles unrelated to the illness—Sustaining some activity that is not illness-related may help family members to maintain a broader perspective on their situation and to continue valuable relationships with others.

Planning for the future—Dealing with, rather than avoiding, some of the realities of the future after the death can help to increase the sense of preparedness and begin to link the family with resources they will need later [18].

Those who wish to assist and support families in which a member is dying can work with them in the two areas outlined above. As the family system realigns itself during the illness, it will often be receptive to integrating other people into the family to help it with its functioning. Indeed, within the extensive "death and dying" literature, perhaps the most consistent point made is that coping with death, loss and grief is clearly assisted by the availability of good social supports. Those caring for or about families of a dying person would do well to become part of and help strengthen the social support systems of these families.

Raphael has summarized clearly the process of coping for families experiencing a member's death:

> . . . if [the family] can handle its loss with feeling and openness, flexibility, strength, and mutual support amongst its members, and support from others, it is likely to rebuild a powerful and unified system to face its new future [3, p. 56].

In observing and working with families one is constantly reminded of the resilience, strength, and potential that exists within family systems. Families in which a member has died indeed have identified some positive outcomes which reflect the new functioning and stability which can come out of loss and crisis [5, 14]. These possible outcomes for families have included:

- an increased appreciation of time as limited
- emotional growth
- greater family cohesiveness
- a redefinition of values and clearer sense of priorities
- a sense of their strength and ability to cope with future crises

This changing, rebuilding, and growth within families is, of course, not simple nor without the pain which accompanies loss and grief. This is illustrated in the words of one young mother whose baby had died and who was asked to reflect on possible positives which had come from this experience. In writing out some of her thoughts, she started by underlining at the top of the page, "*Nothing can take away the pain of my baby's death,* but . . . ," and she went on to list several rewarding changes in herself and her family.

The path for those involved with families in which a member is dying is illuminated somewhat by the words of Bowen:

> Knowledge of the total family configuration, the functioning position of the dying person in the family, and the overall level of life adaptation is important for anyone who attempts to help a family before, during, or after a death [16, p. 86].

Gaining such knowledge requires a willingness to understand the nature of family systems, recognition of the stresses that families experience when a member is dying, appreciation of the strengths within families, and commitment to work with and support family units. Through such efforts, sensitive responses and effective palliative-care practices will be available for families in which a member is dying.

REFERENCES

1. W. Worden, *Grief Counselling and Grief Therapy*, Routledge, London, 1991.
2. D. Shephard, Principles and Practice of Palliative Care, *Canadian Medical Association Journal, 116,* pp. 522-526, 1977.
3. B. Raphael, *The Anatomy of Bereavement*, Routledge, London, 1984.

4. B. Davies, J. C. Reimer, P. Brown, and N. Martens, *Fading Away: The Experience of Transition in Families with Terminal Illness*, Baywood Publishing, Amityville, New York, 1995.
5. F. Walsh and M. McGoldrick, Loss and the Family: A Systemic Perspective, in *Living Beyond Loss: Death in the Family*, F. Walsh, and M. McGoldrick (eds.), W. W. Norton & Company, New York, 1991.
6. A. Hartman and J. Laird, *Family-Centered Social Work Practice*, The Free Press, New York, 1983.
7. C. Detmer and J. Lamberti, Family Grief, *Death Studies, 15*(4), pp. 363-374, 1991.
8. T. Rando, Understanding and Facilitating Anticipatory Grief in the Loved Ones of the Dying, in *Loss and Anticipatory Grief*, T. Rando (ed.), Lexington Books, Lexington, Massachusetts, 1986.
9. F. Scherz, Theory and Practice of Family Therapy, in *Theories of Social Casework*, R. W. Roberts and R. H. Nee (eds.), University of Chicago Press, Chicago, 1970.
10. M. Vachon, Grief and Bereavement: The Family's Experience Before and After Death, in *Care for the Dying and the Bereaved*, I. Gentles (ed.), Anglican Book Centre, Toronto, 1982.
11. S. B. Goldberg, Family Tasks and Reactions in the Crisis of Death, *Social Casework*, pp. 398-405, July 1973.
12. J. J. Spinetta and P. M. Deasy-Spinetta, Talking with Children Who Have a Life-Threatening Illness, in *Living with Childhood Cancer*, J. J. Spinetta and P. M. Deasy-Spinetta (eds.), Mosby, St. Louis, 1981.
13. J. Vernick, Meaningful Communication with the Fatally Ill Child, in *The Child in His Family (Vol. 2): The Impact of Disease and Death*, E. J. Anthony and C. Koupernik (eds.), Wiley, New York, 1973.
14. E. J. Futterman and I. Hoffman, Crisis and Adaption in the Families of Fatally Ill Children, in *The Child in His Family (Vol. 2): The Impact of Disease and Death*, E. J. Anthony and C. Koupernik (eds.), Wiley, New York, 1973.
15. P. Weenolsen, *Transcendence of Loss Over the Life Span*, Hemisphere, New York, 1988.
16. M. Bowen, Family Reaction to Death, in *Living Beyond Loss: Death in the Family*, F. Walsh and M. McGoldrick (eds.), W. W. Norton & Company, New York, 1991.
17. K. Doka, *Disenfranchised Grief: Recognizing Hidden Sorrow*, Lexington Books, Lexington, Massachusetts, 1989.
18. M. Wijnberg and M. C. Schwartz, Competence or Crisis: The Social Work Role in Maintaining Family Competency During the Dying Period, in *Social Work with the Dying Patient and the Family*, E. R. Pritchard et al. (eds.), Columbia University Press, New York, 1977.

CHAPTER 12
Caring for the Dying

Ira R. Byock

INTRODUCTION

Care for persons who are dying is at once simple and complex. Comprehensive care for terminally-ill patients is complex because dying is a multidimensional, multifactorial experience for the person whose life is ending. Therefore, responding to the needs of the dying requires a coordinated, interdisciplinary team effort. Specific problems that develop may each be multifactorial in nature. For instance, the evaluation and management of physical symptoms such as neuropathic pain, intermittent bowel obstruction, or pruritus (itching) individually and collectively are likely to require anatomic, physiologic, and pharmacologic considerations. Similarly, the psychological and medical evaluation and treatment of depression, or of intermittent confusion, in a patient with far-advanced disease may prove intricate and complex. However, each of these clinical tasks are encompassed within a general orientation toward care for the dying that remains straightforward. As modeled by contemporary hospice/palliative care programs, care for people who are dying is being organized around the goals of alleviation of suffering and the enhancement of the person's ongoing quality of life.

This chapter is intended to provide the reader with an understanding of that care. Emphasis will be placed on the processes, qualities, and concepts of care with the hope of providing a solid framework from which the interested reader can build an understanding of the complex details of actual practice. In exploring the principles on which hospice/palliative care is built, the chapter will emphasize both the essential role of ensuring comfort for the dying person, as well as the distinguishing feature of hospice care, which is the recognition and preservation of opportunities for the person and family within the experience of dying. The chapter concludes with a description of a "therapeutic stance" or caring attitude which clinicians from various disciplines can cultivate in striving to best serve their dying patients.

In attempting to provide a clear overview of hospice and palliative care and in focusing on principles and process, it is important that the large number of specific helpful services and skilled personnel who participate in a person's care not be omitted. A typical listing of component services and the roles of various members of the palliative-care team might include the following:

1. the patient's physician and/or the hospice physician who performs a medical evaluation and prescribes medications and symptom alleviating treatments
2. the nurse who assesses the patient's physical and functional status and administers ordered treatments
3. the social worker who undertakes the financial and psychosocial evaluation and accesses sources of support of the patient and family
4. the chaplain who explores the spiritual needs of the patient and provides pastoral support

Yet presenting hospice and palliative care as a survey of services and individual clinical responsibilities risks obscuring the essence of this specialized care within a morass of details. As the marvel of a multi-layer cake could not be captured by a comprehensive list of ingredients and spices, the essence of hospice/palliative care lies in the vision, intention, and synergistic process that brings about the finished whole. The defining features of hospice and palliative care are better conveyed by referring to key concepts, qualities, and processes of care.

PRINCIPLE ONE: HOSPICE IS AN INTERDISCIPLINARY TEAM APPROACH TO TERMINAL CARE

Care for the dying is optimally practiced as a team process and as a coordinated whole. Each member of the interdisciplinary clinical team represents a valuable resource during the procedure of devising and implementing a patient-family centered plan of care. Synergy occurs in the process; the whole is more than the sum of its parts. This phenomenon is consciously recruited in the work of the team.

PRINCIPLE TWO: DYING IS A PART OF LIVING

The most fundamental feature of hospice philosophy is a recognition of dying as a part of living, an important part. While the symptoms and physical needs of the dying person are recognized as requiring expert medical attention, the fundamental nature of dying is understood to be a profound personal experience rather than a set of medical problems to be solved. Viewed from the perspective of the life of the individual, even the multitude of medical problems are dwarfed by the enormity of this final transition.

This underlying philosophical stance toward dying as a personal experience forms a guiding principle in the design of each patient's palliative plan of care and is reflected in the subsequent interventions by members of the clinical team. Whenever possible, the expediencies of medical testing and treatment are subordinated to the personal goals of the patient and family. The patient's and family's priorities dictate the priorities for the plan of care. Family visits, attendance at important family celebrations, such as weddings, graduations, and reunions, and participation in religious and cultural rituals often become the focus of patient's plan of care. Medical services may be employed in creative ways utilizing sophisticated home-based services and novel routes of medication administration in support of these goals. It is this orientation that characteristically distinguishes hospice/palliative care from even the most comprehensive medical model-based care of the dying.

PRINCIPLE THREE: THE PATIENT WITH HIS/HER FAMILY AS THE UNIT OF CARE

Hospice/palliative care recognizes the patient with his or her family as the unit of care. This is another defining feature of the palliative approach to care. Families have always and will always participate in this final transition with the person who is dying. The impending loss of a loved one is as profound an experience in the life of the family as is the coming birth of a new member. Each person in the patient's family as well as the family as a whole is inevitably, inescapably affected. Bereavement support, as a corollary of this principle, thus forms an integral component of hospice care.

PRINCIPLE FOUR: SYMPTOM MANAGEMENT IS THE FIRST PRIORITY

Symptom management is the first priority for the palliative-care team. Pain and other types of physical distress commonly occur during the course of far-advanced illness. Fear of pain is the most often expressed source of dread among patients and families who are facing a life-limiting illness. Indeed, without effective control of severe pain and other sources of physical distress, the quality of life for the dying person will be unacceptable. Whatever resources are needed and the highest level of expertise available must be employed in service of controlling persistent symptoms. The commitment to alleviating suffering must be strong and the clinical approach must be organized, comprehensive, and ongoing. Palliative-care teams, especially the physicians and nurses involved, must remain dedicated to do whatever is necessary to control physical discomfort.

The astounding prevalence of unmet physical distress among the dying and the documented patterns of inadequate medical practice arise from a definable constellation of barriers to appropriate prescribing, especially inadequate medical and nursing education relevant to symptom management [1-7]. It is important to emphasize that there are no biologic or pharmacologic limits on the ability to control physical suffering in the context of far advanced illness, nor any legal or ethical reason for persons to be afforded less than whatever is required to achieve relative comfort as they die. In practice, even severe physical distress usually yields to fairly routine interventions. However, adequate control of symptoms is not always easy and in unfortunate cases can prove to be very difficult. But it is always possible [8]. Barriers to the relief of physical distress are medical, financial, social, and even cultural, but none are insurmountable. As Angell reminded the medical profession,

Pain is soul destroying. No patient should have to endure intense pain unnecessarily. The quality of mercy is essential to the practice of medicine; here, of all places, it should not be strained [9].

PRINCIPLE FIVE: HOSPICE AND PALLIATIVE CARE REPRESENT INTENSIVE CARE

It is axiomatic that dying patients are among the very sickest in the health-care system. While hospice and palliative care are often spoken of in terms of "supportive care," in meeting the needs of the patients and families served, the hospice practice often represents intensive care. The issues of the cost or "aggressive" nature of a proposed intervention should not obviate consideration within the process of decision making regarding palliation of a patient's distress. The intensive nature of the caring interventions—such as neurolytic blocks for unrelenting neuropathic pain or sedation for management of severe terminal agitation—is properly limited only by patient-imposed restrictions.

The clinical evaluation of the dying person begins with listening. The clinicians listen to the story of the person, their current symptoms, various sources of discomforts, their concerns and fears. A focused assessment of the patient's symptoms begins with a history and physical examination. Laboratory and radiologic evaluations may be appropriate to discerning the underlying pathophysiology of the person's discomfort. This information is then processed by the clinician and by the interdisciplinary team. Implementation of the resulting palliative plan of care must be followed by ongoing evaluation of the person's subjective quality of life.

The performance of a medical evaluation on a patient who is dying is analogous to medical training regarding the pediatric well-child evaluation. During the office (or home) evaluation of a newborn and infant, the clinician inquires about each of the young person's bodily functions: How are they eating, sleeping, eliminating? What is the condition of their skin and their oral and perianal membranes? And beyond the physical: How are they spending their time? Who is with them most of the time? What is the quality of their interactions with family, particularly their primary-care providers? Is there nurturing and affection in addition to the basic physical care? For the newborn the question is: Is bonding occurring between the patient and his/her mother and father? For the older infant, developmental landmarks are assessed at each visit and the clinician is taught to evaluate interactions between patient and caregiver(s) including the amount and quality of play. The question the clinician must evaluate is: Are the interactions with and stimulation provided to this little patient sufficient to preserve the person's ability to grow, the opportunity to become all that he or she can be?

The medical encounter with the dying person and family occurs within a similar framework. Meticulous attention to symptoms and the physical details of care is essential, but not sufficient. There is a recognition that this, too, is a critical time within the life of the individual and the life of the family. The multidisciplinary, comprehensive and, when necessary, intensive nature of care is consistent with the recognition.

THE SOCIAL AND CULTURAL CONTEXT OF CARE

In emphasizing the philosophical underpinnings, principles, and qualities of effective hospice/palliative care, it is important to remember that care for the dying always takes place within a "real world" social and cultural context. The prevailing cultural and social milieu within which the dying person lives will present an identifiable set of supportive elements and stresses. Modern health care is changing. People are being discharged sooner; more surgery is being done on an outpatient basis. Decisions about where care should be provided and what supportive services should be utilized are no longer merely the province of patients and physicians. In today's world, pre-approval is required before elective surgery and, similarly, discharge planning from hospitals is often driven by cost considerations and, in the United States, by a patient's insurance coverage and financial status. In contemporary America the costs of care during a progressive illness such as cancer, heart, or pulmonary disease, or HIV infection, often leave the patient utterly impoverished as they are dying. The stress of becoming a financial burden on one's family and the emotional pain of having expended the majority of the family's savings is often voiced in terms of suffering. Such anxieties are well-founded. A study of the impact on the family of the continuing home care of seriously ill loved ones found that 55 percent of the families surveyed sustained one or more of the following major adverse consequences: 29 percent reported the loss of most of the family's major source of income; 31 percent reported the loss of most, or all, of the family's savings; and 20 percent of families reported that a member had to quit work, relocate, delay their educational plans, delay their own medical treatment, or otherwise make a major life change [10].

For the person dying, the social problems involving "health care financing" and "resource allocation" become all too personal. Care for dying defines an interface in which large scale social ills are managed clinically, one person at a time. Financial support services and emotional counseling directed at these psychosocial sources of suffering are, consequently, an important component of modern hospice care.

THE NATURE OF SUFFERING

While symptom management is the first priority for hospice/palliative care, the experience of distress among patients with terminal illness is not confined to physical discomfort. The human experience of distress associated with dying is best termed suffering. Cassell defines suffering as the state of severe distress that is associated with a perceived threat to the integrity of the individual [11]. Personhood in this model is conceived as a dynamic multidimensional matrix of spheres which jointly comprise one's experienced identity or sense of self. The dimensions include one's body (physical self), mind, past, family of origin, present family, culture, spiritual beliefs, political beliefs, roles in family (Mom/Dad, sibling, child), roles at work and organizations, preferences, aversions, habits, and on and on. Cassell stresses that we each have a transcendent dimension of self. This may or may not be experienced in religious terms. Some persons may experience a sense of connection to other enduring constructs, such as wilderness, or one's country, or family which will live on for generations to come.

A sense of meaning about who one is pervades a person's sense of self. Meaning serves as a mesh work through which the process of personhood is woven. Damage to this crucial dimension of self inevitably causes suffering. The person may experience emptiness, joylessness, feelings of worthlessness, hopelessness, anxiety, guilt, and a sense of impending doom.

As death approaches, certain dimensions of personhood are particularly vulnerable. One's occupation comes under early attack. No longer is one the valued coworker or supervisor, handyman, clerk, teacher, or physician. Activities in community affairs, such as team sports, one's congregation, service groups, or local government or a myriad or other interests which had previously given purpose to the person's daily life are, similarly, now relegated to the realm of the past. More poignantly, the dying person no longer experiences himself or herself as the breadwinner of the family or the keeper of the household; no longer feels able to fulfill the responsibilities of husband or wife, parent or child.

The dimension of the future, the person's sense of a future self, is under direct attack. Whereas previously the future was filled with hopes and plans, it now seems empty and bleak. Expressions of suffering commonly are set in the near future: "If my breathing (pain or weakness) gets any worse, I'll not be able to take it."

If suffering occurs when a person experiences himself or herself to be coming apart and if the loss of meaning represents an "ungluing" of personhood, suffering among the dying could be expected to be universal and irremediable. Debilitated by illness, ultimately perhaps, confined to bed, a person's sense of self is clearly assaulted. In hospice experience, however, suffering is neither universal nor beyond our ability to intervene. With careful management of symptoms and adequate general support, the large majority of people cared for by modern palliative-care programs are relatively comfortable even as they die and many achieve a sense of peace by the time their sensorium dims for the last time.

More interestingly, as we shall see, people occasionally experience a heightened sense of well-being despite progressive decline in function, the loss of roles, and the loss of relationships. People who have been hardened frequently soften. Anger that has kept one at odds with a family member or previous close friend commonly gives way to an openness to reconciliation. Those who have long felt isolated may once again—or for the first time—be able to feel loved. The existence of such phenomenon is of profound importance to our approach to the dying; it would be of critical significance even if it occurred only rarely. Within modern hospitals and clinic settings, few dying persons experience an elevated quality of life or, if they do, such experiences remain largely unrecognized [12, 13]. Built on the foundations of illness and inquiry, and the goals of cure, restoration of function and prolongation of life, the prevailing medical model has no place to incorporate experiences of heightened well-being in the context of profound functional decline and impending death.

Modern medicine is by intention a problem-based discipline [14]. Patients come to doctors with problems. The patient's chart is organized by problem lists and the clinical approach is structured through evaluation and intervention directed at each identified problem, physical and/or psychosocial. Dying of progressive illness does present a set of medical problems to be identified and dealt with. The orientation of medical training, protocols, record-keeping, and reimbursement nearly constrains physicians and nurses to approach dying as if it were primarily a set of medical problems to be solved. As a result, experiences of heightened well-being in the midst of physical and functional decline may be dismissed or diminished by the treating clinicians. If we are to maintain a person- and family-centered approach to care, our clinical models must incorporate the full range of the human experience with life's end. If we seek a full understanding of the human experience with dying we must admit that people often change in ways that have value for them even as they die. This is hardly a subtle psychological observation. Accounts of personal change of profound significance for the person dying and his or her family form a common theme within biography, biographical novels and, increasingly, within the palliative-care literature [15-18]. As with suffering among the dying, which for too long has gone unrecognized by modern medicine, subjectively valuable, important personal experience during the process of dying has been ignored in the scientific literature and may be more common than expected.

On the completion of a workshop presentation I had given on end-of-life care, a woman stopped to speak with me and offered me a copy of the last letter her adult son had written to her. She asked that I use it if it seemed meaningful to others.

> Dear Mom,
> This last part of my life could have been very unpleasant, but it wasn't. In fact, in many ways, it has been the best part of my life. I've had the opportunity to get to know my family again, a chance very few people have or take advantage of. I've enjoyed a life full of adventure and travel, and I enjoyed every instant of it. But I probably never would have slowed up enough to really appreciate all of you if it hadn't been for my illness. That's the silver lining in this very dark cloud.
>
> When you get down to it, I'd have to live several hundred years to fulfill all the dreams I've had. I have done pretty well with the time allotted me, so I have no regrets . . .

And the letter closes,

> If anyone ever asks you if I went to heaven, tell them this: I just came from there [19].

A few years ago I received a holiday newsletter from good friends, the Bluestein family, who are well-known folk singers in California's central valley. Within the portion of the letter that had been photocopied and mailed to everyone on their holiday list was the following passage:

At the beginning of last year Jemmy and Cordia were ushering out of life their dear friend and mentor, Virgil Byxbe, proprietor of the famous Sweetsmill Folk Music camp, which has been part of our children's growing up and grown up experience in Fresno. When he became seriously ill and there was no one to take charge they got him to a reliable doctor. When it became clear there was no remedy he wanted to be home, so they carried him home, arranged nursing care, sent out a call across the world to all his friends who needed to say goodbye, and they came. They sat with him, massaged him, lay down beside him, and mostly sang and played for him. It was an incredible passage for him and for all who took part. They had a diary for people to record their feelings, and in July a memorial up at Sweetsmill when they had a ceremonial procession and planting of the ashes [20].

Clinical professionals who care for the dying recognize that a person's impending death can serve as a remarkable stimulus for healing—and for growth. This should not be surprising, because throughout life growth and personal transformation is often spurred by profound challenges, even at times, by pain and suffering.

A number of discernible *opportunities* exist within the realm of the personal lives of the patients and families cared for (see Table 1).

Important communication can take place, the sharing of bad news and sad feelings. A particularly precious opportunity presented by a progressive illness, in contrast to a sudden, "easy" death, is the chance to reconcile previously strained relationships, perhaps between previous spouses, or between a parent and estranged child. Probably before any significant relationship is felt to be completed, both persons in the relationship have a sense that at least five things have been communicated to one another: "Forgive me." "I forgive you." (If it is a significant relationship there will almost always be some element of past hurt.) "Thank you." "I love you." and "Good-bye." This is a common experience we witness—and nurture—in hospice. It is remarkable how the history of a relationship (and family) is transformed when the story of two persons ends well.

Table 1. Preservation of Opportunities

Preservation of Opportunities for:
- Communication
- Resolution
- Closure
- Grieving
- Self-acceptance
- Experiencing the love of others
- Experience of meaning and purpose
- Exploration of the transcendent

Source: Ira R. Byock, M.D.

The process of a person's dying can also present an opportunity for life-review. This a chance to achieve a sense of meaning about one's life. A chance to tell one's stories. And, through this process, to effect the transmission of ones special knowledge and wisdom to others. For families it is a chance to listen and receive. To affirm for the person departing the inherent value of their being, and the treasure of their special contributions and their memory.

Beyond these tasks that can enrich the interpersonal experience, for the person dying there is the opportunity to explore the deeper questions of meaning and purpose that are an inherent component of the human condition. Hospice and palliative-care providers have much to offer the person struggling with existential and spiritual questions. It is not answers that matter; what matters is being fully present—listening—and a willingness to support the person in finding his and her own answers.

In elaborating and exploring specific achievable goals within the process of declining and demise, the phrase "dying well" seems fitting. Unlike the term "good death" the concept of dying well tends—along with the related notion of "wellness in dying"—to preserve the subjective nature and broad variation within the range of personal experience with dying. Dying well can be defined as a personal experience with life's end which embodies a subjective sense of meaning or purpose and a sense of completion, at times even of fulfillment that is of positive value and importance for the person or family.

The specific characteristics of personal experience witnessed in hospice practice vary widely from person to person. The model and the language of lifelong growth and development effectively encompasses the broad range of human phenomenology related to dying [21-23]. The model of human development that has been applied to pediatric behavioral medicine and early childhood educations can be extended to provide a theoretical basis from which to examine end of life experience and shape clinical care for the dying. Focusing on common aspects of the human experience with progressive, far advanced disease has enabled the elaboration of a "working set" of developmental landmarks relevant to life's end. A person's individuality is not diminished by recognition of elemental commonalities within the human conditions as life ends. The end-of-life developmental landmarks and the taskwork that subserve them are intended to represent predictable personal challenges as well as important opportunities of persons as they die. Byock has provided a working set of developmental landmarks and taskwork as an example of how this construct can be applied (see Table 2) [21, 23]. The actual landmarks and taskwork delineated invite refinement and modification. The general developmental approach can provide a valuable map to clinicians through the treacherous landscapes of the dying experience and end-of-life care.

Importantly, within this model one need not sanitize nor glorify the experience of life's end to think of a person as having died well or, similarly, as having achieved a degree of wellness in their dying. Personal growth is rarely easy and a growthful dying may actually be difficult, sweaty, and gritty. The touchstone of dying well— the sense of growing in the midst of dying—is that the experience is valuable and meaningful for the person and their family.

Table 2. A Working Set of Developmental Landmarks and Tasks
for the End of Life

- Sense of completion with worldly affairs
  - Transfer of fiscal, legal, and formal social responsibilities

- Sense of completion in relationships with community
  - Closure of multiple social relationships (employment, commerce, organizational, congregational). Components include: expressions of regret, expression of forgiveness, acceptance of gratitude and appreciation
  - Leave taking; the saying of goodbye

- Sense of meaning about one's individual life
  - Life review
  - The telling of "one's stories"
  - Transmission of knowledge and wisdom

- Experienced love of self
  - Self-acknowledgment
  - Self-forgiveness

- Experienced love of others
  - Acceptance of worthiness

- Sense of completion in relationships with family and friends
  - Reconciliation, fullness of communication and closure in each of one's important relationships. Component tasks include: expressions of regrets, expressions of forgiveness and acceptance, expressions of gratitude and appreciation, acceptance of gratitude and appreciation, expressions of affection
  - Leave taking; the saying of goodbye

- Acceptance of the finality of life—of one's existence as an individual
  - Acknowledgment of the totality of personal loss represented by one's dying and experience of personal pain of existential loss
  - Expression of the depth of personal tragedy that dying represents
  - Decathexis (emotional withdrawal) from worldly affairs and cathexis (emotional connection) with an enduring construct
  - Acceptance of dependency

- Sense of a new self (personhood) beyond personal loss

- Sense of meaning about life in general
  - Achieving a sense of awe
  - Recognition of a transcendent realm
  - Developing/achieving a sense of comfort with chaos

- Surrender to the transcendent, to the unknown—"letting go"

Growth can occur within a family even as sad news is shared and the prospect of losing one another through death is confronted. In the context of progressive illness grieving often begins well before the death of the person. It is a process that both the family and the dying person go through. Grief is misunderstood when it is seen solely as an experience to be endured and outlasted. As May has asserted, "Grief is neither a disorder nor a healing process; it is a sign of health itself, a whole and natural gesture of love" [24].

Relationships with loved ones need not be severed as much as completed. People also can grow inwardly as attention shifts and they have the chance to devote time to reminiscence, life review, and the telling of stories. A sense of meaning about one's life can be achieved. With basic supportive counseling—often consisting mostly of listening with caring intent—people commonly come to develop a deepened sense of self-worth. Often for the first time in their life, a person in the midst of dying may achieve a sense of self-love and, thus, an ability to receive—to feel—the love of others.

The transcendent dimension of personhood commonly assumes greater importance as one nears the end of life. Perhaps this is because one's perspective becomes broader, and attention less diverted by the demands and priorities of a full and busy life. As a person finds who they are in the present is no longer the person who had been defined by long-standing roles, responsibilities, habits, preferences and, even relationships, attention turns to the question, "What endures?" and to the larger questions of meaning of life in general. While death-bed conversions are largely the stuff of fiction, it is quite common for people to express a deepened sense of connection to nature, or to a notion of God, from within their own cultural or religious tradition.

THE THERAPEUTIC STANCE OF THE CLINICIAN

Clinical experience in hospice and palliative care reveals that the end of life can be a time of remarkable opportunity and a time of profound richness and depth for the patients and families. The magnitude of the growth clinicians witness is often surprising to both the patient and family. Furthermore, care providers in hospice or other palliative-care settings recognize that the opportunity for growth cannot only be preserved, it can also be nurtured. Protocols and practice algorithms can be helpful but will not suffice; to be effective the clinical work of palliative care must be highly individualized. Palliative care is practiced one patient and one family at a time. Through the skillful effective management of symptoms, opportunity is preserved and through skillful sensitive counseling, growth can be facilitated.

Although training and experience are always valuable and while competence within the relevant disciplines is essential, the main characteristic of clinicians providing palliative care can be thought of as a "therapeutic stance" from which team involvement and direct clinical interaction can occur. Critical attributes of this caring orientation and attitude include the following:

Reliability

Patients are dying in an inherently chaotic period of time and process. Health-care providers must make preparations for predictable problems but also develop contingency plans for the unpredictable problems that will arise. Doing so requires a systems approach. There must be enough resources and skillful, experienced personnel in the health-care system to handle any emergency or contingency. Achieving this end requires education on subjects of relevance not only to hospice/palliative-care staff, but also to area nursing home staff, hospital-based providers and even to the emergency medical services (EMS) providers within the community.

Honesty

Truth-telling is a fundamental principle of medical ethics—and it is certainly applicable here. Patients have a right to be offered available information about their condition and the treatment options available. Withholding bad news in an attempt to shield the person dying from the truth is virtually always a mistake and frequently arises from a misguided desire to protect the holders of the information whether they are family members or professionals. Secrets tend to isolate people at the very time when closeness is most needed [25].

Non-Attachment

Non-attachment refers, first, to outcomes. Despite the very best of palliative care, sometimes, bad things happen. The world in which patients live, and therefore die, is imperfect. By maintaining reliability and making certain that competent caring attention is always available, palliative-care clinicians will have done everything for their patients that one human being can do for another.

Non-attachment also refers to maintaining a non-judgmental attitude toward our patients regarding their emotions and reactions. Even the very best care during this trying time of life may provoke displaced anger toward professional care givers. Alternatively, expressions of love and devotion toward care givers may be out of proportion to services rendered. The challenge for professionals is to absorb these emotions—somewhat like a sponge—while not reacting in overly personal ways to either.

Authenticity

In contemporary, colloquial shorthand, authenticity is referred to as "being real." It refers to openness and emotional availability. This feature of the palliative clinician's therapeutic stance initially may seem antithetical to the quality of non-attachment, yet the willingness to take action while acknowledging the tension between the desire to flee through emotional detachment on the one hand and the seductive draw of personal involvement on the other hand is what imbues the professional's clinical practice with authenticity. At its best, authenticity refers to a willingness to engage the patient in a personal non-objectified manner. It is a willingness to extend friendship while maintaining professional standards of human interaction.

This invites true compassion—which from its roots means not simply sympathy or kindness but a willingness to "suffer with" the other. To see the dying patient as a person to be met in friendship, shoulder to shoulder on a journey neither would choose, invites this meaning of compassion. Excellence of medical care almost inevitably follows.

Dr. Francis Peabody, one of the fathers of modern American medicine, said:

> The significance of the intimate personal relationship between physician and patient cannot be too strongly emphasized, for in an extraordinarily large number of cases both the diagnosis and treatment are directly dependent on it. One of the essential qualities of the clinician is interest in humanity, for the secret of the care of the patient is in caring for the patient [26, p. 2].

Authenticity also implies a willingness to say difficult things to patients when necessary—this may include an ability to set limits on inappropriate behaviors or demands. It may also extend to the clinician sharing with the patient his or her own feelings of frustration, disappointment, and sadness.

Authenticity is not merely an attribute that is valuable to the recipients of care; within authenticity lies the rewards for care providers. Clinicians who make home visits to hospice patients and their families have been known to remark on an ambience that often surrounds home deaths that is wonderful—it is notable how frequently the word sacred is used—even though the experience is stressful and always exhausting for the family.

Participation in such experiences is the legitimate, earned privilege of the caring professions. The clinician's commitment to education and training and the demonstrated willingness to be present at the most difficult times with the intention of serving carries with it the opportunity to share in some of the most meaningful and intimate experiences in the life of the person and family served.

Imagination

Clinicians should avoid declaring to a patient, "I know what you're going through," for it is callous to assume that one person could really know the intimate experience of another. However, if the clinician has taken the time and invested the emotional energy to actually do so, the statement, "I can only imagine how difficult this must be for you," can communicate empathy. This process involves what may be termed the receptive imagination. From within this therapeutic stance the clinician endeavors to listen to the patient's story as if one were the speaker and to look at the world as if through the patient's eyes.

The clinician caring for patients in their dying can also draw upon a creative capacity, the generative imagination and, in so doing, contribute tangibly to achieving a satisfactory outcome [17]. When working with a person who acknowledges that the length of their life is limited and after being confident of a therapeutic alliance, a clinician may invite a patient to look at the events of his or her illness as the middle portion of a poignant biographical novel. The person's imagination can be enlisted to address several questions: "What would be left undone if the hero/heroine of the story died suddenly, today?" More provocative still, given what is known of the main character's history, values, and currently terminally ill condition, "What would success look like?" or "How might the story end in a way that was meaningful and valuable in the person's own terms?"

This use of generative imagination also gives rise to hope. Within the medical model, when there is no longer any realistic expectation of cure, hope is often spoken of as an expectation of comfort. This is tantamount to saying that all people who are living with a terminal illness can hope for is to avoid suffering. If human potential does exist at the end of life, our concept of hope can and must be expanded. The dictionary definition of hope has to do with "a desire for some good, accompanied with at least a slight expectation of obtaining it, or a belief that it is obtainable" [27, p. 875]. By sharing with the patient the information that growth at times does occur in the context of terminal illness—that it is possible, and that the person can be supported in this process—the person is invited to have hope; he or she is presented with a goal that is both valuable and achievable.

CONCLUSION

Modern hospice and palliative care reflects an understanding that dying is more than a set of medical problems to be solved. Dying is fundamentally a profound personal experience for the person and family. It is a time of living—an important time. Pain and other sources of physical distress associated with far-advanced disease can be controlled. With time and skillful listening, even deeply personal sources of suffering among the dying are comprehensible and clinically approachable. In addition to acknowledging the capacity for human suffering at the end of life, hospice and palliative care recognize dying as a time of remarkable opportunity.

Simply by doing what clinicians do best—caring for patients—and by providing care without embarrassment about the inevitability of death, by caring within a team of committed providers, by keeping one's own commitment and that of the team strong, by preparation and education, and by acknowledging the lifelong human capacity for growth and development that exists within each of dying patients and their families, caring professionals can contribute to a healthy reincorporation of the value of dying within the ongoing mystery of life.

REFERENCES

1. T. P. Hill, Treating the Dying Patient: The Challenge for Medical Education, *Archives of Internal Medicine, 155,* pp. 1265-1269, June 26, 1995.
2. C. S. Cleeland, Documenting Barriers to Cancer Pain Management, in *Current and Emerging Issues in Cancer Pain: Research and Practice,* C. R. Chapman and K. M. Foley (eds.), Raven Press. Ltd., New York, pp. 321-330, 1993.

3. K. G. Wallace, B. Reed, C. Pasero, G. L. Olsson, Staff Nurses' Perceptions of Barriers to Effective Pain Management, *Journal of Pain and Symptom Management*, 10(3), pp. 204-213, 1995.
4. C. S. Cleeland, R. Gonin, A. K. Hatfield et al., Pain and its Treatment in Outpatients with Metastatic Cancer, *New England Journal of Medicine*, 330(9), pp. 592-596, 1994.
5. J. H. Von Roenn, C. S. Cleeland, R. Gonin, Physician Attitudes and Practice in Cancer Pain Management: A Survey from the Eastern Cooperative Oncology Group, *Annals of Internal Medicine*, 119, pp. 121-126, 1993.
6. F. M. Marks, E. J. Sachar, Under Treatment of Medical Inpatients with Narcotic Analgesics, *Annals of Internal Medicine*, 78, pp. 173-181, 1973.
7. J. McCormack, R. Li, D. Zarowny et al., Inadequate Treatment of Pain in Ambulatory HIV Patients, *The Clinical Journal of Pain*, 9(4), pp. 279-283, 1993.
8. I. Byock, Consciously Walking the Fine Line: Thoughts on a Hospice Response to Assisted Suicide and Euthanasia, *Journal of Palliative Care*, 9(3), pp. 25-28, 1993.
9. M. Angell, The Quality of Mercy, *New England Journal of Medicine*, 306(2), pp. 98-99, 1982.
10. K. Covinsky, L. Goldman et al., The Impact of Serious Illness on Patients' Families, *Journal of the American Medical Association*, 272(23), pp. 1839-1844, 1994.
11. E. J. Cassell, The Nature of Suffering and the Goals of Medicine, *New England Journal of Medicine*, 306(11), pp. 639-645, 1982.
12. S. B. Nuland, *How We Die*, Alfred A. Knopf, New York, 1994.
13. R. Peschel and E. Peschel, Sisyphus and the Triumphs of Medicine, *Psychological Reports*, 64, pp. 891-895, 1989.
14. G. E. Nelson, S. M. Graves et al., A Performance-Based Method of Student Evaluation, *Medical Education*, 10, pp. 33-42, 1976.
15. C. Saunders, *St. Christopher's in Celebration*, Hodder & Stoughton, London, 1988.
16. P. Kelly and M. Callanan, *Final Gifts*, Poseidon Press, New York, 1992.
17. I. Byock, When Suffering Persists..., *Journal of Palliative Care*, 10(2), pp. 8-13, 1994.
18. M. Kearney, Palliative Medicine—Just Another Specialty? *Palliative Medicine*, 6, pp. 39-46, 1992.
19. C. Goethe, personal communication.
20. E. Bluestein, personal communication.
21. I. Byock, Growth: A Paradigm for Hospice Care (workshop presentation), *IXth International Congress on Care of the Terminally Ill*, Montreal, November 3, 1992.
22. I. Byock, Growth: The Essence of Hospice, *American Journal of Hospice Care*, 3(6), pp. 16-21, 1986.
23. I. Byock, The Nature of Suffering and the Nature of Opportunity at the End of Life, *Clinics In Geriatric Medicine*, 12(2), pp. 1 5, May 1996.
24. G. May, For They Shall Be Comforted, *Shalem News, Vol xvi:* p. 2, June 1992.
25. C. Saunders, On Dying Well, *The Cambridge Review*, February 27, 1984.
26. K. J. Isselbacher et al. (eds.), *Harrison's Principles of Internal Medicine* (13th Edition), McGraw-Hill, Inc., New York, 1994.
27. *Webster's New Universal Unabridged Dictionary* (2nd Edition), Simon & Schuster, New York, 1983.

CHAPTER 13
Nursing Care of the Dying

Reena McDermott

Dying is a natural part of life. It is the one life experience that is common to all. Rich or poor, famous or unknown, all colors and creeds, no one is excluded from this final life experience. Yet we approach it as if it was somehow unexpected, an intrusion into our lives. Our society, which embraces and glorifies health and vitality reinforces this notion, that death and dying not only forces itself upon us, but we must try, with great energy, to avoid it, at least, for as long as possible.

Advances in modern science and technology, new and emerging treatment modalities, are adding more and more time to life for people living with life-threatening illnesses. People who have illness such as cancer, amyotrophic lateral sclerosis (Lou Gehrig's disease), acquired immune deficiency syndrome (AIDS), congestive heart failure, chronic obstructive lung disease, kidney failure, to mention a few, are living longer than those diagnosed with the same illnesses even ten or twenty years ago. Too often people develop a false hope that this "extra time" means they have beaten the odds. Instead of embracing this time as a opportunity to prepare, and experience the final phase in the journey of life to the fullest, the attitude of avoidance of the unexpected intruder is reinforced again.

An alternative approach to this attitude of avoidance of dying and death is palliative care. Palliative care is a philosophy of care which combines active compassionate therapies to comfort and support people and their families who are living with life-threatening illness. It focuses on the physical psychosocial and spiritual needs and expectations, while remaining sensitive to individual, cultural, and religious values, beliefs, and practices. Care is planned and delivered by an interdisciplinary team which includes the patient and family. Integral to effective palliative care is patient/family control and an emphasis on maintaining or enhancing quality of life.

The interdisciplinary team consists of many professionals and trained volunteers (see Figure 1). The complexity of dealing with life-threatening illnesses, the various treatments, the effects and side-effects, and the impact of all of these on the quality of life of the patient and family, challenges the care providers and requires the

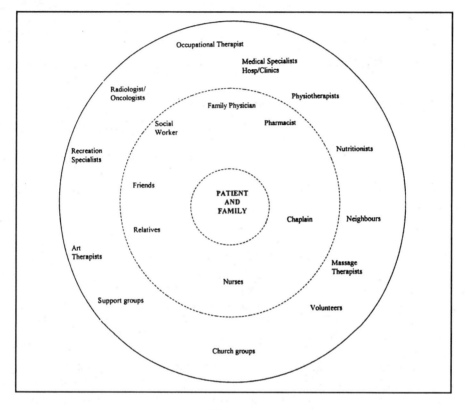

Figure 1.

combined knowledge and skills of many professionals. The nurse is an essential key member of the palliative-care team. This chapter will focus on the role of the nurse in caring for the dying.

Nursing care has two distinct aspects; clinical and hands-on care which focuses on the physical impact of the disease on the body, and the art of nursing which focuses on impact of the disease on the whole person. Many writers have written about the "hands-on" care in which they describe the tasks such as dressing, treatments, and general care of the body which is the responsibility of the nurse. Few have written about the art of nursing which although distinct is interwoven throughout all nursing care.

In this chapter, I will share some thoughts with you on this special aspect of nursing which I call the art of nursing. The reason I'm taking this focus is because of the belief, borne out of thirty years experience, that the relationship between patient and nurse is only therapeutic if they each bring to the situation not just professionalism and illness and neediness but each gifts the other with his/her person. In such a relationship, even in a life-threatening situation, growth and healing takes place.

The art of nursing often goes unnoticed and is taken for granted and yet it is central to patient care. The art of nursing is a humanistic approach to care which has as its central core a helping relationship. Palliative care endorses a humanistic approach, and the helping relationship between patient and nurse plays a central role.

The nurse, more than any other team member, has the privilege of spending the most time with the patient. S/he often functions as the team leader, but always is a catalyst in implementing the care plan and advocating on the patient's behalf.

The patient relies on the nurse to explain the sometimes confusing, and often overwhelming, health-care system. He/she interprets unfamiliar language, takes time to listen to the patient's story, explains possible choices, affirms choices already made, finds out what the patient's wishes are with regard to care and in a supportive way facilitates access to resources to meet his/her goals and expectations. Such interactions are usually invisible and go unnoticed but they form the basis of a helping relationship. One of the definitions of nurse, in Webster's Dictionary, is "to manage skilfully" [1]. Caring for someone who is dying, and supporting the family during the dying process and after the death, requires a high level of skillful management. The nurse caring for the dying wears many hats: care provider, communicator, facilitator, problem solver, planner, confidant, and companion.

As care provider the nurse brings to the care of the dying person general nursing-care knowledge and skill which involves "hands-on" care such as bathing, dressing, medication administration, skin care, mouth care, bowel care, and nutritional care. Part of "hands-on" care also includes creating an environment that is safe and comfortable for the patient. Compassionate competent care is the right of every person faced with a life-threatening illness.

The palliative-care nurse brings additional training in symptom management to care of the dying patient. The concept of total pain described by Twycross and Lack, is the foundation for effective symptom management (see Figure 2) [2].

Effective symptom management begins with the patient's description of the symptom and its impact on his/her daily living. This information combined with the nurse's own knowledge, medical/test reports, the nurse's observations and the family's story of the illness, forms the basis for the patient's care plan. In planning care it is essential that the patient and family are involved. While gathering the background information the nurse not only listens to what is being said but he/she must be sensitive to, and observe, the hidden messages. Body language, the interaction between patient and family members, voice inflections, facial expressions, all present clues to patient and family coping, as well as to patient/family relationships.

Each individual brings to his/her illness unique lifelong coping strategies. It is very important that the nurse recognize what those strategies are. It is not the nurse's responsibility to take control and "fix" everything. A healthy therapeutic relationship between nurse and patient is one in which each respects the other. The nurse as care provider encourages the patient to take control and is there to assist, guide and support, rather than take over. Nursing care focuses on the impact of the disease and treatments on the patient and family. Knowing the importance and meaning of pain and other symptoms to the patient and family is just as important as knowing the

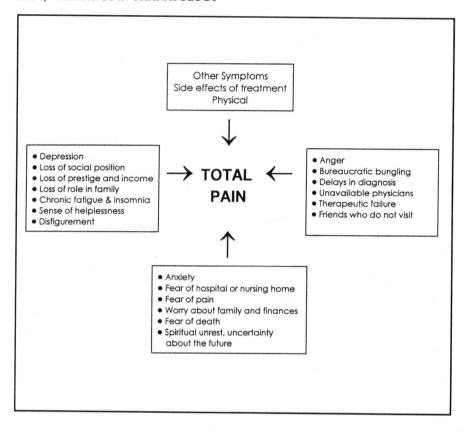

Figure 2.

cause of the symptom and how to treat it. Knowing what the patient's goals and expectations are, is essential to an effective care plan.

The nurse cannot enter into this type of helping relationship without bringing his/herself as a person. This means the nurse enters the relationship giving up some of the power inherent in a professional relationship. Taking up the challenge of caring for the dying means the nurse commits to receiving as well as giving. The nurse as expert offers his/her knowledge and skill to the patient who, in turn, shares this awesome life experience, and both have an equal opportunity to experience quality of life.

In order to create a therapeutic environment the nurse must have excellent communication skills. Besides knowing how to listen and observe, he/she needs to know how and when to speak, to convey non-verbal messages that are appropriate and effective, to interpret what is said and articulate it to other team members. Communication also involves allowing the patient and family to express positive and negative feelings, desires, and wishes. It involves knowing the value of silence, or the touch of a hand, or a hug.

As a facilitator the nurse is a key player in the interdisciplinary team effectiveness. The nurse is usually the person who presents the patient/family problems to the other team members. He/she shares the information, assessment, and the patient/family goals and expectations. As the team begins the process of problem solving the nurse collaborates with the other experts in developing a care plan.

In problem solving and planning care the nurse articulates the patient/family goals and expectations. He/she advocates on behalf of the patient/family to ensure that quality of life issues are respected and control does not shift from the patient to the team. This kind of team interaction involves a delicate balance of sharing and compromise.

Although each discipline independently applies their expert knowledge and skill in the care plan each compliments and supports the other. The nurse implements and monitors the care plan and keeps the patient/family involved and informed as much as they wish.

Patients and families always choose a significant member of the team as their special confidant. Their choice need not necessarily be a professional, and in my thirty years experience, they choose that confidant not because of a professional role, but because of a special personal response or bond they feel with that person. Often the nurse is picked perhaps because he/she is there and has been collecting data and monitoring the care. Whatever the reason, the role of confidant is a privilege and a big responsibility.

People faced with death explore the meaning of life, review achievements, failures, and generally seek to "put their life in order" so to speak. As confidant the nurse is required to listen, affirm, and generally act as a sounding board. Confidentiality is a sacred trust between the patient and confidant and information may not be shared without the express permission of the patient.

The role of companion on this important journey is one that is interwoven throughout the nursing care of the dying. One of the greatest fears of dying patients is dying alone, being abandoned by family and friends whose sorrow at the thought of losing a loved one often keeps them away.

At the very beginning, in the first meeting, the nurse promises to accompany the patient right to the end. That promise is taken very seriously by both patient and nurse. It is this part of care that is hardest to hand over. I have known nurses who stayed late or switched time off in order to be with the patient at the end.

In the past twenty-five years there has been an ever-growing body of knowledge and research in care of the dying. Numerous clinical techniques and resources have been developed to manage symptoms. Education opportunities for nurses and other disciplines have increased. The one constant has been the recognition of the importance of the interpersonal relationship between the patient and his/her care provider. The palliative-care nurse must possess not only clinical knowledge and expertise, but also he/she must, bring to the dying person the gift of him/herself as a person. Without the personal interaction this final experience of life cannot be experienced to the fullest.

Today in our society there is much debate about euthanasia. Euthanasia comes from the Greek and means strictly "good death." Taken in that sense that is what every nurse wants for his/her dying patient. A good death can be achieved when the journey toward death is taken in the company of people who love and support the person who is dying, and when there is opportunity to live life to the fullest, comfortably, and with dignity.

REFERENCES

1. *New Webster's Dictionary and Thesaurus*, Book Essentials Inc., New York, 1991.
2. R. G. Twycross and S. A. Lack, *Therapeutics in Terminal Cancer*, Churchill, Livingstone, 1990.

BIBLIOGRAPHY

Saunders, C., *Hospice and Palliative Care: An Interdisciplinary Approach*, Edward Arnold, Great Britain, 1990.
Doyle, D., *Caring for a Dying Relative: A Guide for Families*, University Press, Oxford, 1994.
Stoddard, S., *The Hospice Movement: Updated and Expanded A Better Way of Caring for the Dying*, Vintage Books, New York, 1992.
Ley, D. and Van Bommel, H., *The Heart of Hospice*, NC Press Limited, Toronto, 1994.
Spilling, R., *Terminal Care at Home*, Medical Publications, Oxford, 1989.
Hanratty, J. F. and Higginson, I., *Palliative Care in Terminal Illness*, Radcliffe Medical Press, Oxford and New York, 1994.
Hanson, E. J. and Cullihall, K., Images of Palliative Nursing, *Journal of Palliative Care, 11*(3) pp. 35-39, Autumn 1995.
McDermott, R. and Russell, J., *Palliative Care: A Shared Experience*, London Accell Printers, 1994.

CHAPTER 14
The Role of Social Work in Palliative Care

Andrew M. Feron

Social workers have had a role in working with the dying and their families since social work practice began in hospitals at the start of the twentieth century. This role was reaffirmed in the *Palliative Care Service Guidelines* published by Health and Welfare Canada in 1989 [1], which identified social work as one of four core-team members essential for meeting the physical, psychosocial, and spiritual needs of palliative-care patients and their families. These guidelines note that social work in palliative care provides leadership in the supportive aspects of the program including practical assistance and emotional support for the patient, grief counseling (pre- and post-death) to the family as well as some aspects of staff support. Counseling, organizational, facilitative, teaching, and team skills are also an important part of the social workers role.

Social work is an integral part of palliative care. Both are based on philosophies of caring and concern for others. The principles of social work include: starting where the patient is; developing trust; a belief in the patient's right to self-determination; and respect for a patient's worth and dignity. These are congruent with the principles of palliative care which view the patient as a whole person, the patient and family as the unit of care, and supports the right of personal autonomy.

Palliative care also reaffirms social work values of seeing a patient as part of a family, community, and society. Palliative care social work practice includes:

- an individual approach which focuses primarily on the personal concerns of the patient;
- an interactional approach which deals with family interaction; and
- a systems approach [2].

Within these approaches, a variety of skills—such as individual, family, and group counseling; crisis intervention; and casework—are utilized.

Although palliative care initially focuses on a patient's specific physical symptoms, it is not complete without also addressing emotional and psychological issues. These issues are most often psychosocial, systems related, or instrumental and apply equally to both patient and family. More specifically, psychosocial issues involve depression, denial, anger, fear, anxiety, sadness, blame, and issues of loss. Systems issues include: the lack of coordination of the care plan, dissatisfaction with care, lack of social support, placement issues and the need for education or information. Practical or instrumental issues include legal and financial concerns, as well as community referrals [3]. In addressing these issues, palliative care social work focuses on the achievement of specific tasks which serve to enhance a patient's quality of life.

Pilsecker identifies four tasks for helping palliative-care patients and their families, which are the same as those which pervade all of social work.

1. helping patients and families to get in touch with their feelings and understand their behaviorial options;
2. assisting patients and families to develop or maintain meaningful communication;
3. assisting patients and families to locate and utilize other community resources as needed; and
4. helping health professionals involved with the patient/family to get in touch with and acknowledge their own feelings, and to understand and respect patient/family needs and to meet them in a sensitive manner [4].

In order to achieve these tasks, a social worker plays a variety of roles which are reflective of traditional social work roles and include the following:

- assessment
- counseling
- advocacy
- collaboration/consultation
- education
- practical assistance
- team support
- research
- policy development

In playing these various roles, social workers are given an opportunity to journey with palliative-care patients and their families, and to participate in a very personal process.

ASSESSMENT

Social workers are the logical choice for completing the psychosocial assessment in that they are trained in understanding the milieu of the person, including psychological, social, and interpersonal components [5]. Each patient/family is unique and is the product of their culture, values, racial and ethnic origins, spiritual beliefs, developmental age, families of origin, socioeconomic status, and numerous other factors. A psychosocial assessment captures this uniqueness and serves as the groundwork for intervention while also helping the palliative-care team understand each patient/family system.

Lusk identifies a framework for a comprehensive assessment which includes a social and developmental history, assessment of the family system, and physical and environmental resources. Included in the social and developmental history are cultural, educational, and psychological issues prior to the illness, focusing especially on coping skills associated with loss. Assessment of the family system includes both nuclear and extended families as well as the social-support network: its size, capabilities, structure, stability and ethnicity, the roles various members play, its strengths and vulnerabilities. It also includes assessing for mental status, mood and affect, appropriateness of behavior, patient and family's reaction to the illness, defense mechanisms and coping strategies, the relationship between the patient, care giver and other family members, altered communication patterns, how family roles have been affected by the illness, and how their roles and responsibilities have been reallocated and accepted by others. Assessing for physical and environmental resources refers to such things as adequacy of the home environment, health, and capability of the care giver to provide necessary care, financial status, and the need for referral to community agencies for equipment or other services [6, 7].

In assessing the patient, it is important to establish what changes his/her illness has brought, how his/her life has changed since the illness, and who currently supports him/her. It is also important to understand the patient's reaction to the illness and to identify any practical or emotional unfinished business s/he may have. The patient needs to be placed within the context of his/her family, in order to assess the strengths and difficulties of a family and understand how it works. The normal patterns of communication, support, and conflict in the family, and the extent to which they have been disrupted by the illness need to be explored. The family in turn, needs to be placed within the context of their community and social network. It is important to understand a family's ethnic, cultural, and religious background and the potential impact of these influences on the patient and his/her illness. It is also important to inquire about informal and formal helping systems available to the family within its community, such as churches, social groups, and schools [8].

A Plan for Intervention/Care Plan is subsequently developed from the psychosocial assessment which can help the patient sustain present coping abilities or develop strategies to cope with stress [9]. The Plan for Intervention/Care Plan can also help the patient develop problem-solving techniques, and establish communication with the family and the palliative-care team.

The interventions that come from the care plan are supportive, and patient/family centered. The resolution of specific problems and the provision of appropriate resources are primary aspects of intervention. Some of the specific interventions which have been utilized in palliative care include:

- facilitating the expression of strong feelings [4]
- validating the patients strengths
- promoting the patients' optional coping and well-being [9]
- encouraging the patient to focus on presenting problems and helping him/her formulate specific plans of action [10].

Interventions are aimed at patients and families who need help in order to cope with their situation. Typically they need help because they do not have the information they need, they cannot communicate sufficiently with each other to reach a solution, they lack the confidence to act, or they do not have the resources they need [8].

In operationalizing a Plan for Intervention/Care Plan, social workers utilize skills in a variety of approaches, including crisis intervention, adjustment therapy, psychotherapy, short-term casework, longer-term therapy, and bereavement counseling.

COUNSELING

The social-work role in counseling consists of encouraging patients and their families to express their feelings, while also helping them focus on the presenting problems. They are encouraged to utilize their strengths to cope with existing stressors, and are thereby helped to formulate a specific plan of action. Helping patients/families to express their feelings, and convincing them that this expression is acceptable and appropriate can reduce many of the negative feelings associated with a terminal illness. There may not always be answers or solutions to the emotional anguish expressed by dying patients but they can be helped by being heard. Sharing the problem is sometimes enough to provide relief. It is not necessary to approve what the patient says or does, it is important to show understanding of the feelings behind the patient's words and actions [8].

In providing supportive counseling, the social worker provides a therapeutic environment based on understanding, concern, and acceptance, within which the patient is empowered to make positive changes in his/her situation while also increasing his/her self understanding and emotional independence. A social worker will have a repertoire of approaches and styles to draw upon in providing counseling. Some of the essential skills that are utilized include: information giving, information receiving, clarifying, probing, empathy, confronting, sharing, reassurance, listening without speaking, giving alternative frames of reference, interpretation, acceptance/affirmation, giving feedback, and supporting [11].

The provision of counseling to patients during the dying process and to families through the grief process is important. Vachon, in a study of palliative-care patients and families, found that one-quarter to one-half of them wanted or needed help in dealing with their situation. Many, however, would not ask for this help. Vachon asserted that counseling should be immediate, action-oriented, and have limited goals [12].

Addressing the needs of family members is an important component of counseling. Wijnberg and Schwartz identified two tasks that family members must undertake when a member is dying. The first is being able to be helpful to the dying patient and the second is adjusting to the disruption in their personal life [13]. In providing counseling to the family, it is important to recognize the responsibilities they carry as care givers as well as the significance of the terminal illness for them, the nature of the pain and loss they are experiencing, and their encounters with grief prior to and after the death of the patient [14].

The social-work role in counseling also includes facilitating communication between the patient, the family, and the palliative-care team. The family conference is one vehicle through which this communication occurs. One of the goals of the family conference is to meet the needs of the patient/family, needs for information, and the opportunity to safely express and share feelings. Another goal is to emphasize that care is family-centered and that members of a family cope best in a crisis when they support each other. Meeting a patient alone, and meeting family members without the patient present, tends to split relationships and emphasizes the isolation of the patient [11].

Recognizing the importance of continuity of care, counseling does not end at the time of a patient's death, but extends to include bereavement follow-up work. In bereavement counseling the social worker helps the bereaved explore and express thoughts and feelings which are difficult and painful. By listening, understanding, responding without being judgmental and being able to tolerate unpleasant feelings, the social worker can prevent the bereaved from feeling overwhelmed, and hopefully help them move toward adjustment [15]. Bereavement follow-up includes addressing anticipatory grief issues, assessment of risk factors, crisis intervention, support groups, education, ongoing counseling, a referral service, and supervision of volunteers who do much of the bereavement follow-up for those experiencing normal grieving patterns [5].

ADVOCATE

Social workers have traditionally been known as advocates for the oppressed and underprivileged. In the role of Advocate, social workers ensure that patients are heard and that they have choices in their care as well as a right to refuse care. It is important to assist patients in maintaining as much control over their lives as possible [5]. Patient advocacy is frequently required in palliative care since few patients are physically able to act on their own behalf, and family members are busy caring for the patient, having neither the time nor the energy to work through red tape and bureaucracy [16].

In addition, social workers are expected to be advocates by becoming a liaison between the patient and needed community resources. A social worker uses his/her experience for the patient's benefit, thus ensuring that the patient receives the services s/he is entitled to, and that these services are provided in a manner that safeguards his/her dignity. As an advocate, a social worker becomes the spokesperson for the patient by presenting his/her case. The social worker will argue, bargain, negotiate, and manipulate the environment on behalf of the patient [10].

COLLABORATION/CONSULTATION

The roles of collaborator and consultant are demonstrated in the interactions between a social worker and members of the palliative-care team. In order to provide quality care, social work, along with other members of the interdisciplinary team, must function as a cohesive unit, utilizing the expertise and resources of each discipline represented, both professional and nonprofessional. Although each profession in palliative care has core skills and knowledge, there is overlap, particularly in the emotional aspects of care. This overlap will only be fruitful if all professionals have a clear idea of their own role and an appreciation of what other professions can offer [17].

A social worker's training in group work and systems approach is an asset to team functioning and helps to facilitate the camaraderie and cooperation that are essential. Weekly formal team meetings are utilized by social work in its consultative role to review each patient/family situation, to discuss possible changes in the approach to problems, and to revise the care plan if appropriate. Informal conferences, which occur almost daily among team members, are another vehicle through which social work attempts to keep everyone informed and updated on each patient/family situation.

Social workers need to be confident enough in their role, to be comfortable with a degree of role blurring. It is important to recognize that no one member of the interdisciplinary team holds the exclusive rights to the psychosocial aspects of a patient's care. Patients and their families will share their feelings and concerns with whoever they choose, whenever they choose. This may or may not be a social worker, or at a time when social work is available. It is therefore essential that social workers work collaboratively with other members of the palliative-care team, and be comfortable extending their role into non-traditional areas including some aspects of nursing care and pastoral care.

EDUCATION

The social worker's role with respect to education in palliative care involves professional development, teaching patients/families, and community education. In terms of professional development, social workers have a responsibility to keep abreast of new developments and knowledge within their profession and the palliative-care field. Social work in palliative care is still a relatively new specialty in a fast developing area of care. Although there is no formal training in Canada which qualifies social workers specifically for palliative care, there are short courses, as well as palliative-care conferences and workshops, from which knowledge and skills can be obtained [17]. Social work plays a role in teaching patients and families to understand their own emotions and anxieties. Each patient's and family's entire social network is dealing with loss, changes in family roles and relationships, and fluctuating emotions. Increasing awareness and understanding of these issues within the family helps to reduce fear, isolation, loneliness, conflict, and misunderstanding.

Social workers also have a responsibility to participate in community education. Palliative-care programs provide a valuable practicum experience for social work students at both the undergraduate and graduate levels. Even students planning a career outside the health field can learn much about helping people deal with loss and change, which are universal issues encountered in any area of professional or private life [16]. Supervised practicum experiences with a palliative-care team provide an opportunity to work in-depth with dying patients and their families, and to test skills and attitudes. No classroom experience can match this, provided there is proper supervision [17].

As palliative-care social work develops into a specialty field, there is an increasing expectation of experienced palliative-care social workers to become teachers for their own profession, as well as other health-care professionals, and voluntary groups. Social workers are now beginning to take an active role in teaching courses on the psychosocial aspects of palliative care at the university and college level, and are also playing a larger role in presenting papers and conducting workshops at regional, provincial, and national palliative-care conferences.

PRACTICAL ASSISTANCE

One of the most important roles for social workers is the provision of practical assistance. Referrals to other institutions or community services, providing resource information, coordinating available services, discharge planning, accessing insurance or disability plans, arranging a funeral, and obtaining financial and legal assistance are just a few of the many tasks completed by social workers. Social workers are experts in community resources and facilitate contacts with these resources. Knowing the scope of services, prices, and compatibility with the patient's needs can be a great asset [5].

TEAM SUPPORT

As a result of the personal demands that palliative care makes on the individuals who provide it, the social work role often extends to include providing emotional support to team members. Because working in palliative care involves the use of self in relationships with patients and families, members of the palliative-care team are sometimes subjected to inordinate stresses. These include repeatedly experiencing feelings of sadness, loss, and helplessness. By virtue of their professional training and experience, social workers are specifically qualified to offer the necessary support and assistance to help combat these stresses [3]. Social workers are also best able to assist other team members to admit and accept emotional disequilibrium, not only in patients and families but also among themselves. People facing loss awaken powerful feelings in the professionals who meet them. We cannot listen properly to the loss of others if our own losses, actual or feared, are unexplored and unresolved [8]. Staff support may be provided to the palliative-care team as a whole or on an individual basis. Impromptu conversations, ward rounds, staff meetings, and educational programs are vehicles for social work input [4].

The emotional demands experienced by a palliative-care social worker in providing support to the palliative-care team as well as patients/families can be stressful. Coping with these demands requires continuous development of self-awareness in order to understand one's feelings and responses to dying and bereavement and thus to control them. Without this self-awareness, one may either over-identify with the patient or family and be overwhelmed by their grief, or avoid anything more than superficial involvement and minimal helping efforts [18].

RESEARCH

Because the role of palliative-care social work is relatively new, research has been limited, and is an area that requires further development. Research is needed to help define which specific social work interventions involved in palliative care are most helpful for which patients, and under which circumstances. Social work needs to be involved in developing a better understanding of the psychosocial aspects of palliative care, and in the implementation of new ways of caring for patients and their families [8]. In order to support the work that social workers do in palliative care it is important to "validate" that it is effective [5]. Social workers can also broaden the body of knowledge in palliative care by developing and completing research in such areas as program evaluation and consumer satisfaction, prevention of staff burnout, characteristics of persons who work in palliative care, the role of environment in reducing anxiety, and the relationship between anxiety and pain or other symptoms [16].

POLICY DEVELOPMENT

It is important for social workers to keep abreast of current palliative care and social work issues, while also playing a role in the development of policies, procedures, standards, and guidelines which are responsive to emerging issues and trends. The best link for this is to belong to the national and provincial palliative-care organizations, and to participate in the development of palliative-care regionally, nationally, and internationally. Social workers should seek roles on advisory committees and offer their expertise in helping to define the future of palliative care [8]. Social workers, knowledgeable of the community as a whole, its strengths and weaknesses, it resources, and its cultural components, can include this knowledge in discussions of policy issues and program development.

Social workers should also maintain active membership in professional social work organizations. As a profession, social work needs to look at the development of a national registry of Canadian palliative-care social workers. Efforts toward this were taken in October 1995 at the 6th Canadian Palliative Care Conference in Halifax where social workers from across the country met for the first time as a formal interest group. This was an important step in giving psychosocial care a clear voice, while also providing the foundation for future networking, education, and collaborative research. Palliative-care social workers need one another and should be meeting together to process their feelings and experiences. Meeting as a group helps to reduce isolation, and provides an opportunity to discuss difficult cases, raise ethical issues, engage in problem solving, and to provide peer support. Developing mentorship programs and arranging for social workers to shadow one another in their respective settings are just two ways of broadening the understanding and support of social work practice in palliative care. Social work still has far to go in its efforts to establish itself as an integral part of every palliative-care program. A 1988 survey by Rodway and Blythe showed that half the palliative-care facilities in Canada do not employ social workers. Clearly this demonstrates that we have a lot to do in terms of further developing our role in palliative care.

Although the role of social work in palliative care encompasses a variety of specific roles, the challenge is to creatively and skillfully juggle these roles in a way that is sensitive and responsive to the needs of patients and their families. In order to effectively do this, social workers working in palliative care need to be caring, flexible, knowledgeable of others and themselves, able to skillfully apply professional methods and techniques, and have the capacity to individualize their work [19].

There is a deep sense of satisfaction and meaning that comes from palliative-care social work and the privilege of sharing in, and being a part of the final days of a patient's life. Valuable lessons about living are learned from those who are dying. The courage of patients and families, and the love they share helps to diminish the emotional drain and stress often associated with working in this specialty area.

REFERENCES

1. Palliative Care Services, *Report of the Subcommittee on Institutional Program Guidelines/Guidelines for Establishing Standards,* Health and Welfare Canada, p. 17, 1989.
2. L. Quig, The Role of the Hospice Social Worker, *The American Journal of Hospice Care,* p. 22, July/August 1989.
3. M. R. Rodway and J. Blyth, Social Work Practice in Palliative Care, in *Social Work Practice in Health Care Settings,* M. J. Holosko and P. A. Taylor (eds.), Canadian Scholar's Press, Toronto, p. 403, 1989.
4. C. Pilsecker, Terminal Cancer: A Challenge for Social Work, *Social Work in Health Care,* 4, pp. 373-374, 1979.
5. K. Brandt and C. Cody (eds.), *Guidelines for Social Work In Hospice,* The National Hospice Organization Council for Hospice Professionals Social Work Section, p. 6, 1994.
6. N. Millett Fish, Social Work Practice in Hospice Care, in *Social Work Practice in Health Care Settings,* M. J. Holosko and P. A. Taylor (eds.), Canadian Scholar's Press, Toronto, p. 389, 1989.
7. M. Lusk, The Psychosocial Evaluation of the Hospice Patient, in *Health and Social Work,* 8, pp. 210-218, 1983.
8. B. Munroe, Social Work in Palliative Care, in *Oxford Textbook of Palliative Medicine,* D. Doyle, G. Hanks, and N. MacDonald (eds.), Oxford University Press, Oxford, p. 566, 1993.

9. D. M. Dush, Psychological Research in Hospice Care: Toward Specificity of Therapeutic Mechanisms, *The Hospice Journal,* 4(2), pp. 9-36, 1988.
10. V. Sadkadakis, R. Bonar, and M. MacLean, The Role of the Social Work in Terminal Care with Institutionalized Elderly People, *Journal of Palliative Care,* 3(2), pp. 19-25, 1987.
11. P. Kaye, *Notes on Symptom Control in Hospice and Palliative Care,* Hospice Education Institute Inc., Connecticut, p. 94, 1992.
12. M. Vachon, Counselling and Psychotherapy in Palliative/Hospice Care: A Review, *Palliative Medicine,* 2(1), pp. 36-50, 1988.
13. M. Wijnberg and M. Schwartz, Competency or Crisis: The Social Work Role in Maintaining Family Competency during the Dying Period, in *Social Work with Dying Patient and the Family,* E. Prichard, T. Collard, B. Orcutt, A. Kutscher, I. Seeland, and N. Lekowitz (eds.), Columbia University Press, New York, pp. 97-98, 1977.
14. B. Rusnack, S. McNulty Schaefer, and D. Moxley, "Safe Passage": Social Work Roles and Functions in Hospice Care, *Social Work in Health Care,* 13(3), p. 9, 1988.
15. R. J. Dunlop and J. M. Hockley, *Terminal Care Support Teams: The Hospital—Hospice Interface,* Oxford University Press, New York, p. 36, 1990.
16. N. Millet, Hospice: A New Horizon for Social Work, in *Hospice Care: Principles and Practice,* C. A. Corr and D. M. Corr (eds.), Springer Publishing Company, New York, p. 139, 1983.
17. F. Sheldon, Education and Training for Social Workers in Palliative Care, in *Oxford Textbook of Palliative Care,* D. Doyle, G. Hanks, and N. MacDonald (eds.), Oxford University Press, Oxford, p. 794, 1993.
18. C. Germain, *Social Work Practice in Health Care: An Ecological Perspective,* The Free Press, New York, p. 196, 1984.
19. D. E. Stark and E. M. Johnson, Implication of Hospice Concepts for Social Work Practice with Oncology Patients and Their Families in an Acute Care Teaching Hospital, *Social Work in Health Care,* 9(1), pp. 63-70, 1983.

CHAPTER 15
Home Care

John Hinton

There is a well-recognized apparent paradox that an ever-increasing proportion of deaths take place in hospitals but most people say they would like to die at home. How does this come about?

The figures are clear enough; for example, in Britain 65 percent of all deaths now occur in hospitals and similar institutions, or 68 percent of cancer deaths [1]. Attention was drawn to the rising trend in the 1960s as concern grew over the quality of care dying people received. At that time, about a half died in hospitals whereas a century earlier it had been less than a tenth [2]. The tendency was world-wide. In the United States the available statistics showed the proportion of hospital deaths to be rising by about 1 percent annually, from 50 percent in 1949 to 61 percent in 1958 [3]. In southern Australia, figures obtained from funeral directors indicated that home deaths had fallen from 57 percent in 1910 to 26 percent in 1970 [4]. Various explanations are given for why even more people die in the hospital; the tenacious wish of patients to be cured and of staff to cure, an acceptance of increasingly technical methods in medicine, an inability to "give up," the assumption by professionals and others that serious illness means hospital treatment, the inadequacies of home-based care, fewer people available to give care in today's smaller family units, an aging population, no adequate arrangements or plans for home care or support, and so on [5].

There are arguments against so much terminal care taking place in the hospital. Dying in institutions may bring unnecessary discomfort because professionals strive for unrealistic goals while patients suffer indignity, the side-effects of a barrage of treatments, and the risk of intercurrent infections. All too easily, patients lose their individual status, with their personal preferences ignored and their unhappiness only partly relieved by hospital visits which can be awkward and limited. In contrast, dying at home can meet personal needs and the disease is not the central focus. People belong in their own home, they can have privacy and pleasures, can enjoy the company of their family or friends with their familiar surroundings, objects and pets, be independent or show affection, and sleep with their partner. Many homes and relationships, of course, are not that ideal, but they may still be preferable to substandard or unaffordable hospital care.

About the late 1950s public indifference to much unnecessary suffering in terminal illness began to be replaced by a growing motivation to give better care to those with but a short time to live. It may have been influenced by the powerful war-time memories of altruism and compassion contrasted with callousness and the abuse of power, which fostered a post-war reaction against injustice and inequality. Such feelings when focused on the needs of the dying found two main directions for its thrust. In the United States much of the impetus came from outside the traditional caring professions. Some reacted against the unnecessary reticence about the subject and the frequent indifference to an individual's personal values when dying. They sought to re-educate people that dying and death should be openly recognized as part of life's cycle. The movement in some cases carried a sense of blaming medical attitudes. In Britain, however, the emphasis was more than a few doctors, social workers, nurses, and others sought to clarify what did or did not happen to people with terminal illness and then find ways to make improvements. Moving back toward good home care for people with cancer was an important arm of that thrust. It became clear that this involved more than ensuring people had sufficient relief of pain, vital though this was. The renaissance of home care merits reviewing because it gives insights into many issues concerning death and dying.

THE DEVELOPMENT OF HOME CARE

Before this century the sick and helpless, including the dying, were normally cared for at home by other members of the household; the family doctor attended and so might nurses of varying skill and reputation. Alternatively, they might enter the hospital for special treatment or be in institutions, including work-houses and wards for the chronic sick. Home care is no new invention, but has recently taken on the meaning of giving more expert palliative care in the home setting. Formerly, professional carers were guided by example and experience, which reinforced both good and bad precedents. Apart from religious writings, little was written specifically about care of the dying until Worcester's book on *The Care of the Aged, the Dying and the Dead* in 1935 [6].

In the 1950s the earliest surveys of what did happen to people dying at home were published. Incurable cancer received particular attention because its outcome was clear and it was a notorious cause of suffering. In Britain, not long after the National Health Service was implemented in 1948, the Marie Curie Foundation and Queen's Institute of District Nursing gathered answers to nurses' questionnaires about the current state of 7,050 patients with cancer distributed throughout the country [7]. At least two-thirds suffered moderately or severely, both physically and mentally, and over half were bed-ridden. Most were cared for by relatives, but the elderly couples and the 7 percent living alone often endured great hardship. The report concentrated on many material needs, meals, domestic help, night nursing help, laundry, dressings, and money. The frequent lack of basic household amenities at that time may now seem a little out-dated, but nevertheless much in this pioneering report still applies. Quotations from the nurses' notes described relatives' suffering and the patients' despondency because the condition was incurable and no one apparently took any interest in their treatment (at this time many convalescent and nursing homes did not accept "cancer patients"). The report concluded by recommending more residential homes but commented on other aspects of care including recreation, congenial company and, last, religion.

A second survey was conducted throughout the British Isles in 1956 and showed that 49 percent of deaths then took place in people's own homes where there were wide variations in practice and generalized deficiencies in the availability of district nurses, local authority support, or suitable hospital beds [8]. The other half died in institutions of different types. There were the "Homes for the dying" which too often came as a shock to the patients who had been transferred from other care unprepared. The "Homes run by religious orders" showed more devotion than sufficient nursing skills and amenities. Other modified "Homes" (and grand houses) provided more comfort and plenty of furniture from previous inhabitants, but had fewer suitable facilities when residents reached a terminal stage. The nursing homes varied from near-hospital standards to a more homely atmosphere. Finally, there were the National Health Service hospitals where 41 percent of deaths took place. This important group of deaths frequently took place in long-stay units which the report criticized for their poor standards, insufficient staffing, and depressing surroundings; they were often set in old buildings which had been Victorian public assistance institutions. Hughes recommended improving the administration and provision of various services for in-patients and also measures to facilitate care at home, including (way ahead of his time) some payment for relatives who cared for their kin [8].

These two extensive surveys in this decade were complemented by two smaller but more intensive studies by social workers who enlarged on the personal aspects of what was going on at home [9, 10]. Both noted that many patients received generally satisfactory care but there was still some physical suffering. They also pointed out that patients had mixed views on wanting to stay at home or be admitted to "their own" hospital, but not to a "chronic ward." The problems of gaining admission when required were not always resolved. Some dissatisfaction with medical care surfaced, particularly regarding people's psychological needs and the poor or misleading communication which patients received. A third of the relatives were strained to their limits. The families appreciated the continued interest shown by the investigators and would discuss with them, or any carers who stayed in touch, their coming to terms with the situation. The interplay between previous family or social problems and the current situation was also noted. Rereading these early reports reminds one that many elements in palliative care are frequently being rediscovered. The sequence of the reports also reflects in an intriguing way the pattern of initially aiming to meet the urgent requirements to relieve physical suffering and a subsequent shift in emphasis to include people's social and psychological needs.

The early 1960s saw further deficiencies exposed. A considerable proportion of people who died in the hospital were found to suffer considerably, both physically and mentally [11, 12]. Death for old people in residential homes could also be bare of comfort. There the dying were often moved out of sight so that their unfortunate death should not disturb the glacial pretence that death did not exist [13]. These various reports and other writings strengthened the recognition that people with terminal illness needed more help and the will to see that they received it. Particular attention was then focused on the treatment of physical suffering, notably pain. Pain relief had not been thought out, was often poorly organized and based more on habit than pharmacological knowledge. The places or manner of care were also regarded as in need of some change, but it was unclear what should be done.

Care at home was an obvious option, but without changes it often did not meet people's needs. An early venture was published from New York in 1962 describing the care of patients with cancer or with severe heart failure who were treated in the Montefiore Hospital Home Care Program [14]. In appropriate cases the doctors, nurses, and social workers visited people at home in collaboration with various community agencies, especially a Visiting Nurse Service. The results of five years experience indicated that the service was appreciated by patients and family and was usually successful and often—not always—cost less then admission. Much of the momentum for home care subsequently came from other directions rather than hospitals.

Voluntary and charitable bodies concerned for people with cancer played an early, highly significant role. In the United Kingdom, the Marie Curie Memorial Foundation followed up their 1952 report by providing not only residential homes but by introducing in 1958 a day and night nursing service to complement the more general district nursing service. The National Society for Cancer Relief (founded by Douglas Macmillan in 1911) expanded its role and in 1975 financed its first nurse to supplement average domiciliary care with a greater expertise derived from previous community experience and a training in the care of the dying. Meanwhile those in the primary-care services pointed out they already achieved much and would like to do more. A general practitioner in Sheffield, England, reported from a survey conducted locally in 1963 that 55 percent of people dying from malignant disease did stay at home, cared for by family doctors and district nurses [15]. Most patients appeared satisfied, although 15 percent had periods of over six weeks when nursing was difficult. Dr. Wilkes, the author, recommended improvements in terminal-care facilities and he later played a major part in founding a center for day care, St. Luke's Hospice.

Clearly many threads of information and the motivation to improve home care were converging, but it was the modern hospice movement which provided the major impetus in weaving them together. St. Christopher's Hospice in London was conceived by Dr. Cicely Saunders and opened in 1967. There was an out-patient clinic from the start and in 1969 a specialist home-care team was formed to meet the needs of patients who had improved sufficiently with hospice in-patient treatment to be able to return home for a while and perhaps to die there [16]. Some continued supervision had proved necessary to maintain support for patients and families who often felt cut off from the hospice staff on whom they had come to rely. It ensured that medication which had been carefully stabilized in the hospice was not misunderstood or mistakenly altered, and that instead of people having to phone the ward for reassurance, staff visited the home. There was a twenty-four-hour on-call system and readmission would be arranged at once, if necessary.

Once the service was in place, an increasing number of patients were referred directly to the St. Christopher's out-patient clinic and the home-care team for advice. The team monitored the care but emphasized the continuing primary role of the local general practitioners and district nurses. This avoided the failures to integrate hospital and primary care that a contemporary survey had found in nearly half the patients with malignant disease when discharged from the hospital [17]. That report described many patients as being shuttled to and fro with neither adequate analgesic prescriptions, attention to other distressing symptoms, nursing help, nor any counseling. In contrast, the hospice home-care team could continue to provide support and open discussion to patients and relatives during their regular visits. They also unobtrusively guided and educated other professional colleagues with whom they collaborated [18]. The idea caught on and spread. Senior doctors with administrative responsibility recognized the need to plan for about half of the population to die at home and estimated, for example, that 10 percent would require specialist care, preferably by small units close to where they lived [19].

When the revitalized concept of hospice and home care reached North America it met the gathering strength of the movement to re-educate people about death and dying. The more open attitude about death had recently been boosted by the way the public imagination had been caught by Kübler-Ross' book [20] and lectures which had provided a simplified model of people negotiating a series of stages on the way to full acceptance of dying. "Death education" and the "hospice approach" had sufficient common ground to start the development of home-care units. The first hospice home-care team in United States opened in New Haven, Connecticut, in 1974 and included a doctor who had worked at St. Christopher's Hospice. A hospital-based palliative-care unit, which undertook consultative visits to patients at home, was set up in Montreal in 1975.

Back in Britain in 1975, the first Day Hospice was opened in Sheffield to provide a service to complement the care that relatives and others gave to patients at home. The Marie Curie Nurses continued their valued role of supplementing the hands-on skilled nursing care mainly provided by the district nurses employed by Health Authorities. The Macmillan nurses, funded by the National Society for Cancer Relief, now began their important role of providing more specialized advice and support on a domiciliary basis. The exact pattern of home-care services varied according to local circumstances. For instance, the Christchurch unit in southern England, set up in a hospital site in 1975 to serve the local community, practiced making a first domiciliary visit by the Macmillan nurse and medical consultant jointly. Subsequently members of the home-care team would continue visiting and monitoring the situation regularly as required. This same team also organized a day hospital and took an active role in teaching [21]. In nearby Southampton a National Health Service funded unit opened in 1977 combining twenty-five in-patient unit beds and a home-care service which became a twenty-four-hour service soon after [22]. A similar approach led to a Macmillan Home Care Service opening alongside the St. Columba's Hospice in Edinburgh, also in 1977 [23]. It was a time of rapid change.

A center in Bath pioneered a compromise pattern of local development that illustrates what has now become familiar. First, the community perceived the need to improve care along hospice lines for people with a terminal illness, but no health authority funds were currently available. The leading spirits registered a charity in 1976, the Dorothy House Foundation [24]. The need was great, the finance limited and so the service started with one trained, experienced nurse providing a specialist domiciliary service from her own home; the house was later also used as a social center and then for day care. The service needed to expand and the National Society for Cancer Relief gave a grant which, with other charitable sources, helped to finance a larger domiciliary team. They then obtained a house which could be converted to provide a necessary small in-patient unit and an administrative center. Perhaps the arrangement was not ideal but each step improved the care available, the value of the service became more widely recognized and more donations followed. The National Health Service began to contribute funding as well as advice and the original intention that a voluntary endeavor should complement and hopefully improve pre-existing resources finally came to fruition. Many have followed the pioneers along similar routes, according to the perceived needs of a particular community, the views of the local advocates (and opponents) and the opportunities available. Where economic necessity has forced a palliative-care service to start with a home-care service only, its success has often reinforced the staff's opinion that home care is preferable wherever possible, regardless of financial savings. The early workers also discovered the need for flexibility, "what works well in one part of the country may be completely wrong for another. Death and dying is different in each person, each street, each town or city" [25].

Improvements in standard home care continued to be initiated by a few hospitals. In Vancouver in 1974, an early hospital discharge system with a medical adviser arranged a home-care service in collaboration with the family practitioners and community health nurses, physiotherapists, homemakers, meals-on-wheels, and Red Cross Loan supplies [26]. It aimed to give full physical, emotional, and psychological support to patients and apparently met their needs sufficiently; many had a period at home and a third remained there until they died. In Sweden the usual care pattern was for patients to receive medical advice or treatment at a hospital or a primary-care center rather than at home, and so most people with acute or chronic debilitating illness were cared for in hospital or similar situation; 85 percent of deaths took place there. In 1977, the Motala Hospital organized a hospital-based home-care team, initially for its geriatric clientele but then extended this until about one-third were patients with terminal cancer who wished to be at home [27]. The doctor and nurse planned their visits according to the needs of the patients and relatives, who were given the phone number of a permanently manned office and promised help within thirty minutes if required. Other medical and paramedical services could be consulted or used as necessary. St. Thomas' Hospital in London, started a hospital support service in 1978 to advise on palliative care for patients in the wards and, if appropriate, continued the consultation service for patients who had returned home.

The 1970s therefore demonstrated a recognition and an ability to enable some people to die at home in comfort, in keeping with the current phrase "death with dignity." In-patient hospices in Britain, however, were multiplying so rapidly that an authoritative Report from the Standing Medical Advisory Committee in 1980, the Wilkes Report on terminal care [28], was moved to recommend that further development of in-patient units should be limited in favor of an integrated system of improved care at home by the primary teams of family doctor, community nurses etc., with the local general hospitals, and more day care units. The existing specialist terminal care units, including the hospices, should have a particular role in research and teaching. The committee's recommendations to slow the increase of in-patient units for terminal care had as much effect as Canute's command to the waves, but more home-care teams and day units did come into existence. In 1980, twenty-three home-care services were identified in Britain [29], and in 1995 there were 384 [30].

HOME-CARE TEAMS: STRUCTURE AND FUNCTION

The growing experience of specialist home-care teams gradually clarified what was required, but the considerable range in apparent needs and the ways of meeting them argued against imposing any one pattern. Some principles were established, however.

Nurses have a leading role and it is generally agreed that recruits to home-care teams should have had prior community work experience and training in palliative care although their particular skills are honed by subsequent involvement in active practice. An early paper suggested that each specialist domiciliary nurse should care for at least sixty patients/annum—a case load of fifteen to twenty patients at any one time [31], but the same author later reported that she found the referral rates/annum varied between thirty-three and 182 per nurse in eight different teams [32]. Another study of twelve hospice-based home-care teams pointed out that two basic models could be differentiated. First was a *participatory model*, in which an initial visit by the hospice doctor was followed by the home-care nurses maintaining regular contact, monitoring progress, sometimes sharing in practical nursing care, while the hospice doctor continued supervising at a clinic or the home and supplied medication. Second was an *advisory model* which could cover more patients by appropriate members of the team making an initial assessment and then advising the primary-care team. The latter were responsible for coordinating subsequent care, but they could call upon the specialist home-care team for support, advice or further visits as required [33]. The twelve teams, in fact, shared a number of other variations in their staffing and working patterns.

After nurses, doctors are next most frequent professional members of home-care teams. Their part again varies with circumstances, especially whether or not health services provide a local family doctor to be the patient's primary physician. If so, the home-care team doctor will usually act as consultant, assessing the patient, taking part in the home-care team's discussion of optimal management and advising the general practitioner. Someone will need to act as the patient's advocate regarding the need for further investigations or hospital treatment in the full knowledge of the potential gains or losses of such moves, including the physical and mental stresses involved. The roles of the palliative-care specialist and general practitioner overlap here. Where the health system provides no family doctor, the home-care doctor's responsibilities are likely to include both primary and specialist functions. Specialist home-care teams therefore need to liaise closely with the family doctors and district nurses. They also have to ensure that members of their own team liaise adequately, usually by frequent meetings to discuss new patients or current case problems, and so coordinate their efforts and develop mutual trust [34]. Periodically, they need to review their aims and functioning because they now carry broad responsibilities. Probably two-thirds of patients with cancer in Britain currently make contact with specialist home-care teams at some point in their progress [35].

Home-care team staffing depends on its functions. The need to control unpleasant symptoms, particularly pain, has deservedly been given considerable priority. Intense physical suffering can swamp all other feelings. Earlier reports emphasized the extent of unrelieved physical suffering and recent surveys have shown that despite improvements in treatment, patients and relatives still find that physical suffering is high, if not the highest, in the list of problems encountered [36]. Therefore, home-care teams must include someone among the available staff with up-to-date specialist knowledge in the treatment of physical symptoms.

Carers should also be able to meet the needs of people when serious disease causes disability. Many patients report that the ensuing restrictions, helplessness, and dependency, for them, prove worse than any other symptoms. Weakness, limited movements, paralysis, rapid exhaustion, and so on may prevent them working, managing domestic activities, and eventually self-care. The last calls for physical nursing. The family usually bears the brunt of this, but nurses are needed to advise, encourage, teach, and sometimes relieve the family over routine tasks especially when patients are confined to bed. Nurses also need expertise in dealing with more specialized problems such as giving advice on managing a colostomy, supervising certain dressings, or setting up and maintaining a syringe driver for symptom control. One survey of the care given to patients dying at home in Belfast reported that three-quarters of the patients received daily nursing which included advice on self-care, injections, dressings, enemas, suppositories, skin care, help with turning, and general supervision [37].

Home-care teams may have other specialists available to assist people to cope with their physical dysfunctions; which also improves their morale. Physiotherapists and occupational therapists may be among day unit staff or available from other sources. Equipment, be it a wheel-chair, commode, hospital bed, or a whole range of devices up to the latest electronic marvel can make a great deal of difference to patients' and carers' problems. Bitter experience has taught that the organization must be geared to provide the equipment as soon as the need arises, not when the problem or the person has passed on to another phase [23].

Other practical needs involve a widening circle of care givers; aides to help the patient bathe, people to sit in during the day or the night to allow the caring relative to rest or get the shopping, a meals-on-wheels service, ambulance services, and so on. The necessity of domestic help has long been recognized, even in the first special report in Britain, 1952 when 8 percent were assisted by home-help services [7]. Such help is usually supplied by organizations other than the health services and can be hard to come by because, although willing, they themselves are often overworked and understaffed [18]. Nevertheless, liaison between the various home carers, as for example in the Vancouver early hospital discharge arrangement described in 1974, can free relatives from domestic tasks sufficiently that they can give nursing care to their own kin or take a needed rest [26]. It was one service that clearly did increase between parallel 1969 and 1987 surveys in Britain, being provided to 10 percent and 24 percent respectively, with more to those over sixty-five years or living alone [38].

A survey of all the palliative-care services in Britain and Ireland in 1990 showed that 43 percent of the 321 existing home-care teams were attached to in-patient or day care units (26% to both) [39]. Most teams consisted of about two to five nurses, 46 percent had a doctor, 37 percent a social worker, 22 percent a chaplain, 18 percent a physiotherapist, 16 percent an occupational therapist, and 50 percent a secretary. The median caseload per nurse was nineteen and was usually between ten and thirty, not far from Ward's estimate ten years earlier [31]. The staff figures confirm what has often been said, palliative care involves many disciplines. If the patients do attend a day care unit other sorts of help may be available, including hairdressing, chiropody, various complementary therapies, and help from volunteers including transport to and from the unit [40]. In a recent survey of palliative care in Britain and Ireland the types of assistance available at day centers had extended to include speech therapy, dietary advice, hypnotherapy, relaxation, yoga, massage, aromatherapy, treatments using art, pottery, music and writing, and reflexology [41].

Most of the work of home-care teams described so far has been within the practical and traditional functions of professional care. Nevertheless, there has always been some professional recognition that the care of the dying requires more than bare logic and medical science. Some of the critical accounts of doctors "overtreating" dying people arise from narrow concentration on ways of defeating disease and a distortion of logic. A proportion of those treating patients with incurable conditions shut their minds to the psychological or spiritual aspects of care, perhaps because they regard it as someone else's duty and possibly because the attitude protects their own way of functioning. Unfortunately, their patients may well feel that they themselves are not getting the consideration they should receive. The Marie Curie report of 1952 commented that many patients, relatives, and the nurses faced with looking after them summarized their rejected status as "sent home to die" [7]. Most now actively participating in palliative care recognize that mortally ill people and their families often need more than the alleviation of symptoms, important though this is. Some need counsel or support in their coming to terms with the physical, emotional, and spiritual consequences of what is happening to them.

Moreover, the total care of dying people includes an opportunity to do something more positive than just fight a rear-guard action against unkind fate. It can seek to make this period of life positively enjoyable, potentially rewarding, and perhaps contain a sense of completion. All of these elements are open to different ways and levels of interpretation.

An early publication from Dr. Cicely Saunders, then speaking from her experiences in teaching hospitals and terminal-care homes, gave practical advice about meeting people's medical, nursing, emotional, and spiritual needs and indicated that these elements needed to go hand-in-hand when planning suitable care facilities [42]. She and others pointed out that many patients were well aware that they might be dying and that care should include a more adequate professional response than was usually forthcoming [12, 20].

Hospices and home-care units gradually gained further experience of ways to support patients and families to cope with personal problems. The need for this aspect of care became more exposed as distress from pain and other physical symptoms was better controlled. The unproductive arguments about "telling" and "not telling" patients about their prognosis were led into more sophisticated pathways by contributions from various sources including sociologists [43], social workers, and those concerned with ethics. The word "communication" became fashionable. The point was confirmed when home-care teams began to ask people what help they wanted or had found useful. Their answers were by no means confined to symptom control. In one early unit the help that patients appreciated most was the friendship and moral support, more than the drugs and treatment advice or the explanation of illness [24]. The relatives' views were similar, putting moral support first, then ready availability, awareness of problems, and ability to talk honestly.

Since then other more systematic analyses have been conducted. The help wanted by patients and by families can differ. For patients prompt symptom control and being treated as a whole person have ranked high in importance, while families have given high priority to information; the need for spiritual care has depended on previous religious affiliation [44]. A recent review of various reports summarized that besides physical symptoms, many patients experienced psychological and financial problems for which they needed help and that families as a whole could feel stressed and want support and counseling at various stages [45]. The nurses' viewpoint of their role when caring for people with terminal illness has also been the subject of an extensive review in which the author noted that much nursing practice in this area had grown from anecdotal evidence [46]. This review included the unpublished findings of a nursing opinion survey that their work, as well as monitoring symptoms and physical care, entailed teaching patients about their illness and helping them cope, and talking with them about death and dying. The nurses' role similarly included talking with relatives about death and dying and also "sorting out social problems" [47].

"Sorting out social problems" is a phrase with a rather naive quality, whereas most experienced nurses and other professionals working in palliative care recognize this to be a complex field. Patient's and relative's lifelong psychological difficulties may well come to the fore during terminal illness. Moreover, even "average" families have their own explicit and implicit "rules" about relationships and behavior which may or may not meet this crisis adequately. They may adapt their previous patterns successfully by themselves or benefit from outside help. Each member of the family also has his or her own values, beliefs, and ways of coping. Help by listening can be recommended generally; the sharing itself often aids adjustment. There are times when skilled and effective intervention would be beneficial and times to hold back. It should be noted here that, of course, bereavement and spiritual values are highly relevant to palliative care at home, but these aspects are discussed elsewhere in this book.

Home-care teams have more than front-line clinical duties. Day-to-day administration may not seem a very rewarding activity but when patients and families are so dependent on doctors and nurses to shield them from lurking distress, they are made additionally vulnerable if planned or promised help does not materialize. Lapses are likely to result in anxiety or resentment and sometimes allow physical distress to be unchecked. The much appreciated benefits of available telephone support and an on-call service often rely upon the contribution of an efficient, diplomatic secretary. Patients need to see some consistency in their treatment, not a see-saw policy according to which carer happens to visit. Teams have to organize continuity by means of adequate clinical notes as well as sorting out any differences in approach in regular meetings. This liaison function extends outside the team. Besides discussing cases with the community nurses and general practitioner, home-care teams link with other services such as hospital clinics, radiotherapy units and other hospital consultants as well as contacts with volunteer organizations, clergy, ambulance services, home help services, and so on. They may slip into the role of providing the main liaison between various bodies in default of anyone else being willing or able.

Teams also need to maintain their own integrity. Problems over team leadership may need to be resolved in order for them to function well [35]. Mutual support is often required when empathy with patients and families hurts too much, when treatment apparently achieves nothing or when sound advice is unjustifiably rejected and people suffer in consequence. Such support usually comes about through friendships within the team and in their regular meetings. In some circumstances help or guidance from someone outside the regular team is beneficial. This may be either regular or occasional and is usually with the whole team. Now and again individuals need their own outside help.

As specialists in palliative care, team members take part in nurse training and the education of other colleagues. The intention of palliative-care specialists is not to usurp the field and allow the skills of other participants to wither, but to raise standards of care in the community and in hospitals. A great deal of unobtrusive teaching occurs during consultation, but explicit training is also needed. At least one-third of general practitioners in one survey said they frequently had difficulties in controlling patients' pain and other symptoms and more found it difficult to cope with patients' and relatives' emotional distress. Over half of these doctors thought that further training in symptom control, communication, and bereavement counseling would be very helpful [48].

Conscientious teaching soon exposes the need for more knowledge. We need further research into symptom causation, ways of improving therapeutic skills and devising the best practical ways of applying what is already known. Senior members of home teams also contribute to policy decisions and take part in relevant committee work [49]. Someone has to guide health services into making positive plans for palliative care, provide funds, and not lose sight of this need among the urgent demands of acute medicine and curative treatments. The medical recognition in Britain in 1987 of palliative care as a specialty was a sign of its advance and carried a commitment to appropriate training and the maintenance of professional standards [50]; a local milestone in a worldwide change.

HAS PALLIATIVE CARE AT HOME PROVED EFFECTIVE?

An ambition of many home carers is that patients should stay in their own surroundings, be treated effectively, and eventually die at home. The case has been set out on the grounds that dying in hospital is associated with unsuitable or inadequate care, greater anxiety, loneliness, and indignity and that it contradicts people's stated preferences. There is also a broader ethical objection that death should not be hidden away. Nevertheless it is generally conceded that many do need hospital admission, especially after long periods of illness with the brunt of care falling on relatives who cannot get sufficient domiciliary help [51].

The generally assumed view that most people wish to die at home when the time comes, is less clearly established than has been supposed. It depends on how and when the enquiry is made: an automatic answer by healthy people has debatable value. For example, one group of patients with terminal cancer could differentiate clearly where they would prefer to die given ideal circumstances as distinct from their currently existing situation. The ideal preference to be at home rose slightly to 70 percent as patients came nearer to death; the realistic preference for home care fell to 49 percent, with the remainder almost equally divided between hospital and hospice in-patient care [52]. Another retrospective study asked the caring relative if the place of death had been right for the patient and for the carer. They thought that home was clearly better than hospital for the patient, but from their own viewpoint they were roughly equally divided between home and hospital deaths [53].

If, in ideal circumstances most patients would want to die at home and the home care services have improved, surely fewer deaths should now be taking place in hospital. Either the statistics are inaccurate or misleading, or the premises are mistaken. The trend for more deaths to take place in hospitals and other institutions, however, continues its well-established increase. In an extensive review by Mor in 1986 he summarized that only 15 to 20 percent of patients with cancer then died at home [54]. Local factors had an influence. For example, in the U.S. National Hospice Study it was observed that a hospice home-care program did improve the chances of dying at home if there was someone there to give care [55]. A counter-influence was that the percentage of home deaths fell if the hospice had beds [56], as had been noted in England [32].

A partial explanation of why improved care might not alter the place of death came when studies of home-care programs established that they lengthened the period at home rather than changed where people died [57]. Various units periodically claim that far greater proportions of their patients die at home. It is hard to evaluate these reports when patient groups differ, as may their family carers (if any), the availability of beds or professional bias against or for admitting patients nearing death if they or their carers near the limits of tolerable discomfort at home. There are problems over how such statistics are compiled. Reports often fail to state if all the referred patients have been followed until they die; over-prompt claims which do not include those in care for longer periods can produce a higher proportion of home deaths. Having more time at home is a gain in itself, on personal and perhaps financial grounds. Some enquiries have confirmed that expanding the home-care program could reduce the number of days in hospital and the expense [58]. Reports have conflicted however, over the extent of financial savings as they depend on the type of treatment provided—extensive home-care services may be little if any cheaper than in-patient care [59]. There are also problems over which costs should be included in the calculations.

Studies of other aspects of home care have not always demonstrated the hoped-for benefit that people expected to see. For example, some thorough studies have failed to find significant improvements in patients' quality of life scores. Professional carers have reported elements of care where their own or other people' skills, attention or facilities clearly fail to meet patients' and families' needs. Such results should not be dismissed unless clearly invalid. Ignoring the unpalatable does not improve care, only misses opportunities to discover explanations or correct mistakes.

Surveys of general practitioners have reported that they are dissatisfied with their own ability to control symptoms such as pain, breathlessness, insomnia, constipation, anorexia, or confusion [38]. They have felt uneasy about communication with relatives and patients [38, 60] especially if relatives say "don't tell" him or her. A Gallup Poll of general practitioners found that many still spoke with relatives but rarely with the patients about dying [61]. Family practitioners have also commented more generally that some of their colleagues do not give patients sufficient attention and that their medical training in this area has been deficient, although the latter is improving [61, 62]. Not infrequently the doctors have been found unaware of their patients' problems [38].

General practitioners have found deficiencies in services other than their own. They report a lack of adequate communications from hospitals about their patients, a third in one survey [38]. They have also had great difficulty in getting patients admitted even when their need was great. General practitioners had cases where there was insufficient nursing time available, especially at night [48] although they usually felt there was good understanding between themselves and the district nurses [63]. They have mixed views on the value of specialist palliative-care services, although their opinion is more positive if they have such a service available locally [64].

The district nurses in the wide survey in Britain of care in the last year of life mostly thought nursing care in general had been adequate, but a quarter did not [65].

They revealed more difficulties when they were asked specific questions. They often had insufficient nursing time, especially for talking with patients and families. They also reported inadequate communication with hospitals, but this had improved between 1967 and 1987, the dates of the two parallel surveys. Relationships with the general practitioner did not, in their opinion, always run smoothly. They thought that doctors generally referred dying patients for nursing help later than they should. This was reported by 14 percent in 1969 but rose to 48 percent in 1987. The apparent worsening could, like some other findings, be a favorable sign that standards may be rising. District nurses may be more aware of what can be done by getting to know patients earlier. There were, however, clear cases where symptom control or the strain on carers had reached a crisis level which could well have been averted. There were also some deficiencies in what general practitioners had told nurses either about necessary treatment or what patients or relatives had been told. The doctor's management of pain control was criticized in some cases.

The recipients of care, although generally appreciative of the help they receive, have had cogent criticisms. For instance, in Cartwright's second survey in Britain 80 to 90 percent felt that the general practitioner was easy to talk to, but the rest did not, sometimes commenting he appeared to have insufficient time [66]. There was a disappointing fall in the number of home visits since the similar survey eighteen years earlier. Most praised their doctor for the care he or she gave, but 7 percent retrospectively felt the care had been poor. They cited instances of lack of interest, or failure to visit or examine and there were some bitter comments over delay in diagnosis.

The same two surveys also indicated that little had changed regarding the apparent frequency of physical symptoms over the eighteen years. Another rather different retrospective survey of cancer patients only, however, did sound a more optimistic note over pain control [67]. The caring relatives reported that although 70 percent had experienced pain, only 4 percent had no relief. The patients' other symptoms had proved more resistant; nausea, vomiting, dyspnea, dysphagia, and confusion were insufficiently relieved in 25 percent. One-third of the carers of these patients with cancer in south-west England would have liked more domestic support and others would have been helped by some relief from night care duties and an earlier supply of equipment and incontinence pads. Many relatives had not been informed of the financial relief that was available. Results do vary from survey to survey, and a retrospective assessment in the Greater London area reported that pain was insufficiently relieved in as many as half of the patients at home and some other physical symptoms in a third or more [68]. Two-thirds of patients were said to have felt "low" or miserable at some time in their last year and a fifth were anxious in the last week. This report stated that about a third needed more nursing help, and confirmed the frequent need for more domestic assistance and help with patients' basic activities, such as bathing and dressing. This group also often wanted more financial aid.

Clearly there is a difference between what can be done in home care and what some people—or even the "average" person—receive. There is insufficient evidence, as yet, to demonstrate that home care has achieved a convincing widespread improvement. It follows, therefore, that the national figures on the proportion of home deaths cannot yet be expected to change. Is there any clear evidence that home care benefits patients at all? A few comparisons of hospital, hospice in-patient, or home care have been conducted to see if the place of care has made a significant difference in the qualities of people's life near the end. Before quoting some results some limitation of research methods in this field should be noted.

To show convincingly that one form of treatment is better than another usually requires prospective studies which conform to a randomized controlled design with subjects taken from a widely representative population. In terminal care such projects are almost impossible to complete for both ethical and practical reasons [69]. Compromises are necessary and so conclusions become uncertain, and this can deter researchers and hinder publication. Retrospective studies can conform more readily over choosing comparable samples, but the data are more suspect because they are delayed and indirect. Palliative care is to improve how people feel and such data are imprecise. The scientific community, with good reason, prefers data which can be accurately measured. Quantitative material is more suitable for orthodox scientific methods than qualitative if the measurements are demonstrably reliable and can be reproduced by different observers. Some quantitative data in this field are doubtfully valid, however, because the desired uniformity of measurements can lead to distorting or discarding key elements which cannot readily be fitted into approved scales or stereotyped categories. So when reading research reports into palliative care, it is as well to retain some scepticism over simple extrapolations from any single study, because methods are as yet imperfect and values differ so widely. Where a number of enquiries using different approaches arrive at similar conclusions, then there is a better basis for evaluation and planning.

Only three examples of comparisons are mentioned here, very different studies. Two are early reports that included patients from the pioneer hospice, St. Christopher's, and one from the United States. The first was a retrospective comparison of home and hospital which found that relatives reported *more* pain in the terminally-ill patients at home. Those at home, however, were less likely to be confined to bed or confused [70]. The other early London study used current data and different subjective criteria. It compared four groups of patients in a radiotherapy ward, a Foundation Home, the hospice in-patient unit, and its home-care service [71]. Judged by the patients' general satisfaction with medical/physical treatments they did not differ significantly. In their degree of satisfaction over the level of discussion with members of staff, the patients expressed most praise for the more open communication in the hospice groups. The general relationships with the staff had their highest ratings from the group of patients at home. Home-care patients also gave the most positive confirmation that they were where they wished to be (as judged on the realistic level). This was despite the fact that hospice home-care patients were rather more anxious and irritable than the hospice in-patients (both hospice groups had less emotional disturbance than those in the other two settings).

The massive 1986 U.S. National Hospice Study, like Parkes' retrospective enquiry, found that there was rather more persistent pain and fewer hospice patients without pain when cared for at home than in hospital-based hospice care, but both hospice groups did a little better than those in conventional care [72]. Apart from this observation, the hospice care patients at home or in hospital gave equally satisfactory results, although more home-care patients died at home and their care cost less [56]. A battery of standardized quality of life measures failed to demonstrate many differences between the groups. A later secondary analysis of some available National Hospice Study data estimated a "quality of death" as judged by the previously ascertained views of patients and carers about their last three days of life [73]. The desires they had given earlier included such elements as having certain people present, physical independence, freedom from pain, peace/happiness, and so on. According to these criteria, hospice patients whether at home or hospital, did better than those in conventional care.

These and other reports, descriptive or comparative, have produced very mixed results. Some findings showed that different types of care, including home care, can be quite successful. More widely representative surveys, however, find that many needs still go unanswered. Why? Unfortunately, delay in applying research findings is only too common. It can be due to justifiable caution or to other reasons, including simple reluctance to change. At present, fortunately, palliative care appears to be advancing—up to a point. Some results from the various surveys and treatment comparisons disappoint those who have witnessed or given good care. In many cases the poor survey results appear to be due to "simple" failure to deliver care that is widely known, accepted, and even readily available. This opens up a whole field of human motivation and behavior. Lapses can be ascribed to ignorance, carelessness, indifference, what people consider important, the way we regard other people in general or selectively, what a nation or an individual is willing to pay for or can afford, and many other overt and covert reasons.

For those who accept that the care of dying people is important, some guidelines emerge from time to time. Some are based on descriptions by successful home-care teams, others on research findings and treatment trials. Recommendations emanate from leading individuals, authoritative committees as well as those who still labor in more ordinary circumstances and witness the common lapses as well as the achievements of care. One example is a set of guidelines developed by district nurses and others in the light of survey results in their region [74]. They include: (1) having an identifiable and accessible team; (2) the team should meet and coordinate care; (3) time should be provided to listen and assess; (4) symptoms should be controlled; (5) domestic, financial, moral, and professional support should be available; and (6) the patients and carers should feel involved in care, taught to help themselves, and made aware of the help available. Such guidelines are open for discussion and may be improved upon, but their conscientious delivery could well improve care.

Other guidelines may focus on different, although complementary aims. The example above recommended an approach which pointed out ways of improving the care process while, on the whole, keeping within the constraints of the facilities already available. Another set of recommendations has emphasized the need for increased services and finance to keep patients at home, more nurses, more night sitters, more home visits by general practitioners, greater availability of physiotherapists, occupational therapists, etc., and more equipment there when the patient needed it [75]. Many proposals have common ground, especially over the suggestions that palliative-care training be improved. Professional attitudes should benefit from better teaching at medical schools and there should be more postgraduate training posts for doctors and for nurses. They should learn to pay as much attention to the family, especially the immediate carers, as to the patient. The current standards of communication between staff and patients should improve further, so should liaison between hospitals and other carers. Professional attitudes toward death, particularly the view that death is a failure, need modifying [62].

The relevance and force of such recommendations would be greater if we had a better grasp of what does happen to people during terminal care, what changes take place, and why so many continue to leave their home to die in a hospice or hospital bed. It was this aim that led to my embarking on a fairly detailed prospective study of the patients' and carers' perception of what happened if they were given competent home care, with in-patient care available whenever they chose. At a different level it also led to my receiving the invitation to write this chapter with its selective review of some widely-based information and a final section on some of the project's findings and relevant research limitations in palliative care [76, 77].

HOSPICE HOME CARE AND
THE PROGRESS OF PATIENTS AND RELATIVES

Ways of measuring progress during terminal cancer include symptom check-lists and such rating scales as are suitable for repeated assessments, e.g., quality of life scales. Despite their advantages, because they predetermine what is deemed relevant or shape the form that answers may take, they were largely unsuitable for this sort of exploration. Consequently the assessment interviews started with an open-ended enquiry to give patients and relatives an opportunity to volunteer what they thought important. The semi-structured interviews went on to include a few regular assessments chosen because they were either intrinsically important to the aims of total care, e.g., the degree of acceptance of dying, or because they invited the recipients to say to what extent they were satisfied with their care. One recognized quality of life scale was included for comparative purposes. Some assessments had multiple functions, e.g., mood and anxiety levels could indicate if people's needs were being met, or if adjustment was going well or if there was emotional distress that might need direct relief. The patients and relatives were interviewed separately and although some commented this was unnecessary because they both felt alike, in fact their individual views quite often differed.

Assessments were made weekly and continued throughout the terminal illness, except that for those living more than two months—most did not—the intervals were lengthened. The wish to continue assessment into the later stages was another reason to avoid using questionnaires or rating scales which demanded more than very ill people could manage or even be asked to do. It has been shown that interviews may be managed when other ratings cannot [78]. The methods chosen therefore, gained in flexibility but lost the advantages of standardization. As subjective data are imprecise and open to bias, this study largely relied on making comparisons between different stages in the same subject(s) or between paired subjects and used the same interviewer/assessor throughout, which should even-out many imperfections. Obviously the subjects were not a randomized sample from the whole population, but samples need to be chosen according to the question or hypothesis being considered. This had to be a purposive sample because it deliberately set out to minimize or exclude failures due to recognizably sub-standard care. It sought, among other things, to see where a reasonable standard of care needed further modifications. The conclusions drawn from such a sample regarding, say, the differences between various stages of illness or the differences between particular patient subgroups may still be generalized to some extent. The particular percentages should not be extrapolated uncritically to the general population.

These particular patients had been referred to St. Christopher's Hospice home care unit which has an established reputation for its standard of care and could arrange admission whenever it was required. The sample came from the 428 patients who were referred over a two-year period, but 16 percent had no caring relative, 6 percent were already unable to converse, and 21 percent died or were admitted within the first week. The facts themselves indicate problems liable to arise when patients are at home. The one in three randomized sample therefore yielded seventy-seven patients and relatives who could be assessed regularly until the patient's death. Only 29 percent eventually died at home, although in 18 percent admission was for only one day and a further 12 percent for two or three days. So one question was answered; even when given competent home care, if appropriate in-patient care was also available a large proportion came to be admitted before the end. It was noteworthy, however, that following referral individuals did spend a median of 90 percent of their time at home. Focusing solely on the place of death gives a misleading impression of where people spend most of their terminal illness.

The problems these people volunteered during this testing time were most often the patients' physical symptoms, but also included their psychological symptoms, the carer's emotional and physical state and various social difficulties. In an average week about a third reported no physical discomfort. The physical symptoms, such as pain, were usually by this stage either established persistent problems which were then relieved or at least made tolerable, or they were new (perhaps earlier) problems which erupted and were usually brought under control. Most symptoms, except weakness, were present for less than 5 percent of the week and rarely more than 25 percent. Only 6 percent of patients had a physical discomfort that reached a level where it was described as causing distress (usually pain, breathlessness, or weakness) and 4 percent had some emotional distress. Persistent distress was uncommon, but when it did threaten or occur it usually lead to admission for further treatment. These figures may seem low compared with those given in many other reports and are to some extent a tribute to the quality of care they received. When comparing results from different surveys, however, note carefully the definitions of the statistics. The figures given here for this study are based on the weekly prevalence levels and many reports are based on symptom incidence over a long period of terminal illness. In the latter, one or two acute episodes may give a misleadingly poor impression of people's suffering. Also note that it is unjustifiable to equate data based on retrospective views with that from current accounts [79, and further results from this study now in press].

Charting the progress of this group of home-care patients over the last eight weeks showed that pain did not generally become worse or more persistent despite worsening illness. Mental confusion did increase in the last weeks. Depression in patients actually decreased over the last two months but conversely the relatives became more sad or depressed. Relatives experienced more anxiety than patients throughout this period. Patients tended not to mention their milder levels of anxiety spontaneously but would reveal it on more direct enquiry. Each week most patients and relatives were assessed to be equable, with 20 to 25 percent saying, with some conviction, that they felt cheerful and were enjoying life.

Almost two-thirds of these patients said they were well aware that they were probably or certainly dying. (In assessments I have conducted since 1959, awareness levels have steadily risen.) Less than a tenth were non-committal or said they were expecting to improve. The relatives declared yet more awareness of the probable outcome and grew more certain still as the condition progressed. Acceptance of dying could be assessed in those indicating their awareness. The patients as a group (but not necessarily as individuals) showed increasing acceptance until by the last interview half fully accepted they were dying. Two-thirds of caring relatives reached full acceptance. Some could not, and 4 percent of patients and 9 percent of relatives were unaccepting and troubled. During the terminal illness people coped in different ways. Conscious thinking about the outcome ranged from preoccupation to the opposite, about a quarter of the patients knowingly suppressed their awareness and 8 percent showed clear "denial." The relatives were not dissimilar in this respect although only 2 percent maintained denial near the end. Many people were just realistic, especially the relatives. About one in six patients expressed optimism and a similar proportion expressed hopeless, even despairing, feelings. Some patients expressed their intention to fight to get better but the proportion fell from 19 percent to 8 percent over the last two months.

Most recipients of care were very appreciative (the assessor took no part in their care). About 60 percent each week thought their care from all sources had been excellent or very good and only 5 percent were just satisfied. An important change came about in the preferred place of care. All had started off wanting to stay at home. As the state of patients—or the carers—changed, an increasing proportion came to prefer in-patient care. At the last interview obtained (usually in the final week of the patient's life) only 54 percent of patients said home care was still their realistic preference. The relatives' view often changed a week ahead of the patients' and, when last assessed, 45 percent gave a home care preference. Between the last interview and the death a few more were known to have opted for admission. The message was clear, for optimal care both home and in-patient care were wanted.

The total experience of these patients and relatives seemed to convey that this pattern of care was largely considered acceptable (more details and quotations have been published). It often finally entailed admission. Why? The stated reasons for the final admission were frequently multiple and usually included the need for symptom control or that the patient's condition had seriously deteriorated and/or that the demands on the caring relative had become too great. Intermediate periods of in-patient care were usually for symptom control, especially for special treatment techniques, and a quarter were to give the relatives respite. Behind these explicit reasons lay a series of contributory causes and predisposing factors.

The effect of some demographic features became apparent when the outcome for all 415 patients referred over the two years was analyzed. Living alone meant a 95 percent chance of dying in the hospice as compared with 70 percent if a competent adult was at home. Being over seventy, or female, only marginally decreased the chances of dying at home. Particular diagnoses had a greater effect on the place of death; stomach cancer favored death at home, breast cancer in the hospice or hospital. The carers' age, sex, or relationship appeared to have only a minor influence but if their physical fitness was impaired, as it was in many of this age group, it significantly reduced the patients' chances of staying at home. As the period of home care lengthened the chances of dying at home noticeably fell. In-patient deaths rose steadily from 34 percent in the first three days to 86 percent of those in hospice care for more than three months.

The severity or type of problem existing when first referred had little association with the eventual need for admission. How problems subsequently progressed did. Repeated assessments showed trends which anticipated or matched the given reasons for admission. In the week before admission over 90 percent of patients reported they were troubled in some way (notably by weakness or pain) and 26 percent had moments of distress, figures considerably higher than the average. There was greater mental impairment in those admitted. Anxiety and depression was more marked in both patients and in the caring relatives just before admission, but which was cause and which effect was hard to tell. More easily interpreted and relevant to management was the greater degree of fatigue in relatives in the week or two before patients were admitted. The standardized Quality of Life Index fell steadily throughout the whole period and dropped further in the admitted group, but there was no particular admission threshold [80].

Some of the attitudes assessed in this prospective study of patients and relatives were shown to link with whether patients subsequently died at home or not. At the first interview the patients' attitude toward their condition was a better guide to the place of death than their symptoms. Patients who were more aware of dying and coped in a realistic manner were much more likely to die at home. For those who were optimistic, still fighting to overcome their illness and suppressing or denying thoughts of dying, death at home was relatively uncommon. Their defensive attitudes tended to give way a week or two preceding admission. Some quietly re-evaluated their situation and moved toward greater acceptance before admission. A few persuaded themselves that their admission was to get better and a few suffered a painful collapse of this psychological defense and needed help. Among the relatives a sizable subgroup could not initially accept that the patients were dying and some of these were still striving to save the patient at the last assessment interview. All of this group were admitted for just the final day.

There was a rather contradictory aspect to patients and relatives intercommunication. Many spontaneously expressed some relief if they had partaken in a significant sharing of knowledge or feelings. In the regular assessments, however, about half stated that they deliberately concealed or were reticent in expressing their feelings, usually to avoid upsetting the other or themselves. The outcome, as far as staying at home was concerned, was that those relatives who had shown such reticence throughout were significantly more likely to continue looking after the patient at home to the end; an advantage to the stiff upper lip? Admissions were quite often preceded by relatives revealing their emotions more than usual, an observation having ambiguous implications. It is a complex field and no simplistic rules can decide what is best for each individual.

Like much research, the results raise as many questions as answers. It was reasonably clear that where the choice between home care and suitable in-patient care was readily available, admission was accompanied by a recognition that it had now become the preferred option. Most relatives also felt retrospectively that the patient had died in the best place. As stated initially, there are many advantages for patient and family when care can be completed at home and there is good reason to try and make it possible for more to do so. The wish to die at home, the need to die in comfort and the avoidance of undue physical or emotional strain on relatives, however, are three separate aims which can come into conflict. As yet, professional knowledge and skills cannot always meet all the patients' and carers' needs at home. It is not defeat to choose the option which gives the greatest over-all comfort.

REFERENCES

1. Office of Population Censuses and Surveys, *Mortality Statistics: 1992*, H.M.S.O., London, Series DH1, no. 27, Table 7, 1994.
2. A. Cartwright, L. Hockey, and J. L. Anderson, *Life Before Death*, Routledge and Kegan Paul, London, 1973.
3. M. Leer, When, Why and Where People Die, in *The Dying Patient*, D. G. Brim, H. E. Freeman, S. Levine, and N. A. Scotch (eds.), Russell Sage Foundation, New York, pp. 5-29, 1970.
4. R. W. Hunt, M. J. Bond, R. K. Groth, and P. M. King, Place of Death in Southern Australia: Patterns from 1910 to 1987, *Medical Journal of Australia, 155*, pp. 549-553, 1991.
5. J. A. Billings, Why Dying People and their Families Seek Home Care, in *Outpatient Management of Advanced Cancer*, J. A. Billings (ed.), J. B. Lippincott, Philadelphia, pp. 285-292, 1985.
6. A. Worcester, *The Care of the Aged, the Dying and the Dead*, C. C. Thomas, Springfield, Illinois, 1935.
7. Joint National Cancer Survey Committee of the Marie Curie Memorial and the Queen's Institute of District Nursing, *Report on a National Survey concerning Patients with Cancer Nursed at Home*, Marie Curie Memorial, London and Edinburgh, 1952.
8. H. L. Glyn Hughes, *Peace at the Last: A Survey of Terminal Care in the United Kingdom*, Calouste Gulbenkian Foundation, London, 1960.
9. J. Aitken-Swan, Nursing the Late Cancer Patient at Home: The Family's Impressions, *Practitioner, 183*, pp. 64-69, 1959.
10. M. Bailey, A Survey of the Social Needs of Patients with Incurable Lung Cancer, *The Almoner, 11*, pp. 379-391, 1959.
11. A. N. Exton-Smith, Terminal Illness in the Aged, *Lancet, 2*, pp. 305-308, 1961.

12. J. M. Hinton, The Physical and Mental Distress of the Dying, *Quarterly Journal of Medicine, 32*, pp. 1-21, 1963.
13. P. Townsend, *The Last Refuge*, Routledge and Kegan Paul, London, 1962.
14. I. Rossman and W. L. Kissick, Home Care and the Cancer Patient, in *The Physician and the Total Care of the Cancer Patient*, American Cancer Society, New York, pp. 161-169, 1962.
15. E. Wilkes, Terminal Cancer at Home, *Lancet, 1*, pp. 799-801, 1965.
16. B. McNulty, Discharge of the Terminally Ill Patient, *Nursing Times, 66*, pp. 1160-1162, 1970.
17. M. Skeet, *Home from Hospital*, The Dan Mason Research Committee of the Florence Nightingale Memorial Committee, London, 1970.
18. B. McNulty, Continuity of Care, *British Medical Journal, 1(844)*, pp. 38-39, 1973.
19. K. R. O. Porter, Four Recurring Themes, *British Medical Journal, 1(844)*, pp. 40-41, 1973.
20. E. Kübler-Ross, *On Death and Dying*, Macmillan, New York, 1969.
21. A. Newbury, The Work of the Domiciliary Service at the Macmillan Unit, Christchurch, in *Macmillan Seminar on Domiciliary Care 1980*, National Society for Cancer Relief, pp. 16-18, 1981.
22. P. Debney, The Work of the Domiciliary Service at Countess Mountbatten House, Southampton, in *Macmillan Seminar on Domiciliary Care 1980*, National Society for Cancer Relief, London, pp. 14-15, 1981.
23. D. Doyle, Domiciliary Terminal Care: Demands on Statutory Services, *Journal of the Royal College of General Practitioners, 32*, pp. 285-291, 1982.
24. P. Clench, *Managing to Care in Community Services for the Terminally Ill*, Patten Press, Richmond, 1984.
25. F. Copperman, Care of the Dying Patient at Home, *Nursing Focus*, pp. 133-134, May 1982.
26. S. Malkin, Care of the Terminally Ill at Home, *Canadian Medical Association Journal, 115*, pp. 129-130, 1976.
27. B. Beck-Friss and P. Strang, The Organization of Hospital-Based Home Care for Terminally Ill Cancer Patients: The Motala Model, *Palliative Medicine, 7*, pp. 93-100, 1993.
28. E. Wilkes, *Report of the Working Group on Terminal Care*, Standing Medical Advisory Committee, D.H.S.S., H.M.S.O., London, 1980.
29. B. Lunt, *Terminal Cancer Care: Specialist Services Available in Great Britain in 1980*, University of Southampton, 1981.
30. Hospice Information Service, *Hospice Facts and Figures*, Fact Sheet No. 7, St. Christopher's Hospice, London, 1994.
31. A. Ward, Standards for Home Care Services for the Terminally Ill, *Community Medicine, 4*, pp. 276-279, 1982.
32. A. Ward, *Home Care Services for the Terminally Ill, A Report for the Nuffield Foundation*, University of Sheffield Medical School, 1985.
33. K. Boyd, The Working Patterns of Hospice Based Home Care Teams, *Palliative Medicine, 6*, pp. 131-139, 1992.
34. P. Smith, The Complementary Home Care Team, in *The Management of Terminal Malignant Disease*, C. Saunders and N. Sykes (eds.), Edward Arnold, London, pp. 248-253, 1993.
35. A. M. Smith and A. Eve, Access to Specialist Palliative Care, *British Medical Journal, 308*, pp. 273-274, 1994.
36. I. Higginson, A. Wade, and M. McCarthy, Palliative Care: Views of Patients and their Families, *British Medical Journal, 301*, pp. 277-281, 1990.

37. P. M. Reilly and M. P. Patten, Terminal Care in the Home, *Journal of the Royal College of General Practitioners, 31*, pp. 531-537, 1981.
38. A. Cartwright, Changes in Life and Care in the Year Before Death 1969-1987, *Journal of Public Health Medicine, 13*, pp. 81-87, 1991.
39. A. M. Smith, A. Eve, and N. P. Sykes, Palliative Care Services in Britain and Ireland 1990—An Overview, *Palliative Medicine, 6*, pp. 277-291, 1992.
40. L. Hockey, St. Columba's Hospice Home Care Service: An Evaluation Study, *Palliative Medicine, 5*, pp. 315-322, 1991.
41. A. Eve and A. M. Smith, Palliative Care Services in Britain—Update 1991, *Palliative Medicine, 8*, pp. 19-27, 1994.
42. C. Saunders, *Care of the Dying*, Macmillan, London, 1959.
43. B. G. Glaser and A. L. Strauss, *Awareness of Dying*, Aldine, Chicago, 1968.
44. L. J. Kristjanson, Quality of Terminal Care: Salient Indicators Identified by Families, *Journal of Palliative Care, 5*, pp. 21-30, 1989.
45. M. L. S. Vachon, L. Kristjanson, and I. Higginson, Psychosocial Issues in Palliative Care: The Patient, the Family, and the Process and Outcome of Care, *Journal of Pain and Symptom Management, 10*, pp. 142-150, 1995.
46. A. Bergen, Nurses Caring for the Terminally Ill in the Community: A Review of the Literature, *International Journal of Nursing Studies, 28*, pp. 89-101, 1991.
47. F. Bunn, An Exploratory Study of the Role of the Macmillan Nurse, unpublished B.Sc. project, 1988, in A. Bergen, Nurses Caring for the Terminally Ill in the Community, *International Journal of Nursing Studies, 28*, p. 94, 1991.
48. A. Haines and A. Booroff, Terminal Care at Home: Perspective from General Practice, *British Medical Journal, 292*, pp. 1051-1053, 1986.
49. A. Nash, The Role of the Macmillan Nurse, *Nursing Standard, 5*, pp. 33-37, 1990.
50. R. Hillier, Palliative Medicine: A New Speciality, *British Medical Journal, 297*, pp. 874-875, 1988.
51. A. Bowling, The Hospitalisation of Death: Should More People Die at Home? *Journal of Medical Ethics, 9*, pp. 158-161, 1983.
52. J. Townsend, A. O. Frank, D. Fermont, S. Dyer, O. Karran, A. Walgrove, and M. Piper, Terminal Cancer Care and Patients' Preference for Place of Death: A Prospective Study, *British Medical Journal, 301*, pp. 415-417, 1990.
53. J. M. Addington-Hall, L. D. MacDonald, H. R. Anderson, and P. Freeling, Dying from Cancer: The Views of Bereaved Family and Friends about the Experiences of Terminally Ill Patients, *Palliative Medicine, 5*, pp. 207-214, 1991.
54. V. Mor and S. Masterson-Anderson, Quality of Life Outcomes, in *Hospice Care Systems*, Springer, New York, pp. 142-150, 1987.
55. V. Mor and J. Hiris, Determinants of the Site of Death among Hospice Cancer Patients, *Journal of Health and Social Behavior, 24*, pp. 375-385, 1983.
56. D. S. Greer, V. Mor, J. N. Morris, S. Sherwood, D. Kidder, and H. Birnbaum, An Alternative in Terminal Care: Results of the National Hospice Study, *Journal of Chronic Diseases, 39*, pp. 9-26, 1986.
57. C. M. Parkes, Terminal Care: Evaluation of an Advisory Domiciliary Service at St. Christopher's Hospice, *Postgraduate Medical Journal, 56*, pp. 685-689, 1980.
58. J. McCusker and A. M. Stoddard, Effects of an Expanding Home Care Program for the Terminally Ill, *Medical Care, 25*, pp. 373-384, 1987.
59. H. Taylor, *The Hospice Movement in Britain*, Centre for Policy on Ageing, London, pp. 14-15, 1983.

60. A. C. Blyth, Audit of Terminal Care in a General Practice, *British Medical Journal, 300*, pp. 983-986, 1990.
61. W. G. Keane, J. H. Gould, and P. H. Millard, Death in Practice, *Journal of the Royal College of General Practitioners, 33*, pp. 347-351, 1983.
62. E. Wilkes, Terminal Care: How Can We Do Better? *Journal of the Royal College of Physicians London, 20*, pp. 216-218, 1986.
63. A. Cartwright, The Relationship between General Practitioners, Hospital Consultants and Community Nurses When Caring for People in the Last Year of Their Lives, *Family Practice, 8*, pp. 350-355, 1991.
64. D. A. Seamark, C. P. Thorne, R. V. H. Jones, D. J. P. Gray, and J. F. Searle, Knowledge and Perceptions of a Domiciliary Hospice Service among General Practitioners and Community Nurses, *British Journal of General Practitioners, 43*, pp. 57-59, 1993.
65. C. Seale, Community Nurses and the Care of the Dying, *Social Science Medicine, 34*, pp. 375-382, 1992.
66. A. Cartwright, *The Role of the General Practitioner in Caring for People in the Last Year of Their Lives*, King Edward's Hospital Fund, London, 1990.
67. R. V. H. Jones, J. Hansford, and J. Fiske, Death from Cancer at Home: The Carer's Perspective, *British Medical Journal, 306*, pp. 249-252, 1993.
68. J. Addington-Hall and M. McCarthy, Dying from Cancer: Results of a National Population-Based Investigation, *Palliative Medicine, 9*, pp. 295-305, 1995.
69. I. R. McWhinney, M. J. Bass, and A. Donner, Evaluation of a Palliative Care Service: Problems and Pitfalls, *British Medical Journal, 309*, pp. 1340-1342, 1994.
70. C. M. Parkes, Home or Hospital? Terminal Care as Seen by Surviving Spouses, *Journal of the Royal College of General Practitioners, 28*, pp. 19-30, 1978.
71. J. Hinton, Comparison of Places and Policies for Terminal Care, *Lancet, 1*, pp. 29-32, 1979.
72. J. N. Morris, V. Mor, R. J. Goldberg, S. Sherwood, D. S. Greer, and J. Hiris, The Effect of Treatment Setting and Patient Characteristics on Pain in Terminal Cancer Patients: A Report from the National Hospice Study, *Journal of Chronic Diseases, 39*, pp. 27-35, 1986.
73. K. A. Wallston, C. Burger, R. A. Smith, and R. J. Baugher, Comparing the Quality of Death for Hospice and Non-Hospice Patients, *Medical Care, 26*, pp. 177-182, 1988.
74. R. Jones, Primary Health Care: What Should We Do for People Dying at Home with Cancer? *European Journal of Cancer Care, 1*, pp. 9-11, 1992.
75. G. Thorpe, Enabling More Dying People to Remain at Home, *British Medical Journal, 307*, pp. 915-918, 1993.
76. J. Hinton, Can Home Care Maintain an Acceptable Quality of Life for Patients with Terminal Cancer and Their Relatives? *Palliative Medicine, 8*, pp. 183-196, 1994.
77. J. Hinton, Which Patients with Terminal Cancer are Admitted from Home Care? *Palliative Medicine, 8*, pp. 197-210, 1994.
78. B. J. Lunt, The Assessment of Symptoms and Mood in Terminally Ill Cancer Patients, in *Psychosocial Issues in Malignant Disease*, M. Watson and S. Greer (eds.) Pergamon Press, Oxford, p. 27, 1986.
79. S. Ahmedzai, A. Morton, J. T. Reid, and R. D. Stevenson, Quality of Death from Lung Cancer: Patients' Reports and Relatives' Retrospective Opinions, in *Psychosocial Oncology*, M. Watson, S. Greer, and C. Thomas (eds.), Pergamon Press, Oxford, pp. 187-192, 1988.
80. W. O. Spitzer, A. J. Dodson, J. Hall, E. Chesterman, J. Levi, R. Shepherd, R. N. Battista, and B. R. Catchlove, Measuring the Quality of Life of Cancer Patients: A Concise QL-Index for Use by Physicians, *Journal of Chronic Diseases, 34*, pp. 585-597, 1981.

PART III

Introduction: Bereavement

Grief is primarily the realization that the world that is, and the world that "should be" are different—that we live with broken dreams. There have been several models of the grief process, the emotional, physical, intellectual, behavioral, and spiritual manners of adjusting to the loss of someone or something of personal value. While grief has been mentioned in literature from classical times, and Freud applied his basic view of ambivalence both to life and to each other to the grief process, grief theory as we know it today begins in the 1940s.

Eric Lindemann, a psychiatric resident in Boston, interviewed the families of those who died in the Coconut Grove fire, a dance held after a college football game. Lindemann described the following characteristics of the bereaved: sensations of somatic distress occurring in waves lasting from twenty minutes to an hour at a time, a feeling of tightness in the throat, choking with shortness of breath, need for sighing, and an empty feeling in the abdomen, lack of muscular power, and an intense subjective distress described as tension or mental pain.

Grief theory advanced when the British psychiatrist, John Bowlby, postulated his attachment theory. According to Bowlby, each child engages in attachment behaviors. These attachment behaviors are rooted in the need for survival so that the child can find and trust adults who would care for him/her. These attachment behaviors consist of smiling, eye contact, etc. When the child was deprived of the attachment figure, e.g., the parents go out for an evening and leave the child with a sitter, the child would protest by crying and clinging. Often, this protest behavior was successful. Parents might change their plans. This, according to Bowlby, is the root of grief. Grief is primarily the protest we make when a person who is significant in our lives is no longer available to us.

We live in a death denying culture. Ours has become a four- or five-generation society. Such longevity creates a picture of eternal life on earth, supporting a notion that one will be here forever, along with one's parents and children. Our longevity, combined with our limited personal exposure to death, our sense of the uniqueness of the individual, and our sense that we have control over the forces of nature has allowed us to develop the view that death will always happen in someone else's family.

Dr. Colin Murray Parkes, perhaps the foremost researcher and clinician dealing with bereavement, believes that grief is reaction that we undergo when a significant attachment has been broken, usually through death. Our response to grief is rooted in the success of the attachments we have made as children. Failure to make strong attachments as children produce clinging behavior, or pseudo-independent behavior, or learned helplessness. These life patterns have consequences later in life which are exacerbated by the death of someone significant.

Mr. Richard Paul believes that the last part of the twentieth century has witnessed the devaluation of funeral rituals along with the deterioration of traditional support systems for the bereaved. For many years North Americans have been artificially isolated from the care of sick and dying loved ones by the specialists of institutional medical intervention and then have been mere spectators in the funeral process. Having little experience or understanding of dying, death, funerals, and bereavement, people have been ill-equipped to understand the value of funeral rituals to meet their emotional, psychological, sociological, and spiritual needs. This chapter reviews the historical background to current funeral practices, addresses specific criticisms of these practices, and offers an understanding of how funeral rituals and funeral directors serve as a resource to grief management.

Dr. Kenneth Doka who first researched disenfranchised grief discusses that topic. Most of the literature has concentrated on grief reactions in socially recognized and sanctioned roles: those of the parent, spouse, or child. There are circumstances, however, in which a person experiences a sense of loss but does not have a socially recognized right, role, or capacity to grieve. In these cases, the grief is disenfranchised. The person suffers a loss but has little or no opportunity to mourn publicly. Up until now, there has been little research touching directly on the phenomenon of disenfranchised grief. In our society, this may occur for four reasons. *1. The Relationship Is Not Recognized. 2. The Loss Is Not Recognized. 3. The Griever Is Not Recognized. 4. The Death Is Disenfranchising.*

Having examined some aspects of grief, we now offer some suggestions about the care of those grieving. Dr. Rose Marie Jaco tells us that an empathetic heart and a compassionate spirit are necessary characteristics for an able counselor to possess, they are not sufficient to ensure effective practice. Counseling is a discipline which requires practitioners to have knowledge about human personality and development, skills in communication and relationship-building and a set of attitudes that allows them to work in the best interests of the client without having their personal values interfere in the process. Because of the unique needs of bereaved and dying people, care givers need some preparation in order to observe that first principle which guides people involved in the work of helping others—*at least do no harm.*

Dr. Silcox gives specialized information about the treatment of those persons suffering from a complicated form of grief. The form and intensity of grief experienced is the result of a complex interplay between *trauma* and *traumatized*— between all of those factors inherent to the loss itself and all of those strengths and weaknesses inherent in the individual experiencing the loss. Disease or distress states in general have usually been seen as the result of clashing forces—the destructive forces of the invader vs. the resistive forces of the host. This medical model, which draws heavily on combat as an analogue, sees the *offensive player as loss* and the *defensive player as the bereaved*. The current abuse literature reframes this same dynamics as *traumatic agent vs. recovering host*.

Mrs. Peggy Anderson, a bereavement counselor in London Ontario, shows us how the death/grief denying culture in which we live impacts on a bereaved widow. She discusses the therapeutic work of groups in general and in particular the work with groups of widows. She developed the "Alone and Growing" model which she shares with us. Grief impacts on the emotional, physical, mental, spiritual, social, sexual, and economic aspects of living; in other words, in every way.

Mr. Tom Golden is a social worker in private practice who has developed an expertise in working with men in crisis. He believes that the key to understanding a man's orientation is to examine the man's perception of himself on a hierarchy. To understand a man's hierarchical nature we must know what this thing called hierarchy is and how it came to be. We can see the need for hierarchy in the situation which men faced. This can be contrasted with the gatherer roles that women tended to enact. Some interesting gender differences can be linked to this hierarchy/relational schema. Men are known to have better skills at mentally rotating three-dimensional objects in space. Some theorize that this is due to the thousands of years men spent hunting, where their lives were dependent on visually tracking three-dimensional objects. The men relied on a designated hierarchy while the women probably had more of the luxury of deciding together what they would do.

Another group affected particularly by death is that of children who have aged parents. Mrs. Miriam Moss and Mr. Sydney Moss believe that the bond between a parent and a child is significant over a lifetime. Each is unique and irreplaceable for the other. Parents and children have a common history. They have spent decades sharing experiences and developing joint views of reality. The child's very identity is formed within the context of his relationship with his parents. In middle age there tends to be increasing independence and interdependence. There is also a sense of generational continuity in which each symbolizes "family" for the other, both biologically and psychosocially. Although many themes in the relationship may change over time, the parent remains a parent and the child remains a child throughout life. When a parent dies the child is faced with the loss of a highly significant person. The parent death is significant is that it is a point of transition in the life of the child. It has the potential to affect the middle-aged child in areas of self, family relations, and overall worldview. An increased understanding of parent death may provide a model for the understanding of other family deaths such as sibling, spouse, and child.

CHAPTER 16

Bereavement: What Most People Should Know

C. Murray Parkes

Bereavement is the life situation that results when an attachment ends. The term is commonly reserved for people who have suffered a loss by death and this is how we shall use it here. It is worth remembering, however, that the lessons to be learned from bereavement by death are relevant to many other types of loss.

Grief is the emotional reaction to loss. It results from bereavement and, because people can anticipate a loss, it can precede it; we then term it Anticipatory Grief. Anticipatory Grief differs from the grief which follows bereavement in that, whereas grief after bereavement tends to grow less as time passes and the tie to the lost person is severed, the grief which precedes bereavement tends to increase in intensity and to be associated with increased closeness and a strengthening of the tie to the person whose life is threatened.

Mourning is the public face of grief, the way in which people behave after bereavement. As such it is very much influenced by social and cultural factors. Thus, in some societies everyone affected by bereavement is expected to weep openly and without reserve, in others grief is only expressed in private or not at all. Social custom usually dictates where, how, and who is to grieve. Thus, in most societies women are expected to grieve more freely than men. *Rituals*, such as funerals often provide people with opportunities to grieve and in parts of China professional mourners may even be employed to lead the way. In other parts of the world, including much of the West, funerals have no such function and participants may be under considerable pressure to control their feelings and "put on a good face to the world."

Religious faiths give meaning and explanations for death and often promise the hope of a life hereafter for the deceased. Membership of a religious community can ensure the support of like-thinking people who may give comfort and support to the bereaved. On the other hand there are many who lose their faith when faced with the injustice of an untimely or painful death and there are others who feel under considerable pressure to accept the will of God and that any expression of grief is a betrayal of faith or a kind of selfishness. Clearly religious faith is a complex thing and we should not be surprised at the results of research which seldom show that people who subscribe to a particular religion are therefore less vulnerable to bereavement than others. Systematic cross-cultural studies are few but there are some which indicate that, although people from societies in which grief is expressed openly have more emotional problems in the short run, they are, in the long run, less likely to suffer psychosomatic problems and lasting psychological difficulties.

GRIEF AND ATTACHMENTS

Grief is part of the range of thoughts, feelings, and behaviors that attach people to each other and are found in all social animals. The function of these attachments are to keep us safe in the world and they develop, in human beings, in the course of the first year of life. Babies are born with a propensity to cry vigorously if they are frightened or their needs are not being met. Within the first few months of life they learn to distinguish their principle care giver (usually their mother) from others and from then on their attachment behavior is directed primarily to her. She becomes the main object of their smiles, cuddles, and coos when she is present, and it is she who evokes their tears and anger when she stays away too long or when they are fearful or uncomfortable.

By the end of the first year of life most children are firmly attached to one person and will accept few substitutes. During the second and subsequent years they begin to broaden their range of attachments to include father, older siblings, baby sitters, and others. Hopefully, by the time adolescence is reached, they will have learned to trust a variety of people and also to trust their own ability to survive when separated from their parents. This sets the scene for the major transition that takes place when they leave home and develop new couple relationships, usually in the setting of a sexual relationship. When children are born the cycle starts again and the attachments which the parents bring to the relationship with their own children reflect the attachments which they made to their principle parent in childhood.

Although these attachments are rooted in instinct, like all instinctive mechanisms, they are modified by learning from the time of their first inception. Important work by John Bowlby (a psychiatrist and the father of Attachment Theory) and Mary Ainsworth (a noted American psychologist and pupil of Bowlby) has demonstrated clearly that the patterns of attachment which grow up between the principle parent and child in the course of the first year of life tend to persist and to influence all future attachments. If the baby is fortunate to have a parent who is sensitive to their needs, responsive to their bids for attention, present when needed and who protects while encouraging them to explore the world and to develop their own autonomy, they will grow up securely attached and with a reasonable degree of trust in themselves and others. If, on the other hand, their principle parent is insensitive to their needs, ignoring or punishing their bids for attention, frequently absent when needed, inconsistently protective or over-protective so that they are discouraged from exploring the world and discovering their own potential; we should not be surprised if the child is insecure and its development is held back.

It is not only parental rejection that causes problems, over-anxious or over-controlling parents can do just as much harm to the developing child. Ainsworth has distinguished three patterns of insecure attachment which tend to persist and to cause problems later in life. These are (1) the clinging or "anxious/ambivalent" attachments which tend to arise when the child gets the idea that it is necessary to cling to mother if they are to survive in a dangerous world; (2) the apparently detached (or "pseudo-independent") behavior of the child whose parents cannot tolerate closeness and who punish bids for attention; and (3) the inconsistent and confused behavior of the child whose parents are inconsistent in their responses so that the child grows up with no confidence in its ability to cope (this can be seen as "learned helplessness") [1].

The particular problems which tend to occur in later life are (1) the "anxious/ambivalent" person often has difficulty in separating from their parent in adolescence. Their tendency to cling often leads to the very thing that it is intended to prevent, rejection. When they succeed in making relationships it is often with (2) "pseudo-independent" people who need to be the adored "strong" partner in a strong/weak relationship to reassure them of their own loveability and strength. These relationships succeed because they provide both partners with the security that they need, but serious problems may emerge when one or other partner dies. It is easy to understand how difficult it must be for the dependent partner to cope with life on their own and it is not surprising that they often seek for someone else to depend on, often an older person, a doctor, or some other caring person. Until such a person is found they tend to suffer from *chronic grief,* an intense type of grief which persists for much longer than is normally the case.

"Pseudo-independent" (or "compulsively self-reliant") people often try to cope by avoiding grief. They keep busy, put away reminders of their loss and avoid anything that will remind them of what has happened, for a time they may appear to be a "tower of strength." But sooner or later problems emerge. They may develop an illness that bears a strong resemblance to that of the person who died (*identification symptoms*) or they may start to experience feelings of loss and despair at night or at other times when their defences are down. These *delayed or inhibited grief* reactions reveal the fact that their independence of other people is more apparent than real.

Finally there is the person whose experience of learned helplessness has left them with very little confidence in their ability to cope and very little trust in others. They tend to react to bereavements, as they do to all major challenges, by *depression.* They withdraw into a relatively safe place and give up all attempts to get out of the rut of misery into which they have been sucked.

Before considering what can be done to help people through these difficult bereavements let us take a look at the nature of grief and the psychological components that go to make it up.

COMPONENTS OF GRIEF

In the early stages of bereavement people tend to swing back and forth between the so-called pangs of grief and attempts to put grief aside and get on with the many tasks that face them. They are in a state of conflict between (1) the urge to cry aloud and search for the lost person which, as we have already seen, is a normal part of the reaction to any separation from the people to whom we are attached; and (2) the need to control, inhibit, and avoid grief, which reflects the social pressures and habits of thought that we have learned from early childhood (almost the first thing a mother says to her child is "Don't cry!"). As time passes they become aware of a third component, (3) the need to discover how their identity and assumptions about the world have got to change in the light of the psychosocial transition that they now face.

The pangs of grief are often the most severe psychological pain that people have experienced and they are accompanied by feelings of intense anxiety and all the physical symptoms to which this can gives rise. These include dryness in the mouth, heaviness in the limbs, aches and pains reflecting tension in the muscles, headaches, palpitations, diarrhea, frequency of urination, difficulty in getting to sleep, tiredness, difficulty in concentration and impairment of memory and judgment. Given that these are occurring at a time when the world suddenly seems to have become very dangerous and people have lost their accustomed sense of security, it is not surprising that they are often misunderstood. The person whose husband has died of a heart attack begins to worry that she too may have heart trouble, the more she worries the worse her palpitations become and before very long her heart is racing and she has gotten caught in a vicious circle of escalating fear and worsening symptoms. Similarly the elderly widow whose concentration is impaired by her grief may imagine that she is dementing or the controlled person who keeps bursting into tears may think that he or she is heading for a "nervous breakdown." It is important to recognize that all of these symptoms are, in fact, normal features of grief. The normal heart beats faster at times of anxiety; it is not possible for people who fear danger to pay attention and remember routine things (they have more important things on their minds); and the person who does not express grief is at greater risk of mental illness than the person who "breaks down."

Anger is a normal reaction to bereavement and is an understandable consequence of untimely deaths. Unfortunately it often gets misunderstood or directed inappropriately at the people who are closest to hand. Anger may alienate potential sources of help and split families. It is only too common for the "Never-darken-my-door-again" situation to arise at this time.

Along with anger feelings of *guilt* and self-reproach are common. These often take the form of "if onlys": "If only I'd pushed him into having that operation he'd still be alive today," or, "If only I'd stopped him from having that operation he'd still be alive today." You can't win.

Anger and guilt are particularly likely to create problems for the bereaved when the relationship has been a very ambivalent one. In such cases people may cling to their grief as a kind of punishment, as if, "I didn't love him enough when alive, now

I will make it up to him by grieving forever." One can detect self-punitive grieving from such statements as "Why should I be happy now that he is dead?" as if the bereaved had no right to happiness.

SEARCHING

Despite the fact that the intelligent person knows that it is illogical to cry aloud and to search for a dead person, newly bereaved people have a strong impulse to do just that. What emerges is a reflection of the conflict within us. The urge to cry becomes stifled into a sob and the urge to search is seen in the way in which bereaved people revisit places associated with the dead person, treasure possessions and other reminders of them, and go over in their minds the events leading up to the loss as if, even now, they could find out what went wrong and put it right.

At times the search may seem to be rewarded. The widow sees her dead husband coming toward her in the street and it is only when the other person gets closer that she realizes that she has made a mistake. Sights and sounds are easily misinterpreted and bereaved people frequently report having heard the dead person's key in the lock or heard them call out. At times when people are in a drowsy state of mind they commonly experience "hypnagogic hallucinations" in which the dead person is seen with great clarity standing at the foot of the bed or in some similar situation. These "hallucinations" disappear rapidly when the bereaved person "wakes up." They may be a cause of anxiety to people who associate hallucinations with mental illness and it is important to recognize their normality. Most common of all is a sense of the presence of the dead person near at hand or in certain places that come to have a special importance. For some this is the grave, for others it may be a favorite chair or other place. Many societies designate a specific location for the dead, thus, in traditional Buddhist belief in Japan, each household has its family shrine which can become a kind of "hot-line" to the dead. Japanese bereaved people find this shrine a source of comfort. In Western society a photograph and a bunch of flowers in a special place at home often serves a similar function.

INHIBITION AND AVOIDANCE

Nobody can grieve all the time and it seems necessary for people to swing back and forth between confronting and avoiding the full reality of bereavement. At the immediate impact of a loss, particularly if it is unexpected, the reaction is often one of numbness and incomprehension. People experience a strong sense of unreality and, although they seldom deny the literal truth of what has happened, they still say "I can't believe it is true." This reaction seems to protect people from the full impact of an event that threatens to overwhelm them and it may help them to carry on with the various important tasks of calling an ambulance, phoning the family, looking after the children, arranging the funeral, etc.

Numbness seldom lasts for more than a few hours or days but people continue to attempt to limit the full reality of their loss by distracting themselves, shutting themselves away from people who will express sympathy and shutting up clothing and other articles that will bring the dead person too powerfully to mind. Some find that they can escape from grief by going straight back to work, others escape to the pub and attempt to anaesthetize themselves with alcohol. None of these methods can be relied on to succeed for long and sooner or later "grief will out." When grief that has been "dammed up" does emerge it is often in a more intense and embarrassing form than would have been the case if it had been expressed from the start.

In emergencies and times of war it may be necessary to inhibit grief for extended periods of time. This may explain the relative lack of grief in the concentration camps and among soldiers, policemen, and doctors who experience bereavement in the course of their day-to-day life. It is notable that those societies that value their prowess in war often play down the importance of grief; Apache Indians, for instance, never mention the names of their dead and a major attenuation in the customs of mourning in Britain took place in the course of the first world war and was reinforced during the second.

THE PSYCHOSOCIAL TRANSITION (PST)

Psychosocial transitions occur whenever people undergo a major change in their lives which requires them, in a short space of time, to revise basic assumptions, habits of thought and behavior that have been learned over many years and which we tend to take for granted. A wife who loses a husband not only loses a loved person outside herself but she suddenly becomes a widow. She has no idea what that means or how to behave and it will be many months before she has discovered the many changes to her ways of thinking and behaving that are now appropriate to this stage of her life.

Each train of thought seems to lead into a blind alley and bereaved people are often surprised at the number of ways in which the dead person continues to penetrate their lives. A widow will come downstairs in the morning and lay the table for two, or she will catch herself thinking "I must ask my husband about that." Often the person who has died is the person to whom we would have turned at times of trouble. Yet here we are, with the biggest trouble we have ever experienced, repeatedly trying to turn to someone who is not there. Some of the changes reflect the need to take over roles formerly performed by the dead person. This is most likely to be a problem if there was a strict division of roles between the partners. On the other hand individuals who, as a couple, have shared their decision making and roles, will find it much easier to cope if one or the other is gone.

Other problems arise from the changes in the bereaved person's view of the world. A married person may have achieved high status through their association with a powerful or much-loved partner. When that partner is gone they not only lose status, they may become an object of pity. People whom, in the past, we looked down upon, suddenly start patronizing us and there is a subtle change and reshuffling of the hierarchy in which each one of us is embedded.

Changes of this kind are hard to adapt to and people may be tempted to cling to a view of the world and of their place within it that is now obsolete. "I don't think of myself as a widow," they may say or they may refuse to take training courses or jobs that would imply admission of the fact that their world has now changed. Some try to preserve their house exactly as it was when the person died as if it was still possible for them to return and resume life as if nothing had happened. Queen Victoria is a good example of this "fossilisation." After Prince Albert died she had all of the rooms in her palaces photographed to insure that everything would be replaced in the right place after cleaning. Visitors to Osborne Palace on the Isle of Wight will find it still as it was on the day in 1861 when Albert died.

This kind of thing would not, perhaps, matter if it was not for the fact that it is seldom possible to live in two worlds at the same time. Sooner or later the demands of reality come into conflict with the maintenance of the fantasy world and the bereaved have to decide whether they can bear to give up a dream.

BEREAVEMENT AND HEALTH

There is good evidence that bereavement can have harmful effects on both physical and mental health. The most obvious and common example is the effects caused by anxiety and stress. These were described above and need not be repeated here. They explain many of the calls which bereaved people make upon doctors and they respond well to proper explanation and reassurance.

More serious are the problems which can arise when a bereavement aggravates a pre-existing health problem. Thus the effects of bereavement on the heart have been described above and most of the time these are not serious. But if a person already has heart disease this may be aggravated and there is even evidence of an increased risk of death. One might suppose that the risk would be greatest in people who get emotionally upset. If that were the case we would expect that the risk would be greater in women than in men since women, as we have seen, are more likely to react to bereavement by overt grief. In fact it is men rather than women who are most at risk of death from heart disease after bereavement and there is other evidence that the inhibition of grief is more damaging to the heart than its expression. Fortunately it is possible to minimize the influence of emotions on the heart by means of a group of drugs termed "Beta Blockers" and many physicians now prescribe these as a preventive measure to people with known heart disease who suffer a bereavement.

Bereavement has been shown to impair the body's Immune Response System and this may increase the risk of infections and cancers. Here the evidence suggests that it is the intensity of depression rather than grief itself that has the most profound effect.

Rheumatic and arthritic conditions can also be aggravated by bereavement and these are the commonest cause of medical consultations among bereaved elderly people. Youngsters are more likely to consult their doctors with psychological symptoms.

Practically any psychiatric problem can be aggravated by bereavement, but the most common reasons for people to seek psychiatric help are anxiety states, panic syndromes, and depression. Pathological grief reactions such as the chronic grief, delayed grief, or conflicted griefs described above also occur. When they arise it seems that the normal oscillation between confrontation and avoidance has broken down, the bereaved then remain either in a state of chronic preoccupation with the loss or in constant attempts to avoid it.

One other condition that can complicate grief is Post-Traumatic Stress Disorder (PTSD). This condition can be caused by any unexpected and horrific life experience, particularly when associated with threat to ones own life or to the lives of loved persons. It is characterized by the repeated recollection of horrific or painful memories of the loss event which tend to haunt the sufferer and to evoke severe feelings of anxiety and fear. These memories may return as "flash-backs" as the person relives again and again the events in question, as if it were being replayed on video-tape. They also occur in the form of recurrent nightmares that may be so unpleasant that the bereaved person is afraid to go to sleep at night.

The memories are triggered by any sights or sounds that remind the sufferer of the trauma and are so unpleasant that people will go to great lengths to avoid such reminders. They may stop work, shut themselves up at home and refuse to talk or think about what has happened.

When the traumatic experience has led to a bereavement the avoidance interferes with the task of grieving. In the normal course of grief happy memories of the dead person soon begin to outweigh the painful memories. People treasure photographs and other mementoes which bring pleasure and help the bereaved to find a new place for the dead person in their hearts, as many put it "He (or she) lives on in my memory." Following traumatic bereavements, however, this cannot happen. The painful memories of the loss event seem to drive out the happier memories, photographs are put away, cupboards closed, and friends placed under strict injunction not to mention the death or the dead person. This leads to a stagnation in the grieving process so that several years later people who have suffered a traumatic bereavement still have difficulty in believing that the death has happened while simultaneously being unable to forget it.

THE ASSESSMENT OF RISK

Most bereaved people do not need help from outside their own families and their network of friends. This, after all is what families and friends are for and there is a possibility that these important people will back off if the "experts" move in when they are not needed.

On the other hand there is a significant number, estimated at about one-third of those who suffer a major bereavement (such as the death of a spouse, partner, or child), who will benefit from additional help from outside the family. It is often possible before, or at the time of a bereavement, to identify those people who are most likely to be at risk and in need of this help. These are listed in Table 1 from which it will be clear that the greater the number of risk factors, the greater the risk. Most of these factors have already been described above but it is worth looking more closely at a few of them. Personal vulnerability is not usually difficult to assess though it requires sensitivity and tact to ask questions on these issues. The person needs to understand that such questions are not idle curiosity but reflect a sincere recognition of the stress which the person may be facing along

Table 1. List of Factors Influencing Bereavement Risk after Major Bereavement

1. Personal Vulnerability
    Previous history of psychiatric disorder or suicidal threat.
    Insecure attachments in childhood.
    Ambivalent or clinging/dependent attachments.
    Compulsive self-reliance (pseudo-independence).
    Low trust in self and/or others.
    Poor health, particularly known heart disease.

2. Traumatic Bereavements
    Sudden, unexpected, and untimely bereavements.
    Witnessing horrific events.
    Possible personal culpability.
    Bereavement by murder or manslaughter.
    Bereavement by suicide.
    Multiple losses.
    Personal long-term care of dying person.

3. Lack of Support Systems
    Family and/or friends absent.
    Family and friends seen as unhelpful.

with a wish to be of help. If the person is reluctant to give information on such matters we should not press them but should rely on our own gut feeling about the vulnerability of this person.

Traumatic losses are usually very obvious, but the newly bereaved person who has suffered such a loss may be reluctant to accept any help that is offered for fear that they will be forced to confront issues which threaten to overwhelm them. Again sensitivity and tact is required to insure that they realize that would-be helpers will respect their wishes and not ride rough-shod over their defenses.

Losses which follow a long illness in which the survivor has been a principal care giver constitute a risk because of the extent to which the bereaved person has come to center their life on the person now dead and because of the feelings of personal responsibility for the death that are likely to be felt by the survivor. This is particularly the case when it is a sick child who has died.

Raphael has found that people who perceive their families as "unhelpful" are at greater risk after bereavement than do those who see their families as "helpful" [2]. It is important to note that she also found that this group, more than any other, benefitted from bereavement counseling.

HELPING THE BEREAVED

Problems are much more likely to follow sudden unexpected and untimely bereavements than those that have been anticipated. It follows that those who are in a position to warn people about a possible coming bereavement should do their best to do so. Anticipatory grief does do something to prepare people for the losses that are to come and it enables those whose relationship is problematic a last chance to put things right. They are then less likely to blame themselves later. A vigil at the bedside of an unconscious person may not do the dying person any good but it may be most important for the relatives who need this opportunity to prove their devotion before it is too late.

In helping people to prepare themselves for bereavement we need to provide them with emotional support as well as information. This may not be easy because as long as the patient is alive the family will tend to deny their own needs for support. This said, those who work in hospices or other settings where people die, will have many opportunities to stay close to the family and to convey to them our recognition of their needs as well as those of the patient. In such circumstances it is the family (which includes the patient) who are the unit of care rather the patient (with the family as an optional extra that we take on if we have the time).

The traumatic impact of death can be minimized if doctors take time and trouble when they break bad news. A few words of kindness at this time will be remembered for the rest of the bereaved person's life and may do more than anything else to counteract the horrific memories that so easily come to dominate the bereaved person's life.

In general most people appear to be at peace when they are dead and the viewing of a dead person is usually experienced positively by the bereaved. Viewing provides them with a chance to make real the fact of the death and to say "Goodbye." On the other hand there are times when viewing a dead person can add to the trauma of a traumatic bereavement and trigger the horrific memories of PTSD. This is most likely to happen when people are unexpectedly confronted with sights, smells, and other sensations of an horrific nature. Even the experience of viewing someone who appears peacefully at rest can be spoiled if the bereaved are not expecting them to feel ice cold when kissed.

It follows that viewing the dead is an important act that needs to be planned beforehand. People should be warned of anything likely to surprise or shock them and no pressure should be brought to bear to persuade them to view. Children, who are often very sensitive to the emotions of adults, should be accompanied by an adult who can be relied on to remain in control and the adult should explain beforehand exactly what the child should expect.

It is now standard practice in obstetric wards to take photographs of stillborn babies. This provides an image for the mother who may have decided not to view the dead baby but who may subsequently regret this decision and for the mother who wants to take with her some evidence that her intrauterine child was a real baby. There is good reason to take similar photographs whenever people, for one reason or another, have been unable to view the body of a loved person.

Funerals can be wonderful celebrations of the life of a valued person or monstrous ordeals which add to the trauma of bereavement. They too need to be planned carefully in consultation with the bereaved family. There is a world of difference between the production-line cremation service in which an unknown cleric repeats the same words, at half-hour intervals throughout the day, over a series of dead people of whom he knows nothing, and the lovingly-thought-out ceremony in which priest and bereaved together have chosen the prayers, hymns, and tributes that can enrich the funeral service and point up its poetry.

However beautiful a funeral can be it comes far too soon to set a period to mourning. In many societies it is believed that the spirits of the dead remain earth-bound for a period of time after death. During this time the living have an obligation to pray and to mourn for them. There is then a second ritual following which the spirits go to their final resting place and the bereaved can stop mourning and move forward into the next chapter of their lives. Whatever our beliefs about a spirit world may be, the idea of a second ritual that marks the end of overt mourning can be of great help to the bereaved. A memorial service, requiem mass, or stone-setting ceremony can all perform a similar function, marking the passage of time and instigating the end of obligatory mourning. This does not mean, of course, that grief will come to an abrupt halt at this point. Bereaved people regularly report that, even years later, meeting someone who knew the dead person can evoke another pang of grief and, in this sense, it does not end. On the other hand it does help to know when our duty to the dead is done and we can be permitted to seek new relationships and responsibilities.

In all of these rituals the clergy are the "ritual experts" and they continue to play an important role in support of bereaved people. In the secular West, however, few people now seek help from the church and its clergy; rather it is doctors, nurses, social workers, and counselors who have become the experts on bereavement. Grief is now seen as an illness to be recovered from rather than a normal transition. Sedatives, tranquilizers, and antidepressants are used in its treatment. This tendency to medicalize normal life crises encourages people to depend on their medical attendants to a questionable degree and, while doctors do have a role to play in treating the medical complications of bereavement, they should beware of encouraging people to adopt sick roles. In most instances they can do more good by reassuring them that they are *not* sick than they can by prescribing treatment.

There are, of course, times when a doctor is needed. This is particularly the case if the bereaved are suffering from severe depression or at risk of suicide in which case an anti-depressant may save a life. But tranquilizers and sedatives are all habit forming and, while they do little harm if taken intermittently, it is only too easy for bereaved people to become dependent on them. It has also been claimed that they interfere with the course of grief if taken regularly although the evidence for this claim is not conclusive.

Support for the bereaved given by selected and trained volunteer counselors backed by professional psychologists or social workers, has been shown, in random-allocation studies, to be effective in reducing the bereavement risk in high-risk groups and reducing the utilization of General Practitioner services. Self-help (or

Mutual-help) groups such as "The Compassionate Friends" (for parents who have lost a child) and "Gay Bereavement" (for homosexuals who have lost a partner), are also popular but have not yet been subjected to the test of scientific evaluation. People who join such groups meet others who are "in the same boat" and can, therefore, be expected to understand. Problems in leadership within self-help groups can arise and, in some cases, it has been possible for the most disturbed or paranoid members of the group to take control.

In the United Kingdom the organization "Cruse—Bereavement Care" offers a nationwide network of trained volunteer bereavement counselors. In the United States and many other countries these are confined to hospice-based bereavement services. This creates the anomaly that the people most likely to get effective help after bereavement are those who have lost a family member by cancer. Yet deaths from cancer, because they are predictable and provide families with opportunities to prepare themselves for bereavement, are associated with a lower bereavement risk than most other illnesses. The implication of this is not that hospices should stop providing care for the bereaved, their services have been shown to be effective, but that similar services should be provided for a wider range of bereaved people.

Despite the existence of these various types of special help it is to their *friends and family* that most people will and should turn at times of bereavement and it is worth considering what the ordinary person can do to help in these circumstances. The answer to this question can best be summed up as follows:

> The bereaved may need permission and opportunities to grieve, they may also need permission and opportunities to stop grieving and get on with their lives.

In the early stages they need reassurance that it is alright to cry and to rage and they need sympathetic people at hand who will provide them with a shoulder to cry on. Those who cannot cry should not be pressured to do so. For many it is sufficient to talk through the implications of the loss without overt expression of emotion and people who have been reassured that they do not *have* to cry may feel secure enough to do so once they have come to trust us.

The psychosocial transitions which follow bereavement require people to review their lives in great detail and to rethink their basic assumptions about themselves and their world. They will do this best by talking about the situation and their feelings about it. When people are explaining themselves to us they are also explaining themselves to themselves, taking stock and discovering what they must give up and what they can hold on to. This takes a great deal of time and effort. A good listener is of more value than someone who attempts to give answers to the numerous problems that emerge. In the long run, it is the answers that the bereaved figure out for themselves that are likely to meet their individual needs and stand the test of time. It also helps to restore their self-esteem if they can make their own decisions rather than being told how to run their lives.

FURTHER READING

It has not been possible in the space available to provide scientific justification for the assertions and recommendations that have been made in this chapter. Numerous studies of the psychology of loss and grief have been conducted in recent years and those dealing with loss by death in adult life are summarized in the third edition of my book *Bereavement: Studies of Grief in Adult Life* [3]. For a more comprehensive review which includes losses in childhood as well as in adult life Raphael's *Anatomy of Bereavement* [2] is recommended. Full details of the types of counseling that can be given by members of the caring professions and by volunteer counselors when people are dying or bereaved are given in *Counselling in Terminal Care and Bereavement*, by Parkes, Relf, and Couldrick [4], and in Worden's book *Grief Counselling and Grief Therapy* [5]. For those who would like to learn more about the way people from different cultures across the world cope with death and bereavement I suggest the book *Death and Bereavement across Cultures*, edited by Parkes, Laungani, and Young [6], and for the medical reader who wants to obtain a psychiatrist/physician's perspective Jacobs' book *Pathologic Grief* [7]. For a wide-ranging consideration of the research into human and animal attachments which includes several review articles see, *Attachment Across the Life Cycle*, edited by Parkes, Stevenson-Hinde, and Marris [8].

REFERENCES

1. M. D. S. Ainsworth, Attachments and Other Affectional Bonds Across the Life Cycle, in *Attachment Across the Life Cycle,* Chapter 3, C. M. Parkes, J. Stevenson-Hinde, and P. Marris (eds.), Routledge, London and New York, 1991.
2. B. Raphael, *The Anatomy of Bereavement,* Hutchinson, London, 1984.
3. C. M. Parkes, *Bereavement: Studies of Grief in Adult Life* (3rd Edition), Tavistock/Routledge, London; Pelican, Harmondsworth; and International Universities Press, New York, 1996.
4. C. M. Parkes, M. Relf, and A. Couldrick, Counselling in Terminal Care and Bereavement, *British Psychological Society,* Liecester, 1996.
5. J. W. Worden, *Grief Counselling and Grief Therapy,* Tavistock, London and New York, 1982.
6. C. M. Parkes, P. Laungani, and W. Young (eds.), *Death and Bereavement Across Cultures,* Routledge, London, 1996.
7. S. Jacobs, *Pathologic Grief: Maladaptation to Loss*, American Psychiatric Press, Washington, D.C. and London, 1993.
8. C. M. Parkes, J. Stevenson-Hinde, and P. Marris (eds.), *Attachment Across the Life Cycle,* Routledge, London and New York, 1991.

CHAPTER 17

Funerals and Funeral Directors: Rituals and Resources for Grief Management

Richard J. Paul

> ... he who can look on the loveliness of the world, and share it's sorrow, and know something of the wonder of both ...
> —Oscar Wilde

The words and symbols employed in any discussion of funeral rituals and practices may well evoke past experiences, media images, and/or previously formed judgments. The subject is emotionally imbued and objectivity may be clouded by subjective notions. The reader is encouraged to be aware of associations and preconceptions as they arise in order to remain open to new information and concepts.

INTRODUCTION

As a director on the board of a mental health agency I was attending a joint board and staff development workshop focused on establishing the organization's mission statement. The facilitator had stated that it was important for us to know clearly what business we were in and, as a preamble, had asked each of us to introduce ourselves by saying what business we were in as individuals. Only too familiar with the stereotypical responses to my role as a funeral director, I was searching my mind for a unique way to say I was in the "funeral business." When it was my turn to speak I declared that I was "in the business of grief management."

A well-known maxim in the area of grief psychology is the expression, *"either you manage your grief, or your grief will manage you."* This phrase states categorically that if you are not equipped and informed to be the master of your grief, then you will be a victim or a slave to your emotions. The funeral director can provide information and facilitate ritual experiences that will lead the bereaved to a deeper understanding of, and support in, the grief and growth process.

> *Definition:* Grief management may be understood as working with the personal manifestations of bereavement through an informed awareness towards a healthy reconciliation of the loss and redefinition of a relationship that has been permanently changed.

Funeral directors assist grieving people to ritualize, and so to recognize and begin to reconcile, an individual's death. One person's death represents a loss, or many losses, unique to everyone touched by that life and death. However, each individual's death diminishes humanity at one, or perhaps more than one, level. So funeral rituals, and funeral directors as resources for this process, serve all humans in the acceptance of death as a part of the human experience.

In the closing decade of the twentieth century death is slowly coming back out of the closet. Humanity's evolving world view over the course of the last 100 years first removed the natural ebb and flow of the birth, life, and death cycle from the human experience. Now, human perspective is gradually awakening to the reality that acceptance of mortality is an essential element in a full and balanced participation in, and appreciation of, life.

Another influence of humanity's developing belief system has been a pendulum swing from total acceptance of the status quo to a close scrutiny and an occasional devaluation or outright rejection of traditional values, institutions, and rituals. North American society's inexperience with death combined with the dissolution of familiar and meaningful ritual practices is a primary cause of the recent depreciation and misapprehension of funeral customs.

Funeral customs and practices are connected with human death and the final disposition of the body. Like other rites of passage, funeral observances are a distinctly human trait. In addition to marking the death and dealing with the body, these observances are also closely tied to accommodating and satisfying social, spiritual, psychological, and emotional needs of the bereaved. Frequently the funeral traditions of a particular culture have arisen to assist the bereaved in adapting to life without the deceased.

Funeral traditions and practices within a culture reflect not only its history but also its current religious beliefs, community values, social framework, education level, and degree of government intervention. The investigation of a particular society's funeral customs can provide theological, psychological, and sociological insights to that culture. British Prime Minister Gladstone responded to a cartoon criticism of funeral directors which ran in the January 1885 issue of London's *PUNCH* with the statement, "Show me the manner in which a nation or community cares for its dead and I will measure with mathematical exactness the tender sympathies of its people, their respect of the laws of the land and their loyalty to high ideals" [1, p. 35]. North American funeral practices have emerged to include a broad spectrum of activities which indicate specialization, cultural diversity, flexibility, and a focus on the individual, both the bereaved and the deceased.

HISTORICAL PERSPECTIVE OF FUNERALS

Activities and ceremonies following, and related to, a death are performed globally and can be traced to the earliest societies. However, what constitutes a funeral practice must, by the very nature of humankind, be very diverse and broadly defined. "The first known deliberate burials were those of early Homo sapiens groups. Archeological evidence indicates that one of the early groups, the Neanderthals, stained their dead with red ochre—a possible indication of some belief in an afterlife" [2]. The only consistent feature of humanity's response to the death of an individual throughout history has been that generally some form of funeral ritual is followed.

What would be considered compliance with local religion, custom, and practical considerations among one group would be considered a violation of the sensibilities and represent an indignity to the human body by another community.

> The modern Parsees expose the bodies of their dead to be devoured by vultures because they consider this method most appropriate and satisfactory, for, in accordance with Zoroaster's teachings, they consider fire too sacred to be put to any such ignoble use, and the burial of the dead as a defilement and an injury to the earth, which they consider as the mother of mankind [3, p. 13].

The wide variation of human motivations and funeral practices is the basis for misunderstanding and subsequent minimization or criticism both between, and within, societies.

The first North American pioneers brought with them a European perspective and experience regarding funerals based primarily on the Christian religion. Living often on remote farms, isolated even from neighbors, the extended family was responsible for all aspects of the funeral for a family member. Traditionally, men would tend to the male and women would care for the female dead body. The "laying out" would simply involve bathing, closing the mouth and eyes, dressing and placing the body in a simple, homemade container or coffin. A process of "keeping vigil" followed when the coffin was placed in the parlor of the home and someone stayed by the body around the clock for one to three days. During this time relatives, friends, and neighbors within traveling distance would arrive to pay their respects by the coffin. Part of the purpose for a long "vigil" or "wake" period was to watch for any signs of life. Limited medical tests of the time could miss vital signs of a deep coma and an extended wake was deemed necessary to avoid burying someone alive.

If the death occurred in a hot season and ice was available, the body would be packed in ice to delay decomposition and allow people to arrive from any distance. During the "wake" the bereaved family were in fact hosts to their visitors and much of their time was spent on preparing meals and accommodating those who had traveled far from their own home. The obligations of hospitality often deprived the principal grievers from fully appreciating the reality of the death and benefitting from the support of their visitors.

On the third or fourth day after the death a funeral service followed either in the home or in a local church if one was available. When a church was accessible a funeral procession would leave the home with men either carrying the coffin or driving it in the back of a wagon to the service. Following the service a similar parade would travel to the cemetery. Burial was practiced almost exclusively among the early settlers based on the Christian belief that "For the trumpet will sound, the dead shall be raised up imperishable" [4].

The phrase "rugged individualism" is often used to describe the survival characteristic of the first European settlers in North America. Families were primarily self-reliant and every waking hour was spent on the essentials of existing in a harsh and undeveloped environment. In this setting, the time taken for a funeral was a precious commodity and when the service was over it was crucial that everyone get back to work. There was no time for extended mourning. Fragments of this "rugged individualism" still influence the attitudes toward bereavement, and the grieving practices, of many modern North Americans.

As communities developed and the economy could support some specialization in the provision of merchandise and services, the jobs of cabinet maker and the livery owner followed. The role of the modern North American funeral director is based on these particular vocations. When a death occurred the local cabinet maker was called upon to build a casket for the body. The European "coffin" shaped slightly triangular was wider at the shoulders and narrower at the feet. A "casket" in those times was a rectangular chest built to contain valuables. Perhaps the cabinet maker was asked to build a "casket" to contain the human remains because, as a tangible symbol of the individual, the body was still deemed valuable. Or it may be that the four-sided structure of the casket was more practical to make than the six-sided coffin. In any case the casket is considered a North American structure and the coffin is distinctly European.

The livery stable owner became involved by having a specially designed horse-drawn wagon called a "hearse" to carry the casket from the home to the church and then to the cemetery. By repeated first-hand exposure to previous funerals the livery owner and the cabinet maker became more knowledgeable than most in their communities about both the related practices and requirements of funerals and burials. This familiarity was the basis for these two vocations becoming a resource to be consulted at the time of a death.

With the advent of the industrial age North Americans had less time to attend to their own dead. Gradually the special knowledge of someone to "undertake" the funeral and burial arrangements evolved from a part-time role of the cabinet maker or liveryman into the role of a full time "undertaker." From the convenience of having the "undertaker" provide his parlor for the wake or visiting period prior to the funeral service the phrase "undertaking parlour" or "funeral parlour" emerged to describe a building "exclusively designed and equipped for this particular work and for the comfort of the bereaved" [3, p. 38]. By transferring to the funeral director the responsibility for the care of the dead body and the organization of the visitation period, funeral service and burial, the mourners were then freed up to attend to their grief and receive the support of their friends and relatives without unnecessary work or distraction.

Prior to the introduction in North America of embalming as a service of the undertaker, burial had to be conducted near the place of death. When a death occurred far from home, transportation was impossible. Early embalming in the United States, like that in Europe, was first practiced in the preservation of anatomical material. During the Civil War in the United States, Dr. Thomas Holmes was commissioned in the Army Medical Corps to embalm many of the army officers who had been killed in battle, allowing their bodies to be transported back to their home communities for a funeral and burial. Gradually the training and licensing of undertakers improved and embalming the body developed into an accepted practice to facilitate the funeral process.

Embalming permits a delay in the final disposition of the body allowing details to be confirmed without undue haste and leaving distant family and friends time to attend the funeral proceedings. The process of embalming involves introducing a preservative and disinfectant into the body. The purposes of embalming are to sanitize, preserve, and restore the dead human body. Sanitization renders the body clean, safe, and inoffensive to be near or touched. Preservation prevents rapid decomposition which in turn allows time for funeral arrangements to be made and people to gather. Restoration leaves the body at once familiar and peaceful in appearance. The process known as embalming helped further distinguish and establish the funeral director as a specialist and a professional.

As government regulations such as death registration, burial and cremation requirements, licensing of funeral directors and funeral homes, were imposed on funerals, the profession of funeral director became entrenched as a resource to be consulted at the time of death. Over the first half of the twentieth century very little changed in North American funeral practices.

In the meantime, families were usurped from the care of their sick and dying by advancing medical technology and intervention. People rapidly lost contact with both the process of dying and the event of death. In the same way, society as a whole lost touch with the care of the dead and ritualizing the loss. Funeral directors literally developed from consultants to the bereaved into purveyors and perpetuators of the status quo in funerals. In effect, funeral directors and funeral homes became mysterious repositories of death and funeral practices in North America. The profession became less involved as a resource for consultation and more a dictator of etiquette, telling the bereaved what they should do and what was required.

Within the activities comprising a funeral many therapeutic and healing features remained. However, funeral practices became increasingly rote with the bereaved relegated to spectators, or meekly doing what they were told by the funeral director and the church.

CRITICISMS OF MODERN FUNERAL PRACTICES AND PRACTITIONERS

In the early 1960s, dissatisfaction with the status quo swept North America and funeral customs were exposed to the same critical eye as almost every other ritual and institution on the continent. Unfortunately, critics of established funeral practices are products of the self-same culture that has all but eliminated their exposure to, and experience with, death. Consequently, the people who are criticizing funeral practices have stepped forward from the North American population that is not generally in touch with the birth to death continuum and this "partially accounts for a widespread (North) American tendency to deny death and the need for funerary rituals" [5, p. 176]. As a result there has been a tendency to "throw out the baby with the bath water" and to write off the benefits that accrue both from established funeral rituals and from genuinely caring funeral directors.

Complaints of some people have ranged from general griping about funerals—they are too impersonal, traumatic, morbid, anxiety-provoking, artificial, or expensive—right through to Jessica Mitford's accusations of exploitation in *The American Way Of Death* [6]. The censure surrounding modern North American funeral practices focuses primarily on the funeral director "who has been the scapegoat of death since ancient times" [7]. Ironically, the funeral director is in the unique position of being criticized for discharging exactly the tasks he or she is supposed to perform.

The funeral service profession in North America has some culpability in society's stereotyping of funeral directors and traditional funeral practices and its detachment from, and discontent with, the death experience. Dissatisfaction with North American funerals may be traced in part to the sense of powerlessness, and simply being relegated to the role of passive observer, that many principal grievers have experienced during the funeral of a loved one. By taking over every aspect of caring for the dead body and arranging every detail of the funeral and final disposition of the body, funeral directors have compounded the sense of chaos and impotence that naturally occurs following death. This expropriation of responsibility has been done by the funeral director "specialist" with the best of intentions, to relieve the bereaved of unnecessary distractions and details. Unfortunately, being deprived of all control makes the bereaved even more of a victim than they already are through the death of their loved one. Frequently arising from victimization is a sense of anger and, when coupled with the anger which can develop from grief, the funeral director and the funeral are an obvious target.

Some of the blame for defining and maintaining inaccurate and harmful stereotypes lies in North American funeral directors losing touch with the roots of their vocation. Requests for some personalization or customization of the funeral process have been met with responses such as, "That's not how we do things around here."

Recognizing that it is in the best interest of the bereaved to have command of their situation funeral directors are returning more to an orientation of resource and consultant. By identifying the questions that need to be asked, and the options to answer those questions, the funeral director is assuming the role of walking beside the mourners rather than leading them. This has the therapeutic effect of placing some power back in the hands of the bereaved.

Another criticism of current North American funeral customs and funeral directors is that the facilities, vehicles, caskets, and procedures are more elaborate than necessary. One visitor from South Africa recently stated that he felt the North American approach to funerals was excessive. He added, "If one of my Zulu friends die, his family will simply lay his body out on the kitchen table and anyone who wishes may come and pay their respects before the burial." There were two points not understood by our South African visitor. First, any North American who wished to have their relative's body laid out on their kitchen table could organize that to happen, but it is unlikely that very many people would find that arrangement desirable. Second, the North American funeral director and funeral home are a distinct vocation and facility arising out of a society that is characterized by specialization. In contrast with other societies, North Americans are more mobile and defined by information, innovation, and technology. Within the economy of time, specialization has become a necessity. When an individual becomes a consumer of funeral services that person normally has little previous experience with death, or the time and motivation to learn. The tendency, like that in any other crisis or problem, is to seek out a specialist.

The biggest single complaint is that funerals are too expensive. Not taken into account in this analysis is the overhead for providing, on a twenty-four-hour-a-day basis, 365 days a year, specially trained people, comfortable and expressly designed buildings, vehicles, equipment, and sundries of a funeral home. Also it is not commonly understood until in consultation with a funeral director, that the consumer has the freedom to choose from a wide range of options and prices for services and merchandise as mandated by government.

> It is of interest here to mention that statistics suggest that people are prepared to pay for a wedding, on the average, twice what they pay for an average funeral, and this without benefit of "wedding insurance." We know of only one published statement condemning the uneconomical behavior of parents at this festive occasion and know of no charges publicly made of exploitation by the dress-making industry, catering industry or Brewer's Association of America in connection with the wedding [7, p. 171].

A familiar charge is that the bereaved consumer of funeral services and merchandise is vulnerable to exploitation due to the influence of their bereavement. The fallacious conclusion is that, since the funeral director has the opportunity to capitalize on the defenseless mourner, he or she will necessarily take advantage of the situation. Every vocation does have the rare bad apples who abuse their influence with clients. They receive extensive bad press, which in turn paints the whole profession with the same brush. Funeral service is no exception.

Statistics show that consumers of funeral services express far less discontentment with the performance of funeral directors than the vocal critics would have everyone believe. In Ontario, Canada, statistics show that following approximately 332,500 deaths during the four-and-a-half-year period of January 1, 1991, to June 30, 1995, the Board of Funeral Services, responsible for licensing and disciplining Ontario funeral homes and funeral directors, received only 193 complaints. Out of all the opportunities for dissatisfaction with funeral service only 0.051 percent of consumers expressed a problem.

Generally speaking, individuals who take on the responsibility of becoming a modern licensed funeral director do so with some conviction that they will be able to make a difference in peoples' grief experience and from that interaction will have a modicum of "job-satisfaction." In response to the frequently asked question, "Why did you become a funeral director?" the general content of the answer is, "Because I wanted to help people" [9, p. 9]. The focus of funeral service is on assisting people to ritualize their loss so that through those rituals they may be better equipped to manage their grief. With the assistance of the funeral director the bereaved are enabled to manage their grief and begin the process of adjusting to life without the deceased.

FUNERAL RITUAL AND BEREAVEMENT MANAGEMENT

Throughout most of history it was believed that the deceased needed the funeral prayers and rituals of the survivors to assist the spirit on its journey to the afterlife. Perhaps it is a remnant from those days, but a persistent misunderstanding about the purpose of funerals is that everything done is for the benefit of the one who died. In fact the opposite is true.

> The overriding function of a funeral is to serve as a rite of passage. Transitions into different states of being are celebrated throughout life in all cultures. Major changes such as birth, puberty, marriage, and death all have rituals to help individuals and society adapt to the changed state and cope with the disequilibrium that occurs during transition [5, p. 179].

The funeral is *about* the person who died, but it is *for* the living.

> *Definition:* Ritual may be understood as an organized, purposeful, time-limited, flexible, group-centred response to the most significant transitions in life.

People do not send flowers, or make charitable donations, for the dead person, but rather for the survivors. People do not visit the dead body, but instead they view the body and visit and support the bereaved. People do not stop what they are doing and interrupt their lives to arrange a funeral for the benefit of the deceased, they do it for themselves. And in the making and implementing of funeral arrangements, the bereaved are in the process of managing their grief.

Funeral activities meet several needs and serve various purposes. They assist the survivors to confirm the reality of a death at a profound level. Viewing the body is perhaps one of the most contentious aspects of modern funerals and it is unique to the last part of the twentieth century. This issue would have been a "non-starter" 100 years ago. People did, and still do, look at the dead body of a loved one because they need and want to. Again, the generally pervasive lack of familiarity with death in modern society has rendered the dead body mysterious and undesirable to some.

A word occasionally misused when describing an individual's revulsion toward viewing the dead body is that the practice is "barbaric." In fact the barbarians did the opposite of civilized people. They simply left the dead bodies of both their comrades and victims where they dropped. Critics of viewing the body postulate that it is an illogical and therefore unnecessary exercise. The implication is that simply being informed of the death is all that any rational person needs to immediately begin adjusting to the loss. It is further implied that primitive and less sophisticated peoples may need to see the body, but not an intelligent person. This position can be directly linked to the denial that is generated by the remoteness of death from the daily lives of the majority of North Americans. Not viewing the body also flies in the face of the fact that humans are at heart "doubting Thomas'," and that "seeing *is* believing." Accepting the reality of a death is not just a function of a logical deduction, it is also more importantly an emotional adjustment demanded of a heart that does not want to be separated.

It is because seeing the dead body is so challenging to our senses that we need to push past the resistance and face the reality. Dr. Alan Wolfelt has coined the phrase that the bereaved need to "lean into their grief" and suggests that "we must remember that through the process of moving toward pain we move toward eventual healing" [9, p. 140]. This is in direct conflict with our society's philosophy of pain avoidance. Yet, viewing the body is irrefutably facing the fact of the death and the repetition of exposure aids the gradual process of emotional acceptance of the truth.

For many people, there is a natural anxiety and resistance to the first viewing of the body. If the last time the person was seen alive they were healthy, it is normal not to want to see the individual dead. Or, if the bereaved witnessed the death, the last image of the deceased may not have been particularly pleasant or flattering. However, funeral directors can cite many examples of how the demeanor of the bereaved has relaxed, even lightened, during their various opportunities to witness the dead body.

> Viewing the body is often quite helpful as it challenges the normal desire to deny the loss while promoting acceptance of the death. Participating in the funeral ritual—standing at a wake and repeatedly looking at the deceased in the casket, attending a funeral service, accepting the condolences of others, witnessing the casket at the grave—graphically illustrates to the bereaved that the death has indeed occurred. Even if it cannot be emotionally accepted at that time, the memories of these experiences will later help to confirm to the bereaved the reality of the loss of the loved one. Viewing the body has been criticized in recent years, as some mourners have wished to avoid the painful reactions that seeing the body can engender. However, it is precisely the impact of the finality of the

loss that viewing seeks to promote. Clearly the body of the deceased is the best symbol of the individual and therefore the most effective one to focus upon in attempting to perceive the deceased in a new relationship, as someone who is no longer alive and will only exist in memory. The custom of viewing the body not only promotes realization of the loss, especially after sudden or accidental death, but also, through proper preparation and restoration of the body, assists in recall of the individual prior to any disfigurement from pain, accident, or violence. This preparation is not designed to make the deceased look alive, but to provide an acceptable image for recollection of the deceased. The presence of the body provides an immediate and proper climate for mourning and is a natural symbol to stimulate discussion and expression of emotion about the deceased [5, pp. 180-181].

From the basis of viewing the body, funerals support the bereaved in confronting denial, the first barrier in grief management and reconciliation.

Recently, a clergy friend moved to the West and wrote to tell me, "The biggest adjustment by far is around the rituals (or lack of them) around death. The lack of visitation means that I don't get to see anybody except the immediate family prior to the funeral. One funeral I performed I found the lack of visitation particularly hard—a fourteen year old killed in a car accident." Death at any age may be a challenge to accept, but a young person's death just goes against the grain of what we expect as summarized in the teaching of a Zen Buddhist story that concludes, "Grandfather die, father die, son die."

Viewing the dead body is not intended to provide enjoyment, but rather acceptance of a painful reality. A father whose sixteen-year-old son was killed on a motorcycle described the agonizing hour that elapsed between first hearing of the accident and finally arriving at the hospital. The attending nurse asked the father if he wanted to see his son's body and without hesitation he went into the emergency room where he lay. I asked him how that was for him and he replied, "I know it sounds strange, but I felt a sense of relief." My theory is that the parent had invested so much emotional energy into denying the truth (i.e., it was all a mistake and someone had borrowed the motorcycle, or someone was wearing his son's coat, or it was the passenger and not his son who was killed) that when he saw the reality of the death, he didn't have to pretend any longer.

A comment frequently ridiculed is, "Doesn't he look good." The obvious negative response is, "How can they say he looks good, he's dead!" Until someone has been at the accident scene or at the bedside while a dying loved one takes their last breath it may be difficult to understand how comforting it is to see the body reposed, free of suffering. The purpose of viewing the body is to facilitate acceptance of the death. A concern I have heard expressed is, "I want to remember her as she was." The implication is that viewing the body will supplant all previous memories. From my own experience I have learned the opposite is true. Until the reality of the death is accepted and any unfinished business is settled, it is difficult, if not impossible, to move into a relationship based on memories. It is literally as if the mind cannot accommodate the transition from a physical relationship to a memory relationship until the emotions have acclimatized to the death.

The funeral process facilitates social validation of the bereavement and expression of the community's concern and consolation. A funeral was described by Howard C. Raether as "An event to which no-one is invited, and everyone is welcome" [10]. Mourning was defined by Alan Wolfelt as "grief gone public" [11]. By having family and friends witness their mourning, the bereaved are at once ratified that they are moving through their grief and also are supported in that journey. The grievers receive validation that their loss is legitimate by attendance of their supporters during visitation and the funeral. The very presence of the supporters attests that the life and the loss of the deceased is important. Through the exchange of tributes and stories during the visiting and funeral service, the bereaved have the opportunity to create a treasure trove of memories. In this way grievers are assisted in the necessary change from a relationship of the physical to a new relationship based on the memory and spirit of the one who has died.

Death frequently jolts the survivors from a sense of predictability in their lives into feeling out of control. The funeral director gently restores some sense of predictability to the bereaved by consulting with them and offering alternatives to create a meaningful structured activity called a funeral. This is contrary to the rote practices of some earlier funeral service providers wherein they provided the setting and accoutrements of a "traditional funeral" and at best hoped the bereaved had a healthy grief experience. Now the dedicated funeral director, skilled in active listening and knowledgeable about grief, although more specialized, is actually closer to the original roots of the profession, as a resource and a consultant. The funeral director walks with the bereaved through an exploration of possibilities for bringing together activities, symbols, people, and rituals that will reflect the life of the deceased. This aids in accurately remembering the deceased which in turn assists in healing and completing the grievers' relationship with the one who died.

By the very nature of our youth-worshipping, technology-driven, materially-oriented society where death is "out of sight and out of mind," most people live as if they always have tomorrow. Death is not there to remind us of our limited time on earth contrary to a North American Native philosophy which is paraphrased, "My own death is my best friend, he walks one step behind me, ready to tap me on the shoulder and remind me to do what is important today." With little evidence of "the shortness and uncertainty of human life" it is very easy to put off until tomorrow what we are uncomfortable with doing today. As a result, when a death occurs it often leaves the survivors with unfinished business. And unfinished business can be a major obstacle to reconciling a death.

When an individual dies, no matter how prepared we feel we are, it interrupts our relationship with that person. The death is similar to someone walking out of the room while you are talking, leaving you in mid-sentence and feeling incomplete. Having unfinished business is like an unfinished conversation in that it is hard to say goodbye to someone when you are not finished speaking with them.

When in consultation with a bereaved person or family, whether before, during, or after a funeral, I introduce them to the concept of unfinished business and encourage them to explore their own unfinished business with the deceased with the following suggestions.

On a blank piece of paper write the titles *Amendments*, *Forgiveness*, and *Other Significant Statements*, i.e.:
Amendments (then write below it)
—"I'm sorry for . . ." (and fill in whatever comes to mind and repeat it)
—"I'm sorry for . . ." (do it again and again until nothing comes out)
Forgiveness (then write below it)
—"I'm angry about . . . (fill it in, but add at the end) . . . and I forgive you."
—"I was hurt when . . . . . . and I forgive you." (repeat it until nothing comes to mind)
Other Significant Statements (then write whatever else is important to say)
—"I love you" or "Thanks for . . . " are frequently sentiments that are left unexpressed

When you have completed the list above, try saying out loud, "Goodbye _____." If you can say goodbye you know you have completed your unfinished business, for now. If not, perhaps you have not been honest with yourself. You may find it useful to repeat this exercise at a later date. I read the entire list out loud at my father's grave, five years after his death, and the relief I felt was incredible. A problem experienced by some people is that they mistakenly believe that the dead (or non-present person) has to physically hear the amendments, forgiveness or other important statements in order to make the resolution of unfinished business complete. We only have control over the change that occurs inside us when we clean up our unfinished business and it is our own quality of life that is improved by this effort [12, pp. 128-129].

The funeral process offers several opportunities for the bereaved to recall and release unstated feelings toward the deceased. At the moment when realization strikes that the person is dead, there is a window of opportunity to express thoughts or "get things off your chest." If this opening is not seized it will delay the griever's ability to achieve some level of closure with the physical relationship that has ended. In the future there will be fewer and fewer moments that will facilitate expression of the unfinished business. The consequence may be that the unfinished business will be carried forever by the mourner. Standing by the casket and talking to the body or thinking the things that went unsaid; writing a letter of unexpressed sentiments and placing it in the casket; telling another person the things that were left unsaid; reading a letter or a poem during the funeral that says what needed to be said; all of these are methods for dealing with unfinished business.

For the mourners and their supporters who hold established religious beliefs the funeral service offers reiteration of those articles of faith which espouse the tenet of an afterlife and a loving God. The setting of the church, with predictable words and familiar procedures, can provide a comfort for those raised in, or practicing, that religion. If a funeral service is going to provide some assistance to each mourner in their grief management there are three basic components which stand out as meeting the needs of the majority: the religious or spiritual; the memory of the deceased; and some grief information. In addition to providing hope of an afterlife and reassurance of a loving God, the funeral should help the mourners remember the deceased accurately and there should be some provision of relevant grief education. Even for those not familiar with the traditions of the officiating clergy, if the service is not treated exclusively as an opportunity to win new converts, the message delivered to the bereaved can be therapeutic and hold some comfort for everyone.

For agnostic or atheistic mourners a humanistic style of service can also fulfill the three components of a comprehensive funeral. From a secular point of view there are many writings and songs that celebrate life. A spiritual point of view can avoid religious doctrine and still support a conviction that life is good and that death is a part of the circle of life. The balance of the service can contain eulogies and activities that are reminiscent of the person who died and the speaker(s) can share their own learning about grief for the benefit of those in attendance.

One funeral director related the example of clients arranging a funeral for a man who had died. They said they didn't believe in funerals and didn't put any stock in rituals. They only wanted to carry the man in a simple casket out to the cemetery and lower his body into the grave. When that was done one of the party played a mariner's chant on a penny whistle, after which they passed around a bottle of Chivas Regal with each participant taking a swig. Then they poured the balance of the bottle over the casket. When they were done filling in the grave, they returned to a house where they shared a second bottle and told reminiscences of the deceased's life. Even in the simple activities surrounding that burial were some of the therapeutic benefits of the ritual known as a funeral.

Tears are not generally an accepted part of social interaction in North America. The setting of a funeral is an exception in that tears are expected, even encouraged. During the funeral one of the most forceful stimuli to elicit tears is the closing of the casket. This activity profoundly emphasizes how the relationship of the bereaved is in transition from a physical association to a memory or a spiritual orientation with the deceased. This is an activity that families can, and should, be invited to participate in, or at least witness, because it gives them another option for control and gives a tangible reality to the finality of the moment. When the casket is not open or even present at a funeral the bereaved are deprived of one more powerful opportunity to express their emotions. Without the physical reality of death in the room there is no focus to the funeral and the event can assume an air of unreality.

The "rugged individualism" of North America referred to earlier serves as an impairment not just to healthy grieving, but to general emotional health. Rugged individualism has been used to describe an attitude of unfaltering strength and machismo where tears and other expressions of emotions have no place. The attitude of "rugged individualism" has created what Alan Wolfelt described as a "grief-denying society" [11]. This translates into a general ignorance and intolerance of grief characterized by such harmful phrases as, "Big boys don't cry." "Pull yourself up by the bootstraps." "You are only feeling sorry for yourself." "Don't you think you have grieved long enough?"

North America in the early years of rugged individualists was literally a place where "when the going got tough, the tough got going." Certainly, there was very limited time to build homes, harvest crops, gather firewood, and other necessities of survival in the developing years of North American settlement by Europeans. Time taken for the rituals and activities surrounding death and grieving was a precious commodity. However, in those early years time was taken to deal with a death when the event occurred.

By contrast there has recently been a steady increase in grieving people choosing to immediately dispose of the body and plan a memorial service for some later date. On the surface this seems like a normal choice to accommodate the hectic and highly mobile life styles we lead. However, a death is not like a wedding that can be planned a year in advance. Death, even anticipated death, severs a physical relationship and so necessarily interrupts the lives of the survivors. If a death is the emotional equivalent of a physical amputation then the time to treat the wound is immediately. Any delay in appropriate treatment may result in emotional scar tissue.

After cremation there is a common request that the cremated remains be scattered. It seems that scattering appeals to a romantic notion of either spreading the ashes to the four winds or placing them in some location of significance. Often this action is prompted by a preference stated by the deceased. In Ontario, Canada, it is against the law to place any human remains in a place other than a licensed cemetery. I have had the feed-back following scattering that the experience was unsatisfactory for the survivors. There is no place marking the deceased's life. Burial of the body or the cremated remains in a cemetery grave or niche provides some focus as a "long-term grief recovery location." The crowds of mourners who daily attend the Vietnam Memorial in Washington are testimony to the value of a specific place where the bereaved can think, pray, talk, and celebrate the life. There is also the value of a sense of history or roots that is satisfied by a marked resting place, not only in the short-term, but also in the decades to come.

One factor that has a direct influence on the increasing tendency to disavow the benefits of a viewing and visiting period, a funeral and a committal service is the common experience of extended periods of illness. Medical, surgical, and pharmaceutical advances have not only sustained life but also prolonged infirmity and dying well beyond what humans could have expected fifty years ago. For the family and friends of someone suffering a terminal illness the protracted threat of death enacts a form of torture. Although it seems rare for families to fully embrace the reality of an imminent death and the opportunity it presents for grief work, people do experience some degree of anticipatory grief. The obstacle this presents is that anticipatory grief is just that, grieving in anticipation of a loss. It is only when the physical death occurs that full grieving begins. However, feeling that they have already "suffered enough" there can be an inclination to discount the values of a funeral to mark the beginning of the grieving process.

BEFORE DEATH–PREARRANGED FUNERALS

When families know that a loved one is dying they can benefit from taking counsel from a funeral director in advance of the death. This is also true for the terminally ill person. By taking the time to prearrange and/or prepay a funeral the individuals involved are afforded some sense of control during the frustrating experience of watching someone die. At the same time, information about anticipatory grief and palliative care can often be obtained from the funeral director. Armed with some knowledge about grief, people can take a proactive approach to the last days of their relationship with someone. It is a demonstration of overcoming denial to prearrange a funeral for a loved one in anticipation of their death.

Making funeral arrangements in advance of death is slowly being recognized as a pragmatic thing for everyone to do. The superstition of avoiding talk of funerals from fear of hastening death has no more grounds than believing that having a current will or adequate life insurance would cause an early demise. The activity of gathering data and setting down some parameters for one's own funeral can be a selfless act and a gift of love to the survivors. Indicating preferences while leaving room for decision making by the bereaved at the time of the death can help restore some sense of control, the only proviso being that inflexible over-planning should be avoided.

One of the most frustrating interviews a funeral director encounters is the situation when the deceased had mentioned some view or desire for their funeral which the survivors feel bound to follow through, regardless of their own needs and feelings. Most frequently the deceased has either minimized the impact of their life and death on their survivors or he/she has been unaware of the importance of funeral ritual to healthy grieving. Consequently, the funeral director has the delicate responsibility of helping the bereaved balance a sense of obligation to the deceased with an awareness of how to meet their own needs. Although it may be unintentional, in this case the deceased can appear self-centered in allowing their vanity to override consideration of the survivors. By dictating, for example, that no one should view their dead body, or any other restrictions on the survivors, the one who died contributes to their family's sense of disempowerment. In very real terms, the deceased will not benefit from the prearranged funeral except to know they have lightened the burden of sorrow for their loved ones. So the potential survivors should be included in any discussion or consultation about the funeral.

CHILDREN AND FUNERALS

It is a direct function of the last part of the twentieth century that the question has been raised as to whether or not children should be part of the funeral process. Before the turn of the century children were as naturally a part of a family funeral as they were part of any other significant family function. Children have become "forgotten mourners." As people, albeit young people, if they have invested love into the person who died they will need to grieve in their own way just as much as adults.

The popular North American view is to exclude children from the rituals of mourning. The belief is that children don't understand death and they will only be traumatized by seeing the dead body and the grief of significant adults. On the contrary, children do grieve and need the reality of the funeral process and the support of family and friends, similar to adults. As well, children will either learn about handling death and grieving from their significant adults or they will derive this information from the media and fill in the gaps with their own imagination.

Dr. Charles Corr, at a King's College conference on children and death, suggested that children need reassurance on three questions: Did I cause it? Will I catch it? Who will take care of me? At the same conference, social worker Bunty Anderson countered several rationalizations often used by adults: "I was never allowed to attend a funeral when I was a child." "And what was it like for you?" Anderson suggests such parents be asked. Some adults are still resentful that they weren't allowed to attend funerals as children, and others developed a great fear of funerals. "They are too young for all that sadness." Anderson's response is that sadness is better than the anxiety of the unknown. "Kids are too young to understand." Her admonition is that the emotional tone in the house is never lost on children. She went on to recommend that fairy tales like "Grandmother with shiny wings," untruths such as "Mother has gone on a long journey," and euphemisms similar to "He went to sleep and never woke up," should all be avoided.

Dr. Earl Grollman has advised that parents explain what the funeral is, what they will see and hear, and why it is being done. "Just as your children cannot be spared knowledge about death, they cannot and should not be excluded from the grief and mourning following a death. They too have both a right and a need to say goodbye" [13, p. 56]. His concern for children is that their parents will prejudice the child's decision to attend a funeral by conveying their own fears or asking a loaded question such as, "You don't want to go to the funeral do you?"

Another aspect of a funeral home that should be investigated is what their policy is toward children and funeral education. What resources and facilities do they have to accommodate children's needs to play and draw and talk and read. Many funeral homes are recognizing that children should be encouraged to attend and participate in the funeral process as part of the whole family.

> The appropriate time to talk about death is when it is part of the child's experience. The proper mood is one of openness and honesty. The important consideration for the adult is that the child's feelings and experiences are quite different from his own and have to be judged accordingly. Then he can share life as far as it can be shared in understanding, and find answers that can be built on as understanding grows. The important relationships that give security to life and love will be protected then, even in times of emotional stress and painful events [14, pp. 32-33].

The death of a significant person, or animal, is an event in a child's life that could be called a "teachable moment." The crisis offers an opportunity that parents and other important adults can build on for a child with the information and resources of the funeral director.

AFTER THE FUNERAL

A facet of modern funeral service, as with hospitals and hospice, that was previously unheard of is the concept of follow-up programs or aftercare services. In the past the common endpoint for the funeral director's services was the conclusion of the graveside or committal service, consolidated only by the payment for the funeral. Knowing that modern life does not offer the same informal support network of former days and that people are generally ill-equipped to understand and optimally work with their grief, funeral directors have responded. The practice of offering assistance after the funeral is completely in line with the concept of funeral homes functioning as resources in the service of grief management.

A visit from the funeral director ostensibly to assist the family in completion of forms and applications can evolve into sitting in counsel with the bereaved. Follow-up services can also take the form of any or all of the following: a questionnaire; a lending library of grief books; newsletters or other support communications; grief support groups; memorial planting of trees; lectures by authorities on the subject of healthy grieving; holidays and grief seminars and services. The existence of some form of after funeral attention can be interpreted as a commitment on the part of the funeral home to genuinely care for and serve the bereaved in their grief journey.

CONCLUSION

Funeral observances have been part of humanity's response to life, death, and loss since the first primitive rituals of our ancestors. North American funeral practices and practitioners have evolved, and will continue to develop, in response to our needs and life styles. Funeral directors have not created the value of funeral rituals, but are involved with the bereaved in creating funeral rituals of value. "Most persons who notify the funeral director of a death and ask him to be of service are in essence saying, 'I have a problem; what should I do?' " [15, p. xvi]. It is in the best interest of the consumer of funeral services to view the funeral director as a consultant in the area of funeral ritual and grief management. From this proactive perspective the bereaved can use the funeral director as a resource to ritualize, and eventually reconcile, the transition that occurs following a loved one's death.

However, there is a "segment of funeral directors who firmly believe that 'funeral directors are not and should not be counsellors' " [16, p. 4]. This group of funeral directors confuse the role of a "counsellor" with the work of a "therapist" and do not wish to stray into this form of human relationship.

Dr. Jackson, the noted psychologist, says, "Funeral directors do not choose as to *whether* or not they will be counsellors. Their only choice is—will they be a good or bad counsellor." He goes on to explain that by the very nature of the caretaking and caregiving services inherent in the duties and responsibilities of a funeral director he assumes the role of counselor not by choice but by his advice, direction, and practice [15, p. 1].

In consideration of the North American public's general lack of knowledge and understanding about death, loss, funerals, and bereavement, Dr. Jackson's statement might also be paraphrased, "Funeral directors do not choose as to *whether* or not they will be *grief educators*." Information about the grief process and how rituals can meet some of the needs of the bereaved need to be disseminated by funeral directors in their role as a resource to grief management.

Since loss and bereavement are irrevocable facets of our human existence it behooves everyone to become an expert, at least in the subject of their own bereavement. As we also will likely find ourselves directly involved in the decision making following another's death it is equally necessary to be an informed consumer of funeral services. All funeral homes and funeral directors are not created equally. It is also true that you do in fact get what you pay for. Taking the time to know local funeral homes and their service philosophy will be a wise investment in demystifying and defusing the emotional impact of a future loss.

The concept of the funeral process and the funeral director assisting the living in the management of their grief is not widely understood or accepted. Everything connected with funerals is still generally associated with death, or the spirit of one who has died, or the dead body and it's final disposition. As knowledge and understanding continue to develop regarding the emotional upheaval of bereavement, the purpose and process of mourning, and the impact of unresolved grief on the individual and society, so to are the true value of the funeral and the contribution of the funeral director being realized.

Through the shock, pain, disorientation and adjustments of loss, the funeral process, by virtue of it's existence, confirms for everyone in attendance the conviction that the deceased's life held value.

> It is important for us to realize that the rites and rituals that we use to mark the end of life are our efforts to say a significant and appropriate "Good-bye." We don't just dispose quickly of the bodies of those we love as if they were worthless. Some remnants of our love are still attached to them, whether we want to admit it or not. We cannot treat what we have loved without loving care without doing damage to all of the other loving relationships in life [14, p. 32].

By the celebration of an individual's life the funeral reinforces the significance of everyone's life and further confirms that although we may well feel pain if we lose someone we love, the life and the love are worth that pain.

Recognizing and accessing the resources of a funeral director is an effective action for the bereaved to augment their knowledge and ability to ritualize and manage their own grief. In order for funeral homes to better serve the bereaved it is necessary for funeral directors to expand their concept of both the funeral director's role and the definition of funeral ritual. Then, as they companion the bereaved in their crisis and assist in the ritualization of their loss, funeral directors can optimize the rare privilege and opportunity to facilitate an appreciation of the deceased's life, the mourners' own lives, and the wonder of life itself.

REFERENCES

1. T. W. Van Beck, *Ethics Handbook for Funeral Service Practitioners,* The Loewen Group, Covington, Kentucky, 1993.
2. Funeral Rites and Customs, Microsoft®, *Incarta*©, 1993, Microsoft Corporation, Copyright, Funk and Wagnall Corporation, 1993.

3. C. G. Strub and L. G. Frederick, History, in *The Principles and Practices of Embalming* (5th Edition), Professional Training Schools, Inc., and Robertine Frederick, 4722 Bronze Way, Dallas, Texas 75236, 1989.
4. *Holy Bible, New International Version,* International Bible Society, Zondervan Publishing House, 1984.
5. T. A. Rando, Funerals and Funerary Rituals, in *Grief, Dying and Death: Clinical Interventions for Caregivers,* Research Press Company, Champain, Illinois, 1984.
6. J. Mitford, *The American Way of Death,* Simon & Schuster, New York, 1963.
7. V. R. Pine, Comparative Funeral Practices, *Practical Anthropology, 16,* pp. 49-62, 1969.
8. R. Fulton, The Sacred and the Secular: Attitudes of the American Public Toward Death, Funerals, and Funeral Directors, in *Death and Identity* (Rev. Edition), R. Fulton (ed.), The Charles Press, Bowie, Maryland, 1976 (b).
9. A. D. Wolfelt, Acknowledging the Need for Interpersonal Skills in the Funeral Home, in *Interpersonal Skills Training: A Handbook for Funeral Home Staff,* Accelerated Development, Inc., Publishers, Muncie, Indiana, 1990.
10. H. C. Raether, personal communication.
11. A. Wolfelt, personal communication.
12. R. J. Paul et al., The Six C's of Christmas and Grief, in *Personal Care in an Impersonal World,* John D. Morgan (ed.), Baywood Publishing, Amityville, New York, 1993.
13. E. A. Grollman, A Parent's Guide for Explaining Death to your Child, in *Talking About Death: A Dialogue Between Parent and Child,* Beacon Press, Boston, 1976.
14. E. N. Jackson, When to Talk About Death, in *Telling a Child About Death,* Channel Press, New York, 1966.
15. H. C. Raether and R. C. Slater, About this Book, in *The Funeral Director and His Role as Counsellor,* National Funeral Directors Association, Milwaukee, 1975.
16. A. D. Wolfelt, Why This Book? in *Interpersonal Skills Training: A Handbook for Funeral Home Staff,* Accelerated Development, Inc., Publishers, Muncie, Indiana, 1990.

CHAPTER 18
Disenfranchised Grief: An Exposition and Update*

Kenneth J. Doka

INTRODUCTION

Ever since the publication of Lindemann's classic article, "Symptomatology and Management of Acute Grief" [1], the literature on the nature of grief and bereavement has been growing. In a few decades following this seminal study, there have been comprehensive studies of grief reactions [2], detailed descriptions of atypical manifestations of grief [3] theoretical and clinical treatments of grief reactions [4, 5], and considerable research considering the myriad variables that affect grief [6, 7]. But most of this literature has concentrated on grief reactions in socially recognized and sanctioned roles: those of the parent, spouse, or child.

There are circumstances, however, in which a person experiences a sense of loss but does not have a socially recognized right, role, or capacity to grieve. In these cases, the grief is disenfranchised. The person suffers a loss but has little or no opportunity to mourn publicly.

Up until now, there has been little research touching directly on the phenomenon of disenfranchised grief. In her comprehensive review of grief reactions, Raphael notes the phenomenon:

> There may be other dyadic partnership relationships in adult life that show patterns similar to the conjugal ones, among them, the young couple intensely, even secretly, in love; the de facto relationships; the extra-marital relationship; and the homosexual couple . . . less intimate partnerships of close friends, working mates, and business associates, may have similar patterns of grief and mourning [6, p. 227].

---

*Much of the material used in this chapter is drawn from an earlier exposition of disenfranchised grief [1].

Focusing on the issues, reactions, and problems in particular populations, a number of studies have noted special difficulties that these populations have grieving. For example, Kelly [8] and Kimmel [9, 10], in studies of aging homosexuals, have discussed the unique problems of grief in such relationships. Similarly, studies of the reactions of significant others of AIDS victims have considered bereavement [11, 12]. Other studies have considered the special problems of acknowledged grief in prenatal death [13, 14], Peppers and Knapp [15], Kennell, Slyter, and Klaus [16], Helmrath and Steinitz [17], ex-spouses [18, 19], therapists' reactions to a client's suicide, and pet loss. Finally, studies of families of Alzheimer's victims [20] and mentally retarded adults [21-23] also have noted distinct difficulties of these populations in encountering varied losses which are often unrecognized by others.

Others have tried to draw parallels between related unacknowledged losses. For example, in a personal account, Horn compared her loss of a heterosexual lover with a friend's loss of a homosexual partner [24]. Doka discussed the particular problems of loss in nontraditional relationships, such as extramarital affairs, homosexual relationships, and cohabiting couples [25].

This chapter attempts to integrate the literature on such losses in order to explore the phenomenon of disenfranchised grief. It will consider both the nature of disenfranchised grief and its central paradoxical problem: the very nature of this type of grief exacerbates the problems of grief, but the usual sources of support may not be available for helpful.

THE NATURE OF DISENFRANCHISED GRIEF

Disenfranchised grief can be defined as the grief that persons experience when they incur a loss that is not or cannot be openly acknowledged, publicly mourned, or socially supported. The concept of disenfranchised grief recognizes that societies have sets of norms—in effect, "grieving rules"—that attempt to specify who, when, where, how, how long, and for whom people should grieve. These grieving rules may be codified in personal policies. For example, a worker may be allowed a week off for the death of a spouse or child, three days for the loss of a parent or sibling. Such policies reflect the fact that each society defines who has a legitimate right to grieve, and these definitions of right correspond to relationships, primarily familial, that are socially recognized and sanctioned. In any given society these grieving rules may not correspond to the nature of attachments, the sense of loss, or the feelings of survivors. Hence the grief of these survivors is disenfranchised. In our society, this may occur for four reasons.

1. The Relationship Is Not Recognized

In our society, most attention is placed on kin-based relationships and roles. Grief may be disenfranchised in those situations in which the relationship between the bereaved and deceased is not based on recognizable kin ties. Here the closeness of other non-kin relationships may simply not be understood or appreciated. For example, Folta and Deck noted, while all of these studies tell us that grief is a normal phenomenon, the intensity of which corresponds to the closeness of the relationship, they fail to take this (i.e., friendship) into account. The underlying assumption is that closeness of relationship exists only among spouses and/or immediate kin [26, p. 239].

The roles of lovers, friends, neighbors, foster parents, colleagues, in-laws, stepparents and stepchildren, caregivers, counselors, co-workers, and roommates (for example, in nursing homes) may be long-lasting and intensely interactive, but even though these relationships are recognized, mourners may not have full opportunity to publicly grieve a loss. At most, they might be expected to support and assist family members.

Then there are relationships that may not be publicly recognized or socially sanctioned. For example, nontraditional relationships, such as extra-marital affairs, cohabitation, and homosexual relationships have tenuous public acceptance and limited legal standing, and they face negative sanction by grief when the relationship is terminated by the death of the partner, but others in their world, such as children, may also experience a grief that cannot be acknowledged or socially supported.

Even those whose relationships existed primarily in the past may experience grief. Ex-spouses, past lovers, or former friends may have limited contact or they may even engage in interaction in the present. Yet the death of that significant other can still cause a grief reaction because it brings finality to that earlier loss, ending any remaining contact or fantasy of reconciliation or reinvolvement. And again these grief feelings may be shared by others in their world such as parents and children. They too may mourn the loss of "what once was" and "what might have been." For example, in one case a twelve-year-old child of an unwed mother, never even acknowledged or seen by the father, still mourned the death of his father since it ended any possibility of a future liaison. But though loss is experienced, society as a whole may not perceive that the loss of a past relationship could or should cause any reaction.

Nor does there have to be any actual contact to experience a loss. For example, many individuals can become quite committed and attached to varied celebrities. Even though they never meet that person, they may be profoundly affected by their death. The public displays of mourning for such diverse individuals as John F. Kennedy, Elvis Presley, or Jerry Garcia, to name but a few, illustrate the intense private grief that individuals may experience.

2. The Loss Is Not Recognized

In other cases, the loss itself is not socially defined as significant. Perinatal deaths lead to strong grief reactions yet research indicates that others still perceive the loss to be relatively minor [6]. Abortion too can constitute a serious loss [27], but the abortion can take place without the knowledge or sanctions of others, or even the recognition that a loss has occurred. It may very well be that the very ideologies of the abortion controversy can put the bereaved in a difficult position. Many who affirm a loss may not sanction the act of abortion, while some who sanction the act may minimize any sense of loss. Similarly, we are just becoming aware of the sense of loss that people experience in giving children up for adoption or foster care [6], and we have yet to be aware of the loss-related implications of surrogate motherhood.

Another loss that may not be perceived as significant is the loss of a pet. Nevertheless, the research shows strong ties between pets and humans, and profound reactions to loss [20].

Then there are cases in which the reality of the loss itself is not socially acknowledged. Thanatologists have long recognized that significant losses can occur even when the object of the loss remains physically alive. Sudnow, for example, discusses "social death," in which the person is alive but treated as if dead [28]. Examples may include those who are institutionalized or comatose. Similarly, "psychological death" has been defined as conditions in which the person lacks a consciousness of existence [29], such as someone who is "brain dead." One can also speak of "psychosocial death" in which the persona of someone has changed so significantly, through mental illness, organic brain syndromes, or even personal transformation (as through addiction, conversion, and so forth), that significant others perceive the person as he or she previously existed as dead [25]. In all of these cases, spouses and others may experience a profound sense of loss, yet that loss cannot be publicly acknowledged for the person is still biologically alive.

3. The Griever Is Not Recognized

There are institutions in which the characteristics of the bereaved in fact disenfranchise their grief; therefore, there is little or no social recognition of his or her sense of loss or need to mourn. Despite evidence to the contrary, both the very old and the very young are typically perceived by others as having little comprehension of or reaction to the death of a significant other. Often, then, both young children and aged adults are excluded from both discussions and rituals [6].

Similarily, mentally disabled persons may also be disenfranchised in grief. Though studies affirm that the mentally retarded are able to understand the concept of death [21] and, in fact, experience grief [23] these reactions may not be perceived by others. Because the person is retarded or otherwise mentally disabled, others in the family may ignore his or her need to grieve. Here a teacher of the mentally disabled describes two illustrative incidences:

> In the first situation, Susie was seventeen years old and away at summer camp when her father died. The family felt she wouldn't understand and that it would be better for her not to come home for the funeral. In the other situation, Francine was with her mother when she got sick. The mother was taken away by ambulance. Nobody answered her questions or told her what happened. "After all," they responded "she's retarded" [30].

In some cases, the way that an individual grieves may not be acknowledged or recognized by others. Doka and Martin suggest, for example, that there is a masculine pattern of grief [31]. They also suggest that many persons may invalidate or disenfranchise that style of grieving.

4. The Death Is Disenfranchising

There are also cases in which the circumstances of the death create such shame and embarrassment that even those in recognized roles (such as spouse, child, or parent) may be reluctant to avail themselves of social support or may feel a sense of social reproach over the circumstances of death. Death from a disease such as AIDS or from suicide or other self-destructive causes (e.g., drunk driving, drug overdose, etc.), or even in certain situations of homicide may all be illustrations of disenfranchising deaths. Each of these circumstances may carry a stigma that inhibits survivors from seeking or receiving social support.

These contexts are not exclusive. In some cases grief may be disenfranchised for a number of reasons. For example, a foster parent who cares for an HIV-positive child that later dies may fit into three categories. Their role as a foster parent may not be recognized. Others may think that in agreeing to care for a child with a life-threatening illness they understand and anticipate the death, thereby minimizing the loss. And foster parents may be reluctant, given the stigma of AIDS, to share with others their experience of loss.

Nor are these descriptions exhaustive. They are merely illustrations of the kinds of losses that may be disenfranchised. Since the publication of Doka's *Disenfranchised Grief* [32], in many different situations including adult children of dysfunctional families [33] and adolescent romantic relationships [34].

THE SPECIAL PROBLEMS OF DISENFRANCHISED GRIEF

Though each of the types of grief mentioned earlier may create particular difficulties and different reactions, one can legitimately speak of the special problem shared in disenfranchised grief.

Disenfranchised grief may exacerbate the problem of bereavement in a number of ways. First, the situations mentioned tend to intensify emotional reactions. Many emotions are associated with normal grief. Bereaved persons frequently are associated with normal grief. Bereaved persons frequently experience feelings of anger, guilt, sadness and depression, loneliness, hopelessness, and numbness [1, 5]. These emotional reactions can be complicated when grief is disenfranchised. Although each of the situations described is in its own way unique, the literature uniformly reports how each of these disenfranchising circumstances can intensify feeling of anger, guilt, or powerlessness [8, 12, 15, 18, 35, 36].

Second, both ambivalent relationships and concurrent crises have been identified in the literature as conditions that complicate grief [5-7]. The conditions can often exist in many types of disenfranchised grief. For example, studies have indicated the ambivalence that can exist in cases of abortion [27], among ex-spouses [18, 19], significant others in nontraditional roles [24, 25], and among families of Alzheimer's disease victims [35]. Similarly, the literature documents the many kinds of concurrent crises that can trouble the disenfranchised griever. For example, in cases of cohabiting couples, either heterosexual or homosexual, studies have often found that survivors experience legal and financial problems regarding inheritance, ownership, credit, or leases [9, 10, 24, 25]. Likewise, the death of a parent may leave a mentally disabled person not only bereaved but also bereft of a viable support system [23].

Although grief is complicated, many of the factors that facilitate mourning are not present. The bereaved may be excluded from an active role in caring for the dying. Funeral rituals, normally helpful in resolving grief, may not help here. In other cases they may have no role in planning those rituals or in deciding whether even to have them. Or in cases of divorce, separation, or psychosocial death, rituals may be lacking altogether.

In addition, the very nature of the disenfranchised grief precludes social support. Often there is no recognized role in which mourners can assert the right to mourn and thus receive such support. Grief may have to remain private. Though they may have experienced an intense loss, they may not be given time off from work, have the opportunity to verbalize the loss, or receive the expressions of sympathy and support characteristic in a death. Even traditional sources of solace, such as religion, are unavailable to those whose relationships (for example, extramarital, cohabiting, homosexual, divorced) or acts (such as abortion) are condemned within that tradition.

Naturally, there are many variables that will affect both the intensity of the reaction and the availability of support. All the variables—interpersonal, psychological, social, physiological—that normally influence grief will have an impact here as well. And while there are problems common to cases of disenfranchised grief, each relationship has to be individually considered in light of the unique combinations of factors that may facilitate or impair grief resolution.

Implications

Despite the shortage of research on and attention given to the issue of disenfranchised grief, it remains a significant issue. Millions of Americans are involved in losses in which grief is effectively disenfranchised. For example, there are more than one million couples presently cohabiting [37]. There are estimates that 3 percent of males and 2 to 3 percent of females are exclusively homosexual, with similar percentages having mixed homosexual and heterosexual encounters [38]. There are about a million abortions a year; even though many of the women involved may not experience grief reactions, some are clearly "at risk."

Disenfranchised grief is also a growing issue. There are higher percentages of divorced people in the cohorts now aging. The AIDS crisis means that more homosexuals will experience losses in significant relationships. Even as the disease spreads within the population of intravenous drug users, it is likely to create a new class of both potential victims and disenfranchised grievers among the victims' informal liaisons and nontraditional relationships. And as Americans continue to live longer, more will suffer from severe forms of chronic brain dysfunctions [39]. As the developmentally disabled live longer, they too will experience the grief of parental and sibling loss. In short, the proportions will rise rapidly in the future.

It is likely that bereavement counselors will have increased exposure to cases of disenfranchised grief. In fact, the very nature of disenfranchised grief and the unavailability of informal support make it likely that those who experience such loss will seek formal supports. Thus there is a pressing need for research that will describe the particular and unique reactions of each of the different types of losses; compare reactions and problems associated with these losses; describe the important variables affecting disenfranchised grief reactions;[1] assess possible interventions; and discover the complicated grief reactions, such as masked or delayed grief that might be manifested in such cases. Also needed is education sensitizing students to the many kinds of relationships and subsequent losses that people can experience.

Kammerman reminds that there are complex costs to enfranchising the disenfranchised griever [40]. Some are economic. Liberalizing bereavement-leave policies for non-family losses have both economic cost to companies and are difficult to monitor and enforce (e.g., what is a casual acquaintance compared to a good friend? etc.) He also suggests that the needs of family mourners may be lost in the countervailing claims of others who demand their right to grieve.

Yet the work of disenfranchised grief expresses simple truths. Human beings have a great capacity to attach—to a wide variety of others, in our past or present, to people we do not even know, even across species. And when there is a loss to that attachment, we grieve.

REFERENCES

1. E. Lindemann, Symptomology and Management of Acute Grief, *American Journal of Psychiatry, 101,* pp. 141-49, 1944.
2. I. Glick, R. Weiss, and C. M. Parkes, *The First Years of Bereavement,* Wiley, New York, 1974.
3. V. Volkan, Typical Findings in Pathological Grief, *Psychiatric Quarterly, 4,* pp. 231-250, 1970.
4. J. Bowlby, *Attachment and Loss: Loss, Sadness and Depression,* Vol. 3, Basic Books, New York, 1980.
5. W. Worden, *Grief Counselling and Grief Therapy,* Springer, New York, 1982.
6. B. Raphael, *The Anatomy of Bereavement,* Basic Books, New York, 1983.
7. T. Rando, *Grief, Dying and Death: Clinical Interventions for Caregivers,* Research Park, Champaign, Illinois, 1984.
8. J. Kelly, The Aging Male Homosexual: Myth and Reality, *The Gerontologist, 17,* pp. 328-332, 1984.
9. D. Kimmel, Adult Development and Aging: A Gay Perspective, *Journal of Social Issues, 34,* pp. 113-131, 1978.

---

[1] As has been stated, some of these variables will be common to all losses. Others, such as the degree to which a loss is socially recognized, publicly sanctioned, openly acknowledged, or replaceable, may be unique to certain types of disenfranchised grief.

10. D. Kimmel, Life History Interview of Aging Gay Men, *International Journal of Aging and Human Development, 10,* pp. 237-248, 1979.
11. A. Heinemann et al., *A Social Service Program for AIDS Clients,* paper presented to the Sixth Annual Meeting of the Forum for Death Education, October 1983.
12. S. Geis, R. Fuller, and J. Rush, Lovers of AIDS Victims: Psychosocial Stresses and Counselling Needs, *Death Studies, 10,* pp. 43-54, 1986.
13. R. J. Corney and F. T. Horton, Pathological Grief Following Spontaneous Abortion, *American Journal of Psychiatry, 131,* pp. 825-827, 1974.
14. J. Wolff, P. Nielsen, and P. Schiller, The Emotional Reaction to a Stillbirth, *American Journal of Obstetrics and Gynaecology, 101,* pp. 73-76, 1970.
15. L. Peppers and R. Knapp, *Motherhood and Mourning,* Praeger, New York, 1980.
16. J. Kennell, M. Slyter, and M. Klaus, The Mourning Response of Parents to the Death of a Newborn Infant, *New England Journal of Medicine, 283,* pp. 344-349, 1970.
17. T. A. Helmrath and G. M. Steinitz, Parental Grieving and the Failure of Social Support, *Journal of Family Practice, 6,* pp. 785-790, 1978.
18. K. Doka, Loss upon Loss: Death After Divorce, *Death Studies, 10,* pp. 441-449, 1986.
19. S. Scott, *Grief Reactions to the Death of a Divorced Spouse,* paper presented to the Seventh Annual Meeting of the Forum for Death Education and Counselling, Philadelphia, April 1985.
20. W. J. Kay et al. (eds.), *Pet Loss and Human Bereavement,* Arno Press, New York, 1984.
21. P. S. Lipe-Goodson and B. I. Goebel, Perception of Age and Death in Mentally Retarded Adults, *Mental Retardation, 21,* pp. 68-75, 1983.
22. R. Blyman, C. Green, J. Rowe, C. Mikkelson, and L. Ataide, Issues Concerning Parents after the Death of their Newborn, *Critical Care Medicine, 8,* pp. 215-218, 1980.
23. R. B. Edgerton, M. Bollinger, and B. Herr, The Cloak of Competence: After Two Decades, *American Journal of Mental Deficiency, 88,* pp. 345-351, 1984.
24. R. Horn, Life Can be a Soap Opera, in *Perspectives on Bereavement,* I. Gerber et al. (eds.), Arno Press, New York, 1979.
25. K. Doka, Silent Sorrow: Grief and the Loss of Significant Others, *Death Studies, 11,* pp. 455-469, 1987.
26. J. Folta and G. Deck, Grief, the Funeral and the Friend, in *Acute Grief and the Funeral,* V. Pine et al. (eds.), Springfield, Illinois, 1976.
27. B. Raphael, Psychosocial Aspects of Induced Abortion, *Medical Journal of Australia, 2,* pp. 35-40A, 1972.
28. D. Sudnow, *Passing On: The Social Organization of Dying,* Prentice-Hall, New Jersey, 1967.
29. R. Kalish, A Continuum of Subjectively Perceived Death, *The Gerontologist, 6,* pp. 73-76, 1966.
30. H. Goldstein, private communication.
31. K. Doka and T. Martin, *Taking it Like a Man: Masculine Patterns of Grief,* paper presented to the Annual Meeting of The Association for Death Education and Counselling, Portland, 1994.
32. K. Doka, *Disenfranchised Grief: Recognizing Hidden Sorrow,* Lexington, Massachusetts, 1989.
33. C. E. Zupinak, Adult Children of Dysfunctional Families: Treatment from a Disenfranchised Grief Perspective, *Death Studies, 18,* pp. 1183-1195, 1994.
34. M. Kaczmarek and B. A. Blackbond, Disenfranchised Grief: The Loss of an Adolescent Romantic Relationship, *Adolescence, 26,* pp. 253-259, 1991.

35. K. Doka, *Crypto Death and Real Grief,* paper presented to a symposium of the Foundation of Thanatology, New York, March 1985.
36. L. Miller and S. Roll, A Case Study in Failure: On Doing Everything Right in Suicide Prevention, *Death Studies, 9,* pp. 483-492, 1985.
37. I. Reiss, *Family Systems in America,* Holt, Rinehart and Winston, Lexington Books, New York, 1980.
38. J. Gagnon, *Human Sexualities,* Scott, Foresman, Glenview, Illinois, 1977.
39. R. Atchley, *Social Forces and Aging* (4th Edition), Wadsworth, Belmont, California, 1985.
40. J. Kammerman, Latent Functions of Enfranchising the Disenfranchised Griever, *Death Studies, 17,* pp. 281-287, 1993.

BIBLIOGRAPHY

Bowling, A. and Cartwright, A., *Life After a Death: A Study of the Elderly Widowed,* Tavistock, New York, 1982.

Parkes, C. M. and Weiss, R., *Recovery from Bereavement,* Basic Books, New York, 1983.

CHAPTER 19
Using Counseling Techniques to Help Bereaved and Dying People

Rose Marie Jaco

INTRODUCTION

As human beings we cannot live our lives without coming to some understanding of death. The very process of living teaches us essential facts about the end of our lives, observations that are confirmed by research and writing in the field of thanatology. Through our own experience we understand that a loss associated with a death "is a transactional process involving the dead with the survivors in a shared life cycle that acknowledges both the finality of death and the continuity of life. Coming to terms with this experience is the most difficult challenge we confront in life" [1, p. 30]. Because our daily lives are so closely and significantly interwoven with those of other people, the fact that death inevitably intervenes to break our ties with them is the greatest source of pain and distress known to humankind. Interpersonal counseling is one powerful method of helping people cope as effectively as possible with their own death or the death of a loved one, at a time when they must learn how to live well in a world forever changed.

My purpose in writing this chapter is to provide a general overview of the nature of counseling, and to describe how counseling techniques can be used to help bereaved and dying people cope with the tasks they face. My assumption is that this chapter will be read by many whose professional education has prepared them well to counsel others about problems in living, but they now wish to acquire more specific knowledge about how to help the bereaved or dying person. For them, much of this material will be a review of earlier learning.

Other readers will be new to the field of counseling, and are seeking basic information about how the process works, perhaps with a view to assessing their own level of interest in entering this area of counseling. I further assume that readers will have sufficient knowledge of theories about attachment, loss, grief, mourning, bereavement, and the dying process so that these terms and concepts can be referred to in this chapter without great elaboration. Although space does not permit more than a general examination of the nature of counseling and its theoretical foundations, this chapter will explore the goals of counseling bereaved and dying people, the basic values, attitudes and communication skills which effective counselors need, and some specific interventions which have proven helpful to these clients. References are provided for those who wish to deepen their understanding of particular areas of the field.

GENERAL ASPECTS OF COUNSELING THE BEREAVED AND DYING

Although an empathetic heart and a compassionate spirit are necessary characteristics for an able counselor to possess, they are not sufficient to ensure effective practice. Counseling is a discipline which requires practitioners to have knowledge about human personality and development, skills in communication and relationship-building and a set of attitudes that allows them to work in the best interests of the client without having their personal values interfere in the process. In answer to the question of who does bereavement counseling, Parkes indicates that there are three categories of people likely to be involved [2]. The first consists of health and mental health professionals whose education has already trained them in the skills of counseling. They are psychiatrists, psychologists, social workers, pastoral care workers, marriage and family therapists, and therapeutically-trained nurses and physicians. The second group involves volunteers who are trained specifically for this work by professionals, and who may work in a team setting where consultation is available. The third group is composed of bereaved people who offer each other mutual support and encouragement in a variety of self-help settings where professional guidance may or may not be available. Because of the unique needs of bereaved and dying people, each group needs some special preparation in order to observe that first principle which guides people involved in the work of helping others—*at least do no harm.*

It is well to distinguish here between the terms "counseling" and "therapy." Both approaches have as their aim the strengthening of a person or family to cope with the demands of their life situation, but "counselling is more likely to emphasize activities that involve supportive, situational, problem-solving, conscious awareness, present-time and short-time concerns; and psychotherapy is more likely to emphasize activities that are reconstructive, depth emphasis, analytical, past-focused, and long-term" [3, p. 4]. Both disciplines deal with serious issues in people's lives, and both have healing or therapeutic aspects, but therapy is designed to help people make profound changes in their personality, family structure or relationships in a way that counseling cannot achieve. Worden distinguishes between "grief counselling" and "grief therapy" in the following way.

> Counselling involves helping people facilitate uncomplicated or normal grief to a healthy completion of the tasks of grieving within a normal time frame. I reserve the term *grief therapy* for those specialized techniques . . . which are used to help people with abnormal or complicated grief reactions [4, p. 37].

Counseling and therapy are two dimensions on the interpersonal helping continuum, overlapping somewhere in the center of the line, and it is difficult to separate them clearly, as therapists counsel, and counselors intervene in ways that are therapeutic. As counselors, it is well to bear in mind that it is not helpful for people, and may in fact be harmful to them, should we try to do more than our training has prepared us for, and we need to be alert to the fact that some of our clients may require the deeper work of therapy when their reactions are extreme, negative, and entrenched.

The kind of complicated mourning which will likely require therapy rather than counseling involves one or more symptoms from the following four categories: *chronic grief reactions* in which people are so immersed in feeling the tragedy of their loss that there appears to be no way to conclude the grieving process, and they have little energy or will left to resume the normal business of living; *exaggerated grief reactions* which include such symptoms as clinical depression, panic attacks, phobic behaviors, post-traumatic stress disorder or substance abuse; *masked grief reactions* expressed as a physical illness without organic foundation, or as delinquent or acting-out behavior; and finally, *delayed grief reactions* where a death which was not adequately mourned at the time may invest a subsequent life event with the strong feelings attached to the first loss, for example a divorce, the death of a pet, or even a theatrical production [4].

The theoretical base of counseling is marked by diversity in the way its core areas of interest are described and explained. These include the nature of human personality and social interaction, the goals and objectives of counseling, and the techniques which counselors should use [3]. No one perspective seems to offer enough variety, sensitivity to situation, and flexibility to enable counselors to draw upon a single theory to help every client they encounter. This fact obliges counselors to develop and integrate their own personal model of counseling from the pool of possible approaches available in the counseling field. The model counselors develop should be congruent with their beliefs about people and the role the counselor should play, be soundly based on current theories and research in the treatment field, and relate closely to the needs of clients in a problematic area. Most counselors use theories about counseling in an eclectic way, drawing from them the pieces that best fit the needs of their client at that point in the helping process, and which are most in keeping with the counselor's personal style of communication and interaction. As well as undertaking this thoughtful process of model-building, the personal formation of the beginning counselor requires supervision and guidance from people experienced in the field and this resource should be sought in whatever situation the counseling occurs. Seasoned counselors as well as beginners need the opportunity to consult with knowledgeable colleagues in situations where they are confused about an assessment, uncertain about which of several directions to take or aware that emotional reactions might be obscuring their judgment.

Since counseling usually takes place within some kind of structured setting—hospital, hospice, agency or voluntary organization, consultation ought be available from professional counselors or experienced volunteers. Ideally, each of these settings should have a set of policies which guides the provision of bereavement and palliative counseling, including training, group conferencing of cases, and supervision of new workers. To add to the challenge of this work, counseling is offered to clients in a variety of ways—to individuals, couples, families, and groups. With these different configurations of people the basic principles of helping and the goals of intervention remain the same, but counselors need to learn a variety of communication and interview techniques to deal with clients alone, or in company with others.

GOALS OF COUNSELING BEREAVED OR DYING CLIENTS

Rando provides some general guidelines for the treatment of complicated mourning, which would be equally effective in all forms of grief work [5]. Of the twenty-one points she lists, the following core directions emerge. Counselors need to encourage, support and normalize the mourning process with their clients; to help them accept the reality of the death and affirm the legitimacy of their affect, cognitions, and symptoms; to assist them in working through their grief by identifying the full range of their emotional response and expressing these feelings in some appropriate form; to examine any resistance they may have to the grieving process, and to complete unfinished business with the deceased in some symbolic manner.

These guidelines provide a cognitive map for the counselor, whose overall purpose in working with the bereaved is to enable them to use their innate strengths of intellect, judgment, will, and spirit to cope as effectively as possible with their loss and the many demands life is placing on them as a result of it. As a helping endeavor the field of counseling provides general goals which are most compatible with the aims of helping the bereaved. George and Cristiani state that, whatever theoretical orientation the counselor might have, five distinct goals of counseling are commonly defined in the literature [3]. These are to facilitate behavior change in clients, to enhance their coping skills, to promote sound decision making, to improve the quality of their relationships, and to help them grow in ways that develop their potential. All of these objectives are appropriate ones for working with bereaved or dying persons, but must be adjusted to conform to the unique needs these situations create. For example, it would be fitting to add to this list the goal of helping bereaved and dying people find spiritual solace to support them as they struggle to answer the ultimate question of what life and death mean to them.

Transforming the goals of counseling into actions that will meet the specific requirements of bereaved, grieving, and dying clients requires that a counselor achieve a deep understanding of how people experience these situations. We can gain in our appreciation of what the experiences of mourning and dying mean to people by reflecting on some theoretical models of these states which enable us to see common themes among the many variations human life provides.

One model is offered by Worden, who conceptualizes the demands bereavement places on people as "tasks of mourning" which need to be worked through to completion [4]. The first task facing a grieving person is *to accept the reality of loss,* the opposite of which is to deny the fact and finality of the death, or to minimize its meaning. The second, very demanding task is *to work through the pain of grief* so that it will not "manifest itself in some symptoms or other forms of aberrant behavior" [4, p. 13]. Third, the bereaved person needs to *adjust to an environment in which the deceased is missing*. Adjustment means that the bereaved must take on some of the roles played by the dead person, redefine themselves as individuals, and find meaningful life goals that do not include the living presence of the other. The fourth task, which Worden believes to be the most difficult one to accomplish is *to emotionally relocate the deceased and move on with life.*

This challenge of emotional relocation involves survivors in finding a fitting space in their inner world of mind and spirit so that they can place their attachment to the deceased person in such a way that they can retain the valued relationship in memory, but are free to make connections with others and to invest themselves in new activities. Failure to complete this task results in people becoming entrenched in their grief, in a sense being frozen in time, without the capacity to find meaning in their existence other than that associated with the deceased. Using this somewhat linear approach of tasks to be completed, a counselor would assess the manner in which the mourner was working through his or her grief, knowing that in reality it could not be conducted in a straight line, as the tasks interweave and overlap. The counselor would choose techniques designed to help mourners attain the successful completion of these tasks, with the goal of their achieving a state of adjustment whereby "people regain an interest in life, feel more hopeful, experience gratification again, and adapt to new roles" [4, p. 19].

Other models of grieving have been developed, for example the "pathways" concept of Martin and Elder. Viewing grief as a process, rather than a set of tasks, these authors have plotted the mourner's passage on connected double circles designed to depict various stages of grief, and surrounded by figures representing people found in the social surround of the bereaved [6]. The lower circle contains the responses to loss of protest, despair, and detachment, and the upper circle their opposites—exploration, hope, and investment. The work of mourners, often helped by others, is to experience the emotions associated with the stages in the lower circle and through gradual growth, to become capable of adopting the attitudes depicted in the upper circle, and in the process be enabled to rejoin life.

As the model is circular in nature, there is no real beginning or end point, but the person enters at whatever stage he or she has reached, is helped to assign personal meaning to the death, and finally enters a state of mind where redefinition is possible and "the loss (is seen) as a challenge and a change that can be managed. It is the redefinition of the event that propels people from one circle to the other" [6, p. 77]. This model is valuable because it respects the unique response each person has to grief, acknowledges people's movement back and forth between stages, and validates the natural flow of emotions and uneven growth patterns found in real life. If counselors choose to be guided by this model their role would be to facilitate the person's progress through the stages, holding out as a goal the resolution of crippling grief, but acknowledging the need to work and re-work significant losses throughout life.

Because a family is a system composed of interrelationships which hold different meanings for each person involved, the death of a family member reverberates throughout the group unevenly, resulting in individual differences in grieving. Simultaneously the loss of a family member affects the family system itself in a way which tends to destabilize it, requiring the family to undergo a restructuring process. In McGoldrick's view, families must go through four stages of mourning similar to those outlined by Worden [7]. These consist of the family members collectively acknowledging that death has occurred; sharing their experience of the life and the loss and giving these meaning within the family's context; reorganizing the family system by shifting roles, focus or connections, and reinvesting in other relationships and pursuits. In recognition of the delicate re-balancing tasks which a family faces after a death, McGoldrick provides sound directions to take for both families and their counselors.

> When family members communicate openly about a death (no matter what the circumstances) and participate together in culturally meaningful rituals such as funeral rites and visits to the grave, death becomes easier to integrate . . . Tolerating differences in reaction to death, including the inevitable ambivalent feelings toward the dead, is essential. When family loyalty demands a certain response that does not fit with true feelings, the mourning process is delayed or, in some cases avoided completely. Until family members can mourn, they remain—to a greater or lesser degree—stuck [7, p. 51].

When a person is known to be dying, counselors can aid family members, and the person him/herself, to prepare for death through the process of anticipatory grief. Here those who are about to die or become bereaved are helped to acknowledge that fact in appropriate ways so that they can begin the work of letting go and mourning before the death occurs. Worden again applies his four task model to this work, but adds the concept of helping people complete any unfinished business they may have with each other prior to death through giving them permission to talk about what is important to them, particularly those emotionally-laden subjects which have been previously avoided in the interest of maintaining the appearance of family unity [4].

In his reflections on how to help dying people cope with their impending death, Pattison rejects the notion that there are stages in the dying process, and replaces it instead with the concept that dying occurs in three phases [8]. The first is the acute crisis phase of discovering that death is approaching, during which people feel "bewilderment, confusion, indefinable anxiety and unspecified fear" [8, p. 146]. This is a time for counselors to offer emotional support combined with problem solving around the real issues the impending death raises in the life of the person, his or her family and loved ones. The second phase is termed "the chronic living-dying phase" during which the person will face many fears. Pattison lists eight common fears of the dying including loneliness, loss, pain, and regression and he proposes specific approaches to help deal with each fear [8, pp. 162-166]. In general terms, the counselor's role in this phase is to help people cope with each fear as it emerges. For example, enabling dying people to deal with their fear of loneliness and loss would involve them in the paradoxical, but achievable task of drawing strength from their current attachment to loved ones while at the same time preparing to permanently separate from them; coping with the fear of loss of control by enabling clients to make as many decisions about their medical and living situation as possible, and countering the fear of a lost identity by working with them to develop their personal philosophy of life in ways that give meaning to both their unique lives and to their deaths.

Given this type of support "the dying person may then accept the surrender to the internal self, allow himself to turn away from life, and seek reunion with the world out of which he or she has sprung. Then psychic death is acceptable, desirable and at hand" [8, p. 152]. The terminal phase begins when body mechanisms begin to fail and the person withdraws psychologically. The contribution a counselor can make at this time involves not abandoning the person, but talking and touching in ways designed to comfort and support, so that he or she is aware of being cared for until life ends.

Whether we choose a task, pathway, phase, or some other model to help us grasp the complex ways in which mourning and dying are played out in individual lives, our role as counselor should conform to the image encouraged by the counseling discipline itself. Counselors have the privilege of being invited to share briefly in the lives of people for the sole purpose of enhancing the quality of those lives. This kind of interpersonal helping must be based on a deep sense of respect for the differences and unique responses we encounter. Counseling bereaved or dying persons means that, in a sense, they have invited us to become traveling companions on their journey, beginning where they are and allowing them to set the pace while we offer support, encouragement, information, and challenge. As well as facilitating their efforts, we need to avoid behaviors that are known to hinder the helping process, such as providing solutions, moralizing, criticizing, or giving false reassurance [3].

THEORETICAL FOUNDATIONS OF COUNSELING

Theories in the field of human behavior are attempts to capture truth or reality by describing what is observed, explaining these phenomena in an organized way, and predicting what might occur in certain circumstances. As George and Cristiani note, theories in the counseling field provide the practitioner with a "systematic approach to dealing with a problem," and allow counselors who are confused about what might be helpful in a specific situation "to turn to theory to enlarge their perspective about the various alternatives" [3, p. 108]. Theories are infinitely useful to the counselor because they present both a framework for understanding human behavior, and guidelines for selecting the interventions most likely to be helpful in a particular situation. The following discussion of theory is based on ideas drawn from Ivey, Ivey, and Simek-Morgan [9] and George and Cristiani [3].

Ivey et al. identifies the three major forces which have shaped the field of counseling and psychotherapy as psychodynamic, cognitive-behavioral, and existential-humanistic. Psychodynamic theory, originally based on Freudian perspectives of human nature, has since expanded to include many advances in understanding such as ego psychology, the developmental theories of Erikson [10] and Miller [11], the object relations theory of Klein [12], and most important for the bereavement counselor, the attachment theory of Bowlby [13-15]. Theories from the psychodynamic perspective help us to be conscious of the shaping power of early life experiences; to understand and access the strengths inherent in the adaptive functions of the ego, (principally thinking, perceiving, and remembering); to appreciate the fact that life transitions and developmental stages present the person with specific tasks to be accomplished, and to work with the mechanisms of defense which people use to protect themselves against uncomfortable feelings, particularly the anxiety associated with loss, both current and past.

When counselors draw understandings about people from the vast body of psychodynamic literature, they are prepared for the complexity of human behavior, based as it is on both unconscious and conscious forces and are ready to take into account developmental influences, especially those of childhood. In bereavement and palliative work counselors will find the following understandings from psychodynamic theory useful. Because of the theory's strong emphasis on the degree to which the past influences the present, they will expect that history will probably repeat itself and that clients will likely deal with death using the approaches they learned in their families of origin. Counselors will therefore encourage their clients to reflect on previous losses in the family, and talk about how these were dealt with, within the context of the ethnic and cultural background of the family.

If, for example, the counselor is working with a client who has problems expressing sorrow about death and discovers that there was a family pattern of denying the feelings associated with loss in the interests of "getting on with life," the counselor might choose the following interventive direction. The client would be encouraged to see if there is a connection between responses learned in the family and his or her present reactions; to re-experience some of the buried feelings associated with losses of the past; to re-frame the experience of loss as one which needs to be shared and talked about, and to redesign his or her own method of grieving or facing death without feeling that family values are being betrayed in making such a change. Although early traumatic experiences and the shaping power of the family of origin are important concepts in psychodynamic theory, it offers many other rich insights into human nature, in particular its focus on the mechanisms of defense.

The second force in shaping the counseling field is cognitive-behavioral theory, which involves approaches such as the rational-emotive therapy of Ellis [16], the behavioral counseling of Bandura [17], Beck's cognitive-behavioral treatment of depression [18], Glasser's reality therapy [19, 20] and others. Although behavioral change is a major focus of this perspective, the role of thoughts and feelings in shaping the behavioral choices people make is now emphasized by theorists. Counselors using this theory encourage people to become observers of themselves in their social environment and to note events which precede and follow their actions. This is termed an A-B-C analysis, (antecedent-behavior-consequence) and is undertaken as a means of helping people interrupt and change what is usually a unconscious patterned behavioral reaction by consciously altering the way they perceive others and events. As a result of deliberately changing their perceptions, people are set free from automatically adopting a cognitive or affective response which leads to a predictable action, and are enabled to select alternative behaviors with a better sense of being in control of their lives.

Useful contributions from this school of thought to bereavement and palliative counseling include an awareness of the ways in which thinking, feeling, and behaving are linked, and the potential for introducing positive change through intervening in any one of these three areas. For example, a bereaved person may genuinely believe that any chance for having a meaningful life has ended because of the death of a spouse. As a consequence of this belief, the person carries around a sense of emptiness and sorrow. Behavior is affected because his or her desire to interact in a sociable way with other people is blighted by these feelings, and so conversations and activities with others are avoided. Increasing isolation feeds the belief that life now lacks meaning, reinforces feelings of emptiness, and results in a more entrenched avoidance of others.

The counselor who draws on cognitive-behavioral theory for guidance in helping a client in this position may begin by gently challenging the belief that all meaning in people's lives is lost when a person significant to them dies, and proposing instead an alternate belief that a loved one's life is honored by the willingness of his or her survivors to live their lives fully. When a person is gradually helped to change a limiting belief system, feelings of being hopeless and helpless are also likely to change, and the person is more likely to act in ways that result in meaningful activities and interactions. Because the behavioral approach encourages action as well as the changing of dysfunctional thoughts and feelings, the counselor might simultaneously encourage some activities, even such simple ones as joining workmates for coffee or learning relaxation techniques. Any shift, no matter how small, will begin to make a difference in people's perception of themselves, and is used by the counselor as a lever to encourage the resumption of a fuller life. Emphasizing the circular interplay of beliefs and attitudes, feelings and actions is a major contribution of cognitive-behavioral theory to the counseling field, and one that offers many entry points for introducing positive change in the lives of the bereaved and dying.

In Ivey's analysis the third force affecting the field of counseling is based on existential-humanistic theory, which includes the person-centered approach of Rogers [21, 22], the gestalt therapy of Perls [23, 24], and the existential work of Frankl [25, 26], and Yalom [27]. These theoreticians emphasize respect for the uniqueness of each individual, belief in the person's drive to become fully what they are in potential, focus on self-integration, awareness of the connection of mind and body, and the need people have to find meaning in their particular existence in the world. Borrowing from existential-humanistic theory, counselors working with bereaved or dying persons would offer themselves as warm, empathetic listeners, very interested in the story the bereaved client has to tell about the loss of a loved one, or what the dying client has to say about the life and people he or she must leave. According to this theory, the process of being fully heard empowers clients to determine what meaning and significance lies in the relationships and events of their lives as they describe them, and then to take action where needed to ensure that that meaning remains congruent with their hopes and vision about themselves. "Clients speak; therapists listen carefully and attempt to understand clients' perceptions of the world. Having been heard and understood, clients can move forward" [6, p. 302].

In the existential-humanistic framework the general emphasis is on helping clients see tragic events in a light that is growth-producing rather than limiting. Using techniques such as reframing or re-constructing the interpretation of events, focusing on the future rather than the past, and attending to new goals and the needs of others rather than remaining self-absorbed, counselors help their clients focus on the future. An additional perspective in the existential-humanist school is gestalt theory, which encourages counselors to use such techniques as making people aware of the feelings and bodily sensations they are experiencing in the immediate present, helping them to gain deeper understandings of themselves through dialogue with conflicted parts of the self, or assisting them in gaining insight through undertaking imaginary conversations with significant others or writing letters (not necessarily sent) to the absent person.

Counselors in bereavement and palliative care might base the following approaches on the existential-humanistic set of theories. The counselor remains very real and present with their client, encouraging the person to tune in to their inner world of feeling and sensation; to reflect on areas of pain and discomfort, and discuss actions that might be appropriate in relieving these feelings. One important outcome of increased self-awareness is that clients are helped to take responsibility for getting their needs met in a straightforward manner, without manipulation or inappropriate dependency, and according to their own expectations. A long-term goal of therapy within this model is the achievement of personal integration, which occurs when "the person functions as a systematic whole comprising feelings, perceptions, thoughts and a physical body whose processes cannot be divorced from the more psychological components. When one's inner state (emotions) and behavior match, little energy is wasted and one is more capable of responding appropriately to meet one's needs" [3, p. 71].

Counseling is a field which is constantly changing in its basic understanding of human beings and how to help them achieve their full potential among the vicissitudes of life. Space does not permit a full review of new developments in the field, but two emerging theories which are profoundly affecting counseling practice are multicultural theory [28, 29] and feminist theory [30, 31]. These theories illuminate the importance of age, gender, ethnicity, religion, socioeconomic status, and cultural roots in the formation of personality, as humans interact with forces in their social environment. Both multicultural and feminist theories call into question what are seen as the narrow explanations of personality found in earlier theories. Critics operating from these perspectives claim that some widely accepted notions about personality are based on an unspoken assumption that the white, male, middle-class experience of the world represents a universal truth shared by all. The case is strongly made that counselors need to be aware of the strong impact on personal development that is exerted by the biological and socially different life experiences of males and females. In addition, counselors need to be sensitive to the effect that belonging to a cultural minority has in shaping an individual or family's response to life events, including death and dying. Both multicultural and feminist theories emphasize relationships with others as a major source of meaning in life, interdependence in contrast to independence, connection as opposed to pure individuality and self-determinism.

The number, diversity, and contrasting features of the many theories which inform the discipline of counseling might seem confusing or intimidating to those approaching it for the first time. It is reassuring to know that there are common features found in all of these theories which contain the essence of the helping process. Guided by this central core of characteristics and goals, counselors can select additional understandings and interventions from specific theories, as required, to meet the client's unique needs. Marmor has identified seven common factors shared by the major theories in the field [32]. All counseling incorporates the client-counselor relationship as an important feature; the release of emotional tension on the part of clients; the attainment of a deeper understanding of the meaning of their life situation; a corrective emotional experience provided by the warmth and acceptance of the counselor; the opportunity to use the counselor as a role model, particularly around values and perspectives; the exposure of clients to influences exerted by the counselor toward changes in thought and behavior, and opportunities to rehearse these changes prior to incorporating them in the client's daily life.

BECOMING A COUNSELOR

Whatever the theoretical foundations upon which counseling is based, there is one fundamental human truth that underlies the process. That is the fact that in the course of our interaction with others we exert influence in ways that affect the thoughts, feelings, and behaviors of each person involved. The natural encounters we have with other people result in a type of mutual influence which continually affects our perceptions and our actions in ways that are both overt and subtle, intended and accidental, but which construct a good part of the fabric of our lives.

Interpersonal counseling depends upon this inherent aspect of human interaction by providing the influence of a skilled person whose specific role is that of helping another individual at a time when he or she must cope with a crisis, loss, relationship conflict, or a problem-in-living. A counselor, in a certain sense, can be thought of as an artificial presence in another person's life, because he or she is not part of a natural social network, but enters the client's world for a specific, time-limited purpose. Because counseling is essentially the work of helping strangers, this very distance from the daily life of the client benefits the process by enabling the counselor to be objective in assessing the client's situation and impartial in selecting interventions designed to bring about positive change. In addition, the counselor's detachment from the client's natural life makes it easier to implement two of the cardinal principles of counseling, which are that the goals to be achieved must be those of the client, not the counselor, and that their relationship cannot be a reciprocal one, in that counselors cannot seek help to solve their own problems from their clients. An exception to this particular help-seeking principle is found in the self-help movement, where helping is explicitly achieved through the mutual process of sharing experiences, such as loss and grief, and seeking support from other mourners.

Because of the emotional intensity attached to work in this field, Pattison recommends that helpers, particularly those who work with the dying, cultivate an attitude of "compassionate detachment" as,

> To respond to the fears and human condition of the dying person will always involve responding to ourselves. We face a continuing tension within ourselves to be in touch with the meanings of death for ourselves so as to be empathically sensitive, and yet to be able to maintain our psychic composure and objectivity so that we can respond to the dying person as he or she is in life [8, p. 136].

Two distortions of this attitude need to be avoided. The first is that of exaggerated detachment, where dying people become objectified in the sense that they become targets of rigid programs so strongly rooted in theory that an individual's responses risk being discounted as abnormal, and the second is that of exaggerated compassion, where there is a sense of "psychological fusion" with the dying. This leads to the helper using his or her experience with the dying person to do personal work with unresolved issues from the past, as well as some anticipatory grieving about deaths yet to come [8]. Clearly in counseling the client's needs supersede the needs of helpers, but that does not mean that people working in this field must disregard their own needs. In order to avoid burnout, or "compassion fatigue," (a condition of emotional emptiness which particularly affects conscientious and dedicated helpers), they need to arrange their personal lives in such a way that they draw satisfaction from many sources other than their work with the bereaved and dying.

THE ETHICS OF COUNSELING

There are some who will find the use of the term "influence" disturbing, containing as it does the possibility of control and dominance. Because the practice of counseling does have the potential to harm clients through manipulating or exploiting them at a time of special vulnerability in their lives, it must be guided by a set of ethical principles designed to protect the client from a misuse of power by the counselor. Practitioners who belong to an established profession are already guided by a code of ethics, a distinguishing characteristic of all professions. All professional codes of ethics are composed of principles designed to protect the rights of clients, to ensure confidentiality, to set forth standards of practice, to regulate the keeping of records, and to ensure that professionals remain current in their knowledge and skills.

Usually the first and guiding principle in a code of ethics is the assertion that all actions taken must be for the well-being of the client, and that every effort must be made to ensure that no harm will come to that person because of his or her interaction with the professional. This precludes the forming of what is termed a "dual relationship" with the client, meaning a relationship in addition to the counseling one, such as a sexual or business connection. Confidentiality is promised under certain conditions, and the reasons for breaking confidentiality must be grave indeed to set aside this basic protection of the client's reputation and privacy. However, the sharing of information is certainly necessary among members of a team and is mandatory with child welfare authorities should there be any question of child abuse.

Counselors are also instructed that they should break the bounds of confidentiality in the interest of protecting their client's life, if the person is actively suicidal, and to protect the life and safety of another person, should the client reveal aggressive intentions toward others. It is important for workers in the field of death and dying to clarify the ethical constraints that prevail in their setting, and for those workers without a prior professional affiliation, to heed the advice of Kennedy, who instructs non-professional counselors to "follow the model of professional helpers" when it comes to ethical behavior [33, p. 53]. It is because counselors have the ability to intentionally influence others at times of great vulnerability in ways that can have either positive or negative outcomes for people, that they are obliged to understand and follow the guidelines for ethical practice.

Influence consists of many elements which are not commonly thought of in this way, such as listening, questioning, responding, providing emotional support, understanding, giving information and clarifying options, as well as certain techniques specifically designed to result in client change. Influence is exerted by means of specific communication and interviewing skills, and is channeled from the helper to the client through a special relationship which is intentionally encouraged and created by the counselor. This relationship is formed when a counselor constructs a climate of psychological safety for the client by offering him or her self in a warm, empathetic, concerned and non-judgmental manner, somewhat in the manner of a caring friend or relative, but with the understanding that the encounter is taking place for the explicit purpose of helping the client cope as effectively as possible with the demands life is placing upon them.

CORE HELPING CONDITIONS IN COUNSELING

Counselors need to come to terms with the fact that they themselves are the major tool used in the counseling process. Their own personality, beliefs, attitudes, emotions, experiences, social, and communicative skills are the instruments used to help people in need. This means that counselors need to think very carefully about how best to refine their personal instruments so that their work is genuinely helpful to others. The question of "what makes help helpful?" has long intrigued researchers. This has led to the identification of what are called "core conditions" or attributes which counselors should possess in order to be effective in their work of helping strangers [34, 35]. Carkhuff and his associate confirm through research that the degree to which counselors display the four characteristics of genuineness, empathy, positive regard, and concreteness directly affects their ability to be helpful to clients [34]. Based on the fact that possessing these facilitative attitudes will make our counseling work more effective, we need to learn the elements of each condition, incorporate them into our personal style in a manner which is valid and comfortable, and if need be, alter our communication style to reflect these attributes.

Genuineness or congruence refers to counselors allowing themselves to be known as real people, not hiding behind a professional or false facade. This requires us as counselors to be constantly aware of our own reactions, values and belief systems, so we will know where we stand in relation to the client's situation and responses. It means that clients do not need to wonder whether or not we are emotionally moved by their situation, whether we are puzzled, worried, or annoyed. Our words and body language match in a congruent way, and they are clearly displayed to the client. However, prudence dictates that there are some reactions which we should keep to ourselves on the basis that we always work for the client's well-being and we must do nothing that weakens or diminishes a client. If, for example, we are working with a person who has lost the good will of his or her family members through irresponsible behavior in the past, it will not enable him or her to cope better with social isolation if we add our blaming voice to the chorus. We may genuinely believe that this person played a major role in creating a rupture in the family, but rather than immersing them in extreme self-blame we recognize that there will be a more positive outcome for the client if we help them acknowledge their feelings of responsibility for the past and then move on to examining what they might now do differently to change their situation. Being genuine and congruent means that we are never false in our responses, but it does not require us to be open books. Rather, we need to be selective in what we reveal to a client, always reacting on the basis of what will best help this person, at this moment, to attain his or her goals.

Empathy is the ability to enter the world of other people, see that world through their eyes, understand their frame of reference and accurately identify their feelings. To be empathetic does not imply that the counselor must agree that clients are correct in their perceptions or actions, but it does mean that the person must be accepted as they are without being judged adversely. Empathy involves both affective and cognitive skills, in that the counselor needs to tune in correctly to the other person on an emotional level, while at the same time thinking about the realities of his or her situation. Responding empathetically is challenging in that it requires counselors to leave their personal world, to some extent, in order to freely enter the world of the other, yet they must remain well rooted in their own values and perceptions to protect their sense of identity, and thus be able to provide clients with a solid reference point. Accurate empathy on the part of the counselor enables clients to feel fully heard, understood and accepted, and from this position people are often able to imagine possibilities and thus introduce change into their lives.

Positive regard toward people which contains respect for their unique value as human beings, non-possessive warmth of feeling, and a deep belief in the fact that people have strengths that they can use in the pursuit of their goals in life. These characteristics form the cornerstone of Roger's "person-centred" therapy [21], but Ivey et al. point out that "Positive regard is a concept basic to all counselling and therapy theory. If you as a therapist cannot believe there is something positive and valuable in the client, there is little hope for client change" [9, p. 25]. Having an attitude of positive regard for clients does not necessarily mean that a counselor would like to have them as friends. Counselors work with all types of troubled and difficult individuals and families whom they might well avoid in their natural lives, but they are guided by a piece of wisdom in the culture of counseling which says "to understand all is to forgive all." With their heightened ability to understand the complex forces that create human beings, counselors also increase their ability to understand, accept and forgive the people they help.

What this means for a client is that he or she feels (perhaps for the first time), a sense of respect, warmth, acceptance, and appreciation directed toward them from another person, and the relationship which is formed as a result can be used by the client for support as he or she begins to make positive changes in thought and behavior. This does not imply that a counselor must accept abuse or manipulation from troubled people in order to serve clients well. That would not be positive for either the counselor or the client. Through developing a clear understanding of the boundaries and conditions which make a counseling relationship possible, and communicating this message to clients by words and actions, counselors convey the limits of the association

The core characteristics of *concreteness and immediacy* refer to an orientation on the part of counselors which directs their conversation with clients from remote and abstract considerations to talking about events and relationships in the here-and-now. It has been found that people are much more likely to institute change in their lives if they examine the details of their recent discussions, interactions, and decision-making efforts, focusing on their own behavior and reality, rather than engage in talk about generalities. We need to be extremely sensitive in using this approach, however, as some people prefer the comfort gained by distancing themselves somewhat from their own lives, and we may also be working with people from cultures where a more indirect type of discussion is valued, as with persons of Asian and African background. It is clear that the core conditions which facilitate good counseling practice are interrelated. In summary, as counselors we need to be genuine and congruent people in order to offer our clients warmth, respect, and positive regard in a manner they know to be authentic.

COMMUNICATION TECHNIQUES
USED IN COUNSELING

The core facilitative conditions of the counseling relationship are expressed by means of a variety of verbal and non-verbal communication skills that can be learned through study, discussion, practice, and supervision. As these skills involve the counselor's tone of voice, choice of words, facial expressions, and body language, it is wise for beginners to obtain feedback on their communication skills by conducting some of their practice where it can be observed by an experienced counselor, through the use of audio and video-tapes, one-way mirrors, and role-plays in the classroom. Basic counseling skills have been identified, categorized, and tested for effectiveness by Ivey and his associates over many years [9, 36] and are found, with some variations in terminology, in other current texts on counseling [37-39]. Three main groupings of skills have been distinguished—those of attending, listening, and influencing [9]. The use of these techniques should be tailored to the age, mental state, and cultural expectations of clients.

The first and most important set of skills for connecting with a client are those of *attending*. The fact that we are paying careful attention to the people we are conversing with is conveyed to them by maintaining appropriate *eye contact; a body posture* that leans slightly in their direction, (but is neither distant nor invasive); the use of *responsive facial expressions* and *speaking* to them in a warm and varied tone of voice. This cluster of body language skills can be consciously developed by a counselor and integrated into their style in a way that becomes natural for them. *Active listening skills* are used concurrently with attending skills to form a communication style which facilitates our clients' ability to share and trust, and enables them to move forward in dealing with their issues in a purposive way.

In the Ivey framework, *listening skills* are comprised of the following behaviors: the ability *to ask both open and closed questions* in a suitable and timely manner in order to draw out clients' stories; the capacity *to respond* verbally and non-verbally in ways that encourage and support clients as they work through difficult passages in their lives; proficiency in *selecting and repeating back key words and phrases* in order to clarify precise meanings; competence in *reflecting feelings* accurately and *responding* to these with empathy and finally, the ability to *pull together many confusing themes* in clients' lives in a way that offers a meaningful summary of their reality and affords a sense of direction for growth and change. There is a large element of art as well as knowledge involved in using this array of skills, because the counselor must constantly observe the interaction between the self and the client, and almost intuitively select the listening skill that will be most beneficial at that precise stage of the interview.

Although this combination of attending and listening skills does influence clients to see their situation more objectively, to discover new paths to follow and possible changes to make, counselors can add to their effectiveness by choosing from a set of *influencing skills* specifically designed to move clients in the directions they wish or need to go. Ivey et al. notes that these skills enable us to share ourselves and our experiences more deeply with clients, but goes on to say that "Influencing skills are complex, and often are more effective if used sparingly, and in careful concert with listening skills" [9, p. 55]. Influencing skills include the powerful one of *reframing or re-interpreting* the client's world in a different light, in a way that enables people to reconstruct their view of reality and thus change the thoughts and feelings that have robbed their lives of meaning. Counselors may *give directives or suggest actions* that would benefit clients, such as the following directive given to an anxious client: "It would be helpful for you to limit the amount of time you spend in worrying, and set aside a particular part of the day, perhaps a ten minute period, where you can concentrate on the things that really concern you." Clients usually respond well to practical recommendations that are clear and precise.

Advice may be given on matters that involve information known to the counselor, for example in the management of children's behavior or a client's eligibility for a particular program. *Self-disclosure* is sometimes helpful when the counselor's personal experiences or knowledge of how other people cope is pertinent to the client's situation. *Feedback* allows clients to hear how they and their actions are perceived by the counselor and the technique of *logical consequences* permits counselors to review the possible outcomes of various options their client might choose. A highly controversial but useful technique is that of *confrontation,* in which the counselor points out a discrepancy between what clients say are their goals, and the actions they choose. Since this type of communication has the power to hurt people, it must be used with great care, when the level of trust between counselor and client is high, and the intervention comes out of a genuine caring for the client's growth, and not as a way for the counselor to express his or her own frustrations [3].

All of the communication skills and choices listed above can be used when working with individuals, couples, families or groups, although a counselor will need some special study and supervision to develop expertise in all four areas. The major differences in working with configurations of clients in contrast to an individual is this: the counselor needs to take into account the interaction between or among the people present as a real factor in the helping process. Sometimes, when the exchange between the couple or among family or group members is positive, it can be amplified to increase the support and momentum a client or family needs to act on the implications of an insight they have gained, or to plan for new kinds of behavior. When the interaction is conflicted or negative in nature, it can often be used by the counselor as additional information to clarify a situation, to illustrate the logical consequence of prior words and actions, or as a source of energy from which people can move toward more positive ways of being together. Working in a multiperson format also requires the counselor to ensure that people have the opportunity to express themselves according to their needs, to respond to the others present, to be heard and understood, and to have a voice in problem-solving discussions.

Working with a client usually involves an interview of some type. Interviews can range from the brief, informal contacts often made in hospitals and institutions, to structured and planned sessions conducted in the home or office, or a mixture of both. With the exception of self-help group sessions, most interviews with individuals, families, or in counseling groups follow the five-stage model Ivey, Ivey, and Simek-Morgan has identified. These stages are:

1. establishing rapport and outlining some structure, such as the interview time frame;
2. outlining current concerns and problems; searching for client strengths and resources;
3. clarifying client values, goals, and objectives;
4. generating solutions to problems, directions for growth, and identifying influences of the past and of the client's personal style that need to be taken into account; and
5. transferring new learning and directions into actions to be taken in the clients life [9].

For counselors to have this structured model as a template against which to measure and design their interviews with clients does not mean that they are locked into a set of mechanical moves. It does, however, provide some security to counselors to know that there is a reliable framework for the helping interview which they can re-shape as the situation demands, spending more or less time on various aspects, according to the nature of the client's situation.

SPECIFIC INTERVENTIONS FOR COUNSELORS

As well as the approaches already mentioned, the literature on working with bereaved and dying people contains many creative ideas which counselors can use to enable clients to move forward with their work of acknowledgment, suffering, resolution, and acceptance. Much needs to be taken into account when guiding people toward these specific activities, including such factors as their age and mental condition; their capacity to be self-reflective; whether they are faced with social stigma around the cause of death, and the presence or absence of a support network in their natural lives. Counselors can obtain guidance for helping clients in particular situations by consulting the many specialized books available, such as those on the death of infants or children [40, 41]; death by suicide [5] or AIDS [5], sibling or spousal death [42], and violent or accidental death [5].

Among the most effective of interventions is the ritualizing of the loss [7, 43]. Rituals are "composed of metaphors, symbols and actions in a highly condensed, dramatic form" which can be used to "mark the loss of a member, affirm the life lived by the person who has died, facilitate the expression of grief in ways that are consonant with the culture's values, speak symbolically of the meanings of death and ongoing life, and point to a direction for making sense of the loss while enabling continuity for the living" [43, p. 207]. Rituals can be as simple as lighting a candle in memory at a Christmas dinner, toasting the absent member at a wedding, or looking through family picture albums on the anniversary of a death.

The major ritual associated with death is the funeral, and it represents a valuable opportunity for both dying people and their survivors to mark the life and death of the deceased person in a meaningful way. As counselors, we may have opportunities to raise the question with survivors of what type of funeral they would find most comforting, and with the dying, discover what sort of commemoration they would like to have, including music, religious elements, burial or cremation, and post-funeral gathering. One youthful man, dying over a period of some months, gave a great deal of thought to choosing selections from his favorite classical music to be played at his funeral. His widow and children found comfort in feeling his presence through the music he had chosen.

Rituals perform three major functions for the bereaved. Through some deliberately chosen ceremonial action mourners are helped to acknowledge and grieve their loss, are given ways to symbolize their incorporation of the deceased person into their ongoing lives, and are provided with a marker which symbolizes their intention to re-invest in living [7]. Rando offers detailed guidance to counselors for the development of appropriate rituals in cases of complicated mourning, but the approach she proposes would be useful in all cases of grief. She says:

> Therapeutic ritual sanctions and validates the mourner's expression of feeling. In cases where there is personal or social conditioning against expression of affect, participation in therapeutic rituals—especially those prescribed by an authority figure such as a caregiver—provides both the forum and the means by which emotions can be released without violating previous conditioning . . . [5, p. 315]

As an example of a simple ritual which addressed the denial of grief by the father and the isolated grief of the mother, one family was helped by a counselor to mark the death of their infant daughter and sister, dead of a rare congenital condition at the age of seven days. The father wished to move on with life, and concentrate on the well-being of his two remaining sons, while the mother felt that the life of her child had not been recognized as important, and struggled with times of deep depression, coupled with anger at what she saw as her husband's lack of feeling. Father had been bereaved of his own mother at the age of eight, a loss that he had never been allowed to grieve, and because he could not face reactivating that old sorrow, chose to believe that the best way to cope with his daughter's death was to ignore it and bury himself in work. However, he was very concerned about his wife, and on the third anniversary of the baby's death, agreed to mark her life in a special way for the first time. The whole family visited the cemetery together (in previous years the mother had gone alone) and when they returned home they examined the contents of the box in which the mother had placed the baby's photograph, the hospital identification band, baby clothes, and the cards and letters sent both at her birth and death. Many tears were shed as the parents answered the previously unasked questions of their children, but each member of the family felt comfort and relief to be able to share their sadness with each other. This ritual has been conducted for the past two years as the birthday celebration for the lost baby, but may well be modified as the needs of the family members change. The mother no longer feels the deep sadness and isolation she had struggled with over the years, and responds well to the fact that her sons now talk quite easily about their sister, and she and her husband have reconciled their differences in mourning behavior in a way that has strengthened their emotional bond.

There are several types of intervention designed to assist mourners in accepting the reality of their loss, and to help them work through the suffering phase of their grief. These interventions can be either reflective or active in nature. For people who have a capacity for self-reflection, writing about their inner experiences can be therapeutic. This can be done through keeping a journal of their journey through grief, or by writing letters to the deceased which can be kept in a special place, burned as a symbol of the person's completion of the separation stage of their process, or buried in a corner of the cemetery plot as a permanent memento of the relationship. Clients are often helped by being taught techniques of relaxation, meditation, and thought control. The latter approach involves two dimensions. One is the conscious stoppage of negative or intrusive thoughts which are often self-blaming and guilt-inducing, and their replacement with positive self-talk, whereby people are instructed to recall the benefits they had during the life of their loved one, remember the joyous moments they experienced together, and think in terms of living the remaining years of their life as fully as possible, as a fitting tribute to the deceased.

The use of a technique known as "guided imagery" can be used to help people work on many of the tasks they need to complete when a loved person dies. In essence, it gives the client an opportunity to re-grieve their loss in a present time framework, and in a protected setting. Because this is a powerful intervention, it should be planned and carried out with great care, and should not be used with emotionally unstable or mentally ill people, or by beginning counselors in the field. An explanation is given to the client that by using their imagination and your guidance, they could go back in time to dialogue with the person they have lost, and tell them about their thoughts and feelings. Among the many benefits of this technique are the mourner's ability to acknowledge the finality of the loss, differentiate himself from the deceased, express tears and rage, deal with ambivalence and misdirected anger, tease apart interlocking grief reactions, emancipate himself from unspoken binds, reveal secrets and deal with unfinished business, express love and forgiveness, and get permission from the "presence" of the deceased to look for new relationships and options, especially those that seem to flow naturally from what the deceased would have wanted for the bereaved [44].

Actions may take many forms including making memorial donations in recognition of the dead person, establishing services or awards to acknowledge his or her life, or finding a unique expression of sorrow that matches the values and culture of the family. In one case a counselor helped a survivor of the Holocaust to commemorate the lives of his parents, who were killed in a concentration camp, their burial site unknown. This inability to pay respect to his parents in their final resting place had remained as a source of pain to the client for the fifty years since their death. In his advancing years he planned to make a final visit to the small town where he and his forebears had lived for generations, and although there were no longer relatives living there, he had kept in touch with some old family friends over the years. He was encouraged to have them arrange for a marble marker to be placed on the family plot, with information about his parents' lives, and the cause of their death, a well as a beautiful biblical inscription. This stone was blessed in a small ceremony which gave immense comfort to the client, who now felt he had performed his obligation to honor his parents, and so allowed him to place some closure on their deaths.

The technique of helping people find a final resting place in some internal space in their heart and spirit for their lost loved one involves the client in both cognitive and emotional restructuring. To accomplish this task clients needs to have completed the acceptance stage, and be at least partially through the stage of experiencing the pain of their grief. It is necessary for them to crystallize and distill the memory of the loved person in a way that allows that person to be incorporated into the clients' own identity, so that the image can be retrieved at will, according to the needs of the moment. This does not imply that mourners are constantly preoccupied with the deceased person, but in fact places them in control of their memory by giving them assurance that they can connect with their loved one whenever they wish. This relieves anxiety about possibly forgetting the person, and seems to provide a sense of security and comfort.

A case example of how this approach was successfully used involved a woman client in her fifties, whose husband had died suddenly from an undiagnosed heart condition. At that point, the family froze in their developmental path, and neither of the adult children was able to move on in their lives, largely because of their mother's unresolved grief. She had lost her identity as the wife of an exceptional man, her role as homemaker in a perfect home, and she could not bear to allow her children to go on to the next step of marriage and leaving home. Although these children were in their twenties, mother's pain at the prospect of losing them spoiled their interactions with possible marriage partners, and neither child felt free to give their affection to a potential mate. When mother entered counseling to deal with her depression and grief, she moved rather slowly through the process, although it had been three years since her husband's death. However, she gradually became more forward-looking in her approach, and was at last able to travel away from the home which she had been unable to leave because it symbolized the happy times in her life. As she began to live with more freedom from her grief, one of her daughters became interested in a man, and raised the question of marriage with her mother. At first the mother said she couldn't possibly attend a wedding without her husband, but as she had begun to do some work on incorporating his image into her daily existence, she reached a stage where she was actually able to escort her daughter down the aisle, believing that her husband was walking with them because she carried his essence within her.

CONCLUSION

Although we are reminded by Rando that "Once bereaved, always bereaved" [42, p. 115], it is our hope for our clients that they will move through their work of mourning to achieve a good quality of life, free from oppressive sadness and pain. Counseling is a most effective way of helping them attain this goal, and for the counselor is extremely rewarding work, although the challenges are many. Becoming an effective counselor to bereaved and dying people requires careful preparation in gaining knowledge and perfecting skills, as well as the experience that only time and the exposure to a wide variety of situations can provide.

REFERENCES

1. M. McGoldrick and F. Walsh, A Time to Mourn: Death and the Family Life Cycle, in *Living Beyond Loss: Death in the Family,* F. Walsh and M. McGoldrick (eds.), W. W. Norton & Company, New York, pp. 30-49, 1991.
2. C. M. Parkes, Bereavement Counselling: Does it Work? *British Medical Journal, 281,* pp. 3-6, 1980.
3. R. L. George and T. S. Cristiani, *Counselling Theory and Practice* (4th Edition), Allyn and Bacon, Boston, 1995.

4. J. W. Worden, *Grief Counseling and Grief Therapy: A Handbook for the Mental Health Practitioner* (2nd Edition), Springer Publishing Company, New York, 1991.
5. T. Rando, *Treatment of Complicated Mourning*, Research Press, Champaign, Illinois, 1993.
6. K. Martin and S. Elder, Pathways Through Grief: A Model of the Process, in *Personal Care in an Impersonal World: A Multidimensional Look at Bereavement*, J. D. Morgan, (ed.), Baywood Publishing, Amityville, New York, 1993.
7. M. McGoldrick, Echoes From the Past: Helping Families Mourn Their Losses, in *Living Beyond Loss: Death in the Family*, F. Walsh and M. McGoldrick (eds.), W. W. Norton & Co., New York, 1991.
8. E. M. Pattison, The Living-Dying Process, in *Psychosocial Care of the Dying Patient*, C. A. Garfield (ed.), McGraw-Hill Book Co., New York, 1978.
9. A. E. Ivey, M. B. Ivey, and L. Simek-Morgan, *Counselling and Psychotherapy: A Multi-Cultural Perspective* (3rd Edition), Allyn and Bacon, Boston, 1993.
10. E. Erikson, *Childhood and Society* (2nd Edition), Norton, New York, 1963.
11. A. Miller, *The Drama of the Gifted Child*, Basic Books, New York, 1981.
12. M. Klein, *Envy, Gratitude and Other Works, 1946-1963*, Hogarth, London, 1975.
13. J. Bowlby, *Attachment and Loss*, Vol. I, Basic Books, New York, 1969.
14. J. Bowlby, *Attachment and Loss*, Vol. II, Penguin Press, Harmondsworth, United Kingdom, 1975.
15. J. Bowlby, *Attachment and Loss, Sadness and Depression*, Vol. III, Basic Books, New York, 1980.
16. A. Ellis, *Humanistic Psychotherapy, The Rational-Emotive Approach*, Julian Press, New York, 1973.
17. A. Bandura, Behavior Modification Through Modeling Procedures, in *Research in Behavior Modification*, L. Krasner and L. Ullman (eds.), Holt, Rinehart & Winston, New York, 1965.
18. A. T. Beck, *Cognitive Therapy of Personality Disorders*, Guilford Press, New York, 1990.
19. W. Glasser, *Reality Therapy*, Harper Collins, New York, 1965.
20. W. Glasser, *Take Effective Control of Your Life*, Harper Collins, New York, 1984.
21. C. Rogers, *Client-Centred Therapy*, Houghton-Mifflin, Boston, 1951.
22. C. Rogers, *On Becoming a Person*, Houghton Mifflin, Boston, 1961.
23. F. Perls, *Gestalt Theory Verbatim*, Real People Press, Moab, Utah, 1969.
24. F. Perls, *In and Out of the Garbage Pail*, Real People Press, Moab, Utah, 1969.
25. V. E. Frankl, *Psychotherapy and Existentialism*, Simon and Schuster, New York, 1967.
26. V. E. Frankl, *The Unheard Cry for Meaning: Psychotherapy and Humanism*, Simon and Schuster, New York, 1985.
27. I. D. Yalom, *Existential Psychotherapy*, Basic Books, New York, 1980.
28. P. Pederson (ed.), *Handbook of Cross-Cultural Counseling and Therapy*, Greenwood Press, Westport, Connecticut, 1985.
29. D. Sue and D. Sue, *Counseling the Culturally Different* (2nd Edition), Wiley, New York, 1990.
30. A. Lukas, *Meaningful Living*, Schenkman, Cambridge, Massachusetts, 1984.
31. J. Jordan, A. Kaplan, J. B. Miller, I. Stiver, and J. Surrey (eds.), *Women's Growth in Connection*, Guilford Press, New York, 1991.
32. J. Marmor, The Psychotherapeutic Process: Common Denominators in Diverse Approaches, in *The Evolution of Psychotherapy*, J. K. Zeig (ed.), Brunner/Mazel, New York, 1987.

33. E. Kennedy, *Crisis Counseling: An Essential Guide for Nonprofessional Counselors,* Continuum Press, New York, 1986.
34. R. R. Carkhuff and B. G. Berensen, *Beyond Counseling and Therapy* (2nd Edition), Holt, Rinehart and Winston, New York, 1977.
35. C. B. Truax and K. M. Mitchell, Research on Certain Therapist Interpersonal Skills in Relation to Process and Outcome, in *Handbook of Psychotherapy and Behavior Change: An Empirical Analysis,* A. E. Bergin and S. L. Garfield (eds.), Wiley, New York, 1971.
36. A. E. Ivey, M. B. Ivey, and L. Simek-Downing, *Counseling and Psychotherapy: Integrating Skills, Theory and Practice* (2nd Edition), Prentice Hall, Englewood Cliffs, New Jersey, 1987.
37. H. Hackney and S. Cormier, *Counseling Strategies and Interventions,* Allyn and Bacon, New York, 1994.
38. G. Corey, *Theory and Practice of Counseling and Psychotherapy* (4th Edition), Brooks/Cole, Pacific Grove, California, 1991.
39. D. Hutchins and C. Cole, *Helping Relationships and Strategies* (2nd Edition), Brooks/Cole, Pacific Grove, California, 1992.
40. T. Rando, *Parental Loss of a Child,* Research Press, Chicago, 1986.
41. S. Ilse, *Empty Arms: Coping with Miscarriage, Stillbirth and Infant Death,* A. Applebaum (ed.), Wintergreen Press, Maple Plain, Minnesota, 1990.
42. T. Rando, *Grief, Dying and Death: Clinical Interventions for Caregivers,* Research Press, Champaign, Illinois, 1984.
43. E. Imber-Black, Rituals and the Healing Process, in *Living Beyond Loss: Death in the Family,* F. Walsh and M. McGoldrick (eds.), W. W. Norton & Co., New York, 1991.
44. F. T. Melges and D. R. DeMasco, Grief-Resolution Therapy: Reliving, Revising and Revisiting, *American Journal of Psychotherapy, 34*, pp. 51-61, 1980.

CHAPTER 20
Complicated Bereavement

Jo Ann Silcox

Remember your creator in the days of your youth, before the days of trouble come, and the years draw near when you will say:-I have no pleasure in them-;
Before the sun and the light and the moon and the stars are darkened and the clouds return with the rain;
In the day when the guards of the house tremble, and the strong men are bent, and the women who grind cease working because they are few, and those who look through the windows see dimly;
When one is afraid of heights and terrors are in the road; the almond tree blossoms, the grasshopper drags itself along and desire fails; because all must go to their eternal home, and the mourners will go about the streets;
Before the silver cord is snapped and the gold pitcher is broken at the fountain, and the wheel broken at the cistern,
And the dust returns to the earth as it was, and the breath returns to God who gave it.
Vanity of vanities, says the Teacher; all is vanity.
Ecclesiastes 12:1-9

INTRODUCTION

Not even the wealthiest and most successful of Israel's chosen kings was, toward the end of his life, spared the agony of loss and the torment of grief—and neither shall we, regardless of our circumstances.

Loss begins with our birthing and ends with our own deaths, punctuated by a thousand intervening cycles of death and rebirth as our very development as human beings depends upon mastering the art of cleaving, letting go, cleaving, and then letting go again.

The wondrous joy of attachment, we know, will be followed inevitably by the agonizing emptiness of abandonment and though we bravely advert that "It is better to have loved and lost than never to have loved at all," at times of loss all of us, to one degree or another, rail against the unfairness of it all.

Our death-denying North American culture is in fact a loss-defying culture—one determined, despite all of the millennia of evidence to the contrary, to market the myth that individual prowess can secure in life that which is not only abundant but eternal, this side of the veil!

It is little wonder, then, that we struggle, unlike Charlie Brown, against the concept of good grief and instead tend to view all loss as failure, all sorrow as weakness, all bereavement as complicated and therefore pathological grief. In our cult of perfect health, we have rendered and integral of the cycle of life aberrant and applied to it a *disease model*.

In truth loss is inevitable, developmental, and unique for each human life.

HISTORICAL BACKGROUND

From Freud's earliest attempts to define bereavement as the process of decathecting the libidinal attachment to a lost object, care givers across many professions have struggled to define normal grief and to differentiate it from its pathological or complicated variants. Even earlier, the father of modern medicine, Hippocrates, worried that passions could not only influence the function of the body but also cause disease. Poets and artists through the centuries have dramatized the morbidity associated with enlarged grief, warning of the mortality associated with a broken heart.

In 1944, the sociologist Lindemann described bereavement on a massive scale in the wake of the disastrous Coconut Grove Fire from which study emerged the Pentateuchal signs of bereavement: somatic disturbance, preoccupation with the image of the dead, guilt, hostility, and disorganized behavior [1].

Homes and Rahe, responding to the growing clinical apprehension regarding containing this new disease, published in the late 1950s their now immortalized Life Change Units Scale—a consumer-beware guide to the disastrous mental, physical, and social illness which would flow from allowing too many events of transition to accumulate in a calendar year [2]. It has taken nearly forty years for researchers, grounded in systems theory and whole person assessment, to correct that scale and to recognize that the meaning that a particular life event has for the individual needs to be taken into account and not simply its occurrence as such.

In 1976, the American psychiatrist Valliant, sagely reminded us all that Grief hurts, but does not make us ill [3]. We forget that it is the inconstant people who stay in our lives who drive us mad, not the constant ones who die. We forget that it is failure to internalize those whom we have loved, and not their loss, that impedes adult development. Development is not inhibited by loss but enabled by loving.

LOSS, GRIEF, BEREAVEMENT

Bereavement is the process of separation from that to which we have attached value. Loss may be real, anticipated, or imagined. That which is lost may be relational, material, mental, emotional, spiritual, mythical, constitutional, individual, or communal.

Grief is the emotional or affective response to the absence (real or feared) of a valued object, person, or situation. It may be immediate or significantly delayed. It may be short-lived or chronic. It may be suppressed, partial, or life-consuming.

Mourning is the process by which we apprehend the presence of loss, mourn the absence of the valued other, and move on to re-attach to the world in new commitment, armed with an internalized representation of what which was lost.

STAGES OF DYING

Theorists from many disciplines have attempted to understand the process of letting go by studying first the ultimate loss—death. Elisabeth Kübler-Ross, in her seminal studies of the dying, described five sequential or occasionally recurrent stages in the journey of unwinding this mortal coil [4]. Kübler-Ross characterized the dying patient as progressing through a quintet of progressive adaption to loss which included: denial, anger, bargaining, depression, and acceptance.

1. The Stage of Denial
   Initial news of untreatable disease is frequently accompanied by a shutting down of both emotions and cognitive functions—both of which are replaced by a state of shock in which even the possibility let alone the probability of death is vehemently denied. *It cannot be true!*

2. The Stage of Anger
   As denial begins to lose its grip, persons facing death typically deal with rising hostility towards the impotence of self, family, friends physicians and God himself, to stem the relentless tide of disease. Some individuals vent a full range of feelings of bitterness, rage and envy while the anger of others may be much more muted. Typically the latter group are introverted with low self-esteem, strong guilt reactions, or self-destructive personalities—often viewing death as deserved punishment.

3. The Stage of Bargaining
   Hope in individual power re-emerges during this stage of arguing with the inevitable. The dying person debates with God in a series of rituals which often have strong magical overtones. Reverting to the beliefs of childhood that thoughts and wishes can in some way affect reality, many persons return to the religious orientations of their past, or begin to search for the first time in their lives for a power beyond themselves—one able to overcome death and illness. The patient promises a change in personal lifestyle or in disposition of his goods in exchange for renewal or prolongation of life.

4. The Stage of Depression
   The fourth stage really has two phases: *preparatory grief* and *final grief.* During the stage of *preparatory grief* the patients finally detach themselves from their surroundings, relinquish their wider social relationships and family responsibilities, and begin the process of mourning the anticipated cessation of

emotional bonds. Even patients who have been separated from their families for a long period of time will begin reflecting about these past relationships and may even try to rectify wrongs that they have committed long in the past.

During the stage of final grief, the patient is increasingly preoccupied with the loss of his own life. This period os often filled with reflections about the total meaning of life and existence and all degrees of depression may be seen.

5. The Stage of Acceptance

In this final stage, the patient is seen to embrace the inevitability of his impending death and often requests that his last hours be spent either alone or in the presence of a beloved few [4].

STAGES OF GRIEF/BEREAVEMENT

It was a short step from the study of the dying patient himself to a plethora of theories which attempted to describe the reactions of individuals and collectives alike to the experience of loss, regardless of its magnitude.

For, in fact, societal focus began to shift inevitably to the burden of shattered dreams borne not by the deceased, but by those whose lives his loss impacted:

> Parting is all we know of heaven
> And all we need to know of hell.
> Emily Dickinson [5]

PHASES OF GRIEF

Not surprisingly, the phases of grief envisioned bear significant similarity to those of Kübler-Ross.

1. The Phase of Protest

This first phase of mourning is characterized by frantic attempts on the part of the bereaved individual either to maintain the relationship with the lost person or object or to recover it. The initial reaction is that of disbelief or denial. *I don't believe it. It can't be happening.* This stage may be momentary or it may become intense and prolonged resulting in a place of fixation and complicated grief.

Bereaved persons in this phase may not be able to accept in any way that the person is dead or the object lost and will continue to behave as if nothing has happened. In a yet more severe form—that of *shock*—there seems to be dulling of all senses and function—as if time had stood still until restitution could recur.

> There is a pain—so utter—
> It swallows substances up—
> Then covers the Abyss with Trance—
> So Memory can step
> Around—across-upon it—
> As one within a Swoon—

> Goes safely—where an open eye—
> Would drop him—Bone by Bone.
> Emily Dickinson [5]

The bereaved may attempt to shake or talk the deceased back onto life. *Weeping* characteristically is profuse and may represent both a protest and an attempt to recover the lost person, much as lost children wail to alert temporarily out-of-sight parents to return to their aid. Considerable *anger* and *hostility* may characterize this early phase—directed at caregivers, surviving relatives, self, or the deceased in a chorus of indictments. *How could you do this to me? What have I done to deserve this?*

2. The Phase of Disorganization

This second phase of bereavement represents a time of awakening—a growing apprehension of the certainty and irreversibility of the loss. Described in graphic detail by Lindemann of the bereaved relatives of the 500 victims of the Coconut Grove Fire in 1944, this phase is one of overwhelming human angst.

Affective responses include profound *sadness*, deep yearning for the lost loved one, diffuse *anger*, overwhelming *guilt*. The surrounding world seems deprived of meaning and hope but in limited grief, in contrast to depression, the bereaved person's self-esteem is still intact.

Somatic responses are plenteous in this period including digestive disturbances, loss of appetite, tightness in the throat, choking sensations, sighing respirations, feelings of weakness, lack of energy, physical exhaustion.

Behavioral changes include disorganized aimlessness and restlessness, reduced concentration, mechanical actions, social withdrawal, distractibility.

Mental changes typically include irritability, temporary memory lapses, confusion preservation with images of the deceased, periodic hallucinations, tormenting dreams, intrusive memories.

Social behavior alternatives between marked withdrawal from and intense clinging to those whose presence is evocative of the deceased.

C. S. Lewis, who documented his own journey of the dark night of the soul in the loss of his beloved wife, Joy, in *A Grief Observed* wrote of this phase:

> For me at any rate the program is plain. I will turn to her as often as possible in gladness. I will even salute her with a laugh. The less I mourn her the nearer I seem to her. An admirable program. Unfortunately, it can't be carried out. Tonight all the hells of young grief have opened again; the mad words, the bitter resentment, the fluttering in the stomach, the nightmare unreality, the walled-in tears. For in grief nothing stays put. One keeps on emerging from a phase, but it always recurs. Round and round. Everything repeats. Am I going in circles, or dare I hope I am on a spiral. but if a spiral, am I going up or down it? [6].

3. The Phase of Reorganization

In this final phase, the bereaved begin to reinvest their energies and interests in the world. Depending on the previous experience of loss, the intensity of the attachment, their present strengths and supports, this phase may take months or years or a lifetime.

Gradually they begin to give up the intensity of investment in the lost person—slowly pushing themselves to put away those pictures and possessions which have heretofore daily provoked floods of remembrance. The intensity of last memories begin to fade and imperceptibly shift into longitudinal memories or life and sharing colored by the return of pleasure and affection.

New activities are begun and old relationships renewed—but with great caution and not inconsiderable guilt as the demon of survivor guilt often slows this phase—"Why should I be enjoying this person or that even when the deceased no longer can?" (e.g., Primo Levi).

Some aspects of the old relationship are always maintained—*memories, fantasies of reunion* (supported by religious beliefs in an after-life, communication with the dead, reincarnation, etc). Finally the relationship is maintained by a process of identification—the individual taking on some of the projects, beliefs, attitudes, or behaviors of the deceased.

> The distance that the dead have gone
> Does not at first appear—
> Their coming back seems possible
> For many an ardent year
>
> And then, that we have followed them,
> We more than half suspect,
> So intimate have we become
> With their deserved retrospect.
>
> Emily Dickinson [5]

Out of all of this come new adaption, new growth, new liberty, new mastery—as in every other stage of the developmental life cycle. New *values, attitudes, talents, and coping mechanisms* emerge with which not only is the individual equipped to face life alone but with which he is better prepared to embrace the next phase of attachment and subsequent loss.

> As with Solomon's grief, so with ours, the night is always darkest before the dawn:
> For everything there is a season, a time for every matter under heaven;
> A time to be born and a time to die;
> A time to plant, and a time to pluck up what is planted;
> A time to kill, and a time to heal;
> A time to break down and a time to build up;
> A time to weep, and a time to laugh;
> A time to mourn, and a time to dance;

A time to throw away stones and a time to gather stones together;
A time to embrace and a time to refrain from embracing;
A time to seek, and a time to lose;
A time to keep, and a time to throw away;
A time to tear and a time to sew;
A time to keep silence and a time to speak;
A time to love and a time to hate;
A time for war and a time for peace.

Ecclesiastes 3:1-8

FACTORS AFFECTING THE OUTCOME OF BEREAVEMENT

No two grieving individuals think, feel, behave, or believe in exactly the same way—despite apparent similarities in loss sustained.

What Factors Determine the Unique Manifestations of Individual Mourning?

The form and intensity of grief experienced and displayed is the result of a complex interplay between "trauma" and "traumatized"—between all of those factors inherent to the loss itself and all of those strengths and weaknesses inherent in the individual experiencing the loss.

Disease or distress states in general have usually been seen as the result of clashing forces—the destructive forces of the invader vs. the resistive forces of the host. This medical model, which draws heavily on combat as an analogue, sees the offensive player as loss and the defensive player as the bereaved.

The current abuse literature reframes this same dynamics as traumatic agent vs. recovering host.

Traumatic Agent

Death or loss is the offensive player in this scrimmage. Its virulence is measured in terms of its ability to cause disequilibrium in the following spheres:

biological integrity
psychological integrity
social integrity
spiritual integrity

The potency of the loss is heightened by its:

1. *global nature*—the greater the number of target areas attacked, the greater the devastation. Losses which leave the bereaved compromised physically, guilt-ridden, deprived of primary support sources or systems, and questioning life's ultimate meaning—are more likely to produce long-term sequelae than those which interfere transiently in only one sphere of functioning.

2. *intensity*—Loss which produces profound complications (e.g., multiple non-reversible injuries) likewise predisposes to chronic grief or dysfunction.
3. *unpredictability*—Sudden, unexpected loss is usually more traumatic than gradual loss which allows pre-mourning.
4. *social acceptability*—Death by suicide, homicide, secondary to substance abuse, in the course of violent crime etc., leaves the bereaved to deal with imputed shame and a certain degree of social shunning.

Defensive Host

The victims of loss are clearly not only the dying but also the bereaved who must continue to cope long after death has ended the struggle for the dying.

The impact of that then solitary journey is dependent on the current state of equilibrium of the mourner at the time of the real or anticipated loss. As with the impact of the traumatic agent itself, equilibrium is dependent upon each of the four primary spheres of whole person functioning:

biological integrity
psychological integrity
social integrity
spiritual integrity

Biological Equilibrium

Any present unstable current physical illness is likely to be aggravated by the particular global stress of loss—e.g., cardiovascular deaths are frequent in the face of traumatic loss.

Concurrent use of a prescription sedative or mood-altering drugs on a self-administered basis (e.g., alcohol, tranquilizers, sleeping pills, pain killers) may significantly interfere with the grieving process leading to delayed or distorted grief reactions.

Disease or injury associated with the loss itself (e.g., survivors of AIDS, accidents) may lead to either survivor guilt or extreme hostility—each interfering with the global healing process.

Psychological Equilibrium

Confidence in one's ability to withstand and overcome loss is dependent upon:

- current self-esteem and self-worth
- confidence in the reliability of previously learned adaptations to change and loss
- absence of disorganizing major mental illness
- freedom from ambivalent, hostile, or unresolved issues with the deceased
- personal existential view of the nature of the loss process itself (e.g., crime-based, AIDS)

Social Equilibrium

Courage to withstand loss will be influenced by:

- the stability and past reliability of proffered support systems
- the specific sensitivities of family, friends, and others to the nature of the loss itself
- the absence of concomitant complicated grief responses in significant others (e.g., hostility)
- availability of need-specific support systems at various stages of grief
- the availability of life-affirming roles in relationship other than those shared with the deceased (e.g., friend, mother, secretary—not just wife)

Spiritual Equilibrium

Resolution is facilitated by the individual's ability to find existential meaning in the life lived by the deceased and in the coping mechanisms learned during the loss by the bereaved.

Bereavement brings, initially, a questioning of ultimate purpose and meaning and may shake existing belief systems. Recovering is dependent upon finding meaning in a new world view.

CULTURAL BEREAVEMENT AS A SOCIAL ANALOGUE OF MASSIVE LOSS

Eisenbruch, an Australian Medical Research Council Fellow, has recently explored massive loss, using the refugee experience of cultural bereavement as a paradigm. This parallels similar work by the American psychiatrist Judith Herman in comparing the experience of survivors of childhood sexual abuse to survivors of the Holocaust, of war, and of cultural displacement—all phenomena which disrupt the fundamental supports and beliefs systems of the bereaved at every level.

Massive suffering of this nature must be understood in the light of being uprooted, of losing one's family, one's primary social and economic structure, and one's basic sense of cultural meaning.

The term *nostalgia* has been used in the literature to describe the overwhelming disorientation caused by such core losses.

The global nature of the losses inherent in such uprooting are often compounded by the absence of a culturally sensitive support system to accommodate the process of grief, and many studies have suggested that the apparent tendency of refugees, or the disenfranchised, to *ghettoize* is an adaptive mechanism—to allow grief to occur among one's kind—before attempting the yet more difficult step of adaption to a new culture.

In a similar fashion, such displaced persons may be subject to recurrent grief at times of subsequent alienation—e.g., advancing age, personal bereavement, physical illness, social isolation—thereby reactivating the trauma of the original uprooting.

Uprooting disrupts the individual's *concept of self*. The anxieties of change center upon the struggle to defend or recover a meaningful pattern of relationships. Some exiles, in anticipation of light from their homeland, perform *rituals* aimed at preserving the images about to be lost. When coupled with the lack of a community of supportive compatriots, cultural bereavement leads to *intense guilt, withdrawal, social isolation, and depression*. The intense clinging to past culture, with an inability to form new attachments is similar to the mummification and overidealization of the deceased seen in complicated individual bereavement. An entire community of uprooted people, by extension, can be seen to be experiencing *complicated collective grief*.

This concept has ramifications for later intervention recognizing that the *global nature of loss* and the particular *language and symbols of grief peculiar to a particular culture* must be recognized and honored by anyone attempting to make meaningful contact with victims of this level of loss.

Constructs which must be explored in counseling the culturally bereaved include: memories of family and homeland, continuing experiences of family and past, ghosts and spirits from the past, dreams, guilt, clarity of recall of the past, structuring of the past in the homeland, experiences of death, response to separation from the homeland, comfort from religious belief, and comfort from religious practice.

LINKS BETWEEN GENERAL AND CULTURAL BEREAVEMENT THEORY
(see Table 1)

The ramifications of massive social upheaval in bereavement counseling are obvious. Cultural bereavement exercises a profound effect on the uprooted person's state of mind and the clinician needs to take this into account together with a careful understanding of cultural-specific expressions of grief before making pathological diagnoses.

Such an awareness may allow counselors to go beyond restrictive North American concepts of appropriate grief to an active search for intercession from traditional hierarchies within the patient's local community (e.g., shamans, priests, traditional healing ceremonies).

Group participation in *traditional ceremonies* does more than simply treat the grief of individuals. The group participation promotes restoration of the patients' old culture and acts as an antidote not only to their cultural bereavement but also to that of the entire community of victims of cultural bereavement.

Many studies, in fact, strongly emphasize that the contemporary decline in accepted ritual guidance at the time of loss is a major factor in the emergence of complicated grief syndromes in the last four decades.

A prime lesson from such sociological studies is the importance of *maintaining or recreating known culture* for the bereaved. Pressures to accommodate to change and to new beginnings may in fact prolong the grief process rather than relieving it.

COMPLICATED BEREAVEMENT AND MOURNING

What is It?

In response to overwhelming loss, certain individuals are unable to come to terms with the loss, either to acknowledge it consciously, or to give up yearning for the person. Its form varies in

intensity—too little vs. too much
onset—premature vs. vastly delayed
duration—eclipsed vs. chronic
focus—hostile ambivalence vs. canonization
locus of control—somatization vs. acting out
reality contact—depression vs. psychosis
resolution—fixated vs. partial

How Common is It?

About 12 to 14 percent of bereaved persons suffer from decompensation resulting in some degree of shorter- or longer-term survivor disability.

Who Are its Victims?

While all of us are prone in the face of overwhelming loss to periods of dysfunction, four groups or survivors have been identified as being particularly prone:

survivors of sudden or unexpected loss
survivors of dependent relationships
survivors of ambivalent relationships
already compromised individuals

What Are its Manifestations?

Unexpected Loss Syndrome

The explanatory model for this syndrome proposes that the mode and onset of the dying itself has pathogenic effects—in both its unnatural and unpredicted aspects. Unexpected loss commonly qualifies as a traumatic stressor that would evoke signs and symptoms of distress in almost everyone. The mode of death is seen to be so fearful and overwhelming as to preclude assimilation and accommodation. Instead a dysfunctional syndrome follows that reflects the incomplete and fragmentary resolution.

Typically this *post-traumatic stress syndrome* includes startle reactions, explosions of anger, recurrent intrusive recollections of dying (nightmares and flashbacks), compensatory psychic numbing, constriction of affect and social functioning, and loss of sense of control over one's own destiny.

When unexpected loss is associated with unnatural causes (e.g., accident, homicide, suicide), the bereaved is further traumatized by forensic and judicial

Table 1. Links between General and Cultural Bereavement Theory

Constructs from General Bereavement Theory	Cultural Bereavement Constructs	Areas of Exploration in Bereavement
Thoughts and perceptions of the past	Memories of family	What is thought about? What triggered the thoughts? What is the response to memories?
	Continuing experiences of family and past	Is there a sense of presence? What communication occurs with the dead? Does the dead person exhort? What is the emotional response to contact?
	Ghosts or spirits from the past	Do the spirits exhort? What action is taken in response? Is there physical contact? What triggers contact? What is the emotional response to contact?
Survivor guilt	Dreams	What is the trigger? What is the dream scene? Is there exhortation by actors in the dream? What is the outcome? How does the dreamer respond to the dream?
	Guilt	What were the reasons for the flight from the homeland? Was it wrong to flee? How does the person rationalize the flight now?
Survivor guilt	Clarity of recall of past	Does the person have difficulty recalling images of the family? Does the person fear difficulty of being recognized? What is the response to these fears? Are there available souvenirs? What is the response?

Table 1. (Cont'd.)

Constructs from General Bereavement Theory	Cultural Bereavement Constructs	Areas of Exploration in Bereavement
Violence of separation or death	Structuring of the past in the homeland	What contrast of memories exists before/after loss? How are memories structured? Does the person transfer feelings to host country?
Absence of leave taking	Experiences of death	Who died? What were the causes of death? How certain is person that relative died? Did person participate in the deaths? Whose fault was it that the deaths occurred? Were there leave-taking rituals? Is there any expectation of reunion? How does the person yearn for the dead?
Anger/ Ambivalence	Response to separation from the homeland	What understanding was there of the flight? Who instigated it? Was there anger at the time of separation? Does the anger persist now? What fear of violence/war? What is the political context of this fear?
Antidotes to cultural bereavement	Comfort from religious belief	Which beliefs (Christian, Buddhist, pantheistic other?) provide comfort? Is there permission to express these? What impact did war/revolution have on person's beliefs?
	Comfort from religious practice	Which religious practices are helpful? Why does the person participate in ceremonies? How does the person feel as a result?

investigations and media intrusion as well as public voyeurism. *Social isolation and imputed shame* adds to the intolerable burden as does the often solitary search for *vindication, justice or explanation* in the face of public or professional indifference or avoidance. The *violation of the sacred* in these kinds of deaths is often mocked by the accompanying public shunning to which its survivors are exposed out of communal fear of contagion.

Dependent Loss Syndrome

Dependence in this instance refers to a relationship of relative non-differentiation in which one's image of self is contingent upon the availability of another. This dependence demands continuing interchange as a requisite for maintaining an image of self as whole or acceptable.

The death of the figure with whom the bereaved was dependent initiates a pathogenic shift in self-image from that of being strong, caring, and worthwhile to discrepant images of being weak, uncaring, and incompetent—there being often no concomitantly available relationship in which the role of equivalent centrality can be quickly reinvested.

This model presupposes that these pathologic self-images are potent compelling organizers of perception that independently deform the thoughts, feelings, and behavior of pathologic grief—but a major cause may equally be the re-emergence of earlier self-images and roles prior to the emergence of the recently lost dependent relationship. These pathogenic self-images may have evolved during earlier developmental stages of self-differentiation and the lost relationship may have a temporary buffering effect creating an image of worth and competence. Persons so characterized often bear the diagnostic description of *dependent, borderline or narcissistic personalities*. This dynamic creates a bereavement pattern of *immediate overwhelming pining and chronic grief*.

Conflicted Grief Syndrome

This syndrome follows the death of an ambivalently valued figure in which the ambivalence cannot be psychologically tolerated. The ambivalent investment in the lost other produces conflict in the bereaved and is experienced as *guilt, self-blame, and self-accusation*.

Freud initially viewed this dynamic as the basis of depression in which the self is viewed as bad and worthless, in contrast to mourning in which the external world is impoverished. Clinically, this form of grief often presents as an *absent or minimized early response* followed months or years later by a *delayed intense pining or rage*.

Secondary Grief Syndromes

In individuals already compromised at the time of loss, precipitation of latent disease states, or perpetuation of ongoing states may be anticipated. These characteristically represent decompensation in one or more areas of individual functioning:

Behavioral

Behavioral changes in the both extremes are noted. Social withdrawal syndromes are common with schizoid, dysthymic, or avoidant behavior. Similarly acting out syndromes may emerge as with substance abuse, violence, excessive spending, sexual acting-out, eating disorders, or other impulse states. More rarely emergence of phobic or panic states may be seen.

Cognitive

Contained decompensation may manifest in the emergence of obsessive-compulsive or ruminative thoughts. In more extreme situations delusional material or ideas of reference signal the onset of a psychotic decompensation (schizophrenia, involutional melancholia, paranoid states, transient psychoses, etc.).

Affective

Prolonged or profound loss plus a vulnerable survivor combine to heighten the risk of a clinical depression in which the hopelessness of the outside world now invades the soul of the survivor. This may manifest as a chronic dysthymia, a unipolar depression, a bipolar depression, a cyclic depression, an involutional state, or a suicidal conviction.

Dysthymia is characterized by a persistently low mood and accompanying negativistic attitude with energy loss, low self-esteem, and difficulty in decision making.

Bipolar illness is characterized by altering periods of profound depression and extreme elation with accompanying congruent changes in behavior and cognition (suppression or release phenomenon).

Major depression is characterized by a primarily affective syndrome, differing in character from the individual's pre-loss functioning and typified by at least five of the following symptoms:
- depressed or irritable mood most of the day, nearly every day
- markedly diminished interest in almost all of the activities of the day, nearly every day
- significant weight loss or weight gain, when not dieting, or decrease in appetite
- insomnia or hypersomnia nearly every day
- psychomotor agitation or retardation nearly every day
- fatigue or loss of energy nearly every day
- feelings of worthlessness or excessive inappropriate guilt (which may be delusional) nearly every day
- diminished ability to think or concentrate, or indecisiveness nearly every day
- recurrent thoughts of death, recurrent suicidal ideation without a specific plan, or a specific plan for committing suicide.

Depression vs. Grief Reaction
Depressive reaction is characterized by:
- guilt and self-blame
- more than six month's duration
- functional incapacity
- suicidal thoughts and plans

Grief reaction is characterized by:
- sadness and external blame
- less than six month's duration
- persistent social functioning
- absence of suicidal actions

Suicidal risk is elevated by:
- social isolation
- ambivalent ties
- dependent ties
- previous history of depression
- previous history of psychosis
- substance abuse
- concomitant debilitating illness
- survivor guilt
- family history of suicide
- family history of violence
- unemployment
- lack of overriding belief system
- recent separation or divorce or job loss
- previous significant unresolved history of loss

Psychosomatic Illness and Accidents

Epidemiological studies show that bereaved persons are more prone to physical decompensation and accidental injury in the first two years following loss. Psychosomatic illness affecting all systems (cardiovascular, gastroenterological, immune, metabolic, endocrine, musculoskeletal, genitourinary, respiratory, neurological, etc.) are more prevalent. In addition independent disease states known to have a depressive overlay may be accentuated:

- Cushing's disease, Addison's disease, Diabetes Mellitus, Hypoparathyroidism, Hyperthyroidism
- Rheumatoid Arthritis, Temporal Arteritis, Polymyalgia Rheumatica
- Infectious Mononucleosis, Hepatitis, Herpes Zoster, Tuberculosis
- Cancer of lung, brain, head of pancreas
- Parkinsonism, Cerebrovascular accident, Multiple Sclerosis, Alzheimer's disease
- Drug interactions: Steroids, Betablockers, Reserpine, Alcohol, Minor Tranquilizers, Barbiturates, L-Dopa

REFERENCES

1. E. Lindemann, *Beyond Grief: Studies in Crisis Intervention,* Jason Aaronson, New York, 1979.
2. T. H. Homes and R. H. Rahe, The Social Readjustment Rating Scale, *Journal of Psychosomatic Research, 11,* p. 213, 1967.
3. G. E. Valliant, *Adaptation to Life,* Little Brown, Boston, 1977.
4. E. Kübler-Ross, *On Death and Dying,* Macmillan, New York, 1969.
5. T. H. Johnston (ed.), *The Complete Poems of Emily Dickinson,* Little Brown Co., Boston, 1957.
6. C. S. Lewis, *A Grief Observed,* The Seaway Press, New York, 1963.

CHAPTER 21

Working with Widows in Groups

Peggy M. L. Anderson

This chapter will focus on widows and groups. To begin, it will look at how widows experience grief. Next, it will explore how losing a husband in a death-denying society impacts negatively on women. Factors which bring healing to women grieving spousal loss will be considered. The therapeutic nature of groups in general and the value of grief support groups for widows in particular will follow. The chapter will conclude with a comprehensive explanation of "Alone and Growing," a structured grief work support group model. This group, which the author piloted for widows in London, Ontario, in 1987 continues to run three times yearly, facilitated by Peggy Anderson who is a writer, grief counselor/consultant in private practice, and a widow herself.

THE WIDOW AND THE EXPERIENCE OF GRIEF

The death of a husband is something for which we can never be fully prepared! Whether it comes after sudden trauma or protracted illness, death is a jolt. The reality of any close death is mind-challenging and gut-wrenching; the death of a spouse challenges and wrenches in special ways. When a husband dies, a part of us dies too. Many women claim they feel empty after the death of a spouse. In fact, the Sanskrit word for widow is "empty" and it defines us very well. Part of who we are goes with our mate. Another reality for the widow is that once her spouse dies, she feels her own mortality. Women who experience the death of a partner know as never before that we too will die. We also know that others we love are vulnerable. No one is exempt. Small wonder that grief for the widow feels a lot like fear. Grief for my lost husband; grief for my lost self; fear that death may happen to others I love; fear of my own death: these are all part of the package presented to a wife upon entering widowhood. It is hard at first to see the gift in this package.

ASPECTS OF A WIDOW'S GRIEF

When we think of bereavement we think immediately of its emotional nature.

> Grief is the experiencing of all the emotions connected with a loss from the shocked stage through to acceptance and eventually to finding joy again in one's life.

This is a useful basic definition of the grieving process. But in the case of grief after spousal death this definition is not enough. Grief has several other components which must be understood if we are to be able to relate to the grief experienced by the widowed woman. Her grief has physical, mental, spiritual, social, sexual, and economic components as well as the emotional one. Each of these aspects of grief, though discussed separately here, operates concurrently in the life of a widow, making the grieving process for women after spousal loss complex and exhausting.

Emotional

Going though grief means going through all of the emotions we know are associated with the grief process initially explained as stages by E. Kübler-Ross [1]. These emotions include numbness or shock, denial, bargaining, anger, guilt, sadness to depression, fear to panic, determination, rejuvenation, and acceptance. Going through grief is not linear as the stages theory suggests but rather erratic, like a roller-coaster ride, out of control. Grief lasts for years, not months, and is unpredictable. The path through one's grief is unique to each individual and at times seems overwhelming. One moment we feel too much; the next we steel up and feel nothing. For many, widowhood feels so different from our usual way of being we think we must be going crazy! Grief for the widow is certainly emotional.

Physical

Grief after a husband's death has its physical component too. It exhausts us yet we feel we must keep busy. Many of us do not sleep well, yet we are bone weary. Some of us do not want to eat. Some of us somatize our grief into aches in the body. Pain from this source is real and often manifests itself physically in places where our spouse was hurt or ill. For example, my husband died of cardiac arrest. Soon after his death, I experienced heart pains which, of course, I checked out with my physician. When I learned there was no physical reason for my pain, it soon disappeared. My developing this pain was a normal physical response, a somatizing of my grief. Because grief affects us physically we need to remember to look after ourselves, to eat well and to get adequate rest during this time or our physical selves will suffer.

Mental

Our grief is also mental. Loss is a shock to the brain as well as to the body. We cannot concentrate, cannot remember, totally forget some things and remember others out of all proportion to their importance. In a sense we are "not in our right minds" but somewhere else. Our focus is entirely on what we have lost. Time, too, is out of whack for many of us. A minute seems like an hour, an hour—a day. Each day is far too long and the thought of getting through a weekend seems impossible. We really must think in terms of "one day at a time" as a survival mechanism during this period. Anything else seems beyond our comprehension.

Spiritual

Many widows face a crisis of faith after a husband dies. While a strong faith may have helped her in the past, after death, especially if the loss was untimely, unnecessary or characterized by pain and suffering, a widow may reject her faith. She may become angry with her God. Certainly our faith is put to the test through the death of a spouse. From the stories of women I have researched, spirituality tends to return and change as grief heals.

Social

One of the most difficult aspects for the grieving widow to face is the social one. We live in a "coupled" society and many of us have been in partnership for a long time. To suddenly be single without a husband makes us the odd one at the table, the fifth wheel with our coupled friends, a supposed threat to marriages, a visible reminder that death could interrupt the comfortable couplehood around us. We eventually may be avoided or excluded from our old social network. This change is unexpected and is hard to accept. For us it is another loss to integrate into our already shattered lives. We have strong feelings of abandonment or anger as a result and may vent feelings inappropriately at the very friends we long to keep. We may also feel abandoned by our spouse and be angry at him for leaving us in this predicament.

Sexual

But leave us he has. We do not have his shoulder to cry on when we feel alone and we miss his support and companionship. We miss intimacy and physical touch. We miss loving. This is an aspect of being widowed that is not often acknowledged. There is some shame attached to still feeling sexual after a husband's death. When we do not deal with the issue of sexuality we may repress our sexual desires after a spouse dies to the extent that we never want to mate again. Or sometimes we move into indiscriminate liaisons because we need touch and holding. For a while, this feels like love. Most of us find we want a healthy relationship again after a spouse dies and after we grieve our loss fully.

Then for some, fear around both dating and becoming sexually involved again looms large. When we are able to openly share these fears and expectations with others the associated stress fades. Conflict over our own sexuality is another aspect of widowhood.

Economic

A widow will certainly face some kind of readjustment financially after a husband's death. She may now have to take over all of the business matters of the family. If the family has relied on a husband's income alone, a widow may panic when she realizes that she has a family to feed and no income—no prospects. On the other hand, a widow may suddenly find herself inheriting life insurance and may feel guilty about spending any of it when she and her husband had saved for so long for their dream retirement. Fear and guilt characterize this practical aspect of a woman's grieving period.

WIDOWS, SUPPORT, AND HEALING

Dealing with all of the aspects of loss facing us after becoming widowed challenges us. To meet the challenge we need to find inner resources such as courage, tenacity, and creativity. We must trust in ourselves believing that we will, in fact, thrive again and feel whole once more on our own. Can we find such inner resources when our resistance is low and our self-esteem ebbing? Women can, and women do. The great secret is that when we have support, we can and do find what we need more readily.

Society and Support for the Widow

After the death of a spouse, a widow generally finds herself well supported by family, friends, and community. This support begins at the death of her spouse and continues during and after the funeral period for a few months, often while the widow herself is still in shock. Just as her numbness begins to wear thin and she starts to feel again, her support system, believing her to be better, drifts away. Too often when the widow needs support most, it is not there for her. In fact, if she still continues to exhibit grief behaviors after this time her family and friends may judge or berate her. Collectively we do not understand grief well and we don't know how to help the bereaved. It is an unfortunate truth that after two decades of grief education, society still lacks the training, the resources and the compassion to deal with loss in a supportive and healing manner.

How Can We Help?

Several things can help the newly bereaved widow over the course of her loss. It will help her to have family, friends, and a community which understands the enormity of her loss and the complexity of the grieving process. It will help for her to have many resources to chose from in healing her own grief. This may range from books to a church group to good conversation with a trusted friend or mentor. Most important from my experience is having the opportunity to interact with other widowed women. From them we will believe in our own ability to heal because they have done so before us.

How Groups Help

Groups provide the opportunity to be with others and to grow because of it; they show us we are not alone, help change behavior and attitude, develop in us new socializing techniques, instill hope, allow for catharsis (the healing release of emotion), impart information, promote altruism, and facilitate a search for the meaning of life. All of these are important therapeutic factors at work in group dynamics, says group therapy expert Yalom in his book *The Theory and Practice of Group Psychotherapy* [2]. All of these factors will be at work in a well run grief support group.

The Group Process and Widows

Isolation is a widow's curse. Isolation and lack of support exacerbate any grief process; support makes the grieving process lighter. If support from family members, friends, or a community is wearing thin or is unavailable, groups can help fill the support gap. Groups organized with the widow and her grief work in mind, provide a place in which to meet, and interact with others who share with us a common bond. A support group where all members have been widowed has a very special quality. Because members of widows' support groups have all lost a spouse/partner to death, trust is almost automatic.

Our loss has moved us in many ways; one result is that it forces us into an existential crisis. What is the meaning of life?—his life?—my life? When we are alone this search for the meaning of life tends to be internalized. In a group the search becomes externalized. We quest together in a widows' support group for the meaning of life. Also unique to this group is that by seeing the same crisis in another person we become less angry, sad, panicked, or guilty. Group draws its members out of morbid self-absorption and gives to each participant a new perspective and sense of purpose. We begin to care about others. Finally, we become deeply supportive of one another. The "helper-therapy" principle is at work here: this is the principle which says that by helping others we help ourselves. That rich dynamic is very much at work in a grief support group for widows.

A widow will benefit from participating in a group. Provided the group deals with grief honestly and fully in a safe environment with skilled and experienced facilitators, the group will lead to healing and growing. Simply put, groups work.

THE "ALONE AND GROWING" GRIEF WORK SUPPORT GROUP MODEL

Getting Started

When my husband died there were no grief work support groups around. I was not coping well. I had no social life, my work was draining, my parenting was abysmal, and I was depressed. I had no ideas about grieving, what was normal and not or who to turn to for help. Worst of all for me was that I had no one I could talk to about it all. I felt incredibly isolated. It was the isolation that propelled me into action. I searched for and found a young widow who like myself had been left to single-parent four children and who tried to understand her grief and wrote about it. Her name was Betty Jane Wylie [3]. Next, I began to collect other women's stories with an aim to help newly widowed women like myself. Doing that research was unexpectedly therapeutic for me. I found the mutual sharing exciting and inspirational. I knew that the simple process of one-on-one sharing could work for any one of us. So I called together several widowed women from my book project in order to start some kind of group that would give us this opportunity.

We began by brainstorming. What did we want most from this group? Ideas came thick and fast. We wanted to stop feeling isolated; we wanted to get out of the house, meet other adults and relate again in a meaningful way. We wanted to be able to express our pain, not repress it. We wanted to be able to express all of our feelings, our anger and guilt and hopelessness. We wanted to share what had happened to us and hear what had happened to others. We wanted to interact with other women who really understood what it was we were living through and who cared about us. Desperately we wanted to stop feeling depressed. We wanted to feel better about ourselves, to get the joy back into our lives. Finally, we wanted to move on into a new, full, and meaningful life alone.

Knowing what we wanted was a start. We also were pretty clear about what hadn't helped. Drop-in widow-to-widow groups where there was no structure, no consistency of membership, and no planned grief work, became little more than crying and coffee sessions. Groups led by professionals who had not addressed their own personal issues of loss didn't move us into our own grief work fully because we felt their discomfort with our loss. The interaction remained supportive but no grief work was done. Now, knowing what was needed and what to avoid in a support group for widowed persons, I came to some conclusions about the necessary group format for "Alone and Growing" [4]. To be effective the group must have a leader or leaders with adequate life experience who had done their own grief work. The group should be time limited and should have grief work as its focus. Its membership should include only widowed persons and its framework should be structured. In order to maximize its potential the group should be therapeutic, deal honestly with death and grief issues and aim to promote individual healing and growth. I called this group "Alone and Growing" to describe that focus.

The Group Format

To repeat, then, the "Alone and Growing" model of a widowed persons' support group which I use is a

1. facilitated
2. time-limited
3. grief work oriented
4. supportive and
5. structured group.

1. Facilitated

A grief work support group must have a leader. The ideal leader for such a group is one who has been widowed in the past, has competence and credibility as a group leader and who is passionately committed to the idea that groups help. This leader should be willing to be a participant as well as a facilitator in the process. Often, it is her years of experience and knowing which become an inspiration for newer widowed persons. This leader should have a caring spirit, an ability to organize, an ability to be flexible, a desire to keep the confidentiality of the group, a genuine understanding and respect for the bereaved, an understanding of the group process, a desire to continue learning about his or her own grief, and finally, a willingness to empower the bereaved.

Co-facilitating, in which two people partner to lead, is very effective. I have always co-facilitated the "Alone and Growing" groups for several reasons. First, two leaders can share the responsibility and chores involved in running the group. They can also diffuse the emotional burden which can come with the processing of deep grief. There is often initially a lot of sadness in the group. Working in partnership with another who understands this and is mutually supportive diffuses the responsibility for holding that emotion which we as leaders sometimes feel. Also, the experience of two leaders gives to group members a greater variety of options to consider. Two leaders can alternate roles, one leading, one modeling; that is, one introduces an idea for discussion and the other "models" it to the group. Modeling to the group members teaches them about sharing and about extending their own boundaries in a non-threatening but creative way. Though I have found that groups facilitated by leaders who are also widows and participants work best, the combination of a widowed volunteer and a professional also works effectively. Most important is that the need for a group be filled in the community and that it be organized by individuals who have a good combination of knowledge and experience.

2. Time-Limited

The "Alone and Growing" group is time-limited as opposed to being open-ended. A group traditionally runs seven consecutive Tuesdays or Thursdays from 7:30–9:30. The same members participate each week; no new members are added during the group's duration, i.e., the membership is closed. When the groups first began, both Jane, my co-facilitator, and I were working full time at other things. I had three children at home. Committing seven Tuesdays in a row to group work was all either of us could handle. Similarly, most newly bereaved women often feel over-loaded with chores and decisions which they must handle alone for the first time. Committing to attend meetings one week night per week for a longer period of time often seems like too much. Interestingly, from member feedback I know that our meeting nights become the high point of their week and as the group moves to its close members don't want the sessions to end, would like to see the groups run longer, twelve weeks maybe, or a whole year. My feeling is that many women simply could not commit initially to such a long run. Having a seven-week time-limited group allows for members to accept endings and to return to a place of independence. It is important that the support group members not use the group to avoid returning to their own personal world and the people in it. Of course, in groups many deep friendships do form and these carry on beyond the group time and become part of member's real and ongoing support system.

To accommodate members who want to continue to work together but want leadership, I have facilitated some "Continuation" groups with "Alone and Growing" graduates. Usually these groups do not focus on grief work but on personal growth and self-actualization, are much less structured and vary in length.

It is also important to note that several groups may want to continue to meet informally on their own after the group terminates officially, becoming a permanent and valued source of support and friendship. While occasionally I meet with one or another of these "old" groups my involvement as facilitator is over and I am simply another friend who has been widowed when I am with them. They seem to care about me still and I them. It's a nice result of doing the hard work with widows. I meet so many very wonderful, resourceful, and caring women!

3. Grief Work Oriented

Our groups are "grief work" oriented. We are not just a group which gets together to talk at random or to cry together or to socialize, although we do cover all of those things in the course of the seven weeks we share together. Our group focuses on doing "grief work," described as the "perhaps the hardest work we will have to do in our lives." Grieving is work, and it is not something that can be circumvented. We all have to go through our grief. "Grief work" includes looking at how we feel about our lives now, what life was like in the past with our partners and telling about our partners' illness, death, and funeral/memorial/cremation service. Always, discussion of these things in group unleashes the many deep feelings we are experiencing around the death of our partner and the pain of being alone which follows. That is grief work.

We must confront and talk about the past and feel the present, including the emotions aroused in us by this exploration, in order to let go of our past, to move on and heal. We end our seven weeks positively, by looking to the future. Work in this group model is cumulative and moves from difficult to easier issues each night and over the entire seven-week duration from present to past to future. Grief work in our group also includes beginning to care again for oneself and others, and beginning to feel joy once more in our day to day living.

4. Supportive

All members of our group including the facilitators are widowed persons. Sharing that common experience creates an instant bond among the members. To give substance to this bond we require that each member of the group agrees to three things:

1. to wish every one in the group good will,
2. to be present for each of our meetings, and
3. to keep in confidence everything that is said in the group.

This agreement helps make our group a safe place in which to share. This honesty nurtures growth as expert, Yalom, states:

> It was clear to me (and demonstrated by empirical research) that the members of the group who plunged most deeply into themselves, who confronted their fate most openly and resolutely, passed into a mode of existence that was richer . . . [2, p. 100].

Though open sharing is modeled by the leaders and encouraged, no pressure is put on the participant. Decisions to participate in any activity or verbal sharing is always optional. Empowering the individual to be in charge of her own grieving process is paramount.

I have found that age and time elapsed since the death of the spouses matters little in creating a cohesive group. In fact, it is an advantage to mix age and time widowed. Group members help one another more fully because of their widely diversified age and life experience. The main criteria I use for bringing a person into the group is that the person is clearly motivated to participate. (It also should be her own motivation, not a motivation driven by family or friends, which propels her into the group.) If she is feeling isolated and wants the group, even if she is very close to the time of death of the spouse, good can come out of a group experience for that person. Interestingly, I have had many people come to the group several years after a death of a spouse, simply because they have not had the time or have not allowed themselves to grieve earlier. That, too, is fine. Grief which has been repressed will come out in a group devoted to doing grief work openly and honestly. To reiterate, our groups are built of a strong base of mutual respect and support which comes out of the shared experience of the death of a spouse.

Some End Notes

Just a few notes about participants in a grief group such as this. First, they are a very vulnerable population. There may be considerable depression and some talk of not wanting to live by group members. While talk such as this is normal, a skilled group leader must know about pathology and danger signals and be ready to refer a participant to another professional if necessary. Some facts to remember here: loss of a husband precipitates more psychological problems in women than loss of wife for men; where the relationship has been poor or worse grief is more complicated. Before each group begins I do one pre-group hour-long interview with each prospective member. In it I discourage women with unusually worrisome signs of grief from moving too soon into group work and make referrals at that time.

I have found that many grieving widows often feel considerable anger at the medical profession. While much of the anger is justified, some of it is not. In groups we need to hear the anger without taking sides. I have also found that widows do not want their grief compared with that of separated and divorced persons. Some issues which they do want to discuss are children and single parenting, family conflicts, sexuality, socializing again, and planning for the future.

Finally, I want to emphasize that working with women after the death of a spouse is the kind of work which requires integrity. When we discuss their husband's dying and death and their own responses to those life changes, we move into very private space. This is a privileged task and is awesome work. A gentle hand and a loving heart must be with us as we facilitate sharing in this sacred space with others.

5. *Structured*

The "Alone and Growing" support group is structured. Structure facilitates the grief work process. Of course, within the structure there has to be flexibility. No group member should be required to do or say anything that does not feel comfortable for her. Also, each group is different. Each group has a unique personality according to its membership. It follows that each group will address its own collective issues.

Important to each unique group is that the facilitator of it understands the grief process and is able to facilitate so that each member participates (not necessarily verbally) in the process and begins his/her own healing. I begin preparing group members early in the pre-group interview already mentioned where they can ask any question of me, vent fears, and give me their loss history. I want to give them some idea of what's expected of them as they participate and to do that I discuss with them some of group's "ground rules."

Different groups have different ground rules; here are ours:

- we will start and end on time
- we will keep the confidentiality of the group
- we wish everyone good will
- we will attend all meetings
- we will not rescue someone who cries
- we will pass the kleenex
- we will listen as one person speaks
- we will not judge
- we will not discount anyone's feelings
- we will not cross-talk or interrupt another speaker
- we will not give advice
- we will try to stay on topic

The manual I have written to help others facilitate support groups is called *Alone and Growing: How to run a grief work support group for widowed persons* [4]. It includes step by step lesson plans for each of the seven-week group meetings. From these plans it is possible for any person, professional or non, to facilitate a grief work support group. Everything from set-up, to materials, to resources and questions are included in the booklet. The reader may choose to follow the plans provided in the booklet word for word. Some who have already worked with groups use these plans in a supplemental way. While the "Alone and Growing" model for a widowed person's support group is only one way to do grief work in a group context, I have experienced it to be an extremely effective way.

CONCLUSION

I am, as you have probably already ascertained, a strong proponent of grief work support groups. I also firmly believe that when one is dealing with new, raw grief, grief work will happen only if the agenda is carefully structured, the leadership of a certain quality and commitment and the participants all individuals who have had a husband die. Extremely important also is that facilitators have done sufficient personal grief work; otherwise the group could be compromised. Although I have already stated this earlier, I must repeat that I know groups work. I have been present to see the process succeed within the seven structured weeks of my "Alone and Growing" groups [4]. I have also met after the groups are finished with former group participants, sometimes years after their doing a group, who strongly validate their group experience. I see there has been healing and growth.

It is truly awesome to experience the power that people have to heal themselves and to help others in the process. It is my hope that this chapter and perhaps your future work in the field of death, dying and bereavement may combine to provide resources for the bereaved in our society.

REFERENCES

1. E. Kübler-Ross, *Living with Death and Dying*, Macmillan, New York, 1981.
2. I. D. Yalom, *The Theory and Practice of Group Psychotherapy* (3rd Edition), Basic Books, New York, 1970.
3. B. J. Wylie, *Beginnings: A Book About Widows* (3rd Edition), McClelland and Stewart, Toronto, 1988.
4. P. M. L. Anderson, *Alone and Growing: How to Run a Grief Work Support Group for Widowed Persons*, Sophia Publications, London, 1994.*

BIBLIOGRAPHY

Anderson, M. L., *Wife after Death: Women Coping and Growing after the Death of a Partner*, Fitzhenry & Whiteside, Markham, Ontario, 1993.
Parkes, C. M., *Bereavement: Studies of Grief in Adult Life*, Penguin, Baltimore, 1986.

---

*This manual may be ordered from: Sophia Publications, Attention: Peggy Anderson, 83 Victoria Street, London, Ontario, Canada N6A 2B1. Purchase price is $15.00 plus $3.00 postage, Canadian funds. Please make checks or money orders payable to: Peggy Anderson.

CHAPTER 22
Men and Grief

Tom Golden

GENDER DIFFERENCES

We are beginning to understand gender differences relating to the way men and women communicate. This information has been popularized by Deborah Tannen's book *You Just Don't Understand* [1]. This information is fascinating, but it doesn't go quite far enough. While it is informative about the communication differences, it doesn't explain the difference between a man's and woman's nature in processing feelings. This chapter will examine some of the findings of gender difference research and then take that extra step to theorize how these differences affect men and women in their grieving.

Physical Differences

The underlying nature of men and women is different in many ways. A good place to start are the physical differences. It has been recently theorized that the hormone prolactin is related to a man's having less access to the use of emotional tears. Prolactin is a hormone that is instrumental in emotional tear production. It seems that levels of prolactin drop at about the time a young boy enters adolescence. It is theorized that this drop makes it more difficult for boys (and later men) to access their tears in grief due in some part to physiological reasons. I can remember the distance I had from emotional tears as an adolescent. I can now understand this in a different way, knowing that a part of that change was probably physiological. This difference can be seen around the world in various cultures and is not limited to North America. Men tend to cry less following a loss.

Another physical difference is provided by research which indicates that men and women have significant differences in brain structure. One of these differences was reported in *Time Magazine* in an article which described the corpus callosum as thicker in women's brains than in men [2]. The corpus callosum is a structure that connects the two hemispheres of the brain. One hypothesis theorizes that this difference gives a woman a greater connection between her verbal capacity and her feelings, and leaves a man less able to verbalize feeling states. If this hypothesis is true, it would help explain why men tend toward activity in engaging their grief. It would also help us in understanding the perennial problem in relationships where women are left baffled about why their men don't talk as freely as they do about their feelings. If you listen to a man talking about his grief, he will generally describe his grief not in terms of feelings but in terms of his own body, i.e., a heaviness in the chest or stomach. We will see in this section how a man's activity connects him to his body and to his feelings.

Psychological Differences

One important difference in men and women on a psychological level has to do with a man's need for autonomy. It stems from many factors, one of which is the difficult separation a boy experiences from his mother at about age four. At that time the mother feels that it is no longer appropriate for the young boy to have the "unlimited access" to her which he had when he was an infant and probably a toddler. He is told not to touch certain parts and is not allowed to enter the bathroom when his mother is there, even though he sees his sister doing so. This is the initial separation which young boys experience, a pulling away of the mother from the son, which the young girls don't have to go through. The young boy learns how to be autonomous and to alternate between periods of autonomy and periods of intimacy. This pattern continues in his relationships as an adult male in which he tends to move back and forth with his partner from intimacy to autonomy. The man needs periods away from his spouse in order to be ready to approach his spouse for intimacy. This pattern also can be seen in the way a man grieves. Men will tend to move in and out of their grief, finding things, places, or activities to serve as mechanisms for this movement.

Men and the Hierarchy

Men tend toward a hierarchical nature, viewing the world in terms of who is governing whom. Women, on the other hand, tend to view the world through the lens of who is relating to whom. Tannen points out that men live in a hierarchical world that is characterized by having the consciousness of who is "one up" or "one down" [1]. Conversations are seen by men as a place to maintain their image and to avoid being put into a one down position, with the goal of maintaining their independence. It is easy to see this developing in boys as they learn in grade school to put each other down. A great deal of effort and energy goes into creating and remembering put downs in order to be ready for the word battle that goes on between boys. This is the beginning of hierarchy. It can also be seen in the knowledge that each young boy has about who in his class can kick the farthest, run the fastest, etc. The hoped-for goal of the boy and later the man is to appear to be on top of things and, above all, maintain independence. Women, however, tend to live in a network of support. Their concern is not so much to appear independent but to seek connection with their peers, not from a hierarchical standpoint but from a position of being equal. Their negotiations are more for closeness, both seeking and giving confirmations of support, rather than maintaining status. The keyword for women is "intimacy," which is a measure of the degree that women are related to each other. Men have a keyword of "independence." The object of their striving in the hierarchy is to maintain and enhance their independence and position.

Hierarchy

To understand a man's hierarchical nature we must know what this thing called hierarchy is and how it came to be. Many people have theorized about the origins of the hierarchy. One explanation looks at the hunter/gatherer roles that have been our ancestry. The men were those who usually hunted. In order to hunt they needed to depend on each other. A part of this dependence was the hunters' capacity to be quiet and to communicate to one another without making a commotion. One can imagine a group of men hunting together using hand signals to express the complex movements and actions needed to stalk and kill the prey. There was a need for an identified leader, someone who would decide when and where to act. The hunt was no place for a group decision or gathering the thoughts and feelings of others before coming to a decision. Thus, there must have been some hierarchical strata that aided men in working together. They needed to be quiet and follow the directions of one man who lead. If the leader was killed during the hunt, there was probably a man already designated to take over his role, and then a third and fourth. We can see the need for this type of hierarchy in the situation the men faced.

This can be contrasted with the gatherer roles that women tended to enact. In gathering the needed foods, women many times worked in groups to gather or to clean and make preparations. It is easy to imagine groups of women talking and communicating with each other as they completed their tasks together. This type of activity also lends itself to group decisions and deciding together what to do, rather than having to depend on a specific woman for leadership and direction.

Some interesting gender differences can be linked to this hierarchy/relational schema. Men are known to have better skills at mentally rotating three-dimensional objects in space. Some theorize that this is due to the thousands of years men spent hunting, where their lives were dependent on visually tracking three-dimensional objects. A man also throws and runs differently than a woman. These skills also seem related to our ancestry of hunting. Men had to pursue prey and throw spears in the hunt. Over the years the men who threw well and ran quickly were more likely to survive and have children.

With these histories it is easy to assume that the men were more practiced at stealth, strength, and quiet within a hierarchical network, while the women tended to be more relational and democratic with each other during their work. The men relied on a designated hierarchy while the women probably had more of the luxury of deciding together what they would do. While in their village, the men were probably responsible for providing for the community and protecting the rest of the group. The expectation must have been that the man would sacrifice his safety for the safety of others.

Hierarchy at Work and Play

It is easy to see how these ideas manifest themselves in a man's work. Firefighting, for example, has long been a male-dominated profession, and maybe the ideas mentioned above have something to do with that. A fireman expects to put himself at great physical risk as he performs his job of protecting the community. He does this within a hierarchy designated by rank. Similarly, policeman put themselves at risk to protect their community, also within a hierarchy of rank. With both of these professions it is easy to see the similarity to the hunters of old, putting themselves at risk for the safety of their community, designated to provide, protect, and sacrifice. It is interesting that the men who are involved in this sort of work tend to report that they easily bond with the men with whom they work.

We find a similar process in the armed forces. Men are in a hierarchy with the goal of protecting the community. They are stratified by a complex system of rank, and the hierarchy of the organization is reflected in all that goes on. The chain of command is a sacred issue, with men honoring the rank above them with respect and obedience.

The construction business offers another example. One only has to observe a construction site for a short time to see how the men work together. There is remarkably little interaction or talking. Much of the time hand signals and gestures get the point across as these men work together under the direction of the foreman.

The same hierarchical ideas tend to also dominate a man's play. Think of a baseball or a football team. Signals pass between the pitcher and the catcher, and the quarterback signals changes in the play at the line of scrimmage. Also note the hierarchy and leadership on a sports team. As the team goes into a huddle it is only one man who gives the next play, the entire team follows along, rarely speaking out against the call.

Competition of all kinds is related to the hierarchy. Competition is merely a means of placing oneself in the hierarchy, a result of the desire to be one or more rungs higher on that ladder. Whether it involves a trout fishing tournament, the Super Bowl, or a job at the office, competition is a ritual which most men have played out repeatedly. A boyhood example of this is choosing sides for a ball game. Someone always has to be first and last in the order of choosing. It is often a painful identification of where you stand on the ladder, how high or low you are in the eyes of your peers. I can remember the relief I would feel as a boy if I could maneuver myself into a position of choosing the sides rather than being chosen. In this way the pain of being chosen in the middle or near the end was avoided. It is hard to imagine little girls choosing sides to play house.

Hierarchy is also present in relationships. Men, having become sensitized to hierarchical arrangements, can easily misinterpret requests as being "ordered around" by their wife. I have seen this cause trouble repeatedly in relationships. The wife will ask the man to do something for her, and he, feeling she is not asking but commanding, will respond in a negative fashion. Many times he is feeling as if his wife assumes that she is above him on the hierarchy. The woman is unaware of the dilemma and assumes that the man just doesn't care about her. Both the man and the woman end up feeling hurt by this.

Gender Difference and Grieving

What does all this have to do with grief? These basic differences lead to dramatically different strengths and paths in processing emotions and, therefore, in the way men and women grieve. Both men and women are affected by the cultural avoidance of death and grief, but this avoidance has a different effect on the two sexes. A woman generally has an easier time in dealing with this prohibition in that she probably has a system in place in which intimacy is the keyword. This network of friends or family will often encourage the sharing of grief as a means to connect and therefore become more intimate. A man many times has no such system. He highly values independence and autonomy and sharing grief could be perceived as a threat. By revealing his grief to another man, he would be putting himself one or more rungs down on the hierarchy. The hierarchy values action and what can be done about things, not emotional connection. The hierarchy is interested in product, efficiency, action, and outcome.

For a man to share his grief, he needs to know that he is respected. For a woman to share her grief, she needs to know that she will be related to. The reason for this need for respect is the result of the hierarchy: in the hierarchy respect is a keyword and is intimately related to one's position on it. This can be easily observed in groups of men who are healing their grief. The work of talking about their grief is usually put off until the men know that they have the respect of other men.

The men tend to naturally avoid talking about their grief for another reason. They see their grief as a burden and don't want to lay that on anybody. In the hierarchical arrangement where product and output are of importance, grief is seen as an impediment to product and output and is therefore not something men want to "share" with others. This can be contrasted with woman's more natural fit with grief being connected with her leaning toward increasing intimacy. Men see grief as being something that is a problem and a burden, and within an hierarchy you don't place a burden on someone who has no responsibility for it. To express this to another man or to a woman would be, first, an admission that he was unable to handle his problems by himself (a sign of a lack of independence) and second, a dumping of a negative pile of stuff onto someone else who had no responsibility for it.

Using Action to Heal Grief

So what do men do with their grief? We have found that men tend to value autonomy, independence, and action. We have also found that men are less efficient in processing feelings verbally. How do men deal with their grief? They use their strengths of action. Action is valued in the hierarchy, and men use this as a catalyst to their grief. This action usually provides a place or thing and something to do with their bodies. A simple example is the activity of looking at a family picture album. Many men use this activity as a means of entering their grief. It is an action with a beginning and an end; you pick up the book and when finished put it back on the shelf. This beginning and end help to mark the boundaries of the experience for a man. Bill's wife had died six months prior, and sometimes after he got the kids to bed he would take out the picture album. He would sit in his chair while leafing through the book. His tears would flow as he looked at the various pictures. It was this action (as opposed to interaction for women) that helped Bill put himself into the space of grief, becoming more aware of his memories and his body's reaction to the loss.

Another example of how this works is a man whose high school-age son died in a car accident. In the first month or two after the death the man started to put together a book about his son. This was not a book that he intended to publish, but basically a book of memories. He did this by coordinating many of his son's friends and teachers in bringing this product about. Many hours were spent working together, gathering items that would become a part of the book, planning and talking about what should go into it. Teachers were involved in the process, and the young man's coaches, ministers, girlfriends, and ex-girlfriends. It was a community affair, and during this process this man spent a great deal of time talking with others about his son's life and listening to the stories others had to tell. This interaction was very similar to what might have happened had the man gone into a therapy group, but it was different in some significant aspects. All of his interactions were connected with a product—the book. He was the editor and producer of this product, and in this way he maintained his independence. His interactions with others relating to his son's death were connected to the production of this book, but they were no less healing than someone who chose to relate their grief to another person without the accompanying action. The man found healing for his grief through action that was harmonious with his need for independence and his orientation toward producing a product.

When looking at a man's grief from this perspective, it is easier to see why men tend to grieve in a private and quiet manner. They don't want to be a burden to others, they want to maintain their interdependence, and they want to use their strength of action in dealing with a very powerful force such as grief. Much has written about the pathology of a man's tendency to grieve alone but when seen in this vein it can be understood as a personal choice the man makes rather than a step into pathology.

The fact is men and women grieve differently. Following the death of a child, for instance, a mother will grieve by crying and talking with her close friends and family. The father, more hierarchical in nature, is more inclined to relate to events through physical action rather than feelings. The grieving father may perform some sort of action such as creating a book, starting a scholarship in the name of the child, or raising money for a special interest the child had. He will want to do something to connect with his grief.

This difference many times leads to misunderstandings. Men and women tend to be suspicious about the other's mode of grief. He may think that she is "overdoing it" as she emotes in the presence of those close to her. She may feel that the man is not really grieving because he grieves in private or through action, not sharing his tears in the same way she does. Yet both styles need to be honored because both, when used effectively, accomplished the same goal—coming to terms with the loss.

It is important to note that the use of action in healing grief is not exclusive to men; some women use action-oriented healing and use it well. In the same vein, many men are able to use relational skills to heal their grief. When a man relates his grief to others, particularly to men, it can be a powerful healing. We are painting with broad strokes when we attempt to link men with action and women with relating. In general, men tend toward action as a primary mode in healing their grief while using relating as a secondary mode, and women are the opposite. A man's action can serve as a ritual container for grief if he forms a conscious link between the action and the loss. Each time he performs the action it activates the grieving process and moves it toward healing. Men honor and acknowledge their grief by connecting it to their actions and preparing a specific place that allows the grief to emerge.

REFERENCES

1. D. Tannen, *You Just Don't Understand*, Morrow, New York, 1990.
2. C. Gorman, Sizing Up the Sexes, *Time Magazine*, pp. 42-51, January 20, 1992.

BIBLIOGRAPHY

Frey, W. H. *Crying: The Mystery of Tears*, Winston Press, Minneapolis, Minnesota, 1985.
Tanenbaum, J., *Male and Female Realities*, R. Erdmann Publishing, Costa Mesa, California, 1990.

CHAPTER 23

Middle-Aged Children's Bereavement After the Death of an Elderly Parent

Miriam S. Moss and Sidney Z. Moss

Most people live longer than their parents, and thus they experience their parents' deaths. Although some persons may suffer the death of a parent when they are young children, or in the years when they are completing their education or beginning to build a family, the death of a parent is much more likely when the child is middle-aged. In the United States, only one in ten children has lost a parent by age twenty-five. By the age of forty-one half have lost one parent, and by the age of forty-eight three-quarters have lost one parent. Looked at differently, by age fifty-four half have lost *both* parents, and by age sixty-two three-quarters have lost both parents. This pattern occurs largely because death comes mainly to persons who are elderly. In the United States, 72 percent of all deaths are of persons aged sixty-five and over. Most older people have living children, thus on their death they are survived by middle-aged sons and daughters. It has been suggested that the death of an elderly parent is the most common death of all family deaths.

Overall, it has been estimated that each year 5 percent of people in the United States have a parent die. Although the death of an elderly parent is a common occurrence in middle age, there has been relatively little theoretical, clinical, or research literature that examines this normative experience.

PARENT DEATH: WHY IS IT SIGNIFICANT?

As mentioned above, parent death is a normative occurrence. It is an expected and meaningful experience for most adults, and as such its meanings and impact should be understood.

The bond between a parent and a child is significant over a lifetime. Ties between parent and child are often among the longest of the life course. Each is unique and irreplaceable for the other. Parents and children have a common history. They have spent decades sharing experiences and developing joint views of reality. Attachment begins in infancy when the close tie is integral to dependency on the parents for protection, nurturance, affection, and guidance [1]. The child's very identity is formed within the context of his relationship with his parents. In middle age there tends to be increasing independence and interdependence. There is also a sense of generational continuity in which each symbolizes "family" for the other, both biologically and psychosocially. Although many themes in the relationship may change over time, the parent remains a parent and the child remains a child throughout life. When a parent dies the child is faced with the loss of a highly significant person. As we will indicate, there is evidence that the attachment continues beyond the parent's death.

Another reason that parent death is significant is that it is a point of transition in the life of the child. It has the potential to affect the middle-aged child in areas of self, family relations, and overall worldview. As we shall see, the effect can be both positive and negative.

Finally, an increased understanding of parent death may provide a model for the understanding of other family deaths such as sibling, spouse, and child. Although much of bereavement theory has been rooted in widowhood, we will suggest that major themes in parent death augment that theory and may be relevant to many other family losses.

WHY HAS THE MEANING AND IMPACT OF THE DEATH OF AN ELDERLY PARENT BEEN SO LITTLE EXAMINED?

Although most people who die are elderly, the two fields of gerontology (study of the lives of older persons) and thanatology (study of death, dying, and bereavement) have consistently skirted the area of death in old age. They have found little common ground [2]. Neither has integrated the literature of the other into its own. We suggest that each of these fields focuses on an area that itself is feared and devalued in our culture: old age or death. Each feels threatened if it becomes wedded to another devalued area, and may wish to avoid furthering negative perceptions of the field. Our focus here is on that doubly devalued interface.

There are other reasons for the lack of attention to parent death as well. There may be a tendency to ignore life tasks of middle-aged persons, a time when a large number of parent deaths occur. Rather, there is an emphasis on other tasks of middle age such as maintaining a satisfying marital relationship, meeting career goals, and coping with problems of launching children into young adulthood.

Generally grief for an elderly parent does not involve the intensity of emotional response that is evoked by the death of children or of younger persons. A few studies have compared groups of bereaved adults who have lost a parent, a child, or a spouse. In general, when differences were found the intensity of response was greater for the death of a child than for a spouse, and greater for a spouse than for a parent. None of the studies however, suggest that parent death has an insignificant impact.

Conversely, the dearth of attention to this loss may be a way of protecting ourselves from the deep, meaningful, and pervasive impact of this loss. Authors, often middle-aged themselves, may wish to distance themselves from the threat of the reality of parent death. Thus, they avoid potential pain, regrets, and unfinished business in relation to the parent.

A major factor in the lack of attention to death of parents of middle-aged persons is the societal devaluation of the very old. Ageism systematically stereotypes and stigmatizes older persons. They are often seen as senile, rigid, and withdrawn from the world. If the lives of older people are of little value to society, then their deaths will have less impact, and the bereavement and grief of the surviving child may be less socially supported. Death of an old person has been thought by many to be the least tragic of deaths. It is as if advanced age itself is a legitimization of the rightness of the death. Often when a person dies, the first question that is asked is "How old was she?" Learning the age of the deceased may guide one in judging the fairness or the rightness of the death. If the deceased was relatively young it may suggest the need for considerable social support for the bereaved survivors. On the other hand, if the deceased was very old it may imply that the mourner needs little comforting. The death may be seen as "on time," and may represent a smaller social loss. There is some evidence that families mark the death of an old person with fewer funeral rituals.

The bereaved child of a deceased elderly parent may thus feel that his or her grief is socially disenfranchised [3]. The loss may be seen as minimally significant and thus not socially validated. Even cross-cultural studies of death and dying pay little attention to the adult child's loss of a parent. The social and cultural devaluing of the parent's death may lead the surviving child to control and modify the expression of bereavement [4].

MAJOR THEMES AROUND THE DEATH OF A PARENT

Bereavement for the death of a parent is a process, not an event. Dying or the expectation of death often covers an extended period of time. Chronic long-term illness is the cause of death for most older persons. Thus the death of old persons tends to be expected and anticipation of the death frequently occurs [5]. Participants in our ongoing study of 212 sons and daughters (age 40 to 65) whose parent had died six to ten months previously were randomly selected from death records. Only 8 percent of these adult children indicated that they had not thought about the possibility of their parent's death beforehand. Sixty percent said that they and their parent had talked about the parent's dying. Further, 64 percent indicated that they had begun to grieve for their parent before she died, and one-fourth said that before she died there were times when they were so overcome with grief that they couldn't say or do some of the things they would have liked. Thus, anticipation of the death has both cognitive and affective components.

Next we move to examine aspects of bereavement for a parent. Each of the themes we will examine can be relevant to a time period prior to the death as well as after the death.

Overall the bereavement process is multidimensional. Major aspects include emotional upset, shifts in sense of self and in the family, a sense of acceptance, and a pervasive tie with the deceased parent. These are neither stages nor phases, but interrelated responses to parent death that tend to be significant for many surviving children.

EMOTIONAL RESPONSE TO THE DEATH

A number of studies have examined the child's grief, or emotional response to parent death. Although there is variation in the intensity of upset, research has generally shown that adult children often feel a deep sense of loss and sadness after a parent has died.

Scharlach recruited 220 adults from newspaper ads [6]. Each had a parent (average age 74 years) die a median of two years earlier (range from 1 to 5 years). Mail questionnaires were used. About one-third said they "still get upset when I think about the person" and over half said "At times I still feel the need to cry for the person." A subgroup of study participants were subsequently interviewed and 60 percent were found to experience emotional reactions such as anxiety, fear, depression, or suicidal ideation.

Moss, Moss, Rubinstein, and Resch held qualitative interviews with a convenience sample of 107 daughters (age 40 to 65) [7]. Their widowed mothers (mean age 81) had died three to six months earlier. In a supplementary self-administered questionnaire, three-quarters of the daughters indicated that "Losing a parent is one of the hardest things I've ever had to deal with," and almost half said they "still get upset when I think about my mother."

Umberson and Chen analyzed a large national sample of adults ranging from twenty-four to ninety-six years old [8]. Participants were interviewed twice over a two-and-half-year period. Two hundred and seven adults had experienced the death of a parent during that time. This study allowed for a comparison of characteristics of the adult child before and after the parent's death. Compared with adult children who were not bereaved, the bereaved children had a significant increase in psychological distress (defined as depression), as well as an increase in alcohol consumption and a decline in physical health.

These results should be seen in the context of findings of another study by Norris and Murrell [9]. In their longitudinal survey of a large probability community sample, they located fifty-eight persons whose parent had recently died. They detected no transient or persistent changes in depression from the initial levels. Differences in the size of samples, and in the measures and analyses in the above studies may explain some disparities in their findings.

IMPACT ON THE SELF

Parent death has been found to affect the self in a number of ways. Robbins held lengthy qualitative interviews with ten middle-class daughters (age 35 to 55) recruited from women's networks [10]. She found that their mother's death led to the daughter's greater sense of individuation and thus increased the daughter's positive view of herself and the world.

Umberson, however, in analyzing the large longitudinal study above, reported little change in world view over time for bereaved children [11]. There was no significant change in a sense of personal vulnerability, a sense of justice, fatalism, or self-esteem although there was a decline in mastery for bereaved children vis-a-vis the non-bereaved children.

Other studies of parent death have examined the way surviving children describe their personal sense of finitude and attitude toward death [6, 12]. The death of a parent also can be seen as the loss of a buffer against the child's own death. Without the parent, the child may increasingly feel the need to face her own mortality. Douglas found this to be true in her qualitative study of forty middle-aged children [12]. Also, over half of the daughters in the Moss study agreed with the statement: "Since my mother died, the possibility of my own death has become more real to me," and 40 percent agreed, "Since my mother's death I feel that I am closer to death" [7].

IMPACT ON THE FAMILY

When an older person dies, he leaves a bereaved family. If he is the first parent to die, he is survived by his widow as well as adult children, children-in-law, siblings, and grandchildren. If the deceased parent played a central role such as a kin-keeper or head of the clan, the loss is likely to have a ripple effect in the same and younger generations. We know of no research that has examined the impact of the death on the family as a whole.

Scharlach and Fredrikson examined change in the child's relationship with kin [13]. They found that the relationship with the surviving parent became closer for 38 percent, and more conflictual for 14 percent. For the marital tie, 31 percent became closer and 25 percent more conflictual. Sibling ties tended to change as well, 39 percent closer and 26 percent more conflictual. Finally, 35 percent reported that ties with their own children became closer, and only 6 percent became more conflictual.

Umberson, using her large longitudinal national sample, found that bereavement was not associated with changes in the child's relationships with a surviving parent, with the adult child's own children, or with other kin [11]. She did report however that marital relationships were negatively affected. Other clinical and research studies have reported this as well. Umberson also held qualitative interviews with forty-two married children to explore the factors associated with this decline in marital quality [11]. In general the marriage suffered because of the spouse's lack of empathy, inability to talk about the loss, inability to allow for shifts in family roles during the period of bereavement, and the spouse's general failure to support and comfort the surviving child.

ACCEPTANCE OF THE DEATH

Overall, sons and daughters have indicated that they have accepted their parent's death. Only rarely did daughters in the Moss study [7] indicate "I cannot accept my mother's death" (9%). Bower, using sociolinguistic methods in an ethnographic study of parent death examined acceptance and delineated some of its central themes [14]. In part, acceptance is seen as cognitive understanding of death as a physical fact (e.g., "Well sure I've accepted it because I know he's dead"). It can be couched in philosophical terms (e.g., "I've accepted my father's death because I know everyone has to die.") or spiritual terms (e.g., "I think it was God's time. He wanted her."). Often it is seen as the inevitable result of a terminal medical condition, or is justified because of the parent's advanced age. Acceptance, further, is facilitated by the parent's wish to die and respect for the parent's autonomy (e.g., [she] wouldn't have wanted to live that way that she was living in the last year of her life"). Finally, acceptance is associated with the maintenance of the tie with the deceased parent (e.g., "I've accepted it, you know, because . . . she lives on in my memory").

MAINTENANCE OF THE TIE WITH THE PARENT

A major theme that recurs in research on parent death is the dialectic between letting go of the parent (often exemplified by acceptance and relief from the burdens of care giving) and holding on to the tie. In the view of traditional bereavement theory the grief process necessitates separation and decathexis from the deceased. Clinical work and research, however, has emphasized the maintenance of the tie as significant for most bereaved persons [15].

Themes of holding on include feeling that memories of the parent are comforting and provide solace to the child. Additionally, it is not unusual for children to continue to interact with their representation of the parent, as well as to think about a future in which they will be reunited. Two-thirds of the daughters of mothers in our research said that "Thinking of her is comforting to me" [7]. In the same study, over half of the daughters agreed, "I still talk to or communicate with my mother," and four-fifths agreed, "I think I will be with my mother again some day."

CHARACTERISTICS OF PARENT AND CHILD ASSOCIATED WITH BEREAVEMENT

We have paid little attention to the ways that the five central themes previously discussed are associated with such factors as background characteristics of the parent and child, or with the quality of the parent-adult child relationship, or with the context of the parent's last year of life. We next turn to a summary of selected findings that help to explain similarities and differences in the experience of bereavement around parent death.

Background Characteristics

Age of the child has been found to be associated with intensity of grief, that is younger children tend to express more grief than older children. Scharlach found this was true only of children of mothers, not of fathers [6]. A study of daughters of mothers found that younger children also experience more somatic difficulties, are less accepting of the death, and less comforted by thoughts of the deceased parent [7]. A study of children whose parent died after living in a nursing home found a similar association between age and emotional upset [16]. Younger children in that study also expressed a greater sense of relief after their parent's death. Overall, older children may be less emotionally upset about their parent's death because they often have witnessed their parents decline and have more time to anticipate the death. Also they have become socialized to the likelihood of parent death because many of their age peers have experienced that loss. Conversely the younger children tend to have younger, more healthy, and independent parents and thus death may be seen as more untimely or sudden, violating the assumptions of parent's invincibility and the expectation of continuity of habitual interaction with the parent.

The gender of the child tends to be consistently related to emotional expression, specifically daughters express more sadness and upset than sons. Ongoing research by the authors indicates that daughters not only express more grief, but they have more somatic responses to the death, less acceptance, and maintain a stronger continuing tie with the deceased parent. This may reflect a tendency for men (sons) to control their expression of grief in order to preserve their sense of manliness and self-esteem. Although developmental theory suggests that the mother-daughter tie is the closest in many respects, there is an interesting tendency in several studies for daughters of fathers (vis-a-vis daughter-mother, son-mother, and son-father) to express the most intense grief. Many of these gender differences tend to reflect the overall cultural tendency for women to be more emotionally expressive than men and for women's lives to be more imbedded in social relationships [4].

Higher socioeconomic level of the children has been found by some researchers to be associated with greater impact of the parent's death and by others associated with less impact. The former finding is congruent with the idea that those who are economically comfortable deal with fewer life crises and would have assumptions about a benign world, and thus might be particularly vulnerable to the impact of family deaths. Conversely, it has been suggested that persons with greater education and financial resources could find adaptation to the loss less stressful.

Quality of the Parent-Child Tie

Relationships between adult children and their elderly parents are complex and multidimensional. Scharlach found that an adult child's lack of autonomy in relation to his living parent was associated with greater grief after the death [6]. Popek and Scharlach, in examining the quality of relationship of daughters with their mothers found that relationships which were ambivalent, conflictual, or emotionally distant were more likely to result in unresolved grief reactions one to five years after the death. They found that grief reactions were more resolved when the daughter had a close, mutually accepting relationship with mother [17]. In our earlier research, the closer the daughter-mother tie, the greater the grief, and also the more comforting the daughter's thoughts about her mother after the death [7]. Umberson and Chen found that the strain in the adult child's tie with the parent was unrelated to bereavement outcomes [8]. However, negative childhood memories of parents (e.g., alcoholism, violent behavior, mental health problems of the parent) were associated with less distress after the death. Conversely, if there were no such negative childhood memories, there was more distress in bereavement. These seemingly contradictory findings are the product of different data sets, different methods, and different measures of relationship and bereavement. They raise more questions than they answer about the complexities of the association between parent and child and the subsequent bereavement reactions to the parent's death.

Characteristics of the Parent's Last Year of Life

The child's response to a parent's death may be expected to be associated with the quality of life of the parent over his or her final year. In a series of research studies by the authors, three groups of families were recruited: light or non-care givers (for parents who had lived independently in the local community), heavy care givers (who co-resided with their parents who had lived in a nursing home for much of the final year), and children of parents who had lived in a nursing home for much of the final year [7]. As would be expected, the parents in the nursing home group had lower quality of life and poorer cognitive functioning than the other two groups, and the independent parents were higher in functioning than the other two groups. In comparing the bereavement outcomes of the three groups we found that children of independent parents expressed more intense grief and less acceptance of the death than children of parents who had lived in a nursing home for most of their final year. Heavy care givers did not differ significantly from either of these groups. This is congruent with other studies which found that deaths which were more sudden, and less anticipated by the adult child are more upsetting and less acceptable. The three groups did not consistently differ on other measures such as somatic responses to the death, sense of personal finitude, and the tie with the deceased parent. These findings demonstrate the value of distinguishing between multiple dimensions of bereavement outcomes and analyzing how each is expressed in different contexts of parent death.

Bass and his colleagues studied a group of fifty-five care-giving adult children from the time their parent was alive and receiving their care to a follow-up interview an average of six months after the death [18]. They found that the child's appraisal of care giving was associated with her reactions to bereavement: greater care giving strain was associated with more difficulties perceived in bereavement. This pattern is similar to that reported by Pruchno et al. who studied the impact of a parent's death after living in a nursing home [16]. She reported that a child's feeling upset at baseline about having a parent live in a nursing home was a major predictor of the child's sadness after the death.

This series of studies suggests that it is important to consider the context of the last years of life of elderly parents in order to increase our understanding of parent death. Further, they suggest that the child's difficulties in adjusting to earlier aspects of the parent's life are associated with more subsequent stresses in bereavement.

DISCUSSION AND IMPLICATIONS

Overall we have reviewed some of the major themes that have recurred in studies of the impact of parent death on a middle-aged child. There appears to be profound grief and sadness, some tendency for children to step back and look at themselves in relation to their lives and their personal finitude, some tendency for shifts to occur in the family, particularly in child's marriage when spousal expectations are not met. There is a recurrent theme of continuity, of maintaining the tie with the parent yielding a sense of comforting memories and frequent thoughts of eventual reunion. Additionally, the themes tend to emphasize a sense of transition—from being a child with a living parent to being a child whose parent has died. Transition implies change, rather than homeostasis (or returning to the ways of life that occurred prior to the death). We are suggesting that a viable theory of bereavement must somehow integrate continuity and transition.

Parent death at any age involves not only bereaved children but a wide range of bereaved kin. Each survivor is imbedded in a changing family world and it is important to consider the implications of the death for the whole family. The death of the first parent may involve factors such as widowhood that distinguish it from the family process of bereavement for the last parent.

Different religious, ethnic, and nationality groups often have their own special way of viewing life and death [19]. Without understanding the beliefs of different groups we are limited in understanding how individuals in those groups respond to their parent's death.

In summary we have suggested that the death of elderly parents can have profound significance for their surviving children and the way they view themselves, their family and their world. Just as parents continue to maintain aspects of their role as long as they live, the child continues to find meaning in the tie with the parent well beyond death.

REFERENCES

1. J. Bowlby, Attachment and Loss, Vol. 1, *Attachment*, Basic Books, New York, 1969.
2. V. W. Marshall and J. Levy, Aging and Dying in *Handbook of Aging and the Social Sciences* (3rd Edition), R. H. Binstock and L. K. George (eds.), Academic Press, New York, pp. 245-260, 1990.
3. K. J. Doka, Disenfranchised Grief, in *Disenfranchised Grief*, K. Doka (ed.), Lexington Books, Lexington, pp. 3-11, 1989.
4. J. Klapper, S. Moss, M. Moss, and R. L. Rubinstein, The Social Context of Grief Among Adult Daughters who have Lost a Parent, *Journal of Aging Studies, 8,* pp. 29-43, 1994.
5. M. S. Moss and S. Z. Moss, Anticipating the Death of an Elderly Parent, in *Ethical Issues in the Care of the Dying and Bereaved Aged*, J. D. Morgan (ed.), Baywood Publishing, Amityville, New York, pp. 111-129, 1996.
6. A. E. Scharlach, Factors Associated with Filial Grief Following the Death of an Elderly Parent, *American Journal of Orthopsychiatry, 61,* pp. 307-312, 1991.

7. M. Moss, S. Moss, R. Rubinstein, and N. Resch, Impact of Elderly Mother's Death on Middle-Aged Daughters, *International Journal of Aging and Human Development, 37,* pp. 1-22, 1993.
8. D. Umberson and M. D. Chen, Effects of a Parent's Death on Adult Children: Relationship Salience and Reaction to Loss, *American Sociological Review, 59,* pp. 152-168, 1994.
9. F. H. Norris and S. A. Murrell, Social Support, Life Events and Stress as Modifiers of Adjustment to Bereavement by Older Adults, *Psychology and Aging, 5,* pp. 429-436, 1990.
10. M. A. Robbins, *Midlife Women and Death of Mother,* Peter Lang, New York, 1990.
11. D. Umberson, Marriage as Support or Strain? Marital Quality following the Death of a Parent, *Journal of Marriage and the Family, 57,* pp. 709-723, 1995.
12. J. D. Douglas, Patterns of Change Following Parent Death in Mid-Life Adults, *Omega: Journal of Death and Dying, 22,* pp. 123-137, 1990-91.
13. A. E. Scharlach and K. I. Fredrikson, Reactions to the Death of a Parent during Midlife, *Omega: Journal of Death and Dying, 27,* pp. 307-319, 1993.
14. A. Bower, The Adult Child's Acceptance of Parental Death, *Omega: Journal of Death and Dying,* in press.
15. D. Klass, P. Silverman, and S. Nickman, *Continuing Bonds: New Understandings of Grief,* Taylor and Francis, Washington, D.C., 1996.
16. R. A. Pruchno, M. S. Moss, C. J. Burand, and S. Schinfeld, Death of an Institutionalized Parent: Predictors of Bereavement, *Omega: Journal of Death and Dying, 31,* pp. 99-119, 1995.
17. P. Popek and A. Scharlach, Adult Daughters' Relationships with their Mothers and Reactions to their Mothers' Death, *Journal of Women and Aging, 3,* pp. 79-95, 1991.
18. D. M. Bass and K. Bowman, The Impact of an Aged Relative's Death on the Family, in *Gerontology: Perspectives and Issues,* K. F. Ferraro (ed.), Springer, New York, pp. 333-356, 1990.
19. R. A. Kalish and D. K. Reynolds, *Death and Ethnicity: A Psychocultural Study,* Brooks/Cole, Los Angeles, 1976, republished Baywood Publishing, Amityville, New York, 1981.

PART IV

Introduction: Children and Death

The confrontation of the ideas of *children* and *death* challenges our basic understandings of life, death, and God. In this section we examine the meaning of death to children, the care of dying and bereaved children and their families, as well as the particular needs of adolescents and the particular circumstances of black children.

Our basic philosophical orientation is that we live in a neat predictable world. We believe that the universe is governed by God for our benefit. However, there are two flaws in this model. First of all, only a limited part of the human experience can be thought of as orderly. In particular, death is not evenly distributed. The second limitation of this model is that we often do not adjust our beliefs to fit reality. For example, there is nothing in the nature of things that demands that the older generation outlive the younger. We all know that infants, children, and young adults can and do die, but we often act as though children were born with a guarantee that they will not die until their seventies. The death of a child calls into question our feelings of security and control, including our belief in God as the benevolent guide of the universe.

Mrs. Eleanor Deveau does two things. First of all she presents a simple overview of what children know about death at various phases of their lives. Using the themes of irreversibility, nonfunctionality, universality, and causality, Mrs. Deveau tells us how children understand death at various points of their lives. Second, she applies these age specific data to the grieving situation. She reminds us that children grieve differently than do adults. They may grieve in shorter spurts, but for longer periods of time. Grief is rooted in broken attachments. Children, by their very immaturity, are much more dependent on attachments than are adults. In addition, Mrs. Deveau points out the importance of gender differences in grieving children as well as differences caused by family dynamics and roles.

Dr. Barbara Anschuetz shows us that grief is a normal part of the adolescent's life. The teenager is in a process of grieving the world s/he knew as a child and fearing the world of adulthood which awaits. The bereaved adolescent is disenfranchised. S/he is told that s/he must take the loss as an adult; that s/he must be there for their parents or younger siblings. If we add this disenfranchisement to the peer pressure which every adolescent feels, the bereaved adolescent is particularly distressed. The teenager cannot openly cry, a child might, yet does not have the loss experience of adults. By very nature, the teenager has fragile defenses. Bereavement challenges these defenses even further. Dr. Anschuetz discusses the particular dynamics which come with the death of a parent or the death of a sibling, or the death of a friend. She ends with concrete ways of helping the bereaved adolescent.

Dr. Ronald Barrett speaks about the unique experiences of bereaved black children. The characterization of Black families as matriarchical, dysfunctional, culturally deficient, etc., give the Black child much to grieve and feel sorrowful about. Consequently the Black child may come to question the value of the Black family experience and grieve experiences the child believes he/she was suppose to have had. Ironic Realizations—"Black is Beautiful" and "Black is Stressful." The experience of loss is understandably influenced by the status of health in the Black experience. The manifestation of inequality and subsequent poverty is most visibly evident in the differential status of health among Blacks as compared to Whites. According to the results of a report from the Task Force on Minority Health, the general health of ethnic minority groups in the United States is poorer, with few exceptions than that of Whites.

CHAPTER 24

The Pattern of Grief in Children and Adolescents

Eleanor J. Deveau

> An ungrieved loss remains forever alive in our unconscious, which has no sense of time [1].

It is as much an emotional necessity for children to grieve as it is for adults. Though we may fail to acknowledge the fact that all children grieve, they still experience a multitude of feelings and reactions associated with the death of someone close to them. Even infants are aware of the absence of a mother's or father's familiar voice and feel the presence of different arms that now hold and try to comfort them. When children's grief is acknowledged, many adults mistakenly assume that they do not experience grief as deeply and, because of their resilience, are able to easily forget what has happened. Attig emphasizes that bereaved children and teens are "vulnerable to the dismissal of the significance of their losses" [2, p. 52]. When a sibling dies, Davies points out that the effects of losing a brother or sister are "long-lasting and pervasive" [3, p. 97]. When a parent dies, an integral and stable part of a child's world suddenly disappears. He or she is left feeling insecure and wondering if the surviving parent will also die [4].

The death of someone close often leaves bereaved children with vivid memories of the events surrounding the death and changes the course of their lives forever. The expected is no longer possible because their mother, father, or sibling has died. Grief is a highly individual, cognitive, and emotional process that is not limited by time and does not necessarily have an ending [5]. Children do not "get over" their grief. Their search for meaning concerning the death of a family member becomes a part of their lives as they grow, mature, and acquire more information about the world around them. Miller points out that the process of bereavement "weaves the experience of the death, the meaning of the loss, and a changing relationship with the deceased into the fabric of their lives over time" [6, p. 100]. The death may influence their choices in life and the career decisions that they make. For example, some may enter medicine to find a cure for the cancer that killed a parent, others may pursue a particular profession to fulfill the dream of a deceased sibling.

The purpose of this chapter is to examine the pattern of grief in children and how it differs from adult grief. Many of the internal and external factors that influence children's understanding of death and the manner in which they grieve are explored. This chapter concludes by addressing the tasks that bereaved children and adolescents need to accomplish and includes guidelines for adults to help them through this process. The reader is referred to other chapters in this book that address specific emotional and behavioral reactions and coping strategies used by bereaved children and adolescents.

THE PATTERN OF GRIEF IN CHILDREN

It is generally agreed that bereaved adults do not follow specific stages of grief. Over time, they develop coping strategies, reorganize their lives, and change activities and routines in order to go on with life without the person that died [7]. For the most part, it is acknowledged that feelings associated with grief last much longer than previously believed. However, the expectation in Western society remains that bereaved individuals should be over their grief in six months to one year following the death of a loved one [8, 9]. Balk and Hogan point out that American society still continues to underestimate the characteristics, intensity, and duration of bereavement [10].

Is there a predictable or typical pattern of grief during childhood? Just as with adults, children and teens do not appear to follow specific, fixed stages of grief. Hence, my use of the more common definition for the word "pattern" may be a misnomer because the manner in which children grieve is not bound by a regular or sequential order. For lack of a better term, I have chosen to use the less common definition of "pattern" which refers to a random combination or order and, therefore, allows for the vacillation in children's understanding of what death means to them and their reactions during bereavement as they grow, mature, and acquire more information.

We know that children are in a state of transition as they grow and mature, but what is often unclear is how a death experience affects them at any given time as well as over a long period of time. If we consider the definition of transition as an emotional process that involves coming to terms with losing what is familiar and integrating what is new, then children's understanding of death and their pattern of grief undergoes a transition as they acquire new information and question old beliefs and understanding. The ability of children and teens to express and cope with their grief following the death of a family member is influenced by (1) their understanding of what death means to them at that point in time and (2) many internal and external factors that affect their understanding as well as their ability to grieve.

Children Grieve Differently Than Adults

Though there are similarities between the grief responses of children and adults, children are more vulnerable and at a greater disadvantage when they must face the death of a loved one. In the literature they are frequently identified as disadvantaged grievers [11, 12]. Children have a cognitive necessity to understand death and how it impacts on their lives, yet most lack the life experiences that can help them acquire such understanding. In contrast to adults, children's reactions are significantly influenced by age, developmental phase, cognitive ability, and many other factors that directly impact on their world. Children grieve for different reasons because their grief is directed at the losses of the many roles that were fulfilled by a deceased parent or sibling.

Krupnick and Solomon identify three questions that are on the minds of children who experience the death of a parent. These questions would also be of concern to children whose sibling has died:

1. "Did I make this happen?" Young children think in terms of cause and effect and often believe that they said or did something wrong to cause a relative's death.
2. "Will I die too?" Children closely link their fate to that of other family members. When a mother, father, or sibling dies, they may believe that they will also die.
3. "Who will take care of me?" When family members are in turmoil and routines dramatically change, children's lack of a sense of security may cause them to worry that no one will be available to take care of them [13].

In contrast to adults, children cannot sustain grief reactions for long periods of time [9]. Younger children, in particular, tend to deal with their grief in small amounts, wavering back and forth between crying one minute and playing the next. They need time to go away, to play, and then to come back to ask their questions when they are ready. Death is a learning experience for children. Part of this learning requires them to ask many questions, some of which may be very difficult to answer. Repeating the many circumstances surrounding a particular death can be painful and exhausting for most parents. However, this repetition helps children to understand what has happened and to establish the reality of the loss in their minds.

Natural limitations in their ability to express emotions and describe experiences also put bereaved children at a disadvantage. Younger children frequently turn to play activities and drawings to express their difficult feelings. Play provides a safe neutral forum for bereaved children to release feelings and work through anxieties, either alone or with other children. Drawings, on the other hand, offer a simple medium of expression through which children can portray their thoughts and feelings without the use of language. Such drawings can provide adults with unique insights into the world of children, including their understanding of death and what the death of a loved one means to them [14].

As children grow and mature, their understanding of the world around them changes—naturally, this process includes changes in their understanding of death. Over time, they need to re-visit and talk about the experience of the death of someone close in order to make sense of what happened in the past and fit it into their understanding of what death means to them now. Several months or even years later children and adolescents may ask more questions about the person that died and voice their anxieties and concerns. Though it may be very difficult for adults to recount such memories, it is important to realize that children are just trying to update their understanding based upon their present level of development and cognition.

Children's Grief May Be Delayed

The initial reactions of children to the death of someone close may not be as immediate or obvious as those of adults. Many are not sure how they should react [15]. It is not unusual to see young children resume play activities or appear to be relatively unaffected following the news of the death of someone close. Unfortunately, such limited reactions may reinforce adults' beliefs that children do not understand and, therefore, do not experience grief as deeply.

Children take their cues from their parents [16]. If parents are extremely upset and in a great deal of turmoil following a death in the family, children may try to ignore or bury their own feelings in order to avoid hurting or upsetting their parents any further. If this turmoil and instability persist, children will continue to internalize or put off their own grief. Without the permission to grieve, they may develop physical problems such as headaches, stomach-aches, insomnia, and enuresis. Or, they may experience difficulties which include repeated nightmares, problems with school work, and trouble establishing and maintaining friendships with peers.

When children and adolescents cannot address their concerns following the death of a loved one, they often carry difficult "grief secrets" such as unfinished personal business with the deceased and feeling responsible for the death [17, p. 92]. If they continue to postpone or suppress their grief they may experience serious emotional difficulties when they reach adulthood and must face the death of someone else [18]. For example, Joelle was eight years old when her mother died of cancer. They had been very close and her mother spent considerable time with her during the terminal stage of her illness. Following her mother's death, Joelle was not allowed to attend the funeral. She yearned for her mother but was not permitted to talk about her or share her difficult feelings with anyone. She believed that she must have been responsible in some way for her mother's death. She still remembers relatives telling her friends that her mother was just away for a while when anyone would ask where she was. At twenty-six, Joelle's cousin died. Gradually, Joelle withdrew from social activities, lost considerable weight, experienced many sleepless nights, and was anxious, sad, and angry much of the time. A counselor helped her realize that her difficulties were the accumulation of many years of grief over the death of her mother. With someone willing to listen, Joelle was able to talk about her mother, reconstruct the events before and after her death, discuss her feelings of helplessness and guilt following her death, and slowly come to terms with her loss.

FACTORS INFLUENCING THE PATTERN OF GRIEF IN CHILDREN AND ADOLESCENTS

Many factors come together to influence significantly the grieving process during childhood. The next section of this chapter will address a number of these factors, specifically those listed below.

- age, cognitive ability, and developmental level
- personality and emotional maturity
- gender differences
- the communication pattern in the family
- the amount and kind of emotional support that is available
- the family's cultural and religious beliefs and practices
- the relationship with the person that died
- the nature of the death
- life experiences
- other external factors

There are no simple predictors or guidelines to follow when trying to assess what children and teens understand about death and how they feel about the death of someone close. The challenge for adults and professionals is to consider all the possible factors that may interconnect to influence children's and adolescents' understanding of the meaning of the death of someone close and their ability to integrate that meaning into their lives as they try to cope with their grief. Only when we are able to identify and understand the many factors that impact on the pattern of grief in children and teens, will we be better prepared to help them through the bereavement process.

AGE, COGNITIVE ABILITY, AND DEVELOPMENTAL LEVEL

Chronological age is one major factor that is frequently used to determine children's understanding of death and their pattern of grief. However, knowing a child's age is not enough to tell us what a particular child understands about death [19]. Cognitive ability and developmental level are other major factors that must be considered. Piaget's model focuses on understanding the cognitive development of children in general, but does not specifically address their conceptions of death [14, 20, 21]. Erickson's psychosocial model addresses levels of development, but again does not relate directly to children's understanding of death [22]. An eclectic model developed by the Lombardos describes different conceptions of death by matching children's ages with Piaget's four stages of cognitive development [23].

Nevertheless, trying to incorporate children's understanding of death into specific cognitive and developmental levels does not easily or consistently conform to any particular chronological age [14].

Though childhood development models can be helpful when trying to determine children's understanding of death, DeSpelder and Strickland caution that we should only use them as guides. The authors draw an interesting analogy between maps and models of childhood development explaining that they "can be useful for guiding one's way . . . but the particular features of the landscape will always possess a uniqueness that cannot be fully described by a map" [24, pp. 90-91]. In other words, each child possesses distinct characteristics which cannot be easily captured or understood if one only uses a model approach and does not consider the interplay of many other factors in the child's personal environment.

Recently, studies have encouraged a different approach to determining children's levels of understanding of death [19, 21, 25, 26]. The focus of the research is to assess children's understanding of death in relation to a presumed mature adult concept of death [19, 21]. This concept of death is complex and consists of a number of distinct subconcepts or components [19]. Speece recommends "an individualized and component-based approach to predicting a particular child's concept of death" [19, p. 20].

Four key bio-scientific components, universality, irreversibility, nonfunctionality, and causality, form the basis for a mature concept of death [19]. Universality (inevitability) refers to the ability of children to conceptualize that death is universal and inevitable and will happen to everyone, including themselves. Irreversibility (finality, irrevocability) refers to the fact that dead people do not come back to life after they have died. Nonfunctionality (cessation, dysfunctionality) refers to children's ability to conceptualize that all functions of life, i.e., biological, sensational, emotional, and cognitive, have ceased [21]. Causality refers to the ability of children to understand the objective and biological causes of death [25, 27].

Speece suggests further investigation of four other components, i.e., noncorporeal continuation, animism, disposition, and decomposition. Together, these eight components form the framework for a mature concept of death. He stresses the need for further study to standardize and define these components and establish reliable and valid instruments that can measure children's concepts of death [19].

Conclusions from the research suggest that the attainment of a mature concept of death, which encompasses an understanding of all its subconcepts or components, probably occurs much earlier in most children than previously anticipated. Lonetto points out that a death experience "can stimulate the development of more mature concepts about death that do not follow a prescribed pattern" [28, p. 186]. In the midst of these findings and ongoing research, clinicians and educators are challenged to find useful ways to integrate the present inconclusive information into their work when they try to determine what bereaved children and adolescents are thinking and feeling concerning the death of someone close to them [14].

Though we must be careful not to stereotype individual children in specific age or stage categories, it is helpful to group them to some extent in order to appreciate the many changes in their cognitive ability, developmental level, and understanding of the concepts of death over time. Since the following age ranges are broad and somewhat arbitrary, they may not adequately address those children whose understanding develops more rapidly because of other factors and, therefore, have a more advanced concept of death at an earlier age. Using common age ranges, the following paragraphs provide a condensed version of information concerning the four subconcepts of death in relation to cognitive ability and developmental level. The reader is directed to another chapter [14] written by the author for more detailed explanations.

Infancy to About Two Years of Age[1]

In this age range children rely on touch, movements, and the physical manipulation of objects. When someone dies they sense that things have changed. They recognize that the arms that hold them are different, that some of the voices have changed, or certain people are no longer there. They may be more fretful and anxious and their eating and sleeping patterns may change. There has been limited research in this age group regarding understanding of death but it is generally accepted that children less than two years of age do not have an accurate understanding of death.

Their anxieties tend to focus primarily on a fear of separation from their mother. Some researchers theorize that children under three years of age react to separation from a parent, especially a mother, as if that separation was a death [29].

Children from About Two Years Up To and Including Six Years of Age

For most of these children death is temporary, reversible, and not universal. Since they expect the dead person to eventually return, they may show very little emotion after someone close to them has died. Many children associate death with sleep and believe that the dead live on somewhere else and that they can see, talk, eat, and walk around. One three-year-old child wanted to know where Grandpa's ladder was so that he could climb out of his coffin, do his shopping, and find someone to do his cooking for him [30].

Children in this age range usually believe in cause and effect. Many think that death is caused by bad acts and, therefore, assume that they said or did something that caused the death of someone close to them. Though these children believe that most people die of old age, they include accidents, monsters, killings, bad acts, and separation from mother as other causes of death.

These children weave magic and fantasy into their thoughts and explanations of the world around them. They tend to ask many direct and often blunt questions such as, "What happens to the dead person in the ground?", "Why is the person buried so deep?", and "Can bugs get into the coffin?" Their attention span is short, they

---

[1] This section from Infancy to Adolescence provides a summary of information found in the author's chapter, *Perceptions of Death Through the Eyes of Children and Adolescents* [14].

frequently go off and play, and they cannot sustain prolonged grief reactions. For these children, their predominant anxiety still focuses on a fear of separation from their mother. There is a strong association between being left alone and being dead.

Children from About Six Years Up To and Including Eight Years of Age

Many children in this age range begin to recognize that death is universal though some remain uncertain [28]. They move toward believing that death is irreversible. They acknowledge nonfunctionality through their understanding that the dead do not move, see, talk, breathe, or eat. However, television programs (that often portray death as temporary) and medical procedures (that appear to bring people back from the dead) may convince some children that death is reversible [31]. Other children externalize death and personify it as a monster that "can rob you of your life," but if you see it coming you can escape its grasp [28, p. 92; 32]. They believe that death happens to people who are old and occasionally acknowledge that a child may die. Their other explanations for causes of death include a monster that can be avoided, accidents, and killings [14, 28].

These children focus less on separation from their mothers and concern themselves more with a fear of bodily injury or mutilation. Death is believed to be scary and frightening. Children become interested in the ceremonies and rituals associated with death [28]. They may exhibit feelings such as sadness, anger, and anxiety for short periods of time. Play continues to provide them with a forum where they can act out their anxieties and feelings.

Children from About Nine Years Up To and Including Twelve Years of Age

During this age range, children begin to think in more abstract terms. They know that death is universal and that everyone eventually dies. They understand nonfunctionality because they know that all body parts cease to function after death. Though they acknowledge that death may be irreversible, advances in medical technology that halt or reverse the dying process raise questions and create some uncertainty about the distinction between life and death [31]. They believe that most deaths happen because of old age and some acknowledge that death can occur at any age, including the very young. Other deaths result from a full range of external and internal causes including illness, accidents, disasters, and suicide [14, 28].

Mutilation anxiety continues from their younger years, and now there is a concern with suffocation anxiety, i.e., the fear of being buried alive. Other anxieties focus on what will happen when and after they die, including issues of pain, suffering, and whether the body will go to heaven or hell. They also wonder how the death will affect their families. Many describe death as full of darkness and gloom. They continue to be interested in, and concerned with, the rituals of death and burial [28].

Adolescence

Teens incorporate abstract thought and reasoning into their understanding of death and know that it is universal. Some teens, who challenge this universality and defy the reality that they may die if they tempt fate, engage in risk-taking behaviors such as drug abuse and reckless driving [33]. They know that death is irreversible and that all body functions cease. However, questions concerning irreversibility and non-functionality result from advances in medical technology that can maintain the body in a life-like state. Accounts of life-after-death experiences and ethical and legal debates regarding organ transplants, genetic engineering, and euthanasia increase their uncertainty [31]. Teens know that death can occur at any age. They identify a full range of internal and external causes including accidents, drunken driving, suicide, natural disasters, and war [14, 28]. Teens may doubt certain accepted causes of death because some medical conditions are no longer fatal. Adolescents who believe that medical advances will eventually eradicate other terminal diseases may question and challenge all four key components of a mature concept of death [14].

Adolescent anxieties include fear of suffering a painful death and fear of the unknown after death. Their thoughts turn to existential concerns about what happens to the soul or spirit after death. Death is often equated with sadness, loneliness, and uncertainty [28]. Teens who experience the death of someone close may contemplate suicide as a means of escaping their own emotional pain [33]. Some may turn to alcohol and drugs, while others may act out or withdraw.

PERSONALITY AND EMOTIONAL MATURITY

Personality and emotional maturity combine with age, developmental level, and cognition to influence the way in which children and adolescents react to the death of someone close. An individual's personality is an important factor in how he or she responds to life experiences. Robert Kastenbaum explains that "thoughts about death are intertwined with the total pattern of personality development right from the beginning, influencing and being influenced by all the child's experiences" [34, p. 106]. Hummer and Samuels point out that one should not underestimate the amount of ego strength as a factor in coping when a death occurs [35]. Generally, individuals with more self-esteem and a stronger self-concept tend to cope better in stressful situations. Balk reported that teens with higher self-concept scores coped better following the death of a sibling [36]. Hogan and Greenfield found that the duration of lingering grief reactions in adolescents was associated with self-concept, i.e., the lower the self-concept, the longer the duration of grief symptoms and vice versa [37]. Silverman and Worden found that bereaved children with lower self-esteem experienced more behavioral difficulties following the death of a parent [15].

Bereaved children who are more expressive tend to move toward people in order to talk, ask questions, and voice their concerns. Others instinctively move away because they are quiet and shy, do not want to talk, prefer to be alone, or are more comfortable internalizing their feelings [15]. Shannon, age five, was very quiet and withdrawn for many months before her parents realized that her behavior was associated with the unexpected death of her baby brother. No one noticed any difficulties until she became increasingly anxious, tearful, and clinging when it was time to go to school or to be left with a baby-sitter. Other children may rebel or protest against the death of someone close to them, often acting out their hurt, anger, and fears in aggressive and sometimes destructive ways. Jason, age twelve, stopped playing sports, got into fights in the school yard, and fell behind in school after his father's accidental death. Before this tragedy, Jason had been a popular student and very active in hockey [30].

It should not be assumed that a child's or adolescent's level of emotional maturity can be equated with his or her level of physical development and/or cognitive ability. Greenberg cautions against using these as guides to determine if children and teens have the emotional maturity to cope with the death of someone close [38]. Janet, who appeared older and more mature than her seventeen years, was expected to stay close to her younger brother and sister during the memorial service for her father. Instead, Janet quietly changed positions to be beside her aunt, holding on to her during and after the service. For several months, she continued to cry frequently and preferred to stay at home where she felt more secure.

GENDER DIFFERENCES

Coupled with personality and emotional maturity, gender differences influence how children and teens respond to a death. Traditionally in Western society there has been a tendency to socialize males to become "more independent, assertive, dominant, and competitive," and females to become "more passive, loving, sensitive, and supportive in social relationships" [39, p. 533]. In addition to these qualities, boys are expected to suppress their emotions and take control of difficult situations. On the other hand, girls are expected to outwardly express their feelings and exhibit anxiety in stressful situations. One recent American study addressed the attitudes and feelings of elementary school children toward violence and war (children in this study did not have any direct exposure to war). The findings, which were gender and age-specific, indicated that girls opposed war more often and expressed more negative emotions concerning the aspects of war. As grade level increased, boys became more tolerant of war and violence as compared to girls [40].

Stillion cautions that current patterns of socializing male children are putting them at higher risk for difficulties when they must cope with death and bereavement [41]. Silverman and Worden found that bereaved boys who were older than twelve years of age were expected to behave more like adults [15]. This is very much in keeping with the "stiff upper lip" syndrome associated with males in our society. They also found that boys were "less comfortable with their feelings and were more likely to get reinforcement from their support network to contain these feelings" [15, p. 102]. In the same study, girls were more apt to share their feelings and talk to their friends about the death of a parent. Hogan and Greenfield suggest that the tendency for male children and teens to suppress their grief increases their level of vulnerability during bereavement [37].

THE COMMUNICATION PATTERN IN THE FAMILY

Children quickly learn which subjects are open to discussion and tend to follow the pattern established in the family. The choice of communication pattern, which is partly determined by parental attitudes concerning death, sets the stage for how bereaved children and adolescents cope with their grief. Will they talk about the person that died or will they keep difficult feelings to themselves in order to avoid upsetting their parents? Children and teens who know that they can talk openly are more likely to express their feelings and their need for emotional support [42].

The pattern of communication within the family usually influences how much children and adolescents are told prior to an anticipated death or following a sudden death. However, circumstances surrounding certain deaths may alter established patterns of communication. Mayer states that "when AIDS is the cause of death, children are further silenced. Discussing death with children is difficult, but discussing an AIDS death is even harder" [43, p. 115]. The stigma attached to a death by homicide, suicide, or AIDS may leave parents struggling to protect their family by withholding information concerning the cause of death. Unfortunately, the need for secrecy inhibits their ability to be open and honest with their children.

Some parents weigh their degree of honesty and openness in communication with their need to maintain the innocence of childhood. In other words, they believe that the more they tell their children, the less they are able to protect them from the harsh reality of the pain and suffering that death engenders [14]. Others believe that children should be protected from the truth because they are too young, they are unable to understand what has happened, and/or they lack the experiences that will help them cope with the truth. But, how will they acquire the experiences and understanding, if they are denied the opportunities to voice their concerns and ask their questions?

Parents who do not know what to say, feel too uncomfortable to talk about death, or worry that they will not have the "right" answers tend to adapt a closed or guarded pattern of communication. Even when parents do not have "the answer" they can still give a response [44]. It is more important that parents are willing to talk with their children and provide support and reassurance when they voice concerns [45, 46]. When information is withheld and communication is very limited, children and adolescents may feel isolated and rejected. They may also misinterpret the lack of discussion to mean that the life of the deceased was not valued or important to other family members.

In an atmosphere of closed communication where questions are not encouraged, many parents mistakenly assume that children do not want to know any details. Unfortunately, if children are left on their own with little or no information concerning the death of someone close to them, they will use their imagination to interpret the events and construct elaborate and sometimes frightening explanations [45].

Often, these include the assumption that they were somehow responsible for the death. Children who move through childhood without any opportunities to discuss their concerns and share their grief may experience difficulties similar to those of Joelle who was mentioned earlier in this chapter.

Generally, when a pattern of open communication is established, encouraged, and maintained in the family, children and adolescents are better able to adapt to difficult life experiences [47]. Essentially, all of the literature favors openness and honesty in communication regarding issues related to death. Openness allows for communication in both directions—from parent to child and from child to parent. It provides children with the permission to talk freely, ask questions, discuss difficult issues, and feel that they are an integral part of the family. Families who can maintain openness in communication facilitate opportunities for members to come together to understand and support each other in the midst of any crisis. This ability to come together as a family also allows children and teens to observe mourning behaviors. Grollman describes tears as "wordless messages" that are "a vital part of grieving" for all bereaved individuals [46, p. 12]. Parents who show their tears and talk about their feelings, provide children with role models which teach them that expressions of grief are normal and expected.

Talking with children about the death of a loved one does not have to be anxiety-provoking and frightening. Rather, such open discussions can dispel fears, release difficult feelings, and promote reassurance, security, and trust, in spite of the pain that may be generated by the information. However, this openness should not assume that parents must "tell all" and that they must tell it all at one time. Children should not be overburdened with every detail to the point where they are overwhelmed with too much information. Instead, discussions should be tailored to the child's level of understanding based on age, development, and cognitive ability. The best way to maintain a balance is to let the discussion be guided by the child's questions and concerns. Before parents can begin to talk with their children about death, it is critical that they understand their own feelings and come to terms with their fears and anxieties concerning such matters [14, 22, 48].

THE AMOUNT AND KIND OF EMOTIONAL SUPPORT THAT IS AVAILABLE

Provision of adequate emotional support requires consistency and stability. Given the many stresses and demands of daily living, maintaining consistency and stability can be a considerable challenge for most parents. When a family member dies, the shock and disbelief alone can undermine the most stable families and leave other families in complete turmoil. The amount and kind of emotional support that is available to family members is influenced by a family's dynamics including the roles identified and assumed by family members; the established pattern of communication; parent-child relationships; support available from extended family; availability of, and willingness to access, community support; and child-rearing practices. Often the emotional support that could be provided by grandparents and other relatives is not possible because extended family members tend to live at a distance.

Parents have their own interpretations of what it means to provide children and teens with adequate emotional support. Some parents believe that they must protect their children from undue pain and suffering. These parents assume that sending their children off to a relative or close friend after a death in the family will provide stability and shield them from the grief in the household. Though time away may provide immediate respite from the profound sadness at home, it excludes children from grieving with their families. Other parents immediately try to resume routines and carry on with family activities as if nothing has happened. Reestablishing family routines helps contribute to feelings of security and control, but may carry the message that the death was not that significant and again denies children and teens any opportunity to grieve because they are expected to quickly get on with their lives.

Though parents may prefer that adolescents spend more time with family, teens need their own space and access to peers. Unfortunately, friends may not be very helpful in sorting out difficult feelings because they lack similar life experiences and may be too anxious or uncomfortable to talk about death. However, peers can provide an important source of "time out" or respite [49] as well as emotional support by "being there" for bereaved teens [50, p. 138]. Seventeen-year-old Jason, whose only sibling died, said, "I know they don't understand how I feel but they phone me and we hang out together. They look out for me so I feel like I have a bunch of big brothers."

Marital problems, serious financial difficulties, and dependency on alcohol and drugs tend to consume parents and preclude adequate emotional support. Such problems often create an atmosphere of confusion and instability which becomes exaggerated after the death of a family member. When roles are not clearly defined, routines frequently change, and boundaries remain inconsistent, bereaved children and adolescents cannot receive the emotional support they require.

Death of a Parent

From the research literature, Edelman identifies two requirements for bereaved children following the death of a parent: (1) "a stable surviving parent or other caregiver to meet their emotional needs" and (2) "the opportunity to release their feelings" [51, p. 8]. Unfortunately, in some families where one parent has died, the surviving parent and other family members look to older children and adolescents for emotional support. Children and teens may accept such comments as, "You are my pillar of strength," or "Now you must look after your mother and your little brother," to mean that they are expected to assume the roles of protector, nurturer, and provider for their families. Unfortunately, older children and teens who shoulder such unreasonable expectations and engage in role reversals to look after their surviving parent and siblings are denied the opportunity to grieve, receive little, if any, support for their own grief, and feel isolated and rejected.

Where there was continued conflict between separated parents, bereaved children and teens may receive little, if any, emotional support and acknowledgment of their loss from the surviving parent. These children may be provided with limited information concerning the circumstances of the estranged parent's death, be discouraged from asking questions, and may not be permitted to participate in the funeral.

In families where domestic violence is the norm, children and teens have already accumulated many losses and receive little, if any, emotional support [52]. Such violence breeds anxiety and fear and does not acknowledge individual needs and concerns. The death of the abuser or the abused parent leaves children and adolescents extremely vulnerable and exposed to heightened uncertainty concerning who will take care of them. Often they must struggle with difficult feelings concerning the circumstances of the death of their parent and contend with complicated grief reactions.

Death of a Child

Parents who are completely distraught over the death of one of their children may expect the surviving child or adolescent to walk in the shoes of the deceased child. Such role changes place undue stress on the surviving sibling and cause considerable guilt, frustration, anger, and rejection of their own self-worth. As a result, these children and adolescents cannot garner the emotional support that they require because their own needs and concerns are not acknowledged and supported.

Complicated Deaths

A death from suicide or AIDS carries its own stigma which restricts emotional support and imposes additional stress on all family members. When a parent or child commits suicide, surviving family members are plunged into a state of shock and must contend with debilitating feelings of guilt and failure for not being able to prevent the death. A parent's or child's death from AIDS often leaves surviving family members struggling with difficult feelings of guilt, shame, anger, and uncertainty [43]. The circumstances surrounding these deaths not only hinder open communication but seriously limit a parent's abilities to provide adequate emotional support and acknowledge children and teens' needs.

Simultaneous multiple deaths within a family shatter the family unit creating total disruption, instability, loss of control, and tremendous uncertainty. Too many roles need to be filled by too few family members who are overwhelmed by their losses. As a result, fewer relatives are available to provide much needed emotional support to surviving children and teens.

THE FAMILY'S CULTURAL AND RELIGIOUS BELIEFS AND PRACTICES

Cultural and religious beliefs and practices may significantly affect the way in which children understand the world around them, including their understanding of, and adjustment to, the death of someone close. These beliefs influence the pattern of communication established within the family as well as the amount and kind of emotional support that is available to bereaved children and adolescents. Cultural and religious beliefs and practices may become more evident and may hold more importance for family members during critical life cycle events such as a death [38]. Usually, there is considerable overlap between cultural and religious beliefs and practices making it difficult to separate them. Simply stated, culture provides traditional behaviors and social norms whereas religion offers rituals that deal with life and death events.

Rituals

For both adults and children, rituals provide structure, encourage and facilitate participation, establish a means to commemorate the death of someone close, and help to promote the grieving process. Silverman and Worden found that children and teens who attended their parent's funeral believed that their attendance helped them to acknowledge the reality of the death, honor their parent, and receive comfort and support from others [15]. Weeks explains that death rituals "provide a means of attaching young people to their families and to their wider circle of social and cultural environments" [53, p. 147]. Though the use of rituals is common in most non-Western cultures, there is a need to renew ritualization in Western society as a means of acknowledging the deceased and maintaining ties to each other and to relationships in the past [5, 54].

Cultural Influences

Death and bereavement are handled differently in various cultures because each has its own values, meanings, traditions, and rituals. For instance, some cultures view death as an accepted part of the life cycle, whereas others consider death as a punishment [24, 55, 56]. As a result, children's understanding of death will be influenced by their family's own beliefs and practices. In some cultures, mourning rituals begin prior to an expected death, yet discussion concerning the death is not allowed. In such a milieu, children's understanding of what is happening is limited to the rituals that they observe because they are not permitted to ask questions or express their concerns [38].

In addition to a family's own established beliefs, a variety of cultural attitudes are communicated through television programs, films, and media reports of tragic deaths and disasters. Children listen to these accounts and observe the responses of actors, actresses, victims, and commentators. Cultural attitudes that are conveyed may not be congruent with their own family's beliefs. As a result, they may experience confusion and difficulty as they try to interpret what they see, hear, and read and integrate it into their understanding of what death means to them in the context of their own family's beliefs. Such confusion and difficulties are more common when the topic of death is not open to discussion in the family.

Religious Influences

Balk and Hogan point out that religion can provide a means of coping with death and bereavement [10]. However, religious beliefs do not necessarily make it easier to cope with a death. Though these beliefs may provide comfort and meaning for some families, they may provoke anger and create confusion and anguish for others. For younger children, abstract religious concepts concerning death and the afterlife are confusing and difficult to understand. Euphemisms, such as "God took your sister to be one of his angels" or "God took Mommy to a better world," often frighten and anger children rather than comfort and console them.

The granting of adult privileges and responsibilities varies with cultures, religions, and ethnic groups. With many, religious status is conferred during early adolescence. As a result, teens are suddenly expected to behave as adult participants in religious customs and rituals concerning death. Though adolescents think and reason differently than children, they still are not adults. Death shatters any fantasies of immortality that may still linger from childhood and forces teens to confront the possibility of their own death [33, 49]. It "violates the ideals of fairness, justice, and goodness," and challenges God's existence [33, p. 26; 58].

There is evidence to indicate that religion can be beneficial for some bereaved adolescents [10, 50, 57]. Karl, a fifteen-year-old, explained, "because religion gives me the belief that there is something on the other side, I'm not so scared about death." Balk reports that many adolescents grieving the death of a sibling found that "religion became increasingly more important in their lives" [10, p. 68]. Usually by two to three years after a sibling's death, more religious teens reported that their feelings of grief had subsided as compared to non-religious teens who felt more depressed and confused about the death [10, 57].

THE CHILD'S RELATIONSHIP WITH THE DEAD PERSON

Another factor which impacts on children and adolescents' ability to cope with bereavement is the type and significance of their relationship with the person that died. Attig explains that the "distinctive features of relationships with the deceased make bereaved children and adolescents uniquely vulnerable" [2, p. 54]. If the relationship was very close, they tend to experience more difficulties adjusting because of the permanent void created by the death of the loved one. If there was conflict, and this conflict was not resolved prior to the death, children may be plagued by feelings of guilt over what they said or did when the person was still alive. More difficult or conflicted relationships tend to leave children and teens with more problems during bereavement.

Sibling Death

Siblings identify closely with each other and often link their fate to one another. When a sibling dies, the surviving child must deal with the loss of a playmate, friend, competitor, rival, confidant, and protector [49, 58, 59]. Since their brother or sister died, they realize that it is quite possible that they may also die. Their sadness and distress may combine with other difficult feelings such as guilt from a belief that they were somehow responsible for the death, anger at the sibling for leaving them, relief at not having to compete for attention any longer, and even more guilt for feeling angry and relieved. Such a mix of emotions can be extremely difficult to manage for many bereaved children and adolescents.

When an only sibling dies, their role as a brother or sister ends and they may face greater feelings of loneliness and emptiness. They have lost the life that they shared together as well as the future plans and dreams that they imagined together. In a study by Davies concerning children's grief seven to nine years after a death, she found that almost half of the siblings still thought about their dead brother or sister on a daily basis [60].

The manner in which bereaved parents cope with the death of a child directly impacts on how surviving children and teens manage during bereavement [50]. Some parents may become so overprotective and nurturing that surviving children and teens have difficulty maintaining their own identities and continuing their participation in activities outside the home. Conversely, some parents may reject affection or demonstrate resentment toward the surviving child or teen. Still others may make unfavorable comparisons to the deceased child or attempt to cast the surviving child in the image of the deceased. All these reactions create confusion and directly impact on the self-concept of the surviving child or teen [3, 60]. Some may feel that they must try to compensate for the death of their brother or sister by over-achieving in school or, in the extreme, taking on the identity of the child that died. If parents continue to be completely focused on their own grief, the surviving child's feelings of rejection and poor self-image may combine with feeling guilty that he or she is alive instead of his or her sibling.

Bereaved parents need to find a balance in which they keep the doors of communication open and gently nurture, protect, and support surviving children and teens. They need to be aware that difficult feelings such as guilt and anger will continue to surface, often unexpectedly, as children grow into adulthood. For example, anxieties may appear when they reach the age at which the sibling died. Special occasions such as a graduation or wedding may bring a flood of emotions including a yearning for lost opportunities that could have been shared together.

Death of a Parent

The death of a parent overwhelms children and adolescents with conflicting thoughts and emotions and impacts on most aspects of their lives [15, 61]. In order to understand how children and teens cope during bereavement, Silverman and Worden point out that we must consider "the context in which the death has occurred," i.e., the social and family system as well as the personal characteristics of the family members [15, p. 94]. Many bereaved children and teens must contend with the loss of the love, security, nurturing, protection, and role modeling offered by the deceased parent. Conversely, others, who lived in an environment of domestic violence or drug and alcohol abuse, must cope with the negative and difficult feelings left behind by hurtful relationships with the deceased parent. As previously mentioned, when the surviving parent was the abuser, children's lives are further complicated with uncertainty, fear, and anger.

Children, who were very young when one parent died, may yearn for the years that they could have had a relationship with that parent. Others retain a lingering sense of never having known the deceased parent. Even years later, many of these children actively pursue their need to fill in the picture of the parent that they never knew [24]. One eighteen-year-old, whose father died when he was an infant, stated, "This question just keeps rolling around in my head all the time about my Dad... about who he was and if I'm anything like him?"

The death of a parent during adolescence creates considerable difficulties for teens as they strive for independence and the freedom to make their own choices and decisions. The emotional turmoil surrounding a parent's death may cause many teens to temporarily regress into childhood where the expression of feelings is more comfortable, especially for males [33]. A parent's death may create considerable insecurity and family instability which makes it more difficult for adolescents to gain control over their lives. Older teens who are encouraged or expected to assume roles left behind by their deceased parent may struggle with their own identity and independence. Their ability to cope with their grief may be compromised as they focus on filling the shoes of their dead parent. Such responsibilities leave little time for them to spend with peers, maintain activities outside the home, and pursue personal career goals.

The findings of Silverman and Worden indicate that a mother's death causes the greatest number of changes and difficulties in the lives of children and teens [15]. When one parent dies, the ability of the other to assume the necessary roles of a single parent influences how well children and adolescents cope during bereavement [15]. Other important factors include the surviving parent's ability to maintain open lines of communication and provide opportunities to reflect and remember the dead parent. Maintaining a connection to the deceased parent will be discussed in the next section concerning the tasks of grieving.

THE NATURE OF THE DEATH

The literature suggests that the more sudden the death, the greater the impact, the greater the intensity of the emotional responses and the stress experienced by all family members [7, 62]. The circumstances surrounding a sudden or anticipated death also create additional difficulties for bereaved children and adolescents.

Sudden Death

A sudden death by accident, heart attack, disaster, suicide, or homicide brings forth overwhelming shock that has no forewarning and leaves family members totally unprepared for the intensity of their reactions. They have more difficulty absorbing the reality of their loss and their grief may be more complicated. Sudden death usually increases feelings of guilt for not somehow preventing the death and leaves survivors with a need to blame someone for what has happened. There is a sense of helplessness which is often linked to anger and rage directed at the believed perpetrator, as well as an increased need to try to make sense of what has happened [7]. Rando points out that sudden death diminishes the capacity to cope and violently shatters the bereaved person's assumptive world. There is no opportunity to say goodbye and take care of unfinished business [63]. Shock may persist, emotional reactions are often heightened, and a post-traumatic stress reaction may occur [63-65].

When there is a sudden death by homicide or suicide, adults may receive very limited information concerning what actually happened. When there is no body for family members to view, this prolongs the shock, enhances the unreality of the death, and enforces the possibility that there may be a mistake. Sometimes, legal and medical aspects surrounding the death prolong the process to such an extent that families are "stuck" waiting for explanations and cannot get on with their grief. Even when information is forthcoming, many parents and adults choose not to talk openly and honestly about such deaths with children and teens because of the stigma, anxiety, and fear that may be generated. All these factors impact on how much information is transmitted to children at the time of death and during the months that follow. Unfortunately, this does not prevent children from creating their own explanations. If they believe that the circumstances are so terrible that no one can talk about what happened, then their imaginations have every opportunity to run wild often fabricating more frightening and anxiety-provoking explanations than the actual truth.

Most relationships have some element of conflict from time to time. Children and teens who may have thought or said that they wished a parent or sibling were dead may experience overwhelming guilt when that relative suddenly dies. If we do not share information with children and provide them with opportunities to ask questions and express their concerns we may further enhance their belief that they are somehow responsible for the death. Or, we may give them the message that we are denying the value of the life of the person that died, especially if the death occurred as a result of suicide or homicide.

Anticipated Death

In contrast to sudden death, the anticipated death of a loved one provides time—time for family members to come together to participate in the care of their dying relative, to take care of unfinished business, to say goodbye, and to engage in anticipatory grief. Rando defines anticipatory grief as a process that covers three time intervals in which there is grief for the physical and psychosocial losses that have already occurred in the past, those that are ongoing in the present, and those that are yet to come [63]. Though anticipatory grief offers opportunities that are not possible following a sudden death, Rando emphasizes that children who are aware that their relative is dying are not at any particular advantage when compared to children who are already bereaved. Rando lists many variables that identify these children as disadvantaged grievers (see [63, p. 17] for a complete listing).

The impending death of a parent or sibling brings its own difficult, often complicated, situations. However, anticipated death allows family members to assume helpful roles, integrate the meaning of the illness, and observe the physical decline and increased dependency of the dying relative. Prior to including children during terminal care, they must be provided with information concerning their relative's illness that is easily understood and appropriate for their developmental level [63]. During the process of terminal care, children and teens need to know what to expect and must be kept informed of changes as they occur.

Though watching a parent or sibling deteriorate physically can be painful and distressing, it allows children and teens time to gradually integrate the reality that someone they love is dying. It provides them with opportunities to ask questions, express concerns, acknowledge feelings, and participate in care giving. Generally, clinical and research findings indicate that children and adolescents tend to cope better when they are allowed to participate in the care of their dying parent or sibling [49, 66]. Lauer and associates reported that siblings identified that their own involvement in the care of their dying brother or sister was the most important aspect of their experience during terminal care [67].

One important opportunity during terminal care is the possibility of taking care of unfinished business [7, 63, 68]. Rando stresses that "children need to achieve closure as much as adults" [63, p. 33]. They need to be able to resolve any differences, talk about things that matter to them, express feelings, share memories, and say goodbye.

As previously mentioned, certain circumstances surrounding an anticipated death may create additional difficulties for children and adolescents. The knowledge that a parent or sibling is dying of AIDS or attempted suicide may severely compromise the existing relationship between the child or teen and the dying relative. Difficult feelings are further complicated by the stigma associated with AIDS or suicide and the family's need for secrecy and privacy [43]. Teens may have problems participating during terminal care and prefer to spend more time out of the home. Others may act out their hurt, anger, and frustration in more aggressive ways.

LIFE EXPERIENCES

Life experiences help to underpin children's understanding of the world around them and contribute to shaping their beliefs, values, and attitudes. For younger children, the death of a pet or other animal may be their first encounter with death. Though there is a greater tendency toward open discussion concerning death, many parents and adults still believe that talking about death threatens the innocence of childhood [2, 14]. Adults who are able to take advantage of early "teachable moments" begin to lay the groundwork and provide a framework for children to build upon as they learn about life and death events [69, p. 457]. Such early encounters often bring many questions and afford teaching and learning opportunities for both children and parents to talk openly and honestly with each other about what happens when someone dies and how they cope with difficult feelings. These experiences must be fitted into the context of the child's world and take into account many variables including age, cognitive ability, developmental level, the family's cultural and religious beliefs, and parental attitudes. Gordon stresses the importance of laying a foundation early in childhood and cautions parents not to wait until adolescence to begin death education [33].

When children and teens must cope with the death of someone close, they draw from any earlier life experiences to help them make sense of what is happening now. Children who have experienced previous deaths tend to have a greater maturity concerning their level of understanding. However, this does not necessarily mean that they will be better able to cope with bereavement. Their age, developmental level, the manner in which previous experiences were handled, and many other factors contribute to how well they are able to cope now. Did the child have any opportunity to talk about the previous death, ask questions, express concerns, attend the funeral, and participate in the rituals of death? Or, was the child given little, if any, explanation and excluded from the events surrounding that death? The latter situation would suggest that the child was not given the opportunity to grieve the death and now may find that he or she is trying to understand and cope with both deaths at the same time.

Other life experiences, such as wars, persistent racial or religious communal conflict, and man-made or natural disasters can significantly complicate children and adolescents' abilities to understand and cope with death and bereavement. For example, how does exposure to devastating military destruction in war-torn areas such as Sarajevo affect children's understanding and attitudes concerning death? Studies indicate that children faced with experiences of war reach a more mature level of understanding concerning death as compared to children who are not subjected to such violence [26, 27, 70]. Does repeated exposure to the deaths of relatives and friends in refugee camps [70] or during communal conflict desensitize them and, perhaps, help them cope better or differently with repeated losses? Or, do such experiences increase their vulnerability and instill fear, insecurity, and helplessness, as well as an inability to comprehend and come to terms with the numerous losses in their lives? For many of these children and teens, such repeated violence and multiple deaths have lasting impacts and contribute to difficult feelings including survivor's guilt and post-traumatic stress reactions [65, 71, 72]. Man-made disasters, such as the senseless bombing in Oklahoma City, invoke fear and anger and leave adults and children struggling with the sombre reality that such sudden, violent deaths can happen to anyone, anywhere.

OTHER EXTERNAL FACTORS

I have discussed some of the external factors that limit or enhance children and adolescents' ability to understand death and cope with bereavement. One external factor that can have a pervasive influence on children's perceptions of death and their attitudes toward bereavement is the information that is transmitted through the media, in particular television. Television serves many positive roles in relaying news, political and scientific information, education, music, and entertainment. However, much of the daily entertainment on television contains many acts of violence and death [73]. There is a fine line between fantasy and reality in the portrayal of death by the media. Cartoon characters never stay dead and many programs deliver a message suggesting that death is only a temporary condition. Many prime time programs imply that death is impersonal, violent, and destructive [33, 73]. Such views are also supported by Western society which has attempted to maintain the denial and distancing of death. More difficulties arise for children and teens when programs convey messages that are contrary to parental values, attitudes, and cultural beliefs.

Many questions come to mind. What is the long-term impact on children and teens when they are regularly exposed to conflicting values concerning violence and death? Does witnessing frequent episodes of violence and death desensitize them to the reality of death? Does the sensationalization of murder and suicide in news reports have a negative influence on children and teens' beliefs and attitudes concerning death? Can such sensationalism alter their thinking regarding the tolerance of violence and promote less respect for life? It is known that children are increasingly desensitized when they view television violence [73]. Perhaps repeated viewing of violence on television is another variable that contributes to children's increased tolerance of violence in relation to war.

Keeping the focus of this chapter in mind, the critical question is: To what extent does television viewing of violence and death influence how children and teens react to the death of a loved one? Wass points out that violent portrayals on television "contribute to the acquisition of behavior traits beginning early in childhood" [73, p. 97]. When a family member dies, which role model does a child choose? The obvious answer should be the parent. However, not all parents foster open communication concerning death-related issues. Fewer parents use television as a teaching tool to distinguish between fantasy and reality. Children who lack such education, support, and guidance, particularly younger children and those with lower self-concepts, may pattern their behavior after what they view on television or they may be too confused to know how they should react.

In Summary

Space does not permit the discussion of all possible factors that interconnect and influence the manner in which children and adolescents grieve the death of a loved one. Some of the factors that have been discussed have a direct bearing on how children develop an understanding of a mature concept of death. Others address important issues that influence their pattern of grief. The reader is encouraged and challenged to consider the full range of possible factors and identify those which put children and teens at risk versus those that are nurturing in nature and contribute to positive reactions during the bereavement process.

As we move on, it is important to keep in mind the many factors discussed and their impact within the context of a bereaved child's or adolescent's life. The next section addresses the tasks that children and teens need to accomplish during bereavement and provides guidelines for adults to help them through this process.

THE TASKS OF GRIEVING

Grief or mourning, which is the adaptation to loss, involves four tasks. These tasks, as described by Worden, provide a helpful overview of the grieving process (see [7] for a complete description):

1. to accept the reality of the loss
2. to work through the pain of grief
3. to adjust to an environment in which the deceased is missing
4. to emotionally relocate the deceased and move on with life.

There is no particular order that must be followed to accomplish these tasks and at times they may be achieved simultaneously. Since they are not self-limiting, certain life events and developmental transitions may cause a resurgence of grief reactions [74] which in turn provide a need to work through some of these tasks again.

Children and Adolescents

As children grow and mature, they already have many tasks that they must accomplish. The process of grief may become more difficult or complicated as they are challenged to try to accomplish both the tasks of growing up and those of grieving. Bereaved children and adolescents may need assistance to avoid putting developmental and cognitive tasks on hold while they are grieving. As previously mentioned, adults must understand that children grieve differently for many reasons. The many factors discussed previously will also influence the manner in which they work through the tasks of grieving. Sandra Fox identified the following four psychological tasks for bereaved children and adolescents which are similar to those delineated by Worden for bereaved adults [75].

Task 1: To Understand

Many factors including age, developmental level, cognitive ability, and parental attitudes interconnect to determine how children accomplish this task. They need to understand what has happened to the person that died and to make sense out of the death. Fox believed that there are at least three reasons why this is the most challenging of the four tasks [75]. First, is the manner in which we define and explain death. Younger children, in particular, need careful, honest explanations which clearly state that the person is dead and his body has totally stopped working. The use of euphemisms, such as "Daddy has gone on a long trip," establishes the anticipation that Daddy will eventually return, or, "Your brother is gone and won't be coming back" creates confusion and anger toward the sibling for leaving. Discussions concerning what happens to the soul or spirit after death should avoid confusing abstractions and be grounded in the parent's own cultural and religious beliefs.

Second, we need to be aware that children's magical thinking and their belief that they can cause bad things to happen may interfere with their understanding of the cause of death. Adults should take their cues from bereaved children and not assume that they know what they are thinking and feeling. It is important to let them talk freely about the death and what it means to them. We need to listen carefully to their questions and verify with them what they understand concerning what we have said. It is critical that adults match their answers and explanations to the child's developmental and cognitive level of understanding.

Third, adults must keep in mind the fact that children's understanding of death changes over time as they grow and mature. Knowledge of children's development and cognitive abilities at different ages allows adults to appreciate what children can understand at any given point in time.

Task 2: To Grieve

Bereaved children and adolescents need to be able to grieve and to work through their difficult feelings. Parents and other adults who try to protect them from the pain and suffering of bereavement often complicate, delay, or halt their grief reactions. Children and teens need to be able to express their feelings and concerns in an atmosphere that is non-judgmental and promotes feelings of security, trust, and reassurance. Adults need to be aware that children's grief is not limited by time and that their understanding of what the death of a relative means to them changes as they acquire more information about the world around them. When a death occurs early in life, children need to be able to re-visit that death in order to make sense of it and integrate the information into their present level of understanding.

As discussed earlier in this chapter, reactions to death, especially in young children, may be quite different from what adults typically expect. Adults and professionals must be prepared to accommodate these differences and not assume that children who appear relatively indifferent to a death are not as deeply affected by their loss as children who exhibit more of the expected emotional responses associated with bereavement.

Grief support groups provide a milieu in which children and teens are given the permission to grieve by experiencing and expressing their losses in the presence of peers who are also grieving (see [76-79] for specific information concerning support groups for children and adolescents). Participation in these groups helps bereaved children and teens understand the grief process, integrate the death into their lives, and resolve difficult emotional issues that may otherwise linger into adulthood.

Task 3: To Commemorate

Though this task appears to vary from the one defined by Worden, part of "adjusting to an environment in which the deceased is missing" can also involve ways that commemorate or preserve the memory of the person that died.

Children and teens need to find ways to remember and honor the death of someone close. Participation in rituals, such as the funeral or a memorial service, the planting of a tree, writing a poem, journal or memory book, or drawing pictures, are helpful ways to commemorate a person's death and to say goodbye. Attendance at the funeral also assists children and adolescents to understand the reality of the death. There is no magical age for deciding when it is appropriate to include children in the funeral services. Careful explanations will prepare them for what to expect and allow them the opportunity to make choices regarding their degree of involvement.

Over the years, children should be encouraged and supported to continue this commemoration at other occasions such as special anniversaries and celebrations. Commemoration is necessary to teach children and teens that all lives have value [75, 80]. However, commemorating the life of a person that died from suicide, AIDS, or was the victim of domestic violence or a drunk driver may be difficult for many reasons. If handled appropriately, the causes of these deaths can provide realistic insight and valuable teaching opportunities for bereaved children and teens [81-83]. In the case of suicide, the commemoration should focus on honoring the life of the person that died versus the manner in which he or she died. Otherwise, romanticizing such a death may appear to support suicide as a solution for those who are emotionally struggling with life [83].

Task 4: To Go On With Life

Children and adolescents need to go on with their lives and develop an identity which is based on life without the person that has died. Usually, going on with life takes place once they understand, express their grief, and commemorate the death of their loved one [75]. Children need to know that it is okay to be happy and to live on without the person that died. Older children and teens may require more reassurance that they can go on living without the person that died because they are more inclined to contemplate their own death by suicide as a means of dealing with their pain, confusion, sadness, and overwhelming sense of loss.

Maintaining a Connection with the Deceased Person

The bereavement literature has supported the belief that detachment from the deceased is a necessary process for recovery from grief [8, 9, 84]. Others have indicated that such connections create potential areas of difficulty for bereaved adults and children [85, 86]. Contrary to these opinions, more recent findings suggest that going on with life does not mean that bereaved individuals must detach themselves and forget the person that died.

Silverman and Worden report that children and adolescents, during the early months of bereavement, try to maintain a connection to their deceased parent. Though the parent has died, the relationship has not ended [15]. Balk and Hogan's findings also indicate that an ongoing attachment continues in the lives of bereaved adolescents [9]. These findings are in keeping with studies of bereaved parents which report that remaining connected to their deceased children is a necessary part of the bereavement process [87, 88].

One follow-up study during the first year of bereavement, reported that children and teens develop an "inner construction of the dead parent" which gradually changes over time as they mature [5, p. 294]. These findings suggest that children and adolescents need to maintain a connection with the deceased parent. This connection to, or accommodation of, the dead parent in their lives is an active attempt to make sense of their loss and helps them to go on living [5].

Such findings suggest that we need to rethink our understanding of the bereavement process in order to focus on helping children maintain a connection to their deceased parent or sibling rather than encouraging them to detach or let go of the relationship. Silverman and associates stress the need to help children and teens develop a "common language for talking about the death and the person that died" and believe that the use of rituals can help to legitimize their connection to the deceased relative [5, p. 502].

CONCLUDING REMARKS

Children can learn to cope with what they know and understand. It is the unknown which can be truly terrifying for them [89].

We know that grief is a cognitive and emotional process full of transitions. We also know that the death of a loved one changes life forever. Children and adolescents who experience the death of a parent or sibling will hurt, will need to adapt to many changes in their lives, will have some difficult times, will be changed by the experience of the death, and their grief will go on for a long time and may, in fact, be timeless. However, studies clearly indicate that experiencing the death of a loved one does not necessarily mean that they will be psychologically damaged [5, 9, 15, 90].

We must acknowledge the uniqueness of each child and adolescent. Such acknowledgment requires us to be more perceptive concerning the many factors that impact on a bereaved child's or adolescent's world. Attig emphasizes the need to respect bereaved children and teens. Such respect requires an understanding of their individual experience with death, an appreciation of their relationship with the deceased, and a sensitivity to their vulnerabilities concerning their loss [2].

Time and what we do with that time will help children and adolescents cope with bereavement and accomplish the tasks of grieving. We need to provide a stable environment in which they are not judged or left on their own but rather given the space, love, and security that allows them to work through their grief in their own time and in their own way. We need to be available to children and teens to answer their questions honestly and be willing to listen, share, and learn from them. We also need to pay attention to the thoughts and feelings that bereaved children portray through their drawings and writings. Artwork, poems, and stories provide unique insights into their understanding of death and the meaning of the death of someone close to them [14].

Helen Keller said that the only way to get to the other side is to go through the door. In our need to protect children and teens from the pain and suffering that death engenders we may try to close the door or encourage them to go around it. Instead, we need to help children and adolescents go through the door of grief by providing them with the tools to understand death, cope with bereavement, and complete the tasks of grieving.

REFERENCES

1. B. G. Simos, *A Time to Grieve: Loss as a Universal Human Experience*, Family Service Association of America, 1979.
2. T. W. Attig, Respecting Bereaved Children and Adolescents, in *Beyond the Innocence of Childhood: Helping Children and Adolescents Cope with Death and Bereavement*, Vol. 3, D. W. Adams and E. J. Deveau (eds.), Baywood Publishing, Amityville, New York, pp. 43-60, 1995.
3. B. Davies, Long-Term Effects of Sibling Death in Childhood, in *Beyond the Innocence of Childhood: Helping Children and Adolescents Cope with Death and Bereavement*, Vol. 3, D. W. Adams and E. J. Deveau (eds.), Baywood Publishing, Amityville, New York, pp. 89-98, 1995.
4. R. Buckman, *I Don't Know What to Say: How to Help and Support Someone Who is Dying*, Key Porter Books Limited, Toronto, Ontario, 1988.
5. P. R. Silverman, S. Nickman, and J. W. Worden, Detachment Revisited: The Child's Reconstruction of a Dead Parent, *American Journal of Orthopsychiatry*, 62(4), pp. 494-503, October 1992.
6. M. A. Miller, Re-Grief as Narrative: The Impact of Parental Death on Child and Adolescent Development, in *Beyond the Innocence of Childhood: Helping Children and Adolescents Cope with Death and Bereavement*, Vol. 3, D. W. Adams and E. J. Deveau (eds.), Baywood Publishing, Amityville, New York, pp. 99-113, 1995.
7. J. W. Worden, *Grief Counselling and Grief Therapy: A Handbook for the Mental Health Practitioner* (2nd Edition), Springer Publishing, New York, 1991.
8. C. M. Parkes and R. S. Weiss, *Recovery from Bereavement*, Basic Books, New York, 1983.
9. J. Bowlby, *Attachment and Loss: Loss, Sadness, and Depression*, Vol. 3, Basic Books, New York, 1980.
10. D. E. Balk and N. S. Hogan, Religion, Spirituality, and Bereaved Adolescents, in *Beyond the Innocence of Childhood: Helping Children and Adolescents Cope with Death and Bereavement*, Vol. 3, D. W. Adams and E. J. Deveau (eds.), Baywood Publishing, Amityville, New York, pp. 61-88, 1995.
11. T. A. Rando, *How to Go on Living when Someone You Love Dies*, Bantam Books, New York, 1991.
12. R. R. Ellis, Young Children: Disenfranchised Grievers, in *Disenfranchised Grief*, K. Doka (ed.), Lexington Books, D. C. Heath and Company, Lexington, Massachusetts, 1989.
13. J. L. Krupnick and F. Solomon, Death of a Parent or Sibling During Childhood, in *The Psychology of Separation and Loss*, J. Bloom-Feshbach, S. Bloom-Feshbach and Associates (eds.), Jossey-Bass Publishers, San Francisco, California, 1987.
14. E. J. Deveau, Perceptions of Death through the Eyes of Children and Adolescents, in *Beyond the Innocence of Childhood: Factors Influencing Children and Adolescents' Perceptions and Attitudes Toward Death*, Vol. 1, D. W. Adams and E. J. Deveau (eds.), Baywood Publishing, Amityville, New York, pp. 55-92, 1995.
15. P. R. Silverman and J. W. Worden, Children's Reactions in the Early Months after the Death of a Parent, *American Journal of Orthopsychiatry*, 62, pp. 93-104, 1992.
16. D. W. Adams and E. J. Deveau, *Coping with Childhood Cancer: Where Do We Go From Here?* (New Rev. Edition), Kinbridge Publications, Hamilton, Ontario, 1993.
17. K. Braza, Permission to Grieve: Developing a Children's Grief Support Group, in *Young People and Death*, J. D. Morgan (ed.), The Charles Press, Philadelphia, Pennsylvania, pp. 92-98, 1991.

18. T. Rodabough, Helping Students Cope with Death, *Journal of Teacher Education*, Vol. XXXI, pp. 19-23, 1980.
19. M. W. Speece, The Search for the Mature Concept of Death: Progress on Its Specification and Definition, *The Forum Newsletter*, 6(XXI), pp. 1, 20-23, November/December 1995.
20. J. Piaget, *The Child's Conception of the World*, Harcourt, Brace, New York, 1929.
21. M. W. Speece and S. B. Brent, Children's Understanding of Death: A Review of Three Components of a Death Concept, *Child Development*, 55, pp. 1671-1686, 1984.
22. E. Erickson, *Childhood and Society*, W. W. Norton, New York, 1950.
23. V. S. Lombardo and E. F. Lombardo, *Kids Grieve Too!* Charles C. Thomas Publisher, Springfield, Illinois, 1986.
24. L. A. DeSpelder and A. L. Strickland, *The Last Dance* (3rd Edition), Mayfield Publishing, Mountain View, California, 1992.
25. A. Lazar and J. Torney-Purta, The Development of the Subconcepts of Death in Young Children: A Short-Term Longitudinal Study, *Child Development*, 62, pp. 1321-1333, 1991.
26. D. J. Schonfeld and S. Smilansky, A Cross-Cultural Comparison of Israeli and American Children's Death Concepts, *Death Studies*, 13, pp. 593-604, 1989.
27. S. Smilansky, Different Mourning Patterns and the Orphan's Utilization of his Intellectual Ability to Understand the Concept of Death, *Advances in Thanatology*, 5, pp. 39-55, 1981.
28. R. Lonetto, *Children's Conceptions of Death*, Springer Publishing Company, New York, 1980.
29. A. K. Gordon and D. Klass, *They Need to Know: How to Teach Children About Death*, Prentice-Hall, Englewood Cliffs, New Jersey, 1979.
30. D. W. Adams and E. J. Deveau, *Children's Understanding of Death at Different Ages and the Pattern of Grief in Children and Adolescents*, workshop presentation at the Children and Death Conference, King's College, London, Ontario, May 1992.
31. M. W. Speece and S. B. Brent, The "Adult" Concept of Irreversibility, in *Young People and Death*, J. D. Morgan (ed.), The Charles Press, Philadelphia, Pennsylvania, pp. 11-28, 1991.
32. M. Nagy, The Child's Theories Concerning Death, *Journal of Genetic Psychology*, 73, pp. 3-27, 1948.
33. A. K. Gordon, The Tattered Cloak of Immortality, in *Adolescence and Death*, C. A. Corr and J. N. McNeil (eds.), Springer Publishing Company, New York, 1986.
34. R. Kastenbaum, The Child's Understanding of Death: How Does it Develop? in *Explaining Death to Children*, E. A. Grollman (ed.), Beacon Press, Boston, Massachusetts, pp. 89-108, 1967.
35. K. M. Hummer and A. Samuels, The Influence of the Recent Death of a Spouse on the Parenting Function of the Surviving Parent, in *Childhood Bereavement and its Aftermath*, S. Altschul (ed.), International Universities Press, Connecticut, pp. 37-43, 1989.
36. D. E. Balk, Adolescents' Grief Reactions and Self-Concept Perceptions following Sibling Death: A Study of 33 Teenagers, *Journal of Youth and Adolescence*, 12, pp. 137-159, 1983.
37. N. S. Hogan and D. B. Greenfield, Adolescent Sibling Bereavement Symptomology in a Large Community Sample, *Journal of Adolescent Research*, 6(1), pp. 91-112, 1991.
38. M. L. Greenberg, The Impact of the Hospital System on Dying Children and their Families, in *Beyond the Innocence of Childhood: Helping Children and Adolescents Cope with Life-Threatening Illness and Dying*, Vol. 2, D. W. Adams and E. J. Deveau (eds.), Baywood Publishing, Amityville, New York, pp. 211-236, 1995.

39. E. M. Heatherington and R. D. Parke, *Child Psychology: A Contemporary Viewpoint* (4th Edition), McGraw-Hill, New York, 1993.
40. G. R. Cox, B. J. Vanden Berk, R. J. Fundis, and P. J. McGinnis, American Children and Desert Storm: Impressions of the Gulf Conflict, in *Beyond the Innocence of Childhood: Factors Influencing Children and Adolescents' Perceptions and Attitudes Toward Death*, Vol. 1, D. W. Adams and E. J. Deveau (eds.), Baywood Publishing, Amityville, New York, pp. 109-121, 1995.
41. J. M. Stillion, Gender Differences in Children's Understanding of Death, in *Beyond the Innocence of Childhood: Factors Influencing Children and Adolescents' Perceptions and Attitudes Toward Death*, Vol. 1, D. W. Adams and E. J. Deveau (eds.), Baywood Publishing, Amityville, New York, pp. 29-43, 1995.
42. S. Hetzel, V. Winn, and H. Tolstoshev, Loss and Change: New Directions in Death Education for Adolescents, *Journal of Adolescence, 14*, pp. 323-334, 1991.
43. R. R. Mayer, The Legacy of AIDS: The Untold Stories of Children, in *Beyond the Innocence of Childhood: Helping Children and Adolescents Cope with Death and Bereavement*, Vol. 3, D. W. Adams and E. J. Deveau (eds.), Baywood Publishing, Amityville, New York, pp. 115-135, 1995.
44. C. A. Corr and D. M. Corr, *Responding to Children's Questions about Death*, plenary session, International Conference on Children and Death, King's College, London, Ontario, 1995.
45. E. A. Grollman (ed.), *Explaining Death to Children*, Beacon Press, Boston, Massachusetts, 1967.
46. E. A. Grollman, Can You Answer Children's Questions? in *Beyond the Innocence of Childhood: Factors Influencing Children and Adolescents' Perceptions and Attitudes Toward Death*, Vol. 1, D. W. Adams and E. J. Deveau (eds.), Baywood Publishing, Amityville, New York, pp. 9-13, 1995.
47. J. J. Spinetta, D. Rigler, and M. Karon, Anxiety in the Dying Child, *Pediatrics, 52*, pp. 841-845, 1973.
48. R. Kastenbaum, Childhood: The Kingdom where Creatures Die, *Journal of Clinical Child Psychology, 3*, pp. 11-13, Summer 1974.
49. E. J. Deveau, The Impact on Adolescents when a Sibling is Dying, in *The Dying and The Bereaved Teenager*, J. D. Morgan (ed.), The Charles Press, Publishers, Inc., Philadelphia, Pennsylvania, pp. 63-77, 1990.
50. N. S. Hogan and L. DeSantis, Things that Help and Hinder Adolescent Sibling Bereavement, *Western Journal of Nursing Research, 16*(2), pp. 132-153, 1994.
51. H. Edelman, *Motherless Daughters: The Legacy of Loss*, Addison-Wesley Publishing Company, Reading, Pennsylvania, 1994.
52. B. C. Zick, Domestic Violence, Children, and Their Losses, in *Beyond the Innocence of Childhood: Helping Children and Adolescents Cope with Death and Bereavement*, Vol. 3, D. W. Adams and E. J. Deveau (eds.), Baywood Publishing, Amityville, New York, pp. 153-165, 1995.
53. O. D. Weeks, The Renewal of Ritualization: Funerals of the 1990s, in *Beyond the Innocence of Childhood: Factors Influencing Children and Adolescents' Perceptions and Attitudes Toward Death*, Vol. 1, D. W. Adams and E. J. Deveau (eds.), Baywood Publishing, Amityville, New York, pp. 145-161, 1995.
54. S. M. Silverman and P. R. Silverman, Parent-Child Communication in Widowed Families, *American Journal of Psychotherapy, 33*, pp. 428-441, 1979.
55. M. M. Stevens, Palliative Care for Children Dying of Cancer: Psychosocial Issues, in *Beyond the Innocence of Childhood: Helping Children and Adolescents Cope with Death*

and Bereavement, Vol. 3, D. W. Adams and E. J. Deveau (eds.), Baywood Publishing, Amityville, New York, pp. 181-209, 1995.
56. M. M. Stevens, Family Adjustment and Support, in *Oxford Textbook of Palliative Medicine*, D. Doyle, G. W. C. Hanks, and N. MacDonald (eds.), Oxford University Press, Oxford, England, pp. 707-717, 1993.
57. D. E. Balk, Sibling Death, Adolescent Bereavement, and Religion, *Death Studies, 15*, pp. 1-20, 1991.
58. S. P. Bank and M. D. Kahn, *The Sibling Bond*, Basic Books, New York, 1982.
59. W. Furman and D. Burhmester, Children's Perceptions of the Qualities of Sibling Relationships, *Child Development, 56*, pp. 448-461, 1985.
60. B. Davies, Long-Term Follow-Up of Bereaved Siblings, in *The Dying and Bereaved Teenager*, J. D. Morgan (ed.), The Charles Press Publishers, Philadelphia, Pennsylvania, pp. 78-89, 1990.
61. A. Samuels, Parental Death in Childhood, in *Childhood Bereavement and Its Aftermath*, S. Altschul (ed.), International Universities Press, Connecticut, pp. 19-36, 1989.
62. C. M. Parkes, Determinants of Outcome Following Bereavement, *Omega, 6*, pp. 303-323, 1975.
63. T. A. Rando, Anticipatory Grief and the Child Mourner, in *Beyond the Innocence of Childhood: Helping Children and Adolescents Cope with Death and Bereavement*, Vol. 3, D. W. Adams and E. J. Deveau (eds.), Baywood Publishing, Amityville, New York, pp. 5-41, 1995.
64. T. A. Rando, *Treatment of Complicated Mourning*, Research Press, Champaign, Illinois, 1993.
65. W. Yule and R. M. Williams, Post-Traumatic Stress Reactions in Children, *Journal of Traumatic Stress, 3*(2), pp. 279-295, 1990.
66. B. Davies, After a Sibling Dies, in *Bereavement: Helping the Survivors*, M. A. Morgan (ed.), Proceedings of the 1987 King's College Conference, London, Ontario, pp. 55-65, 1987.
67. M. Lauer, R. Mulhern, J. Bohne, and B. Camitta, Children's Perceptions of their Sibling's Death at Home or Hospital: The Precursors of Differential Adjustment, *Cancer Nursing*, pp. 21-27, February 1985.
68. E. Kübler-Ross, *On Death and Dying*, Macmillan Publishing Company, New York, 1969.
69. C. A. Corr, C. M. Nabe, and D. M. Corr, *Death and Dying, Life and Living*, Brooks/Cole Publishing Company, Pacific Grove, California, 1994.
70. S. Smilansky, *On Death: Helping Children Understand and Cope*, Peter Lang Publishing, New York, 1987.
71. N. Dubrow, N. I. Liwski, C. Palacios, and M. Gardinier, Traumatized Children: Helping Child Victims of Violence, in *International Responses to Traumatic Stress*, Y. Danieli, N. S. Rodley, and L. Weisæth (eds.), Baywood Publishing, Amityville, New York, pp. 327-346, 1996.
72. P. Valent, *Child Survivors: Adults Living with Childhood Trauma*, William Heinemann, Melbourne, Australia, 1994.
73. H. Wass, Appetite for Destruction: Children and Violent Death in Popular Culture, in *Beyond the Innocence of Childhood: Factors Influencing Children and Adolescents' Perceptions and Attitudes Toward Death*, Vol. 1, D. W. Adams and E. J. Deveau (eds.), Baywood Publishing, Amityville, New York, pp. 95-108, 1995.
74. B. Raphael, *The Anatomy of Bereavement*, Basic Books, New York, 1983.
75. S. S. Fox, Helping Children Deal with Death Teaches Valuable Skills, *The Psychiatric Times*, pp. 10-11, August 1988.

76. B. S. Wolfe and L. M. Senta, Interventions with Bereaved Children Nine to Thirteen Years of Age: From a Medical Centre-Based Young Person's Grief Support Program, in *Beyond the Innocence of Childhood: Helping Children and Adolescents Cope with Death and Bereavement*, Vol. 3, D. W. Adams and E. J. Deveau (eds.), Baywood Publishing, Amityville, New York, pp. 203-227, 1995.
77. S. Elder, Support Groups in the Schools, in *What Will We Do? Preparing a School Community to Cope with Crises*, R.G. Stevenson (ed.), Baywood Publishing, New York, pp. 147-167, 1994.
78. C. Johnson, Adolescent Grief Support Groups, in *Beyond the Innocence of Childhood: Helping Children and Adolescents Cope with Death and Bereavement*, Vol. 3, D. W. Adams and E. J. Deveau (eds.), Baywood Publishing, Amityville, New York, pp. 229-240, 1995.
79. E. Ormond and H. Charbonneau, Grief Responses and Group Treatment Interventions for Five- to Eight-Year-Old Children, in *Beyond the Innocence of Childhood: Helping Children and Adolescents Cope with Death and Bereavement*, Vol. 3, D. W. Adams and E. J. Deveau (eds.), Baywood Publishing, Amityville, New York, pp. 181-202, 1995.
80. M. M. Metzgar, What Do We Do with the Empty Desk? in *Beyond the Innocence of Childhood: Helping Children and Adolescents Cope with Death and Bereavement*, Vol. 3, D. W. Adams and E. J. Deveau (eds.), Baywood Publishing, Amityville, New York, pp. 167-180, 1995.
81. R. G. Stevenson, Questions and Answers, in *What Will We Do? Preparing a School Community to Cope with Crises,* R. G. Stevenson (ed.), Baywood Publishing, New York, pp. 183-191, 1994.
82. R. G. Stevenson, Special Crisis Section, in *What Will We Do? Preparing a School Community to Cope with Crises,* R. G. Stevenson (ed.), Baywood Publishing, Amityville, New York, pp. 193-208, 1994.
83. R. G. Stevenson, Teen Suicide: Sources, Signals and Prevention, in *The Dying and Bereaved Teenager*, J. D. Morgan (ed.) The Charles Press, Philadelphia, Pennsylvania, pp. 125-139, 1990.
84. S. Freud, Mourning and Melancholia, in *The Standard Edition of the Complete Psychological Works of Sigmund Freud*, Vol. 14, J. Strachey (ed. and trans.), Hogarth Press, London, pp. 237-258, 1957.
85. E. Furman, Children's Patterns in Mourning the Death of a Loved One, in *Childhood and Death*, H. Wass and C. A. Corr (eds.), Hemisphere Publishing, Washington, D.C., pp. 185-203, 1984.
86. D. R. Dietrich and P. C. Shabad, *The Problem of Loss and Mourning*, International Universities Press, Madison, Connecticut, 1989.
87. D. Klass, *Parental Grief: Solace and Resolution*, Springer Publishing, New York, 1988.
88. S. S. Rubin, The Resolution of Bereavement: A Clinical Focus on the Relationship to the Deceased, *Psychotherapy: Theory, Research, Training and Practice, 22*, pp. 231-235, 1985.
89. J. Katzenbach, *The Traveller*, G. P. Putnam's Sons, New York, 1986.
90. J. L. Krupnick, Bereavement During Childhood and Adolescence, in *Bereavement, Reactions, Consequences, and Care*, M. Osterweiss, F. Solomon, and M. Greene (eds.), National Academy Press, Washington, D.C., 1984.

CHAPTER 25
Adolescent Grief*

Barbara L. Anschuetz

The adolescent is no longer a child and not quite an adult, yet exhibits characteristics of both and neither. As the adolescent attempts to leave childhood and begin his journey toward adulthood, the search for his identity and "niche" in the world becomes a major focus.

The early adolescent (12 to 14 years) is testing his boundaries. The family is still socially and emotionally important, and he requires love and acceptance as he struggles with self-worth. Social acceptance by peers is paramount. The middle adolescent (15 to 17 years) is more aware of his sexuality and peer group activities place more emphasis on opposite-sex relationships. Social skills are more developed and conflict with parents is more likely. During late adolescence (17 to 21 years), relationships with parents are operating at a more adult level. Sexual maturity is occurring as relationships include more commitment and less fantasy. The peer group has less influence as self-confidence and a stronger identity develop.

Even in his expression of grief, the adolescent is different from children and adults. Different from the child, who can only grieve in very short spurts, and the adult whose grief follows accepted societal rituals, the adolescent grieves in a unique manner. "The adolescent, unlike the child, has a greater maturity and capacity to understand the meaning of death. The ability to grasp abstractly the meaning of death and the future brings the adolescent into a new anxiety-laden attitude toward death" [1].

Death affects many areas of the adolescent's life. Through death, the adolescent learns that the daily existence which was taken for granted in the original family and social group has a potential for radical alteration [1].

Fleming and Adolph state that

> during adolescence, the loss of a profound relationship—whether an internalized object or a person in the external world—may interfere in what seems to be the natural progression of intellectual-emotional-psychological "growing up."

---

* Throughout this chapter, the masculine personal pronoun is used. This convention has been used here for ease of discussion.

Changes that are normally expected may be averted, avoided, or may not even take place [2, p. 102].

Death of a significant person during adolescence can affect interpersonal relationships and the developmental tasks. This includes independence-dependence, peer identification, role models, physical and social self-image, social skills, and bonding [3]. The developmental tasks may be affected by many factors—the nature of the relationship, the adolescent's personal coping style, peer relationships, other experiences with death, personal development, and the extent and nature of the adolescent's social support system.

According to Kastenbaum, the confrontation with death in adolescence, in actuality or in prospect, overwhelms the fragile defensive structures at this time of life, often leading to extreme reactions [4]. He also states:

> It is in adolescence that we glimpse for the first time what we and the world might be. Intellect and feeling are united in the same quest, albeit one subject to confusion and misdirection. The life and death questions we raise in adolescence create a sense of vulnerability that we spend most of our adult years trying to conceal and forget [4, p. 13].

Kastenbaum found the adolescent to have a very low tolerance for death-connoting stimuli and to view the end of his life with fear and distaste [5]. Adolescents are very concerned with the meaning of life and how to fit into the expected roles and find their own niche and accountability in the world. Dealing with a death can make the meaning of life more precarious, as is evidenced by the high number of adolescent suicides. Jackson, in his role as a pastoral counselor with adolescents, believed that emotional injury during adolescence may last a lifetime unless there is wise and skillful intervention, as self-destructive behavior is quite common as a mode of resolving grief among teenagers [6]. Gordon indicated that the adolescent's awakening knowledge of death can create an overwhelming sense of doom [7].

Raphael described some common behaviors among adolescents who have lost someone close to them [8]. These behaviors, similar to adults', included identification with the dead person; continuous and intermittent mourning, which is often delayed or private because of other pressures (school and adolescent development); withdrawal from relationships; depressed feelings; care-eliciting behaviors, very often aggressive acting out; and difficulty with sexuality issues (loss of a source of sexual identification, sexual acting out).

Nothing experienced previously can prepare youth for the feelings that accompany a personal loss [7]. If the death of the loved one is by suicide, the conflict can become even greater and put the adolescent "on hold" in one stage of his development, thus affecting his ability to meet subsequent stage-appropriate demands. In addition, adolescents are especially prone to symptoms associated with post-traumatic stress reactions including acting out, truancy, delinquency, violent behavior, and substance abuse [9].

In general, the death of a significant person during adolescence can affect the developmental stages and the growth of the emerging adult. Factors specific to the type of death (death of a parent, grandparent, sibling, or peer) can also impact the adolescent's physical, emotional, spiritual, and sexual well-being.

DEATH OF A PARENT

A review of some early literature on the effects of parental death during adolescence [10], linked the death to a number of psychological difficulties. The effects of parental death on the adolescent ranged from depression [11-14], avoidance of intimacy [8, 15], and developmental delays [2, 16].

Research shows that adults who suffered early parental death spontaneously generated significantly more death themes and suicide ideation than those who did not lose a parent prior to adulthood [1, 14, 17, 18].

Furman's research concluded that the death of a parent is considered the most significant loss that an adolescent can experience and one which can continue through the developmental stages, and even throughout life, as certain traumas, and anniversaries trigger painful memories [16].

The adolescent is already facing a struggle in trying to separate emotionally and physically from his parents. Although fighting for autonomy, the adolescent needs the emotional, spiritual, and financial support of his parents. In addition, the adolescent is attempting to gain control over his/her sexuality and develop social and sexual intimacy. These needs, while attempting to become an individual, enhance his state of conflict and turmoil. When a parent dies, all processes can become overwhelming and even older adolescents will want to revert back to the security of childhood.

Tara was eighteen years old, and in her final semester of high school, when her mother died within days of contracting hepatitis. In a poignant letter to her father, she stated "at times, I am unable to cope with even the simplest situations. I can't answer all the nagging questions. Why my mom? Why couldn't she get better? Why doesn't anyone understand? Why me? . . . I hope that one day I will see the world through those same eyes again, and life will seem as exciting and adventurous as ever, but for now I feel all of these other emotions . . ." [personal communication].

Even, without death, adolescents are experiencing a process of mourning, according to Sugar [19], as they deal with separation from their parents. In his view, normal adolescent mourning is broken into three stages: (1) separation protest phase, (2) disorganization phase, and (3) reorganization phase. The first phase is characterized by disequilibrium and the urge to recover the loss of the love object. The second phase is characterized by antisocial behavior and mood swings. At this stage the adolescent is adapting to the change, as well as looking back at the past longed-for objects in search of reunion. In the third stage of reorganization, the adolescent is more calm and has many other issues to explore and settle while adapting to the object loss.

He also noted that this process of normal adolescent mourning is intensified and complicated by a permanent loss, as in the death of the love object (parent). Hankoff concurred that adolescents who passed through this period in a setting of family or social difficulty in disorganization are apt to have the normal adolescent struggle made more difficult [1]. Furman noted that bereaved adolescents, developmentally at the point of leaving the parents, may experience difficulty moving away from the surviving parent or in following the dead parent's path into adulthood [16].

DEATH OF A SIBLING

Although most of the early research on adolescent loss through death was centered on the death of a parent, recently emphasis has been placed on the significance of sibling death [20-24].

Experiencing the death of a sibling during adolescence, as with the death of a parent, may also affect developmental levels and interpersonal relationships. According to Raphael, the loss of an older sibling may be seen as the loss of someone who represented a source of security and identification with adulthood, thus leading to great insecurity in this area [8]. The loss of a younger sibling may be considered a fantasy to the adolescent, and the grief will be for the fantasy child. The bereaved sibling may also feel a double loss, i.e., that of the parents as well as the deceased sibling. Sometimes parents are so preoccupied with their own grief that the remaining siblings are ignored.

Janine was fourteen years old and in the first months of high school when her twenty-year-old brother, Bill, died. Socially and emotionally, she felt isolated from the all-important peer group, at a time when developing new peer relationships was so necessary as part of "fitting in." She stated that "surviving siblings have many things to deal with. They must deal with a new set of unknown, often scary emotions, as well as peer pressure, school, work, and looking after their parents. A bereaved sibling may grieve in silence for a very long time. For two and one-half years, I roamed the halls of school, growing in a shell" [personal communication].

Krell and Rabkin described three types of clinically identifiable children observed in families who have suffered the loss of a child [25]. The "haunted" child is one who is left in silence and shielded from the pain of loss, usually due to guilt on the part of the parents. The "bound" child is overprotected and fails to develop autonomy. The "resurrected" child is one who, in the parents' eyes, must replace the lost child.

According to Adams and Deveau, bereaved siblings have great difficulties finalizing the death as they have shared so much, including love and hatred for each other [20].

Davies conducted follow-up research on fifty-eight families who participated in a home health-care program in Minnesota, for children who were dying of cancer [26]. Her findings indicated that the surviving siblings thought about their deceased brothers and sisters on a regular basis. They also explored a range of feelings, including being different, lonely, and withdrawn. Some of the surviving siblings also indicated that they experienced maturity or psychological growth, especially around "death" events. This finding concurred with the research by Balk [22, 27], who also studied bereaved adolescents who had lost a sibling through death. His findings showed that sibling bereavement did not adversely affect all areas of psychological growth and development, as the bereaved adolescents found several adaptive responses regarding important dimensions of self-concept. Other bereaved siblings in Davies' study felt that their self-concepts were lowered with a feeling of "not being enough," especially to ever make their parents happy again.

More recently, Davies, studying the long-term follow-up of adolescent sibling bereavement, indicated the four following positive aspects of sibling death: (1) an ability to face death, (2) this ability allowed them to help others who were experiencing death, (3) an understanding of the meaning of life, and (4) a good feeling about themselves (from adversity had come the impetus for psychological growth) [23]. Countered with this finding her study also indicated some of the negative aspects of adolescent sibling bereavement which included: (1) a seriousness to life which separated them from their peer group (peer attitudes seemed trivial and irresponsible), (2) a long-term loneliness and liking to be alone, and (3) a feeling of being less socially competent (due to their isolation).

DEATH OF A FRIEND

The death of a friend causes a sense of doom for the future as the adolescent realizes the fragility of life. Death of a peer threatens the adolescent's belief in his invincibility and immortality.

Chantelle and Jonathan were both vibrant, beautiful, popular friends. They were killed within four months of each other in very similar automobile accidents. Friends who had just started to recover from the shock of Jonathan's death, felt themselves to be especially vulnerable after Chantelle died. Nothing was secure for them, especially life. As one close friend commented, "Chantelle and I drove together to Jonathan's funeral. Then I drove alone to Chantelle's funeral? What lies ahead for me? Am I next?" [personal communication].

Raphael points out that the loss of a peer with whom the adolescent has had an intense relationship can deeply affect the surviving friends [8]. According to Gordon and Worden the death of a peer forces a confrontation with one's own death at any time [7, 28].

OTHER SIGNIFICANT DEATHS

The death of other significant people in the life of an adolescent can also have an important effect on the adolescent's well-being. The death of a grandparent, which may be the adolescent's first encounter with death, can make the adolescent especially vulnerable. The loss of a grandparent who was distant can take on a symbolic meaning, such as the theme that the adolescent's parents and he/she are now vulnerable. If the grandparent relationship was close, and in some cases, had replaced the role of the parent, the loss can be substantial [8].

The loss of a teenage pregnancy through abortion, miscarriage, or even adoption, can also be a very difficult loss to grieve as it is often masked in shame, guilt, or secrecy. According to Joralemon, adolescent mothers and fathers can experience grief reactions, and this grief for the "lost" child can even include grief for their own lost childhood [29].

HELPING THE BEREAVED ADOLESCENT

Seen as a method of assisting bereaved adolescents in the process of working through grief, successful intervention strategies include individual and group counseling, and death education. Rando [30] and Worden [28] emphasized the encouragement of overt expressions of grief to counteract delayed or avoided grief responses.

Non-therapy oriented bereavement counseling groups with specific goals and activities to aid in the bereavement task, and geared to the developmental needs of the adolescent have recently been introduced through the education system [10, 31-33]. Death education, as an ongoing process that is part of a framework for total family and life education, can also assist children of all ages in handling death [34, 35].

Beyond the introduction of classroom activities and school-based support groups, youth hospice training programs and medical center-based grief programs support adolescents who have had to face the death of a peer or sibling [36, 37].

Support groups for grieving adolescents provide a forum for care and nurturing by their peers without the threat of dependency on adults [38]. The adolescent's need for bereavement counseling includes a non-threatening, safe environment in which they can meet with other adolescents in a similar situation, in order to talk about the death, learn to cope with the death, and express feelings related to the death [2, 10]. As they bond with the other adolescents because of their common grief, they develop a sense of security. Rando considers developing secure relationships necessary as part of the adolescent's recovery from grief [30].

A very poignant memory of trust and security within a peer group occurred with an eighteen-year-old male, named Chris, who was grieving the death of his mother. For his item of sharing with the group members, he brought in his mother's recipe box. For ten minutes he pulled recipes out of the box and talked about the memories of his mother baking. His senses were very acute during this exercise. He talked about returning home from school to the taste and smell of whatever his mother was baking, and described the visual memory of the box sitting on the kitchen table, which indicated that something special had been cooked that day. This led to a discussion of how his father single-handedly prepared Thanksgiving dinner, and an acknowledgment that his dad was really trying to keep the family together. All of the other group members, as well as the group leaders had tears in their eyes throughout this sharing exercise.

Adolescents need to talk about the person who died; they need to build a legacy through "grateful memories," stories, and linking objects; and they need to initiate rituals [2, 10, 39].

The author conducted a study of sixteen bereaved adolescents who had recently lost a significant person in their lives. The deaths were either of a parent, grandparent, close relative, or friend. Almost all of the deaths had occurred within ten months of the study. The adolescents in the study ranged in age from fourteen to eighteen years, and all attended public high schools, which were used as the forum to conduct the counseling groups. The sixteen bereaved adolescents who comprised the three bereavement counseling groups represented a varied range of experiences as to the type of death, relationship with the deceased, and circumstances surrounding the death. The results indicated a range of feelings expressed by the bereaved adolescents, including shock, numbness, relief, guilt, confusion, depression, fear, loneliness, emptiness, and anger.

Shock and numbness were expressed as the initial response in the hours and days immediately following the death. Relief was experienced in all cases in which the deceased had been in great pain and the bereaved adolescent had watched the suffering. Experiences of feeling guilty were expressed intensely by the bereaved adolescents. The most common expression was guilt for not having done more and a sense of being selfish. Since selfishness and egocentrism are necessary components of early adolescent development, this was a difficult emotion for the adolescents to resolve.

Confusion was mostly related to the unknown about death and funerals. The bereaved adolescents were universal in their feelings of discomfort at the difficulty and rituals of a funeral. There was also a common sense of being unprepared for what to expect. They were confused as to the role they were expected to play, as well as the range of emotions expressed by different people.

Loneliness was a feeling experienced by all of the adolescents in the study. It was always associated with sadness and was felt when visiting a home or room of the deceased, during special days and anniversaries, and when doing activities related to the deceased.

All of the participants in the study experienced emptiness and described it as a physiological response with words like "a big hole" and "something missing inside."

Anger was the most repeatedly expressed feeling of the grieving adolescents toward death and in almost all cases the anger was deflected toward others.

Depression was a difficult word for the bereaved adolescents to pinpoint in terms of feelings. Depression for them implied withdrawal and inactivity and related much more to physical symptoms normally associated with grief, than emotional or cognitive responses normally associated with depression. Robinson and Fleming who researched cognitive reactions of grief, concluded that "grief" and "depression" are usually not similar in terms or extent of pathology [40]. According to their findings, depression associated with grief is usually benign and without cognitive distortion.

Fear was one of the most extensive emotions reported by the adolescents. Three major themes developed around fear. The first was a fear of their own mortality, especially death by the same cause as the deceased for whom they were grieving. According to Worden, increased personal death awareness is a common source for fear or anxiety for those left behind after a death [28]. The second theme revolved around the fear of losing others through death. The third theme was the fear of forgetting; not just forgetting the deceased, but the physical features that fade with time. This fear was expressed the most by those who had experienced the death the longest.

Throughout the entire study, the feelings that were expressed most frequently by the bereaved adolescents were anger, fear, and guilt. Worden acknowledges that these feelings are often not recognized or felt to the degree they need to be in order to bring about effective grief resolution [28].

Explaining the importance and normalcy of expressing feelings is an integral part of death education. Fleming and Robinson, called this the educational component of grief therapy and stated that "although educating the bereaved will not result in the elimination of their anguish, it can normalize many of their unpredictable and painful emotional responses, and thereby reduce feelings of anxiety and helplessness" [41, p. 13].

Grieving adolescents may also experience significant changes in family relationships, school, and friendships, as the result of the death of a significant person [10]. During the grief process, school can become a low priority, with so many other stressors. Negative changes can be seen in school attendance, behavior, motivation, and/or performance. Another significant area of change can be in family relationships, especially if the grieving adolescents feel they cannot talk about the death with family members or if family members did not encourage the expression of feelings.

Friendships, which can have a powerful and important influence on the lives of adolescents, can also be adversely affected by a death. Grieving adolescents can feel jealousy toward their friends who have not experienced a death, and were going home to "normal" lives. Thus it becomes more difficult to talk to peers about the death [10].

The adolescents in this study indicated that the most helpful part of the bereavement counseling group for them was meeting other people in a similar situation, talking about the death, learning how to cope with the death, and expressing feelings related to the death. Johnson, in her review of adolescent grief support groups, also included testimonials from adolescents indicating that the ability to share feelings and thoughts was the most important aspect of the group [38].

In addition to research supporting the importance of adolescents being able to talk about their feelings, either on an individual basis or in support groups, adolescents also need to mourn for the deceased in their own way [39]. Adolescents use different mourning rituals than adults to express their grief and say "goodbye" to the deceased. Gordon also noted that adolescents reject traditional funeral rituals of which they have little experience [7].

Music and linking objects are very important components of adolescent grief rituals. Grieving adolescents tend to congregate in groups, either at school, at an assigned meeting place, or even in the parking lot of the funeral parlor. They listen to music, openly express their grief and provide support and solace for each other, usually isolating themselves from adults.

One group of adolescents, who held a memorial service at their high school after the death of a friend, brought cases of iced tea, the favorite drink of the deceased. Each adolescent took a can of the drink, and they formed a large circle on the stage. One-by-one they stood in the center of the circle and recounted a memory of their friend, and made a farewell toast, as the others linked arms and swayed to the hard rock music playing in the background.

According to Miller, the memorial service, which is usually entirely arranged by the gathering adolescents, can symbolize the transition, healing, and continuity [42]. She notes that rituals have a clear purpose, beginning and end, and provide a measure of safety for all participants during an emotionally-charged event. Weeks considers death rituals as one means of attaching young people to their families and environment in order to decrease their isolation and increase their social awareness [43].

Religion can also play an important role in helping the bereaved adolescent perform rituals, as well as provide a forum for healing and continuity. In a review of research on the effects of religion and spirituality on bereaved adolescents, Balk and Hogan cite numerous studies in which religion was a significant factor in helping bereaved adolescents deal with death [44]. Even something as simple as "knowing I will see him again in heaven," helped some grieving adolescents find peace and meaning in the midst of their pain. Others developed a deeper understanding of the meaning of human existence and their role.

SUMMARY

The adolescent grief experience is different from that of the child or adult. In order to effectively understand adolescent grief, it is important to understand adolescent development. The death of a significant person during such a tumultuous time of growth and change, can have serious implications for the adolescent's rites of passage into adulthood. It can also have a major impact on school, family, and peer relationships.

Effective bereavement intervention needs to incorporate adolescent needs and feelings; in other words, "meet them where they are." Adolescents will shun many traditional adult mourning rituals in favor of their own memorials and expressions of spirituality. They need to be able to share their many feelings with their peers in a safe, secure environment, free of adult roles and expectations.

REFERENCES

1. L. D. Hankoff, Adolescence and the Crisis of Dying, *Adolescence, 10*(30), pp. 373-387, 1991.
2. S. J. Fleming and R. Adolph, Helping Bereaved Adolescents: Needs and Responses, in *Adolescence and Death*, C. A. Corr and J. N. McNeil (eds.), Springer, New York, pp. 97-118, 1986.
3. S. Calvin and I. M. Smith, Counselling Adolescents in Death-Related Situations, in *Adolescence and Death*, C. A. Corr and J. N. McNeil (eds.), Springer, New York, pp. 215-230, 1986.
4. R. Kastenbaum, Death in the World of Adolescence, *Adolescence and Death*, C. A. Corr and J. N. McNeil (eds.), Springer, New York, pp. 4-15, 1986.
5. R. Kastenbaum and R. Aisenberg, *The Psychology of Death*, Springer, New York, 1972.
6. E. N. Jackson, The Pastoral Counselor and the Child Encountering Death, in *Helping Children Cope with Death: Guidelines and Resources*, H. Wass and A. C. Corr (eds.), McGraw Hill, Toronto, pp. 89-97, 1982.

7. A. K. Gordon, The Tattered Cloak of Immortality, in *Adolescence and Death*, C. A. Corr and J. N. McNeil (eds.), Springer, New York, pp. 16-31, 1986.
8. B. Raphael, *The Anatomy of Bereavement*, Basic Books, New York, 1982.
9. S. Elder, Helping Bereaved Children and Adolescents Cope with the Aftermath of Suicide, in *Beyond the Innocence of Childhood: Helping Children and Adolescents Cope with Death and Bereavement*, Vol. 3, D. Adams and E. Deveau (eds.), Baywood Publishing, Amityville, New York, 1995.
10. B. L. Anschuetz, *The Development and Implementation of a Group Counselling Intervention Model with Bereaved Adolescents*, unpublished doctoral dissertation, University of Toronto, Toronto, Ontario, 1990.
11. J. Bowlby and C. M. Parkes, Separation and Loss Within the Family, in *The Child in his Family*, E. J. Anthony and C. Koupernik (eds.), Robert E. Kreiger, Huntington, New York, pp. 197-223, 1979.
12. H. Finkelstein, The Long-Term Effects of Early Parent Death: A Review, *Journal of Clinical Psychology*, 44(1), pp. 3-9, 1988.
13. G. Nelson, Parental Death during Childhood and Adult Depression: Some Additional Data, *Journal of Social Psychiatry*, 17, pp. 37-42, 1982.
14. D. A. Taylor, Views on Death From Sufferers of Early Loss, *Omega*, 14(1), pp. 77-81, 1983.
15. B. Lipinski, Separation Anxiety and Object Loss, in *Bereavement Counselling: A Multidisciplinary Handbook*, B. M. Schoenberg (ed.), Greenwood Press, Westport, Connecticut, pp. 146-169, 1980.
16. E. Furman, Studies in Childhood Bereavement, *Canadian Journal of Psychiatry*, 28(4), pp. 241-247, 1983.
17. D. W. Adams, *Childhood Malignancy: The Psychosocial Care of the Child and His Family*, Charles C. Thomas, Springfield, Illinois, 1979.
18. J. Birtchnell, The Relationship Between Attempted Suicide, Depression, and Parent Death, *British Journal of Psychiatry*, 116, pp. 307-313, 1970.
19. M. Sugar, Normal Adolescent Mourning, *American Journal of Psychotherapy*, 22(2), pp. 258-269, 1968.
20. D. W. Adams and E. J. Deveau, Helping Dying Adolescents: Needs and Responses, in *Adolescence and Death*, C. A. Corr and J. N. McNeil (eds.), Springer Publishing, New York, pp. 79-76, 1986.
21. B. Davies, Long-Term Effects of Sibling Death in Childhood, in *Beyond the Innocence of Childhood: Helping Children and Adolescents Cope with Death and Bereavement*, Vol. 3, D. Adams and E. Deveau (eds.), Baywood Publishing, Amityville, New York, 1995.
22. D. E. Balk, *Sibling Death During Adolescence: Self Concept and Bereavement Reactions*, doctoral dissertation, University of Illinois at Urbana, Champaign, Illinois, Dissertation Abstracts International, 8203397, 1981.
23. B. Davies, Long-Term Follow-up of Bereaved Siblings, in *The Dying and The Bereaved Teenager*, J. D. Morgan (ed.), Charles Press, Philadelphia, Pennsylvania, pp. 78-89, 1990.
24. A. Guerriero, *Adolescent Bereavement: Impact on Physical Health, Self-Concept, Depression, and Death Anxiety*, unpublished masters thesis, York University, Toronto, Ontario, 1983.
25. R. Krell and L. Rabkin, The Effects of Sibling Death on the Surviving Child: A Family Perspective, *Family Processes*, 18(4), pp. 471-477, 1979.

26. B. Davies, *Long-Term Bereavement in Siblings Following Child's Death from Cancer*, American Cancer Society, California Division, Psychosocial Oncology, San Francisco, California, 1986.
27. D. E. Balk, Adolescents' Grief Reactions and Self-Concept Perceptions Following Sibling Death: A Study of 33 Teenagers, *Journal of Youth and Adolescence, 12*(2), pp. 137-161, 1983.
28. J. W. Worden, *Grief Counselling and Grief Therapy: A Handbook for the Mental Health Practitioner*, Springer Publishing, New York, 1982.
29. B. G. Joralemon, Terminating an Adolescent Pregnancy: Choice and Loss, in *Adolescence and Death*, C. A. Corr and J. N. McNeil (eds.), Springer Publishing, New York, pp. 79-76, 1986.
30. T. A. Rando, *Grief, Dying and Death: Clinical Intervention for Caregivers*, Research Press, Champaign, Illinois, 1984.
31. L. Allen, Teenagers and Grief, in *Children and Death: Proceedings of the King's College Conference*, G. H. Paterson (ed.), King's College, London, Ontario, pp. 121-126, 1986.
32. G. Baxter and W. Stuart, Bereavement Support Groups for Secondary Students, in *The Dying and the Bereaved Teenager*, J. D. Morgan (ed.), The Charles Press, Philadelphia, Pennsylvania, pp. 108-120, 1990.
33. J. G. Corazzini and T. M. May, The Role of the Counselling Centre in Responding to Student Death, in *New Directions For Student Services: Coping with Death on Campus, 31*, pp. 39-50, 1985.
34. G. M. Giacolone and E. McGrath, The Child's Concept of Death, in *Bereavement Counselling: A Multidisciplinary Handbook*, B. M. Schoenberg (ed.), Greenwood Press, Westport, Connecticut, pp. 195-212, 1980.
35. J. D. Morgan, Death Education: Where Do We Go From Here? in *Children and Death: Proceedings of the King's College Conference*, G. H. Paterson (ed.), King's College, London, Ontario, pp. 121-126, 1986.
36. L. Lister and D. Ward, Youth Hospice Training, *Death Studies, 9*, pp. 353-363, 1985.
37. B. Wolfe and L. Senta, Interventions with Bereaved Children Nine to Thirteen Years of Age: From a Medical Center-Based Young Person's Grief Support Program, in *Beyond the Innocence of Childhood: Helping Children and Adolescents Cope with Death and Bereavement*, Vol. 3, D. Adams and E. Deveau (eds.), Baywood Publishing, Amityville, New York, 1995.
38. C. Johnson, Adolescent Grief Support Groups, in *Beyond the Innocence of Childhood: Helping Children and Adolescents Cope with Death and Bereavement*, Vol. 3, D. Adams and E. Deveau (eds.), Baywood Publishing, Amityville, New York, 1995.
39. P. R. Silverman, S. Nickman, and J. W. Worden, Detachment Revisited: The Child's Reconstruction of a Dead Parent, *American Journal of Orthopsychiatry 62*(4), pp. 494-503, 1992.
40. P. Robinson and S. Fleming, Differentiating Grief and Depression, *The Hospice Journal, 5*, pp. 77-89, 1989.
41. S. Fleming and P. J. Robinson, The Application of Cognitive Behaviour Therapy to the Bereaved, in *The Challenge of Cognitive Therapy: Applications to Novel Populations*, M. Vallis and J. Howes (eds.), Plenum Press, New York, 1990.
42. M. Anderson Miller, Re-Grief as Narrative: The Impact of Parental Death on Child and Adolescent Development, in *Beyond the Innocence of Childhood: Helping Children and Adolescents Cope with Death and Bereavement*, Vol. 3, D. Adams and E. Deveau (eds.), Baywood Publishing, Amityville, New York, 1995.

43. O. D. Weeks, The Renewal of Ritualization: Funerals of the 1990s, in *Beyond the Innocence of Childhood: Factors Influencing Children and Adolescents' Perceptions and Attitudes toward Death,* Vol. 1, D. Adams and E. Deveau (eds.), Baywood Publishing, Amityville, New York, 1995.
44. D. Balk and N. Hogan, Religion, Spirituality, and Bereaved Adolescents, in *Beyond the Innocence of Childhood: Helping Children and Adolescents Cope with Death and Bereavement,* Vol. 3, D. Adams and E. Deveau (eds.), Baywood Publishing, Amityville, New York, 1995.

CHAPTER 26

Bereaved Black Children

Ronald K. Barrett

In order to understand and appreciate the unique experience of bereavement in Black children, it is important to note that in some fundamental ways the bereavement experience of Black children is very similar to that of children in general. However, there are some principal distinctions in the experience of Black children that impact the nature and scope of their grief and bereavement. The primary objective of this chapter is to carefully explore the relationship of the Black child's experiences and their influences on experiences of grief and bereavement in Black children.[1] In addition, considerations of other relevant dimensions of loss that Black children grieve, the implications of the growing victimization of Black children as "secondary victims" and its consequences, as well as historical and contemporary rituals of mourning of Black children will be addressed.

BLACK CHILDREN AND LOSS

Death educators estimate that less than 6 percent of children and adolescents in the United States experience the death of a parent or significant other before reaching eighteen years of age [1]. The death of a pet is a more common universal first encounter with death for most developing children in the world. There is little empirical data on the extent of loss for Black children. Estimates of the nature and frequency of loss affecting Black children is at best inferential. Similarly little empirical evidence documents the consequences and impact on the welfare (e.g., displacement, orphanage, financial consequences, etc.) of Black children experiencing loss. For many Black children losses are numerous and one loss may have far reaching consequences that impact the welfare and subsequent course of bereavement.

---

[1] The discussion of the bereavement of "Black Children" is inclusive of all children of people of African descent (e.g., African American, Caribbean, etc.) residing in the United States.

Black Family Life

Most younger Black children are very content with their family life experience and only become aware of the "shortcomings" of their families when they grow older and begin to move more in the mainstream of American society and encounter the biased perception of Black families represented in White American society. There are considerable intracultural differences that exist among Black families— poor families differ from middle- and upper-class families, rural Black families may differ significantly from urban Black families. The prototypic Black Family does not exist [2].

In spite of this reality there is a tendency to characterize Black family life in negative stereotypical terms. Similarly in spite of the many strengths that have assured the survival of Black families through overwhelming odds (e.g., the institution of slavery, socioeconomic circumstances, unemployment, welfare, etc.), the characterization of Black family life in the research literature and in the media gives the Black child a somewhat distorted and imbalanced view that is typically more negative [3]. African-American families are currently stereotyped as female headed households, having high unemployment of African-American men who are often absent and inattentive, and resulting in a relatively high divorce rate [4, 5]. The disastrous consequences of the Black family isolation, declining social supports, and other socioeconomic stressors questions the survival of children and the Black family [6]. However in the context of the supportive resource of the kinship bonds of traditional extended families [3] in spite of these shortcomings, Black children generally have warm regard for their families and have rarely felt unloved.

With the contrasting comparisons to White families and White family life experience as portrayed in the popular media (e.g., television, movies, etc.) the Black child may adopt and internalize the majority culture's biased and stereotyped perception of Black family life. The characterization of Black families as matriarchical, dysfunctional, culturally deficient, etc., give the Black child much to grieve and feel sorrowful about. Consequently the Black child may come to question the value of the Black family experience and grieve experiences the child believes he/she was suppose to have had.

Ironic Realizations– "Black is Beautiful" and "Black is Stressful"

Most young Black children confidently will grow up loving the Black experience and never question its value or merit. For the Black child their initial contact with the White brings additional dilemma in reconciling the Black experience and often contracting White world view, value system, and biased perception of the Black experience.

The Self-Concept of Black Children

The self-concept has been suggested as one of the most important and influential factors in the development of the child. The self-concept of the Black child has been demonstrated to be correlated with virtually countless behaviors from academic achievement to socioeconomic circumstances [7] and what children come to think about themselves is influenced by the manner in which others think and regard them. Racism and oppression by the predominant Anglo culture can hinder and make the maintenance of a healthy self-concept in Black children difficult. An enduring legacy of the Black Power movement of the seventies for Blacks has been an internalized view of "Black is Beautiful." In spite of the efforts of Black parents, families, and institutions to instill a positive self-concept in Black children the continuing American traditions of racial prejudices and discrimination, racial stereotypes, and cultural hegemony makes is difficult for Black children to cultivate a secure and healthy self-concept void of stress and distress [8]. Racial discrimination has been identified as the number one mental health problem of Black people in America [9].

"Personal Effectance" in the Black Experience

For the Black child, particularly in preadolescence reconciling the observation of a positive orientation toward work, adaptability of roles, religion and educational achievements, most Blacks continue to be plagued by many ethnocentric biases in employment, hiring practices, differential pay, monocultural educational modes, poor housing, facilities, and limited access to health care and social services. Few Blacks have been absorbed into the predominant Anglo society. In addition the current resurgence of political conservatism as civil rights legislation and affirmative action gains have been reversed are contemporary trends that few Black youth interpret as optimistic trends. The observance of these and other chronic acts of bias serve as sources of chronic stress and indicators of limited chances of realizing one's need for a sense of "personal effectance" in the American society. Personal effectance as originally defined by Robert White is a universal motivational need of all people to achieve a sense of control and effectance in their affairs in relation to one's environment [10]. If one assumes that personal effectance is a fundamental prerequisite for mental health and a sense of well-being, then the absence of personal effectance would understandably predict any number of problems in well being and functioning (e.g., health, achievement, income, self concept, homicidal violence, suicide, alcohol and substance abuse, and related self-destructive acts, etc.).

Research of racial differences in delinquency report that ethnic minority adolescents have a higher incarceration rate than White adolescents. Juveniles arrested for violent crimes often have poor and unstable employment records and hold unskilled lower paying jobs, and are at greater risk of drug and alcohol abuse as adults. Black juvenile delinquents are reported to have higher rates of depression than their White counterparts and their symptoms are frequently undetected, undiagnosed, and untreated. White youth with similar symptoms were more likely to be referred for treatment whereas Black youth were more likely to be channeled into the juvenile justice system [11, 12]. Diminished family income, erratic family employment records (especially of the father), substandard living conditions, family violence, and abuse and neglect place Black youth are at a greater risk to become involved in violent crime. Participation in violent acts as a child often continues into adulthood (e.g., violent confrontation with peers, domestic violence, and battering, etc.) Juveniles arrested for violent crimes are also more likely to have fewer employment prospects as adults.

The "Culture of Poverty"

Conditions of chronic unemployment, poverty, and illiteracy are correlated with decreased access to health education, preventive services, and medical care, resulting in an increased risk for disease [13]. The current gaps between the income of Blacks and the rest of the American population remains as wide as reported some thirty years ago by the Kerner Report in the 1960s [14]. According to the Census Bureau while child poverty is down, inequality in the distribution of income has increased substantially [15]. Thirty percent of African Americans live below the poverty level. Half of African-American children under six years of age live in poverty as compared to 17 percent of White children. Given that 51.8 percent of African-American families with children under eighteen years of age are female headed [16], this characterization has meaningfully contributed to the feminization of poverty that affects Black children in America [17]. African Americans are disproportionately over represented in numbers in the homeless population in the United States [12].

While poverty and socioeconomic circumstances of African American influence their quality of life and health status (e.g., restricted access to health promoting environmental resources, lack of access to comprehensive health care, substandard housing, inadequate nutrition and diet, etc.), there is more to the problem than mere socioeconomics. If it were possible to set aside the effects of socioeconomics alone, cultural orientations along with the "culture-of-poverty mentality" may have a significant effect on health and the quality of life of African Americans [17, 18]. According to this perspective individuals who are so impoverished are often so conditioned that their behaviors as somewhat self-limiting even in the absence of socioeconomic constraints. The socioeconomics of poverty and its devastating consequences for conditioning those affected by chronic poverty can have a significant impact on health, interpersonal dynamics (i.e., homicidal violence) and the quality of life.

Health and Premature Deaths of Blacks

The experience of loss is understandably influenced by the status of health in the Black experience. The manifestation of inequality and subsequent poverty is most visibly evident in the differential status of health among Blacks as compared to Whites. According to the results of a report from the Task Force on Minority Health [17], the general health of ethnic minority groups in the United States is poorer, with few exceptions than that of Whites. The most recent empirical data from the National Center for Health Statistics and the Centers for Disease Control report that while some of the gaps in White and ethnic health are closing, others are widening. In 1991, for example the CDC reported that life expectancy among

African Americans was again declining from its peak during the 1970s. Deaths due to tuberculosis (TB), cancers of the breast, cervix, and prostate gland; acquired immunodeficiency syndrome (AIDS); and homicide are increasing for the United States populations, especially among young nonwhite teens and adults [19-21].

An historical trend of a higher infant mortality rate for Blacks twice that of Whites [22] suggests for many Black children the experience of loss is confronted early in life with the risk of losing siblings. African Americans make fewer annual visits to physicians than do whites and African-American mothers are twice as likely as White mothers to receive no health care, or care only in the last trimester of their pregnancies [17]. The continued decline and status of poor health of Blacks attenuate the probability of premature deaths among Blacks and appreciably reduces the life expectancy of Blacks [17]. Since 1970 statistical reports from the National Center for Health Statistics in the United States have documented a disparity between the health status of White and Black populations. In 1991, White male life expectancy was 73.4 years, as compared to 65.6 years for African-American males [23, 24]. Obesity is a problem for 44 percent of African-American women aged twenty years and older.

Theoretical explanation of the higher risk of poor health and premature deaths among Blacks has been linked to a number of factors that have been identified as contributors to the declining life expectancy including nutrition, diet, poverty, and accessibility to health care which may effect a wide variety of conditions from a higher infant mortality rate to higher premature mortality rates for Blacks in later life. In addition, Dixon reported similar findings from a study conducted by the National Center for Health Statistics comparing the level of risk for Blacks and Whites for the major cause of death in the United States for the year 1988 [25]. Blacks were found to have a higher level of risk for virtually every category.

However, researchers studying racial differences in longevity and aging report an ironic phenomena of a "White/none White mortality crossover" in the later years (ages 75 to 80) with Blacks having a higher likelihood of living longer than Whites [26, 27]. Quaye reported that African Americans are more likely to be uninsured than Whites regardless of income status [17]. In 1986, 23 percent of African Americans had no private medical insurance as compared with 14 percent of Whites [17, p. 12]. The effect of socioeconomics on poor health, premature deaths as well as the experience of chronic illness often represents a significant loss for Black children who are either personally victimized or emotionally distressed via their concerns about significant others and the consequences of the illness upon their welfare and survival.

HIV/AIDS and Infectious Diseases

Currently in the United States the fastest growing health issues in ethnic communities are the infectious diseases, including TB and HIV/AIDS. Between 1985 and 1992, TB rose by 26 percent among African Americans while rates dropped among Whites. Between 1990 and 1992 the HIV rates among Blacks increased by 19 percent as compared to the relatively stability of HIV incidence among Whites [21].

However, estimates are that by the year 2000 approximately ten million children worldwide are projected to have been orphaned because their parent died as a result of HIV infection. In the United States 18,500 children and adolescents have already been orphaned according to Dr. David Michaels, an Epidemiologist at City University of New York Medical School and Carol Levine, Executive Director of the Orphan Project in New York City. By 1996, this number will increase to 45,600 and by the year 2000 to 100,000 orphans in the United States [28]. Since 1992, HIV/AIDS has been the fourth leading cause of death among women aged twenty-five to forty-four in the United States. By 1993, HIV/AIDS became the leading cause of death in the United States among all persons aged twenty-five to forty-four. In 1991, HIV/AIDS had become the leading cause of death for African-American and Hispanic males aged twenty-five to forty-four. While African-American and Hispanic women make up 21 percent of all women in the United States, these two groups accounted for 77 percent of the AIDS cases reported among women in 1994. In 1994, the AIDS case rate per 100,000 population was 3.8 for White women and 62.7 for African-American women. As of 1993 HIV/AIDS is the leading cause of death of African-American women aged twenty-five to forty-four [13]. There is little current empirical evidence to estimate the consequences and impact on Black children who are/will be infected or affected (e.g., experience significant other losses, be abandoned, orphaned, displaced, institutionalized, etc.) by this epidemic.

Currently the largest population of AIDS cases in the United States are people in their thirties who are believed to have been infected in their late teens or twenties [29]. While only a very small percentage of the cumulative cases in this country have occurred among adolescents ages thirteen to twenty-one, this finding masks the true risks faced by this age group. It is believed that many young people who are infected with HIV while teenagers were not diagnosed with AIDS until much later, due to the long incubation period for the disease. Furthermore the escalating incidence of heterosexual transmission of HIV in the United States is especially pronounced among young people. The largest proportionate increase in reported AIDS cases in 1993 took place within the thirteen to twenty-four age group—and was mostly attributable to heterosexual contact [30]. While many factors have been identified as influential in this alarming increase among adolescent youth, an attitude of invulnerability commonly seen in the young is particularly problematic. There has been little empirical study of attitudes of fatalism and resignation among youth who feel that they have little to look forward to—"so why play it safe?"

In 1989, Edelman reported that Black children constitute more than half of all reported cases of AIDS for children younger than age thirteen [31]. The pandemic of HIV infections and AIDS has challenged the "natural order of things" in the Black community as more and more Black parents and grandparents are burying their young. Young Blacks are confronted with the reality of the deadly consequences of HIV infection and are challenged to come to terms with this reality in making responsible choices to assure their survival. Young Blacks have lost a sense of security in the assured health and well-being to live the normal life expectancy. Young Black youth witnessing the death of peers and other family members to HIV/AIDS are increasing, confronted with the reality of their vulnerability and mortality. Black youth who grieve the premature death of their peers and also experience a loss of a sense of personal security may understandably have feelings of resignation and fatalism amidst the HIV/AIDS epidemic.

Homicidal Violence among Blacks

The American epidemic of urban adolescent homicidal violence is significantly changing the very nature of childhood for a growing number of children who reside in the inner cities of America [32, 33]. Homicidal violence is currently the leading cause of death of Black males aged fifteen to nineteen [21]. The rates of homicidal violence in the Black community has been consistently so elevated that it has appreciably contributed to the statistical reduction of the total life expectancy of Blacks as a group and justifiably should be regarded as a public health concern [34].

While many factors are believed to influence the current rate of homicidal violence in the Black and inner-city communities, the role of socioeconomic circumstances has been identified as a significant contributor to the contemporary trend of escalating urban homicidal violence [34]. Poverty and economic inequality contribute to the risk of child violent deaths in America. Poor children have a higher mortality risk than children from middle- and upper-income families and socioeconomic circumstances. Experts estimate that nearly one million adolescents between the ages of twelve and nineteen are victims of violent crimes each year. In 1992, violence took the lives of 2,428 children, and in 1994 child abuse and neglect alone killed 1, 271 children [35]. The American Medical Association estimates that as much as two million children annually personally experience physical abuse and neglect. Teenagers are twice as likely to be assaulted as persons twenty years old and older. The victims and perpetrators of violence are likely to be adolescent youths [33]. While numerous studies have begun to suggest a demographic profile of the victims and perpetrators to be more likely urban nonwhite (i.e., Black and Hispanic) adolescent males [34]. The more recent empirical evidence suggest both the victims and perpetrators are increasingly younger. While this trend of elevated violence is affecting nearly every segment of American society it is most visibly manifest in the Black communities of American inner cities. The trend of escalating violence among adolescent youth has been on the rise since 1970. Adolescent homicide rates have reached the highest levels in American history.

Homicidal Violence and its "Secondary Victims"

The epidemic of chronic community violence in the inner cities of America is producing a growing population of young children and teens who personally escape physical injury but who subsequently are permanently scarred emotionally and psychologically becoming "secondary victims." These secondary victims are often children from the inner cities and all too often Black children [32, 33, 36]. Estimates suggest approximately ten million children ages three to seventeen are at risk of exposure to domestic violence each year [37]. Estimates are that one-in-ten teenagers between the ages of ten and nineteen has fired a gun at someone or been shot at, and about two-in-five say they know someone who has been killed or wounded by gunfire. The psychological impact of the threat of personal victimization by lethal violence and the witness of chronic acts of violence are having a major impact on a growing number of inner-city American children who reside in communities under siege by violence. There is very little empirical study or clinical evidence on the scope and nature of the impact of chronic exposure to homicidal violence on the mental health and perception of death and dying of such young children.

While there is a growing body of empirical evidence to document this trend of escalating lethal violence, in the absence of empirical data we can only speculate about the numbers of youth who are "secondary victims" as their witness of chronic community violence has permanently changed their lives and robbed them of the carefree innocence associated with childhood. Many understandably loose a sense of safety in the world and fear for their personal safety and well-being as well as that of other significant others (e.g., parents, siblings, peers, etc.).

Young children who are exposed to chronic community violence have been observed to be affected both emotionally and psychologically, oftentimes suffering from symptoms of depression and post-traumatic stress disorders [38]. Approximately 3.3 million children each year witness parental abuse, ranging from hitting to fatal assaults with knives and guns. Domestic violence occurs in 20 to 40 percent of the families of chronically violent adolescents [39]. Witnessing violence in one's family of origin is the most consistently demonstrated background factor among men who abuse women, more common than being a victim of child abuse [40]. Violence undermines the development of self-esteem, competence and personal effectance, autonomy, and can trigger dysfunctional coping responses [41]. One study found that children growing up in violent homes are 74 percent more likely to commit crimes against another person; twenty-four times more likely to commit sexual assault; 50 percent more likely to abuse dugs and/or alcohol, and six time more likely to commit suicide [42]. The familiar pattern of children experiencing violent trauma is characterized as one of seemingly emotional distance and indifference and loss of caring or concern, a possible correlate of post-traumatic stress for children overexposed to trauma associated with violence and unresolved loss.

Educators have reported a significant decline in academic performance, mental concentration, and positive interpersonal behaviors (e.g., increased intimidation, aggression and violence, and a disrespect for others, especially those in positions of authority). Children who are exposed to incidence of chronic violence that often starts at home, that is pervasive in their communities and all too often a characteristic part of the school experience, are at risk. A growing number of inner-city Black children have an understandable concern about their victimization via violence. Consequently, inner-city schools are reporting increasing numbers of children bringing weapons to school, out of fear for their personal survival. Many youth impacted by violence suffer from low self-esteem and a sense of hopelessness and fatalism. For most children who experience the chronicity of traumatic violence have very real concerns about their own safety and vulnerability to become primary victims and consequently loose and grieve a sense of safety and security. Having lost so much, many seem to feel there is not much to look forward to. Since violent deaths are unnatural and often stigmatized losses, children experiencing traumatic violent loss are more at risk of complicated grief and bereavement. Homicide survivors are more at risk of having a more complicated course of grief recovery often due to overwhelming feelings of anger and sometimes survivor guilt. Male children and teens often tend to express that anger via a repetition of violence, therefore increasing the cycle of violence. Some impressionistic evidence seems to suggest male children are more likely to externalize their anger during bereavement while females are more likely to internalize their anger and are more at risk of depression during bereavement [43]. Consequently, children who witness chronic acts of violence are at risk of becoming perpetrators of violence, potential gang recruits, or engaging in criminal acts and yielding to the comfort and escape afforded to them by early alcohol and drug use and abuse.

Wildings, Drive-Bys, Retaliatory Hits, and Adolescent Mourning

Barrett argues that the phenomena of explosive and indiscriminate urban adolescent homicidal violence may in fact be an expression of grief and mourning—shaped and learned (via modeling, reinforcement, etc.) as an acceptable form of self-expression in the urban adolescent American male sub-culture [43]. While violence has been identified as a "rite-of-passage" for some inner-city males to manhood, a violent response is often a sanctioned and expected response of a growing number of inner-city males in response to being hurt or disrespected (i.e., "dissed"). Buss and Durkee's study of hostility and depression reported that African-American male patients indicated they would respond with verbal or physical attack if they felt their rights were violated [44]. The observation of an increased risk of violent crime in Black and non-White youth is curiously correlated to the fact that this segment of the population is also more at risk of being victimized by unemployment, substandard living conditions, family stress and domestic violence, abuse and neglect.

The developing child who witnesses violence as a common response to problem solving and self-expression is more likely to imitate the behaviors modeled at home, at school and in the child's community as well as the larger society. The average American pre-schooler watches more than twenty-seven hours of television per week with an estimated 25 to 30 percent incidence of violence per hour on children's programming. During prime time viewing hours there are five to six violent acts per hour [45]. While simple modeling may explain some violence the causal mechanism is unclear and is at best may be more complex than it appears. Viewing violence the American Psychological Association asserts may increase the mistrust of others and stimulate self-protective behaviors. The over-exposure and the trauma of chronic violence as in secondary victims may also desensitize individuals resulting in apathetic attitudes and increased appetites for becoming involved with violence or exposing themselves to violence. According to both the social learning and sociobiological perspectives, the prevalence of violence in the American cultural experience reinforces violent behavior and the prescription of violence as an esteemed value especially among males who regard violence as essential for survival in a violent social and cultural context.

While a sense of mourning about blocked circumstances for a piece of the American dream is a significant condition to nurture rage and violent behaviors, the inner-city youth's encounter of violent traumatic loss, threats and its accompanying grief may understandably engender violence. For example, in the inner city, the death of a significant other (e.g., family member or a "homie," etc.) due to an act of violence obligates other home boys (and girls) to retaliate to avenge the death as a part of a group covenant of loyalty that honors the deceased and also gives some measure of reassurance and safety in maintaining social control in the "hood." Strategic drive-by shootings are commonly witnessed as a retaliatory act of lethal aggression in response to the tragic death of a member of one's posse, gang, or reference group. Consequently, the participated violence in response to a traumatic death of an inner-city youth's significant other becomes a ritual of mourning during the time of bereavement. The retaliatory act of violence that flows from the experience of anger during one's bereavement and also comes to represent an attempt for control and empowerment but often simply widens the circle of violence. There has been little empirical study of the dynamics in the cycle of homicidal violence among Black inner-city youth. There is much to be learned about the contemporary phenomena of urban adolescent homicidal violence from the careful and systematic study of gang rituals and dynamics in relationship to their experience of bereavement.

There is little study or empirical evidence to document the extent of the psychological and emotional impact of exposure to chronic community violence and unresolved issues of loss in developing inner-city children. There is some impressionistic evidence to suggest that one of the impacts on this generation of youth is a loss or a sense of hopefulness. The irony is a that our youth who are our hope for the future, have little hope for their future. While Kalish and Reynold's 1981 research reports pre-need funeral planning as more characteristic of older Americans, local inner-city funeral directors all across America are reporting urban teenagers showing increasing interest in planning their own funerals [46]. While there are some limited efforts to address the needs of children mourning who have experienced trauma, grief, and loss, there are few if any resources to meet the emotional and survival needs of a growing number of American children who are secondary victims of an unprecedented pattern of escalating violence in American society—particularly in the inner cities of America.

Black Suicide and Self-Destructive Acts

While younger Blacks are at risk of intramural homicidal violence (i.e., Black on Black violent crime), Blacks have not been traditionally characterized as being at risk of suicide. Some report concerns about an increasing rate of suicide among Blacks [47]. While it has been noted that the suicide rate of Blacks is lower than Whites, the suicidal behavior for Black adolescents is increasing though not surpassing their White counterparts [48]. Gibbs warns that the actual suicidal behavior may be masked by acting out and high-risk behaviors, thereby making suicidal intent more difficult to assess [48]. Reynolds, Kalish, and Faberow's cross-ethnic study of suicide attitudes reported that the majority of Blacks (89%) perceived White Americans as more likely to commit suicide than members of other ethnicities and tended to not perceive suicide as being a major concern of their ethnic group [49]. In addition, Black Americans and Mexican Americans in this study tended to see suicide as an act of a mentally ill person, whereas White Americans and Asian Americans tended to perceive suicide as a reaction to stress.

In spite of many stressors that would predict high rates of suicide among Blacks, Early and Ayers report the paradoxical finding of low suicide rates among Blacks [50]. According to Durkheim's reference to "fatalistic suicide" and slavery and the conditions of Blacks one would expect high suicide rates [51]. Similarly anomie theory's reference to blocker opportunities and the social disadvantages of Blacks would also suggest higher suicide rates. While Blacks are characterized as having a disproportionate rate of dysfunctional families, unemployment, poverty, powerlessness, high illegitimacy rates, the suicide rate among Blacks is less than that of Whites [51]. According to Early and Ayers the supportive influence of the extended family systems, the Black church and Black spirituality and anti-suicide cultural values serve as buffers against suicide [50]. While Blacks are not characterized as being at risk for suicide, there is a growing concern about a growing trend toward apparent self-destructive acts among Blacks (e.g., alcohol and drug abuse, crime, irresponsible health limiting life styles, etc.).

Alcohol and Substance Abuse among Blacks

Alcohol and substance abuse is a growing concern in the Black community. The increase in substance abuse takes a toll on the sellers and abusers as well as the total community that ultimately is impacted by a growing cycle of crime and related violence that is related to an increase in substance abuse. While alcoholism and substance abuse have been identified as mental health problems facing the Black community, not enough attention and empirical study has focused on these problems as possible symptoms and manifestations of deeper issues and concerns. It is reasonable to assume that ethnicity plays a significant part in the substance abuse pattern in the Black community. Harvey, in forecasting an increase in drug and alcohol usage in the Black community argued that the increase was significantly influenced by the oppressive conditions and ethnocentric biases that prevail in the dominant Anglo society [52]. Kaestner, Rosen, and Appell conclude that the pattern of drug use among Black males was significantly linked to their world view and their personal experiences with their social and physical environments [53].

While national surveys report that African-American youth between fourteen and seventeen years of age use alcohol to a lesser degree than their White counterparts and have fewer alcohol-related consequences, African-American males over age thirty are more prone to heavy drinking at a rate of 32 percent compared to 20 percent of White males. Likewise, there were substantial differences between Black men and White men with regard to binge drinking (4% versus 1.6%), symptoms of physical dependence (29.5% versus 9.9%) and symptoms of loss of control (17.2% versus 11.2%). African-American women report fewer alcohol-related problems than their White counterparts and they reported higher abstinence rates (46% versus 34% of White women) [12].

Although there has been little study of alcohol and drug abuse of African-American youth, findings from the National Household Survey of Drug Abuse found differences in drinking between African-American and White youth [54]. African-American youth age twelve to seventeen reported use of alcohol at least once in 38.8 percent of the sample compared to 60.7 percent of Whites and 44.1 percent of Latinos. African-American females across all age groups are consistently characterized as being a low risk of alcohol abuse as compared to White females.

A growing body of research evidence makes a strong case that the stress of coping with poverty, unemployment, discrimination, and inadequate housing could contribute to substance abuse [12]. The consistent finding of sex differences in the rate of abuse of alcohol and drugs suggest Black males are more likely to abuse alcohol and drugs as a means of coping than Black females. It is reasonable to assume reinforcers in the male subculture and the larger society promote and reinforce alcohol and drug abuse more in males than females. In conclusion, there is a consistent body of evidence that suggest homicidal violence, suicide and related forms of self-destructive behaviors are more at risk for male than females as a means of resolving personal dilemmas.

SUMMARY

The mention of childhood bereavement typically brings to mind experiences of grief and bereavement associated with a death and loss of a significant other. However, the experiences of bereavement for the Black child often includes additional concerns. While death and dying are common motifs in the Black experience, Blacks are more likely to die of premature deaths from most of the leading causes of death in the United States. The leading causes of death and concern in the Black experience are homicidal violence, infectious disease, and self-destructive behaviors including alcohol and drug abuse. With premature deaths come concerns of chronic illnesses and dysfunction that represent real concerns for Black children and their significant others. The grief and bereavement of Black children may be further complicated with concerns about their personal safety and welfare as a consequence of the illness and premature death of siblings and other significant others. While many Blacks are doing well, for nearly one-third of African-American families with young children, socioeconomic circumstances of poverty and substandard living conditions are ongoing realities and sources of distress. For many Blacks the harsh reality of racism and ongoing racial discrimination makes is hard to maintain a sense of self-esteem and personhood in a hostile cultural context that is not affirming. For a growing number of Black males the distress associated with grieving the loss of hope and possibilities of realizing one's potential for personal effectance can be overwhelming and quite stressful. The significance of this aspect of loss for developing adolescent Black children has been argued as a source of influence on relationships to other (i.e., homicidal violence), and one's self (i.e., self-destructive behaviors) and could serve a contributor to health and well-being. There has been little if any research and study of the impact of these concerns which may represent significant losses and sources of grief for developing Black children.

CONCLUSION

Blacks have been observed to be more likely to experience a myriad of losses and be at greater risk of experiencing physical health and mental health problems, yet least likely to utilize institutional care resources. Those Blacks who do seek institutionalized resources are also more at risk of dropping out at a rate as high as 50 percent due to feelings of alienation, cultural mistrust, and anxiety about institutions that tend to over pathologize their conditions, internalize blame, and often ignore the role of their sociocultural circumstances in White-American society [9, 54]. The findings from one study reported that psychiatrists are likely to recognize and treat serious psychopathology in aggressive antisocial White adolescents but tend to dismiss similar signs and symptoms in Black adolescents as culturally appropriate or evidence of character pathology and thus candidates for institutionalization [56]. The statistics on the differential rate of institutionalization of Black and White juvenile delinquents bear this out.

Just as Black adults have learned to cope independent of the resources of institutionalized care providers often seeking assistance from natural care providers, Black children are understandably inclined to do the same. This increases the challenge for care providers doing outreach to this at risk population. The situation of bereaved Black children coping with a variety of loss issues is further complicated by their reality like all children, in that they are too often left to themselves to cope and make sense of their experiences. Black children, like all children in America are the disenfranchised mourners. It is imperative that care providers understand and appreciate the ramification of loss in working with Black children and teens and most importantly be sensitive to the multiplicity of losses that Black children are sensitive to and grieve a way so different from their White counterparts. Similarly it is important to understand the role of culture and situational factors play in the establishment and maintenance of coping mechanisms. Respecting those influences and designing creative alternatives for Black children and teens as well as advocating for deeper systemic change is long overdue.

In our respective roles as adult care takers and care givers of children (e.g., counselor, educators, parents, etc.) we must do more to assist and enable bereaved Black children. Understand the observation of Webb that children are very sensitive about pain [56]. We cannot protect the young from loss or pain. Perhaps a first step is simply begin to appreciate and acknowledge their pain and suffering. Bereaved Black children may need help in finding appropriate expression of their pain in a society that often denies the reality of their pain of often shows a callous indifference. For the bereaved child each loss and hurt is real, though not significant for the adult. The ultimate challenge is to help the bereaved Black child understand the challenge to grow in spite of the loss and pain. In working through feelings and growing through loss rather than letting loss destroy us, we take a fundamental step toward building a more feeling and competent self. It is important that bereaved

Black children understand their feelings regarding their losses and their options for responding to those losses. We need to understand how bereaved Black children make sense of loss.

ACKNOWLEDGMENTS

Student research assistants—Jean Pierre Dumas, Mark Dalal, and Jamal Jones.

REFERENCES

1. W. Smith, *Dying in the Human Life Cycle*, Holt, Rinehart and Winston, New York, 1985.
2. H. K. Ho, *Family Therapy with Ethnic Minorities*, Sage Publications, Newbury Park, California, 1987.
3. N. Boyd-Franklin, *Black Families in Therapy*, The Guilford Press, New York, 1989.
4. P. Glick, Demographic Picture of Black Families, in *Black Families* (2nd Edition), H. McAdoo (ed.), Sage Publications, Newbury Park, California, pp. 111-132, 1988.
5. H. McAdoo, Family Values and Outcomes for Children, *Journal of Negro Education, 60*, pp. 361-365, 1991.
6. L. Roger-Rose, *The Black Woman*, Sage Publications, Beverly Hills, California, 1980.
7. L. G. Baruth and M. L. Manning, Counselling the Child, in *Multicultural Counselling and Psychotherapy*, Macmillan, New York, 1991.
8. E. Barnes, The Black Community as the Source of Positive Self-Concept for Black Children: A Theoretical Perspective, in *Black Psychology* (3rd Edition), R. Jones (ed.), Harper and Row Publishers, New York, pp. 106-130, 1980.
9. C. Bell, I. Bland, E. Houston, and B. Jones, Enhancement of Knowledge and Skills for the Psychiatric Treatment of Black Populations, in *Mental Health and People of Color*, J. Chunn, P. Dunston, and F. Sheriff (eds.), Howard University Press, Washington, D.C., pp. 205-238, 1983.
10. R. White, Motivation Reconsidered: The Concept of Competence, *Psychological Review, 66*, pp. 297-333, 1959.
11. J. T. Gibbs, Personality Patterns of Delinquent Females: Ethnic and Sociocultural Variations, *Journal of Clinical Psychology, 38*, pp. 198-206, 1982.
12. J. Aponte, R. Rivers, and J. Wohl, *Psychological Interventions and Cultural Diversity*, Allyn and Bacon, Boston, 1995.
13. M. Norris, The Black Church and the AIDS Crisis, in *HIV/AIDS Ministries Network Focus Paper #29*, Health and Welfare Ministries Program Department, General Board of Global Ministries of the United Methodist Church, New York, 1995.
14. O. Kerner et al., *Report of the National Advisory Commission on Civil Disorders*, U.S. Government Printing Office, Washington, D.C., 1968.
15. National Center for Children in Poverty, *Five Million Children: 1992 Update*, Columbia School of Public Health, New York, 1992.
16. B. Schiller, *The Economics of Poverty and Discrimination*, Prentice Hall, New Jersey, 1989.
17. R. Quaye, The Health Care Status of African Americans, *The Black Scholar, 24*(2), pp. 12-17, 1994.

18. J. Inclan and E. Ferran, Poverty, Politics, and Family Therapy: A Role for Systems Theory, in *The Social and Political Contexts of Family Therapy*, M. P. Mirkin (ed.), Allyn and Bacon, Boston, pp. 203-204, 1990.
19. Centers for Disease Control, *HIV/AIDS Surveillance, Year End Edition: United States AIDS Cases Reported through December 1990*, Department of Health and Human Services, Atlanta, January 1991.
20. Centers for Disease Control, *HIV/AIDS Surveillance, Second Quarter Edition, United States AIDS Cases Reported through December 1992*, Department of Health and Human Services, July 1993.
21. C. Cummings and D. Dehart, Ethnic Minority Physical Health: Issues and Interventions, in *Psychological Interventions and Cultural Diversity*, J. Aponte, R. Rivers, and J. Wohl (eds.), Allyn and Bacon, Boston, pp. 234-249, 1995.
22. H. F. Giles, Differential Life Expectancy among White and Non-White Americans: Some Explanations during Youth and Middle Age, in *Minority Aging*, R. C. Manuel (ed.), Greenwood Press, Westport, Connecticut, 1982.
23. U.S. Bureau of Census, *Statistical Abstract of the United States: 1993* (113th Edition), U.S. Government Printing Office, Washington, D.C., 1993.
24. U.S. Department of Health and Human Services, *Health Status of Minorities and Low Income Groups: Third Edition*, U.S. Government Printing Office, Washington, D.C., 1991.
25. B. Dixon, *Good Health for African Americans*, Crown Publishers, New York, 1994.
26. J. J. Jackson, *Minorities and Aging*, Wadsworth, Belmont, California, 1980.
27. K. G. Manton, Differential Life Expectancy: Possible Explanations During the Later Ages, in *Minority Aging*, R. Manuel (ed.), Greenwood Press, Westport, Connecticut, 1982.
28. T. Woodson, Zero Parent Homes: Where will all the Children Go? *Successful Black Parenting*, KLS Communications, Philadelphia, pp. 10-13, 1995.
29. D. Hu, P. Flemming, M. Mays, and J. Ward, The Expanding Regional Diversity of the Acquired Immunodeficiency Syndrome Epidemic in the United States, *Archives of Internal Medicine, 154*, pp. 654-659, 1994.
30. R. Crooks and K. Baur, *Our Sexuality*, Brooks/Cole Publishing, Pacific Grove, 1996.
31. M. W. Edelman, Black Children in American, in *The State of Black America*, Allyn and Bacon, New York, pp. 63-67, 1995.
32. J. Garbino, N. Bubrow, K. Kostelny, and C. Padro, *Children in Danger: Coping with the Consequences of Community Violence*, Jossey-Bass, San Francisco, 1992.
33. W. Lee, Behind Smiles and Laughter: African-American Children's Issues about Bereavement, in *Bereaved Children and Teens*, E. Grollman (ed.), Beacon Press, Boston, pp. 93-112, 1995.
34. R. K. Barrett, Urban Adolescent Homicidal Violence: An Emerging Public Health Concern, *The Urban League Review*, Carfax Publishing, New Brunswick, New Jersey, pp. 67-75, 1993.
35. D. Weis and D. Darow, *Current Trends in Child Abuse Reporting and Fatalities: The Results of the 1994 Annual Fifty States Survey*, National Committee to Prevent Child Abuse, Chicago, 1995.
36. R. K. Barrett, Mourning Lessons: Learning to Cope with Loss can Start at an Early Age, *The Director, LXVII*, (4), The National Funeral Directors Association Publications, Milwaukee, Wisconsin, pp. 24-63, 1995.
37. M. Straus and R. Gelles, Societal Change and Change in Family Violence from 1975-1985 as Revealed by Two National Surveys, *Journal of Marriage and the Family, 48*, pp. 465-479, 1986.

38. R. Pynoos, Children Traumatized by Witnessing Acts of Personal Violence: Homicide, Rape or Suicide Behaviour, in *Death: Current Perspectives*, Mayfield Publishers, Mountain View, California, pp. 248-260, 1995.
39. J. Fagan and S. Wexler, Family Origins of Violent Delinquents, *Criminology*, 25, pp. 643-669, 1987.
40. D. Finklehor, G. Hotaling, and K. Yilo, *Stopping Family Violence: Research Priorities for the Coming Decade*, Sage Publications, Newbury Park, California, 1988.
41. R. Emery, Family Violence, *American Psychologist*, 44, pp. 321-328, 1989.
42. Family Violence Coalition, *Broken Bodies Broken Spirits: Family Violence in Maryland and Recommendations for Change*, A Report to the Community, Baltimore, Maryland, 1991.
43. R. K. Barrett, Trauma, *Violence and Loss in Children and Teens*, Keynote Presentation at the Trauma, Violence and Loss in Children and Teens Conference, sponsored by Valencia Community College, Orlando, Florida, November 1995.
44. A. H. Buss and A. Durkee, An Inventory for Assessing Different Kinds of Hostility, *Journal of Consulting Psychology*, 24, pp. 343-349, 1957.
45. American Psychological Association, Violence and Youth: Psychology's Response, *Summary Report to the American Psychological Association Commission on Violence and Youth*, Washington, D.C., 1993.
46. R. Kalish and D. Reynolds, *Death and Ethnicity: A Psychocultural Study*, Baywood Publishing, Amityville, New York, 1981.
47. R. K. Barrett, African-American Homicide and Suicide: A Closer Look at Who is at Risk, *The American Black Male*, 3(2), pp. 4-8, April/May 1991; 3(3), pp. 4-6, June/July 1991.
48. J. T. Gibbs, Mental Health Issues of Black Adolescents: Implications for Policy and Practice, in *Ethnic Issues in Adolescent Mental Health*, Sage Publications, Newbury Park, California, pp. 21-25, 1990.
49. D. Reynolds, R. Kalish, and N. L. Farberow, A Cross-Ethnic Study of Suicide Attitudes and Expectations in the United States, in *Suicide in Different Cultures*, N. L. Farberow (ed.), University Park Press, Baltimore, 1975.
50. K. Early and R. Ayers, "It's a White Thing"—An Exploration of Beliefs about Suicide in the African American Community, in *The Path Ahead: Readings in Death and Dying*, Mayfield Publishers, Mountain View, California, pp. 191-210, 1995.
51. E. Durkheim, *Suicide: A Study in Sociology*, The Free Press, New York, 1951.
52. W. M. Harvey, Drug Use in the Black Community, in *Black Psychology*, R. Jones (ed.), Harper and Row, New York, pp. 384-397, 1972.
53. E. Kaestner, L. Rosen, and P. Appell, Patterns of Drug Abuse: Relationships with Ethnicity, Sensation Seeking, Anxiety, *Journal of Consulting and Clinical Psychology*, 45, pp. 462-468, 1977.
54. D. Huizinga, R. Loeker, and T. P. Thornberg, *Urban Delinquency and Substance Abuse: Initial Findings*, Office of Juvenile Justice and Delinquency Prevention Research Summary, U.S. Department of Justice, Washington, D.C., 1994.
55. D. Sue, *Counselling the Culturally Different: Theories and Practice*, Wiley and Sons, New York, 1991.
56. D. Lewis, O. Balla, and S. Shanok, Some Evidence of Race Bias in the Diagnosis and Treatment of the Juvenile Offender, *American Journal of Orthopsychiatry*, 49, pp. 53-61, 1979.
57. N. B. Webb, *Helping Bereaved Children: A Handbook for Practitioners*, The Guilford Press, New York, 1993.

BIBLIOGRAPHY

Barrett, R. K., Children and Traumatic Loss, in *Children Mourning, Mourning Children*, K. Doka (ed.), Taylor and Francis Publishing, Washington, D.C., pp. 85-88, 1995.

Barrett, R. K., *WHAT ABOUT THE CHILDREN? Prescriptions for Managing the Grief and Mourning Adjustment of Children in HIV/AIDS Client Cases*, presentation at 1995 National Skills Building Conference, Los Angeles, 1995.

Black, D., The Bereaved Child, *Journal of Child Psychology and Psychiatry, 19*, pp. 287-292, 1978.

Black, D. and M. A. Urbanowicz, Family Intervention with Bereaved Children, *Journal of Child Psychology and Psychiatry, 28*, pp. 467-476, 1987.

L. Costa and D. Holiday, Helping Children Cope with the Death of a Parent, *Elementary School Guidance and Counselling, 28*(3), pp. 206, 213, 1994.

Davis, C. B., The Use of Art Therapy and Group Process with Grieving Children, *Issues in Comprehensive Pediatric Nursing, 12*, pp. 269-280, 1989.

Heiney, S. P., Sibling Grief: A Case Report, *Archives of Psychiatric Nursing, 5*(3), pp. 121-127, 1991.

Kranzler, E., D. Shaffer, G. Wasserman, and M. Davis, Early Childhood Bereavement, *Journal of American Academy of Child and Adolescent Psychiatry, 29*(4), pp. 513-520, 1990.

Mishne, J., The Grieving Child: Manifest and Hidden Losses in Childhood and Adolescent, *Child and Adolescent Social Work Journal, 9*(6), pp. 471-489, 1992.

Perkowski, S., Some Observations Concerning Black Children Living in a Residential Care Agency, *International Journal of Social Psychiatry, 20*(1-2), pp. 89-93, Spring-Summer 1974.

Smith, I., Preschool Children "Play" Out their Grief, *Death Studies, 15*, pp. 169-176, 1991.

PART V

Introduction: Questions of Values

One cannot live without values. Each time we open our mouths we commit ourselves to what we consider essential in life as well as to a theory of knowledge and truth. Unfortunately we can live without articulating our value commitments in a consistent manner. In this section we examine the values to which we commit ourselves as we make death-related decisions.

Dr. James Kow examines the question of patient autonomy. He says that we have become accustomed to individual moral autonomy—patient autonomy—as the default position in bioethics and modern medicine. The notion of autonomy has tinged all bioethical discussions. But in the case of the dying patient, autonomy will leave its indelible marks, but we now realize that we have to equip ourselves with other concepts in order to understand this patient's unique situation. Crucially we have to be open to the experience of the dying patient in order to explain the role appropriate to autonomy in her care. Other values besides the good of individual choice are humanely important at the edge of life, goods that contribute to the integrity and well-being of the person who is the dying patient.

Dr. Gilbert Brodie holds that it is often assumed by the general public that a competent, intelligent appraisal of a court judgment on the constitutionality of a law would require a great deal of legal training and expertise. A significant move toward this demystification has been made by the courts themselves in recent years. This can be seen in the way in which they the judgments are being written. It becomes clear in reading judgments, particularly in charter cases, that the justices are not writing only for other justices and lawyers. One can only conclude that the courts increasingly want to make their reasoning accessible to the broader audience of those who are willing to invest some time and effort to understand them. The purpose of Dr. Brodie's chapter is to engage non-lawyers in the debate that took place in the Sue Rodriguez case in the Canadian Supreme Court. When the arguments on which the case was decided are set out, many readers may be surprised to find out that they are not at all technical legal arguments. The court's judgment's, both the majority and the minority, are in fact based on what can only be characterized as "moral" arguments.

Dr. John Morgan examines the question of immortality. "Immortality" has several meanings. According to Lifton, aside from the philosophical, literal sense of "not subject to death," there are also the biological, the theological, the artistic or creative, and the natural. Morgan uses the term in its literal sense, the idea that some aspect of the human person is not subject to death. Morgan believes that Plato and Aristotle, Augustine and Aquinas were correct when they argued that an examination of the human mind shows that the human person is not necessarily subject to death at the death of the body.

Rev. Dr. Ronald Trojcak works from the latest biblical scholarship to present a reinterpretation of the Christian view of resurrection, both the Resurrection of Jesus and the resurrection in which His followers believe. Trojcak rejects that Jesus' resurrection was the last and greatest miracle that Jesus performed. He also rejects that the Resurrection occurred as an impetus to faith. On the contrary, Trojcak believes that the Resurrection was a consequence of faith, the faithfulness that Jesus had in His duty to God and the faithfulness that God has shown, first to the Maccabees, then to Jesus, and finally promised to all who live faithfully.

Dr. Jaroslav Havelka shows us that the views that we have in the West are not the only ways of viewing death and bereavement. He believes that the major difference between East and West is the view of the ego. In the West we rejoice in our individuality. In the East, the ego is considered to be the foundation of the difficulties we have with death. Western philosophy is rooted in the subject-object distinction, that is, that the thinking subject differs from the object known. Eastern thought begins with a different assumption, namely, the unity of the knower and known.

CHAPTER 27

Autonomy and the Person in the Dying Patient*

Jim Kow

We have become accustomed to individual moral autonomy—patient autonomy—as the default position in bioethics and modern medicine. The notion of autonomy has tinged all bioethical discussions. But this economical approach has started to abate.

In the case of the dying patient, autonomy will leave its indelible marks, but we now realize that we have to equip ourselves with other concepts in order to understand this patient's unique situation. Crucially we have to be open to the experience of the dying patient in order to explain the role appropriate to autonomy in his care. Other goods besides the good of individual choice are humanly important at the edge of life, goods that contribute to the integrity and well-being of the person who is the dying patient.

PART 1: PATIENT AUTONOMY

In bioethics and modern medicine the notion of patient autonomy has achieved a dominant position. My present purpose is to relate the notion of autonomy both conceptually and morally to the dying patient. In Part 1 I will discuss the nature and conditions of autonomy. Part 2 will examine the role of autonomy in the treatment of competent and incompetent patients. Finally, in Part 3 I will explain the significance and the limited role of autonomy in the situation of the dying patient.

Historically, our modern understanding of what is good arises from the fear of a great evil: violent death! Death makes life appear to be unconditionally good. Our nondetached understanding of this good—life—is attached to our deep fear of death.

---

*Throughout this chapter, the masculine personal pronoun is used. This convention has been used here for ease of discussion.

This stress on death reveals the individual to be an absolute bearer of rights, and his principal right is the right to self-preservation. From this premise flows our ideal of individual liberty and rights.

Turning to medicine, we see the concept of individual liberty and autonomy expressed in the legally originated doctrine of *informed consent*. Traditionally medicine has been practiced paternalistically. The physician acted in what he judged to be his patient's best interests. Rothman has described how this practice has changed, how the center of decision making has shifted from physician privilege to patient autonomy [1]. In general the increasing depersonalization of modern medicine, the growth of impersonal institutions, and the diverging interests of patients and physicians, have made patients aware of the need to assume responsibility for their own treatment. Legally, according to the pivotal *Canterbury* ruling: "[e]very human being of adult years and sound mind has the right to determine what will be done with his body . . ." [2, 3]. The physician has a duty to disclose material information regarding the patient's proposed treatment to the patient. Thus while patient autonomy has expanded, physician autonomy and therapeutic privilege have been contracted.

I will now focus on the bioethical aspects of autonomy that underwrite the legal notion of informed consent. What is autonomy? Originally autonomy referred to the political state that governed itself in making its own laws. This ideal of self-governance has migrated to bioethics, where the patient is deemed to be entitled to decide what interventions should be undertaken in regard to his well-being. Autonomy furnishes moral substance to the claim that an individual owns his own life. He shapes his life through his personal decisions. Consequently he has rights: he has valid claims; he possesses certain entitlements.

Is autonomy equivalent to *privacy* [4, 5]? An individual can, of course, use his autonomy to control access to his private life, and to information pertaining to it. But autonomy and privacy differ. For example, a patient can autonomously choose to give up his right to privacy without giving up his autonomy. Or his privacy can remain intact, while his autonomy is violated: he can be misled by a clinician (therapeutic deception) without his privacy being violated.

Interestingly, neither is autonomy identical with *liberty*. Liberty is the ability to act in a free and voluntary manner. Such free action is consciously self-initiated, without undue coercion or duress. When an individual is able to think for himself, and able to choose to pursue what he desires, he is at liberty. Liberty so described is compatible with an absence of privacy. An individual without knowing that he is under surveillance has his privacy violated, but his liberty of action is unaffected. But importantly, his autonomy is diminished. Or, an individual can autonomously decide to surrender his liberty to make judgments in particular situations. Consequently liberty and autonomy differ. In sum: although autonomy presupposes privacy and liberty as initial conditions, these conditions can subsequently be waived.

What is the positive content of autonomy? Autonomy can be construed as authenticity: autonomous actions are judged to be consistent with an individual's attitudes, values, and life [6]. Autonomy lies deeper than the discrete expression of a desire or a preference. It is the integral and continual expression of the individual's life; it marks him out as a person who is self-possessed, and consistent in his choices and actions. Further, such autonomy includes effective deliberation. The individual must have knowledge of a sufficient range of options, and of the weighting of these options, and their consequences, thus enabling him to assess critically his own values and preferences. And to ratify this just mentioned condition, autonomy requires the inclusion of moral reflection. The individual must be able to accept and affirm the moral values that he acts upon. Lastly it is crucial that he also be able to act so as to realize what he has chosen.

Is autonomy an equivocal concept? Is it fragmented, or is it unitary? Methodologically, it is best to treat autonomy in a unitary manner. It is helpful to interpret it, not as an abstract fragmented notion, but as a process of decision making in the face of a concrete problem in a specific situation. Since its exercise always occurs in a particular situation, the exercise of autonomy is a matter of degree. It cannot be realized in an ideal and complete fashion. In experience the decisions of individuals are never fully autonomous, but they can be autonomous in the relevant sense. Two reasons make autonomy valuable: first, autonomy gives the patient the power to control his life, which is a necessary and general condition for his sense of self-worth; second, autonomy recognizes the patient as the norm in medicine and in bioethics.

What are the formal conditions of autonomy [7, 8]? *Competence* is the first formal condition. Issues around competence tend to emerge when a patient and clinician disagree over a treatment decision. Then a threshold determination—competency is not a matter of degree—has to be made as to whether the patient is competent to make the decision in question. The determination of an individual's competency assesses his capacity to make a decision in regard to a specific task. The wisdom of his decision is not being evaluated. Competence is determined by the presence in an individual of the capacity to decide autonomously, not by whether his best interests are protected by his decision. An individual is permitted to be mistaken about what is best for his well-being. As an autonomous agent he has the right to make what appears to others to be a wrong decision!

Respecting the incompetent patient requires that we help him to regain as much autonomy as possible. This positions him to exercise an optimal amount of control in his decision making, or as much as he desires. A genuine attempt should be made to limit the liberty of the incompetent individual as little as possible. The incompetent individual should be cared for and treated in the least intrusive manner [8].

Second, the clinician is obliged to obtain informed consent for all interventions from the patient. *Disclosure* is a part of our moral obligation to treat the patient respectfully. The determination of what information is relevant has shifted from the physician (and care givers) to the patient. The information to be provided is not what clinicians consider appropriate according to their professional standards and practices. To follow a professional practice standard would undermine patient autonomy.

The information to be disclosed to the patient should include the diagnosis, the prognosis, the frequency of risks and benefits, and alternatives to the proposed treatment. This can be framed as the *reasonable person standard of disclosure:* what information should be disclosed is determined by what the reasonable person in the patient's position would want to know. Moreover, the clinician has an obligation to know his patient. He must embrace the unique subjectivity of the person he is treating. This modifies the reasonable person standard of information disclosure; it individualizes it along subjective lines.

The third condition of autonomy is *understanding*. Does the competent patient understand and appreciate the proposed intervention and its consequences? Now the focus shifts from the physician's obligation to disclose information to the quality of the patient's understanding or consent. The competent patient's understanding should not be critically defective. Positively put, he should hold true beliefs about his situation, and should have drawn valid conclusions from a correct understanding of it. He should have assigned the appropriate weights to the benefits and burdens of the proposed treatment. The fourth condition of autonomy is *voluntariness*. A decision is voluntary if no internal or external factors unduly prevent the competent patient from acting on his understanding of his situation. It is true that illness, or depression, or ignorance, or coercion, can levy temporary pressures. But if, despite these conditions, a patient can make a decision, and also act upon it, then he is able to assume responsibility for his own well-being.

In sum: if a patient is competent, understands the information disclosed, and is able to make a voluntary decision and act upon it, then no one should attempt to control or to constrain him. That attempt would be coercive. If the intervention in question is medically necessary, the clinician is permitted (not morally obliged) to try to persuade the patient. Such persuasion is compatible with a respect for the patient's autonomy. But if an autonomous patient does refuse consent, he should not be treated with the expectation that in the future he will retroactively approve of, and so validate, the treatment. A predicted future consent is not an actual present consent to treatment.

Paradoxically, a patient can autonomously choose to reject a part of his personal autonomy. He can choose not to choose; he may decide to allow someone else to make decisions for him. Using his second-order autonomy (the capacity to choose to act or not to act) he can surrender his first-order liberty of deciding to act [9]. In such waivers, the patient voluntarily foregoes his right to give an informed consent, thus relieving the physician from his obligation to obtain informed consent. The patient's consent has been given, but it is not informed. If patient self-determination includes both the liberty of first-order desires and actions, and the autonomy of second-order desires (that one desires to have, or not have, certain desires), then autonomy is not self-determination. Instead autonomy is the capacity for full self-determination, not the realization of it. So an individual can choose to have less than full self-determination. He can decide to yield his liberty, while reserving the right to reclaim his liberty of action if he chooses to.

In other instances, the patient may decide to revise a prior choice, to choose differently from how he chose previously. The question here is whether he has autonomously revised his former choice? To determine this we should ask: does his action fulfill the four formal conditions of autonomy? We may also be inclined to ask whether his decision fits into the pattern of authentic autonomy, into the pattern of his life? His actions are more likely to be viewed as autonomous if they are in character. But acting in character is not a necessary condition of autonomy, for our characters can change markedly.

Finally, an informed consent is the *autonomous authorization* by a patient of a particular medical intervention. This is more than the patient acquiescing to, agreeing with, or complying with a proposal. The patient must actively own or author the proposed intervention through his informed consent. He takes responsibility. Informed consent or autonomous authorization can be interpreted either as an event, or as a process. As an event—the model most frequently used—it is a discrete act. However, it is more accurate to characterize informed consent and autonomous authorization as a process. An actual consent culminates and completes an ongoing process of disclosure, understanding, deliberation, and making a decision. It is temporally stretched. This avoids the common erroneous view that a signed consent form constitutes a sufficient condition for informed consent.

PART 2:
COMPETENT AND INCOMPETENT PATIENTS

Although autonomy articulates an attractive notion of moral independence, the state occasionally intervenes paternalistically in an individual's life. It overrides his autonomy and liberty, and makes decisions for him in order either to benefit him, or to prevent harm to him. Hence paternalism may be justified when the state is endeavoring to help individuals (perhaps more than we care to admit), who are not fully rationally free, to become more rationally free. On this account, paternalism can support individuals in developing their capacity to make their own decisions. Paternalism can serve as a condition for autonomy [10]!

What is the substantive content of a patient's autonomy? This is a vexing question. If autonomy presupposes that an individual owns his body and life, then presumably he can decide to terminate his life via either euthanasia or assisted suicide. The argument has been pressed that an individual has the right to have someone else terminate his life, and that the appropriate individual—a physician is suggested—has a moral obligation to respond positively to such a request. But does the claimed right to euthanasia and assisted suicide constitute a valid claim? Is it a legitimate expression of autonomy?

It is highly debatable whether one individual can obligate another individual to terminate his life, or to help him to do so. But maybe others are permitted to respond positively to his request for death. Such permission is a softer form of autonomy; a right is a harder expression of autonomy. Both cases present autonomy as a kind of consumer choice. Alternatively, euthanasia and assisted suicide could be seen as "victimless crimes," and therefore permissible. Yet undeniably, they are consented to adult killings! They extend the right of individual autonomy to the point of risking serious harm to the common good, let alone the individual's own good. Euthanasia and assisted suicide are social acts. In the case of suicide, although one can choose the time of one's death, this is a permission, not a right. "Rights" talk here misleads us since the law is silent. This silence does not imply that the act is condoned, or that the individual has a right to it, let alone a right which obligates others.

Then there are patients who are suffering and dying. It would be unreasonable to argue that everything that can be done technologically in medicine for them must be done. No. We do not always have to treat, although there is a *prima facie* obligation to try to relieve pain and suffering. Thus the patient in pain and suffering has the autonomous right to refuse treatment which, while life-saving or life-sustaining, is gravely burdensome. It is commonly accepted that life-prolonging treatments are contraindicated when burdens are judged to outweigh benefits significantly.

It is a difficult question whether a non-terminally ill patient should be allowed to die, whether treatment can legitimately be withheld or withdrawn. Literally speaking, such a patient cannot be allowed to die if he is not already dying! Instead he is being killed! However in practical terms the right of a non-terminally ill competent patient to refuse life-saving or life-sustaining treatment is sanctioned. This is considered to be neither euthanasia, nor assisted suicide, since the intention in such selective non-treatment is to avoid a grave burden, not to terminate the patient's life.

Interestingly, Caplan comments that while society strives strenuously to respect the incompetent person's autonomy, it ignores the competent person [11]. Then, society turns around and plots the autonomous rights of incompetent patients on the grid of the autonomous rights of competent patients! If society is unclear about the autonomy of competent patients, this lack of clarity will surely contaminate any discussion of the supposed autonomy of incompetent patients. As we will see, it does.

In the famous "Quinlan" case the court decided that an incompetent patient did not lose her autonomy and rights, and that others could express these for her [12]. Even a patient who is in a permanently vegetative state possesses autonomy and rights; she is merely unable to articulate her preferences. Therefore we must respect the autonomy and rights of an incompetent patient in the same manner in which we respect the autonomy and rights of a competent patient. Since a competent patient has the autonomous right to refuse treatment, an incompetent patient also has the same autonomous right to refuse treatment. Otherwise we would be discriminating against the incompetent patient. That there may be a morally relevant difference between the two kinds of patients seems to have eluded the court. What is humanly and medically asymmetrical is treated as legally symmetrical.

Of course some individuals who become incompetent have made prior autonomous decisions regarding how they want to be treated during their incompetency. These decisions are expressed either orally, or in some written form—often a living-will. This is seen as a prime exercise in patient autonomy [13]. Typically, emergency situations are considered to suspend these expressions of autonomy. Even this is changing; the discretion to treat in emergencies is being circumscribed [14]. Arguably, the clinician is obliged to treat, until the patient's instructions refusing treatment can be verified.

The notions of autonomy and rights have been stretched beyond the conscious competent patient to a time when he is unable to make a competent decision. But even here he exercises a ghostly control. This underscores the importance placed upon the moral principle of autonomy as the basis of legal informed consent or informed refusal to treatment. So incompetent patients—who are congenitally so, or who have never clearly expressed their treatment preferences—are considered to have the exact same autonomy and rights as competent patients. Since they are unable to exercise their autonomous rights a surrogate (proxy decision maker) must assume this responsibility. Not to exercise these rights would be to deprive the incompetent patient of the right to decision making merely because he is no longer (or has never been) autonomous and able to decide! The surrogate represents the incompetent patient.

How should the surrogate decision maker reach a decision regarding the treatment of an incompetent patient? Two criteria have been advanced. First, the *substituted judgment standard.* In the case of Quinlan, the court sought to protect an autonomy right for a person who could not assert her rights because of her permanent vegetative state. It authorized her father to infer her wants and needs from her life as a competent person, and told him to judge what she would have chosen if she had been able to make a decision.

It is somewhat awkward that the substituted judgment standard contains a fictional ingredient. An incompetent person cannot literally make competent autonomous decisions. While it may be desirable to treat incompetent persons as autonomous, this diverges from their actual situation. On the other hand, it is assumed that to treat them as they are, would be to treat them as nonpersons! This is correct if and only if one defines personhood as the ability to exercise one's rationality, and one also accepts that it is rationality which defines personhood.

But if there is no autonomy involved, then perhaps the standard of substituted judgment should be rejected for never-competent patients, and patients who have never expressed their preferences. It is obscure how substituted judgment proponents can establish the moral relevance of autonomy for such patients. This standard is designed to promote individual autonomy. So it veers toward the notion of precedent autonomy, namely, the competent individual's choices expressed in prior statements and behavior should determine the treatment of a presently incompetent patient [15]. Sadly this neglects the person who the presently incompetent patient is, and neglects his interests precisely as an incompetent person. And frequently in the case of once competent patients, they have never exercised their precedent autonomy [16]. Consequently the substituted judgment standard is a legal and conceptual fiction: no judgment exists to substitute for. In place of the substituted judgment standard a *best interests standard* has been proposed. This objective standard (the hypothetical reasonable person standard) purportedly focuses on the individual patient in his specific situation. Upon what he—as a reasonable individual—would want to have done if he were able to decide about his treatment. Unfortunately, this version of the reasonable person standard is unsuitable for determining the incompetent patient's best interests. Instead it absorbs the actually incompetent person into an hypothetical person that he is not. Why not simply look at the incompetent patient as he is? Why not measure the best interests standard by the well-being of the actual incompetent patient, not by the hypothetical reasonable person? Do incompetent patients not have interests that need to be protected? For example, an interest in avoiding pain, and in enjoying pleasure, and so on.

Whom should we protect? Should we not protect actual persons? Thus we might have the obligation to shield the person in the now incompetent patient from the competent individual he was, because the decisions of the previous individual (rooted in his precedent autonomy) might pose a severe risk of harm to the present person the incompetent patient now is. If an incompetent patient retains significant interests in his own life, then it would be precipitous to overlook his contemporaneous well-being. For example: how he experiences treatment or nontreatment? Doubtlessly, quality of life judgments will have to be made, but the focus should be on the value of the quality of life of the patient to himself, not the value of his life to anyone else [16].

Both proposed criteria for decision making for incompetent patients depend upon the principle of individual rational autonomy. The assumed goal is to avoid being categorized as nonautonomous, as a nonperson. However, despite the attraction of the principle of autonomy, it appears incoherent to try to employ it to encompass nonautonomous patients. Why? This distracts us from considering the *subjectivity* of the demented, the permanently vegetative, and the comatose patient, from considering what moral obligations we have to these patients precisely because of the conditions they have, not in spite of these conditions.

PART 3:
AUTONOMY AND THE DYING PATIENT

In order to know who the dying patient is, for whom we are responsible we need to determine who is dead. But death epitomizes uncertainty, and society finds this uncertainty intolerable—sudden death has been redefined as a treatable disease [17]! In order to dodge it, society endeavors to transform death into a technological phenomenon [18]. This move ushers in the specialization, and the fragmentation of medical care, making death not less of a moral phenomenon, but more of one. For specialization and fragmentation are themselves morally problematic. Medical technology dissects death. Symbolically, in the ICU [19], a communal fight occurs to prevent death, but when defeat eventually ensues, there is no gracious communal surrender to the inevitable. There is no failure of rights here, but a profound failure of human rites and rituals to mark the passing of a unique person. Dying is a living human drama, not a techno-medical fight to the death. With all the specialization and fragmentation, does anyone actually attend to the dying patient as dying? Is it not impossible to die a personal death in such impersonal surroundings? Indeed has anyone even sensed that a person is dying [20]?

To return to my original question. The dead are the legally whole brain dead. Society has decided that they are no longer persons. Some have also argued that neocortical death is sufficient for declaring that a person is dead, the presumption being that personhood is given by society. Whomever society recognizes as a person is a person with rights. This approach to death is grafted onto the fear that most people have of a loss of control and self-determination, which they fear more than being treated as nonpersons when they become incompetent. What preoccupies them is the possibility of pain and suffering. And so society maintains that the relief of pain and of suffering to be the highest good. For pain and suffering diminish our control and autonomy.

Yet to what lengths ought we to go to try to relieve suffering? Surely we are not obliged to try to relieve all suffering. Medicine can only attempt to relieve problems of pain and illness. It cannot dispel the mysterious suffering of life itself! The powerful drive to eliminate suffering—via euthanasia or assisted suicide—may inadvertently result in using a quicker death to deny the suffering at the heart of our life, dying, and death! We hurry to death by avoiding dying. We wish to die in an accelerated fashion, subverting the natural rhythms of our biological, psychological, and spiritual departure. Is this an attempt to deny death by futilely trying to control it? Yes. Why? Because we experience a void in suffering; and we disbelieve in eternal life.

We polish the illusion of absolute autonomy in the face of dying and death. We refuse to acknowledge that all our wants cannot be satisfied, that our world comes to an end. Instead of accepting this finality, we panic and reach out desperately in contradictory directions: either seeking an accelerated dying, or demanding that everything that is technologically possible be done. Caught in these imponderables it may be that informed consent and autonomy are transition concepts [21]. This is owed to a realization that rights and autonomy language brooks no compromise. It is a winner take all language, which is highly adversarial, with the upshot that we overlook the possibility that having a right does not mean that it must be exercised. Of course disregarding the patient also produces an adversarial relationship, and it is disturbing that paternalism has been the norm for clinicians. Still, extreme paternalism and extreme autonomy are two sides of the same coin.

The centrality given to autonomy has inflated it unduly; it lacks articulate boundaries. Its putative rationality is really an unquestioned subjectivity; and this rationality imprisons the individual in his individuality, and more tellingly isolates him as a dying person. The autonomy model applied to the dying patient is still caught within the traditional acute cure goals, and biophysical disease model, of allopathic medicine. Dying happens *in* the patient; it is due to a biological cause. To forestall it, the rational individual contracts with his clinician for treatment. This assumes that the patient's self-identity is constituted in complete fashion prior to his illness and dying. In himself he is independent of his illness and dying. He is not a dying patient; he is a patient who accidentally happens to be dying. But why are dying and death excluded from the patient's self-identity? Because they are perceived to be ultimate assaults upon, and insults to, his autonomy, and to the notion that his life is his own. If the clinician sees through this incoherence, he will discover that his ethical and professional responsibilities are ill defined by a patient's autonomous rights. His relationship with the patient is not a contractual relationship. In principle, the patient's needs may legitimately trump his rights as an individual.

The ethical and relational obligations present in dying and death transcend the morality of individual rights and choices. Talk about rights and autonomous choices in the case of a dying patient conceals his dying and death. Why? We cannot master our own bodies medically; we do not have the self-knowledge to master ourselves completely [22]. The only mastery permitted to us is the mastery of moderation, that definitively circumscribes the putatively unlimited principle of autonomy. Individual autonomy and rights do not provide the real answers to the mystery of the dying and death of a person. To echo Thomas Merton, we have to rescue the person in the dying patient from the individual! We must try to prevent the loss of the person in the patient while he is dying. How? By being available to the self that abides in the dying patient. Yet we also have to let the dying patient go when he is dying, so as to protect him in his dying and death.

Lest we forget, autonomy does remain a morally relevant characteristic of the dying patient. However, since autonomy is planted in personal relationships, we need to transcend the bare principle of respect for autonomy. We ought to recognize that the dignity and self-respect of the dying patient are more important than autonomy *per se*. For while autonomy may help a dying patient refuse treatment, it cannot by itself help him to secure care. Autonomy is a means, rather than an end in itself. The principle of respect for autonomy expresses the subjective dimension of the moral agent's choice. Yet inordinately strengthening the autonomy of the dying patient may have the unintended effect of weakening obligations to him, and responsibilities for him.

Should the dying patient's autonomy be promoted? My answer is indirect. We find it difficult to see any human action that does not originate in an explicit choice. We assume that all morally worthwhile conduct is chosen, that the exercise of autonomy is the sole source of human dignity. But perhaps we are less rational than we think. Indeed can what guides reason also be the product of reason? A more fruitful way to appreciate the relationship between autonomy and dying patients is to recognize their determinate singular expressions of autonomy. We should not commensurate what is incommensurable: making decisions while living within life, and making unprecedented decisions at the edge of life. The autonomy proper to dying patients places them beyond mere considerations of justice. Here we transcend both the substituted judgment and the best interests standards in decision making for dying patients, which center on autonomy, and so upon the claims and wants of the competent rational individual. But the ethical situation is more ambiguous than this two track model.

Our moral obsession with individual autonomy blinds us to the fact that an individual cannot shape his life by himself. What self-transcending uses autonomy is put to is more important than the achievement of autonomy in satisfying individual preferences. We believe and act as if we can never have too much autonomy and choice. And so we err on the side of excess. The lion's share of popular advocacy literature assumes the primacy of the principle of autonomy in medical relationships. Patients have become clients, and the dying patient is a special kind of client. The clinician's relationship with this client is predicated on a calculus of possible threats and harms, and risks and benefits to him. But by relocating the focus on personal autonomy, we may discern that the real issues are those of promises and caring, availability and responsiveness, not risks and benefits, and choices. In sum: the vulnerable dying patient needs more than autonomy and rights; he needs care; he needs other persons to share in his experience.

We may be responsible for respecting the dying patient's autonomy in recognizing a good for him that he himself does not register. In such circumstances we owe a greater moral sensitivity to the dying patient than the formalistic requirements agreed to in a fictional contract. How should we judge in these situations? Prudently and virtuously. Is there a method? No. But there is an art of human kindness and sensibility and humanity that alone can protect what is precious in the dying patient's person, including the appropriate expressions of his autonomy. For the dying patient is not only living all the way up to the moment of his death, but he is also *giving!* Unless we acknowledge and try to receive what he can give to those of us who remain, we do not share in his process of self-surrender and self-transcendence that transpires on the front edge of human life.

It is important to return to the issue of the autonomous right to euthanasia and assisted suicide in situations of suffering. Logically the right to euthanasia and assisted suicide, based on the principle of autonomy, is an unlimited right. But it is unclear whether a self-chosen death is the rational way to deal with suffering. Is this not the unavailing attempt to control fate totally? Is this not the notion that the individual in his complete self-assertion can determine all the aspects of his dying and death? This does not make the individual a fuller person. His challenge is rather to accept and to be open to what he cannot control: his fate and limitations. He has to learn to let go in life, to give up his very own life. His life is not his own! This realization runs counter to all that permeates our culture.

The argument for the right to die is an exceedingly bold *in rem* claim against nature, a claim to the inevitable. But the individual also belongs to his intimates. To be close to others is no longer to own one's own life unequivocally. Other persons depend upon the person in the dying patient. He cannot do just as he pleases, as if no one close morally matters. He may belong to his family for instance. The family's interest in the common good, including the dying patient's good, stands in tension with his autonomy. The individual is more than an individual; he is a person in relationships of lesser or greater ethical density; he is autonomous precisely because of those relationships.

We should see the dying patient in closer solidarity with the living. The autonomy of the person, not merely the individual, shares in and contributes to the common good even on the margin of life. Such a person-centered autonomy cannot be neutral to the good of the community it inhabits. The common good of the community for the person is a nondetached good, not an optional good, nor an option right. If this good were detachable, then society would have the right to detach itself from the dying patient; it would have the right to abandon him.

In moral theory, autonomy has been focused too narrowly on the individual's independence from other persons, while underestimating the importance of his intimate and dependent relationships. But individual moral life cannot be reduced to an untrimmed autonomy. We live in our deepest humanity beyond what we can continually, *per impossible*, exercise control and choice over. Such a choice saturated life would be inhumanly destabilizing. It would lack the habitual constants which we depend upon, so as to be able to make crucial decisions. A more responsible deployment of autonomy would situate it in relation to the constant stable goods we live within. Thus our choices are not self-affirming, but affirmed by what is beyond choice.

Some writers equate personhood with the expressions of rational personality [23]. However, this fails to respect the inherent personhood of the dying patient. For while his personality might be submerged in neocortical brain death, in coma states, in vegetative, and in demented states, these states do not indicate in any way that his personhood has been eradicated [24, 25]. Rational autonomy is not self-evidently the core of personal being. The weight placed upon rationality in modern personhood can mislead us into respecting the individual's autonomy (or the abstract principle residing in the surrogate), while overlooking the concrete submerged personhood of the dying patient. Consequently respect for the principle of autonomy includes more than respect for rational self-determination. It includes the whole embodied person.

Respect requires more than nonintervention in the affairs of the dying patient; it includes the obligation to sustain his capacity for making autonomous choices. That does not mean the maximum of decision-making power, but optimal decision making. In the case of competent dying patients, accenting autonomy may not respect them as autonomous persons since dying patients are not caught up with autonomy issues [11]. What they want and prefer and choose at this stage is not unambiguous, because they are wandering on the borders of life as we know it. They are *Unheimlich*. Caring is knowing when to help the dying, and also knowing when individual autonomy is not the issue, but empathy and compassion are.

The choices of the dying patient must be taken with the utmost seriousness. Normal decision theory employs a game theory model of choice. But dying and death are the ultimate end-game, involving mysteries, not problems, practical finalities, not theoretic resolutions. Respect for the autonomous dying patient (in contrast to respect for the principle of autonomy) permits care givers, on occasion, to try to influence the patient's care, with the proviso that the patient must be able to identify with the choice as meaningful. Respect for the competent dying patient means enabling him to choose and act in an expansive manner. This will vary from person to person. Only prudence and sensitivity to the person within the dying person can guide the care giver.

The principle of respect for autonomy in the case of the dying patient is not the only moral good present. Rights and duties cannot fully protect such a unique patient. Respecting the dying patient means that one acknowledges that his life has been lived not solely by self-possession, but by self-transcending direction, hope, and trust. The relevant good in the care of the dying patient is the person himself. It also includes the caring pattern of actions, when both treatment and the attempt to cure have bid a sad but necessary farewell. Healing and wholeness are possible even if cure is not. If these are not attended to, the dying patient can be harmed. This complex matter embraces a number of goods: the remaining good of the art of intensive palliative care; the dying patient's own perceived good; the good for him as a person; and the Good. We care for the whole person, while the individual is dying; we care for the person because there is a whisper upon the wind that the dying person is now bidding us farewell [26].

If the goods at the end of a unique human life cannot be reduced to rights and entitlements, that is because all of us are only temporarily competent and able-bodied. To be a person is to be more or less needy. We share common vulnerabilities. In dying we experience our ultimate neediness and dependence. This does not mean that the dying must be given special rights. Rather we the living should appreciate our common dependency with those who are dying, who are striking out ahead of us. Their independence stands revealed, as does ours, in the completion and culmination of their lives, as a function of a deeper creative interdependence and dependence. In other words, the desires and needs of the dying patient do not give rise to rights as a sovereign individual, but to special responsibilities and obligations on our part as a community. For the dying deserve more than rights; they deserve to be accepted in solicitude.

Unfortunately in a rights-based society the dying and dead are rendered invisible. A surrogate has to exercise their autonomous rights. Oddly, support is lent to shore up the autonomous right of the individual to die, but the dying person appears to get lost in the process, and loses his own dying and death. We are well-intentioned in trying to ease the passage of death, but it cannot be completely eased. Pain can be handled, but the unresolved problems of a singular life may linger. Some dying patients will be unable to rise to their dying and death. Should we help them to avoid this sad conclusion? I do not think that we ought to act paternalistically so as to deny the patient this last opportunity for reconciliation with his life. Dying is the most personal event each of us will undergo, that each of us will suffer: it will be my dying and my death. No one way to die exists; no universal method and no technique to manage death exist [27, 28].

The bioethical notion of autonomy obtains its ballast from a detached rationality. But in the case of the dying patient the care giver must try to be attached so as to receive from him what the patient can give as an ultimate affirmation of the preciousness and irreplaceability of his personal being. Dying patients as unique persons have everything to give at the culmination of their lives, since they have nothing to possess anymore. Their lives are not their own.

Dying and death are hard for all of us. We are wounded; we hurt; we are afraid for ourselves, and for those we love. Autonomy has no words to speak; claims fall silent; desire dwindles. That dying and death wound us so unspeakably is a measure of our deep love for this person who was. And love cannot comprehend why she, why he, why this person cannot be with me forever. Death, love, forgiveness, suffering, joy, and memory—all these place us beyond the pale of autonomy. They delimit autonomy, while we try to locate autonomy, while we try to hold ourselves together.

In dying and death, we are so attached, yet we must surrender and let go, undergoing and suffering through our own powerlessness and unconditional vulnerability. Each man and each woman remains an autonomous person, but their autonomy is rooted in a mysterious ground. The trajectory of autonomy is ultimately dependency. Do we experience this utter powerlessness in dying and death as a being gently and mysteriously guided [29]? The dying patient needs to negotiate with his dying, not to fight it, but to welcome it, to be hospitable to this last guest and friend in his life: death. Why? In order to transform his actions into passions, his activity into receptivity, his motion into rest, his matter into the pure form and substance of what he always was meant to be and now is on the verge of. Such is the autonomy of self-transcendence born in the self-surrender of dying. It is an autonomy, not independent, but born in dependence.

Human autonomy is a participated in, dependent autonomy. We are compromised before we become dying patients! For suffering is the human condition. We live with the shiny illusion of an unsituated autonomy, but it is only an illusion; for dependency is a non-accidental feature of the human situation. It is strikingly true that autonomy cannot be achieved autonomously; neither can it be achieved independently.

REFERENCES

1. D. J. Rothman, *Strangers At The Bedside,* Basic Books, New York, 1991.
2. Canterbury v. Spence, U.S. Court of Appeals, District of Columbia; May 19, 1972. 464 Federal Reporter, 2nd Series, 772, reprinted in *Contemporary Issues in Bioethics* (4th Edition), T. L. Beauchamp and L. Walters (eds.), Wadsworth Publishing Company, Belmont, California, pp. 142-144, 1994.
3. Reibl v. Hughes, (1980), 2 Supreme Court Reports 880, reprinted in *Readings in Biomedical Ethics,* E. W. Kluge (ed.) Prentice Hall, Scarborough, Ontario, pp. 131-139, 1993.
4. G. Dworkin, Autonomy and Informed Consent, *The Theory and Practice of Autonomy,* Cambridge University Press, Cambridge, pp. 103-109, 1988.
5. H. Gross, Privacy and Autonomy, *Nomos XIII,* J. Chapman and J. Roland Pennock, Lieber-Atherton, New York, pp. 169-182, 1971.
6. B. Miller, Autonomy and the Refusal of Lifesaving Treatment, *Hastings Centre Report, 11*(4), pp. 167-176, 1981.
7. T. L. Beauchamp and J. F. Childress, *Principles of Biomedical Ethics* (4th Edition), Oxford University Press, pp. 132-170, 1994.
8. M. Silberfeld and A. Fish, *When The Mind Fails: A Guide To Dealing With Incompetency,* University of Toronto Press, Toronto, pp. 44-118, 1994.
9. G. Dworkin, The Nature of Autonomy, *The Theory and Practice of Autonomy,* Cambridge University Press, Cambridge, pp. 14-20, 1988.
10. G. Dworkin, Paternalism, *Philosophy of Law* (4th Edition), J. Feinberg and H. Gross (eds.), Wadsworth Publishing Company, Belmont, California, pp. 230-239, 1991.
11. A. Caplan, Can Autonomy be Saved? *If I Were a Rich Man Could I Buy a Pancreas?* Indiana University Press, Bloomington, Indiana, pp. 256-281, 1992.
12. In the Matter of Quinlan, an Alleged Incompetent. 1976, Supreme Court of New Jersey, 70, N.J. 10, 335 A. 2d 647.
13. Advance Directives: Are They an Advance? Advance Directives Seminar Group, Centre for Bioethics, University of Toronto, *Canadian Medical Association Journal, 146*(2), pp. 127-134, 1992.
14. L. Emanuel and K. V. Iserson, and N. O. Tatum, Ethical Dilemmas in Emergency Medicine, *Patient Care, 28*(13), pp. 138-151, 1994.
15. R. Dworkin, Autonomy and the Demented Self, *Milbank Quarterly, 64*(suppl. 2), pp. 4-16, 1986.

16. R. Dresser, Autonomy Revisited: The Limits of Anticipatory Choices, *Dementia and Aging*, R. H. Binstock, S. G. Post, and P. J. Whitehouse (eds.), The Johns Hopkins University Press, Baltimore, pp. 71-85, 1992.
17. M. C. Greengold, Sudden Death, *Journal of the American Medical Association*, 273(19), p. 1496, 1995.
18. E. J. Cassell, The Sorcerer's Broom, *Hastings Centre Report*, 23(6), pp. 32-39, 1990.
19. R. Zussman, *Intensive Care*, University of Chicago Press, Chicago, 1992.
20. D. C. Thomasma, Mercy Killing of Elderly People with Dementia: A Counterproposal, *Dementia and Aging*, R. H. Binstock, S. G. Post, and P. J. Whitehouse (eds.), The Johns Hopkins University Press, Baltimore, pp. 104-105, 1992.
21. R. Veatch, Abandoning Informed Consent, *Hastings Centre Report*, 25(2), pp. 5-12, 1995.
22. D. Callahan, *The Troubled Dream of Life*, Simon and Shuster, New York, p. 37, 1993.
23. D. Brock, Justice and the Severely Demented Elderly, *The Journal of Medicine and Philosophy*, 13(1), pp. 73-99, 1988.
24. R. E. Cranford, The Persistent Vegetative State: The Medical Reality (Getting the Facts Straight), *Hastings Centre Report*, 18(1), pp. 27-32, 1988.
25. M. Howell, Caretakers' Views on Responsibilities for the Care of the Demented Elderly, *Journal of American Geriatrics Society*, 32(9), pp. 657-660, 1984.
26. J. Hamilton, Dr. Balfour Mount and the Cruel Irony of Our Care for the Dying, *Canadian Medical Association Journal*, 153(3), pp. 334-336, 1995.
27. H. Hendin, Selling Death and Dignity, *Hastings Centre Report*, 25(3), pp. 19-23, 1995.
28. E. Latimer, Caring for the Seriously Ill and Dying Patients: The Philosophy and Ethics, *Canadian Medical Association Journal*, 144(7), pp. 859-864, 1991.
29. H. J. M. Nouwen, *A Letter of Consolation*, Harper Collins, San Francisco, pp. 45-53, 1989.

BIBLIOGRAPHY

Aries, P., *Western Attitudes Towards Death*, P. Ranum (trans,), The Johns Hopkins University Press, Baltimore, 1974.

Bernat, J. L., How Much of the Brain Must Die in Brain Death, *The Journal of Clinical Ethics*, 3(1), pp. 21-26, 1992.

Callahan, D., Autonomy: A Moral Good, not a Moral Obsession, *Hastings Centre Report*, 14(5), pp. 40-42, 1984.

Callahan, D., Bioethics: Private Choice and Common Good, *Hastings Centre Report*, 24(3), pp. 28-31, 1994.

Childress, J. F., The Place of Autonomy in Bioethics, *Hastings Centre Report*, 20(1), pp. 12-17, 1990.

Devettere, R. J., The Imprecise Language of Euthanasia and Causing Death, *Journal of Clinical Ethics*, 1(4), pp. 268-274, 1990.

Dworkin, G., *The Theory and Practice of Autonomy*, Cambridge University Press, Cambridge, 1988.

Guidelines on the Termination of Life-Sustaining Treatment and the Care of the Dying, A Report by the Hastings Centre, Indiana University Press, Bloomington, Indiana, 1987.

Herbst, H., J. Lynne, A. C. Mermann, and J. Rhymes, What do Dying Patients Want and Need? *Patient Care*, 29(4), pp. 27-39, 1995.

Hill, T. E., *Autonomy and Self-Respect*, Cambridge University Press, Cambridge, 1991.

Jonas, H., The Burden and Blessing of Mortality, *Hastings Centre Report*, 22(1), pp. 34-40, 1992.

Kübler-Ross, E., *On Death and Dying,* Collier Books, New York, 1970.
Latimer, E. and J. McGregor, Euthanasia, Physician-Assisted Suicide and the Ethical Care of Dying Patients, *Canadian Medical Association Journal, 151*(8), pp. 1133-1136, 1994.
Martin, R. J. and S. G. Post, Human Dignity, Dementia, and the Moral Basis of Caregiving, in *Dementia and Aging,* R. H. Binstock, S. G. Post, and P. J. Whitehouse (eds.), The Johns Hopkins University Press, Baltimore, pp. 55-68, 1992.
McCue, J. D., The Naturalness of Dying, *Journal of the American Medical Association, 273*(13), pp. 1039-1043, 1995.
Meilaender, G., Terra es Animata On Having a Life, *Hastings Centre Report, 23*(4), pp. 25-32, 1993.
Moody, H., A Critical View of Ethical Dilemmas in Dementia, in *Dementia and Aging,* R. H. Binstock, S. G. Post, and P. J. Whitehouse (eds.), The Johns Hopkins University Press, Baltimore, pp. 86-100, 1992.
Morison, R., The Biological Limits on Autonomy, *Hastings Centre Report, 14*(5), pp. 43-49, 1984.
Nouwen, H. J. M., *Aging: The Fulfilment of Life,* Image Books, Toronto, 1990.
Nouwen, H. J. M., *Our Greatest Gift: A Meditation on Dying and Caring,* Harper Collins, San Francisco, 1994.
Nuland, S. B., *How We Die,* Vintage Books, New York, 1995.
On Life and Death, Report of the Special Senate Committee on Euthanasia and Assisted Suicide, Ministry of Supply and Services Canada, 1995.
Roy, D. J., J. R. Williams, and B. M. Dickens, *Bioethics in Canada,* Prentice Hall, Scarborough, Ontario, 1994.
Veatch, R., *Death, Dying, and the Biological Revolution,* Yale University Press, New Haven, 1976.
Veatch, R., Is Autonomy an Outmoded Value? *Hastings Centre Report, 14*(5), pp. 38-40, 1984.
Veatch, R., The Impending Collapse of the Whole-Brain Definition of Death, *Hastings Centre Report, 23*(4), pp. 18-24, 1993.
Will, G., For the Handicapped, Rights But No Welcome, *Hastings Centre Report, 16*(2), pp. 5-8, 1986.
Yeide, Jr. H., The Many Faces of Autonomy, *The Journal of Clinical Ethics, 3*(4), pp. 269-274, 1992.

CHAPTER 28

Assisting Suicide: An Analysis of the Legal (i.e., Moral) Arguments in Judgments of the Supreme Court of Canada in the Sue Rodriguez Case

Gilbert E. Brodie

The prohibition of assisting suicide has come under challenge in Canada, the United States, and other Western countries. As a legally embodied prohibition, this challenge has been taken up in the courts. Most visibly in the United States are the trials of Dr. Jack Kevorkian, who like Dr. Morgentaler in Canada on the abortion issue, is repeatedly acquitted by juries of blatant violations of the law. Juries regularly acquit when they do not see what the law prohibits as something which is *morally* wrong.

In the case of Sue Rodriguez, a forty-two-year old mother dying of a progressive degenerative disease, the courts were asked to strike down the Criminal Code provisions prohibiting assisting suicide. Eventually her condition would deteriorate to the point where she would not be able to commit suicide without assistance. In anticipation of that, she sought protection for the person who would eventually help her. Her attempt to have the law struck down as violations of the Charter of Rights and Freedoms worked its way through the Canadian Courts to the Supreme Court of Canada where it was decided in late 1993. The Supreme Court decided against her, as had the Court of Appeal of British Columbia. Both decisions, however, were split decisions. In the Supreme Court it was the closest of splits, 5-4.

LEGAL CHARTER ARGUMENTS AS MORAL ARGUMENTS

It is often assumed by the general public that a competent, intelligent appraisal of a court judgment on the constitutionality of a law would require a great deal of legal training and expertise. Surely, it is thought, one must be an expert on constitutional law as are the justices and lawyers who argue before them. The typical reaction of a citizen who is dismayed by a court ruling is not to challenge the court's decision but rather to call for a change in the Constitution. While this mystification of what is involved in deciding a Charter case is sometimes useful for the government in achieving compliance with a court's rulings, in the long run it undermines the function of the judicial system in a society. A significant move toward this demystification has been made by the Courts themselves in recent years. This can be seen in the way in which the judgments are being written. It becomes clear in reading judgments, particularly in Charter cases, that the justices are not writing only for other justices and lawyers. Legal principles, rules, and doctrines which would not need to be explained to a second-year law student are nonetheless explained, albeit briefly. One can only conclude that the Courts increasingly want to make their reasoning accessible to the broader audience of those who are willing to invest some time and effort to understand them. This is not to say that arguments are never presented with a (not-very-thick) veneer of legal terminology, but the assistance necessary to penetrate that veneer is far less than most people presume.

The purpose of this chapter is to engage non-lawyers in the debate that took place in the Sue Rodriguez case in the Supreme Court. When the arguments on which the case was decided are set out, many readers may be surprised to find out that they are not at all "technical legal arguments" comprehensible only to legal experts. The court's judgment's, both the majority and the minority, are in fact based on what can only be characterized as "moral" arguments. Anyone who has been following the debate on suicide and assisted suicide in the philosophical or theological literature will immediately recognize the arguments considered by the court. To say that the court decided this case on moral grounds is not to say that the case was improperly decided. In fact, this is the only way in which the court, *legally*, could decide it.

The general public is accustomed to a sharp division between the law and "ethics" or "morality" (terms which I will use interchangeably). This perception is reflected in such oft-heard statements as "It may be immoral, but it's perfectly legal!"[1] or "Morality and legality are two completely different things." Morality or ethics is seen, generally speaking, as being about the meaning and priority of values, and the reasonableness or unreasonableness of norms or rules restricting our freedom. It asks: "Does this good end justify this particular means to it?" Morality is concerned, as well, about the goodness of individuals, virtues and vices, motives and intentions.

The law, on the other hand, is popularly perceived as looking up provisions or previous judgments in those thousands of uniformly bound volumes which cover the walls in the oak-lined law offices and judges chambers so often depicted in the media. It may well be that many cases are resolved in this manner. Charter cases,

---

[1] When the converse statement is made, namely, "It is illegal, but it is perfectly moral!" you can be certain that this is part of an argument to have the activity de-criminalized.

typically, are not. When a case involves a challenge to a law as contrary to the Charter of Right and Freedoms the answers to the challenge will not be found by examining the provisions of various statutes. The Charter guarantees, within *reasonable* limits, certain rights and freedoms.[2] An example of such a right is the one set out in Section 7, which is the right to "fundamental justice" when being deprived wholly or in part of one's life, liberty, or the security of one's person.[3] Like other rights, the right to fundamental justice in these matters is not itself absolute, but rather is subject to the reasonable limits identified in Section 1. The task before the court is essentially a philosophical, ethical one. It is to determine the meaning and scope of these rights and freedoms (what, e.g., is covered by "security of the person," or what principles are included within "fundamental justice") and, in cases where they are infringed upon, whether it is a "reasonable" infringement. Seeking to determine what is "reasonable" or "just" are precisely what ethics is about.

THE LIMITED ROLE OF LEGAL PRECEDENT IN CHARTER CASES

This does not mean, of course, that the Court does not draw upon the views and arguments of previous judgments, (as do philosophers.) The Supreme Court is not bound, however, by the judgments of lower courts or even, strictly speaking, their own previous Supreme Court judgments. While the Supreme Court is understandably reluctant to reverse a previous decision, the possibility of doing so cannot be *a priori* dismissed. Although there is a legitimate concern not to unduly sacrifice the value of stability in the legal system by frequent reversals, it is ultimately not the *fact* that a previous court has decided in a particular way that is decisive in the case at hand. It is the compelling force of the reasoning or arguments of that (those) previous judgment(s) which the court must weigh. Justice Sopinka recalls this point in relation to the issues in this case in paragraph 24:[4] "The way to resolve these problems is not to avoid the historical analysis, but to make sure that one is looking not just at the existence of the practice itself (i.e., the continued criminalization of assisted suicide) but at the rationale behind that practice and the principles which underlie it." Courts are only bound by the conclusions of higher courts; the Supreme Court is ultimately bound only by the Constitution, which in this type of case amounts to being bound by "fundamental justice" and the "reasonable."

---

[2] The first Section of the Charter states: "1. The Canadian Charter of Rights and Freedoms guarantees the rights and freedoms set out in it subject only to such reasonable limits prescribed by law as can be demonstrably justified in a free and democratic society."

[3] The Section states "7. Everyone has the right to life, liberty and security of the person and the right not to be deprived thereof except in accordance with the principles of fundamental justice."

[4] The Supreme Court has started making its judgments widely available electronically via the Internet (http://www.droit.umontreal.ca./cgi-bin/CSC_list?vol3+1993+EN). This is done through the Faculty of Law at the University of Montreal. To facilitate referencing of downloaded documents, paragraph numbering is now used. I will indicate these numbers with each citation.

Given the essentially ethical or moral nature of the problem faced by the Supreme Court in a Charter challenge to a law, it is not surprising that the arguments debated are the same ones which philosophers have been debating. What else could they be? In this analysis I will show that, at times, these arguments are well-made, but that at other times they are not. The criterion for whether there arguments are well-made or not is not the authority of a reviewing philosopher. It is whether they are rebuttable by a counter-argument to which an alternative formulation of the argument would not be vulnerable. I will suggest some reformulations or alternative arguments which would have provided better support for their conclusions. Finally, I will try to clearly identify the fundamental ethical issue which divides the court and the society. On a broader level, it is hoped that this analysis will help those without formal legal training to realize that they are in a position to understand the court's reasoning and therefore to intelligently concur with or dissent from their decisions.

THE ARGUMENTS

The conclusion of the majority in the Rodriguez case is supported by the following four arguments. The first two are arguments supporting the upholding of the law prohibiting the assistance of suicide.[5] These arguments will be presented along with the reply of the dissenting judgments to them. The third and fourth arguments are essentially replies to arguments raised by the dissenting justices. The arguments can be briefly stated as follows:

I. To allow assistance in suicide contradicts the intrinsic value of human life.
II. The active participation by one individual in the death of another is intrinsically morally and legally wrong.
III. The analogies to other sorts of actions which are legally and morally permitted, namely, not using "extraordinary means" to sustain life, or giving pain-killing drugs which may shorten life, are not valid analogies.
IV. An exceptionless prohibition of assisting suicide is not a fundamentally unjust infringement on the right of the physically handicapped to control over their own body even if it deprives them of the choice to commit suicide possessed by those physically able to commit suicide without assistance.

I. THE INTRINSIC VALUE OF HUMAN LIFE

Argument: To allow assistance in suicide contradicts one of the values which the state has a duty to protect, namely, the intrinsic value of human life or the inherent dignity of the human person.

---

[5] The Criminal Code, Revised Statutes of Canada, 1985 states: "241. Every one who (a) counsels a person to commit suicide, or (b) aids or abets a person to commit suicide, whether suicide ensues or not, is guilty of an indictable offence and liable to imprisonment for a term not exceeding fourteen years.

At Issue (Even for the Dying): The Intrinsic Value of a Living Person

This argument is stated most directly by Justice John Sopinka, author of the majority judgment (concurred in by Justices La Forest, Gontier, Iacobucci, and Major), in paragraphs 10 and 12. In paragraph 10, he is responding to the appellant's [i.e., Rodriguez] argument that "the right to control what happens to her body while she is living" (paragraph 5) which is part of what is meant by the right to "security of the person" would include the right to the necessary assistance to end her life. Sopinka is indicating that he finds more merit in the respondent's [i.e., the Government] reply to this argument:

> [Paragraph 10] I find more merit in the argument that security of the person, by its nature, cannot encompass a right to take action that will end one's life as security of the person is intrinsically concerned with the well-being of the living person. This argument focuses on the generally held and deeply rooted belief in our society that human life is sacred or inviolable (which terms I use in the non-religious sense described by Dworkin [1] to mean that human life is seen to have a deep intrinsic value of its own). As members of a society based upon respect for the intrinsic value of human life and on the inherent dignity of every human being, can we incorporate within the Constitution which embodies our most fundamental values a right to terminate one's life in any circumstances? This question in turn evokes other queries of fundamental importance such as the degree to which our conception of the sanctity of life includes notions of quality of life as well.

Excursus[6]: The Ambiguity of "Human Dignity"

Before proceeding in our discussion of the deep " intrinsic value of human life," it is worth drawing attention to the fact that Sopinka appeals here not only to that value but also to the "inherent *dignity* of every human being." "Inherent human dignity" is a value appealed to by both sides in this debate. Rodriguez's appeal is based, in part, on "the right to live her remaining life with the inherent dignity of a human person" (paragraph 5). When opposing sides in a debate both appeal, without further elaboration, to the same value it is clear that its content or meaning is not clear. Neither side explicitly sets out its understanding of just what "human dignity" refers to or what it is that gives human beings their dignity. Notwithstanding the fact that the other side is also appealing to this most important value, both sides seem to regard its meaning as so obvious that there is no need to spell out how their position protects human dignity and the opposing side's position infringes upon it. What each side understands by "human dignity" can be *inferred* from the context. While a thorough examination of this would turn this into more than an "excursus," the importance we attach to protecting

---

[6] The term used by academics to indicate that they are about to go off on a tangent.

"human dignity" warrants a brief indication of the two different meanings being given to this term. In fact, clarifying this ambiguity will reveal the fundamental difference between the two sides.

Respecting "human dignity" means, in general terms, treating a human being as a human being, that is, treating her or him in a way that acknowledges what makes her or him human. This would be simple were it not for the fact that human beings are not. Human beings are complex, changing beings. We have a variety of different capacities and limitations which increase and diminish over the course of a typical lifetime. It is possible to adopt, particularly implicitly, different meanings for the term "human dignity" by focusing on one capacity or the ability rather than another. To focus on one value is not, of course, to deny the importance of another. The focusing on, or prioritizing of, one value often does lead to the "instrumentalizing" of the other. That is to say, the lower ranked value is seen to have its value inasmuch as it is useful in serving the higher value.

"Human dignity," for the side supporting Rodriguez, focuses on the human capacity to control reality, including oneself. Human beings are truly extraordinary in this regard. To exercise control, a person must first of all have the *freedom* to choose.[7] Thus various forms of liberty (personal, political, and economic), as well as self-determination are given the highest priority. A not uncommon understanding of the history modern civilization is to see it as the history of the extension of various forms of liberty. In addition to liberty, control requires the ability to bring about what one has chosen. Here the sciences, both physical and social, have greatly enhanced out ability to manipulate reality according to our chosen purposes. To be denied control, either by being denied the freedom to choose what we have the ability to do, or by being denied the means to accomplish that which we have freely chosen, is to infringe upon the very quality which gives us our dignity or worth. One of the problems in human life, however, is that it involves a process of gradually maturing and declining, acquiring and losing control. It is in this context that we hear references to the "indignities of old age" or less frequently to the "indignities of youth." The fact that for many the ultimate indignity is the loss of bladder or bowel control probably says something about our culture, but I will leave it to the reader to speculate on what that might be. In any event, this understanding of human dignity sees the value of human life in the effective exercise of freedom.

"Human dignity," for the side opposing Rodriguez, focuses on the human capacity to be self-consciously aware of reality, including oneself. Human beings are truly extraordinary is this regard as well. While many animals are consciously aware of themselves and reality, human beings are conscious of being consciously aware. This creates a number of distinctly human capabilities: the capacity to question, and occasionally to insightfully understand, that of which we are aware; to appreciate

---

[7] Thus it is that B. F. Skinner [2], the behaviorist who argues that human freedom of choice is an illusion which we must get beyond, entitles the book in which he makes this argument: *Beyond Freedom and Human Dignity*.

what we experience and the experiencing of it; to imaginatively place ourselves as being engaged in a variety of courses of action and then to freely choose one of them; to imaginatively make choices and then to decide, in advance, what that choice will be—that is, to promise, and thus to love. We will speak more of human consciousness later in conjunction with the thought of Ronald Dworkin [1]. For the moment it is adequate to point out that the "trajectory" of these human capabilities is not at all congruent with that of our ability to control reality and our bodies as part of it. The very real importance of our ability to control reality is that it sustains and enhances our ability to be consciously present, to know, appreciate, and love others, and ourselves. To destroy our ability to exercise these capacities is to infringe upon the very things which give human life its dignity or worth. This understanding of human dignity sees the effective exercise of freedom as having its value in protecting and expanding our conscious presence to, and the relating of ourselves to, reality.

In most contexts it is not necessary to distinguish which of these two understandings, that is, "human dignity as control" or "human dignity as conscious presence," one has implicitly adopted. In most of life, the exercise of control and the ability to be consciously present go hand in hand in the service of one another. It is only in those contexts where one is in conflict with the other, as is the case with suicide (and the assisting of it), that one must decide which of these two *different* understandings one endorses. What this means is that appeals to "human dignity," not withstanding their rhetorical impact, are essentially "begging the question." To beg a question is to argue for a position in a way that *implicitly* assumes that the position has already been established and accepted. The fact that the argument is going around in circles is hidden until what was implicit is made explicit. The pro-Rodriguez appeal to "human dignity" (as control) implies that the value of being alive is to be found in the exercise of (at least certain) freedoms. In short, the value of life is not "intrinsic" but rather as a platform for the exercise of freedom. The contra-Rodriguez appeal to "human dignity" (as conscious presence) implies that the value of being alive is "intrinsic" and therefore not reducible to, nor wholly dependant on, having an unrestricted freedom to decide not only what, but *whether*, one is going to be. In effect, both appeals to "human dignity" assume that the debate over the "intrinsic value of human life" has already been settled, and settled in their favor. We now return to that debate realizing that it is at one and the same time a debate about two things: the value of life *and* the meaning of "human dignity." Which meaning is adopted will determine whether it is permitting or prohibiting assisted suicide that infringes upon "human dignity." *End of Excursus.*

In paragraph 12, Sopinka is responding to the appellant's further argument that the value of "life" and the protection of it is not even raised or "engaged" in the case of assisted suicide for a terminally-ill person. For the terminally-ill person, the suicide is not a choice of death itself (which the terminal condition has made inevitable), but rather a choice regarding the timing and manner of the death. Sopinka responds:

Death is, for all mortals, inevitable. Even when death appears imminent, seeking to control the manner and timing of one's death constitutes a conscious choice of death over life. It follows that life as a value is engaged even in the case of the terminally ill who seek to choose death over life.

"Intrinsic Value" not "Absolute Value"

It is important to be clear about what this argument does and does not assert. To say that "life" or more precisely "a living human person" has "intrinsic value," "inherent dignity," or even a non-religious "sacredness" or "inviolability" is not to assert that a person's life is an "absolute" value. If it were an absolute value, its preservation would always take priority over all other values with which it may come into conflict.

Are there any absolute values? Various notable thinkers from St. Augustine to Immanuel Kant have argued that maintaining our "virtue," or "moral integrity," or "faith" ought to be recognized as moral absolutes. Certainly the preservation of these has been seen as justifiably taking priority over the preservation of one's life. To make life an absolute value is to assert that there is nothing worth dying for. It would also give the highest priority to the preservation of something which ultimately can not be preserved. We need not ever lose our integrity, but we inevitably will lose our life. It is possible, of course, to make "life" one's absolute value, but this is not what is done by the conviction Sopinka here appeals to which asserts that human life has "intrinsic value" or "sacredness." It is true that in theology, the "Sacred" and the "Absolute" are often equated, but Sopinka refers with approval to a recent British House of Lords judgment (Airdale N.H.S. Trust v. Bland, [1993] 2 W.L.R. 316) that clearly distinguishes the two. In paragraph 38, he states: "Persistence in a vegetative state was found not to be beneficial to the patient and *the principle of sanctity of life, which was not absolute*, was therefore found not to be violated by the withdrawal of treatment" (emphasis added). In the next paragraph he notes, in reference to the same case, that: "Lord Keith stated at p. 362 that though *the principle of sanctity of life is not an absolute one,* 'it forbids the taking of active measures to cut short the life of a terminally ill patient' " (emphasis added).

Sopinka clearly rejects valuing life as an absolute value when he states in paragraph 14: "I do not draw from this that in such circumstances life as a value must prevail over security of the person or liberty as these have been understood under the Charter, but that it is one of the values engaged in the present case." Sopinka also rejects the sometimes implicit conviction of liberalism that the preservation of "liberty" (or "freedom") or "security" as "control" are absolute values. In paragraph 7 he states:

> None of these values prevail *a priori* over the others. All must be taken into account in determining the content of the principles of fundamental justice and there is no basis for imposing a grater burden on the propounder of one value as against that imposed on another.

If the "intrinsic value" or "sacredness" of a person's life does not mean that it always takes priority over other values or that "life is to be preserved at all costs" (as some have mistakenly contended is the position of the majority in this case), then what does it mean?

The Meaning of "Extrinsic" and "Intrinsic" Values

The key term in this argument is "intrinsic." What does it mean in this context? "Intrinsic" or "inherent" value is used in contrast to "extrinsic" or "contingent" value. To say something has *ex*trinsic or contingent value is to say something about the current relationship of a valuing person(s) to it. Simply stated, something has extrinsic value if somebody, in fact, values it. By "valuing" something we mean an inclination to protect, preserve, or reproduce it. Where there is no such inclination, the reality is not (extrinsically) valued. Things extrinsically valued are also referred to as a "contingent value" inasmuch as its value is contingent on someone valuing it. The "marketplace," "supply-and-demand," or "auction" value of a thing would be an example of extrinsic value. If no one is willing to make any "bid" on a thing, then it has no (extrinsic) value.

Most simply put, something has *in*trinsic value when it *ought to be* valued, whether it is, in fact, valued or not. Intrinsic value is not a function of our valuing. It is a function of the properties inherent or intrinsic to the reality itself. We will consider these properties shortly, but first a common misconception regarding intrinsic value needs to be identified.

Intrinsic value is not a function of the extrinsic valuing *of others*, particularly God. This impression is sometimes created because "intrinsic value" is at times associated with the "sacredness" (a term with clearly theological connotations) of life. One who appeals to intrinsic value is not saying: "other people value this" or "God values this" and "therefore, you ought to too." In relation to the question of suicide, the argument would be that while the person committing suicide may not value their own life, others (family, friends, society, God) do value the continuing life of this person and therefore it ought to be preserved for their sake.[8] This would simply be to make the will of others the arbiter of intrinsic value. In regard to other people, we rightly rhetorically respond: "Who are they to decide what has value?" Mistaking "intrinsic value" with the extrinsic valuing of another is more likely to occur with reference to God. People whose understanding of reality includes a personal, willing God, are more likely to accept the proposition that: "God values this, therefore you ought to as well!" Even theologically however, this is a clearly challengeable assertion. The more tenable theological position is that something does not have intrinsic value because God values it, rather, God values it because it has intrinsic value.

---

[8] This is not to say that one cannot argue against suicide on the basis of its impact on others; this is only to say that such an argument would not be the argument from "intrinsic value."

Intrinsic Value as "Being," as "Good"

The very notion of "intrinsic value," the idea that something has value independently of anyone valuing it, rests upon certain convictions about reality and its know-ability. To say something has intrinsic value is to say something about the thing itself. The category "intrinsic value" rests upon the conviction that we can, at least in a partial way, identify the "good." Beginning with the broadest possible definition, classical philosophy spoke of the "good" as "being" and "evil" as "non-being" or absence of something toward which that type of individual is naturally inclined. This understanding of the good goes back far enough that it is contained in one of those pithy Latin sayings that greying philosophers so like to cite: *ens et bonum convertuntur* (" 'Being' and 'good' are interchangeable"). While we are dealing here on a very generalized, and therefore abstract level, the basic ideas can be simply stated. In setting out the basis of good or value we can begin negatively, that is, by stating that if "something" did not exist in any way, it would have no value at all. "Things" may exist in a variety of ways: ideas exist in a mind (rational existence), material objects have a physical existence, and non-physical, non-rational realities (should they exist) would have a spiritual existence. In all of these cases, the first ground of value or "level of perfection" is found in existing at all. As a starting point, then, we can say that everything which exists or has being is "good" or has intrinsic value by virtue of that existence. Obviously, from the fact that everything that exists has intrinsic value it does not follow that everything that exists has *equal* intrinsic value. The point we are heading toward is that the relative intrinsic value of something is a function of what exists in it. A plant has greater intrinsic value than a pebble because in the plant there exists a more sophisticated organization that gives the plant a number of capabilities that do not exist in the pebble. Unlike the pebble, it can assimilate nutrients and reproduce. Plants are thus described as existing at a "higher" level of being and thus having greater intrinsic value than pebbles. As with pebbles and plants, so to with pets and persons. With each increase in sophistication and powers, there is an increase in the "level of being," or "level of perfection" or "good" or "intrinsic value" of the thing.

The intrinsic value of human life, then, is the value it has by virtue of what it is and what sorts of potentials or powers it has. To treat human life as if it had the same intrinsic value as animal life (recall the movie, "They shoot horses, don't they") or even no more value than plant life (recall the movie "Soyent Green") is to fail to value something as it ought to be valued. Recall that Sopinka referred to human life as having a *deep* intrinsic value.

This position that human life as being self-consciously present to the world is of value in itself and therefore ought to be acknowledged in our valuing of it is rejected, at least rhetorically, in the dissenting judgment of Madam Justice McLachlin. To say that "X" without "Y" is of no value, is to say that it is "Y" that has value in itself, not "X." She rhetorically asks: "But what value is there in life without the choice to do what one wants with one's life, one might counter" (paragraph 92).

Intrinsic Value as Limiting Freedom

To acknowledge that anything has a significant intrinsic value is to accept a duty to be willing to pay a significant cost to protect it. Such a duty limits our freedom. The only way to avoid any limitation on our freedom would be to deny that there is intrinsic value in anything. But even this extreme position requires that I make an exception of "freedom" itself, for if freedom has intrinsic value then I am not free to ignore slavery, dictatorships, extortion, and other limitations on freedom itself.

In general terms, the philosophy that has come to characterize Western societies over the past couple of centuries is called "liberalism" because of the priority given to the value of "liberty" or freedom. This is certainly understandable as a reaction to an age of monarchies in which the freedom of the individual was given a very low priority. Every legitimate and necessary reaction runs the risk of becoming an over-reaction. Like the over-correction of the driver drifting toward the ditch on his right, he still ends up in the ditch, but on the left side of the road. The basic question facing Western societies today is whether it has gone so far in its increased valuing of freedom that freedom alone is acknowledged as having an intrinsic value. Other things are valued, not for their own sake, but only instrumentally as supporting freedom. As the only thing with significant intrinsic value, freedom becomes, in effect, an absolute value. Does life, being alive, have a value apart from being a pre-condition for the exercise of freedom? Cases such as the Sue Rodriguez case are the places where this question is raised and, in its judgment, partially answered. It is hardly surprising that it was a split decision.

The majority judgment contends that life, no less than freedom, has intrinsic value. To say that human life or human persons have intrinsic value is to say that they ought to be protected whether or not they have extrinsic value to anyone, including the person him/herself. As noted earlier, the intrinsic value of human life is preeminently in its potential for self-conscious consciousness, which in turn is the basis for all other forms of human fulfillment. It is obviously the potential which is the precondition of all other potentials.

In the majority judgment, Justice Sopinka does not spell out his understanding of the intrinsic value of human life, but he does suggest that the intrinsic value or "sacredness" of human life can be understood in a way that is not necessarily religious, as articulated for example by Ronald Dworkin [1].

Dworkin on Sanctity of Life

A human life, Dworkin insightfully notes, is a terrible thing to waste. While the insight here may initially seem less than monumental, Dworkin probes the assumptions on which this assertion is based. He undertakes to use these probings to shed light on the acrimonious abortion and euthanasia debates. To assert that human life has "intrinsic" value; that it is "sacred" or "inviolable" is to use the vocabulary of the "conservative" or "pro-life" side of these debates. Dworkin contends, nevertheless, that this assertion is in fact at the heart of both sides of these seemingly irreconcilable debates. The divisions arise due to the differences in the interpretation and application of this value, differences rooted in larger or more basic views of life and reality.

The intrinsic value of life, Dworkin contends, is best understood retrospectively, that is, as a function of the "investments" already made in it. "Investment" is obviously understood here in a broadly encompassing way. Two types of investment can, and must, be distinguished. The first type of investment is that of "nature" (and/or, for those who understand reality theistically, "Nature's God.") This "natural" investment is distinguished from a specifically "human" investment, that is, the investment of various individuals, including the person him/herself. Intrinsic value, as understood by Dworkin, is variable. As we noted above, the intrinsic value of something may be greater or lesser than the intrinsic value of something else. The judgment of how great the intrinsic value of a human life is, will be significantly affected by the relative weight given to the natural and human investments. Each of these types of investments needs to be considered.

The Natural Investment in Human Life

Human life, so far as we know, is the pinnacle of the evolutionary processes that have been going on on this planet for several hundred million years and possibly even since that "big bang" started the entire universe. The natural processes that have led to the evolution of self-consciousness have certainly been complex. In completely naturalistic terms, how it is that the *human brain* is capable of generating a *mind* conscious of itself is something which some experimental psychologists speculate may be beyond the ability of the human mind ever to understand. Even if there is no conscious force (i.e., God) directing evolution to some objective, these blind physical forces have produced some intricate complexities. Nothing is more to be marveled at than the complexity capable of yielding consciousness. No consciousness is more marvelous than consciousness conscious of itself. While it is possible that the universe is studded with self-consciousness or even "higher forms of consciousness" which we cannot conceive, it is also possible that only in the human mind has the universe become aware of itself, wondered about its origins, its dimensions, its destiny. When we focus on images of teeming cities with overpopulated masses, it is easy to lose sight of how extraordinary, in the larger context, a human consciousness is. In a sack of diamonds, a single diamond may seem a common thing. Only when seen in a larger context, is the marvelousness of its qualities likely to be appreciated—its intrinsic value perceived. In addition, however, to the investment of Nature (or for the theistic believer, Nature's God), Dworkin also identifies a different kind of investment which also contributes to the intrinsic value of human life, namely the personal investment.

The Personal Investment in Human Life

By the "personal investment" in a human life, Dworkin is referring to the investment of time, energy, resources, concern, and so on that people have made in a given person. This includes not only the investment of others, but also the investment of the person in securing, developing, and protecting their own well-being. The major difference between the natural investment and the personal investment in the person is that the natural (or divine) investment is the same for all, whereas the personal investment will vary, particularly with the age of a person. The personal investment that has been made to bring a newborn to its present state may be considerable, but it is far less than the personal investment that will have been made by a variety of individuals (including the person him/herself) by the time that that newborn is five or fifteen or twenty-five or fifty years old. Again, to say that this personal investment has contributed to the intrinsic value of the person is to say that that person's self-conscious presence *ought* to be valued by the person him\herself and by others whether this is in fact the case or not.

Contradicting the Valuing of a Person

To say that we value a particular ability means, minimally, that we act in a way consistent with preserving these as much as possible for as long as possible. Valuing an ability, for example, does not mean that we will do anything possible to preserve it, including the jeopardizing of other abilities or values. I might refuse brain surgery which might restore one ability but in the process endanger another. Such choices mean only that I value it as one of several values which may unfortunately come into conflict with one another. While it is not a contradiction to valuing these abilities to recognize the ability to preserve them is limited by our physical nature and other values, it would be a contradiction to valuing them to act in a manner the very design and purpose of which was to destroy them. While noting that there is no consensus on specific arguments by analogy (that we will consider in Argument III), Justice Sopinka does see a more general consensus which finds expression in our laws. At the end of paragraph 54 and continuing on to paragraph 55, he notes:

> To the extent that there is a consensus, it is that human life must be respected and we must be careful not to undermine the institutions that protect it.
>
> This consensus finds legal expression in our legal system which prohibits capital punishment. This prohibition is supported, in part, on the basis that allowing the state to kill will cheapen the value of human life and thus the state will serve in a sense as a role model for individuals in society. The prohibition against assisted suicide serves a similar purpose. In upholding the respect for life, it may discourage those who consider that life is unbearable at a particular moment, or who perceive themselves to be a burden upon others, from committing suicide. To permit a physician to lawfully participate in taking life would send a signal that there are circumstances in which the state approves of suicide.

The "human life" which is being valued here is not understood minimally as the cellular life of the human body, nor maximally as full possession of all one's abilities in a "prime of life" condition. Rather it is understood as the ability to be consciously present to oneself, to others, and to the rest of reality. So long as the potential for the exercise of this ability exists, the potential for a human existence exists. Of course we would intensely prefer that all of our abilities could be preserved at their highest levels until we die. Yet there is an intrinsic value to the ability to be self-consciously present even where other abilities are lost or diminished. With this ability and some minimal communication it is possible to love, to value the presence of another and their love for you. Even when one can no longer make dinner or cut the lawn, it is possible to sympathize with another's problems, rejoice with them in their accomplishments and good fortune. It is in our mind, not our muscles, that our greatest potential for fulfillment and contribution to others is to be found.

II. THE INTRINSIC WRONGFULNESS OF "ACTIVE" KILLING

Argument: The active participation by one individual in the death of another is intrinsically morally and legally wrong.

After reviewing the examination of assisted suicide by the English House of Lords and the Law Reform Commission of Canada, Sopinka concludes in paragraph 43:

> It can be seen, therefore that while both the House of Lords, and the Law Reform Commission of Canada have great sympathy for the plight of those who wish to end their lives so as to avoid significant suffering, neither has been prepared to recognize that the active assistance of a third party in carrying out this desire should be condoned, even for the terminally ill. The basis for this refusal is twofold it seems—first, the active participation by one individual in the death of another is intrinsically morally and legally wrong, ...

Misidentification of the Relevant Difference as "Active" vs. "Passive"

The first thing that must be said about this argument is that it is badly stated.[9] The problem is with the use of the qualifier "active." Sopinka obviously uses this term because it is used by Lord Goff in the House of Lords judgment (Airedale N.H.S. Trust v. Bland, [1993]) and in paragraph 43 Sopinka is referring to his views. In this judgment allowing the withdrawal of treatment, Lord Goff draws explicitly on the distinction between "active" and "passive" euthanasia.

Why is it problematic to refer to the prohibited killing as that which involved the "active participation" of a person? The problem is that it misidentifies the relevant consideration as the "activeness" of the behavior. What has been prohibited in a centuries-old moral-legal principle is not "active" killing, but rather the "direct killing of the innocent." What it means to cause a harm, including death, *directly* acquired a precise technical meaning within the tradition that used this terminology. "Direct" killing, may be and often is "active" killing, but it is not its activeness that

---

[9] I am not referring to the reference to a "third" party, where "second" would seem the appropriate numeration.

makes it "direct." As we shall see, it is possible to kill "directly" by omission, or indirectly by action. It is the "direct killing of the innocent" that has been judged to be "intrinsically morally and legally wrong" not "active participation in the death of another." The problem here is not some persnickety concern about historical accuracy. The problem is that in this *misstated* form the principle is indefensible, as the dissenting judgment by Madam Justice McLachlin is quick to point out. After citing Sopinka's formulation, McLachlin replies in paragraph 90:

> The answer to this is that Parliament has not exhibited a consistent intention to criminalize acts which cause the death of another. Individuals are not subject to criminal penalty when their omissions cause the death of another. Those who are under a legal duty to provide the "necessaries of life" are not subject to criminal penalty where a breach of this duty causes death, if a lawful excuse is made out, for instance the consent of the party who dies, or incapacity to provide: see Criminal Code, s. 215. Again, killing in self-defense is not culpable. Thus there is no absolute rule that causing or assisting in the death of another is criminally wrong. Criminal culpability depends on the circumstances in which the death is brought about or assisted. The law has long recognized that if there is a valid justification for bringing about someone's death, the person who does so will not be held criminally responsible.

If this reply constitutes a valid rebuttal of the argument regarding the "intrinsic wrongfulness" of assisting suicide, then it seriously weakens the majority's overall position. A careful, at time line-by-line analysis is necessary to determine its validity. McLachlin's reply does point out the error of Sopinka's misstatement of the principle regarding what has been judged to be "intrinsically morally and legally wrong." It can be shown, however, that McLachlin's reply is not a valid rebuttal of the principle accurately stated. Accurately stated, the principle identifies two morally significant variables in determining the justifiability of the killing: (1) the "innocence" or "guilt" of the person killed and (2) the "directness" of the killing. "Innocence" here is taken as referring either to moral culpability or to material aggression. Capital punishment was justifiable because the person executed was judged to be morally culpable for their crime and thus appropriately punished by an action intended to kill him. Capital punishment, while "direct" is not a violation of the prohibition of the "direct killing of the *innocent.*" The argument was applied to the morally culpable aggressor killed in self- (or other-) defense in hopes of preventing the killing of the apparent victim. Active participation in the killing of the innocent could also be justified, but only where that killing was not "direct."

The Difference Between "Active" Killing and "Direct" Killing

In the context of moral discourse, "direct" has a technical meaning not synonymous with "active." "Directness" refers to the object or end pursued by the employment of the deadly means; the purpose for which the means are used. A killing is therefore "direct" if the means employed have as their immediate objective the death of the person killed. When death is the objective, the means are chosen precisely because of their capacity to cause death. In capital punishment, for example, an injection or electric charge foreseen to be capable of rendering the prisoner paralyzed or comatose or catatonic (but not dead) would not be chosen except by mistake. If such a mistake were made, the injection or voltage would be increased until it was capable of producing death. The action is not "completed" until death has occurred. Thus the form of the old death sentence: "You shall be hung by your neck *until dead*." Certainly in most actions where death is the objective, the only means able to produce this result will require some *overt action* for the simple reason that we are rarely in a vulnerable situation where the *omission* of an action by another has the capacity to cause our death. If such a situation did arise, however, a person who chose not to act *in order to* bring about a person's death would have *directly* killed that person by omission. By altering the facts of an actual case we can see an example of this. Several people out on a yacht drowned when they all decided one night in the middle of a lake to jump overboard for a swim. After the last person had jumped in the water, they realized that no one had remembered to throw the rope ladder over the side of the boat so they could climb back on board. Suppose that we alter the facts slightly so that one person remained on board, realized the situation, but chose to ignore their pleas to throw the ladder over the side although he could easily have done so. The only intended end which could make sense of the choice not to act would be the death by drowning of the people in the water. If in fact this is the intention, we can expect that he will persist in this omission until all have drowned. This person would be no less guilty of murder than if he had caused their deaths by an overt action, say, pulling the ladder that had been thrown overboard back onto the boat while the others were still in the water. Where the objective of employing the means (be it an overt action or an omission) is death, the act is one of direct killing.

McLachlin Rebuttal of Sopinka's Assertion Regarding "Active" Killing

In her reply to Sopinka's assertion regarding "active" participation, McLachlin assumes the irrelevance of the commission-omission distinction in itself by pointing first to a case of omission. She notes: "Individuals are not subject to criminal penalty when their omissions cause the death of another." Here she is referring to the absence in the English common law tradition of an obligation to assist a person to whom a "duty of care" is not owed. Apart from this qualification however, does this statement as a generally true proposition contradict my contention that "direct" and therefore morally and legally culpable killing is possible by omission? To answer this we must first deal with the ambiguity in the statement itself. In doing so we will also see how the use of the terms "action" and "omission" or "active" and "passive" function like the magician's gestures to misdirect our attention.

When Can Omissions be Said to "Cause" Effects?

The term "omissions" can refer to: (A) actions I, without significant obstacle, was capable of doing but which I freely and knowingly chose not to do, or (B) anything else which I did not do, including things which I was not capable of doing, or could have done only at great risk of life and limb, or which I had no right to do, or which it never occurred to me to do, etc. An assertion could be quite reasonable assuming that the speaker had "A-type" omissions in mind, but become quite unreasonable if the term "omission" were understood to refer to those of the "B-type." McLachlin leaves it to us to infer from the context which meaning she has in mind. Before pursuing this, however, let me state that direct killing is only possible by A-type omissions. Recall that "direct" killing is killing where the means are *chosen in order to* bring about the death. It is meaningless to speak of choice were there is no ability to perform the act contemplated, or even more so where the act was never even contemplated. Omissions which are chosen in order to respect the non-interference rights of others would be falsely characterized if they were characterized as having "caused" the consequences of the choices of those not interfered with. This would be to say that by not "marrying off" my child to a "suitable" person, even without my child's consent, I have "caused" the heart-break of the marriage breakup to their own immature choice. Or closer to the case, that by not restraining and inserting a force-feeding tube down the throat of a mentally-competent, adult hunger-striker, I have "caused" the damage to their health or even their death that the hunger-strike, which they have chosen, causes. It is equally absurd to say that I have "caused" consequences of not providing some assistance to another when that person, assuming again that they are a mentally-competent adult, has chosen to waive any right to that assistance, or declined it when offered.

In Justice McLachlin's reply to Sopinka, her assertion regarding "omissions" clearly implies the omnibus "B-type" of omissions with their highly dubious "causalities." In the next sentence (see the citation from paragraph 90, above), she notes that there is no criminal penalty for one who "causes death" by not providing the "necessities of life" due to an "incapacity to provide" them. Of course not. There is no criminal penalty, nor moral culpability, for not doing anything one lacked the capacity to do. This reflects no more than the basic axiom of moral logic: "Ought implies Can." It cannot be read as indicating an inconsistent intention of Parliament regarding the direct killing (even by omission) of the innocent.

McLachlin's second example of someone not being subject to criminal penalty by virtue of a "lawful excuse" for "causing death" by not providing the necessities of life is where this omission is with "the consent of the person who dies." As noted above, this reply relies upon an unsupportable notion of causality. It is to say that we "cause" whatever consequences follow from our not performing actions which would have been our duty had we not been relieved of them by the consent of the person to whom they are owed. If this over-extended understanding of causality were adopted, we would have abandoned the very important distinction between "causing" something and "permitting it." The connection between causality and responsibility is severed, for I can be said to have "caused" something for which I have no responsibility. When someone waives my duty to them, I am relieved of the responsibility to perform it (assuming that it is a duty they have the right and capacity to waive), yet with McLachlin's usage I can still be said to have "caused" the consequences of not doing what I had no responsibility to do. This kind of imprecision in the use of basic concepts like "causality" leads to conclusions like: we all cause everything that happens because of something we did not do even though we had no responsibility to do. In summary, the omissions to which McLachlin refers are in the first case, not a choice at all (because of incapacity), or in the second case, not a "cause" of the death in any reasonable sense. Neither provides a counter-example to show an "inconsistent intention" on the part of Parliament in criminalizing acts of omission chosen in order to cause death.

McLachlin offers another instance to support her contention regarding Parliament's inconsistent intention: "Again, killing in self-defense is not culpable." While killing in self-defense would certainly violate the no "active participation in killing" principle, does it violate the correctly stated "no direct killing of the innocent" principle? Just as "direct" killing may be accomplished by inaction, "indirect" killing may involve overt action or commission. Killing is "indirect" where the act (of commission or omission) meets a number of conditions. First, it is chosen as a means to some other and justifiable end. This means that the death, while foreseen as a certainty or possibility, is not among the ends sought by the means. If the possibility of achieving the objective while avoiding the death unexpectedly arises, that possibility will be seized. This also means that it is not the death itself which produces the end which is sought, for if this were, the death would be one of the objectives (albeit so that it could in turn produce a further objective). Second, the other objective must be of comparable value to the loss of life. For example, the saving of a life or lives would be of sufficient value to accept the loss of life where there was no possibility of saving those lives without a loss of life. Other values, such as the protection of one's bodily integrity, could also be seen to be of such a value to allow the acceptance of a death. In other words, the death is "indirect" when it is the unintended, even if foreseen, yet unavoidable side-effect of the pursuit of a value comparable to the value of life.

Lethal force could be directed at a psychotic gunman shooting into a trapped crowd of people because he posed an immediate physical threat to human lives even though he may not be morally culpable by virtue of his psychosis. The objective here is not his death, but his incapacitation from causing further harm. At first it may seem that this is playing some kind of word or mind games. A moment's reflection comparing this to the case of direct killing in capital punishment reveals the real differences between the two. In the case of the psychotic gunman, if he is paralyzed or otherwise immobilized by the shots of the police without being killed, the action is completed and no further force is employed. In fact, at this point the gunman will be rushed along with the other victims to the hospital in an attempt to save his life. This is the standard police procedure with any violent aggressor because they are assumed innocent until their guilt can be established in court. Only then would punishment, including capital punishment, be indicated. This is also why no violence can be used against an aggressor once she/he has incapacitated herself/himself, i.e., surrendered. Because the objective is solely incapacitation, only sufficient force to assure that is justified. If nothing less than lethal force can assure incapacitation, then lethal force can be used—not because it is lethal, but because it is the minimal force sufficient to incapacitate. In this case, the external action will be indistinguishable for one in which the intent is to kill the aggressor. This does not mean, however, that as *human* actions they are the same, for *human* actions are external actions chosen to some *end* recognized as the *purpose for* choosing the external action. There is a real (although not visible) difference in the purposes (killing vs. incapacitation) making them different as *human actions* even though they are not different as physical events with physical consequences. It is only as human actions (that is as "end-directed") that they are capable of expressing our character or being a part of the pursuit of larger, more encompassing goals. It is only as human actions that activities can have a moral quality, namely, morally right or morally wrong. In short, it is theoretically possible that two physically identical actions with identical physical consequences could have the opposite moral quality by virtue of being directed to different ends. One could be direct killing, the other indirect killing. While there will be differences in what *would* be done if incapacitation were achieved without killing (in direct killing, more force is used until the person is dead; in indirect killing, the person is given what medical assistance is available to prevent death) the opportunity for these differences to become visible may not arise. The legal (and moral) permissibility of "killing in self-defense" does not show an inconsistent intention of Parliament to criminalize the "direct killing of the innocent."

A second category of killings of innocent persons which involve the "active participation" of someone, but which are nonetheless rightly categorized as "indirect," are the killings that can be properly categorized as "collateral deaths." This is the situation where innocent bystanders in close physical proximity to a legitimate military target are foreseeably victims of the weapons aimed not at them but at the target. If the death of these bystanders were intended as a kind of "bonus" to the destruction of the military target then the killing of them would be direct. This type of bombing strategy is unfortunately something of which history can provide many examples. It is possible however that these deaths can be genuinely unintended for they contribute nothing to incapacitating the military capacity of the aggressor. Further, it is not these deaths which causes the destruction of the military target. What external evidence would tend to support the assertion that these deaths really are "collateral" and not intended? The most compelling evidence would be the efforts taken to minimize such deaths, most notably the development of greater precision in the targeting of these weapons allowing a reduction in the warhead size without reducing its ability to destroy its target. If the kind of precision targeting demonstrated during the Gulf War were to become the norm in aerial warfare, it would reduce the number of deaths in the "enemy" population. This would support the contention that they are not intended. Other measures, such as announcing in advance that bombing raids or missile attacks would begin would allow people to avoid being close to military targets as much as possible. This is part of the reason for the traditional requirement that war be declared.

The law in the Western legal tradition has not regarded all killing, nor in the formula adopted by Justice Sopinka "active participation" in all killing as "intrinsically morally and legally wrong." It has, however, regarded all "*direct* killing of the *innocent*" as intrinsically morally and legally wrong. The kinds of killing that Justice McLachlin cites to challenge this argument are either the direct killing of the *guilty*, or the *indirect* killing of the innocent. As we have seen, the decisive element in determining the prohibited killing is the intention.

What would be the application of the properly stated principle to the issue at hand, namely, assisting another to commit suicide. The would-be suicide is neither morally culpable, deserving of punishment, nor an immediate physical threat to anyone, and therefore is "innocent." As innocent, the only killing which could possibly be justified would be *indirect*. However, an act intended to assist in the suicide would be intended to bring about the death of the person (and would not be completed until the person was dead), that is to say, it would be *direct* killing. Thus the principle as Justice Sopinka *should* have cited it *does* support the prohibition of assisting in suicide. It would be prohibited, not because the killing involves "active participation" but rather because it would constitute the direct (intended) killing of the innocent.

As we will develop more fully in regard to the next argument, terminology like "active euthanasia" and "passive euthanasia" misdirects our attention away from the intention. It is as if one were to refer to throwing a non-swimmer into a river so that they would die as "active drowning" and not jumping into the river to rescue the non-swimmer as "passive drowning." At first this may seem like plausible terminology, until we realize that the intention for not jumping in may not have been "so that they would die." If I did not jump in because I am a very weak swimmer and would be very likely to die myself before even reaching the non-swimmer, it is a serious misrepresentation to call my "not jumping in" a case of "passive drowning" of the non-swimmer. On the other hand, if we change the location of our example from a swift flowing river to a wading pool where the non-swimmer is a toddler, throwing the child in and not stepping in to lift the child out may indeed be characterized as "active" and "passive" forms of drowning. The equivalence is based on the fact that, at the side of the wading pool, only an *intention* to have the child drown would make sense of a decision either to throw the child in or not to lift the child out. In short, we are talking about what I called a "Type A" omission. The use of this terminology wrongly suggests that this is true in all cases. The concept of directness is also important in relation to the Court's next argument regarding morally analogous practices to which we now turn.

III. THE REAL DIFFERENCE BETWEEN ASSISTING SUICIDE AND TWO ACCEPTED PRACTICES

Argument: The analogies to other sorts of actions which are legally and morally permitted, namely, not using "extraordinary means" to sustain life, or giving pain-killing drugs which may shorten life, are not valid analogies.

The majority argument here is actually a response to the argument raised in two of the dissenting judgments, that of Justices McLachlin and Cory. It will be simpler to begin with their argument and then consider the reply of the majority. This argument rightly contends that it is *arbitrary* to allow one activity while prohibiting an activity that is the moral equivalent of it.

If Arbitrary, Then Unconstitutional

What would be the Constitutional significance of this argument if it is a valid argument. The significance is to be found in the requirement of Section 7 of the Charter of Rights and Freedoms which states that infringements of our liberty or security of the person be in accordance with the principles of "fundamental justice" and in Section 1 which states that any law which limits our rights and/or freedom, (as this law, like most laws, certainly does) must be a "reasonable limit" on that right and/or freedom; but a law that is genuinely arbitrary could not be regarded as consistent with fundamental justice. Furthermore, while a limited inconsistency with fundamental justice might be found to be reasonable (when applying Section 1), a limit would certainly not be reasonable if the injustice were due to *arbitrariness*. To be arbitrary, i.e., without adequate reason, is the antithesis or any notion of justice and by definition is unreasonable. Madam Justice McLachlin finds the prohibition of assisting suicide to be arbitrary in two ways. The first of these will be dealt with in this argument, the second in Argument IV. Arbitrariness creates an unreasonable inconsistency with fundamental justice. This arbitrariness is to be found, not within a single law, but rather by looking at the result of a set of laws which together constitute a "legal scheme." In this argument she will contend that two facts taken together, namely (1) that "A" (which is equivalent to "B" or "C") is prohibited, while (2) "B" and "C" are not prohibited, constitutes an "arbitrary scheme" of law. In this case the prohibition of "A" would be "arbitrary" unless "B" and "C" were also prohibited (which they are not). The crux of this argument is obviously going to be whether "A" is in fact equivalent to "B" or "C." Justice McLachlin will contend that she can see no difference between them; Justice Sopinka will argue that he can.

The Alleged Arbitrariness

Before responding to it, Sopinka provides a succinct statement of the minority line of argument in paragraph 21:

> It is also argued that the extension of the prohibition to the appellant is arbitrary and unfair as . . .[10] the common law allows a physician to withhold or withdraw life-saving or life-maintaining treatment on the patient's instructions and to administer palliative care which has the effect of hastening death. The issue is whether, given this legal context, the existence of a criminal prohibition on

---

[10] The words omitted at this ellipsis are "suicide itself is not unlawful, and." This refers to the second way in which McLachlin sees this legal scheme as arbitrary. This will be discussed in Argument IV.

assisting suicide for one in the appellant's situation is contrary to principles of fundamental justice.

Justices McLachlin and Cory speak for many people when they contend that they cannot see any morally relevant difference between: assisting a person in committing suicide (hereafter "AS") and not starting or withdrawing treatment that might extend a persons life (hereafter "NT"); or between AS and giving pain-killing drugs which might hasten the end of a person's life (hereafter "PK"). Justice McLachlin, in paragraph 91, states:

> This conclusion meets the contention that only passive assistance—the withdrawal of support necessary to life—should be permitted. If the justification for helping someone to end life is established, I cannot accept that it matters whether the act is "passive"—the withdrawal of support necessary to sustain life—or "active"—the provision of a means to permit a person of sound mind to choose to end his or her life with dignity.

Justice Cory, in paragraph 234, makes the same argument:
> I can see no difference between permitting a patient of sound mind to choose death with dignity by refusing treatment and permitting a patient of sound mind who is terminally ill to choose death with dignity by terminating life preserving treatment, even if, because of incapacity, that step has to be physically taken by another on her instructions. Nor can I see any reason for failing to extend that same permission so that a terminally ill patient facing death may put an end to her life through the intermediary of another, as suggested by Sue Rodriguez.

The reason that Justices McLachlin and Cory do not see a difference between the types of activities that *they* describe is because, morally, there *is* none. However, *their* analogy, while valid, does *not* show the unreasonableness of continuing to prohibit AS while permitting NT or PK because of an ambiguity regarding what NT and PK refer to. That to which McLachlin and Cory draw a valid analogy is not what has been morally endorsed in existing practice. To detect this ambiguity, two things are necessary: (1) Recognition of the basic elements to be examined when seeking to understand and evaluate a human action, and (2) a careful examination of exactly what type of action is being described in these arguments.

1. Basic Elements in Understanding or Evaluating a Human Action: Motive, End, and Means

There are two dimensions to human actions reflecting the two dimensions to human persons. An "internal" or non-physical dimension arising from the mind and will of the person, namely, the "end," "objective," or "purpose" which the person had decided to seek; and an external dimension or physical activity (or inactivity) chosen by the person as the "means" to realize that end in a physical world. A human activity is, of course, an event in the physical world but to be understood *as a human action* it is necessary to examine why or for what purpose it was done. I may be able to project the consequences of a particular activity without knowing why it was done, but I will not understand the action without knowing its "end." Without knowing why this person did this or did not do that, I will not learn anything about the identity or character of the person who acted. It is true that we can sometimes infer, with a high degree of certainty, why an intelligent person would have performed a certain action because the action would only serve a narrow range of ends. But other actions are capable of being the "means" to very different types of ends. Here the inferences will be less certain and the action will have to be examined very carefully to draw an even uncertain inference.

The "end" of an action is often not clearly distinguished from the "motive" for pursuing the "end" to which we choose the "means." Sometimes there is no great harm in lumping "motive" and "end" together, but in other cases the failure to distinguish them leads to a serious lack of clarity. "Motive" is a broader, more encompassing orientation than is an "end." Motives are often identified as generalized sorts of relationships such as greed, revenge, ambition, compassion, jealousy, gratitude, repentance, etc. These generalized orientations are expressed or embodied in the decision to bring about a particular end. For example, because I am greedy I hire a collection agency to re-possess the car you bought from me on credit and on which you have missed a payment. The motive is greed, the end is repossession of this car, the means is hiring. The same action (end and means) could arise as an expression of other motives, say, revenge for something you had done to harm me. The same motive could and probably will be expressed in a variety of other actions. Because motive refers to the general relationship out of which the intending of an end and the choice of a means to that end arises, it is much more difficult to infer the motive of the action than to infer the intended end. While I may be able to infer, even beyond a reasonable doubt, what you intended to do from a careful examination of what you did, this examination will not necessarily produce the same degree of certainty regarding the motive. This is why it is necessary in a murder trial to establish, usually by inference, what is intended but not what the motive was for intending it.[11] This difficulty would become critical if the motive were to determine the criminality of the action. This difficulty is noted by the Law Reform Commission Report which is cited by Justice Sopinka in paragraph 41:

> As in the case of "compassionate murder", decriminalization of aiding suicide would be based on the humanitarian nature of the motive leading the person to provide such aid, counsel or encouragement. As in the case of compassionate murder, moreover, the law may legitimately fear the difficulties involved in determining the true motivation of the person committing the act.

How is it that we are able to infer, with varying degrees of certainty, the end of an action by a close examination of the means chosen in a particular set of

---

[11] While demonstrating the presence of a hostile relationship/motive (e.g., jealousy, revenge, etc.) makes it easier to believe that a person intended a particular harm, a conviction would be appropriate even if the motive were misidentified provided that the intention was correctly identified. There are also "senseless" "random" crimes with no apparent motive.

circumstances? The "end" of the action is sometimes called the "terminus" in the sense that the means will continue to be employed until this state is produced. Before this state is reached, the action is seen as "incomplete;" after it is reached, further action is "superfluous" and, if it continues, must be directed to some further end.

In the expression "mercy killing" we have an identification of both the motive, i.e., "mercy," and the end, i.e., the "killing" of the individual. To achieve this end, some lethal means (action or inaction) will have to be employed until the death of the person results. Until the person is dead, the action is not complete. The means are chosen for their ability to produce the death (the end.). The end of death is sought because one identifies with the suffering person and seeks to end that suffering (a motive of "mercy"). What makes "mercy killing" an anomaly is not that death is the end but rather that mercy (a positively regarded motive) is not typical of the motives which lead people to seek the death of others. What makes "mercy killing" a moral problem is obviously not whether mercy or compassion is desirable; it is whether it makes sense, all things considered, to seek the death of another as an embodiment of that motive.

Both the motives which move me, and the ends the motives lead me to choose, reveal something of my character. Certain motives, for example, compassion and gratitude, are positively regarded because they characterize the sort of person we judge it makes sense to try to be. Other motives such as greed jealousy, or revenge are regarded negatively for the same reason. Further, some motives such as ambition may be regarded as potentially positive or negative depending on the particular type of ends and means it leads the person to choose. It is possible that a positively regarded motive may lead one to choose an action which is without adequate justification. Because I feel compassion for the suffering of my child struggling to complete an assignment, I step in and do the assignment myself. Not every action which arises out of a positively regarded motive is, by virtue of that alone, a justifiable action. The refrain: "Your motives were good, but . . ." has become an all too familiar part of our lives. One of life's challenges is to find intelligent reasonable ways to embody our good motivations.

The question addressed in this third argument is not directly the justifiability of mercy killing or assisting suicide, but rather its moral equivalence to activities already approved and allowed. If they are morally equivalent, then it would be arbitrary to allow one and prohibit the other. Assuming that what is currently allowed is justified, we indirectly justify by analogy, that which we can show is morally equivalent to it.

We noted above that the same motive could be embodied in the pursuit of a variety of different ends, and that the same ends could be sought out of a variety of motives. It is also possible that the same means may be chosen to a variety of ends. This is possible where an activity produces more that one effect. Any one (or combination) of effects may be the end sought, that is, the reason why the means is chosen. Not treating or giving pain-killers are examples of this type of activity (means) where the "end" for which they are done is not always readily obvious. This is particularly significant because for two actions to be morally equivalent, the "end" of each action must be the same. If the ends are different, the actions *as human actions* (which are precisely means *to an end*) are not the same.

2. The Human Actions Compared in the McLachlin-Cory Analogies

When McLachlin and Cory make their argument by analogy they do identify both the means and the "end" or the "purpose" of the action or inaction but this is done almost in passing and without focusing on the moral significance of the purpose. Let us take a close look at both the "means" and the "end" on each side of the analogy.

On one side of the analogy is "AS" assisting suicide. The end here is the death of the person who had decided to commit suicide. The means may vary, but assuming that they are intelligently chosen, they will have a lethal potential and will be chosen precisely because of that potential. On the other side of the analogy we have either "NT," not starting or withdrawing treatment that might extend a persons life; or "PK," giving pain-killing drugs which might hasten the end of a person's life. The critical question here is what is the *end* to which these activities are chosen as a means? Is the end for which these means are chosen the *death* of the patient? The only general answer that can be given is "Possibly 'yes', but not necessarily; so possibly 'no'." The answer is "Possibly 'yes' " because it is possible that treatments are not used, or pain-killers are administered/taken, because of the life-shortening potential of these courses of action. As we said above, any of the foreseeable effects may be the one *on account of which* the action is chosen as a means. When, *but only when*, these are chosen as means to the end of death, NT and PK *are* morally equivalent to assisting suicide. They are morally equivalent because the intention, the intended end, is the same.[12] But the answer is also "Possibly 'no'" because it is not necessary that death is the intended end. It is quite possible that the pain-killers are used because of their pain-relieving potential, not their death-hastening potential. It is possible that the choice is made not to undertake or continue treatments because of the potential of "not treating" to lessen the burdens or pains born by the patient, not its potential to shorten the patient's life. Not only may this death-hastening or life-shortening potential not be the reason for the choice of the means, this potential may be profoundly unwanted and regretted. If a course of action were available to alleviate the pain as effectively without introducing the death-hastening possibility, that course of action would unhesitatingly be chosen because "pain-relief" not "death-hastening" is the end. If life-extending treatments were available which promised benefits to the patient clearly exceeding the costs or burdens they imposed on the patient, they too would be chosen. In short, because both "NT" and "PK" can be chosen to significantly different ends (death vs. pain-relief or burden avoidance)

---

[12]Recall from our earlier example that it was possible (in a "Type A" omission) that I did not jump into the river to save the drowning person *because I wanted them to die,* in which case my *not* jumping in *would be* morally equivalent to throwing the person in the river. But, given different circumstances, it was also possible that my intention for not jumping in was simply not to drown myself.

and as such are significantly different human actions, there is a serious ambiguity as to which human action is being referred to. In fact, which "NT" or which "PK" are being referred to is decisive in this argument because one of the "NTs" *is* analogous to "AS," but the other is not. The same is true of the "PKs." Furthermore, it is the one that is *not* analogous which has been approved in the common law and in medical practice. In order to keep these different actions distinct, let us refer to "pain-killers given in order to shorten the life of the patient" as "PK to death" and "pain-killers given in order to relieve pain" as "PK to relief." Similarly, let us refer to "withholding or withdrawing treatment in order to advance the time of the patient's death" as "NT to death" and "withholding or withdrawing treatment in order to not impose treatment burdens/costs disproportionate to the likely benefits to be experienced" as "NT to unburden." Which NT are McLachlin and Cory referring to when they claim an identity with AS? Note that McLachlin says:

> If the justification *for helping* someone *to end life* is established, I cannot accept that it matters whether the act is "passive"—the withdrawal of support necessary to sustain life—or "active"—the provision of a means to permit a person of sound mind *to choose to end his or her life* with dignity (emphasis added).

McLachlin clearly indicates here that she is thinking of "NT to death," that is, not treating *in order to* help end life. The same is true of Justice Cory, when he states: "I can see no difference between permitting a patient of sound mind *to choose death with dignity by refusing treatment* . . ." (emphasis added). Both justices are correct in what they say. When the intended end of both actions is to bring about death, it does not matter whether the means is active or passive. Cory does not see a difference because there is none. He is correct that it would be arbitrary to approve "NT to death" while disapproving AS, which of it very nature is means chosen "to the death" of the other. The argument fails, however, because of what the Justices assume, namely, that "NT *to death*" is what had been morally defended and legally protected. The same argument would apply to the analogy to giving pain-killing drugs. While "PK to death" is analogous to AS, it is "PK to relief" that is approved. The significance of the intention is recognized by McLachlin and Cory, for it is precisely the correspondence of the intention in "NT to death" and "PK to death" to the intention in AS that forms the basis for the analogy that they assert. By the same token, however, "NT to unburden" and "PK to relief" are not analogous to AS because of the difference in the intention.

The intention, as a mental act, obviously cannot be directly observed. If it is to be known, it must be inferred from the action. There are situations in which two different intended ends will call for identical actions as a means. In these situations, it will not be possible to infer which end is being pursued by the action. In many situations, however, differences in exactly what is done or not done will provide a legitimate basis for inference. For example, is there any observable indication of whether a pain-killing drug is being given for its death-advancing or its relief-providing potential? The most obvious indicator is the extent to which the means is applied. If the drug is given in sufficient quantities to alleviate the pain, but no more than that, this is an indication that pain relief is in fact the end. Of course, it is possible that a person giving or receiving the drugs actually desires the death-advancing effects of the drugs but does not proceed after the pain is relieved for fear of legal consequences given the present state of the law. To know this would require clairvoyance or a believable self-incriminating assertion on the part of the individuals involved. These are difficulties in terms of *proving* which end is intended. While these evidentiary difficulties will restrict what a Court is willing to do, it does not remove the underlying significance of intending one end rather than another. The action itself, which provides enough, but only enough, drug to relieve the pain can be said to be suited to or proportionate to the end of relieving pain. As a means to causing death, it is deficient and therefore ineffective. As a person's condition deteriorates it is sometimes necessary to increase the dosage to provide effective pain-relief. It is possible that these increases would continue until the point where effective pain relief would also be effective in causing death. At this point we have the situation mentioned above where two different ends would both call for the identical means. By observing the action itself it would not be possible to infer which end is being pursued. This does not remove the possibility, however, that only one of the effects being caused is the end being pursued. The fact that the lethal dosage is not used until it is also the minimally effective pain-relieving dosage, is consistent with intending only the end of pain relief and not the foreseeable death.

The determination of "criminality" within the Western legal tradition has always included a determination (typically by inference) of the intention. Generally speaking, without a "criminal intent" a harmful action does not constitute a "crime," although it may still be a "tort" leaving the perpetrator liable to be sued for damages. The courts are thus quite familiar with the crucial difference that the presence or absence of a particular intention may make. It is not surprising that Justice Sopinka goes directly to the intention to identify why permitted pain-relieving drugs were not morally or legally equivalent to the prohibited assisting of suicide. While acknowledging the difficulties in some cases of *proving* which intent is embodied in the action, he stresses the significance of the differences in the intention. In paragraph 52, he explains:

> The fact that doctors may deliver palliative care to terminally ill patients without fear of sanction, it is argued, attenuates to an even greater degree any legitimate distinction which can be drawn between assisted suicide and what are currently acceptable forms of medical treatment. The administration of drugs designed for pain control in dosages which the physician knows will hasten death constitutes active contribution to death by any standard.[13] *However, the distinction drawn here is one based upon intention—in the case of palliative care the intention is to ease pain, which has the effect of hastening death, while in the case of assisted*

---

[13]Here Sopinka seems to recognize, albeit in passing, that contrary to his earlier formulation, it is not the "active participation" in causing the death of another that is inherently morally and legally wrong. If it were, then this palliative care would be wrong. Here he clarifies, without using the term, that what is morally/legally significant is that it is not "direct" (intended) death-hastening.

> suicide, the intention is undeniably to cause death. The Law Reform Commission, although it recommended the continued criminal prohibition of both euthanasia and assisted suicide, stated, at p. 70 of the Working Paper, that a doctor should never refuse palliative care to a terminally ill person only because it may hasten death. In my view, distinctions based upon intent are important, and in fact form the basis of our criminal law. While factually the distinction may, at times, be difficult to draw, legally it is clear. The fact that in some cases, the third party will, under the guise of palliative care, commit euthanasia or assist in suicide and go unsanctioned due to the difficulty of proof cannot be said to render the existence of the prohibition fundamentally unjust (emphasis added).

While this distinction in the intention demonstrates a morally significant difference (and thus invalidates the analogy) between assisting suicide and giving pain-killers *for the purpose of* relieving pain (and not for the purpose of advancing death), Sopinka does not clearly articulate the fact that the same line of argument applies to the other alleged analogy, namely the one to the approved practice of not treating (withholding/withdrawing potential life-sustaining or prolonging treatment).

Not Treating, Intention, and the "Active" vs. "Passive" Distinction

The alleged analogy between AS and NT is subject to the same rebuttal as applied to PK, namely, that while AS is analogous to "NT to death," it is not analogous to "NT to unburden" and it is "NT to unburden" that is morally approved in medical practice. Because this argument from the intention is not developed, the majority judgment relies on the distinction between "active" and "passive" euthanasia—a distinction which will not support the conclusions based upon it. In reading the attempts to explain or defend the relevance of this distinction it is possible, I believe, to detect a defensive, almost apologetic tone. The main argument for basing policy on this distinction seems to come down to the fact that it has been widely used, by governments and prestigious groups, for a long time. This argument from authority and/or tradition is far from persuasive to a large segment of the population and one gets the sense that the Court realizes this. Listen, for example, to the statement of Lord Goff, of the English House of Lords in a recent case, cited by Sopinka in paragraph 39:

> It is true that the drawing of this distinction may lead to charge of hypocrisy; because it can be asked why, if the doctor, by discontinuing treatment, is entitled in consequence to let his patient die, it should not be lawful to put him out of his misery straight away, in a more humane manner, by a lethal injection, rather than let him linger on in pain until he dies. But the law does not feel able to authorize euthanasia, even in circumstances such as these; for once euthanasia is recognized as lawful in these circumstances, it is difficult to see any logical basis for excluding it in others.

The reply to this faint-hearted defense is obvious. If it is indeed hypocrisy, then "the law" should get over its "feeling" of inability and authorize assisting suicide; and if there is no logical basis for excluding non-terminal cases, then it should be extended to them.

Sopinka is also clearly aware of the challenge to the validity of this distinction, as he notes in paragraph 50:

> The distinction between withdrawing treatment upon a patient's request, such as occurred in the Nancy B case, on the one hand, and assisted suicide on the other has been criticized as resting on a legal fiction—that is, the distinction between active and passive forms of treatment. The criticism is based on the fact that the withdrawal of life supportive measures is done with the knowledge that death will ensue, just as is assisting suicide, and that death does in fact ensue as a result of the action taken.

By way of reply to this criticism of the distinctions, Sopinka can only note in the following paragraph that some commentators:

> ... uphold the distinction on the basis that in the case of withdrawal of treatment, the death is "natural"—the artificial forces of medical technology which have kept the patient alive are removed and nature takes its course. In the case of assisted suicide or euthanasia, however, the course of nature is interrupted, and death results directly from the human action taken....

Sopinka anticipates that this appeal to not interfere with the "course of nature" will have limited persuasive force, for he immediately continues with the observation that:

> Whether or not one agrees that the active vs. passive distinction is maintainable, however, the fact remains that under our common law, the physician has no choice but to accept the patient's instructions to discontinue treatment. To continue to treat the patient when the patient has withdrawn consent to that treatment constitutes battery (Ciarlariello and Nancy B., supra).

If a valid analogy, morally or legally, can be established, this requires that both sides of the analogy be judged in the same way. Both may be approved and permitted or both may be condemned and prohibited. Sopinka's observation merely points out that both may not be prohibited, for without the patient's consent the treatment must be withheld or withdrawn. While this is an important point in its own right, it does preclude the other alternative, namely, that the distinction between them is not a legitimate distinction and therefore they should both be permitted.

The reason why AS is not morally equivalent to NT is not the fact that AS is "active" whereas NT is "passive." This fact is obscured by the persistent and widespread characterization of the problem as the distinction between "active euthanasia" and "passive euthanasia." In fact, this terminology was introduced and is maintained primarily by those who wish to discredit the validity of the distinction. It creates a diversion or "straw-man" that is easily demolished and which the comments by Lord Goff and Justice Sopinka suggest is not easily propped up. For the use of the noun "euthanasia" on both sides of the analogy suggests that the actions are the same, save that the means in one are active and in the other passive. As our analysis above in the case of PK indicated, this is only possibly, but not necessarily, the case. The ethically significant difference, where it occurs, is not to be found in a difference of *means* but rather in a difference of *ends*. As we have explained above, while "NT to death" is analogous to AS, "NT to unburden" is not.

As was the case with pain-killers, there are often observable indicators from which a relatively certain inference may be drawn as to which NT is present. That is to say, they are indicators consistent with choosing not to treat in order to shorten life and indicators consistent with choosing not to treat simply to avoid the burdens of the treatment. The criterion to help determine which intention is present has taken on a "life of its own" in medical ethics as the distinction between "ordinary" and "extraordinary" means of caring for our health.

Not Treating, Intention, and the "Ordinary" vs. "Extraordinary" Means Distinction

Although it is not often recognized as such, the distinction between ordinary and extraordinary means of health care is, in fact, a correlative distinction to the distinction of ends we have been discussing and is best understood in conjunction with it. As a morally relevant category, "ordinary" means are typically described as means which provide a prospective benefit proportionate to the costs or burdens it imposes. It is also true that "ordinary" means are means which it would make sense to refuse only if the intention for not treating was to advance the time of one's death. On the other hand, "extraordinary" means are means the non-use of which makes sense simply in terms of the intention of not imposing or enduring the burdens associated with those means. The connection with the intention can be seen by taking examples of treatments which are clearly ordinary or extraordinary. If I, as an otherwise healthy individual, develop the need for a relatively simple and routine procedure with which I would return to normal health but without which I would die (e.g., stopping the bleeding from a severed artery), I would be dealing with a treatment that would clearly fit within the category of "ordinary" means. If I, understanding the benefits and costs of undergoing or not undergoing the surgery, were to refuse the procedure, it would be reasonable to infer that I was doing so because I wanted to die. The greater the excess of the benefits over the costs, the more the refusal can only be made sense of by an intention to advance the time of one death. Conversely, where the burdens of the treatments exceed the prospective benefits, it becomes reasonable to refuse or withhold that treatment precisely because of those burdens. From the desire to live the remainder of one's life without the burdens of treatments promising lesser benefits, there is no basis to infer an intention to bring about one's death. The greater the excess of the burdens over the benefits, the more reasonable it becomes to refuse those treatments simply out of a desire to maximize the quality of the time an individual has left. There is no "choosing death" here, actively or passively. There is only a recognition of the limits of medicine's ability, particularly as a person's condition deteriorates, to provide treatments that offer more than they demand. To acknowledge our mortality is not to seek our death. When the side-effects or other costs of treatment diminish or remove our abilities to do or experience other valuable things and offer in return relatively minor extensions of the time we have left or minor improvement in our condition, it becomes easier to understand the reasonableness of refusing them than accepting them.

The connection between refusing ordinary means and intending death or between refusing extraordinary means and intending merely to avoid uncompensated burdens (and not death) only follows when these categories are understood as they have been explained here, namely, as a function of the relative benefits and burdens. Considerable misunderstanding of positions and arguments occurs when these terms are interpreted as a function of the state of the art of medicine or as a function of what is "natural" or "unnatural." When "ordinary" means are understood as those treatments on that expanding list of established procedures effective in dealing with individual problems, one cannot reasonably infer a desire to shorten one's life from the refusal of them. The difficulty with this way of understanding "ordinary" is that it looks at procedures in reference to relatively isolated problems independently of the patient's overall condition and situation. In this way, the use of a defibrillator is seen as an "ordinary" means of dealing with a cardiac arrest, or the use of antibiotics as an "ordinary" means of dealing with pneumonia. In the benefits-burdens understanding of "ordinary" and "extraordinary" it is impossible to say whether these procedures would be ordinary or extraordinary without knowing the overall condition of the particular patient and what the benefits and burdens would be to him or her at this particular time.

Life and Freedom

In the first section of this chapter we made note of Sopinka's contention that the value of freedom did not have an absolute or *a priori* priority over the value of life. In the categorization of some means as "extraordinary" and the refusal of them as not entailing a choice or intending of death, we see that the preservation of life does not have an absolute priority over the exercise of freedom. Throughout our life, we have the freedom to choose what potentially health-improving or life-extending means we will use. This will include not only "medical" choices in the narrow sense, but our broader "lifestyle" choices. Affirming the intrinsic value of our life does not require that we do everything that could possibly extend our life, regardless of the probability or the cost. It requires only that we do those thing which, given the particulars of our individual situation, hold out the prospect of a benefit which will exceed the cost. This freedom is not lost in the final stages of our life.

IV. THE NECESSITY OF A PROHIBITION WITHOUT EXCEPTIONS

Argument: An exceptionless prohibition of assisting suicide is a reasonable limit on the self-determination of the physically handicapped even if it deprives them of the choice to commit suicide possessed by those physically able to commit suicide without assistance.

This argument is a reply to the dissenting argument stated most fully by Chief Justice Lamer that the law prohibiting assisting suicide creates an unreasonable limitation on a person's Charter right not to be disadvantaged by discrimination based on things such as physical disability. In order to show that a law is unconstitutional because it violates the Charter, it is necessary to show two things: (1) that it limits a constitutionally guaranteed freedom or infringes on a constitutionally guaranteed right, and (2) that this limitation or infringement is unreasonable. Occasionally the Crown will successfully argue that the limitations imposed by a law do not impact upon any constitutionally guaranteed right, but far more often it will be conceded (or at least not contested) that a right or freedom is limited by a law. The Crown then argues that the limitation is a reasonable one. This is the approach adopted by Sopinka in response to Lamer's argument. Sopinka argues that it is not necessary, in this case, to determine whether this law limits the right to be free from discrimination, because even if it does, it is a reasonable limitation on that freedom. Lamer contends, on the contrary, that the limitation is unreasonable.

Criteria for Determining When a Limit is Reasonable

As with all moral or ethical debates regarding what is reasonable, it is necessary to establish the criteria for deciding the question. The Supreme Court of Canada was forced to do this in its earliest Charter cases. The criteria adopted by the Court are quite similar to a revised natural law approach to determining moral justifiability known as "proportionalism."[14] In fact, part of the Court's own set of criteria are often referred to as the "Proportionality Test." These criteria have been formulated and reformulated in a variety of ways, but the following list will convey an accurate sense of them. Simply stated, a limitation is judged to be reasonable when all four of the following criteria are met.

1. The limitation must have as its objective the protecting or securing of an *important value* or interest.
2. There must be a *rational connection* between the objective identified in 1. and the means (laws, limitations) used to achieve it. Limitations which are unrelated to the values or which would be ineffective or even counterproductive in

---

[14] An introduction to this approach can be found in Bernard Hoose, *Proportionalism: The American Debate and its European Roots*, Georgetown University Press, 1987. This book includes an extensive bibliography on this approach.

protecting them would be arbitrarily rather than rationally connected to those values.
3. The means should *impair* the rights and freedoms *minimally*, that is, no more than is required by the objective.
4. The importance of the objective to be achieved must be *proportional* to the significance of the infringement of the right.

It is with regard to criterion 3. (minimal impairment) that Lemar finds the law unreasonable in that an exceptionless prohibition is more than is necessary to protect the vulnerable from coercion. Where adequate conditions are met to ensure that no coercion has taken place and that the choice for suicide is a settled decision, the protection of the vulnerable can be reasonably assured while allowing exceptions to the prohibition of assisting suicide. Lamer proposes an elaborate set of conditions ("safeguards") which he is confident will preclude the potential abuse of the permission to assist suicide.[15] Sopinka disagrees and contends that neither this nor any other set of safeguards could be relied upon to meet the objectives of the legislation prohibiting assisting suicide.

The Objectives of the Prohibition

The nature of these criteria are such that differences in how the objectives of the legislation are understood could easily translate into differences as to whether the second, third, or fourth criteria are met. Given her reading of the objective of the legislation, Justice McLachlin finds a second way in which the current "legislative scheme" is arbitrary and therefore both unjust and unreasonable. McLachlin, in paragraph 85, asks: ". . . does the fact that suicide is not criminal make the criminalization of all assistance in suicide arbitrary?" For McLachlin, the decriminalization of suicide itself means that the objective of continuing to prohibit assisting suicide cannot be the prevention of suicide. The objective must be the prevention of coerced, manipulated, or pressured *consent* to suicide. At this point it is useful to clearly distinguish the two possible objectives for prohibiting the assisting of suicide.

The first is the protection of *freedom* as genuinely free consent. The freedom of one's consent could be compromised in a number of ways. Our freedom to choose can be compromised by powerful emotional states, particularly depression. Emotional states are often temporary and we find that we would choose differently when they have passed. Our freedom can also be compromised by subtle forms of pressure or coercion, or by confusion or mistakes regarding the facts of the situation. The safeguards devised by Justice McEachern and endorsed by Justices Lamer and McLachlin are designed to guard against this kind of threat to our *freedom*. If it is believed that these safeguards would be adequate and that protecting freedom is the

---

[15]These conditions or safeguards are set out in Lamer judgment, paragraph 131 where he is citing Chief Justice McEachern of the Court of Appeal of British Columbia.

only objective, then a total or exceptionless prohibition is more than is necessary, "overbroad," and thereby violates the "minimal impairment" requirement.

The second objective for the prohibition of assisting suicide is the protection of *human life*. Even where a direct prohibition of suicide itself is seen as being ineffective or counter-productive,[16] a prohibition of assisting suicide could be expected to make a contribution to the objective of preventing suicide. While it is true that prohibiting assistance would make it impossible to commit suicide only for those who were not able to do so without assistance, this would still represent a partial contribution to the objective of protecting *human life*. Furthermore, it could be persuasively argued that it would be arbitrary to allow assistance to those who are *physically unable*[17] to commit suicide, while denying assistance to those who are physically able, but *psychologically unable* to carry out the deadly deed themselves. In other words, the prohibition of assistance may prevent suicide among a class broader than the "physically disabled." In regard to those both physically and psychologically able to commit suicide, the prohibition of assistance may still contribute to the prevention of suicide by conveying a valuing of life by the society.

The crux of the issue, then, becomes whether the prohibition of the assistance of suicide is directed toward the protection of freedom or the protection of life. If, as McLachlin contends, it is solely the protection of freedom then the question becomes whether the safeguards are adequate. (The protection of life can be left to other provisions of the criminal code prohibiting murder.) The adequacy or inadequacy of a given set of safeguards is obviously a matter of making projections on the basis of experience. As a matter more of intuition than logic or observable fact, this is an area where reasonable people could easily disagree. Sopinka does not share the confidence of McEachern, Lamer, or McLachlin and notes, in paragraph 48, that neither did the electorates of California or Washington (not notoriously conservative States) when voting on an even stricter set of safeguards than proposed by McEachern.

For the majority, however, the more fundamental disagreement regards the objective itself. Sopinka sees the objective of the prohibition of assisting suicide as including the protection of life. When arguing that a prohibition with no provisions for exceptions is not "overbroad," he states, in paragraph 69,

> There is no halfway measure that could be relied upon with assurance to fully achieve the legislation's purpose; first, because the purpose extends to the *protection of the life* of the terminally ill. Part of this purpose, as I have explained above, is *to discourage the terminally ill from choosing death over life*. Secondly, even

---

[16]For example, being arrested, booked, tried, and convicted for attempted suicide may deepen the depression by adding a public humiliation to it. Allowing for a person to be committed to hospitalization under public health legislation, rather than proceeding under the criminal code, may be a far more promising way of preventing the suicide.

[17]This group is not the *minority* usually thought of in discussions of not discriminating against the "physically disabled." Virtually everyone who does not die a sudden death will spend at least some time before they die in a condition where they cannot commit suicide without assistance. Eventually this "disability" becomes an almost universal part of the human condition.

if the latter consideration can be stripped from the legislative purpose, we have no assurance that the exception can be made to limit the taking of life to those who are terminally ill and genuinely desire death (emphasis added).

Sopinka is saying, that given the basic values we have as a people, we are not neutral as to whether a person chooses suicide so long as they exercise genuine freedom in the choice of it.

CONCLUSION

A careful examination of the arguments found in both the majority judgment of Justice Sopinka and the dissenting minority judgments of Justices McLachlin, Cory, and Lamer confirms the contention that their positions and supporting argumentation are essentially "moral" in character. What divides the court, as it does the nation, is a fundamental moral question: Do we know enough of what is "good" to assert that anything other than freedom is good, and that is ought to be valued and therefore protected. Societies adopting "liberalism" as a basic philosophy begin with the conviction that freedom is an intrinsic value. If there is any value besides freedom which warrants inclusion in this category surely "life" is the most likely candidate. Human consciousness is, of course, a pre-condition for the exercise of freedom and thus may be protected because of a valuing of freedom rather than of life itself. In the valuing of freedom, we have not allowed individuals the freedom to extinguish their freedom as for example, selling one's self into slavery (regardless of the price). In the issue of suicide and the assisting of it we are faced with the issue of whether or not to acknowledge that being alive has a value apart from being a pre-condition of freedom. To Justice McLachlin's rhetorical question "But what value is there in life without the choice to do what one wants with one's life . . ." The majority has implicitly answered "The great value of being humanly present, especially if by 'do what one wants' one means destroy that life." If this is not the case, an even larger question faces "liberal democratic" societies such as our own. Is it possible to build and sustain a human life and society in which freedom alone can be acknowledged as having an intrinsic value?

REFERENCES

1. R. Dworkin, What is Sacred, in *Life's Dominion: An Argument About Abortion, Euthanasia, and Individual Freedom*, Vintage Books, New York, pp. 68-101, 1993.
2. B. F. Skinner, *Beyond Freedom and Dignity* (1st Edition), Knopf, New York, 1971.

CHAPTER 29
Immortality*

John D. Morgan

Ivan Ilych's life was "most simple and most ordinary and therefore most terrible" [1, p. 16]. He served as a public administrator, had a marriage of convenience, and fathered children. Having injured himself in a seemingly minor manner, he was now dying a painful death. His physicians treated him indifferently, not knowing or at least, not telling him a correct diagnosis and prognosis. His wife hated him, saw him as inept and believed that his illness was his own fault and remained aloof. His fellow workers treated him in a merely correct manner. Meditating on the fate that awaited him, we find him: ". . . agonizingly, unbearably miserable. 'It is impossible that all men have doomed to suffer this awful horror' " [1, p. 42].

We see a similar fatalism and despair in the song that Peggy Lee recorded a few years ago entitled *Is That All There Is?* [2]. The song chronicled several events in a young girl's life, each ending in the disappointment exemplified by the question, "Is that all there is?" Just before the end of the song, Miss Lee anticipates our question "Why doesn't she end it all?" with the response that she is not ready for "that final disappointment."

These fundamentally pessimistic views of human existence are not rare. They are common in the work of the French philosopher Albert Camus [3], in his plays, novels and essays. The question "Why not commit suicide?" for Camus means: "what reason do I have to continue living when life simply doesn't make sense?" [3, p. 4]. One looks for some sort of meaning in one's life and expects the world to give an answer. According to Camus, there isn't any meaning in the world. The world is simply there. What is absurd is looking for meaning. The senselessness of life stems, for Camus, from the fact that we demand explanations for the way the world is and while many theories are proposed, none is satisfactory.

---

*Originally published in *Awareness of Mortality,* J. Kaufman (ed.), Baywood Publishing, Amityville, New York, 1995.

"Any thoughtful man might well imagine that he could have devised a cosmic operation less replete with frustration, suffering, and indignity" [4, p. 17]. The purpose of this chapter is to explore the question implicit in the remarks of Albert Camus, Ivan Ilych, and Peggy Lee. Is the fate of humans to live trivial lives, to suffer disappointment after disappointment until that final disappointment, death? Is it possible that life has a meaning, and that death is something other than an *"awful horror?"* **What gives meaning to a life condemned to death?** From time immemorial, theologians, philosophers, and non-professional thinkers alike have thought that some meaning to life is found in immortality—the continued existence of the person after death.

THE MEANING OF THE TERM

"Immortality" has several meanings. According to Lifton, aside from the philosophical, literal sense of "not subject to death," there are also the biological, the theological, the artistic or creative, and the natural [5]. I will use the term in its literal sense, the idea that some aspect of the human person is not subject to death. Thus, the way I am using the term, immortality is natural, as opposed to the Christian sense of resurrection in which a specific act of God occurs to reverse death.

HUMAN KNOWING CAPACITY

When Socrates, Plato's teacher, was condemned to death, rather than plead for mercy as his accusers had hoped, Socrates announced: "Wherefore, O Judges, be of good cheer about death, and know of a certainty that no evil can happen to a good man, either in life or after death" [6, p. 423]. Socrates' response differs from Ilych's, Camus', and from that implicit in Peggy Lee's song because they differ in their views of the human knowing capacity. The ancient philosophers who held that the person is immortal, did so because of epistemological foundations which I believe continue to be sound.

The basic problem of epistemology (theory of knowledge) and thus of all philosophy is what has been called the question of universals. By a universal is meant a knowing awareness that is applicable to two or more instances of the referent of that awareness. For example, the idea "paper" can be used to mean the substance on which these words are written, the thing that is delivered to one's doorstep in the morning, or the thing in which a gift is wrapped. Each of these things are in some sense paper. Yet each specific instance to which the idea "paper" refers is different. To be more exact I will limit myself to paper meaning "a physical object made from wood or other pulp for the purpose of receiving and storing visible character." The way the terms are used, *papers* are individual examples of paper, the generic. *Paper* refers to individuals, paper is the universal, the idea, the generalization. The history of thought has used many expressions for this awareness.

Individuals are "one out of many." What this means is that there are many pieces of paper in the universe, and the one that I see in front of me is "one out of many." There are many pieces of chalk in the world, and the one in my hand in class is "one out of many." The accurate meaning of the word individual is "one out of many."[1] A universal refers to an awareness that "is equally applicable to more that one individual or more than one instance of the same individual." The idea paper applies equally to each of the many individual pieces of *paper* on my desk. The idea mother applies equally to the many persons who are *mothers* as well as to the many experiences that one has of his/her individual *mother*.

Seemingly the only things that come into daily experience are individual things— this piece of paper in front of me, the piece of paper which is a memo from the department chairman, the piece of paper on which the first page of the newspaper is printed. I have experienced only individual pieces of *paper*, but I know intellectually that they all are subsumable under the same definition, or the same idea, *paper*.

A different example might be easier. As strange as it may seem, we have never heard *music*. What we have heard is individual events of "the rhythmic progression of sound." Yet, the question "Do you like music?" is a meaningful question. The hearer is aware of his/her liking music as a whole, not simply the individual experiences which s/he has had. Even such a specific piece of music as Beethoven's Ninth Symphony is a universal. We have heard only individual renditions of that symphony. Thus when asked if we like it, we do not respond that we like the individual sensations we heard, but we like our "universalized" experience of Beethoven's Ninth, or of music.

Plato [6] and Aristotle [7] noticed this aspect about the human mind twenty-five centuries ago when they said that we are capable of perceiving the difference between "white" and "this white thing" [7, p. 701]. There is a difference between knowing the thing and knowing the idea. **The "problem" of universals is this: we experience only individual things, but we think only in universal concepts.**

One of the basic principles of philosophy is that there must be a sufficient reason for every event [8]. This transcending of the limitations of experienced sense data must be caused by, or rooted in something. It doesn't seem as though the physical world can be the reason for generalizations, the world doesn't have *paper-in-general*, or *mother-in-general, music-in-general*, or anything else in-general. The world has *"this paper," "this mother,"* or *"this music."* If this experience occurs and it is not rooted in the thing known, the physical world, then it must be rooted in the knower.

THE SOUL

In order to explain the idea of soul, at least in Western philosophical thought, one has to look at how the Greeks of the Golden Age explained change. A century after Thales asked the questions from which we date the origin of philosophy, thinkers had reached an impasse [Bakewell 9]. Heraclitus, defining the original matter of the

---

[1] Thus when one says that "I am not being treated as an individual," they are in error. To be treated as a sex object, a cog in the wheel of industry, or as gun fodder for the military industrial complex is precisely to be treated as an individual—one out of many. What they are *not* being treated as is a *person*, a unique substance of a rational nature [9].

universe as *fire*, believed that the universe, as is a fire in a fireplace, is in constant change and that stability is an illusion [9]. Parmenides, on the other hand, seemingly the first to arrive at the abstract term *being*, held that all things are a part of one vast all, and that change is an illusion [10]. Plato hinted at a solution to the problem in the Parmenides [10] but his student, Aristotle [11], gave a fuller explanation. Change for Aristotle is explained by the hypothesis, the hylemorphic theory, that there are two fundamental *principles of being*, matter and form. Matter is amorphous, without determination, infinite possibility; form is determination, specification. Thus the piece of paper in front of me is **matter specified by form to be a particular thing**. Change is the infinite potentiality of matter losing one set of characteristics, forms, or receiving others. Thus neither Heraclitus or Parmenides are fully right or fully wrong. The world is stable because matter is stable, the world is in flux, because matter continually loses and receives forms.

We see in our experience two fundamentally different types of things. There are those things which are fundamentally passive, that is, they react to light, react to chemicals and heat, but seemingly do not initiate their own activity. If I want this piece of paper to move from one place on the desk to another, I, or some other external force, have to move it. All the coaxing in the world will not get the paper to move itself. On the other hand, there are things in the world which are self-moving. A plant takes nutrients from the soil and converts them into itself, an animal moves to a sunny window, the person decides to go to university. We call this ability to move oneself *life*, and it is found generically in plants, animals, and persons.

In order to differentiate the specifying agent in a living individual, Plato and Aristotle call this specifying agent *soul*, rather than form. Thus soul in Greek thought refers to the "source of activities of a living thing," or the "form of a living thing." Aristotle's technical definition of the soul is "the first act of a body capable of vital activity" [12, p. 555]. Thus plants are besouled, as are animals and persons.

There is a long history to the idea of a soul and to the human recognition that life differs from non-life. "There appears to be a universal tendency to conceive of each person as possessing a vital substance, and élan vital, that animates his behavior and quickens his body" [13, p. 222]. The word soul is an Anglo-Saxon term referring to the controlling agency, governing the vital principle in humans [14]. The equivalent Greek term is *psyche* or *pneuma* and the latin term is *anima* [15]. The original meaning of the idea "soul" is breath in both Greek philosophy and the Hebrew Bible. In Greek life the *psyche* was a subtle, animating principle which left the body at death; in the rites of Dionysus the *psyche* was for the first time regarded as a principle superior to the body, and imprisoned by it, and the Pythagoreans held the *psyche* to be the "harmony" of the body [15, p. 566].

> From primitive peoples as the Australian aborigines to the most sophisticated of the world religions, beliefs in the existence of an individual "soul" have persisted, conceivably with a capacity both to antedate and to survive the individual organism or body. The persistence of that belief and the factors giving rise to it provide the framework for the problematic of death in the Western world [14, p. 256].

THE CHARACTERISTICS OF SOUL

The person is a unified being. For the sake of convenience, we speak of hands, feet, liver, and other parts, but in reality we are an intrinsic unity such that the fundamental activity of the part would be different apart from the whole than when it is in the whole. Thus for most of our activity, we can say that the whole person acts. However, since a thing can act only to the extent that it is, if we see activities which transcend the powers of the body, then we can hold the position that the soul is acting independently of the body.

It seems that the soul operates independently of the body in thinking. It is true that all the raw material of thought comes through organic senses; however, that does not imply that it remains organic. Body by its very nature is in space and time. What we mean by individuality is occurrence within a specific space and at a specific time. Thus if Aristotle, Plato, and Aquinas are correct that thinking is not individuated, then the thinking capacity of the person is doing something that a body cannot do, generalize. I think that then following examples might be helpful.

1. The statement "Dr. Morgan taught Anselm's argument for the existence of God in San Diego in 1963, in Montreal in 1974 and in London (Ontario) in 1977," is a true statement. What is the mind doing in making that assertion? Does it not seem that the mind is transcending the limits of space and time? The mind can think of itself in Los Angeles thirty years ago, the body cannot present itself as such.

2. Because the mind gets its information from the body while the body has images of reality, we tend to confuse the two. However, the following example may show that the mind is doing something different than does the body. I know the difference between a plane, closed, three-sided figure (a triangle), and a plane, closed, four-sided figure (a rectangle). Because the mind and body operate together when I think of these examples, I think the meanings of triangle and square while my memory (a sense organ) pictures them. However, this is not always the case. I know the difference between a plane, closed figure of 7,312 sides and a plane, closed figure of 7,313 sides—but I cannot picture them. The mind is dependent on the body for information. That does not imply that the mind is dependent on the body for being. I am dependent on a movie screen for information, but that does not stop me from getting up and walking out.

3. The mind can reflect upon itself. Let us use the following as a definition of mind: "that capacity to know in a non-individualized way." Any definition would do, but that definition is consistent with what has been said so far. Who made up that definition of mind? The mind defined itself by reflecting on its activities. I can make one physical thing touch another physical thing; I can make one part of a physical thing (a piece of paper) touch another part of the same thing; but I cannot make the same part bend back on itself. While you can use the tip of the index finger of the right hand to touch anything, including the tip of the index finger of the left hand, what the tip of the index finger of the right hand cannot do is touch the tip of the index finger of the right hand. Physical things cannot reflect on themselves, the mind can. This capacity to transcend the limits of material things is called *spirituality*.

IMMORTALITY

If the soul does something that the body cannot do, think, then there is no reason to think that the death of the soul necessarily entails the death of the body. We can destroy something by breaking it into component parts or destroying that upon which it depends for existence. But the soul has no parts, and as we have seen it is dependent upon body for *operation*, but not for *existence*. As a simple (partless) substance, the soul is intrinsically immortal [15].

What does the soul do after death? "Aye, there's the rub" [17, p. 47]. Speaking without an appeal to faith, we have no knowledge of life after death. Since the soul is dependent on the body for learning, nothing new could be learned after death. Is the soul dependent on the body for remembering what has already been known? In this life we do not remember except through the stimulation of the senses. However, Aquinas holds that in this life the manner of being of the soul is to be united to the body and to operate that way. He does not believe that implies the same thing after death [18]. Maybe disembodied souls operate differently. Aquinas also holds that since the soul's way of being is to be united with a body, God would not have created an intrinsically defective being—a soul without a body [19]. He uses this as an argument for the resurrection of the body.

The Near Death experiences have many common elements,

> an out-of-body experience during which one's body is viewed and conversations are overheard; a feeling of peace; travelling through a tunnel; meeting or seeing a dead relative, beings of light, or historical religious figures; a life review, in which the events in one's life are re-evaluated in the light of greater understanding; experiences in preternatural realms of light; being told to return to life to complete unfinished business; and a deep feeling of sadness upon leaving this blissful dimension [20, p. 73].

In addition, emphasis is placed on seeing medical procedure while one was out of the body and clinically dead. In some cases these experiences were such that they could not have been seen on television medical shows [21]. If such really happen, there is additional evidence for the ability of the human knowing capacity to transcend the limits of the body.

THE HUMAN JOURNEY

Who is the "I" that undergoes death? We are so used to filling out resumes that we sometimes may believe that the "I" that each of us consists of a long series of independent characteristics. Yet someone could know all that objective data about us, and not really know us. We could surprise even those who live with us most intimately. In moments of self-pity, we state that "nobody understands me." But perhaps the reality is that nobody understands anyone, and we face that reality only in such moments. Jose Ortega y Gasset described the person as a "radical solitude" [22, p. 140], that is, at the very root (radix) of us, there is an ultimate incommunicability and loneliness.

This realization that we are not our resume, that no list of characteristics no matter how long can enclose us is called the "subjectivity" [23, p. 15]. Life does not consist of objective characteristics but is a process of creating the person we are to become from the biological raw material as well as the events of biography.

> The unborn child obviously is given an existence he did not request, a heritage and environment he could not choose. He did not select his parents or his race, or the time and place of his birth. He is borne along on the pre-existing currents of family and society. Soon, however, the conscious self awakens and he rises high enough above the currents to accept or fight their obscure forces. Born into a community whose structure was imposed on him, he gradually becomes aware of his personal autonomy. His actions become increasingly independent; the environment that once held him widens; self-consciousness deepens; he realizes more and more his capacity for deepening the type of relationship he wants to maintain with his given situation [24, p. 130].

Life is continual self-development and self-independence. As the human being progresses from conception to maturity the balance between passive response to stimuli and active initiation of activity tips more heavily toward the activity side. Full activity, however, cannot occur while we are still bound by the body since the body provides such powerful stimuli. Full activity, therefore, would seem to be possible only on a departure from the body [24]. In old age the person is preparing to leave an environment no longer capable of supporting his growth. Death finally emerges as: "man's first completely personal act, and is, therefore, by reason of its very being, the place above all others for the awakening of consciousness, for freedom, for the encounter with God, for the final decision about eternal destiny" [24, p. 129]. This is a spiritual journey, the independence of the person from the limits of the here and now. "By *spiritual* I allude to the journey of the soul—not to religion itself but to the drive in humankind that gives rise to religion in the first place" [25, p. 8]. The spiritual is the human striving toward meaning, the search for a sense of belonging [25, p. 8], the sense of belonging in the universe and a vibrant awareness of the oneness of everything. "To love God is to be in love with the universe. This all might be viewed as Idea One of the spiritual path" [25, p. 13].

> The foetus is subjected to the most painful crisis of its prenatal life precisely when it is about to be born: it is squeezed, constricted, almost strangles, and finally expelled, with no knowledge for it of free air, space, light and love awaiting it beyond the passage. Immediately before death, this other great passage, man suffers biological dissolution. As Shakespeare expressed it: "He shuffles off this mortal coil." With no experience of what he is about to become, he fights for air and feels as if he were being expelled from his body. It is clear, therefore, that the positive meaning of this event cannot be revealed by the preparatory phase, the expulsion: the pains of birth are not yet birth itself, and old age and dying are not yet the stage at which the spiritual person is delivered from the material body [26, p. 188].

Departure from the material body in which passivity prevails would appear as a necessary condition of full activity. The meaning of this earthly adventure is to train the spiritual person for that free act whereby he is to establish his own being. Man is incarnated spirit whom is in the act of *becoming* before he attains the fullness of his *being* [26].

The journey which we call life is acceptance of ourself in an eternal now. Failure to do so places our lives outside of ourselves. The unhappy person "is always absent, never present to himself" [27, p. 64].

> He cannot become old, for he has never been young; he cannot become young, because he is already old. In one sense of the word he cannot die for he has not really lived; in another sense, he cannot live for he is already dead. He cannot love, for love is in the present, and he has no present, no future, no past. . . . He has no time at all [28, p. 80].

Too often we are so afraid of dying, that we do not find time for living. Fear or terror is an expression of man's spirituality, of his inability to be content with himself.

We must, in Steven Levine's words, die consciously in order to live consciously. "To let go of the last moment and open to the next is to die consciously" [29, p. 68]. Focusing on death is a way of becoming fully alive. Perhaps the first recognition in the process of acknowledging, opening, and letting go that I call "conscious dying" is when we begin to see that we are not only the body. We see that we have a body but it is not fully who we are. Conscious death is not merely from without; it must also be an act that one personally performs. "More precisely still it must be death itself which is the act and not merely an attitude which man adopts toward death" [24, p. 125].

CONCLUSION

I have attempted to examine the question of meaning in life through the question of the immortality of the person. It is our view that the abstracting power of the mind is an indication that the human person is capable of engaging in an act that cannot be explained by bodily activity. It is our view that the human soul is a spiritual entity which acts in conjunction with the body to gain experience but is not limited to the activity of the body. Since the person is more than a body, the death of the body is not the end of the person's life. Consequently, life takes on a different meaning. The purpose of life is the continual development of the self, a development that will fully occur only after death.

REFERENCES

1. L. Tolstoi, *The Death of Ivan Ilych*, L. Maude and A. Maude (trans.), Health Sciences, New York, 1973.

IMMORTALITY / 483

2. J. Leiber, Is That All There Is? in *Greatest Songs of the 60's*, The New York Times, Quadrangle/New York Times Book Company, New York, 1970 (originally published, 1966).
3. A. Camus, The Myth of Sisyphus, in *The Myth of Sisyphus and Other Essays*, J. O'Brien (trans.), Vintage, New York, 1960.
4. A. C. Outler, God's Providence and the World's Anguish, in *The Mystery of Suffering and Death*, M. J. Taylor (ed.), Doubleday, Garden City, 1974.
5. C. A. Corr, Reconstructing the Face of Death, in *Dying: Facing the Facts*, H. Wass, R. Neimeyer, and H. Bernardo (eds.), Hemisphere, Washington, 1979.
6. Plato, The Apology, in *The Dialogues of Plato*, R. Demos (ed.), B. Jowett (trans.), Random House, New York, 1937.
7. Aristotle, The Metaphysics, in *The Basic Works of Aristotle*, R. McKeon (ed.), Random House, New York, 1941.
8. B. Wuellner, *Summary of Scholastic Principles*, Loyola, Chicago, 1956.
9. C. M. Bakewell, *Source Book in Ancient Philosophy*, Scribners, New York, 1939.
10. Plato, The Parmenides, in *The Dialogues of Plato*, R. Demos (ed.), B. Jowett (trans.), Random House, New York, 1937.
11. Aristotle, The Physics, in *The Basic Works of Aristotle*, R. McKeon (ed.), Random House, New York, 1941.
12. Aristotle, On the Soul, in *The Basic Works of Aristotle*, R. McKeon (ed.), Random House, New York, 1941.
13. D. Landy, Death: I. Anthropological Perspective, in *Encyclopedia of Bioethics*, W. T. Reich (ed.), Vol. 1, Free Press, New York, 1978.
14. D. M. High, Death, Definition and Determination of Conceptual Foundations: III Philosophical and Theological Foundations, in *Encyclopedia of Bioethics*, W. T. Reich (ed.), Vol. 1, Free Press, New York, 1978.
15. W. L. Reese, *Dictionary of Philosophy and Religion: Eastern and Western Thought*, Humanities Press, Atlantic Highlands, 1980.
16. T. Parsons, Death: V Death in the Western World, in *Encyclopedia of Bioethics*, W. T. Reich (ed.), Vol. 1, Free Press, New York, 1978.
17. W. Shakespeare, *Hamlet: Prince of Denmark*, Great Books of the Western World, Vol. 27, Encyclopedia Britannica, Chicago, 1956.
18. T. Aquinas, *Summa Contra Gentiles*, Trans. [reference to life after death and knowledge of the soul], Volume 27, Encyclopedia Britannica, 1945.
19. J. E. Royce, *Man and His Nature*, McGraw Hill, New York, 1961.
20. P. Peay, Back from the Grave, Common Boundary, in *Utne Reader*, September/October 1991.
21. R. A. Moody, *Life after Life*, Bantam, New York, 1975.
22. J. Ortega y Gasset, In Search of Goethe from Within, in *Dehumanization of Art and Other Writings on Art and Culture*, Doubleday, Garden City, 1956.
23. J.-P. Sartre, Existentialism as a Humanism, in *Existentialism and Human Emotions*, Philosophical Library, New York, 1985.
24. G. J. Dyer, Recent Developments in the Theology of Death, in *The Mystery of Suffering and Death*, M. J. Taylor (ed.), Doubleday, Garden City, 1974.
25. J. E. Fortunato, *AIDS: The Spiritual Dilemma*, Harper and Row, San Francisco, 1987.
26. R. Troisfontaines, The Mystery of Death, in *The Mystery of Suffering and Death*, M. J. Taylor (ed.), Doubleday, Garden City, 1974.
27. S. Kierkegaard, *Either/Or*, in Hegel and Existentialism: On Unhappiness, A. Lessing (ed.), *The Personalist*, 49(1), 1968.

28. S. Kierkegaard, Sickness Unto Death, in *The Denial of Death*, E. Becker (ed.), Free Press, New York, 1973.
29. S. Levine, Conscious Dying: It All Begins with Conscious Living, *Utne Reader*, 1991.

CHAPTER 30
Resurrection

Rev. Ronald Trojcak

The scriptures, the liturgy, theology, the teaching of churches, the lives of the saints—in a word, the whole Christian tradition has consistently testified that human destiny is to culminate in the resurrection of the dead. Yet today, belief in the resurrection is explicitly rejected by some theologians and effectively denied in the lives and hopes of many Christians. No doubt there are many factors contributing to this denial. These are some of the most influential: the secularization of culture in the industrialized world; the steady decline in the authority within and of the main-line Churches, and the extraordinary growth of the fundamentalist Christian groups.

I believe this last-named factor is crucial for our purposes, for at least two reasons. The first derives from the very nature of fundamentalism. Christian fundamentalism both in its origin, about 100 years ago, and in its present forms, sets itself in firm opposition to much of what it sees as the leading characteristics of the modern world. However, more fundamentally, fundamentalists also set themselves in opposition to much of what they see going on in the main-line Churches.

The second reason is intimately connected with the first. For the fundamentalists, the Bible provides the basic ammunition for their assault on the failures of the main-line Churches. Better said: it is the fundamentalist way of reading the Bible which most starkly differentiates the fundamentalist from the non-fundamentalist Christian. Whereas main-line mainstream biblical scholarship has been shaped by modern ways of making sense of the world (e.g., awareness that a first century Jew living in the Near-East did not understand the world the way a twentieth century person living in North America does), the fundamentalist objects to this way of seeing things. Indeed, the fundamentalist will invoke the spirit of "worldly learning and secular humanism" as informing this way of reading the texts. The problem for the fundamentalist is that this way of seeing is a betrayal of the sovereignty, and self-evident nature of the biblical texts. The fundamentalist then logically enough claims that they alone read the Bible correctly and are faithful to its meaning. What they ignore, from my perspective, is the indubitable fact that they too "read the text from their place," and that the presuppositionless reading of the text is simply impossible. No one, except perhaps the neonate, comes to any text, indeed, to any experience, without bringing their own reservoir of previous experience and their meanings, to make sense of the new text or experience. Furthermore as we will see in the course of this chapter, the God of the Bible is not a God of magic. In this present instance this means that the biblical God does not suspend the normal, human process of understanding (anything) even in the case of reading the Bible.

But why all this emphasis on fundamentalism? First, the clearest data we have for understanding the resurrection are the biblical texts. So these texts are also the basis for this chapter. Second, the fundamentalist reading of those texts is almost infinitely more public. Thus, even if you feel you know little or nothing about the doctrine of the resurrection, it is most likely that even the little you might know, is the fundamentalist view of it. Finally, because of the pervasive presence of the fundamentalist position on the resurrection, it is necessary to point out and counter their further claim that they alone read the Bible correctly and so I hope this chapter will also be, and be seen as a dialogue with fundamentalist interpretation of the resurrection.

Having said all this it is useful to notice that the fundamentalist way of reading the Bible does set in relief a perennial task for Christianity. From the very beginning, as it split from its Jewish parentage Christianity has had to continually reinterpret itself. This is because Christianity sees itself as a universal religion, mandated by God to incarnate itself in every time and place. Thus it must both speak to every time and place in a way that is intelligible to those times and places. Yet it must do so in a way which also asserts its own uniqueness. This effort has occurred continuously and with varying degrees of success. The fundamentalist however has come to see this task of reinterpretation as a kind of betrayal, especially when this effort entails methods of reading the Bible.

So called "Liberal Protestantism," and more recently, Roman Catholicism, have earnestly attempted to address the world, as well as to recognize their own worldliness (e.g., their membership in the modern world). It is in this latter point that there seems to be a pervasive unconsciousness on the part of fundamentalists and their treatment of the Bible. And because of their energy, intensity, and highly public self-presentation, the fundamentalist understanding of resurrection has greatly contributed to what is at least confusion, if not outright mistakenness regarding the meaning of this belief. It is this misrepresentation of the meaning of the resurrection which has, I believe, alienated many, contributing to the aforementioned rejection, even by Christians. In a word, when the fundamentalist speaks of the resurrection, I propose that they do it a way in which is at certain central points, unfaithful to this belief as it is understood in the Bible. But they also speak of the resurrection in a way in which many contemporary people find on a number of grounds, useless.

The central problem with the fundamentalist understanding of resurrection is that this way of understanding portrays the resurrection as separated from or merely incidental to Jesus' life in the world. As we will see, there are other large religious problems attendant on this one. This detachment implies a radical devaluing of the "this worldly" life of Jesus, and by implication, of our own. It furthers implies a derogation of the world itself (God's creation) within which human life is carried on.

Now it is one of the hallmarks of contemporary, non-fundamentalist Christianity, that it is wholeheartedly engaged in and respectful of "the world," at least to the extent that it does not see much of modern culture an unambiguously God-forsaken. Now any understanding of the doctrine of the Resurrection which does not somehow encompass this worldliness will not be audible to many today. And any view of human life which sees our present existence as merely a testing period, and the world merely an ante-chamber, or waiting room one occupies before going home to God, will not be able to speak of the resurrection as good news.

Let me then illustrate some unworldly, acosmic ways of interpreting the resurrection. This interpretation of Jesus' resurrection claims that, as his final and greatest miracle, the resurrection absolutely proves Jesus' divinity. It thereby also validates His claim that He is the Messiah and the natural son of God. This reading always includes a marked emphasis on the physical aspects of the Gospel narratives of the risen Jesus' appearances. Much significance is given to the descriptions of the risen Jesus eating, talking, walking. According to this view the *meaning* of the resurrection is to be found in its historically probative force, which compels faith. This has also been called the apologetic use of the resurrection. (Apologetic here has the technical meaning of being a defense of the divine origin and the authority of Christianity.)

The problems arising from this way of understanding the resurrection are both numerous and insuperable. It contravenes the normal understanding of the significance of miracle as this is found in the New Testament. There, the miracle is never an incentive to faith, but always occurs in consequence of faith. Precisely from the perspective of faith it is possible to see how the apologetic use of the resurrection separates it from Jesus' life. The apologetic view of miracle sees it primarily as a wondrous act, so that its deepest significance lies in its exceptional, and unexpected and probative character. Jesus, then, or God as acting through Jesus, is virtually a God of magic. But a magical life is not a real life: that is, it has none of the elements which make up genuine human existence. These include above all, continuing relationships. A more accurate reading of Jesus' miracles precisely locates them within the fabric of a real life. The healings, the exorcisms, the raising of the dead: all of these miracles occur within a context of Jesus' relationships with others. In fact, the miracles of Jesus' precisely create relationships. They have as their primary effect, the restoration of the one healed, or exorcised or raised, to their community. As we will see shortly, the matter of relationships is absolutely central to the meaning of the resurrection of Jesus' and so of our own hoped-for resurrection.

There are other grounds, namely logical ones, for rejecting the apologetic understanding of the resurrection. The argument proceeds in this way: to maintain that God raised Jesus' from the dead is itself a claim made by faith. That is, no one can claim that the resurrection of Jesus' is an historical event in the normal meaning we give to history. Simply compare these two assentations, and the difference becomes obvious: Napoleon invaded Russia, and God raised Jesus from the dead. To carry on with the logical difficulty: one cannot logically move from within a position of faith in order to establish that position. The argument is viciously circular. To believe in the resurrection on these grounds is not only beyond reason, it is contrary to reason. Many modern Christians refuse a faith that is irrational.

There is yet another way of understanding Jesus' Resurrection which also has great currency among fundamentalists. This way appears to connect the Resurrection with Jesus' life more closely. But this mode of connection, I hope to show, raises other grave problems. I am referring to a view of the Resurrection which presents is simply as a *reward* the Father gave Jesus for His, i.e., Jesus', good behavior. As I said, to see the Resurrection-as-reward appears to connect the Resurrection with the rest of Jesus' life. But it also creates serious difficulties concerning the nature of God and the nature of the relationship between the Father and Jesus. And, by implication, I suggest it badly distorts our understanding of the relationship between God and the rest of us.

Let me attempt to explain. In the resurrection-as-reward scheme, the climax of Jesus' life was reached when he died in obedience to His Father's will: the Father wanted Jesus' death. Here, let me pause to offer one classic explanation of the seemingly strange desire of the Father. In this explanation, the sin of Adam was understood as being an infinite offense, since an infinite person, God, had been offended. The question then becomes: how can this offense be repaired? If sin is disobedience the remedy for sin is obedience. If the offence of sin is infinite, only a counteract of obedience on the part of an infinite person (Jesus as the Godman) will adequately compensate the offence. So, Jesus' death is depicted as the supreme act and proof of Jesus' obedience. (Happily, this particular explanation has been all but abandoned.)

But to return to the understanding of resurrection-as-reward, note that in this arrangement as well, the death is seen in isolation, disconnected from the content of the rest of Jesus' life. Although the death could be seen as the climatic act of obedience, two grave problems are latent here. First: if Jesus' death is only seen vertically, as some private arrangement Jesus had made with the Father without reference to the way He lived, then we encounter another form of detachment of the Resurrection from the rest of Jesus' life. The Resurrection is here, in another way, decontextualized. But now to the second problem. Without considering the content of Jesus' life, the notion of obedience becomes a purely formal one. That is, obedience would mean mere compliance with the order of another. Neither the nature or content of either the order or compliance are considered. We would be in a world of automatons. The Father's demand for Jesus' death appears to be a high-handed, even arbitrary measure of Jesus' loyalty. Throughout all this, the Father emerges as a despicable autocrat and Jesus' submission to him appears servile, even infantile. The relationship between Jesus and the Father is anything but one of love. And by implication, we too are to be infantilized by the Father, if not enslaved.

Later in this chapter, when we come to speak of the resurrection as a saving event, we'll discover further, unfortunate results of the detachment of the resurrection from the rest of Jesus' life, and our own. But now, in contrast to the above deficient views, here is an alternate one. This one is consonant with what the biblical writers have to say about Resurrection. This more biblical view also connects the Resurrection far more intelligibly both with the Father's will and our lives. We can begin with a simple assertion of what the Father wills for us all. Note that this Will is the same for us as for Jesus: namely that we grow up, that we mature.[1] Religiously, to grow up means that we outgrow our normal self-centeredness so that we become free to respond to (be responsible to) God and my co-humans. The nature of this response will be explained more fully later in this chapter. In the Jewish view, which underlies the Christian one, to be free is precisely to be able to respond to God and to others. Another way of speaking of God's will for Jesus and for us is to say that God, Who is faithful to us, wishes us to be faithful in return. This fidelity is the very perfection of our freedom, for real fidelity is neither automatic nor inevitable. Any faithfulness that is not free is not genuine fidelity but rather compulsion, or, in Paul's language, "slavery." This is true of the Father's fidelity, Jesus' or ours. It is in choosing to be faithful that we construct and achieve our authentic selves. Therefore, God's will is not an extrinsic, arbitrary or alienating pressure on Jesus, or on us, to bring us to "proper behavior." Rather, it is God's desire that His/Her creation fulfill itself. In this perspective, Jesus' death can be seen as the culmination of His life-long growth in fidelity and freedom, and not as His grudging accession to the Father's autocratic desire, despite Jesus' own choice in the matter. In a word, Jesus' death was the culminating moment in his life of growing in freedom and toward His Father.

If we understand the Father's will in this way, to speak of Jesus' Resurrection as a reward is both paltry and trivializing. Certainly, the Resurrection is not a reward in the sense that it was something that Jesus sought in itself, and so only for Himself. Nor was it a reward in the sense that it was a kind of prize God gave Jesus for good behavior, or for doing some unpleasant and onerous, not to say incomprehensible, task. Rather the Resurrection is the working out of what the Jews had always seen as the leading characteristic of God, namely, God's steadfast love. The Resurrection is the Father's response to the steadfastness of Jesus' love both of his Father and of all those with whom he had lived. Just as Jesus' steadfastness brought him to the Cross, so the Father's steadfastness "brought" Jesus beyond death. Thus, the Resurrection is the completion of divine and human love, regularly expressed in the Bible by the metaphor of a wedding banquet. To repeat a point made earlier: there is nothing mechanical, nothing automatic or inevitable here. Rather there is the final and full achievement of Divine and human freedoms. It is, as we will see in greater detail later on, the completion of God's intention in creating, and so the full achievement of human maturity.

This way of understanding the Resurrection avoids the problems mentioned above. Here, the Resurrection is in no way an incidental or extrinsic conclusion to Jesus' historical human career. Instead, it is an inseparable part of His fully human condition. It is the completion of His exigency, as it is ours, to grow to His creaturely destiny.[2]

---

[1] Now there are all sorts of psychologically based notions of maturity. Many, perhaps most of them, are coherent with a religious or theological view, to a greater or lesser extent. I mention this fact here because very often it is either felt or said, as one person put it, "if it's psychologically true, then it's theologically true."

[2] The terms "exigency" and "creaturely destiny" are to be taken in a religious and theological, rather than psychological sense.

Thus the Resurrection makes no sense apart from all the earlier steps and stages in Jesus' life. What Jesus did, how He lived in this world is, therefore, of absolute significance. His years on earth were not just a dispensable and preliminary period preceding the only truly decisive event in His life, the Resurrection. Rather, the years of His life, both chronologically and logically are of the very essence of the meaning of His death and of His Resurrection. As the final stages of Jesus's coming to maturity, the Resurrection is incomprehensible apart from the life He lived, and the death He died. And to reiterate the point: so too is His death incomprehensible apart from the life as well. Thus, the "other worldly" hope of the Resurrection is inseparable from the "this worldly" life.

Many atheist critics of Christianity such as John Dewy and Friedrich Nietzsche have failed to understand this. And such failure has generated their conviction that the Resurrection distracts women and men from earnestly undertaking their tasks in this world. Nietzsche has called Christianity "life-denying," in the sense that, by reason of their belief, Christians seem to be required to be indifferent if not inimical to the world and their own human development. Both Dewy's and Nietzsche's criticism held that Christians believe that this world, and of course, the lives lived here are essentially transitory and without real or enduring significance, or worse, that this world is essentially evil. They claim that the Christians' allegiance is not and must not be to this present world but to the world to come.[3]

However, today such a view of the world and human life is repugnant to many people, including Christians. Moreover, a sense of responsibility for the world is for many the hallmark of an authentic human and Christian life. Evidence for this can be seen in several new "ecological theologies" as well as the work of the liberation theologians who now come from all over the world. And not even the greatness of the distance between our assertions and actions is proof against this sense of responsibility and participation. All of this undergirds and informs what I am proposing as a more adequate basis for understanding the Resurrection.

Up until now we have been speaking primarily about Jesus' Resurrection. It is now time to take a look a some related issues. But this initial focus is appropriate, for any talk about our Resurrection is grounded in the Christian belief that "God has

---

[3] We owe a great debt to the work of such great scripture scholars as R. Bultmann, R. E. Brown, and R. Schnackenburg for providing a more authentic reading of the term "world" as it is used in the Gospel of John. Later we will encounter further problems originating with the Johannine Gospel. For now, I merely point out that the "world," in normal Johannine usage, does not refer to the physical or cultural environments in which all people live their lives. Rather, "world" means any sector of human life which resists God. The apostle Paul, for his part, has a similar usage which in the course of Christian thought and practice, has been similarly misinterpreted. When Paul contrasts the work of the "flesh" with that of the "spirit," he is not distinguishing between body and soul. The "flesh" for Paul, is that part of each of us which resists the activating and enlivening power of God. The normal biblical term for that power, is "spirit." Finally, for the sake of clarity, let me offer two typical misunderstandings of Christian worldliness. A church's hierarchy decries legislative programs or economic programs which further pauperize the poor, and the complaint is made against them that they are interfering in politics. A country's landless peasantry protests against a wealthy oligarchy which rules that country and the peasants and their supporters are dismissed as God-less communists.

raised Him to life" (Acts, 2/24). Now the purpose of this statement in Acts, and made throughout the New Testament, is not just to announce an event or make a claim about Jesus' ultimate destiny. This statement is also the proclamation of good news for humankind. For the Christian, it is in fact the proclamation of the best possible news: that by reason of Jesus' life, death, and resurrection, the human race has been "saved." That is, Jesus' Resurrection is the initial completion of God's saving activity which is to encompass all of us. We come therefore, to the full meaning of the Resurrection only when we understand it as the saving event for us. It is the issue of salvation which we must now consider.

Before we proceed, let me remind you that the matters being discussed, both up until this point and from this point on, are matters of faith. Lest this seems too esoteric and remote a context, it might be useful to recall that most of human life, and surely the most central concerns of human life, are all matters of faith. I *believe* that someone loves me; I *believe* that the physical universe is intelligible; I *believe* that having a bachelor's degree will benefit me in life. Even if we look closely enough we will discover that, having a great deal of money being better than not having it, is also a matter of faith. If all this is true—as I think it demonstrably is—then we should not be surprised that an answer to the largest question of human life is also a matter of faith. Whether one says human existence is either ultimately meaningless or meaningful, is an act of faith. "To be or not to be," is not a rhetorical question. The very fact that the question of meaning arises at all suggests that any answer one gives is a matter of faith.

Now the Christian, standing on the shoulders of her Jewish forbears, believes that life is a gift from a benevolent God. (This is the meaning of the doctrine of creation found, in narrative form, in the first three chapters of the book of Genesis.) Furthermore, she believes that life is to terminate in—thus has as its point and purpose—full companionship with that benevolent Creator and all fellow creatures. (This is the doctrine of salvation which, in one form or another lies at the heart of all religions.) So far, so tidy. But life is anything but tidy. There are multiple uncertainties and difficulties which beset us all. But it is not from these that we are to be saved in the Jewish-Christian view. For the multiple obscurities and complexities which everyone faces, in one form or another, are simply part and parcel of the human condition. They are the human condition. For the Christian, the central problem is that of our disconnectedness from God and from each other, in consequence of which we are also disconnected from our authentic selves.[4] There are many causes for this state of affairs, but the deepest and most pervasive cause is a moral one, as opposed, for example, to psychological or economic ones. Therefore, at the base of human life is sin: the free choice to disconnect oneself from others (by one or other form of violence) from God (by denying our creatureliness and finitude) and from ourselves (by self-deception.)

---

[4] It is essential to realize that, even to see disconnectedness as life's central problem, is itself a matter of faith. The most casual survey of contemporary attitudes reveals that many, perhaps most people choose to see other problems as the central ones.

All of this is essential to understand what the Christian (and Jew) means by salvation. All this is equally essential for seeing the meaning of salvation within the belief that God has raised Jesus from the dead. We are to be saved from our multiform disconnection by means of Jesus's resurrection. Paul expresses this belief summarily when he says that "in Christ, God was reconciling the world to Himself" (II Cor.5/19).

Now the Christian, in faith, sees Jesus as the one who lived a life fully connecting himself to others and to God. (A modern theologian has described Jesus as "the man for all others.") We could as well say that He was the one *with* all others. Thus Christians believe that they see in Jesus the fullest specification both of what they are to be saved from as well as saved for. But this is hardly all. Jesus, in living as he did, radically upset the normal way we humans operate: on the basis of disconnection. Read here all the multiple forms of inequity, along with the violence that attends this condition. Thus, as a force of disorder, Jesus was eliminated. In coming to believe that God raised Jesus from the dead, the Jews believed a number of things: one, that Jesus attained full companionship with God. To put this in terms we used earlier: in raising Jesus, God was being steadfastly loving in response to Jesus' steadfast love. But this means that God saw in Jesus the fullness of humanity which God had in mind when creating humans in the first place. Jesus, in other words, is now believed as the perfect fulfillment of what it is to be human. The Christian believes not only that Jesus achieved the fullness of humanity (Paul speaks of Him as the "new Adam," the new human prototype) but that, in dying, Jesus' career also answers the fundamental question of the meaning of human existence.

It is this that underlies Paul's assertion of the pivotal significance of Jesus' resurrection: "if Christ has not been raised, then our proclamation is in vain and your faith is in vain" (I Cor., 15/14). Now the restoration of one human to God, in Jesus' resurrection, is not simply for Jesus alone. Rather, the risen Jesus acts to restore all of us both to God and to each other. "Don't be afraid" is the archetypal message of the risen Jesus. This means that the great obstacle to our being connected with each other, fear, is overcome in the work of the risen Jesus. Note that the first letter of John puts this very succinctly: "in love there is no room for fear" (I Jn., 4/18). The overcoming of fear-full existence—which is equivalent to being disconnected, and so, humanly dead—is achieved by our being enlivened by Jesus. The New Testament expresses this process using the classic Jewish metaphor for God's enlivening power: Jesus sends the *Spirit,* thereby not leaving us orphaned, alone, disconnected (cf. John, 14/18). To be fully human is thus to be fully fear-free, or to love, or to be spiritual. These are three of the many ways the New Testament writers devise for saying the same thing. This is what it means by Irenaeus' justly famous statement: the glory of God (i.e., the fulfilment of God's creation) is the human being fully alive. The risen Jesus' sending of the spirit is the continuation of His activity of connecting all of us human beings. Again, all this is expressed in a large variety of ways in the New Testament. At Pentecost, the book of the Acts of the Apostles depicts the advent of the spirit as enabling strangers to truly understand each other (Cf. Acts, cp. 2.). Throughout his letters, Paul continually insists that where there is disunity, Christ, is absent (cf. e.g., I Cor. 11, 17-33). Finally, there is a single word which includes all this: Peace. "Peace be with you" is the risen Jesus' greeting in Luke (24/36) and it is Jesus' farewell gift in John (14/27). But here we must beware of psychologizing. Peace, both in the Hebrew Bible and in the New Testament, is never primarily a state of private or individual inner contentment or restfulness. Instead, peace, *shalom* in Hebrew, is the condition which obtains *between* people who are fully and openly connected with each other, and as Paul says over and over, it is the work of the Spirit. And the converse is obvious: those situations are unspiritual where that peace is absent.

Before we move to the concluding section of this chapter, let me briefly return to the critique I proposed earlier of the fundamentalist and apologetic interpretation of the Resurrection. I hope that the meagerness of that way of understanding the resurrection has emerged from the preceding exposition. Above all, I hope that now, the significance of the fundamentalist tendency to separate the resurrection from the rest of Jesus' life, is clear. That significance becomes clear when we see that at least three essential realities of the Christian life are revealed in the analysis I have just offered. Again, I suggest that the human divine-death of these realities better appears when set alongside the fundamentalist understanding.[5]

The three realities I wish to compare are: the understanding of God, of faith, and of salvation. The God implicit in the fundamentalist's view is sovereign in the same sense that He/She is able to suspend all physical "laws," and the resurrection is the fullest instance of such a suspension. This God "convinces" on the basis of the exercise of this *kind* of power. The God who engages humanity in conversation, and who is so extraordinarily respectful of human freedom, the God who *called* Abraham and Isaac and Jacob, is hardly hinted at in the fundamentalist view. Yet this is the God who covenants with Moses, David, the prophets. He/She is precisely the God of Jesus, and the God Who raised Jesus. This God calls, covenants, appeals, rather than acting to impress and overwhelm by performing unprecedented physical feats. And these two differing views of God account for differing views of faith. There is much talk of submission and obedience in the fundamentalist vocabulary for faith: the believer gives into a "force majeur." There is not much room given to human freedom as the capacity to respond to the appeals of God. Faith in the non-fundamentalist scheme is unequivocally a free response to God. Indeed, as I hope I have shown in my analysis of the Resurrection, mutual responsibility between God and the believer comes to be seen as the heart of the matter. Finally, this mutual response-ability is the very meaning of salvation. Perhaps here the most serious inadequacy of the fundamentalist view of salvation becomes apparent, for that view is a notably private and individualistic one. It is one which tends to extricate the believer from the social reality of her world. In a word, the fundamentalist is, at least,

---

[5] Here, let me make a most important point. In making these comparisons, I am certainly NOT making any judgment on the quality or depth of the *lived religiosity* of anyone, on either side of these matters. I am only proposing that my analysis is both more historically faithful to the biblical understanding of the resurrection, and that that understanding illumines to a far greater depth, the meaning of the resurrection. Again, let me insist: a better theology does not inevitably produce a better Christian. But it does allow for the religious search to be carried on in a fuller fashion.

theoretically, less worldly, less firmly situated in the socio-historical realities of their lives. Theirs tends to be a two-storey religious universe, one heavenly, the other earthly. And it goes without saying which of these two is the native land of the believer.

Now we come to speak of the final stage of the meaning of the word resurrection. This stage is the completion of God's saving work in Christ: the general resurrection. As I explained earlier, the resurrection was not just a private affair between Jesus and the Father, having only to do with the salvation of Jesus. Rather, the resurrection is a saving event for the world, the completion of God's promise to the patriarch Abraham that, through him, all the nations of the world would be blessed. The enlivening action of the spirit, sent by the risen Jesus, works here and now to bring us to faith, hope, and above all, to love. The Christian life is a process of transformation of our self-centered and self-preserving humanity into a pattern of Jesus' complete humanity: His steadfast love. Indeed, love is the prime identifier and witness of the Christian, and of the community of lovers called the Church (cf. John, 13/35).[6]

But the power of the resurrection is not exhausted just by its transforming effects here and how. As we have noted several times earlier and in several different contexts, the resurrection is the completion of God's intention in creating: namely, that all humanity constitute a single community, the kingdom of God, the completion of love. Here again Pauline metaphors are most illuminating. He speaks of life "in Christ" as the new creation, and of the risen Jesus as the first fruit of God's ultimate saving action. Paul is alluding to a typical Jewish metaphor, that of the harvest, to speak of God completing the work of creation.

This completion, obviously, takes the form of the resurrection of all human beings, from all times and all places. (The end also includes the process of judgment, and the criterion by which one is to be judged is the quality of one's relatedness to others: "I was a stranger and you took me in, etc." Mt. 26/31-46.) The ultimate state of humanity has been variously called heaven, eternal life, the Kingdom of God, etc.

In concluding, I want to speak about one way of understanding this final condition. It is described in the language of intimate knowing and being known (cf. e.g., John 17, I Cor. 13/12. et al). When God raises all humanity our self-knowledge will no longer be mediated by what we think of ourselves or what we think others think of us. (For the sake of precision: I take it as given that all self-understanding arises from interaction with others.) Rather, we will know ourselves in God, as the one who is loved by God. This means that we will be fully aware of our divinely effected lovableness, and we will know everyone else in the same way. All those deepest yearnings to be loved, to belong, for goodness, truth, and beauty—of whose fulfillment we tend to despair—will be realized. And Love, God, will be all in all. This is the completion of the resurrection, and the meaning of resurrection faith.

---

[6] Perhaps a more sober, modest, and accurate assessment of the historical performance of the Christian Churches, would go like this: the actual witness of the Churches *ought to* proclaim and sustain the faith and hope, that love is possible, and to do so in a world where fear and violence normally appear to have the upper-hand. In regard to the churches' own self-understanding, that witness ought to take the form of a continual act of repentance for their failure to love, together with a constant call for self-reform.

CHAPTER 31
The Problem of Death and Dying in Major Eastern Traditions*

Jaroslav Havelka

For most of us in the Western world, death is the final happening in our diminishment. We appear to be individuals isolated from other beings, from all sense of the eternal and our personal death is the ultimate horror and injustice. Though born of the cosmic process we feel ourselves at enmity with it and the surrounding nature itself is imagined to be a threat to our existence. An overwhelming fear invades our narrowing lives, distorts our vision and strangles our best impulses. We look upon ourselves as often lonely, unhappy, and frustrated. We became fragmentary, tormented by doubts; our original innocence has disappeared and our value-nucleus progressively collapses.

The hectic world in which we live today, the world of anxiety and violence, where we are afraid of everything, suspect everything, and hate most things, is the ordinary life of our ego, hurried and empty. The essence of our tragedy is that we are mostly not aware of our ignorance with its progressive loss of sensitivity, where fear of life is equal to fear of death. The Eastern mind, deeply aware of this general human condition, contemplates for thousands of years human suffering and fear, and offers an invaluable advice: true freedom from fear and death can be reached only by wisdom, the truth that liberates. For the Orientals human mortality is a concrete fact but not a radical limitation, since they accept the patterning of existence as a symbiotic union of life and death. They know that man's real nature of being reaches beyond the confines of physical death. To him the notion of life's continuity beyond death, and thus some variant of immortality, becomes fully evident only to the inward oriented, enlightened mind. The attainment of such an all-important insight

---

*Previously published in *Thanatology: A Liberal Arts Approach*, M. A. Morgan and J. D. Morgan (eds.), King's College, London, Ontario, 1986, and is reprinted by permission of the publisher.

becomes possible through a maturing process of spiritual liberation, potentially available to all of us.

Any Eastern psycho-philosophy keeps warning us that the most serious obstacle to such an attainment is our own ego in its pleasure-seeking, self-centered, and isolation experiencing tendency. The ego is the builder of our own suffering and our fear of death. To overcome such an obstacle is to achieve a state of liberation from the ignorance of our essential human condition. In this sense our immaturity is characterized by a painful bondage to an illusion, while our maturing leads us to a spiritual clarity which is exempted from fear of death.

It should be noted that the Eastern mind considers the solution of the problem of death as related to the awareness of Cosmic Consciousness which we can realize in this life. In this context the Eastern religious philosophy and psychology are closely related. They insist that indeed all levels of human consciousness, including perceptions and emotions, intellectually coordinated complex cognitions, and meditation upon the Absolute, are integrated in order to achieve the entrance upon the path leading to Reality.

Thus liberation, illumination, or enlightenment, so important to Hindu and Buddhist religious thought, are stages of highest mental processes through which a clarity concerning the Truth of human existence can be obtained. And such a high level of psychological understanding reaches its maturity when a person recognizes the precariousness and superficiality of the ego.

HINDU TRADITIONS

In Hindu religious literature, be it the ancient *Vedas, Brahmanas, Aranyakas,* or classical *Upanishads*, one soon realizes the most important orientation of human life: when one is in contact with the universal source of life (*Brahman*), one enjoys vitality and freedom from fear (*Abhaya*). Our nature becomes filled with light and happiness; "Knowing the bliss of Brahman, one doesn't fear anything" (Taittiriya Upanishad .ii.8.). For the first time our soul is no longer lonely or painfully isolated; it merges with the surrounding world and is saved from confusion and despair. "By knowing Him alone, one surpasses death" (Svetasvatara Upanishad. vi.15.).

The road leading from fear (*Bhaya*) is one pointing to the process of "deflation" of the personal ego, which doesn't imply a loss of individuality but on the contrary, an attainment of a purer, more genuine individuality. These classical scriptures offer varied and powerful psychological methods that aim at mastery over one's self-oriented mind.

The above being achieved, these methods eventually lead to experiences essentially more real than those with the objective world. The ego (*Amha*) is clearly pointed out as an obstacle in reaching the ultimate consciousness, the God-consciousness (*Turiya*).

We are told with unique subtlety and pervasiveness, that the ego is the skillful maker of our own fears and anxieties, among which the most painful and damaging is the fear of death. Since we are attached to what is pleasurable and have aversion to what is painful, the fear of death, which appears to be the ultimate privation, is unbearable to the ego.

A growing realization of one's own fundamental nature transcends our fear of death. The temporary physical span of life becomes only a fragment of the life-process, only one side of the coin, while our existence endures beyond the boundaries of our historical personality. Our individual life is a short-lived explosion followed by the implosion of death, followed again by another explosion in that continuous motion of the wheel of births and deaths (*Samsara*). Death of the body is not a terminal stage for a man of real Self-knowledge. This Self (*Atman*), according to the Hindu tradition, transcends the desire-oriented ego and its mortality; it is our cosmically related consciousness that leads us beyond the boundaries of births and deaths.

In it we discover the indestructible fundament, which passing beyond time and space is outside of the dominion of death. Through this real Self, and not through the ego, we are involved in the cosmic life-process (*Prana*). The meaningfulness of our existence is determined by our participation in this cosmic energy. The Hindu tells us that we are individual waves on an immense cosmic ocean. Each of these waves is only a temporary manifestation, only a fleeting bodily form of an Absolute Substance (*Brahman*).

The real "I-Am" is essentially and qualitatively the vital principle itself, Brahman. And this universal vital principle can never be threatened by death and destruction. Only the neuro-biological aspect of ourselves dies and what leaves our physical body at the moment of death is *Jiva* ("that which lives"), the soul in the Christian context. The individual souls enter the world in a mysterious fashion. Like bubbles of air they penetrate the water (cosmos) and then break free into the unrestricted atmosphere of life. They do not die together with their original bodies. *Jiva* after the death of a person passes through an unknown sequence of bodies, to be individualized and subjected to a renewed cycle of birth and death, until eventually liberation is attained and the cycle terminates.

To reach a higher level of the psycho-religious understanding of life and destiny one has to pass through the process of progressive elimination of ignorance (*Avidya*) which obstructs the clarity of our mental vision. The guide offered to mankind by the remarkable Hindu genius are the *Upanishads*, that ancient literature of sublime wisdom. The Upanishads outline a far-reaching and profoundly conceived goal of life, where the fear, the anxiety, and the pain of death will eventually vanish in a moment of bliss. They follow a development of human consciousness that reaches the ultimate state of liberation (*Moksa*) and frees us from misconceptions, incompleteness, and provisional reality proposed to us in a rather illusory fashion by our ego, *Maya*. When the sages of Upanishads asks us to free ourselves from Maya, they are asking us to break the bondage of the low level of satisfactions which are dominating us. Maya is not really an illusion, but rather a veil interfering with a full vision and understanding of reality.

The Upanishads are the perfect embodiment of the preceding oral traditions of Vedic wisdom. The orthodox Hindu views are here presented in a coordinated system of knowledge leading to the discovery of Brahman, the absolute essence of cosmic energy, in which our soul originates and with which it merges, when we pass away as liberated Selves, Atmans. The Upanishads reveal the truth which is unknown to the sense organs, the truth concerning the development of the individual Jivas, their destiny in bondage and in liberation. They contemplate the nature of the Absolute Brahman, the origin of creation, the cycles of preservation and the dissolution of the universe, the nature's changes and modifications (*Prakriti*).

The Upanishads consider the relationships between matter and spirit and ponder with an exquisite tolerance man's preference to a personal God with various attributes (*Saguna Brahman*) or preference to a non-personal God without attributes (*Nirguna Brahman*). The psychological insightfulness of these ancient scriptures is incomparable even in the context of very modern post-Freudian interpretations. Man's personal and social growth is subjected to a detailed analysis of three preliminary stages of psychosocial maturation (*Trivarga*) which precede the higher state of consciousness (*Moksa*) with its metaphysical and spiritual intelligence.

Here in the atmosphere of wise interpenetration of the profane with the sacred, of death and liberation from death, in the heart of all things of the universe is the Brahmanic, eternal universe itself. Brahman alone is devoid of limiting attributes (*Upadhis*), and in contrast with phenomenal objects, this Supreme reality is spaceless and timeless. Brahman is not subject to any causality but independent of it; there is no differentiation in Him, no duality. Duality of anything is only an appearance (*Maya*), a perception taken as real, when the real Truth is hidden.

And such are all empirical experiences including the experience of dying and of death. When the Upadhis of time, space, and causation are destroyed, what remains untouched and permanent is Brahman, the Immortal Reality.

The Upanishads warn us that our immature mind creates a relative world in which the birth and the death, the beginning and the end are considered the only irrevocable reality of our rather disappointing destiny. In this respect our suffering, grief, and fear of death are grave misinterpretations of our existence which is a part of Ultimate Reality which is everlastingly alive beyond the threshold of bodily death. The realization of Brahman removes the pain of death from our life.

In this realization we are led to understand that our individual existence is part of total Being (*Sat*), comprehended through the absolute consciousness of Atman (*Chit*) which allows us to apprehend the non-tragic aspect of our individual death. Chit illuminates all the known and as yet unknown strata of our minds: our states of waking, dreaming, dreamless sleep, and our meditative awareness. When during this period of self-consciousness the Brahman is understood, the resulting Truth is experienced as a unique bliss (*Ananda*).

It is the most perfect tool of our consciousness, the most penetrating agency of our understanding which leads us "from the unreal to the Real, from darkness to light, from death to Immortality" (Brihadaranyaka Upanishad I,iii,28). Atman is our nuclear Self, leading us to the reality of Brahman and to Immortality (*Amritatvam*). Atman is the Conscious Spirit behind the Universal Reality. Already in the Vedas and more so in the Upanishads Atman is being invoked through a sacred symbol A-U-M.

This sacred word elevates us to the all-absorbing consciousness that animates a person's high mental and vital activities. It dwells, spoken or unspoken, in the hearts of all as the most sacred appellation of Atman and of Brahman.

The ignorance of the nature of our inner Self is the cause of our repeated births and deaths, a mysterious process known as Reincarnation or Transmigration (Samsara). According to this doctrine a soul is born and born again in different levels of perfection, depending on the merits or demerits of its actions and intentions. Thus in each next birth it may acquire more understanding, and at the end of the liberating process it attains perfect Self-knowledge and freedom from further reincarnation and from death.

The mechanism which ties the human soul with the moment of liberation is the law of KARMA, the sequence of cause and effect of all human actions leading to moral commitment and responsibility, or to any lack of it. The more liberated a person becomes the more moral will be his/her action and thus the closer s/he will be to the final dissolution of Samsara.

Everyone succumbs to time (*Kala*) and to the Karmic circumstances of individual life; all born beings are subject to death which is an impartial instrument in the service of Karma. Thus true Self-knowledge is the only effective means of dispelling the fear of death and its illusory reality. "Having realized Atman . . . one is freed from the jaws of death" (Katha Upan.I,iii,15). The process toward such a realization of perfect freedom is *Sraddha*, a faith in the reality of Brahman, Atman, and the Immortality of the Self. As the physical body is destroyed by death, so death itself is annihilated by the liberating power of wisdom (*Vidya*).

The Fear of death and the recognition of an immortal Self within ourselves form an awesome polarity which encompass the dramatic potentialities of human life. Nowhere is this existential quest more magnificently expressed than in *Bhagavad Gita*. This sacred book of Hindu literature examines the goal of human spiritual liberation which leads to God and away from the fearful uncertainties of the anxious ego. In the Gita this tragic bondage is exposed and deposed in the growing illumination that floods our existence. Here we read that the knowledge of Self and of God, through the dissolution of the fear of death is the only goal of life; total surrender, and knowingly to "live, move and have our being in God" is central to the Gita's *Yoga*.

These Yogas are expounded in the Gita as a set of unique instructions: how to live mastering the ego and developing a thirst for the Ultimate reality. There are principally four ways of unification with the Divine. First (*Jnana Yoga*) is with its clear distinction between the inferior ego and the superior Atmanic Self-understanding and of its relation to Brahman. In it the initial ignorance is abandoned in illuminated discrimination, and especially in that capacity of turning one's awareness inward to the center of Consciousness. While in Jnana Yoga, the aim is to perceive one's identity with God, in *Bhakti Yoga* the supreme goal is to adore Him with every atom of one's being. Bhakti Yoga (so richly exemplified in essential Christianity) is an undying love for God for no ulterior reason but for love's sake alone.

The third path toward the divine is *Karma Yoga* where all duties of life are performed without any attachment and pleasure seeking. The so-called royal road toward God is *Raja Yoga*, a way of attaining liberation (Moksa) through a variety of subtle psychological experimentations. These experiments are directed toward practicing certain disciplines which lead to progressively higher spiritual conditions. The goal is a mastery of mental and physiological control, meditative self-awareness and self-actualization. At last there emerges in Raja Yoga a state of complete absorption in God, (*Samadhi*). Here the yogi has reached a level of personal revelation, the ultimate proof of Brahman. In it culminates a sense of ecstatic consciousness or a feeling of immediate contact with Ultimate reality, and the unification of the divergent elements of nature. It is a state of clearest apprehension of the non-duality of everything and thus a cancellation of any fear of death. Psychologically a person is aware of a deep insight in which serenity dislodges any feeling of sad longing and loneliness. Samadhi ignites instantaneously a blissful revelation of Reality: "That are Thou" (*Tat Twam Asi*). In the words of Bhagavad Gita, "Those who meditate on me . . . those I soon lift from the ocean of death."

At this level of Samadhi the Raja yogi has learned that the human soul is imperishable and his previous life-preoccupation with death recedes and pales. He knows now that truly wise people do not grieve either for the living or for the dead, since death is transformed at that moment of liberation into a death-life union which then loses its threat and merges with eternity.

The final stage of human psychological and religious maturation is Moksa, sometimes referred to as Samadhi, and in the Gita as Brahma-Nirvana, which means extinction in Brahman, or union in Brahman. These equivalent ideals of perfection are not experiences to be attained only after death, but at any moment of Self-knowledge in this life.

Nirvana-Samadhi implies primarily the extinction of the illusory, the false self, which although is an indispensable early process of mental maturation, never allows a person to become free in Brahman. A Nirvana-Samadhi man continues to live and work not bound anymore to the world of Karma; and when his body dies, he attains what is known as absolute freedom. "At the hour of death, when man leaves his body, he must depart with his consciousness absorbed in me. Then he will be united with me" (Kathamrta Upan. VIII.6.).

Ultimately all people will achieve Moksa and Samadhi regardless of the length of time it takes for the gradual evolution of Self-knowledge. There may be many returns, many reincarnations before the final goal is reached.

Whatever the length of the waiting period may be, it will happen in a given time. Karma is not eternal and thus it cannot be conceived as a part of eternal damnation. The final stage of all existences is the totally benign reconciliation of all conflicts and traumas of our essentially illusory and dualistic experience of reality.

When the boundary of the Karmic bondage is crossed, the night of tribulation becomes a day of Awareness; the tragic notion of death changes into a sacred play of creation (*Lila*) and the thorn of dying and death is removed forever.

Buddhism

Buddhism, although a reform movement of orthodox Hinduism, adheres deeply to the religious and psychological truths of the Vedas, the Upanishads, and the Bhagavad Gita. Gautama Buddha, historically the first Buddha, did not proclaim a new religion, rather he re-interpreted and concretely reinforced the true spirit of *Sanatan Dharma*, the eternal religion. Again like the ancient sages of the Upanishads, but more emphatically so, Buddhism insists on psychological clarity concerning our personal experiences of the inner truth. Indeed the heart of Buddhism is the psychological insight into one's true nature: enlightenment. *Maha Bodhi*, or Supreme Wisdom, is the purpose of all self-examination, of all morality, of all theoretical and practical knowledge. In the end each living being will achieve Enlightenment and thus untold number of future Buddhas (the illuminated one's) are to come.

And similarly as Hinduism, Buddhism teaches that through Self-knowledge one can conquer death. There is no other way of escaping from Samsara, the wheel of birth, death, and rebirth. For Buddhists the essence of enlightenment doesn't lie in dogma or creed, nor in doctrines and theologies, but in personal psychological experiences containing a high level of liberation. And the notion of death, "memento mori," is lodged in the center of these psychological experiences. Perhaps more than in other religions of the world the problem of death in Buddhism is primarily psychological before it becomes a philosophical and a religious problem.

All phenomenal things are products of our mind and thus incompletely perceived. Only from the center of our Self can they be apprehended as pure Reality. The distinct, the discriminable things do change and are in a state of impermanence, and when analyzed, are found lacking and unchanging substance. This is referred to in Buddhism as *Anicca*.

Similarly when this idea is applied to the nature of our soul, there arises a rather surprising but logically consistent notion of "no personal soul doctrine": *Anatta*. Buddhists insist that we do not possess a subjectively unique, individual soul.

This life dwelling in ignorance, this "wheel of existence," was compared by Buddha to dream, sleep, and forgetfulness; as soon as we awake from this unconsciousness, we can reach Nirvana in this very life. As soon as we wake up, the pain of dying and the terror of death do vanish.

Here Buddha proposes the effective and practical strategy of achieving the recovery from the Dukkha (life is suffering) and Tanha (cause of suffering). This way of complete freedom is Nirvana and it can be attained through the guiding principles of "the eightfold Path." This slow road toward infinite peace and liberation is a unique psychotherapeutic course which can handle all problems and difficulties of personal life. It is a rigorous and concrete system of de-habituation designed to release us from the ignorance of this painful existence, and to transform us into new and free beings.

Any maturing candidate for this Path is directed toward recovery by following a system of new approaches to life through Right understanding, Right aspiration, Right speech, Right action, Right occupation, Right effort, Right mindfulness, and

Right absorption. As the individual practices one approach after another, s/he is eventually immersed in a state of Mindfulness in which his/her thoughts are concerned with the negative effects of clinging to objects of impermanency, including his/her own ego.

That process forms an entrance into the last stage, Right absorption or meditation, in which s/he starts to concentrate on spiritual contemplation, in order to be free to transcend all thought and enter into an awareness of Nirvana. At last, s/he sees the problem of death as an air-inflated bubble which ceases to give him/her any uneasiness and thus any need of serious pondering. Now s/he knows that death is only an imaginary obstacle, an illusion, an empty notion.

No doubt Buddhist Nirvana is an extraordinary state of mind in which every earthly craving is viewed in its ephemeralness and triviality. It is a stage far beyond any passion, desire, lust, sorrow, fear, and anxiety. It is a serene awareness of the bliss of deliverance from all the calamities and imperfections of "the wheel of existence."

In it the sage is delivered from the ordinary sensation of time and space, and the immense cloud of restless and mostly trivial thoughts. In its fullness Nirvana contains a nucleus of the precious experience of "nothingness" or "void" (Sunyata), which is a radical absence of any subject-object relationship. In this aspect it resembles the state of Turiya described in the Mundaka Upanishad. Both refer to consciousness without any content, as something essentially unthinkable and inconceivable and yet attainable through a liberated awareness.

Nirvana is a consciousness beyond the reach of death, beyond all experience of relativity and beyond all the obstructions that used to clutter one's everyday life. To attain Nirvana is to break the illusory bondage to death and to awaken to the intuition of the Supreme One. Like the Upanishads, the state of Nirvana points to the ultimate realization of "the unborn, the undying and the changeless." It is a noble vision, where no subject-object interaction exists, where the phenomenal appears to lose its urgency and where intellectual cognition appears to be rather insignificant.

At last the final hour approaches: for a Buddhist this hour of death is not to be spent in last minute repentance, but in a final episode of meditation which purifies the mind fixing it joyfully upon the memory of Buddha, a lifetime of good works (Dharma), and on the ever more luminous rays of Nirvana. Death is felt as a gate through which passes all personal experience, and being consumed, reappears and is transformed into a sequence of new existences, pointing again toward the more accomplished level of liberation. The body dies, but the person's Karma, the result of all previously active causes and effects, lives on. The fundamental energy activating this continuity is the eternal force of internal urgency, leading us irrevocably toward the crystallization of human consciousness in Nirvana.

Tibetan Buddhism

Tibetan Buddhism, perhaps the loftiest expression of the Eastern spirituality, originates in the Mahayana tradition, that leans heavily on the *Tantras* which are the religious scriptures of the Hindu school of mysticism. This branch of Buddhism cultivates an elaborate cosmology and rich rituals including *Mudras* (ritual gestures), *Mantras* (expressions concerning magical powers), and *Mandalas* (diagrams of symbolic meanings). All these aspects seem to form a religion of esoteric mysteriousness and other-worldliness. Yet two central ideas emphasize the warm naturalness and the concreteness of life. One is a wide and deeply conceived compassion and the other is an enlightened approach to dying and death.

One cannot really understand its hierarchical structure and complex ritual without noticing the importance of these two approaches. Compassion can be generally defined as: a cultivation and transmission of a benevolent force or energy through all levels of living. And it involves not only this active force but even a refined capacity of grateful responding. Indeed the whole structure of Tibetan society, from the person of incarnate lama to the humblest peasant in the mountains, is an expression of a complex chain of compassionate interactions.

In this sense Tibet is a tightly knit organization of psychospiritual support. The potentiality of compassion is linked in an unusual and sublime way with thought on death. That benevolent energy and the goodness of human existence are inconceivable for the Tibetan Buddhist without connecting their relationship with the Supreme Good of Nirvana which solves the problem of death. The notion of interaction is basically simple: either one attains Nirvana in this life and then death is dissolved, or one can achieve it passing through the gate of death. To be compassionate in the most elevated fashion is to guide and help other human beings toward this realization.

This singular offering of spiritual compassion is best displayed in a unique book called *Bardo Thodol* (*The Tibetan Book of the Dead*). This ancient text is recited to the dying or already dead person by a TULKU (a man known for compassion, a priest, a guru) with the most solemn intention of restoring to the dying soul the divine truth it has lost at birth and may rediscover while dying or even dead.

Furthermore, this book is a key to the innermost depth of the human mind, a guide for the seeker of existential understanding of the spiritual path to liberation. Every initiate approaching the stage of liberation is bound to pass through the experience of spiritual "death" before s/he can be reborn in freedom.

Symbolically s/he must die to his/her past, to his/her desire-oriented ego, before s/he can attain Nirvanic liberation. Thus *Bardo Thodol* is addressed not only to those who see the end of their natural life approaching, but also to those who begin to realize the fuller meaning of their existence. Buddhists in general, and the Tibetan Buddhist in particular, insist that both birth and death offer unique opportunities of liberation through "turning-about in the deepest seat of consciousness" as *Lankavatara* Sutra puts it, before *Bardo* was written.

Although the understanding of death in *Bardo* is primarily Buddhist, there are also in it important elements originating in Hindu Tantric symbolism and ritual. Such a union of cultic functions with psychological insights shapes an esoteric religious atmosphere that allows the Tulku to prepare and guide the dying or dead person through a mysterious dominion of death. The most important point is held in helping the person to know how to be "reborn" in an enlightened state of consciousness.

The book is divided into three parts: *Chikhai, Chonyid,* and *Sidpa Bardo.* The Chikhai Bardo or the "Transitional state of the Moment of Death" describes the moment of dying and death in which the person is believed to be in a trance-like state unaware of his/her physical body. That is immediately followed by a state of swoon in which the Super-consciousness itself dawns upon him/her and the immensely Clear light of the Void permeates everything. The Void (*Sunyata*) is the realization of the highest aim of all existences. To attain it is to enter forever the All-conscious Buddhahood, the unconditioned *Dharma-Kaya* (The Divine Body of Truth). In it lies the peaceful essence of the universe, including both the Samsara and Nirvana, which in this last instance become identical.

If the deceased recognizes fully and blissfully this Void of Bright Light s/he will instantaneously reach the fullest liberation. So the highest peak, the supreme vision of Reality occurs often just at the beginning of the departure from physical life. If at that particular time s/he misses the great opportunity, if the bliss of Recognition of the Light does not materialize, s/he begins an ever-deepening descent into the inferior regions of his/her mind leading eventually to a new pre-birth experience of the new life of an infant which is immensely remote from the occasion of becoming liberated. A new human individuation takes place and a new cycle of ignorance and desiring, as well as the growth of his/her new ego is again to be endured, before a new opportunity to be liberated presents itself. The person's Karma was not yet exhausted, s/he was not yet spiritually mature and s/he must continue the unpredictable birth-death cycle.

A detailed description of this regress from the moment of a missed opportunity immediately after his/her death, is explained in the second stage, in Chonyid Bardo. In it one becomes again a victim of Karmic illusions which probably originate in the unresolved psychic remnants of previous existences. While regaining a partial object-consciousness the deceased begins to experience anxieties and terrors, originating in his/her renewed egotistic strivings. The terrifying and chaotic feelings are probably equivalent to psychotic states as we know them in the modern context.

According to the Chonyid Bardo, continuously recited by the Tulku, the fear of being destroyed by imaginary wrathful gods are filling the person's frightened mind. Yet the text warns that these appearances are only figments of fearful and disturbed imaginations. They are mental phantoms, not realities.

The terror and darkness of these moments is described in the third part of Bardo, in Sidpa. The deceased begins to hallucinate that s/he has a body. But even in this late state s/he could still rekindle the saving desire of being liberated, since the Tulku keeps reminding him/her that the fearful experiences of the moment are illusory fragments of his/her craving ego. He can still avoid reincarnation by regaining trust in the Absolute Reality which is overriding all his/her anxieties. But if s/he is unable to do so his/her mind becomes even more eagerly attached to a new body and a new place into which s/he keeps rapidly sinking, and into which s/he desires to be reborn. Thus if all psychological instructions fail, reincarnation becomes inevitable and does presumably occur on the forty-ninth day following his/her death.

The Tulku's role is evidently powerfully compassionate and spiritual. He is in constant communication with the dying or deceased persons when they need it most.

He is a spiritual guide as well as a therapist at the most important and pressing moment of their lives, when the most radical decision must be made either trustingly to surrender to the liberating light of the Void or fail and be reborn into a new circle of Karma.

The Tulku's guidance reminds the dying person of the need of being prepared for death during their lifetime, thus never to be unaware of the momentous opportunity of transformation at any moment of their living. The Experience of Bardo brings no eternal rewards or punishments but a mature insight and opening into a new ultimately illuminated life.

Bardo Thodol is to the Tibetan Buddhist the most precious contribution to the understanding of death and dying, of the existence after death and of the clarification of reincarnation. For the Westerner it is a most fascinating and unique book among the sacred books of the world. Perhaps next to the Upanishads and the Bhagavad-Gita, one of the most remarkable works of Eastern religious psychology and wisdom. In it occurs the crystallization of the Mahayana Buddhism and the Yoga psychology. For the mystically oriented, it represents a manual of guidance through the mysterious and mostly unconscious territory of illusions, fears, and horrors as well as the serene and blissful resolution of these predicaments which are taking place between death and birth. In its dramatic insightfulness it sufficiently resembles *The Egyptian Book of the Dead*, which leads us to the assumption that some deep-seated cultural relationships exist between these two masterpieces of human thought.

Zen Buddhism

In a subtle and distinctly non-tragic way the emphasis on life's impermanency and on death permeates the whole Japanese culture. Since its introduction in the sixth century, Buddhism has been an integral part of Japanese life and a formative power of its history. And particularly so through that part of Buddhism known as *Zen*. Zen Buddhism is essentially a product of the Chinese mentality influenced by the Hindu thought and spirituality. In its philosophical roots it contains the mystical essence of Chinese *Taoism*, Buddhist metaphysics, and the social concreteness of *Confucianism*.

But although Zen in China has influenced the philosophy of the Sung dynasty and certain patterns of Chinese art, it never affected the social psychology of the Chinese people as profoundly as it did in Japan. Zen always upholds the priority of personal experiences and radically refuses to commit itself to any theoretical system of philosophy. The facts of experience are accepted in their un-romantic simplicity, primarily as they are, and not as they are thought to be or presumed to be.

Zen is not pantheistic, nor nihilistic or even merely positivistic. It doesn't reject words but never stops warning, that as they are detached from the essential realities by the use of human language, they harden into abstract concepts and become merely labels. And this process of abstraction and conceptualization, so precious to the Western mind, Zen deeply suspects and rejects as unreal.

The ultimate aim of Zen discipline is to realize Satori (in Japanese, Samadhi in Hindu) which usually translates as enlightenment. More specifically Satori is "the state of consciousness in which Noble Wisdom realizes its own nature." This process of Self-realization is the nucleus of insight and relates directly to the Hindu Moksa and Absolute freedom (*Vasavartin*). Although this experience is beyond the realm of words and thus inexplicable, it forms the innermost truth of our experiences. While Satori is essentially incommunicable, in experiencing it we fathom what might be.

We shouldn't think of it as a state of quietude only, or passive tranquilization, but as an inner awareness that has a unique noetic quality of consciousness. Such a consciousness goes beyond any ordinary informative categorization; it is both an understanding of any object and at the same time it reveals its deepest meaning beyond any classification. A distinct sense of "beyond" is present in Satori: one might call it God, Godhead, the Absolute and yet none of these terms conveys the essence of such an experience.

This quality of Self-realized awareness is a most sublime psychological state that captures any moment as carrying an imprint of death. It "eternalizes" every distinct moment and opens a radically new view of life constantly linked with its polarity, death. Thus death mingles with every moment of life and while it underscores its impermanency, it begins to lose finality.

Here the notion of impermanence generates a pervasive climate of Zen tradition as well as Japanese culture. The term used is MUJO, which is equivalent to the Buddhist Anicca. Life and every component of it is always changing, is never static and fixed; it contains in every manifestation an element of the underlying reality of dying. This notion of the ephemeralness of all things signals the passing away of everything. This ever-present change occurs in a continuity which characterizes a "small death" that marks every event of our life and thus exempts us from the fearful expectation of death as that one final and tragic episode of our existence.

This unique feeling becomes deeply imbedded in the Japanese mentality and is a part of their Satori. It eventually opens the way to the feeling of the "great death" (*Daishi*) which is the capacity to meet the end with a sense of peaceful harmony and composure. This serene acceptance of evanescence leads to *Furyu*, the gentle detached enjoyment of everything that has to pass. The spirit of Mujo is present in other related feelings that link serenity and peace with impermanence. *Jaku* is one of those and it does denote in Buddhist literature as "passing away," "extinction," or Nirvana.

Another typical Zen sensitivity centers upon the tranquil atmosphere of a detached aloofness (*Wabi*). It emphasizes the independence of worldly things, and yet it promotes the feeling of rare value. It is essentially a deeply respectful attitude toward everything insignificant, poor, neglected, and lonely.

The term *Sabi*, which relates to Wabi, suggests aging, attenuation, obscurity, and unpretentious taste which appreciates external simplicity yet which is filled by internal richness. A rare gleam of Satori transpires in both Wabi and Sabi generating a non-tragic elegance of inner glow which accompanies everything destined to perish. In this context passing away is not a death-stamp but a sign of the uninterrupted vital flow of everything, including human life, in its approach to eternity. One of the most exquisite manifestation of Wabi and Sabi is present in Zen's sublime tea ceremony, *Cha-No-Yu.*

Somewhat surprisingly for the Western mind Zen's history is closely related to the life of the Japanese warrior, the Samurai. Especially one aspect of Zen exerted a profound impression on these intrepid feudal knights: indifference to both life and death. Closely related to this is Zen's emphasis on directedness, self-reliance, a certain ascetism, and a strong morally motivated will. All these characteristics combine in the Samurai's ideal, *Bushido,* "the way of the warrior."

Essentially Bushido means to be incessantly aware of the presence of death in the middle of life. Indeed to die in the flowering of one's heroically lived life is the most desirable goal of the Samurai. In learning Bushido he is instructed daily that clinging to life is the way of undignified weakness while a defiance of it earns nobility. His sword is invariably on the side of justice, peace, and noble humanity; it doesn't destroy life but corrects inhumanity and egotism. The sword of a Samurai expresses self-sacrifice in any worthy cause, a reverence for a dignified existence, a benevolence and a disregard for death. The nervous and fearful thought centered on the desire of winning is the greatest obstacle in combat, which is always life and death combat.

To be exempted from such a fear one has to mature through preparatory stages for Satori, and this is achieved by developing a sense of *Mushin,* which translates as spontaneity or "no-mindedness." Through it the Samurai transcends the dualistic notion of life and death and keeps on living leaving behind the illusory Samsara and the fear of defeat. In this spiritual ripening he may attain the unattached ego-less experience of Sunyata (emptiness), and with it, the highest degree of freedom. In reaching this freedom, the Samurai is able to discover the "suchness" of things (*Tathagata*) the essential substance in its permanence.

The Bushido is a process of understanding the "great death" as a result of realizing Tathagata which in its permanent pervasiveness defeats the ongoing threat of death. It can happen anywhere and anytime in the most ordinary circumstances, it can even be encountered in the act of suicide. For a Samurai the *Seppuku* or *Harakiri* (cutting open the abdomen) carries along a valiant display of profound indifference to life and death, also a high degree of sensitivity toward any possible disgrace. Through the fatal cut across the abdomen he reveals symbolically that the vital center of the body has remained pure and undefiled.

This fierce act of voluntary death is for the Samurai an ultimate confirmation of his inner strength and indifference to pain and death on an occasion of presumed social error, unwanted captivity, or an impasse of love. Seppuku is not an escape from life's obligation, but an heroic gesture of imperviousness to death with an equanimity of approaching Satori. The concept of death in Zen remains purely Buddhist in that it dissolves in the process of enlightenment and ceases to be a fearful episode awaited with sadness and grief. The "reality" of death is to be intuitively grasped in the process of liberation and thus it is eventually understood more in terms of a growing religious disposition and creativity than of intellectual categorization.

The close ties between the Zen mentality and Japanese art is evident in its form and in its spiritual meaning. For Zen oriented art life is essentially the "life-death" polarity. In all the branching of its noble art Zen discovers a hidden harmony (*Yugen*) through which one attains a glimpse of eternity in things of constant change. In this creative transformation of everything the artist finds a reality that spills over the boundary between life and death. The insight into this unphantomnable reality is "suchness" of all things, that counteract death while uniting with it.

Japanese *Haiku* poetry is an exquisite example of this unique momentary experience, in which one encounters a creative union of life and death in its utmost concreteness. This beautiful poetry detects the meaning of "suchness" even at the roots of death thus cleansing it of any tragic interpretation. The feeling of life's tragic aspect is totally absent in Haiku and if there is in it sometimes an atmosphere of gentle melancholy, it is more a sign of yearning for the eternal in Tathagata. In it the intuition of "suchness" relates to a faith in the ultimate Reality and that in turn to a radical fearlessness.

The Zen spirit awakens the artist to the fact that the only thing to be afraid of is fear itself and not death; when freed from that, one has entered Satori and through it the unchanging eternal Tathagata.

BIBLIOGRAPHY

Bashman, A. L., *The Wonder that was India*, Grove Press, New York, 1959.
Blyth, R. H., *Haiku*, 4 vol. Tokyo, (1947-1952).
Choron, J., *Death and Western Thought*, Collier, New York, 1963.
de Bary, W. T., *Sources of Japanese Tradition*, Columbia University Press, New York, 1958.
Dumoulin, H., *A History of Zen Buddhism*, Beacon, Boston, 1963.
Embree, A. T., *The Hindu Tradition*, Random House, New York, 1966.
Evans-Wentz, W. Y., *The Tibetan Book of the Dead*, Oxford University Press, 1972.
Evans-Wentz, W. Y., *Tibetan Yoga and Secret Doctrines*, London, 1935.
Farquhar, J. N., *An Outline of the Religious Literature of India*, Motilal Banarsidass, Delhi, 1967.
Guenther, H. V., *Buddhist Philosophy and Theory*, Penguin, Baltimore, 1971.
Holck, F. H., *Death and Eastern Thought*, Abongdon Press, Calgary, 1974.
Isherwood, C. (ed.), *Vedanta for Modern Man*, Collier, New York, 1962.
Johansson, R., *The Psychology of Nirvana*, Allen and Unwin, London, 1969.
Nikhilananda, S. (trans.). *The Upanishads*, Harper and Row, New York, 1949.
Organ, T. W., *The Self in Indian Philosophy*, Mouton, The Hague, 1964.
Prabhavananda S. and Isherwood, C. (trans.), *Bhagavad Gita*, New York, 1954.
Prabhavananda, S., *The Spiritual Heritage of India*, Vedanta Press, London, 1979.
Radhakrishnan, S., *Eastern Religions and Western Thought*, Oxford University Press, London, 1940.
Radhakrishnan, S., *History of Philosophy, Eastern and Western*, London, 1952.
Rahula, W., *What the Buddha Taught*, Grove Press, New York, 1962.
Ricoeur, P., *The Symbolism of Evil*, Harper and Row, New York, 1976.
Robinson, R., *The Buddhist Religion*, Dickenson, Chicago, 1970.
Smith, H., *The Religions of Man*, Harper and Row, New York, 1958.
Sri Aurobindo, *The Problem of Rebirth*, Ashram, Pondicherry, 1969.

Suzuki, D. T., *Zen and Japanese Culture,* Princeton University Press, 1959.
Suzuki, D. T., *Essays in Zen Buddhism,* 3rd Vol., Rider, London, 1973.
Swami V., *The Complete Works of S. V. Advaita Ashrama,* Delhi, 1962.
Welbon, G. R., *The Buddhist Nirvana and its Western Interpreters,* Chicago University Press, Chicago, 1968.
Zaehner, R. C., *Hinduism,* Oxford University Press, New York, 1966.
Zaehner, R. C., *Mysticism: Sacred and Profane,* Oxford University Press, New York, 1967.
Zimmer, H., *Philosophies of India,* Bollingen, New York, 1951.

PART VI

Introduction: Suicide

We hear a great deal about suicide. It is the second or third largest killer of adolescents depending on where you live, it is often performed by the very old, particularly men. Why do people choose suicide? Is there anything that can be done to effect a change in these decisions to take "premature exits?" This section of the book looks at these issues.

Dr. Bruce Connell gives us both a theoretical understanding of the nature of suicide and a practical understanding of when a suicide might be immanent. Basing his work largely on Schneidman, he discusses intrapsychic theories, interpersonal theories, physiological theories, psychological theories, and life-span development theories. The commonalities of suicides which he mentions are particularly important for care givers to know.

Mr. Ralph Rickgarn has worked with suicidal college students for many years. Drawing on that experience, he sows us interventions that can help in preventing suicides. When faced with a potential suicide, he advises us to (1) listen carefully to what the person is saying and the emotional context for a complete understanding of the message. (2) Engage in direct questioning about the details of any plans that the individual may have. (3) Do not interject your own reasons as they may be quite disparate from the suicidal individual's. (4) Offer to accompany the suicidal person to the hospital and remain until professional help is present. (5) Do not be drawn into a compact of secrecy. (6) Leave the assessment and analysis to the professionals. (7) Do not be drawn into inappropriate bargaining or manipulative behaviors. (8) Do not promise what you cannot deliver. (9) Do not leave an acutely suicidal person alone. (10) Do not get into a philosophical debate on moral or other issues so suicide. Focus on the problem and leave the debate for a later time.

Once a suicide has occurred, the attention must focus on the survivors. Dr. Robert Stevenson draws on his experience with high school students to teach us the best way to intervene after a suicide. An understanding of the nature of a death by suicide is essential for those who wish to help the survivors. The death is perceived as sudden and violent. Sudden death is more likely to cause complicated grief than is a death that is anticipated. Even when the actual cause of death does not involve "violent" means, the death may well be perceived as violent by the survivors because of the devastating impact it has on *their* lives. Those who attempt suicide see it not as a "problem" but as a solution to some other problem. The death does not necessarily cause these other problems to disappear and they often remain, still unsolved, to complicate the recovery of survivors. Silence imposed by others who mean well and wish to spare the survivors "unnecessary" suffering only magnifies these feelings of guilt and regret.

The last chapter in this section by Dr. Judith Stillion deals with suicide of the elderly. Why we see many headlines about youth suicide, the reality is that more elderly persons proportionally commit suicide. There has been a lessening of suicide across the last half of the century among the younger elderly because more women live to old age than men and because women's suicide rate peaks in middle age. Second, the cohort differences between this group of elderly and those who went before is noted. The younger elderly form the Baby Boom cohort and represent an investment of time and energy in parenting that had hitherto been unknown. Third, there is a powerful influence of economic gain on the rate of elderly suicide. Although the overall rate of suicide among younger elderly has declined, the elderly still have the highest rate of suicide of all age groups. They remain over-represented among suicides. For example, in the early 1980s people over sixty-five constituted approximately 11 percent of the U.S. population but committed 17 percent of the suicides.

CHAPTER 32
Suicide Theories

Bruce Connell

OVERVIEW OF THEORIES

In many respects, the study of suicide is still in its infancy. The etiology of suicidal behavior is not well understood and we still await a comprehensive theory of life-threatening behavior. Nonetheless there is certainly no shortage of suicide theories. Whether the wide variety of suicide theories represents richness or clutter is debatable. However, it is unlikely that one theory could explain even a single suicidal act, let alone the wide scope of suicidal phenomena.

The roots of life-threatening behavior are multi-factorial and multidimensional. While one can describe suicidal behavior from, say, an intrapsychic perspective (as do Sigmund Freud and Karl Menninger) or a sociological point of view (e.g., Emile Durkheim), no single discipline can capture the breadth and complexity of the field.

Moreover, in most cases it is not that one theory is "better" than another, rather that different theories help us to understand actions motivated by different factors. These variables reflect both individual differences and changes that may occur within the same individual at different stages of the life cycle. As well, the continuum of suicidal phenomena ranges from the unremarkable (ideation) to the extraordinary (completions), with a variety of other behaviors (gestures and attempts) that vary greatly in both intentionality and lethality in between.

There are fundamental but often unrecognized differences between the two forms of nonlethal suicidal behavior collectively known as "parasuicide"—gestures and attempts. It is important to clarify the distinction between the two because only the latter are truly suicidal acts. Strictly speaking, suicide attempts refer solely to the behavior of persons who consciously seek to end their own lives by employing lethal means but who fortuitously survive (e.g., through rescue). On the other hand, gestures are acts of low lethality that are essentially behavioral threats rather than deliberate attempts to end life.

Gestures include hesitation cuts to the wrists and the ingestion of low-toxicity dosages of medication. The typical gesturer is a female in her early teens who ingests a non-lethal quantity of pills in front of family members after an argument [1]. By contrast the typical adolescent completer is a male in his late teens who takes his life with a handgun [2]. The theories considered in this chapter will be exclusively those that describe acts of committed suicide or attempts to die by suicide. It should be noted, however, that much of the common knowledge about suicide is derived from studies of people who have made suicide gestures [3, 4]. Unfortunately, the evidence strongly suggests that attempts and gestures are reflective of two different populations [5].

I have chosen to consider those theories of completed suicide that have, in addition to their historical importance, relevance to current notions about the genesis of suicidal acts. These sometimes disparate psychological theories have been organized into four categories: (1) intrapsychic, (2) interpersonal, (3) psychological, and (4) physiological. In addition, two integrative approaches will be described. The first identifies commonalities among suicidal actions at all ages and stages of development, while the second highlights differences in suicidal behavior across the life span.

Interspersed throughout this chapter are excerpts from notes or poems written by suicidal high school students with whom I have worked in my role as a clinical school psychologist. While these will be exclusively the words of adolescents, I believe that their thoughts and feelings bring to life some of the issues and commonalities that pervade the tragedy of suicide. Hopefully they will also illuminate aspects of some of the theories presented in the chapter. One note was written by a teenager who had made life-threatening attempts. Most, however, are from a young man whom I came to know well but for whom life ended at age fifteen by his own hand. In an effort to preclude identification of the young people themselves, their real names have not been used and descriptive details have been slightly altered on occasion.

Intrapsychic Theories

The pioneering work of Sigmund Freud on the psychodynamics of the human mind is still a rich source of theoretical wisdom. Freud viewed suicidal behavior as a manifestation of intrapsychic conflicts [6]. He maintained that there exists a dynamic balance of power between the polar drives—Eros (the life instinct) and Thanatos (the death, aggressive, or destructive drive). According to Freud the ambivalence toward life versus death displayed by many suicidal persons reflects this struggle. In his classic work *Mourning and Melancholia*, written in 1917, Freud describes how both murder and suicide flow from the force of Thanatos [7]. In Freud's view murder represents aggression expressed toward another, while suicide is aggression turned upon oneself. In other words suicide is "murder in the 180th degree" [8, p. 34].

Although it is tempting to view much of Freud's work as somewhat dated, this formulation receives support from a recent study by Leenaars on authentic suicide notes [9]. Leenaars found that suicidal persons are often preoccupied with feelings of loss or rejection by significant others and have ambivalent (hostile and affectionate) feelings toward such individuals. This is consistent with Freud's hypothesis that a suicidal person turns against him/herself a death wish originally directed at another.

Another of Freud's influential ideas is that of the libido—the amount of psychic energy available to an individual. Freud believed that human beings use up libidinal energy by employing defense mechanisms at an unconscious level to protect themselves from painful or threatening memories [10]. By so doing they have less energy left for growth and development and the balance between Eros and Thanatos shifts toward the latter. When Thanatos overwhelms Eros the individual may develop feelings of hopelessness and inability to cope, which in turn can lead to suicidal actions. The terms Eros and Thanatos are thought of more broadly today than during Freud's day. Eros is associated with prosocial traits including humor and altruism while Thanatos is associated with negative characteristics such as jealousy, hatred, and anger.

The internal struggle between the forces of life and death (both suicide and murder) is apparent in the following sentences drawn from a rambling four page note given to me by a seventeen-year-old female client. On one page she writes: "Sometimes I totally love life" while a page later she states: "I wanted to kill myself on May 2nd . . . I wanted to die then especially." On the next page she mentions that she has "taken knives to my mother's throat while she was sleeping." Still later she writes of "love, peace, flowers, laughing."

Karl Menninger, in his enormously important book *Man Against Himself*, further described the psychodynamics of hostility and elaborated upon some of Freud's ideas on suicide [11]. Like Freud he described the contradiction between self-preservation and self-destruction. In addition, Menninger posited three motives for suicide: the wish to kill, the wish to be killed, and the wish to die. He argued that each of these three wishes is present in every suicide, with one predominating in each.

Interpersonal Theories

The interpersonal perspective on suicide is certainly broader than that of most intrapersonal approaches. The most influential of the interpersonal theories are the sociological conjectures which maintain that human behavior must be viewed in its cultural/societal context. Emile Durkheim's *Le Suicide*, published in 1897, is the classic work [12]. It led to an extensive line of research and to the construction of subsequent theories. Durkheim argued that the likelihood of suicidal behavior is related to the strength or weakness of society's control over the individual. In an effort to explain statistical patterns, Durkheim postulated four different categories of suicide.

"Egoistic" suicide applies to individuals who are on the periphery of society and are not well integrated into any social group. The self-annihilation of a loner would fit into this category. "Altruistic" suicide involves people who are overly integrated into society and for whom no sacrifice is too great. The self-sacrificial behavior of Japanese kamikaze pilots during World War II and the willingness to die of some Islamic fundamentalists could serve as examples.

"Anomic" suicide pertains to those whose accustomed relationship to society is abruptly altered (e.g., a renowned astronaut who suddenly must retire) or to those who lack regulation. The drug-related suicides of some young people in the 1960s might have reflected their alienation from mainstream values and led to their subsequent reckless experimentation with potentially deadly drugs. "Fatalistic" suicides involve excessive societal regulation such that the individual's freedom is so severely restricted that the person sees no viable future. The suicidal behavior of slaves or prisoners of war might be indicative of this type of suicide.

While Durkheim's theory was developed almost 100 years ago it still receives sustenance from current demographic data. For example, North American suicide rates are generally higher in urban areas than in rural communities (presumably due to less social integration) and the suicide rate for married men is much lower than for single, widowed, or divorced men [2]. The lack of family integration could account for the latter finding. While interesting and certainly durable, Durkheim's theory has, in my experience, only limited clinical usefulness.

Based on my experience with school-aged children I would submit, as have others, that suicidal behavior is a marker or signal of pathology within the family system [13, 14]. Adolescents at risk for suicide tend to have experienced severe psychosocial stressors including family problems and to have a limited or maladaptive repertoire of coping skills [15]. They typically cope with stressful situations in maladaptive ways, often through substance abuse and other "acting out" behaviors.

In many cases deficits in parenting place such children at risk from the moment of conception. While researchers have long been aware of the importance of early parent-child bonding, only recently has the link between attachment problems and disturbed behavior been clearly delineated. If attachment does not form within the first few years of life, the child may develop a severe emotional problem known as an attachment disorder [16].

Most attachment-disordered children have spent their earliest years in dysfunctional families. These are maltreated children who have come to expect abuse, neglect, or even abandonment from their parents. Although chronically angry these emotionally disturbed youngsters are often unwilling or unable to directly express their anger to care givers as they fear further rejection or abusive retaliation. Through suicidal behavior they may find ways to express their "retroflected rage" or to escape from their dismal circumstance.

I referred in the overview to the suicide of a fifteen-year-old client of mine whom I shall call Brian. Brian was emotionally and physically abused by an alcoholic father with whom there was no emotional bond. His tenuous attachment to his depressed mother was severed at the age of eight when she died of cancer. He left behind several poems, copies of which were given to me by his sister shortly after his death. In Brian's words:

What?!
As I go on living
The pain and sorrow grow more intense
How much longer can I stand this

> I don't know.
> I am longing for something
> But I don't know what
> Maybe just maybe
> I could find someone
> To show me
> Help me find
> What it is I'm looking for
> But I doubt it.
> I am afraid to ask somebody for help
> For the fear of being hurt is too strong
> So I guess I am looking for peace
> And the only peace I know
> Is death!

Disturbances in family structure (e.g., blurring of role boundaries, dysfunctional family alliances across boundaries) may promote suicidal acting out within the family system [17, 18]. Bowen describes the process of "triangulation" and its role in the maintenance of stability in a pathogenic family system [19]. He delineates the ongoing potential for imbalance in triadic relating among a father, mother, and child. He contends that the self-destructive behavior of an adolescent could serve as the focal point for the parents in a discordant marital relationship.

Ironically the disturbed behavior of such a "scapegoated" teenager could help maintain the stability of the marital relationship (and hence the family) by temporarily uniting the parents in a common cause. However, in the extreme the youngster's very life could be in jeopardy. For example, Sabbath writes of the "expendable child" driven to self-annihilation by a pathological family system [20].

Psychological Theories

In my opinion the definitive treatise on suicide is Edwin Shneidman's *Definition of Suicide* [21]. Shneidman, the father of suicidology, was co-founder and co-director of the Los Angeles Suicide Prevention Centre and founder of the American Association of Suicidology.

In his seminal text Shneidman offers an innovative theoretical model of suicide based on ten psychological commonalities associated with suicidal behavior. To illustrate these variables three additional poems written by Brian are interspersed among these commonalities.

1. *The common stimulus in suicide is unendurable psychological pain.* Shneidman conceptualizes suicide as a manifestation of intolerable psychological pain in an individual unwilling or unable to tolerate that pain. He submits that this subjective intrapsychic pain results from the blocking or thwarting of psychological needs.
2. *The common stressor in suicide is frustrated psychological needs.* Drawing from the work of William James, Shneidman argues that human behavior is driven by the desire to satisfy psychological needs [22]. He derives his

taxonomy of psychological needs from the well-known study of personality by Henry Murray and refers specifically to Murray's list of twenty psychological needs (e.g., achievement, autonomy, nurturance) [23].
3. *The common purpose of suicide is to seek a solution.* The suicidal individual is trying to solve a problem or resolve an issue.

> Worry
> Why I have no one
> I am not sure
> Maybe there is something
> Wrong with me
> I am sure there is nothing
> Wrong with anyone else
> Why do people not accept me
> What must I do to gain their recognition
> Should I be funny?
> Should I be sad?
> Will they accept me then?
> Should I be brave?
> Should I be strong?
> Will they accept me then?
> Should I be dead?
> Yes, then I won't have to worry.

In this poem Brian alludes to psychological needs including affiliation, exhibition, and dominance.

4. *The common goal of suicide is cessation of consciousness.* Survivors of failed attempts typically report that they didn't really want to die but that their aim was to stop the flow of their emotional pain.
5. *The common emotion in suicide is hopelessness-helplessness.* In addition to these feelings suicidal individuals often experience overpowering feelings of loneliness.

> Alone
> Why did you leave me?
> Now I am alone
> I see no reason to be here
> The hurt and pain are too much
> You were all my life meant to me
> And when you went away
> You took the most important part of me
> You!

Along with his strong feelings of loneliness Brian writes of his hopeless feelings. The depth of his emotional pain is all too clear.

6. *The common internal attitude to suicide is ambivalence.* The distressed individual is torn between two opposing forces—the desire to end it all and the desire to be rescued.
7. *The common cognitive state in suicide is constriction.* There is a tendency toward dichotomous "black or white" thinking. The suicidal individual may view suicide as the only option.
8. *The common interpersonal act in suicide is communication of intention.* Most suicidal persons leave clues. These signals sometimes represent a "cry for help."

> I can—I am—I want
> I am human
> I have feelings
> I can be hurt
> I can hurt people
> I can back up into a shell
> I can come out loud and strong
> I can live
> I want to be dead!

Again Brian conveys his unmet needs and displays great ambivalence toward life. His last line, however, unambiguously reveals his intention.

9. *The common action in suicide is egression.* To egress means to exit or escape from a distressing situation. The troubled individual seeks to remove him/herself permanently from the predicament. The desire to seek a solution through escape is apparent in Brian's first poem (see pages 516-517). The themes of loneliness and hopelessness flow through all of his poems as does his expressed need to escape his intrapsychic pain.
10. *The common consistency in suicide is with lifelong coping patterns.* Shneidman notes that a human being's pattern of responding to stressful situations over time follows a consistent pattern [21].

Additionally, Shneidman posits that life-threatening behavior results from the synthesis of three factors: acute intolerable intrapsychic pain ("psychache"), overwhelming external pressure ("negative press"), and a high level of upsetness or agitation ("perturbation") [21]. In turn this third factor is comprised of two elements—cognitive constriction and a penchant for action (a push for a conclusion).

Several key aspects of Shneidman's theory of suicide are encapsulated in his widely accepted definition:

> Currently in the Western World, suicide is a conscious act of self-induced annihilation, best understood as a multidimensional malaise in a needful individual who defines an issue for which the suicide is perceived as the best solution [21, p. 203].

It is a popular misconception that disturbed behavior, including life-threatening behavior, is "caused" by a traumatic incident (especially in one's early life). Shneidman refers to this as a "magic moment" theory that seeks to fix the cause of relatively complex behaviours [21]. Instead the causes are multiple and overlapping. Further confusion results from a failure to distinguish among primary causes, exacerbating causes, and precipitating causes. Typically precipitating factors (e.g., emotional rejection, financial failure) are offered as the cause. Suicidal individuals commonly attribute their misery to such external issues or problems and are largely unaware of underlying psychodynamic factors.

Several studies have suggested that depressive illness is involved in at least half of all suicide completions [24, 25]. However, depression is certainly not synonymous with suicide. Aaron Beck and his colleagues argue that depression is related to a disturbance in thinking. According to Beck depressed people typically are pessimistic and prone to making three types of cognitive distortions:

i) **overgeneralization**—they take one unfortunate circumstance or one aspect of an event and apply it broadly to unrelated events.
ii) **selective abstraction**—they focus on negative aspects of a situation and ignore its positive features.
iii) **inexact labelling**—not only do they interpret situations negatively, they exacerbate the situation by labelling themselves as a result of their negative interpretation. They further compound the problem by reacting to the labels rather than to the situation itself [26].

Aspects of such distorted thinking are apparent in the following excerpt from a note "accidentally" left in a high school classroom by a fourteen-year-old client of mine who had made two serious suicide attempts in the previous three months:

> So far I think I am doing nothing good, only bad and making trouble. Everything I do is wrong and nothing I do is right! Sometimes I wish I was dead! Then people would be happy once more because I'd be gone and so would the trouble I caused. Why should I live when all I do in this world is cause trouble and sorrow?

Beck and his colleagues link these forms of twisted thinking to the negative affect or mood associated with depression and suicide. They emphasize the role of cognitive errors and distorted thinking among suicidal individuals [27]. They refer to a "cognitive triad" involving negative thoughts about oneself, others, and the future. In particular they draw attention, as does Shneidman, to the concept of hopelessness. Indeed they view hopelessness as the single most relevant clinical variable.

The critical role of hopelessness is further substantiated by a study by Kazdin et al., which reported that hopelessness was a better predictor of suicidal intent that was generalized depression alone [28]. Farber's Integrative Psychological Theory conceptualizes suicide as a "disease of hope" in which social influences interact with psychological factors to define the hopelessness seen as a precursor of suicide [29]. Victor Frankl describes a state of "noogenic neurosis" wherein people who do not experience a sense of meaning or purpose to their lives are prone to feelings of despair, hopelessness, and depression [30]. Such people are therefore more likely to engage in suicidal acts especially in the face of significant psychological stressors.

Physiological Theories

In recent years attention has shifted somewhat to biological correlates of depression and suicide. The neurotransmitters serotonin and norepinephrine have become the focus of the biochemical postulations. A deficiency of serotonin has been found in the cerebral tissue of some people who have committed suicide and in the cerebrospinal fluid of attempters [31]. Serotonin is involved in the regulation of emotion and has been linked both to depression and impulsive suicide attempts.

A deficiency of serotonin, as measured by one of its metabolic products (5-HIAA) was found in one study of hospitalized suicidal patients to be associated with future suicide completions [32]. However, contradictory results have been reported by other researchers and the concept of biochemical correlates of suicide remains elusive.

Moreover, it is difficult to determine whether the biochemical changes associated with suicidal behavior are a precipitant of such behavior or more simply a byproduct. To illustrate the distinction consider the following analogy. A person who engages in vigorous exercise can be observed to sweat during and after the period of strenuous activity. Nevertheless, one would hardly claim that the sweating caused the person to exercise. Similarly it is difficult to ascertain whether reduced levels of serotonin found among many suicide completers are related causally or more incidentally to the fatal behavior.

Regardless it would appear that there may exist a "final common pathway" whereby loss experiences and other negative life events are transformed into physiological functioning at the chemical level in the brain [33].

Life Span Development

A life span developmental perspective is also important to understanding the etiology of suicidal behavior. For each human being an organized, systematic process of change occurs, marked generally by movement from immaturity to maturity. These life stages involve different developmental tasks and meanings [34]. Along with increasing complexity these changes lead to altered perspectives on the challenges and meaning of life.

External challenges from the environment force human beings to adapt and cope. In turn this struggle frequently leads to more advanced behavior. Many theorists view suicide as occurring in response to a temporary crisis rather than as an aspect of an individual's personality [21]. The implications of this "dialectic" principle are encouraging for it suggests that a suicidal crisis, if resolved positively, can leave the person stronger and more capable of handling stressful situations in the future.

It is interesting to note that the Chinese use two characters to represent the word crisis. Not surprisingly the first character "wei" is equivalent to the word "danger." The second character "ji" is comparable to the word "opportunity." Most models of crisis intervention are based, in part, on this notion. They typically set as their goal the temporary restoration of emotional balance until the distressed individual can once again learn to cope with life's challenges.

There is a current fallacy (fostered in part by media reports) that suicides spring directly from the influence of external events. Such events can include the death of a popular rock singer like Kurt Cobain or rejection by a significant other. It is also commonplace for people to make simplistic statements (e.g., "He killed himself because his wife walked out.") that attribute a suicidal death to a single factor.

Ronald Maris, however, argues that a person's life history or biography plays a significant mediating role [3]. Individuals who are unable to cope with the emotional and physical effects of aging, cumulative losses, and day to day issues over the "careers" of their lives are especially vulnerable to suicide. Models of causality must therefore consider not only the particular circumstances that surround the tragic event but also those "career contingencies" that mediate reactions to stress.

The motivation for suicidal acting out can vary for people at different life stages. For instance, the suicidal behavior of an adolescent is typically motivated by very different factors than if that same individual were to engage in similar behavior at a more advanced age. In particular the period of adolescence introduces significant physical and psychological changes. Teenagers tend to become more egocentric while at the same time they are more susceptible to peer influence as they seek to develop their personal identities. The unique stresses that accompany this stage of development undoubtedly contribute to the incidence of both suicidal and parasuicidal behavior in this age group.

Features common to many suicide attempts may be more salient at one stage of life than another. Maris suggests, for example, that ambivalence may lessen with age while interpersonal factors such as revenge may be more pronounced for young people [3]. Norman Farberow and Edwin Shneidman studied suicide notes and classified their content into Menninger's triad of wishes to be killed, kill, or die. They noted that wishes to die increased with age, while wishes to be killed or kill decreased with age [35]. They too reported that interpersonal motives decreased with age.

Antoon Leenaars performed a detailed analysis of 1200 authentic suicide notes and found out that young adults' notes (and by extension their suicides) differ significantly from older adults in several essential ways [36]. The former display more suicidal ideation, show more inwardly directed aggression, and are more self-critical. For the latter the "pain of isolation" is an important variable. Additionally suicidal individuals have problems establishing and maintaining interpersonal relationships across their lifespans. Leenaars reports that suicidal young adults describe disturbed, unsatisfactory interpersonal relationships significantly more often than do older adults.

The study of suicide among the middle-aged is a neglected area. Yet the peak age for completed suicide for North American women is the middle years and for both sexes the suicide rate is higher than among young adults [37]. Three factors are related to self-destructive behavior among adults in their middle years: alcoholism, emotional disorders (especially depression), and an accumulation of negative life events [38]. In addition, middle-aged adults typically bear greater responsibilities than during any other period of their lives. For some the stresses of balancing responsibility for their growing children and their aging parents can be very weighty.

It is not widely realized that the suicide rate among those over the age of sixty-five is the highest of any age group [39]. Suicide gestures among the elderly are rare with the ratio of attempts to completions approaching 1:1 [38]. Four factors are particularly associated with suicide among the elderly. These are: alcohol and drug dependence, social isolation (loneliness), cumulative losses, and retirement (especially for men) [38]. A self-perception of having outlived one's usefulness to society and a deterioration in physical health are also contributing factors.

Many factors across the various developmental stages of the life cycle contribute to our understanding of the multidimensional etiology of suicide. Suicide represents a stunningly premature end to development. It is to be hoped that through a more thorough understanding of the theoretical approaches to suicide that the human tragedy involved in these unnecessary losses can be allayed.

REFERENCES

1. P. D. Trautman and D. Shaffer, Treatment of Child and Adolescent Suicide Attempters, in *Suicide in the Young*, H. S. Sudak, A. B. Ford, and N. B. Rushford (eds.), John Wright PSG Inc., Boston, pp. 307-323, 1984.
2. A. L. Berman and D. A. Jobes, Adolescent Suicide: Assessment and Intervention, *American Psychological Association*, Washington, 1991.
3. R. W. Maris, *Pathways to Suicide: A Survey of Self-Destructive Behaviours*, Johns Hopkins University Press, Baltimore, 1981.
4. A. L. Berman and R. Cohen-Sandler, Childhood and Adolescent Suicide Research: A Critique, *Crisis, 3*, pp. 3-15, 1982.
5. E. Stengel, *Suicide and Attempted Suicide* (Rev. Edition), Jason Aronson, New York, 1974 (original work published 1964).
6. S. Freud, *The Ego and Mechanisms of Defense*, International Universities Press, New York, 1946.
7. S. Freud, Mourning and Melancholia, in *The Standard Edition of the Complete Psychological Works of Sigmund Freud*, J. Strachey (ed. and trans.), Hogarth Press, London, *14*, pp. 243-258, 1961 (original work published 1917).
8. S. Freud, cited by E. S. Shneidman, in *Definition of Suicide*, Wiley, New York, 1985.
9. A. Leenaars, *Life Span Perspectives of Suicide*, Plenum Press, New York, 1991.
10. S. Freud, Beyond the Pleasure Principle, in *The Standard Edition of the Complete Psychological Works of Sigmund Freud*, J. Strachey (ed. and trans.), Hogarth Press, London, *18*, pp. 7-64, 1961 (original work published 1920).
11. K. Menninger, *Man Against Himself*, Harcourt, Brace, and Co., New York, 1938.
12. E. Durkheim, *Suicide*, J. A. Spaulding and G. Simpson (trans.), The Free Press, Glencoe, Illinois, 1951 (original work published 1897 as *Le Suicide*).
13. G. W. Brown and T. Harris, *Social Origins of Depression*, Tavistock, London, 1978.
14. A. L. Berman, Child and Adolescent Suicide, in *Life Span Perspectives of Suicide*, A. Leenaars (ed.), Plenum Press, New York, 1991.

15. H. Hoberman, Completed Suicide in Children and Adolescents, in *Adolescent Suicide: Recognition, Treatment, and Prevention*, B. Garfinkel and G. Northrup (eds.), Haworth Press, New York, 1989.
16. J. Bowlby, *Attachment and Loss: Attachment*, Vol. 1, Basic Books, New York, 1969.
17. S. Minuchin, *Families and Family Therapy*, Harvard University Press, Cambridge, Massachusetts, 1974.
18. J. Richman, *Family Therapy for Suicidal People*, Springer, New York, 1986.
19. M. Bowen, *Family Therapy in Clinical Practice*, Jason Aronson, New York, 1978.
20. J. C. Sabbath, The Suicidal Adolescent—The Expendable Child, *Journal of American Academy of Child Psychiatry, 8*, pp. 272-289, 1989.
21. E. S. Shneidman, *Definition of Suicide*, Wiley, New York, 1985.
22. W. James, cited in E. S. Shneidman, *Definition of Suicide*, Wiley, New York, 1985.
23. H. A. Murray, *Explorations in Personality*, Oxford University Press, New York, 1930.
24. P. Sainsbury, Depression, Suicide and Suicide Prevention, in *Suicide*, A. Roy (ed.), Williams and Wilkins, Baltimore, pp. 73-88, 1986.
25. C. Pfeffer, *The Suicidal Child*, Guilford, New York, 1986.
26. A. T. Beck, *Cognitive Therapy and the Emotional Disorders*, International Universities Press, New York, 1976.
27. A. J. Rush and A. T. Beck, Cognitive Therapy of Depression and Suicide, *American Journal of Psychotherapy, 32*, pp. 201-219, 1978.
28. A. E. Kazdin, N. H. French, A. S. Unis, K. Esveldt-Dawson, and R. B. Sherick, Helplessness, Depression, and Suicidal Intent Among Psychiatrically Disturbed Inpatient Children, *Journal of Consulting and Clinical Psychology, 51*, pp. 504-510, 1961.
29. M. L. Farber, *Theory of Suicide*, Funk and Wagnalls, New York, 1968.
30. V. E. Frankl, *Man's Search For Meaning: An Introduction to Logotherapy*, I. Lasch (trans.), Washington Square Press, New York, 1963.
31. M. Asberg, P. Nordsrom, and L. Traskman-Bendz, Cerebrospinal Fluid Studies in Suicide, *Annals of the New York Academy of Sciences, 487*, pp. 243-255, 1986.
32. M. Asberg, L. Traskman, and P. Thoren, 5-HIAA in the Cerebrospinal Fluid: A Biochemical Suicide Predictor, *Archives of General Psychiatry, 33*, pp. 1193-1197, 1976.
33. H. S. Akiskal and W. T. McKinney, Depressive Disorders: Toward a Unified Hypothesis, *Science, 218*, pp. 20-29, 1973.
34. D. J. Levinson, C. N. Darrow, E. B. Klein, M. H. Levinson, and B. McKee, *The Seasons of a Man's Life*, Alfred A. Knopf, New York, 1978.
35. N. L. Farberow and E. S. Shneidman, Suicide and Age, in *Clues to Suicide*, E. S. Shneidman and N. L. Farberow (eds.), McGraw-Hill, New York, pp. 41-49, 1957.
36. A. Leenaars, *Suicide Notes*, Human Sciences Press, New York, 1988.
37. A. Leenaars and D. Lester, A Comparison of Rates and Patterns of Suicide for Canada and the United States, in *Life Span Perspectives of Suicide*, A. Leenaars (ed.), Plenum Press, New York, 1991.
38. J. M. Stillion, E. E. McDowell, and J. H. May, *Suicide Across the Life Span: Premature Exits*, Hemisphere, New York, 1989.
39. U.S. Bureau of the Census, *Statistical Abstract of the United States*, U.S. Government Printing Office, Washington, D.C., 1991.

CHAPTER 33
Suicide Intervention

Ralph L. V. Rickgarn

Suicide is not a neutral word, it is not a neutral behaviour. As a word it evokes apprehension and creates a desire to avoid or detach oneself from a discussion. As a behaviour it evokes powerful emotional reactions regardless of the outcome. Fear, anxiety, disbelief and anger are but a few of the emotions that create an atmosphere which impedes a discussion or involvement in the issues of suicide. As a consequence, attitudes and actions of avoidance and indifference occur. However, with adequate information and the creation of realistic expectancies, this avoidance and indifference may be alleviated and replaced with positive actions and reactions [1, p. 1].

This chapter will provide a framework of information, some methods of intervention and some expectations that will enable individuals to engage in the creation of a caring and confrontive community. Individuals who will be alert for signs of suicide ideation or an impending suicidal action and who will be willing to ask, "Are you thinking about committing suicide?"

THE PROCESS/ETIOLOGY OF SUICIDE

There is a general tendency to think of suicide only in discrete terms of suicidal ideation, attempted or completed suicide. These are, however, the result of a multi-dimensional *process* that culminates in an action. That process may have its inception in a number of contributing factors—psychological, physical, social or environmental—that may have been exacerbated by alcohol and other chemical use and abuse or traumas such as incest, rape, physical and mental abuse, family deaths, relationship losses and lack of self-esteem. Contributing factors create a constellation or matrix of risk elements that may manifest themselves in suicidal ideation and behaviors.

Suicidal ideation has a broad range of existence from a simple, passing thought to serious and extensive planning. I would suggest that there are few if any, individuals who have not had some form of suicidal thought, recognizing the statement, "I wish

I were dead" is a suicidal thought. In most individuals these are transitory states. However, for others, the negative concept of their own self-worth and a deficiency of resilience create situations where these contributing factors become larger than the life of the individual. Once an individual has few reasons to live, a single precipitating factor can become the proverbial "straw that breaks the camel's back," resulting in an attempted or completed suicide.

The suicidal process can be represented as a continuum of suicide. Although this continuum can function in a unidirectional manner, individuals will have variations in the intensity of feelings, the time spent within each component, and may move back and forth within the continuum depending upon individual situations and variables affecting their psychological state. The continuum begins with:

> complex number of individual contributing
> factors (the multidemensionality) resulting in
> |
> a depressed individual who is unable to adequately
> cope with the given situation leading him/her to develop
> |
> a sense of hopelessness that s/he will be able to
> do anything to influence
> |
> the loss of control s/he feels as her/his sense of
> control becomes more and more external
> where a precipitating factor can lead to
> |
> suicidal ideation and other suicidal behaviors
> including attempted and/or completed suicide.

Depression will be one of the most commonly experienced factors ranging from a brief, mild state ("the blues") to a severe clinical disorder. Beck has described depression as a cognitive distortion and a negative view of the self, the world, and the future [2]. Seligman has described depression in terms of the development of feelings of hopelessness [3]. Depression becomes a significant factor when an individual's coping mechanisms begin to fail and their view of themselves and the world becomes overwhelmingly negative. Evans and Farberow have stated, "certainly not all severely depressed persons commit suicide; nor do all those who kill themselves suffer from depression. But depression is a warning sign that cannot be ignored" [4, p. 87].

The next factor is hopelessness which "has proved to be perhaps the best predictor across the full continuum of suicidal thoughts and behaviour, including ideation, attempts, and actual completions" [5, p. 138]. Hopelessness is often indicated by statements that have a totally negative context including such words as "never," "no one," "only," and "nothing," combined with anhedonia (the inability to experience pleasure). Hopelessness is a significant and integral part of the continuum.

The final factor is an external locus of control, the individual's perception that s/he has little or no control over her/his life situation. A sense of powerlessness and helplessness pervades the world of the hopeless individual and prevents him/her from exercising, or even perceiving that there are options and alternatives to his/her condition. Instead the individual perceives that there are two alternatives—living or dying. Individuals usually are ambivalent about attempting or committing suicide. When signs of suicide are noted and responded to by a concerned person, the suicidal person usually will choose the alternative of living. Consequently, ambivalence is a vigorous factor in intervention, providing some time and the opportunity to talk about reasons for living and developing an internal locus, tipping the balance from reasons to die and the perceived external controls.

The etiology of suicide is complex. The interactions of risk factors are complicated [6]. Suicide has been called an individualistic and personalized action because, while trends exist, each individual has a variation on the theme. This continues in the final piece of the continuum where actions may range from a very non-lethal gesture, to an attempt, to a completed suicide. While ambivalence exists, the individual will search, each in his or her own way, for someone who is willing to listen to their pain and engage in some kind of intervention that will facilitate movement away from suicide.

Shneidman describes suicide and suicidal crises as "more accurately a more or less transient psychological constriction of affect and intellect" [7, p. 24] that is marked by perturbation, hopelessness, helplessness, and frustrated psychological pain. It is not that suicidal people want to die, it is just that they cannot find a way to live with this pain. Shneidman has called this acute psychological pain "psychache," "the hurt, anguish, soreness, aching, psychological pain in the psyche, the mind" [8, p. 145].

An awareness of the factors in this continuum facilitates the process of intervention, the assessing of suicidal risk and the assuaging the "psychache."

THE MYTHOLOGY OF SUICIDE

Suicide is within the grasp of any individual given certain circumstances. The idea of someone wanting to commit suicide can be frightening and produce avoidance reactions within the potential helper. This can be done through thoughts ("I can't even think about it!"), words ("I can't talk about it!"), and deeds ("I can't do anything about it!"). While intervention can be an intimidating action, it is the desire to avoid painful issues and the possibility of becoming a survivor that inhibits, even precludes many people from engaging in any form of intervention. Part of this highly protective armour is the mythology of suicide. If we believe the mythology we can detach ourselves and avoid emotional and physical involvement. There are nine reasons for accepting the mythology of suicide [9].

> First, by believing the mythology we can detach ourselves from a potentially traumatic situation. We do not have to become involved in any discussion of the value of human life or make any significant commitment about our beliefs relating to life after death. Somehow we hope to bring some order out of the chaos of suicide and to pretend that what is happening is "out there," beyond our comprehension or control.

Second, by believing the mythology we shift the responsibility to someone or something else. As we are very quick to want to blame and to assign guilt, we have to have a target. So, our targets become heredity, individual circumstances, the phase of the moon or whatever else we may conjure. We want to make very certain that this suicidal behavior is not the fault of our friend, co-worker, lover, spouse, or roommate. We want to make very certain that we are in no way to blame, be blamed, feel guilty, or be made to feel guilty. Someone, something else that is totally beyond control is responsible because we have such limited understanding of suicidal person's life.

Third, by believing the mythology of suicide we can believe "nothing can be done." After all, we have a very limited understanding, we don't want to talk about suicide and it is out of our control. If indeed, nothing can be done, we propel ourselves into the fourth myth.

Fourth, by believing the mythology we absolve ourselves of taking any action and avoid contact with the suicidal person. After all, the unfortunate individual is beyond assistance or we simply are not knowledgeable enough to effectively intervene. Or, the only individuals who can intervene are highly trained psychologists or psychiatrists leaving everyone else "off the hook."

Fifth, by believing the mythology of suicide we can maintain taboos and avoid conversations about suicidal person (except in the most gossipy fashion). The longer we maintain the taboos, the longer we can remain protected from any significant encounter with the suicidal person.

Sixth, by believing the mythology of suicide we not only maintain the taboos, we draw very significant boundaries for ourselves and others. By believing the mythology we are able to maintain significant distances to "protect our guts." Usually, we do not put ourselves in situations where we can be hurt. We usually avoid masochistic behaviours. So, if we can avoid any involvement with a suicidal person we assume we can avoid the pain.

Seventh, by believing the mythology of suicide we can maintain those religious, legal, moral, philosophical sanctions, and condemnations that work to exacerbate the psychological pain which the suicidal person experiences. In the process, we can believe that we have done "what is right."

Eighth, by believing the mythology of suicide we can create for ourselves some illusion that everything is all right. We can accept, for instance, that people who talk about suicide don't take suicidal actions. They are "OK" if they are willing to talk about feeling suicidal. If they are "OK" we are "OK" in not taking any action because everyone's "OK."

Ninth, by believing the mythology and believing that we are helpless to intervene, we avoid the pain and frustration following an attempted or completed suicide, but the distancing may permit some lesser degree of grief. This may be the ultimate protection that we are seeking [9, pp. 85-86].

All mythologies contain some piece of truth that facilitates the myth's perpetuation. However, the greatest part of myths relating to suicide is the misinformation and inaccuracy that provide excuses for not intervening. A review of some of the most predominant myths will provide information useful in suicide prevention and intervention and, if we are willing, enable us to drop the excuses and work with those who need our involvement.

SOME PREDOMINATE MYTHS

One of the most common and destructive myths is that *asking "Are you thinking about committing suicide?" will cause the person to consider suicide*. The fact is the suicidal person has been waiting for someone to ask this question so that s/he can finally express what is happening. The question has two merits. First, it is nonjudgmental. Usually, if we do ask about suicide, the question is framed as, "You're *NOT* thinking about suicide, are you!?" The double punctuation is intentional for there is an exclamation of "not" in the question intimating that "Yes" is not the desired answer. Suicidal people are very alert to these innuendoes, recognizing when an individual is not ready to hear their distress and pain. Their response may be, "Uh, no not really." Then they continue to seek someone who will respond positively. Second, the question uses the word "suicide," which is what the suicidal person wants to hear. This clearly states that you are willing to enter into this conversation in a direct manner. The suicidal person has been looking for someone who would ask, care, and become involved.

Another myth is *the suicidal person wants to die*. That being true, why ask if a person is suicidal? If it is inevitable that the individual is going to commit suicide, isn't it best to build up armour plating for our psyches so we won't get hurt too badly? The fact is the suicidal person does not want to die, s/he simply cannot figure our how to continue living with the incredible psychological pain being experienced, the "psychache."

A woman asked if I had ever had a migraine headache. Her description of her pain was to imagine the worst headache I had ever had and multiply that by 100, something I could not comprehend. It did give me a marker to attempt to understand her extreme psychological pain. If the myth were true, there would be no clues of impending suicide, the "cry for help" wouldn't exist.

A popular myth is that *people who talk about suicide rarely attempt or commit suicide and don't seek help*. The fact is that over 70 percent of suicidal individuals do give some verbal or non-verbal clue of their intentions and approximately 50 percent of the suicides have sought medical assistance in the six months prior to their action. Suicidal individuals seek help in a number of ways, even if they are rather oblique. These myths provide a rationale for not inquiring as well as insulation to avoid necessary confrontation and intervention.

There is the myth that *once an individual has attempted suicide, s/he will always be suicidal*. While this myth may give us an "excuse" for the completed suicide, it is not a given fact. Indeed, many individuals make suicide attempts of various degrees of lethality. However, providing appropriate professional assistance may enable the individual to live a highly productive life with the attempt becoming a single, life history incident. There are individuals who do make a number of attempts and those who live a chronic suicidal life style. However, they are not the majority. Even after a number of attempts, the conflicting issues may be resolved and behaviorial patterns changed. The myth contributes to the "I'm helpless to do anything" syndrome. It's not that we are helpless, it's that we choose to act helplessly.

This brings us to the myth that *all suicidal persons are depressed or mentally ill*. However, many individuals would not have been so diagnosed. This myth works against suicide prevention because a potential intervener may decide that depression and mental illness are clearly beyond his/her competency. Consequently, there is no reason to engage the suicidal person in an initial dialogue to ascertain the extent of their problems. If the myth is invoked, it provides another direction for the helplessness syndrome.

One myth borders on elitism, the myth that *suicide is more common in lower socioeconomic groups*. The reverse may be more accurate. Physicians, dentists, and psychiatrists as well as outstanding high school and college students have high rates of suicide. This myth legitimizes a form of pity for the "poor person" and a way to remain distant from their anguish. The boundaries of this myth may make it very difficult to approach a friend who has expressed suicidal thoughts. Should an attempt or completed suicide occur, we may find it difficult to cope with our survivorship and need some other myth to maintain some degree of avoidance.

Another contribution to the concept "nothing can be done" is the myth that *suicidal tendencies are inherited*. If a suicidal tendency is inherited, it's an inevitable process. There are factors that may be inherited and which exacerbate suicidal risk. These include schizophrenia and affective disorders. There are also suicidal patterns in families that have nothing to do with genetics and everything to do with social learning theory. Patterns of maladaptive coping behaviors including abuse of alcohol and other chemicals and family violence including previous suicide attempts or completions may be regarded as appropriate problem-solving methods. The "family secret" (Aunt Millie committed suicide) may contribute to the acceptability. No one in the family talks about this act in negative terms (if it is talked about at all) and a vulnerable individual may find this an invitation and acceptable solution to their problems.

Suicide also may be the "family legacy." On a flight, a passenger confided to me that he was, as the eldest son, "the next person in my family to commit suicide." The eldest son in every generation, as far as the lineage could be traced, committed suicide. He knew family members were talking about him and wondering when he would do it. He had no intention of committing suicide but his family would not be shocked if he did. It was expected. Fortunately he was not valuable and sought counseling on how to cope with his family and later wrote, "I've told them all to go to hell!" If he had been valuable, the family would have already given its consent, indeed to encourage, for his suicide. Learning what is socially acceptable is as damaging as any inherited quality.

Last, there is the myth that *only a mental health professional can intervene and prevent a suicide*. If this were true, there would be significantly more individuals attempting or committing suicide because they would not use the power of crisis centers, hot lines, and other largely lay staffed organizations. In many instances it is the non-professional who asks the questions and responds in a caring manner, enabling the suicidal individual to begin to understand options and to seek professional help to resolve crises. This myth shifts the responsibility to someone else.

A major effect of this mythology is to shift the responsibility to somebody or something else and a constant thread of "it's beyond my capability because. . . ." These excuses may provide some alleviation of the fear of suicide and survivorship. However, being paralyzed by our fears we miss a splendid opportunity to engage another human in their ambivalence. We may find ourselves wondering why we didn't intervene as we feel the trauma of survivorship.

The Chinese ideogram for crisis consists of two ideograms: danger and opportunity. Intervention has its dangers, we cannot ignore that. There is also the opportunity to make a significant difference in the life of another person. The remainder of this chapter will focus on developing an understanding of the signs of suicide and the tactics of intervention. A word of caution—if, for some reason, you believe that you cannot engage in an intervention, *don't do it*. Instead assure the person that you will accompany them to someone who will listen to their pain and assist them. Two examples follow.

Margaret said she could not discuss suicide with the person she accompanied to my office. Privately she said she had a close friend commit suicide less than a year ago. She also had experienced the loss of a close friend in high school. The latest suicide exposed unresolved issues she was exploring with a counselor. Her own issues disallowed an accurate and empathetic hearing of another's pain.

Warren called me to tell me that he was referring a student. He said he knew his personal religious beliefs would make it impossible for him to empathically talk with this student. While he didn't discuss his beliefs with the student, he told me he believed suicide was a sin and people who were considering suicide were defying God and would never be accepted into heaven. He said he knew this would only make matters worse for this student.

Both individuals recognized that an encounter with a suicidal person would not be beneficial because of either the immediacy of suicide or powerful religious beliefs. There are other reasons, not excuses, for referring individuals and if they are present, a referral should be made.

THE SIGNS OF SUICIDE

Often when I am working with a group following a suicide, I hear the phrase, "There just weren't any signs that he would do something like this." Then as I talk about issues of suicide including warning signs, watching the faces in the group I can almost see little flashbulbs go off in their heads as they recognize they simply weren't aware of the signs. This recognition may produce feelings of guilt. It is necessary to emphasize that we are together, learning, so that we can avoid a next time because the clues will be known. Knowledge is definitely power!

As noted before, suicide is not a single, unconnected event or action. It is a result of progression through the continuum from contributing factors to depression, to hopelessness, to an external locus of control and to suicidal ideation or action. I also want to reiterate that most individuals DO give some sign of their suicidal thoughts and impending actions. These can be behavioral (non-verbal), emotional, verbal or a combination of both.

Behavioral

The most significant clues are a rather sudden, unexplained change in an individual's behavioral patterns. This includes any pattern: sleeping; eating; working; studying; recreation; sexual behavior; consumption of alcoholic beverages; smoking; relationships with other people; and other individual patterns. For example, you notice a person who usually liked to be up late in the evening and the "life of the party" is now going out infrequently and seems to be in bed by ten o'clock in the evening (or maybe earlier). Or, the person may have been an early riser who now finds it difficult to drag him/herself out of bed at ten o'clock in the morning or later. Perhaps s/he drank occasionally and now seems to be drinking to the point of intoxication rather regularly. While earlier s/he seemed to have a real zest for life, now s/he seems to find pleasure in few activities (anhedonia). These indicators do not always point toward suicide, but they denote significant changes in a life and it is appropriate to determine the cause.

A word of caution, there is a tendency to describe these behaviors in "always" kinds of statements—"you're always going to bed so early now." These can usually be countered by a truthful "No I'm not!" since there are exceptions. It is important to remain with observable behaviors, explaining what you have seen in very concrete terms. These are not so readily denied and questioning can be phrased as, "I used to see you . . . now I hardly ever see you . . . There seem to be some serious things happening? I would like to help."

While some individuals may exhibit a decreased or total lack of interest in activities in which they normally engage, others might become hyperactive, restless, even impulsive and reckless, exhibiting unexpected aggression. There may be a lack of energy, lethargy or complaints of fatigue. Other individuals may exhibit frequent, unexplained, irrational changes in behaviors. Decreased concentration, a withdrawal from friends, co-workers and family, and somatic complaints may also take place. These are significant variations that require attention. If the person is not suicidal, there would appear to be other major issues that need resolution.

Among adolescents and young adults there is a particular phenomenon, the "living will." These individuals give away their favorite prized possessions to specific persons. A common phrase accompanying the gift is, "I won't be needing this and I wanted you to have it." It is important to ask why the gift is being presented. In many instances, a statement of suicidal intent will follow.

While we all should have a will, insurance and funeral plans to assist survivors, there are times when this planning seems inappropriate or very sudden. Most young adults do not engage in this planning and it is appropriate to ask them, or anyone else, what is happening in their life that has precipitated this sudden interest in will and funerals.

Emotional

There are a number of emotional clues to depression and impending suicidal actions. These include: pronounced mood swings, withdrawal, a sulky mood, feelings of anxiety, and nervousness. There may also be sadness and unexplained crying.

Crying is often exhibited by women but is rather uncommon in men who have ben acculturated from an early age that crying in inappropriate ("Little men don't cry!"). Therefore, unexplained crying by a man indicates a serious situation where emotions overpower learned patterns.

One emotional response that requires attention is part of the pronounced mood swings mentioned above. Individuals who appear to suddenly be very happy following depression may not be exhibiting just a mood swing, but may have made a decision to attempt suicide or commit suicide. The ambivalence is now removed and the individual, comfortable with the decision, no longer is engaged in the turmoil of deciding if s/he will live or die. The decision is made and the plans can go forward.

Statements

There are emotional issues that are expressed through statements. A key indicator of potential suicidal action is the expression of hopelessness. It is not only a stronger factor than depression, but a major predictor of suicidal behavior linking depression to suicide [5, 10]. Individuals who express this hopelessness, feel that they are powerless, out-of-control, isolated, and alienated. Some examples of their statements are:

> No matter what I do, I can't make a difference and it's all out of my hands anyway.
> It's hopeless! (Often followed by a list of "hopeless" issues.)
> Nobody would miss me if I were gone, Nobody cares!

The key to these statements is the use of a superlative such as "always," "everytime," "nothing," "no one," "only," "never," and similar words in a negative context where alternatives are precluded.

Other statements may revolve around issues of guilt, remorse, self-reproachment, low feeling of self-esteem, or unreal expectations of self.

> I can't live up to their expectations so they'd be better off without me.
> I'm sorry! It won't be long before all this pain is gone!

Then there are statements directly communicating the individual's intent to die:

> Did you ever wonder what it felt like to be dead?
> I want to die!
> I'm going to end it all!
> I'm going to commit suicide.

These statements also create the most apprehension in the listener because they speak directly to the risk of death. Hearing this type of statement evokes an internal flight response in some individuals resulting in eviscerated comments like, "Things aren't that bad," or "You'd never do anything like that." These statements also can be discounted with a response of "Things will get better," or "You're NOT thinking of suicide, are you?" neither of which is helpful.

What the suicidal person wants to hear is, "Are you thinking of committing suicide?"

ASSESSMENT OF SUICIDE AND INTERVENTION OF SUICIDAL PERSON

The suicidal person says, "Yes!"

As you catch your breath, you realize you are now involved in a crucial situation and ask, "Now what?" You should become aware of your own physiological changes. Your heart rate has probably accelerated, you are breathing somewhat differently, and your mind is racing to say the "right" thing. These are normal reactions to a stressful situation that can be useful in focusing on the intervention as awareness is heightened. Often there is a concern about saying something that will "push the person right over the edge." Empathic, caring questions and responses will not do this. The following are some valuable tactics (dos and don'ts) for an intervention

Things to do are:

- Listen carefully to what the person is saying and the emotional context for a complete understanding of the message. Check out what you have heard. If you are at all uncertain, repeat back to the person what you believe was said by either paraphrasing or directly asking, whichever is most comfortable for you. This indicates to the suicidal person that not only do you *want* to understand what is being said, but that you also want to understand it *accurately*.
- Try to remain calm and maintain a positive attitude. Appearing shocked at what you hear may confirm what the individual already suspects—s/he is a worthless person who can only think terrible thoughts.
- Engage in direct questioning about the details of any plans that the individual may have. This is crucial to the assessment of the intentionality (how serious is the individual's intent) and lethality (how lethal is the planned method, if one exists) through the following questions.

What has brought you to this decision? (If at all possible avoid the use of "why?" Why questions often sound accusatory and may remind the person of a scolding parent saying, "Why did you do this?"). While a response may begin haltingly, as the individual recognizes you are listening and you do want to know, a more complex constellation of factors will be revealed.

A significant part of the intervention is facilitating in the person's finding *one* reason to live. Unfortunately, we are accustomed to lists of ten items. Usually, the suicidal person will not be able to think of ten reasons which could increase?? her/his suicidal feelings as s/he will sense another failure. Finding one reason to live begins the process of regaining some power. One reason can alter the perceptions of hopelessness, helplessness, and powerlessness as the individual does something for him/herself. Remember, it is their personal reasons that are important. Do not interject your own reasons as they may be quite disparate from the suicidal individual's.

What available resources does the person have? Is there a support system of family, friends, co-workers, or church members who can assist the individual in recovery? Or, is this truly an instance where the individual has alienated him/herself from everyone and is completely isolated? The individual who has little or no support system is at greater risk.

What means are you planning to use? The suggestion of this question often provokes the response, "Oh, I couldn't ask that. It might sound as if I want to give them an idea." You need to know where the individual is located on the range from low lethality (no plans) to high lethality (a firearm immediately available). It is important to attempt to obtain the means from the individual. This may be something as non-lethal as a few aspirins or as potentially lethal as a knife, a rope, a bottle of prescribed medications, or a firearm. Removal reduces the lethality level immediately and exhibits concern for individual's welfare.

What else is happening at this time? Other risk factors that are involved may be the use of disinhibitors that diminish the individual's capacity to accurately perceive what is happening. These can include intoxication (from alcohol or other chemicals), alcoholism, disorientation (from chemicals or psychological factors), confused perceptions of reality, high levels of stress or traumatic events. Any of these factors (or a combination) significantly elevates the risk level.

When are you planning to attempt/commit suicide? This is an important question for it measures the level of intent. If the individual responds that s/he has just thought about it and that's all, that is a low level of intentionality. If, on the other hand, s/he tells you they plan to commit suicide at 8:00 P.M. that evening and it is mid-afternoon, that is a very high level of intentionality.

It is important to remember that the more serious the level of intent and the more lethal the method, the greater need from professional intervention. If the risk is imminent, do no hesitate to dial 911 or another emergency number.

Who is involved? There are times when more than one person may be involved in a suicide situation, such as a pact between two or more individuals to commit suicide. There are also instances where the suicidal individual plans to kill someone else prior to their suicide (e.g., as an act of revenge). This complicates the intervention and requires immediate action by professionals (e.g., police, psychologists, clergy).

Since the suicidal individual often believes that there is no one who cares about them or their well-being, the offer to accompany the person to a clinic or a professional person and remain with her/him as long as s/he feels it is necessary is very meaningful. I have often accompanied individuals to a counseling service. A few times I have sat through an intake interview. Once the individual is in what s/he perceives as a safe place, and the feeling of having some power or control returns, s/he becomes more independent.

Interacting with a suicidal person in a caring and empathic manner precludes most inappropriate actions. However, there are some things that should not be done.

- Do not be drawn into a compact of secrecy that often begins, "I want to tell you something, but you must promise that you will never tell anyone else." If you agree to this proposal and the person tells you s/he is going to commit suicide you are going to feel very trapped. This will significantly complicate intervention. Never promise complete confidentiality. Tell the individual that you want to help them, but you do not have all the answers and may need the assistance of others.
- Do not say, "You wouldn't dare," or "You can't do this." This may sound like a dare and a challenge to their capability, provoking an "I'll show you!" response.
- Do not say, "This is only a phase, it'll go away in a day or so." It is a serious matter requiring considerable time and effort. Leave the assessment and analysis to the professionals.
- Do not be drawn into inappropriate bargaining or manipulative behaviors. These can be very destructive.
- Do not promise what you cannot deliver, for example, saying "I'll keep you from attempting/committing suicide." You may not be able to do this and if an attempt or completion occurs you will find yourself working through a complex of emotions including sadness, guilt, and anger.
- Do not leave an acutely suicidal person alone. If you need assistance, attempt to alert someone or persuade the individual to accompany you to a place where help can be obtained.
- Do not get into a philosophical debate on moral or other issues so suicide. Focus on the problem and leave the debate for a later time.

Intervention with a suicidal individual is a time consuming and energy demanding activity. It is a crisis that has both danger and opportunity. However, with information about suicide and the knowledge of how to develop an intervention, the dangerous aspects can be reduced and the opportunity for a successful intervention increased.

EXPECTATIONS

The usual expectation is that if we do everything right, the individual will be prevented from attempting or committing suicide. However, sometimes, in spite of the best intentions and actions, a suicide attempt or completion will occur. No one should enter into an intervention without knowing their best efforts may be rejected [11]. Both non-professionals and professionals experience suicide attempts and completions that produce personal grief, disruptions of roles, and self-confidence [12]. Regardless of the outcome of the intervention the intervener must have a support system to attend to their needs. Even after a successful intervention, the intervener needs to be able to talk about his/her involvement and the emotions that were evoked. Debriefing and continuing support are essential factors for the mental health of the helper to avoid negative repercussions.

"Interventions will only be as good as the knowledge that we have for understanding the diversity and the complexity of the risk factor matrix and the suicidal process. Interventions will only be as good as the people who are willing to engage their time and energy in attempting to inhibit the suicidal process" [8, p. 162]. Intervention is about individuals who have knowledge and resolve to ask, "Are you thinking about committing suicide?"

REFERENCES

1. R. L. V. Rickgarn, *The Issue Is Suicide*, University of Minnesota, 1983.
2. A. T. Beck, *Depression: Clinical, Experimental and Theoretical Aspects*, Harper and Row, New York, 1967.
3. M. E. P. Seligman, *Helplessness: On Depression, Developement and Death*, W. H. Freeman, New York, 1975.
4. G. Evans and N. L. Farberow, *The Encyclopedia of Suicide, Facts on File*, New York, 1988.
5. M. D. Rudd, M. H. Rajab, and P. F. Dahm, Problem-Solving Appraisal in Suicide Ideators and Attempters, *American Journal of Orthopsychiatry, 64*(1), pp. 136-149, 1994.
6. M. A. Young, L. F. Fogg, W. A. Scheftner, and J. A. Fawcett, Interactions of Risk Factors in Predicting Suicide, *American Journal of Psychiatry, 151*(3), pp. 434-435, 1994.
7. E. S. Shneidman, What Do Suicides Have in Common? Summary of the Psychological Approach, *Suicide: Guidelines for Assessment, Management, and Treatement*, B. Bongar (ed.), Oxford University Press, New York, pp. 3-15, 1992.
8. E. S. Shneidman, Commetary: Suicide as Psychache, *The Journal of Nervous and Mental Disease, 181*(3), pp. 145-147, 1993.
9. R. L. V. Rickgarn, *Perspectives on College Student Suicide*, Baywood Publishing, Amityville, New York, 1994.
10. K. Minkoff, E. Bergman, A. T. Beck, and R. Beck, Hopelessness, Depression and Attempted Suicide, *American Journal of Psychiatry, 130*(4), pp. 455-459, 1973.
11. L. Millen and S. Roll, A Case Study in Failure: On Doing Everything Right in Suicide Prevention, *Death Studies, 9*(5-6), pp. 483-492, 1985.
12. S. M. Valente, Psychotherapist Reactions to the Suicide of a Patient, *American Journal of Orthopsychiatry, 64*, pp. 614-621, 1994.

CHAPTER 34

"All the King's Horses and All the King's Men..." Picking Up the Pieces in the Aftermath of Youth Suicide

Robert G. Stevenson

Case 1: A parent sits with his head bowed and stares at the floor of the therapist's office. He says, for perhaps the tenth time in that session, that his future has been destroyed. He asks, "What could my daughter have been thinking? How can I go on from here?"

A death from suicide can shatter the life of a survivor. If the survivor feels like a shattered Humpty Dumpty, then those of us who are trying to help "pick up the pieces" should not be surprised if at times our task seems hopeless. We may never be completely successful in helping someone to put those pieces together again, but, as the suicide rate increases among today's young people [1] it is essential that we try. This attempt is the main thrust of suicide postvention programs.

Case 2: A principal calls her faculty together on the first day of the school year, three weeks after the suicide of a student. To avoid the possibility of "copycat" suicides, she directs that they *not* speak of the death with any of their classes or address the topic of suicide.

Case 3: A young man hesitates at the entrance of his school. It is his first day back following his attempted suicide. He has no idea what awaits him, but he feels it can't be any better and will probably be worse than when he left.

The topic of suicide, especially adolescent suicide, has received widespread publicity for almost two decades. We have learned that as bleak as life may appear to those making suicide attempts, the fact remains that most of these young people do not wish "to be dead." They do need help to escape the pain or confusion caused by problems and their inability to solve them. There are many groups concerned with finding ways to save these lives which represent so much untapped potential. Parents, educators, health-care professionals, and young people themselves ask a host of questions every time such a death occurs. Many of the questions seek to explain this death and to gain a better understanding of what happened so that lives can be saved in the future. Society has limited resources to give to this topic. Those who seek to help feel time pressure to come up with answers to their questions as soon as possible. Suicide is, quite literally, a matter of life and death.

The larger picture breaks down into three sub-topics: prevention, intervention, and postvention. Suicide prevention and intervention have received the greatest attention. Mental health professionals and educators have joined forces in producing suicide related programs that are school-based. Priority has been given to prevention programs involving all members of a school community and intervention training for staff members.

PREVENTION

Since it is often difficult to identify young people at risk of suicide, school-wide prevention programs are increasingly provided to all students and staff. The Adolescent Suicide Awareness Program (ASAP) is a good example of such a program. It was developed cooperatively by the staff members of a community mental health center and a regional high school [2]. This program involves everyone in a school community and offers outside support from community health professionals. The ASAP program has been implemented in secondary schools throughout New Jersey. Studies of the program show that it has been a success. The number of completed suicides has declined since its introduction while neighboring states saw an increase in deaths from suicide.[1] Even though the program has been a success, it is being accorded less time and funding because of reductions in school budgets. This reduction may also be due to a mistaken belief that the problem of youth suicide has been "solved." If a program that is believed to have saved lives cannot find adequate time and funding, what chance has a school to expand such a program to add a postvention segment?

INTERVENTION

Most schools have developed some plan and trained appropriate staff members (most frequently guidance personnel and school nurses) to act swiftly to assist students who are "at risk" of self-destructive behavior. These plans are approved by a district's board of education. They typically include two parts: a policy statement concerning self-destructive behavior and specific procedures for dealing with the different levels of self-destructive behavior—threatened suicide, attempted suicide,

---

[1] The term "completed" suicide describes a situation in which an individual dies. The term "successful" suicide is seen in professional literature, but to describe a young person who chose death over life as a "success" sends an unnecessarily harmful message.

or completed suicide [2]. If there has been a completed suicide, intervention often includes follow-up through individual student counseling sessions or group meetings. This is an area that overlaps with postvention. However, the intervention component of these meetings seem to focus chiefly on avoiding another suicide attempt in the aftermath of a death.

POSTVENTION

This chapter began with several examples of people in need of help following a suicide attempt. The immediate crisis has passed, but the pain, the confusion, and problems remain and may have even increased as the numbness of the initial event wears off. Postvention programs can be divided into two main areas: those which follow a death from completed suicide and those which follow a suicide attempt. When a member of the school community has died from a completed suicide (or a "suspected" suicide), those who remain are called "survivors" of suicide. We have learned about their unique needs following this type of death. In the wake of an attempted suicide, there must be a procedure which addresses both the needs of the school community as a whole, and a separate component to address the needs of the attempter. It is this last component which is most often lacking in school-based programs of postvention.

Characteristics of a Death by Suicide

An understanding of the nature of a death by suicide is essential for those who wish to help the survivors. When such a death occurs the following characteristics apply.

The Death is Perceived as Sudden and Violent

Sudden death is more likely to cause complicated grief than is a death that is anticipated. Even when the actual cause of death does not involve "violent" means, the death may well be perceived as violent by the survivors because of the devastating impact it has on *their* lives. When the risk of suicide is known (or feared) survivors still say that they were unaware of the immediacy of the threat. On a very deep level, we want to believe that those we love are "safe" from harm and we look for any information to reassure us. Remember, this is one time when the way we see a problem is more important that the "reality" of what we see. Some people deal with anxiety or fear by attempting to avoid facing it.

Suicide Takes Place in the Presence of Other Problems

Those who attempt suicide see it not as a "problem" but as a solution to some other problem. The death does not necessarily cause these other problems to disappear and they often remain, still unsolved, to complicate the recovery of survivors.

Suicide Magnifies Feelings of Regret and Guilt in the Survivors

Survivors constantly replay events and ask "What if . . . ?" or say "If only I had . . ." Silence imposed by others who mean well and wish to spare the survivors "unnecessary" suffering only magnifies these feelings.

Survivors Experience a Feeling of Loss of "Control"

This can cause a delay in reactions or even an inability to act at all. Survivors may well decide that they could not have stopped the suicide attempt because they are actually "helpless." This can mitigate feelings of guilt, but it carries over into other areas of life and can prevent survivors from coping with their grief or with other life issues they face. They may "submit" to what they perceive as overwhelming opposition to their ability to get on with their lives.

Grief Can be Complicated by the Reactions of Society

When people are not sure what to do, what the "right" response is, support systems can disappear. Rituals may be withheld. A school flag is not lowered to half-mast. A school memorial is not held. One northern New Jersey administrator goes as far as to say that *no* death in a school community should be acknowledged. He recommends this in order to avoid a memorial when the cause of death is suicide. He says this will help prevent copycat suicides and suicide clusters. However, his plan may actually magnify feelings of helplessness among survivors and offers no certainty that the death will not be discussed among students in a school. It only guarantees that such a discussion will occur without any support or guidance from teachers or staff members. When silence is imposed, other channels of communication begin to break down. In the school cited in Case 2 at the start of this chapter, the faculty was finally allowed to speak about the episode when an outside consultant was called in to work with the staff over a year after the death. They shared their thoughts, concerns, and feelings in what was, for them, a major catharsis. However, even then there was no parallel opportunity provided for students.

Grief Can be Complicated by the Survivors Themselves

Even when most of the above judgments and actions do not occur, the survivors may still believe them to be true. There may have been options or choices that the deceased were not able to see because they were so focused on their pain. In a similar fashion, survivors may be so focused on their loss, guilt, and regret they cannot have an objective view of their own condition or the actions of those around them [3].

The grief process helps one to recover from bereavement, but to move through it one must face the feelings of loneliness, hopelessness, and helplessness. These emotions are often present in suicides, plus the additional feeling of worthlessness. Thus, any teen who suffers from the loss of someone close may already face a potentially greater risk of suicidal behavior. When the death involves suicide they are at even greater risk because one of their peers has stepped over a boundary that they may previously have seen as an absolute barrier.

It is not only the students who are affected by a suicide. The stress on all members of the school community can be almost overwhelming. This is not the time to try to develop an appropriate response to this tragic event. Such a response must be planned in advance and have variations for a multitude of contingencies. The objection is sometimes raised that such a plan is not necessary and that to develop one can cause people to think about suicide unnecessarily. Such an argument is an "adult" version of magical thinking. That is, to develop a response plan for an event will actually cause the event to happen. This serves only to show the depth of emotion raised by the topic of suicide. Schools regularly drill for fires, and this author is old enough to remember air raid drills. Such preparation helps to save lives and avoid injury, it does *not* cause these things to happen. Experience has shown that many parents *expect* their child's school to have a ready response planned to use in the wake of a sudden tragic death. When a suicide occurs, they are often shocked to find that any response is developed on an *ad hoc* basis. The impact of individual decisions has never been thought out and when asked to explain why something was or was not done, no answer is available.

There are some cases a parent may insist that nothing be done, that no information be shared, that no school response be allowed. These parents are focused on their own needs and those of their family. They may be unable to see that their child's peers also have needs which the school must consider. If there is no plan in place, such a parental action can paralyze an entire district and prevent needed interventions from being made on behalf of other students who are at risk themselves. If the school community is to respond in a positive manner, such a plan must be developed in advance.

A Postvention Protocol

The procedures contained in a postvention protocol must address two different situations: (1) helping all members of the school community in the aftermath of a completed suicide, and (2) helping a student to reenter the school setting after absence due to a suicide attempt or a threat of suicide. Many schools have begun to address the first situation. The second, illustrated in Case 3 at the start of this chapter, has received far less attention.

1. Completed Suicide

- A committee is appointed by the superintendent of schools, with approval of the board of education, to develop, initiate and monitor a response plan, evaluate results, and recommend changes. It is suggested that the committee include a counselor, school nurse, administrator, and one or more teacher representatives. The response plan should have both immediate and long-term components.

Immediate Response:

- A meeting is held for faculty and staff members as soon as possible after the death, but certainly before teachers meet again with students. Whatever is known is shared with all present. If rumors have been circulating these should be addressed, but care must be taken to avoid jumping to conclusions. For example, where people once avoided even speculating about the possibility of suicide after a sudden or traumatic death, some people now assume the death was a suicide even before all the facts are known.
- Faculty members should be allowed to share feelings and to receive support. One standard account of the event is to be agreed upon. This information should be provided to all students in classrooms or small groups. Large school-wide meetings or a public address system are *not* recommended for this notification.
- Staff members should allow students to express their feelings and be prepared to find that some students may say that they don't feel anything. This emotional "numbing" is normal but young people may need reassurance about this. Once feelings have been vented, students will begin to ask many "why" and "how" questions to learn details of the death. Share as much as is known and agreed upon, but do not be afraid to say "I don't know." Young people cope with grief and loss in many ways, among which are: apathy, punishment-seeking behavior, copying the deceased, or "humor." This humor may seem inappropriate or tasteless, but it does allow young people to talk about things they might otherwise keep to themselves. Laughter and tears both release tension. We joke about our fears. Laughter can restore a measure of control.
- Teachers are professionals and in most cases can be counted on to offer effective support to the young people in their care. However, when dealing with a suicide, educators often express uncertainty as to the "right thing" to say or do. In such cases it can be reassuring to have a set of guidelines prepared for distribution. One such set of guidelines included the following points:
  1. Talk about what happened, and allow students to do the same.
  2. Explain the facts as you know them. Answer all rumors.
  3. Promote positive attitudes and positive solutions. Have students list the people to whom they would go if they had a problem.
  4. Acknowledge that a change has occurred, but be careful not to validate the suicidal act.
  5. Do not romanticize the suicide.
  6. Help students to remember the complete person, not just good points.
- Support areas will be established and students should be excused from class to meet in support groups or with individual counselors if they feel the need to do so. Such meetings should be allowed for a specific period of time, typically two to three days. After that, students can meet individually with their counselors, the school nurse, or classroom teachers.

PICKING UP THE PIECES / 545

- Counselors should continue to follow-up with at-risk students. There should be a list of community resource personnel to assist "at-risk" parents. An initial meeting can be offered by school staff to help make referrals, but in-school support groups are beyond the scope of most schools.
- A meeting with interested parents should be scheduled as soon as possible to answer their questions and offer specific ways in which they can be supportive to their children. Two meetings may be needed, one during the day and the other during evening hours, to accommodate working parents.
- Modification of school academic routines should be considered. Classes should still be held. Standardized tests should be postponed. Classroom tests and assignments may need to be modified for a week or longer. Suicide related curricula in health, social science or other classes should be suspended for at least one marking period.
- The media pose special problems. Their reports can reassure a community that their children are being helped or the same reports can inflame community anger and prevent an effective response. One person must be appointed as media spokesperson and the name and contact phone number must be given to all local newspapers, radio, and television news bureaus. Special briefings should be held for the media, but reporters should not be allowed to attend the initial parent meeting or to disrupt classes by attempting to speak directly to teachers or students. Written statements concerning the death and the steps being taken to assist students and their families should be prepared and available for any interested media personnel.
- Students and staff members should be allowed to decide the questions of whether to hold a service/assembly, what form such a meeting should take, or whether to have some memorial to their deceased classmate and, if so, what form it should take.
- Be sure to maintain records so that there can be special vigilance on the anniversaries of deaths.
- Provide support for the professional staff. In the past, few schools have taken time to help the helpers. Staff members are also survivors and may fail to take care of their own needs because of their desire to help their students. Staff members should be allowed to debrief and to make suggestions for improvements in the response plan. There is no one "best" approach for dealing with issues related to a suicide and "experts" who claim that there is should be viewed critically.
- Students may also wish to make suggestions concerning ongoing support. The students in the River Dell High School course, Contemporary Issues of Life and Death, compiled the following suggestions to educators who are trying to help bereaved students. They are in no special order, but they are sincere and may be helpful to concerned educators.
  - Talk about the death and allow students to initiate discussion when they feel the need. We are sometimes so preoccupied in thinking of a response that we do not hear what has been said.

- Provide students with a safe place and allow them to go there when they need to. Feeling "trapped" in a school or classroom can exaggerate the feelings of helplessness which are part of the grief reaction.
- Allow changes in the environment, such as seating and other items which might be changed after the death of a classmate.
- Violence is the outlet that some students choose for their anger. Try to help students to avoid this, but also try to understand it if it occurs.
- At some point it will be O.K. to get on with life, but this point may be different for each student. Don't force the student to make this decision and try to help students not to "judge" each others grief.
- Provide students with a contact point for times when someone might not be available. Open time in the gym can bring people together and let off steam at the same time.
- Look for ways in which students who wish can offer organized help. Doing jobs for others can help deal with feelings of helplessness. It can give a "purpose."
- Listen to your students. They are the ones who know best what they need, even if they can't find the right words to express it. Sometimes the best thing you can do is just be quiet and listen. What may be needed is a friendly "ear" to which they can speak, then they may be able to find answers for themselves.

To the student list, we can add the following suggestions:

- Do not try to shield young people from "life." Explain what you can and remember that TALKING about a problem does not make it worse—it might just help.
- Avoid platitudes. Things may be "all right" some time after a loss but they will never be the same as they might have been. Don't block emotions. Big boys DO cry and so do all adults.
- Establish priorities. After any death academic work may drop, this is especially true following a suicide. Students must be reminded that lower grades do not make one a "bad" person. Remember that life is not always fair, and bad things do not have to be someone's fault. Avoid placing blame.
- Maintain open lines of communication. Be sure everyone involved understands what is really happening.
- Try to promote a greater feeling of control on the part of all students. Allow the teens some flexibility in choosing the time and place to discuss problems.
- Use, or develop, rituals. They can help people to accept the fact that a change has taken place after a loss.
- Be patient. Healing takes time and we cannot rush the process.

2. *Attempted Suicide*

In the wake of a suicide, there is often no plan for a school-wide response. The family of the student may be firm in their desire to have *no* discussion of the event. However, the other students almost certainly know what has happened in a general sense and "rumor" will fill in details if there is no more accurate source of information. How can the needs of the general student body be reconciled with the wishes of the individual student or his/her family? The needs of the student body are no less real after a suicide attempt. However, the support they are offered may be substantially less than following a completed suicide. One part of a response plan must address the apparent conflict between student *rights* (such as the right of the individual to privacy) and the school's *responsibility* to meet the needs of all its students. It is suggested that a protocol be prepared to meet the needs of students who seek information after a suicide attempt.

If there is no plan for reentry after a suicide attempt, the student in Case 3 above may find that things are indeed worse. The student feels that everyone knows what happened but no one is speaking of it. Or, the student may believe that the others do not know yet and worries what will happen when they do find out. If either of these situations occurs and no one reaches out to help, things for that student will indeed be worse.

Even if the suicide attempt is not to be discussed with other than counselors, it can be helpful to have written materials to provide to the returning student and to other students who are concerned about this student's return. Such material can be a starting point for discussing what has happened and it can be reviewed by the student in private as he/she decides what options the future holds. If possible, this handout should be provided to the student and his family before he returns to school. It is important to note that this written material is meant to assist and *not* replace direct human contact. One of the few resources available to provide to such a returning student is a small pamphlet entitled *Hurting Yourself,* by Oliveto and Harper [4]. It addresses the issues of feelings, what other people think, pressure, family suicides, family, taking care of yourself, taking care of your body and making sure there is no "next time." The twenty-four page pamphlet is inexpensive and can be ordered in quantity. It may even be used in ongoing courses, such as psychology or family life.

As with the completed suicide, there are issues which a school must be prepared to address. As identified by Judie Smith [5] these include support and aftercare; the transition from the hospital to school; and behavior review [2]. The following are ways in which a school can address each of these three issues:

Support and Aftercare

- Support groups, drop-in centers and the ability to speak to counselors in emergency situations should be available on an ongoing basis to all concerned students. These will be especially valuable after a suicide attempt.
- Medication protocols must be established and understood by all concerned. Students cannot be allowed to "self-medicate." Only the school nurse should administer medicine and the nurse must review all prescriptions with the student's doctor.
- Teachers should be informed of what has happened so that they can provide support and make modifications in academic requirements if necessary. The school must maintain open lines of communication with the family and, if the

student is seeing a therapist outside of the school, with the therapist as well, if the family approves.

Transition From the Hospital Setting

- The school should appoint a transition team to open and maintain communication with the hospital while the student is in residence there. The hospital should be asked to recommend any adjustments which might be needed in the student's academic schedule or assignments. Make-up work and tutorial help can be offered by teachers on the transition team while the student is hospitalized. These same school personnel can then be added resource people for the student upon return to school.

Behavior Review

- A behavior contract must be written to address the following points: past behavior problems (so that these do not re-occur), a clear list of rules of student behavior, and a clear explanation of attendance requirements with provisions for regular attendance review. Such a contract should be agreed to by administration, guidance, teachers, student, and the student's family.

CONCLUSION

The willingness of schools and community mental health centers to cooperate in developing intervention protocols and suicide prevention programs has produced some positive programs for students in the last decade. The next challenge is to develop similar postvention programs for schools. In this process it is essential that input be solicited from all interested parties in a community and that each district and school develop an individual policy to meet the unique needs of their community, their school, and their students.

REFERENCES

1. Centres for Disease Control and Prevention, Suicide Among Children, Adolescents and Young Adults—United States, 1980-1992, *Journal of School Health,* 65(7), pp. 272-273, September 1995.
2. D. Ryerson and J. Kalafat, The Crisis of Youth Suicide, in *What Will We Do? Preparing a School Community to Cope with Crisis,* R. G. Stevenson (ed.), Baywood Publishing, Amityville, New York, 1994.
3. R. G. Stevenson, *What Will We Do? Preparing a School Community to Cope with Crisis,* Baywood Publishing, Amityville, New York, 1994.
4. E. Oliveto and J. Harper, *Hurting Yourself,* Centering Corporation, Omaha, 1987.
5. J. Smith, *Returning to School Following a Suicide Attempt,* paper presented at the Annual Conference of the American Association of Suicidology, April 1991, quoted in *What Will We Do? Preparing a School Community to Cope with Crisis,* Baywood Publishing, Amityville, New York, 1994.

BIBLIOGRAPHY

Kline, M., D. J. Schonfeld, and R. Lichtenstein, Benefits and Challenges of School-Based Crisis Response Teams, *Journal of School Health,* 65(7), pp. 245-249, September 1995.

Lord, J. H., *No Times for Goodbyes,* Pathfinder Publishing, Ventura, California, 1988.

Stevenson, R. G., Teen Suicide: Sources, Signals and Prevention, in *The Dying and the Bereaved Teenager,* John D. Morgan (ed.), Charles Press, Philadelphia, 1990.

CHAPTER 35

Suicide Among the Elderly: Understanding with Mind and Heart

Judith M. Stillion

THE STATISTICAL PICTURE

Suicide among the elderly is a delicate subject that demands both cognitive knowledge and affective understanding if we hope to address it successfully. In this chapter, I will provide a brief review of elderly suicide from both a cognitive and affective perspective and then suggest some tools that are available to help elderly people cope with the conditions that cause high suicide rates.

Let us begin by acknowledging that the suicide rate among the elderly has declined across the last half of this century. Figure 1 shows the male rate of suicide for three age groups since 1960 while Figure 2 shows the female rate of elderly suicide across the same time frame. Both figures show that there has been a steady decrease in the rates of the elderly suicide for all except the very old since the middle of this century. Moving to a shorter time frame, Figure 3 shows that between 1980 and 1990, the rate of suicide among the young-old stayed approximately the same but the rates among the two oldest groups increased.

There are three possible reasons for the overall decline in suicide across the last half of the century among the younger elderly: first, because more women live to old age than men and because women's suicide rate peaks in middle age, the rate of suicide among the elderly should be lower as the numbers of women compared to men increase in this age group.

Second, we should not underestimate the possible cohort differences between this and previous groups of elderly people. People who are seventy as this is written were born in 1926. They entered kindergarten (those for whom it was available) in 1931, and spent their early school years being shaped by the Great Depression. They turned eighteen in 1944, just in time to see many of the males in their cohort called to serve in the last years of World War II. Their children, mostly born between 1946 and 1963, form the Baby Boom cohort and represent an investment of time and energy in parenting that had hitherto been unknown. Their middle years were spent

552 / READINGS IN THANATOLOGY

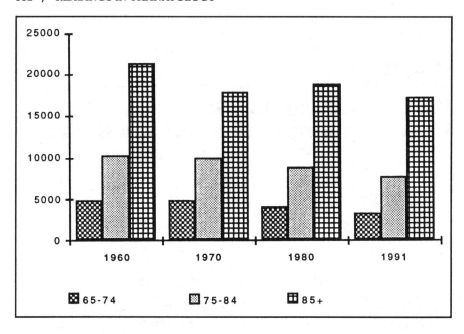

Figure 1. Rates of suicide for males (per 100,000 population).

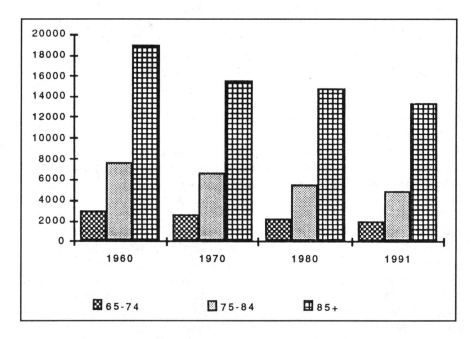

Figure 2. Rates of suicide for females (per 100,000 population).

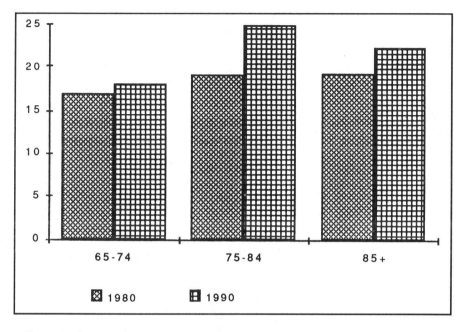

Figure 3. Age-specific death rates for suicide: United States (rates per 100,000).

enjoying the greatest period of prosperity this country had ever known. Largely as a consequence of the time in which they were born, they have moved into old age with more education, better health, and more social benefits of all types than any other previous generation.

Third, we should acknowledge the powerful influence of economic gains on the rate of elderly suicide. One study showed that four things, all economic indicators, predict 90 percent of the variance in suicide behavior among older white men: (1) employment, (2) availability of income security, (3) portion of labor force covered by social security, and (4) average monthly income for husband and wife [1].

Although the overall rate of suicide has declined, the elderly still have the highest rate of suicide of all age groups. They remain over-represented among suicides. For example, in the early 1980s people over sixty-five constituted approximately 11 percent of the U.S. population but committed 17 percent of the suicides [2].

Figure 4 shows the actual numbers of suicide by age and sex for the year, 1991. It is important to remember that these figures represent only those who were known to have committed suicide. Miller has pointed out that the elderly have their own special means of committing suicide, including self-starvation; refusal to follow physician's orders; not taking medications; engaging in hazardous activities; delaying treatments or operations; and voluntary seclusion; all of which may be sub-intentioned suicidal behaviors and would never be counted into the suicide statistics

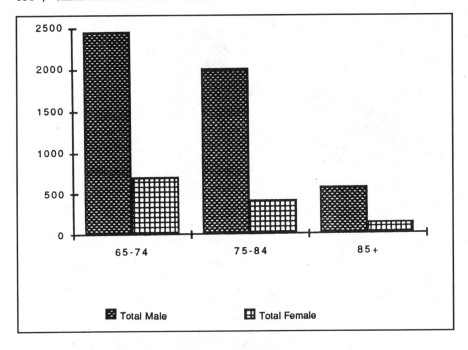

Figure 4. Numbers of deaths by suicide among the elderly in the United States: 1992.

[3]. In fact, there is reason to believe that suicide is even more under reported in this group than in others by at least 40 percent. Moreover, the attempt-completion ratio for elderly people is four-to-one compared to approximately ten-to-one for all other ages combined [4]. This means that elderly people are less likely to engage in suicidal gestures or threats. Their suicide attempts are serious and lethal.

A final generalization about elderly suicide is that the ratio of male to female suicides is higher than in general population: five-to-one compared to three-to-one. In fact, white males in the United States form the great preponderance of the statistics on elderly suicide.

Having looked at the past and the present, let us now turn our attention to the future. Suicide among the elderly is predicted to rise in the twenty-first century. There are several factors fueling this anticipated rise. First, the size of the baby boom population alone will increase the numbers who commit suicide. For example, at present rates of suicide (18 per 100,000), we see 8,500 suicides per year among the elderly. The same suicide rate would result in 12,500 elderly suicides per year by the year 2000; 14,000 suicides annually by the year 2020; and an unprecedented 18,500 suicides annually by the year 2040. However, we may also experience an increase in the rate of suicide since there is some evidence that the larger the cohort, the more likely individuals are to commit suicide at any age [5], perhaps because of the law of supply and demand.

THE SUICIDE TRAJECTORY

Statistics about suicide are informative, but they rarely help us to understand the condition that predispose individuals to take their own lives. Figure 5 shows a model that is designed to promote such understanding. Called the suicide trajectory model, it describes four major categories of risk factors that influence the likelihood of suicide at any age [4]. These categories may interact with each other, each lending its weight to the development of suicidal ideation. There may or may not be warning signs or a triggering event prior to the appearance of suicidal behavior.

There are some commonalities in the risk factors regardless of age. For example, within the biological risk factor category, there is genetic predisposition. We are just beginning to appreciate the fact that there may be a biological foundation for some suicidal behavior. Evidence for this assertion comes from twin studies, in which ten identical twins were located in the literature where both had suicided while no cases of fraternal suicide were found as well as from a study of matched pairs of adopted children [6]. The study looked at fifty-seven suicides who were adopted. Among their biological relatives, twelve had completed suicide. No adopted relatives had taken their lives. In matched group of fifty-seven adoptees who did not commit suicide, only two had relatives who had completed suicide. Once again, no adopted relatives had taken their lives. This evidence is far from

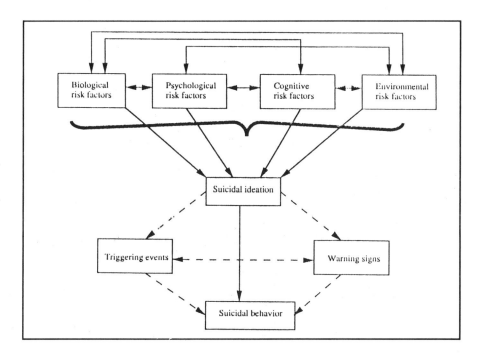

Figure 5. The suicide trajectory.

convincing but it does suggest that there may be a genetic component in some suicides.

Another line of evidence supporting a generic component in suicide is seen in an Amish study, which found that there were twenty-six suicides within the community in the last century—73 percent of them were in four families [6].

One of the most exciting areas of current biological research is that of the physiological correlates of suicide. It appears that people who complete suicide have a lack of serotonin in the neurotransmitters of the brain. In one study, in which a metabolite of serotonin (5-HIAA) was measured, those hospitalized for suicide attempts who had lower levels of the metabolite were ten times more likely to have taken their lives a year later [7, 8]. Whether this lack of serotonin is inherited or comes about as a result of environmental factors is unknown, but it certainly is an important biological finding because it means that some suicidal people may respond to drug therapy.

Still another genetic factor that may predispose to suicide at any age is the presence of the Y chromosome. As early as we can measure them, male babies have higher activity and aggression levels than female babies. This tendency toward activity and aggression may well be part of the inheritance of the Y chromosome. Freud, and his followers believed that some suicides are the result of aggression turned inward. If there is any truth to this concept, inheriting the male chromosome might predispose an individual to suicide. Certainly, the international and historical statistics reported earlier support the assertion that males are at more risk for suicide than are females.

In addition to the biological commonalities found in people of all ages, there are other biological risk factors that apply only to the elderly. These may include such "normal" changes as wrinkling of skin, graying and balding, and loss of teeth. Taken separately, these don't necessarily have much impact, but put together, and placed in a society that worships youth and eschews old age, they have a cumulative effect on the self-esteem of most elderly people. More serious, however, are changes that announce physical decline—including sensory losses. There is growing evidence that severe loss of hearing inclines individuals toward paranoia. Decline in vision increases the frustration involved in everyday living and motor and balance impairment increases caution in the elderly and restricts their freedom of movement. A final category of biological changes includes development of chronic illnesses. Butler and Lewis have estimated that up to 86 percent of all elderly people develop chronic illnesses accompanied by some degree of pain and incapacitation [9]. Miller found that 60 percent of elderly people who complete suicide visit physicians within one month of taking their lives [3]. In addition, two studies conducted in England have found that approximately 60 percent of a group of elderly suicides were medically ill at the time of their deaths [10]. The development of chronic illnesses decreases the comfort level of life and makes suicide an even more attractive option. The role that biological influences may play on suicide within the elderly population is highlighted by the following case study taken from *Suicide Across the Life Span: Premature Exits* [4].

Meet W. D. Henshaw

W. D. Henshaw killed himself on his eighty-first birthday. He carefully spread a newly purchased tarpaulin on the concrete floor of his garage, lay down upon it, and shot himself in the head. The terse suicide note that he left said simply, "It's time."

W. D. was a self-made man. He came from a small dirt farm in the South, worked his way through college and founded an agricultural business that made him a wealthy man while he was still in his thirties. W. D. married a woman from a wealthy family when he was in his mid-thirties and her wealth provided even more security for the business. Although Mrs. Henshaw was thirty-four when they married, they had two children. The Henshaw's appeared to have a stable, if unexciting marriage. However, Mrs. Henshaw developed breast cancer at age fifty-two and died within six months. W. D. never remarried, devoting himself instead almost totally to his business. As W. D. grew older, his son and daughter tried to get him to slow down, to develop hobbies, to take vacations. They had little success. When W. D. turned seventy, his son tried to talk him into retiring. The two men argued violently, and W. D. stayed on the job, although he did cut back his customary work day from fourteen hours to ten.

By age seventy-eight, W. D. was complaining that food had lost its taste and that he could not hear young people's conversations. He began to think that the young executives in his business were conspiring against him. In general, however, his health remained good until he began to have a series of small strokes at age seventy-nine. Between hospitalizations, as his health permitted, he continued to go the office but was aware that it was running well without him and that he could no longer remember many of the details of the business. He had a long talk with his son, admitting his growing confusion and weakness and officially resigned from the presidency of his company. He spent several months putting his affairs in order.

In an uncharacteristic gesture, he invited his family and the executives of his company to a cookout on his eighty-first birthday. His children commented after the party that they had been impressed with W. D.'s renewed energy. His daughter had felt that it was a sure sign of physical improvement, while his son felt it was caused by removal of the stress of the job. After the party, W. D. straightened the house, piled the dishes neatly in the sink, and wrote his two-worded note.

W. D.'s suicide is an example of the profound effect that failing health can have upon an individual—especially one whose entire self-concept is caught up with work.

The second category of risk factors is in the psychological domain, and includes depression, and lack of or collapse of coping skills. Among the elderly, the principle of psychological entropy comes into play. Psychological entropy maintains that "there is an inevitable, progressive disorganization that occurs in living organisms and in physical systems and that leads to the collapse of the steady state system" [11]. Freud put it more succinctly when he stated that the goal of all life is death. We will be exploring the psychological state of mind that characterizes suicidal elderly people in some depth later in this chapter. At this point, to provide a baseline for comparison, perhaps, we should describe some of the psychological qualities of a healthy old age.

There are several variables that make for positive adjustment in old age. These include a zest for life, endurance, a positive self-concept, an optimistic world view, and a strong relationship between past goals and achievements. One of the most useful characterizations of psychologically healthy elderly was that proposed by Erikson who said that a major task of those over sixty-five was to attain a sense of ego integrity [12]. By that he meant, a sense that we have one life to live in one period of history, and that, all in all, we have done the best we could. Contrast this stance with its polar opposite, despair and disgust, and you begin to understand how elderly people can become suicidal.

Peck added substance to Erikson's description of psychological healthy elderly people by stating that there were three tasks that needed to be accomplished during the old age period [13]. The first sub-task is ego differentiation as contrasted with preoccupation with work role. Elderly people need to find multiple ways to remain involved in life, especially as they reach retirement age. The second task is body transcendence vs. body preoccupation. As the body begins to fail, older persons need to find foci for their attention that permit them to rise above the normal signs of age as well as the increasing pains that may accompany the onset of chronic disease. The third task is ego transcendence vs. ego preoccupation. By this, Peck meant that aging people need to find satisfaction in the realization that they have made contributions of some kind to their culture that will live on beyond their finite life spans [13].

Another psychological characteristic of elderly suicidal people is loneliness. Darbonne found that the notes of suicidal elderly included more references to loneliness and isolation than those of any other age group [14]. The final psychological characteristic consists of a triad of depression, hopelessness, and despair. Depression, as we have seen, is rampant among elderly people. Osgood has reported that between 30 and 60 percent of people over sixty are depressed [15, 16].

The third category of risk factors in the trajectory is labeled cognitive risk factors. The body of work produced over the years by Aaron Beck and his associates has shed the most light on cognitive changes among those who are suicidally depressed [17-19]. These researchers maintain that when individuals become suicidal, regardless of their age or stage of development, their thought patterns become rigid. As thought patterns become rigid, people begin to engage in selective abstraction, over-generalization, and inexact labeling. Selective abstraction is the tendency to focus on the negative and ignore or de-emphasize the positives. Overgeneralization is the tendency to view the world pessimistically and to pile negatives upon negatives. Inexact labeling occurs when an individual places a negative label on himself or herself and reacts to the label rather than the situation at hand. Thus, an elderly person like W. D. Henshaw might reason as follows. "I'm not good for anything anymore—no-one wants me around. They all dread my coming to the office (over-generalization). Even though the Board says I am the symbol of the company and the history-bearer, they are just mouthing the words. They really view me as old and sick and incompetent (selective abstraction). I'm just too old to be any good to anyone. I'm just a worthless has-been" (inexact labeling).

Other important cognitive factors affecting elderly people include difficulty in concentrating and poor memory. It is clear that most elderly people decline in some types of learning and in the time it takes to learn new material. There is also an increase in the time it takes to retrieve learned material, especially recently learned material. While these characteristics tend to accompany the thinking of depressed people of all ages, they hold special dread for the elderly who may interpret them as indications that they are developing an organic brain syndrome.

A final cognitive change among older people is in the way death is viewed. Instead of as a threat, for many elderly, death is increasingly accepted as an alternative, which may result in an increased susceptibility or even an embracing of suicide.

The remaining risk factor category shown in the suicide trajectory is that of environmental factors that may predispose a person to suicide, regardless of age. These include turbulent home lives, loss, and the presence of means of destruction, especially firearms.

One specific environmental risk factor that should be explored with suicidal elderly is that of negative life events. Although negative events can occur at any age, the final period of life from age sixty-five onward contains more normative, expected negative changes than any other time of life. In addition to being numerous, the changes are also less reversible or remediable than at earlier periods of life.

Let's just examine a few of these changes. First, widowhood is a normative event for the elderly, often resulting in the loss of the one person who has known and cared for the elderly person across the adult years.

Second, retirement occurs at some time during this period, decreasing both feelings of productivity and opportunities for regular socialization on the job. Elderly retired people often lose status and power as well as health and self-concept as a well and productive person, as did W. D. Henshaw.

Third, cumulative loss becomes a reality. The elderly experience the deaths of long-time friends and relatives, further eroding their social circles. These, coupled with the losses represented by retirement and physical decline, often test the coping of the hardiest elderly person. The timing of these losses is important also since each one comes hard on the heels of the last and there is little time to grieve through one loss before one must cope with the next.

A fourth environmental factor influencing suicide among elderly people is alcohol and drug abuse [16]. It is not unusual for elderly people to use alcohol as a form of self-medication. Because metabolic processes are slower among older people, ingestion of alcohol coupled with prescription or over-the-counter drugs can have toxic effects, exacerbating depression and perhaps becoming life-threatening.

A final environmental factor contributing to elderly suicide is poverty. Poverty seems especially traumatic in old age, especially after a lifetime of seemingly adequate income prior to retirement. As we have seen, Marshall examined the relationship between four different indices of economic well-being among the elderly and the suicide rate for older white men [1]. He found that the four economic indices accounted for over 90 percent of the variance in suicidal behavior and concluded that economic issues are far more important than social or political issues for elderly males. Although the studies are not there for females, there is every reason to believe, that they, too, are negatively affected by poverty. An extreme example may be seen in the following case study.

Elena Mercado

Elena Mercado was widowed after forty-two years of marriage. Her husband, "Merk," who had worked as a machinist for thirty-three years, had died of cancer after a long expensive illness. Elena found herself facing a debt-ridden widowhood. Elena had raised seven children. She and Merk had always taken pride in the fact that he earned enough to permit her to be a full-time wife and mother. Although Elena's seven children were concerned about their mother's financial situation, none of them was able to help very much. Elena gave up her apartment in an effort to cut down on expenses and spent her time divided among the children's homes. She confided to an old friend that she felt like an intruder at every home, because she always took a bed from one of the grandchildren and sometimes felt that she deprived the family of food as well as privacy. Elena actively investigated low cost housing programs, but each one she examined seemed beyond her means. In addition to trying to make small payments on her husband's medical bills, Elena tried to help out with the grocery bills at whichever house she was visiting.

Shortly after Elena moved in with her oldest son for the second time, he lost his job and told her she would have to leave his home. When Elena told her daughter she would have to move in with her sooner than expected, the daughter came to her brother's home to express her unhappiness. The resulting argument between the siblings was bitter. Elena, not knowing what else to do, began to pack. While doing so, she discovered a bottle of old barbiturates left from her husband's illness. Elena left the house, saying she was going for a walk to clear her head. She walked to a nearby park, stopping to buy a coke at the corner deli. She took all of the pills in the bottle. Her body was discovered early the next morning when the police made their routine swing through the park [4].

In Elena's case, the losses of husband and home combined with feelings of helplessness and hopelessness caused by poverty overcame her ability to cope and led directly to suicide.

Taken together, the four categories of risk factors (biological, psychological, cognitive, and environmental) lend their accumulated weight to increase the likelihood of suicidal ideation. The commonalities in suicide ideation include its very nature which is insistent, even becoming obsessive, and the fact that it results in a plan which includes method, place, and time. Generally, with elderly persons, the plan is very specific, highly lethal, and kept as a closely guarded secret [20].

Warning signs that are common across the life span include self-injurious behaviors, verbal threats, and closure behaviors. Among elderly persons, a common warning sign is a visit to a doctor. Studies have shown that as many as 70 percent of the elderly people who complete suicide have visited a physician within one month of the suicide and that as many as 10 percent consult a physician on the actual day of the suicide. Perhaps such a visit serves as a last chance to test whether a professional can offer solid hope for making life more livable.

Triggering events can be viewed as final straw phenomena. The most common triggering event among elderly persons is the diagnosis of a terminal illness for them or for their spouse.

SPECIAL ISSUES IN ELDERLY SUICIDE

Before we move to consider the feelings of elderly suicidal people, we should address briefly some special issues in elderly suicide. The first is the whole question of the right to die with its accompanying issues of passive and active euthanasia and physician assisted suicide. As we will see in a moment, the line between suicide and euthanasia is a very fine one. The second is the issue of widowhood and the question of who is most disadvantaged by it: males or females? A case can be made for either. I would suggest that widowhood is initially harder for males both because they frequently are losing the one person with whom they had been physically intimate across their adult lives and because of the discontinuity in roles. Older males, especially those of the G.I. generation, often have few skills in food preparation or housekeeping since that generation came of age in a time when gender roles maintained that these were "women's work." However, if they are in good health, males have a better chance of marrying again than do females. They can also more easily take an active role in seeking out new companions than is true for females of the G.I. generation. Females, on the other hand, may find more support since in our culture females outlive males by nearly a decade and, therefore, there are more widowed females to support each other. Widowed elderly females may also find comfort in continuing their roles as homemakers. However, women of this generation often have derived much of their identity through their roles as spouses, so their long-term adjustment might be more difficult than would be true of their male counterparts [21].

The third special issue in elderly suicide is that of double suicides. Osgood has reported that between 1980 and 1987, there are ninety-seven documented cases in the United States in which spouses died together: sixty-six were mercy killing/suicide and thirty-one double suicides [16]. One of these was described in this AP Wire Release:

> Highland Park, Texas
> After a loving fifty year marriage and successful medical careers, Don and Betty Morris couldn't bear the thought of some day being separated or finishing their lives in a nursing home.

So the couple, both seventy-six, indulged in scrambled eggs with cheese and lots of bacon, ice cream and corn chips—all of which they had been forbidden to eat. They sipped their favorite sherry and drank lethal doses of a depressant, then lay down in each other's arms until the poison took effect.

The two of them together could function well, but not alone. If Dad had another heart attack, that would have put Mom in a nursing home. They didn't want that. They had seen too many friends who had been placed in nursing homes," said Don Morris, Jr., forty-nine, one of the couple's three surviving children.

The elderly Morris, a semi-retired psychiatrist, and his wife, a retired psychologist, were found dead in their bedroom July 14, by police after the Southwestern Medical School in Dallas, where Morris was a faculty member, received a letter from them describing their suicide.

A pair of suicide notes was found in the couple's bedroom along with a menu of the couple's last meal and a list of poems reflecting on death.

"The problem of many deteriorating old people is obviously a new one—everybody used to die too soon," Morris said in his note. "Therefore, as a society, we have not learned to deal with it in a decent and respectable manner."

The Morris' children said their parents told them they would eventually commit suicide. But in his suicide note, Morris said he regretted taking his life "surreptitiously . . . under cover of darkness."

It is obvious that this case involved the elements of loss of health, interdependence, and desire to avoid worse conditions. It is equally as obvious that this case blurs the line between suicide and active euthanasia. A full discussion of euthanasia and assisted suicide is beyond the scope of this chapter. However, it is an issue that will continue to grow in salience in the near future as the large generation of baby boomers enters their senior years. Economics, ethics, religion, and the medical system will all need their best leaders to address these issues effectively.

FEELING SUICIDAL

Everything we've looked at so far speaks to our intellectual understanding of suicide. But, as people intimately concerned with the lives of elderly suicidal people, we must move beyond the mere intellectual. To really be able to make contact, we have to understand and attempt to experience the inner world of suicidal elderly people. To do that, I invite you to explore with me some dimensions of suicidal state of being in the elderly. For the next few moments, let us become elderly; let us become suicidal—and let's explore all of the dimensions involved.

It's not a unit is it—this state of mind that causes us to consider killing ourselves? To the extent that we can tease out all of the emotions being experienced by elderly suicidal people, we will be more effective in reaching out to them as well as suggesting some possible approaches for reaching them. So let's examine together the A-B-Cs of suicidal depression in the elderly.

First, in all suicidal states, there is an element of anxiety; that formless, free-floating emotion that warns us even in the midst of family, of pleasure, that all is not well. Anxiety causes us to feel tense and to be mobilized to fight or flee at all times. It tests our limits and makes each day a struggle.

The second "A" is anger. While anger is not as prevalent in the suicide notes of elderly people as it is among younger people, there is still some anger present in all suicides. Often people do not understand the source of the anger and have no idea how to direct it. It seems directed at everything and at nothing and in the end it is too frequently directed toward the people we love the most. We don't even find escape in sleep. Anger wakes us up in the middle of the night and we toss and turn trying to discover its source. We review our lives trying to find reasons for being so angry and we can always find some. No one lives a life without some frustration and frustration breeds anger. But such violent anger? Such all encompassing anger? We literally become trapped in it and find ourselves raging against our own existence.

Moving to the "E"s, we become egocentric. Our emotional pain is so threatening to us and so overwhelming that it takes all of our energy to endure it. We have none to use in reaching out to others and the world. Our world narrows until there is nothing but us in it. Even when we're with others, we are alone. Every waking moment is spent thinking about our pain, our problems, our miserable existence.

Exhaustion is another emotion we feel. We can't sleep, don't eat well, and have no peace from the negative emotions that nag at us all day long. Every chore seems to demand too much from us. Exhaustion follows, further weakening our abilities to cope with life. We're just too tired—too tired to live.

Guilt and its twin, regret, are also there, waiting their turn for our attention. We compulsively recite all of our failings and failures, while overlooking our strengths and our successes. We feel guilt for the things we did and the things we failed to do. We remember our youth and the choices we had and we regret the road not taken.

Adding to the guilt and regret is the feeling of helplessness we experience. We are not in control. We cannot change our life circumstances. There is no time—even if we had the energy and the will. We are aware that the sands in the hour glass are falling ever more quickly and that we cannot control their speed or slow their inevitable direction.

And when the strength of the feeling of helplessness reaches its apex, we know without a doubt that it is hopeless, that there is no reason and no way to go on. We know also that tomorrow will not be better—that tomorrow, if it exists, will only bring more pain and suffering; will only see us more diminished; our greatest fears come true. Indeed, we realize that tomorrow is likely to be our worst enemy.

With the ascent of hopelessness comes the inability to feel. Things keep happening in the real world out there. Babies get born, people die, celebrations occur, holidays come and go but they do not touch us. It's as though we're cut off from human experience emotionally. We know that we should feel and sometimes we can feel the faint echo of an emotion, but generally, we are dead inside.

But perhaps the most pervasive emotion of all is a sense of joylessness, an overwhelming lack of pleasure in anything. This inability to feel anything positive adds pain to pain until we come to believe that attempting death may be the only way to feel *anything* again.

And then there is indecision. We, who used to handle a myriad of decisions easily, fluently, without hesitation find that we can barely decide to get out of bed. Small things like what to wear or eat become major struggles. And why not? What does it matter what we wear or eat, when nothing matters anymore? When nothing counts? Our former sureness has evaporated. The faith we had in ourselves, the justness of the world—even our God—are not real anymore.

More threatening than any of these is the loneliness, the isolation we feel. So many of our friends and loved ones have already died, and our children and grandchildren are caught up in their own busy lives. We haven't the time or the energy to make new friends. We are literally separated from our fellow man and we cannot make contact.

A final emotion, especially for us at this stage of life, is resignation. We know that death is coming and that it is coming soon, so why not welcome it, even hurry its appearance?

To bring it all into focus, to sum it all up, suicidal elders are grieving people. They are grieving real losses, experienced or anticipated, but they are also grieving the loss of what life once was and what it could and should be. That loss, generally made up multiple losses of relationships, status, peace of mind, ambition, dreams, etc., ensure that every potential suicide is a person who is grieving.

TOOLS FOR HELPING SUICIDAL ELDERS

Having tried to experience the multiple dimensions of elderly suicidal depression, let's turn our attention now to some of the tools we might use to reach out to those people. Miller has suggested that the difference between an elderly person committing suicide or living out his/her full life span is finding that delicate balance where life is worth living again [3]. Miller put it this way, "Lying dormant within all of us is an extremely personal equation which determines the point where the quality of our lives would be so pathetically poor we would no longer wish to live. He calls this the "line of unbearability" and maintains that once it is crossed, a crisis is triggered. Those who still maintain hope cry out for help. Those who don't are likely to kill themselves quickly and with determination" [3, p. 14].

Shneidman, the father of suicidology, has addressed this same notion with his concept of reducing lethality [22]. He believes that care givers must determine what, if anything, can be done to enable the individual to once again embrace life. One way of doing this is fairly straightforward. We can ask elderly suicidal people under what conditions they would be willing to go on living. Then we can work, however possible, to make their lives more closely approximate those conditions. If the people with whom we work have no suggestions, we may still induce them to re-cross that line of unbearability by using some of the tools available to all of us, regardless of our background or levels of education and training. All of us have such tools. I will suggest only a few that we can utilize as we attempt to bring some hope to the hopeless.

The first and best tool we all have is listening. Each elderly person has a life story, an important one, to tell. It has been said that elderly people are more individual than younger people—because they've had more time to develop their own life patterns. Each of us can focus on the uniqueness of every person with whom we work. Each person is a living miracle. When they were conceived any one of some 400,000 eggs could have ripened and any of several million sperm could have fertilized that egg. Statisticians would tell us that the odds are against any one person being born, living, and growing old. Use this insight to help elderly people feel valued and to get them to tell their stories. We can learn from them what will make a difference in the quality of their lives if we listen and if we will reinforce the values by which they have lived. Finding the threads—emphasizing the values—echoing the meaning—these are the tools of reminiscence therapy—but they are also the tools of those who care about the elderly. Listening also means "being with" and when we remember that one of the major threats to the elderly is loneliness, we begin to appreciate the immense value of being there. Simply by being available to listen, we may move people back across the line of unbearability.

Second, we can take advantage of what I call natural adjunct therapists. Exercise is one—whether it's something as simple as gardening or something much more active, we can encourage the elderly to use whatever physical abilities they have. Even swaying to music in a wheelchair has been shown to have positive effects with elderly people. The truth is that moving deflects depression.

Third, we can introduce the elderly with whom we work to some of the mental tools that are coming on the scene. Particularly for the elderly who may be physically incapacitated, techniques such as imagery, mediation, and self-hypnosis may be helpful. In addition to the benefit inherent in each technique, these activities also give back an element of control, of empowerment to the elderly person who can learn to use them on his/her own.

Fourth, we can encourage our elderly friends to learn something new or to relearn a skill that has languished. Our species has labeled itself "Homo sapiens," in recognition of the fact that learning and knowing are central features of humans. We need to learn like we need to breathe. Mastering a new skill as Grandma Moses did in old age or re-committing to an old lost skill brings zest into life again, fuels our self-esteem, and takes our mind off ourselves.

The fifth tool is laughter. Some say that it is physically impossible to be depressed while you are laughing. Laughing decenters us. We cannot focus only on life's negatives if we can laugh and those who can still laugh in old age are the healthiest of us all. Find funny things to share with suicidal elderly people. If Norman Cousins could laugh his way back to health and enjoy a few more years of productive life, so can the depressed elderly with whom we work. Warn those with whom you work to seek out fellow laughers and to stay away from the somber, the morose, those who would dwell only on the negative.

Sixth, ask those who can do so to give of themselves to others. People who can reach out to help others who are in pain, or need education, or food, find that they cannot long keep their own troubles uppermost in their minds. There are almost always people in worse shape than those you're working with. The world is full of need. And the elderly have had a lifetime of gaining knowledge. Find out what they used to love and find ways to have them share that love again.

Seventh, remember that as Homo sapiens, we are meaning makers, and we need to seek meaning actively. The world's great churches attest to the powerful need to find ways to express our spiritual nature. Whether it is through religion, or some more individual pathway, we need to be active in trying to find the meaning for our lives. While most care givers can't prescribe a given religion unless they work within a denominational framework, we can remember that all humans have spiritual needs and encourage the people with whom we work to explore and express those dimensions of themselves.

Eighth, help the people with whom you work get back in touch with earth and the seasons of earth. We are creatures of this earth, just like the other animals and we lose contact with its rhythms at our peril. Elderly people, in particular, are more likely to have grown up close to nature and more likely, also to have become separated from it in their daily lives as they aged. Help them to re-experience the message inherent in the seasons. Perhaps they will recall that spring brings hope with its promise of new beginnings; that summer teaches us about the richness of our home; that fall's colorful beauty teaches us lessons about harvesting what we have sown and giving thanks for it and that winter can bring a special kind of white, cool peace. Winter can also remind us that even in the coldest of the seasons, the seeds of new life are there—awaiting re-awakening. We need to help our elderly people remember the gifts of the seasons they have already had and to look for personal meaning through re-experiencing them, if only in their memories. The seasons are the most powerful metaphors for our lives as they help us to understand birth, and becoming, aging and death.

Ninth, as those who are concerned about elders, we must remember not to impose our values on those who may be contemplating suicide. If they have irrevocably crossed that line of unbearability into a life of complete hopelessness, loneliness, and physical and psychological pain, and especially if they have accepted death with calmness and grace, if they have celebrated their one life story as Erikson suggests that elderly healthy elderly must do to realize ego integrity, then you may help them most by being willing to talk to them of death and funerals and by being unafraid of their acceptance of the inevitable.

Finally, we need to work together to turn around some of the ageism of modern society. Osgood reports that many elderly feel dejected, degraded, devalued, demeaned, humiliated, useless, and worthless—simply because they are old [16]. My own research on attitudes toward suicide shows that elderly suicide is far more acceptable than is suicide by people of other ages [23]. At some deep level, modern Western societies seem to feel that elderly people are expendable; that their lives are only valued to the extent that they are useful, and that once they reach the stage of being non-productive—they become non-people. Osgood has reminded us that most elderly people who take their lives are not suffering intense physical pain or dying from a terminal illness [16]. Instead, they are leading lives full of loneliness and empty of joy. This is particularly true in our youth-oriented society. We need to work together to try to recover some respect for elderly people—if for no other reason than that they are survivors—and with a little help from us—they can probably help us discover tools for survival. We need to remember also that we are the next elders; that the universal fate of all of us who are lucky to live long enough is to be elderly, and so we must, out of enlightened self-interest, if for no other reason, help our society to understand that life is the scarcest, most precious commodity in the university and therefore deserves utmost respect.

As we work with suicidal elders, we should do so with the understanding that we all have only a limited time to develop our talents, skills, personalities; to learn and to teach, and to become the best person we are capable of being. That realization may help us to work both with individuals and within our society to affirm the process of becoming which is life and to work against those forces that would cut it off prematurely. Old age has its own lessons to be learned—and taught—to those who will follow.

REFERENCES

1. J. R. Marshall, Changes in Aged White Male Suicide: 1948-1972, *Journal of Gerontology, 33*, pp. 763-768, 1978.
2. J. L. McIntosh, R. W. Hubbard, and J. F. Santos, Suicide Among the Elderly: A Review of Issues with Case Studies, *Journal of Gerontological Social Work, 4*, pp. 63-74, 1981.
3. M. Miller, *Suicide After Sixty: The Final Alternative*, Springer, New York, 1979.
4. J. M. Stillion, E. E. McDowell, and J. H. May, *Suicide Across the Life Span: Premature Exits*, Hemisphere Division of Taylor and Francis, Washington, D.C., 1989.
5. P. C. Holinger and C. Offer, The Prediction of Adolescent Suicide: A Population Model, *American Journal of Psychiatry, 139*, pp. 302-307, 1982.
6. S. J. Blumenthal and D. J. Kupfer, Generalizable Treatment Strategies for Suicidal Behavior, in *Psychobiology of Suicidal Behavior*, J. J. Mann and M. Stanley (eds.), New York Academy of Sciences, New York, pp. 327-340, 1986.
7. M. Asberg and L. Traskman-Bendz, Studies of CSF 5-HIAA in Depression and Suicidal Behavior, *Experiments in Medical Biology, 133*, pp. 739-752, 1981.
8. M. Asberg, P. Nordstrom, and L. Traskman-Bendz, Cerebrospinal Fluid Studies in Suicide, *Annals of the New York Academy of Sciences, 487*, pp. 243-255, 1986.
9. R. Butler and M. I. Lewis, *Aging and Mental Health: Positive Psychosocial and Biomedical Approaches* (3rd Edition), Mosby, St. Louis, 1982.
10. B. M. Barraclough and J. Hughes, *Suicide*, Croom Helm, London, 1987.
11. J. Rifkin and T. Howard, *Entropy: A New World View*, Bantam, New York, 1980.
12. E. H. Erikson, *Identity and the Life Cycle*, International Universities Press, New York, 1959.
13. R. C. Peck, Psychological Developments in the Second Half of Life, in *Middle Age and Aging: A Reader in Social Psychology*, B. L. Neugarten (ed.), University of Chicago Press, Chicago, pp. 88-92, 1968.
14. A. R. Darbonne, Suicide and Age: A Suicide Note Analysis, *Journal of Consulting and Clinical Psychology, 33*, pp. 46-50, 1969.
15. N. J. Osgood, *Suicide in the Elderly: A Practitioner's Guide to Diagnosis and Mental Health Intervention*, Aspen, Rockville, Maryland, 1985.
16. N. J. Osgood, *Suicide in Later Life: Recognizing the Warning Signs*, Lexington Books, New York, 1992.
17. A. T. Beck, *Depression: Clinical, Experimental, and Theoretical Aspects*, Hoeber, New York, 1967.
18. A. T. Beck, A. Rush, B. Show, and G. Emergy, *Cognitive Therapy of Depression*, Guilford Press, New York, 1979.

19. A. T. Beck, R. A. Steer, M. Kovacs, and B. Garrison, Hopelessness and Eventual Suicide: A 10-Year Prospective Study of Patients Hospitalized with Suicidal Ideation, *American Journal of Psychiatry, 142*, pp. 559-563, 1985.
20. A. A. Leenaars, Suicide Notes of the Older Adult, *Suicide and Life-Threatening Behavior, 22*, pp. 62-79, 1992.
21. J. M. Stillion, Women and Widowhood: The Suffering Beyond Grief, in *Women: A Feminist Perspective*, J. Freeman (ed.), Mayfield, Palo Alto, California, pp. 282-296, 1984.
22. E. S. Shneidman, Suicide as Psychache, *Journal of Nervous and Mental Disease, 181*, pp. 147-149, 1993.
23. J. M. Stillion, H. White, P. J. Edwards, and E. E. McDowell, Ageism and Sexism in Suicide Attitudes, *Death Studies, 13*, pp. 247-262, 1989.

Contributors

PEGGY ANDERSON is a Bereavement Consultant in London, Ontario. She provides counseling in private practice to individuals and groups, and has been a consultant and speaker to Canadian Mental Health Association branches, Boards of Education, university conferences, churches, and palliative-care conferences. She is the author of the book *Wife After Death* (1991) and *Alone and Growing*—a manual on how to run a grief support program for widowed persons. She also authored *Bereavement in the Schools: A Guide for the Peel County Board of Education*.

BARBARA ANSCHUETZ received her doctorate in Counseling Psychology from the University of Toronto. She has worked with bereaved adolescents for over twenty years. She has provided training and education to mental health specialists and written response guidelines in the area of crisis intervention, grief counseling and therapy, and critical incident stress debriefing. She has a private psychotherapy practice in all areas of grief and trauma intervention for children, adolescents, and adults. She is the Advisor for Bereaved Families of Ontario, York Region Chapter and a member of three trauma intervention teams for emergency services personnel and their families.

RONALD BARRETT is Professor of Psychology at Loyola Marymount University specializing in cross-cultural funeral rites, urban homicidal violence, children and violence, and bereavement burnout. He serves as a consultant to groups locally and nationally as well as a number of school boards in addressing trauma, violence, grief, and loss in young children. He has authored several publications on children, trauma, and violence. In addition to research and public speaking, he is a social activist actively involved with primary prevention efforts via his anti-gang, drug, and crime program for at-risk inner-city youth in south central Los Angeles. He is also involved with research and remedial interventions via his involvements in conducting grief recovery support groups for young children experiencing trauma, violence, grief, and loss.

GILBERT BRODIE is Associate Professor of Religious Studies at King's College in London, Ontario. Dr. Brodie is trained both in theology and in law.

MICHAEL BULL teaches in the School of Social Administration and Social Work at Flinders University of South Australia, Adelaide, South Australia. His practice background covers several areas involving the impact of loss and grief on families, including child welfare, neonatal intensive care, paediatric oncology, geriatrics, childhood bereavement, and family therapy. A graduate of the social work program at the University of Windsor, he worked at Victoria Hospital in London, Canada, for several years before moving to Australia in 1990 where he has been actively involved with the National Association for Loss and Grief.

IRA BYOCK has been involved in hospice work since 1979. He is the Director of the Palliative Care Service and Hospice Medical Director of Partners Hospice, both in Missoula, Montana. He is President of the Academy of Hospice Physicians, and has served as Chair of the Ethics Committee of the Academy of Hospice Physicians and on the Ethics Committee of the National Hospice Association. He is the recipient of the National Hospice Association's prestigious "Person of the Year" award for 1995. In 1996, he was featured in Maysles film, *Letting Go: A Hospice Journey*, which was presented on HBO. His first book, *Dying Well: A Book about Living* will be published by Putnam in 1997.

BRUCE CONNELL is consulting psychologist with the London Ontario Board of Education. He holds a doctorate in Counseling Psychology from the University of Toronto and is an adjunct Assistant Professor with the Faculty of Education of the University of Western Ontario. He is a founding member and former chair of the London-Middlesex Suicide Prevention Council and Co-Chair of the Tragic Events Response Team of the London Board of Education.

ELLIE J. DEVEAU is co-ordinator of program evaluation in the Educational Centre for Aging and Health at McMaster University, Hamilton, Ontario. She is bereavement consultant to Friends In Grief, Inc., Hamilton, Ontario, and a founding member of their board of directors. Ellie is co-author of the book, *Coping with Childhood Cancer: Where Do We Go From Here?* which was the recipient of the Book of the Year award for "Best Books of 1989" from *The Nurse Practitioner: The American Journal of Primary Health Care,* and the recent *Beyond the Innocence of Childhood,* an exhaustive three-volume series on children and death.

KENNETH DOKA is a professor of gerontology at the Graduate School of the College of New Rochelle. In addition he is pastor of Atonement Lutheran Church. His books include *Disenfranchised Grief, Living with Life-Threatening Illness* and *Death and Spirituality* (with John Morgan). He has also published over forty articles and chapters.

ANDREW FERON is a social worker on the Palliative Care Unit at Parkwood Hospital, London, Ontario where he has been working with palliative care patients and their families since 1985. He is a member of the Ontario College of Certified Social Workers, the Canadian Palliative Care Association, and is a former Director of the Ontario Palliative Care Association. He is actively involved in palliative care education through his work as a Social Work Field Instructor for the School of Social Work/King's College, and as a Lecturer/Course Coordinator in the Certified Program in Palliative Care and Thanatology at King's College/University of Western Ontario.

LAWRENCE FRIC received his doctorate in Economics from the University of Toronto and has been a Associate Professor of Economics at King's College since 1971. Dr. Fric's particular research interests are in labor economics and in economic history, as well as his interest in the economic aspects of death-related decisions.

CONTRIBUTORS / 571

THOMAS GOLDEN has been working with men and women in crisis for over fifteen years. He has worked at hospitals and community mental health centers. He has published three booklets on gender and grief: *A Man's Grief, Different Paths Toward Healing*, and *Gender and Cultural Differences in Grief,* and maintains a web page [http://www.dgsys.com/~golden/]. He enjoys presenting workshops in the United States and Canada on the topic of grief and maintains a private practice in Kensington, Maryland.

JAROSLAV HAVELKA teaches Psychology at King's College in London, Ontario. He has published in Switzerland, Sweden, Canada, and Holland where he published his major work *The Nature of Creative Process in Art* (M. Nijhoff, The Hague, Holland, 1968). His scholarly interest is wide but he concentrates on psychology of personality, creative and cognitive functions, humanistic psychology, and the psychology of religion.

JOHN HINTON is Emeritus Professor of Psychiatry in the University of London, England, having been Professor and Head of the Department of Psychiatry at the Middlesex Hospital Medical School, London. His first assessment of Terminal Care was published in 1963 (*Quarterly Journal of Medicine*) with others since, and his book *Dying* (1967) continues re-printing. He has recently conducted an assessment of patients' and relatives' progress while in the Home Care Service of St. Christopher's Hospice, London, and anticipates publishing some papers in the near future from his retirement in the countryside.

ROSE MARIE JACO has taught for over twenty years in the School of Social Work, King's College, London, Ontario, and is now Professor Emerita of the College. Her courses have included social work practice, communication and interviewing skills, family therapy, and social work in health-care settings. She has been active in the London community as a volunteer in social planning, and was a long-term member of a committee working to establish a bereavement service. As well, Dr. Jaco has a practice in counseling and therapy where one of her special interests is helping clients and families with issues of grief and bereavement.

P. ALBERT KOOP received his doctorate in Economics from the University of Southern California. He has been an Associate Professor at King's College since 1970. He is particularly interested in social justice issues in Economics.

JAMES KOW is Assistant Professor of Philosophy at King's College. Born in South Africa, he was educated at the University of Toronto and the Catholic University of America. He has taught at the University of Toronto and King's College and has several publications dealing with ethics and contemporary Christianity.

PITTU LAUNGANI is Professor of Psychology at South Bank University in England. He is coeditor of a recent book dealing with multiculturalism as well as a playwright.

JOSEPH W. LELLA is currently Professor of Sociology at King's College, and Professor of History of Medicine, Faculty of Medicine, University of Western Ontario. He holds a degree in Philosophy and a Ph.D. in Sociology from the University of North Carolina at Chapel Hill. Dr. Lella has been a medical sociologist at

McGill University where he taught both in the Department of Sociology and in the Department of Humanities and Social Studies in Medicine. He served as chair of the later department where he taught behavioral science in medicine, social aspects of medicine, and medical ethics. He has published in all of these areas and has directed, authored, and performed live drama and produced a videotape on medical subjects including the life of Sir William Osler.

REENA McDERMOTT is a registered nurse and an educator. As founder and coordinator of the Palliative Care program at Parkwood Hospital in London, Ontario, she has worked with dying patients and their families for many years. She has also been involved with the palliative-care movement provincially, nationally, and internationally.

JAMES MILLER is faculty of Arts Professor at the University of Western Ontario. In 1988, he organized Canada's first interdisciplinary conference on AIDS and the Arts (*Representing AIDS: Crisis and Criticism*) and curated *Visual AIDS*, a traveling exhibition of AIDS posters from around the world. His anthology, *Fluid Exchanges: Artists and Critics in the AIDS Crisis,* was published by the University of Toronto Press in 1992. He currently teaches courses on medieval allegory, Renaissance aesthetics, and post-Stonewall gay history and culture.

JOHN D. MORGAN is Director of the Centre for Education about Death and Bereavement at King's College of the University of Western Ontario, London, Canada. He has been teaching courses about death and bereavement since 1968 and has coordinated the King's College International Conferences on Death and Bereavement since 1982. He is author of thirty articles or chapters dealing with death and bereavement and has edited or co-edited ten books. He is the Consulting Editor for the Death, Value and Meaning Series published through Baywood Publishing Company. His research interests focus on issues of cultural attitudes related to death and bereavement.

MIRIAM S. MOSS is Senior Research Sociologist at the Philadelphia Geriatric Center, where she has been involved in behavioral research since 1970. She is currently Co-Principal Investigator of a major study of the death of an elderly parent funded by the National Institute on Aging (1982-1992). She is a Fellow of the Gerontological Society of America (GSA), and a member of the Executive Board of its Behavioral and Social Science Section. She was a recipient, with Sidney Moss, of the Richard Kalish Award (1991) of the Behavioral and Social Science Section of GSA for the article "Death of the Very Old." She has published widely on death and aging.

SIDNEY Z. MOSS is a psychiatric social worker and family therapist with a long interest in separation and loss in the family. As a member of the Association of Death, Education and Counseling, he is a Certified Death Educator and Grief Counselor. He is currently involved in a major research study of the death of an elderly parent. He is on faculty of Hahnemann University, Master of Family Therapy Program. He was recipient, with Miriam Moss, of the Richard Kalish Award (1991) of the Behavioral and Social Science Section of the Gerontological Society of America for the article "Death of the Very Old." He has published widely on death and loss in the family.

JOHN ORANGE teaches courses in the novel, Canadian Literature, and film at King's College in the Modern Languages Department. He has published articles and books on Morley Callaghan, P. K. Page, Ernest Buckler, Alice Munro, and Hugh Hood, as well as reviews in most of the leading Canadian Literature journals. He has also lectured in interdisciplinary courses in Women's Studies and Thanatology at King's.

COLIN MURRAY PARKES is Senior Lecturer in Psychiatry at the London Hospital Medical College and Honorary Consultant Psychiatrist to St. Christopher's Hospice, Sydenham. Among his publications are: *Bereavement: Studies of Grief in Adult Life* (2nd Edition); *Recovery from Bereavement* (with R. Weiss); and *Psychological Problems in General Practice* (with A. Markus, P. Tomson, and M. Johnston).

GARY PATERSON is Professor of English at King's College in London, Ontario. He was educated at the University of Toronto and has taught at the University of Manitoba as well as King's College. He specializes in Victorian and children's literature.

RICHARD PAUL is the third generation owner and funeral director of Paul Funeral Home in Powassan, Ontario. In addition to funeral direction, he has taught school and is certified by the Association of Death Education and Counseling as a death educator. He has authored other chapters in this series of books and is often found giving presentations to lay and professional audiences about the roles of the funeral director.

RALPH L. V. RICKGARN has degrees in educational psychology and is currently the Coordinator, Student Behavior, Housing and Residential Life, and Lecturer in the Department of Educational Psychology at the University of Minnesota. He is certified by the Association for Death Education and Counseling as a Grief Counselor and Death Educator. He is chair of ADEC's Government and Professional Organization Liaison Committee and the Suicide Special Interest Group and a Board Member of the Minnesota Coalition for Death Education and Support. He has written a number of journal articles and book chapters on issues of suicide and college students' loss and grief, a booklet *The Issue is Suicide* and the book *Perspectives on College Suicide*. He is the founder of the Death Response Team and a member of the Suicide Prevention Task Force at the University of Minnesota.

JO ANN SILCOX is a psychiatrist in London, Ontario, where she also recently completed a Master's degree in Theology. She is presently in private practice but has also been affiliated with large provincial hospitals as well as a university health service.

ROBERT G. STEVENSON is a secondary school educator in River Dell Regional Schools, Oradell, New Jersey, and is co-chairperson of the University Seminar on Death at Columbia University, New York City. Among his publications are: *Getting to Know Me: A Suicide Prevention Program For Grades 4-5*; "Dealing With the Impact of Community Grief" in *Bereavement: Helping the Survivors*; and *Tips for Principals: Death in the Classroom, It Will Happen; What Will We Do?* His work has been honored by: Bergen County Professional Counselor's Association (Teacher of the Year, 1987); National Council for the Social Studies (Outstanding Dissertation

Recognition, 1985); New Jersey Governor's Award (Teacher of the Year Award, 1988); Bergen Catholic High School (Charter Member—Hall of Fame), and he has received numerous local and national awards for the extracurricular work he has done with high school and elementary school students. He has received Association of Death Education Counseling Certification as a Death Educator and Grief Counselor. His counseling is done at the Centre for Help in Time of Loss, of which he was a founding member.

JUDITH M. STILLION is Professor of Psychology and Associate Vice Chancellor for Academic Affairs and University Planner at Western Carolina University in Cullowhee, North Carolina. She does training of volunteers with Hospice of Jackson County and regularly teaches a course on death and dying at the University. She has served as Vice President, President, and Board Member of the Association for Death Education and Counseling and received their service award in 1992. Among her publications are *Death and the Sexes: An Examination of Differential Longevity, Attitudes, Behaviour and Coping Skills* (Hemisphere, 1985) and *Suicide Across the Life Span: Premature Exits* (Hemisphere, 1989).

RONALD TROJCAK, born in Taylorville, Illinois, began his university career at the University of Illinois as a music student. He was a professional musician until his seminary studies. He received his doctorate in Theology from St. Michael's College in Toronto and has been on the faculty at King's College since 1971. Besides being a practicing theologian and biblical scholar, he has maintained his interest in music and lectures in the relationship between religion and music.

Index

absolute value, 446, 449
acceptance of dying, 217, 229, 231
active euthanasia, 458, 467, 561, 562
Adams, 385-389, 394, 400, 401
adolescent, 279, 282, 339, 367, 368, 372, 380, 384-389, 391-401, 408, 409, 411, 412, 414, 417, 418, 514, 517, 522-524, 539, 540, 567
adult literature, 45
advocacy, 135, 204, 207, 432
Aeneid, 48
African American, 403, 404, 406-408, 411, 413, 414, 416-418
aftercare, 270, 547
age, 11, 14, 20, 23, 25, 26, 34, 35, 40, 47, 51, 52, 54, 65, 68, 69, 79, 80, 83, 94, 107, 108, 111, 112, 114, 120, 122, 139, 143, 145, 146, 150, 160, 170, 205, 232, 258, 264, 282, 294, 300, 302, 303, 317, 335, 340, 344, 347-350, 352, 353, 355, 361, 363-368, 370, 375, 378, 379, 381, 382, 389, 397, 401, 403, 406, 408, 413, 414, 416, 417, 444, 449, 451, 477, 481, 514, 516, 522-524, 533, 551, 553-559, 561, 565, 567
AIDS, 26, 31, 71, 85, 141-160, 197, 223, 263, 265, 276, 279, 280, 282, 302, 316, 369, 372, 378, 383, 387, 407-409, 416-418, 442, 483
alcohol, 246, 316, 324, 350, 367, 371, 375, 405, 410, 411, 413, 414, 523, 525, 530, 535, 559
allegory, 144, 146
Amha, 496

Amritatvam, 498
Ananda, 498
Anatta, 501
Anicca, 501, 506
anger, 36, 37, 51, 169, 173, 186, 192, 204, 242, 244, 260, 279, 303, 304, 311, 313, 319, 321, 328, 329, 332, 335, 366, 368, 372, 374-379, 381, 397, 398, 411, 412, 515, 516, 525, 536, 545, 546, 563
anticipatory, 30-32, 173, 180, 207, 241, 250, 268, 269, 290, 296, 377, 388, 437
anxiety, 12, 27, 31, 35, 37, 43, 76, 121, 141, 151, 159, 160, 170, 173, 186, 204, 210, 223, 224, 226, 227, 229, 231, 232, 243, 244, 245, 247, 248, 260, 263, 270, 290, 292, 300, 305, 350, 362, 365, 366, 368, 370-372, 377, 387, 391, 397, 398, 400, 415, 418, 495, 497, 499, 502, 525, 532, 541, 562
Aquinas, 14, 479, 480, 483
Ariès, 14-17, 19, 25, 30, 138, 437
Aristotle, 17, 477-479, 483
Arnold, 46, 59, 60, 202, 234
ars moriendi, 1, 17, 21, 149
assessment, 63, 184, 201, 204, 205, 207, 219, 226, 229, 232, 236, 248, 287, 310, 494, 523, 534, 536, 537
assisted suicide, 195, 427, 428, 431, 433, 438, 440, 441, 445, 451, 452, 465-467, 561, 562
Association for Death Education and Counseling, 5, 6

576 / INDEX

Atman, 497-499
attachment, 192, 241-243, 253, 281, 285, 289, 291, 292, 306, 309, 310, 314, 347, 348, 355, 383, 385, 500, 516, 524
  non-attachment, 192
attempted suicide, 400, 472, 523, 529, 537, 539-541, 546
attitudes, 1, 3, 4, 11-15, 19, 22, 23, 25, 27, 29, 31, 33, 36, 38, 41, 45, 51, 53, 57, 69, 195, 209, 214, 229, 232, 258, 273, 286, 289, 293, 297, 314, 368, 369, 373, 378-381, 385, 387, 388, 395, 408, 411, 413, 418, 424, 437, 491, 525, 544, 566, 568
  cultural attitudes, 373
  death attitudes, 3, 13, 14, 19, 22, 25, 27
atypical manifestations, 275
Auden, 59
Augustine, 18, 30, 446
authenticity, 192, 193, 424
autonomy, 126, 127, 203, 242, 340, 343, 352, 353, 393, 394, 410, 423-438, 481, 518
avoidance, 110, 168, 197, 233, 245, 247, 248, 263, 293, 322, 343, 393, 463, 525, 527, 530

Becker, 31, 234, 272, 306, 520, 524, 526, 537, 558, 567, 568
balance, 124, 133, 168, 173, 177, 178, 201, 267, 269, 370, 375, 481, 514, 515, 522, 527, 556, 564
Bardo Thodol, 503, 505
bargaining, 311, 328, 536
Beethoven, 62
behavior, 3, 12, 17, 35, 36, 57, 114, 121, 169, 205, 223, 228, 242, 243, 246, 261, 287-289, 291-295, 297-301, 303, 306, 310, 313, 322, 323, 331, 354, 368, 380, 392, 393, 398, 401, 411, 412, 418, 429, 452, 478, 488, 489, 513-517, 519-522, 525, 526, 528, 532, 533, 540, 543, 544, 547, 548, 553, 555, 560
Bellah, 69
bereavement, 1-6, 11-14, 19, 22, 28, 30, 31, 46, 57, 67, 69-71, 73, 123, 140, 179, 180, 183, 206, 207, 210, 223,

[bereavement]
241, 242, 244-253, 256, 258, 261, 262, 265, 271, 272, 275, 276, 279, 281-283, 285-288, 292-294, 305, 306, 309, 310, 312, 313, 315, 317-319, 320, 321, 322, 328, 337, 347-356, 359, 360, 363, 368, 369, 373-376, 379, 380, 382-389, 395-401, 403, 411, 412, 414, 417, 418, 542
  bereaved adults, 348, 360, 381, 383
  bereaved children, 350, 351, 355, 359-361, 364, 367, 369, 371, 373-376, 381-385, 389, 400, 401, 417, 418
  duration of bereavement, 360
Bhakti Yoga, 499
Bhaya, 496
Bible, 1, 16, 30, 273, 478, 485, 486, 489, 493
bioethics, 29, 30, 423-425, 435-438, 483
biological correlates, 521
biological equilibrium, 316
birth rate, 21
black plague, 16, 22
Black children, 403-410, 414-418
black power, 405
body, 4, 5, 12, 13, 18, 19, 22, 38, 43, 48, 50, 51, 56, 58, 65, 73, 80-88, 90-92, 94, 96, 98, 99, 123-125, 127, 131, 133-135, 137, 139, 150, 151, 155, 176, 185, 198, 199, 201, 210, 250, 256-264, 266-269, 272, 291-294, 298-300, 310, 328, 340, 366, 367, 377, 381, 410, 414, 424, 427, 442, 443, 451, 478-482, 490, 497, 499, 500, 502, 504, 507, 547, 558, 560
bonding, 57, 184, 392, 516
boundaries, 70, 74, 172, 177, 299, 333, 344, 371, 391, 431, 497, 517, 528, 530
Bowlby, 242, 281, 292, 306, 355, 385, 400, 524
Brahman, 496-500
British, 33, 69, 71, 73, 76, 79, 98, 104, 215, 253, 256, 305, 400, 439, 446, 471
Buddha, 501, 502, 504, 505, 508, 509
buffer, 351

bureau, 406, 417, 524
burial, 41, 42, 56, 82-85, 86, 87, 92-96,
  98, 100, 102, 257-259, 261, 267, 268,
  292, 302, 303, 304, 362, 365, 366
Bushido, 507

Camus, 70, 75, 475, 476, 483
care, 2-4, 12, 13, 16, 20-22, 25, 27, 28,
  30-32, 53, 68, 80, 84, 101, 103,
  109, 117-124, 126-128, 131,
  133-140, 167, 171-176, 177,
  178-189, 191-195, 197-236, 243,
  249, 250, 252, 253, 257-260
  269-273, 278-280, 282, 286,
  294, 297, 301, 304, 306, 322, 331,
  333, 334, 343, 354, 361, 372, 377,
  378, 387, 389, 392, 394, 396,
  400, 405-407, 410, 415, 416,
  418, 423, 427, 430, 432, 434-439,
  454, 459, 465, 466, 468, 525, 529,
  530, 534, 535, 540, 544, 545, 547,
  565
Carroll, 60
catharsis, 35, 36, 40-42, 72, 331, 542
casework, 180, 203, 206
casket, 90-94, 98, 99, 258, 263, 266, 267
causality, 72, 134, 364, 455, 456, 498,
  522
cemetery, 12, 55, 77, 83, 84, 87, 89-96,
  100-102, 258, 267, 268, 303
censorship, 35, 37, 141-144, 146, 149,
  151, 152, 155, 159, 160
Chikhai, 504
child, 2-4, 12-15, 17, 20, 21, 35, 40, 41,
  42, 50, 53-60, 65, 67-69, 73, 75, 81,
  82, 111, 112, 114, 119, 124, 136, 137,
  145, 154, 155, 167, 168, 170-176,
  180, 184-186, 188, 242-244, 245,
  248-250, 252, 269, 270, 273,
  275-279, 282, 297, 302, 303,
  305-307, 313, 332, 333, 335, 341,
  344, 347-356, 359-389, 391, 394,
  396, 399-401, 403-412, 414-418,
  455, 458, 462, 475, 481, 516, 517,
  523, 524, 545, 548, 551, 555, 557,
  560, 562, 564
Children's literature, 45, 54, 55, 57
Chit, 498
Chonyid, 504

Christian, 1, 16, 18, 46, 82, 154, 155, 257,
  258, 321, 476, 485, 489, 490-494, 497
closet, 145, 146, 147, 156, 256
coffin, 5, 42, 46, 50, 81, 83, 85, 94, 102,
  257, 258, 365
cognition, 135, 323, 362, 367, 502
cognitive ability, 361, 363-365, 368, 370,
  378, 381
cognitive distortions, 520
college students, 25, 31, 530
commemorate, 304, 373, 382, 383
communalism, 69
communication, 37, 120, 122, 130,
  138-140, 169-172, 177, 178, 180,
  188, 190, 195, 200, 204, 205, 207,
  215, 223, 225-227, 229, 232, 278,
  286-288, 297-301, 314, 320, 339,
  363, 369, 370, 372, 375, 376, 380,
  387, 452, 504, 519, 542, 546-548
closed communication, 369
communication pattern, 363, 369
competence, 5, 121, 123, 140, 178, 180,
  191, 192, 199, 229, 230, 232, 282,
  300, 322, 333, 395, 410, 415, 416,
  423, 425-430, 432, 434, 435, 439,
  455
completed suicide, 378, 514, 522,
  524-530, 541, 543, 547, 555
complicated grief, 281, 286, 312, 317,
  318, 372, 411, 541
conceptions of death, 363, 386
concreteness, 297, 299, 503, 505, 508
Confucianism, 505
confusion, 83, 110, 181, 225, 226, 231,
  290, 313, 371, 373-375, 381, 383,
  392, 397, 471, 486, 496, 520, 539,
  541, **557**
conscious dying, 16
consciousness, 12, 13, 15, 18, 21, 26, 29,
  73, 75, 160, 278, 340, 445, 449, 450,
  473, 481, 496-500, 502-504, 506,
  518
control over nature, 14, 25
coordination, 130, 204
coping, 1, 31, 56, 169, 173, 175, 177, 179,
  199, 205, 206, 210, 223, 288, 291,
  307, 314, 317, 331, 348, 360, 367,
  374, 385, 392, 401, 410, 414, 415,
  417, 516, 519, 526, 530, 542, 557,
  559

Corr, 6, 29, 212, 270, 386-389, 399-401, 483
costs, 76, 92-94, 96, 98, 99, 101, 109, 134, 175, 185, 225, 281, 447, 463, 464, 468, 469
counseling, 1, 5, 6, 29, 71, 134, 179, 185, 191, 203, 204, 206, 207, 212, 217, 222, 223, 249, 251, 252, 253, 271, 277, 281, 282, 285-302, 304, 305, 306, 318, 385, 396-401, 416, 418, 530, 535, 541, 544, 545, 547
Creation, 24, 56, 65, 71, 84, 88, 143, 152, 171, 183, 193, 302, 330, 333, 415, 435, 476, 486, 489, 491, 492, 494, 498, 500, 507, 508, 525
crisis, 39, 119, 141-143, 149, 154, 156, 175, 177-180, 203, 206, 207, 212, 223, 226, 261, 270, 272, 280, 290, 295, 306, 329, 331, 370, 389, 399, 416, 481, 521-523, 530, 531, 536, 541, 548, 549, 564
crisis intervention, 203, 206, 207, 522
cultural, 11, 13, 31, 36, 64, 65, 68, 69, 71, 75, 138, 140-144, 153, 155, 156, 169, 176, 183, 185, 191, 197, 205, 210, 241, 242, 256, 292, 294, 300, 306, 317, 318, 320, 321, 343, 349, 353, 363, 372, 373, 379-381, 386, 405, 406, 411, 413-417, 490, 505, 515
cultures, 1, 4, 11, 13, 14, 19, 23-28, 36, 64, 67, 74, 75, 137, 144, 146, 156, 158, 185, 205, 253, 256, 260, 262, 299, 304, 310, 317, 318, 339, 348, 373, 374, 388, 405, 406, 411, 415, 418, 433, 444, 483, 485, 487, 505, 506, 509, 558, 561
culture of poverty, 406

Daishi, 506
Davies, 171, 173, 176, 180, 359, 375, 385, 388, 394, 395, 400
day hospice, 217
death, 1-6, 11-34, 37-43, 45-48, 50-68, 73, 75, 77-87, 89, 91, 94, 96, 104, 106-111, 112, 115, 117-121, 123, 124, 126, 127, 134-137, 140-148, 149, 151, 152, 156, 158-160, 167, 169-173, 175-180, 186, 188, 189, 191, 194, 197, 199, 201-203, 207,

[death] 214-218, 222, 224, 225, 229-236, 241, 247-251, 253, 256-273, 276-283, 285, 287-293, 295-297, 302-307, 309-312, 315, 316, 318-320, 319, 322, 323, 327-332, 334-337, 343, 344, 347-356, 359-389, 391-401, 403, 407-410, 412, 414, 418, 423, 424, 427, 430-438, 442, 445, 446, 452-460, 462-469, 472, 473, 475, 476, 478, 480-484, 488-491, 493, 495-508, 514-517, 522, 527, 533, 537, 539-546, 558, 559, 562-564, 566, 568
death denied, 15, 19, 25
death education, 1-6, 123, 140, 282, 379, 387, 396, 398, 401
death of a friend, 395, 398
death of a parent, 65, 170, 280, 347, 349-351, 356, 361, 367, 368, 371, 375, 376, 378, 384, 385, 393, 394, 403, 418
death of a pet, 55, 287, 378, 403
death of a sibling, 2, 55, 367, 374, 394
death of the other, 15, 18, 19
death of the self, 15, 17, 18
death rate, 78-80
death system, 4, 11-13, 19, 26, 27, 29
death wish, 34, 38, 39, 515
decay, 51, 53, 81, 85, 86, 88, 148
delayed grief, 247, 281, 287
depression, 27, 31, 36, 55, 73, 125, 181, 204, 231, 232, 243, 247, 251, 279, 281, 287, 292, 303, 305, 306, 311-313, 318, 319, 322-324, 328, 335, 350, 385, 393, 397, 400, 401, 405, 410, 411, 426, 471, 472, 520-524, 526, 530-533, 537, 551, 557-559, 562, 564, 565, 567
determinism, 59, 69, 72, 73, 295
Deveau, 359, 385-389, 394, 400, 401
dirge, 48
Dharma-Kaya, 504
distribution of income, 110, 113
direct killing, 452-458
disclosure, 65, 300, 425-427
disenfranchised, 176, 180, 275, 276, 278-281, 282, 317, 349, 355, 385, 415
disorganization, 313, 393, 394, 558
disposal, 19, 81, 85, 90, 96, 98

distribution of income, 406
Doka, 176, 180, 275, 276, 278, 282, 355, 385, 418
domestic violence, 169, 372, 375, 383, 387, 406, 409-411
donation, 87
Donne, 30, 60
drawings, 361, 384
drugs, 22, 131, 149, 222, 247, 279, 280, 316, 324, 367, 371, 375, 405, 411, 413, 414, 418, 442, 458, 460, 463-465, 516, 523, 556, 559,
Dukkha, 501
Durkheim, 513, 515, 523
dying, 1-6, 11-13, 16-18, 21, 22, 24, 26-32, 34, 38, 41, 43, 45, 47, 48, 50-56, 58, 60, 80, 82, 104, 109, 110, 117-120, 123, 126, 130, 134-138, 140, 150, 157, 167-171, 173-195, 197-203, 206, 207, 209-214, 216-218, 220-222, 224-226, 228, 229, 231-236, 249, 250, 253, 259, 264, 268, 273, 280-282, 285, 286, 288, 290, 291, 293, 295-297, 302, 305-307, 311, 312, 316, 319, 336, 337, 348, 349, 355, 366, 377, 378, 385-389, 394, 399-401, 410, 414, 416, 418, 423, 428, 430-439, 443, 446, 475, 481-484, 492, 495, 498, 500, 501, 503-506, 527, 549, 566
Dylan Thomas, 52

East, 81, 95, 485
economic, 1, 34, 68, 77, 78, 80, 98-100, 103, 109, 111, 112, 119, 175, 205, 218, 281, 294, 317, 328, 330, 353, 404, 406, 409, 414, 444, 490, 491, 530, 553, 560
education, 1-6, 15, 20, 22, 25, 36, 59, 80, 114, 123, 124, 126-128, 131, 134-136, 138-140, 156, 159, 183, 192-195, 201, 204, 207-210, 212, 223, 256, 266, 270, 281, 282, 285, 286, 330, 347, 353, 379, 380, 386, 387, 396, 398, 401, 406, 416, 540, 543, 553, 564, 565
Egyptian Book of the Dead, 21, 505
elderly, 20, 21, 30, 119, 122, 134, 138, 212, 214, 244, 247, 283, 347-349,

[elderly]
353-356, 437, 438, 523, 551, 553, 554, 556-567
elderly parent, 30, 347-349, 355
embalming, 5, 15, 21, 26-29, 41, 46, 51, 52, 54-57, 59, 67, 71-73, 84, 91, 94, 95, 259, 273
emotional, 121, 130, 136, 167, 170, 173, 175, 177-179, 185, 190, 192, 193, 203-206, 208-211, 218, 221-223, 227, 229, 230, 233, 241, 242, 250, 256, 263, 264, 267, 268, 270, 272, 279, 282, 287-290, 295-298, 303, 304, 310-312, 320, 328, 333, 339, 343, 348, 350, 353, 359, 360, 362-364, 367-373, 376, 377, 382, 384, 391-393, 397, 398, 410, 412, 471, 516, 518, 520, 522, 524, 525, 527, 531-534, 544, 563
emotional response, 288, 320, 348, 350, 533
empathy, 136, 193, 206, 223, 434
empathetic, 286, 293, 297, 298, 300, 351, 531
Erickson, 363
ethics, 2, 4-6, 120-123, 132, 133, 135, 140, 192, 222, 235, 272, 296, 436-438, 440, 441, 468, 562
ethnic, 99, 148, 205, 292, 355, 374, 405-407, 412, 413, 416-418
euthanasia, 5, 27, 33, 195, 201, 367, 427, 428, 431, 433, 437, 438, 449, 452, 458, 466-468, 473, 561, 562
evaluation, 5, 133, 181, 182, 184, 187, 195, 210, 227, 235, 236, 252
exaggerated grief, 287
existential, 64, 65, 70, 72, 73, 189, 190, 291, 293, 294, 306, 316, 317, 331, 367, 499, 503
exposure, 3, 11, 13, 19, 22, 146, 173, 258, 260, 263, 281, 295, 368, 379, 409-412
extrinsic, 447, 449, 489, 305

faith, 18, 46, 75, 241, 242, 266, 329, 446, 480, 487, 488, 491-494, 499, 508, 564
family, 2, 5, 12, 16-19, 21, 26, 27, 31, 57, 59, 60, 68-71, 73, 75, 76, 81, 88, 91, 97, 101, 110, 112, 114, 119-122, 128, 130, 135-137, 139, 140, 167-194,

[family]
197, 199-201, 203-205, 207, 208, 210, 212-216, 218-220, 223, 225, 229, 233, 235, 236, 245, 248, 249, 250-252, 257, 259, 261, 264, 265, 268-271, 277, 278, 281-283, 286, 289, 290, 292, 298, 301-307, 311, 317, 318, 320, 324, 330, 331, 335, 343, 344, 347, 348, 350, 351, 353, 355, 356, 359-363, 369-373, 375-380, 385, 388, 391, 394, 396, 398-400, 404, 405, 408, 410-413, 416-418, 433, 447, 481, 514, 516, 517, 524, 525, 530, 532, 535, 543, 546-548, 557, 560, 562

family doctor, 214, 219, 220
family problems, 201, 516
family system, 68, 168-172, 174, 175, 177, 178, 205, 289, 375, 516, 517
fantasy, 12, 28, 142, 149, 151, 152, 160, 247, 277, 365, 379, 380, 391, 394
Farberow, 418, 522, 524, 526
fear, 16, 18, 23, 26, 30, 31, 48, 51, 52, 56, 65, 70, 85, 118, 120, 156-160, 173, 183, 204, 208, 244, 248, 249, 269, 270, 290, 291, 320-322, 327-330, 350, 365-367, 372, 376, 377, 379, 392, 397, 398, 410, 423, 430, 461, 465, 482, 492, 494-500, 502, 504, 507, 508, 516, 517, 525, 531, 541
fear of separation, 365, 366
feeling, 12, 19, 29, 45, 56, 59, 61, 67, 70, 71, 118, 121, 124, 126, 133, 135, 136, 151, 167-169, 171, 173, 175-179, 186, 188, 193, 200, 204, 206-210, 214, 220, 231, 233, 241-244, 248, 249, 265, 267-270, 276, 279, 287, 288, 290, 292-295, 298, 302, 300, 303, 304, 311, 313, 320, 322, 323, 329, 332-336, 339-344, 352, 354, 359-364, 366, 368-372, 374-376, 378, 379, 381, 382, 384, 392, 394, 395, 396-399, 409, 411, 415, 416, 467, 480, 500, 504, 506, 508, 514, 515, 518, 519, 521, 526, 528, 531, 532, 533, 534, 535, 542, 543, 544, 546, 547, 559-561, 562, 563

feeling responsible, 362
Feifel, 6, 23, 26, 29, 30, 123
film, 33-41, 43, 62, 142
finitude, 351, 354, 355, 491
Flaubert, 59
Flexner, 124, 125, 138
Foss, 56
fragmentation, 26, 174, 430
free will, 69, 72
freedom, 29, 37, 154, 155, 228, 261, 305, 316, 376, 439, 440, 444-446, 449, 459, 469-473, 481, 489, 493, 495, 496, 499-501, 503, 506, 507, 516, 556
Freud, 322, 389, 513-515, 523, 556, 558
friendship, 57, 193, 222, 277, 334
Fulton, 21, 22, 30-32, 123, 139, 273
funeral, 1, 2, 5, 12, 13, 16, 17, 19, 40, 55, 56, 58, 63, 64, 68, 77, 80-82, 84-87, 89-99, 101-104, 109, 142, 169, 175, 209, 213, 245, 251, 255-273, 278, 280, 282, 290, 302, 330, 334, 349, 362, 372, 373, 379, 382, 395, 397, 398, 412, 416, 532
funeral director, 12, 13, 17, 84-87, 89, 90, 92-99, 104, 213, 255, 256, 258-263, 265, 267-273, 412, 416
funeral rites, 1, 68, 272, 290

gender differences, 339, 341, 353, 363, 368, 387
general practitioner, 216, 220, 223, 226, 236, 251
generation, 113, 412, 530, 553, 561, 562
genocide, 26, 33, 158
genuineness, 297
God, 12, 15-18, 24, 47, 65, 73, 117, 143, 158, 159, 191, 242, 266, 309, 311, 329, 374, 447, 450, 476, 479-481, 486-494, 496, 498-500, 506, 531, 564
Goldscheider, 17, 30
grief, 3-5, 18, 19, 21, 22, 26, 29-33, 45, 48, 56, 61, 67, 70, 75, 167, 169, 171, 173, 176, 179, 180, 191, 203, 206, 207, 210, 241-244, 246-248, 250, 251, 253, 255, 256, 259, 260, 262-273, 275-281, 282, 285-290, 296, 302-307, 309-318, 322, 324, 327-337, 339, 340, 343-345,

[grief]
  348-350, 352-356, 359-363, 366, 367, 369-372, 374-377, 380-386, 388, 389, 391, 392, 394, 396-399, 401, 403, 411, 412, 414, 415, 418, 498, 507, 528, 536, 541, 542, 544, 546, 568
grief responses of children, 361
grief management, 255, 256, 264, 266, 271
grief therapy, 33, 179, 253, 281, 286, 306, 385, 398, 401
grief work, 268, 288, 327, 331-337
grieving, 11, 21, 31, 53, 110, 173, 188, 191, 207, 245, 248, 252, 256, 258, 267-269, 271, 276, 279, 282, 286-289, 292, 296, 315, 316, 327-331, 334, 335, 339, 343-345, 363, 370, 371, 373, 374, 376, 381, 382, 384, 396-399, 414, 418, 564
Grollman, 60, 270, 273, 370, 386, 387, 417
group format, 332
group process, 331, 333, 418
groups, 15, 23, 26, 31, 69, 79, 80, 88, 109, 119, 130, 131, 135, 137, 169, 186, 205, 207, 209, 225, 227, 228, 251, 252, 257, 271, 288, 301, 319, 327, 331-337, 341, 343, 348, 354, 355, 374, 382, 389, 396-398, 401, 406, 408, 414, 417, 466, 485, 530, 539, 544, 545, 547, 551, 553
growing up, 188, 381, 410
growth and development, 65, 131, 132, 189, 194, 395, 515
guilt, 5, 19, 27, 56, 121, 169, 173, 186, 244, 279, 303, 310, 311, 313-316, 318, 320, 322-324, 328, 330, 332, 363, 372, 374-377, 379, 394, 395, 397, 398, 411, 453, 456, 528, 531, 533, 536, 542, 563

habit, 216, 251
Haiku, 508
Harakiri, 507
healing, 158, 188, 191, 198, 259, 263, 265, 286, 307, 316, 318, 327, 330-332, 336, 337, 343-345, 399, 434, 546
health, 2, 5, 13, 19, 25, 27, 28, 31, 75, 78-82, 85, 86, 88, 95, 101, 102, 104,

[health]
  109, 114, 117, 122-124, 126, 127, 131, 133-139, 141-143, 152, 154, 160, 167, 171, 172, 175, 176, 178, 184, 185, 191, 192, 197, 199, 203-205, 209, 211, 212, 214, 215, 217-221, 224, 235, 236, 247, 249, 255, 267, 286, 306, 310, 350, 354, 385, 394, 400, 401, 405-410, 413-418, 455, 468, 469, 472, 482, 523, 530, 536, 540, 545, 548, 549, 553, 557, 559, 561, 562, 565, 567
health care, 27, 80, 109, 117, 123, 124, 126, 131, 134-139, 167, 171, 172, 175, 176, 178, 184, 185, 192, 199, 209, 211, 212, 236, 394, 405-407, 416, 468, 540
heaven, 17, 18, 46, 75, 187, 312, 314, 366, 494
helplessness, 173, 209, 220, 243, 363, 377, 379, 398, 518, 524, 527, 530, 534, 537, 542, 546, 560, 563
Heraclitus, 477, 478
heterosexism, 156
hierarchy, 246, 340-343, 490
high school, 2, 3, 43, 344, 393, 394, 398, 514, 520, 530, 531, 540, 545
Hindu, 68, 75, 496, 497, 499, 502, 503, 505, 506, 508
HIV, 31, 141, 145, 149, 150, 185, 195, 279, 407-409, 416-418
home care, 134
homicide, 33, 279, 316, 319, 369, 376, 377, 407, 409, 411, 418
homophobia, 146, 156-158, 160
homosexual, 159, 275-277, 280, 281
honesty, 192, 270, 335, 369, 370
hopelessness, 186, 279, 323, 332, 410, 515, 518-521, 526, 527, 531, 533, 534, 537, 542, 558, 560, 563, 566, 568
Hopkins, 53, 60, 437, 438, 523
hospice, 3, 13, 27, 31, 167, 181-186, 188, 189, 191-195, 202, 211, 212, 216-219, 224, 227-230, 232, 234-236, 252, 270, 287, 396
hospital, 12, 13, 25, 28, 58, 87, 91, 117-122, 124, 126-128, 130, 131, 133, 134, 139, 148, 157, 171, 174, 192, 212-218, 220, 221, 223-225,

[hospital]
  227-229, 232, 234, 236, 264, 287, 303, 386, 388, 456, 547, 548
human dignity, 432, 438, 443, 444, 445, 473

ideology, 22, 30, 117, 119, 124, 126, 127, 130, 139
Iliad, 48
Ilych, 50, 52, 59, 475, 476, 482
imagination, 41, 160, 269, 304, 369
immortality, 1, 18, 46-48, 52, 54, 193, 194, 217, 374, 386, 388, 395, 400, 475, 476, 480, 482, 495, 498, 499
impact on the self, 350, 375
in-patient, 123, 216-219, 221, 224, 225, 227, 229-233
incompetent, 322, 423, 425, 427-430, 436, 437, 559
India, 20, 67-69, 71, 75, 508, 509
individualism, 36, 37, 69, 70, 75, 76, 258, 267
inheritance, 71, 88, 109, 111-115, 131, 280, 556
inhibition, 245, 247
institutions, 36, 88, 111, 117, 119, 123, 126, 136, 141, 209, 213-215, 224, 256, 278, 301, 405, 415, 424, 451
intensive care, 12, 121, 127, 184, 437, 438
inter-generational claims, 110
interactional approach, 203
interdisciplinary, 181, 182, 184, 197, 201, 202, 208
International Work Group on Death, Dying and Bereavement, 4
interpersonal Theories, 515
intervention, 178, 184, 187, 203, 205-207, 223, 256, 259, 288, 301, 303, 304, 318, 392, 396, 399-401, 418, 426, 427, 489, 522, 523, 525, 527-529, 531, 534-537, 540, 541, 548, 567
intrapsychic theories, 514
intrinsic value, 439, 442, 443, 445-452, 469, 473
invincibility, 353, 395
irreversible, 40, 366, 367

Jackson, 75, 144, 392, 399, 417
Jesus, 142, 486-490, 492-494
Jiva, 497
Jnana Yoga, 499
Joyce, 60
judgement, 244, 288, 429, 432, 493

kala, 499
karma, 72, 73, 499, 500, 502, 504, 505
karma Yoga, 500
Keats, 46
key factors, 13
killings, 39-41, 365, 366, 427, 457
Kübler-Ross, 123, 137, 217, 234, 311, 312, 328, 388, 438

Laurence, 43, 52, 60
law, 1, 4, 35, 36, 38, 59, 72, 73, 82-85, 112, 119, 132, 133, 135, 159, 268, 351, 427, 436, 437, 439-441, 442, 452-454, 458, 459, 461, 464-467, 470, 471, 499, 554
Lee, 56, 59, 60, 139, 417, 475, 476
Leenaars, 6, 514, 522-524, 568
legal precedent, 441
liberal arts, 2, 140, 495
liberty, 314, 424-427, 441, 444, 446, 449, 459
life expectancy, 11, 13, 14, 19, 20, 118, 406-409, 417
life insurance, 88, 110, 111, 112, 269, 330
life span, 13, 16, 21, 22, 180, 514, 521, 523, 524, 556, 561, 564, 567
life span development, 521
Lifton, 123, 476
Lila, 500
Lindemann, 30, 281, 310, 313
linking objects, 396, 398
literature, 1, 3-5, 19, 21, 45, 48, 50, 51, 54-57, 59-61, 64, 85, 87, 123, 136, 141, 167, 169, 170, 179, 187, 235, 275, 276, 279, 280, 288, 292, 302, 315, 317, 347, 348, 361, 370, 371, 376, 383, 393, 404, 432, 440, 496, 497, 499, 506, 508, 540, 555
Little's, 56, 58
loneliness, 46, 56, 70, 208, 224, 279, 290, 367, 375, 395, 397, 480, 500, 518, 519, 523, 542, 558, 564-566
Lonetto, 364, 386

loss of control, 291, 372, 526
love, 33, 37, 48, 65, 68, 81, 85, 144, 146, 152, 188, 190-192, 202, 211, 244, 266, 269, 270, 272, 275, 304, 315, 327, 329, 375, 378, 384, 385, 391, 393, 394, 435, 445, 452, 481, 482, 488, 489, 492, 494, 499, 507, 515, 541, 563, 565

macabre, 144, 145, 147-149, 151, 152, 160
magic, 37, 56-60, 148, 151, 158, 365, 486, 487, 520
Mahler, 64
maintenance of the tie, 352
man, 4, 15, 17, 38, 39, 42, 43, 47, 48, 50-54, 60, 267, 282, 302, 305, 340-345, 379, 435-437, 468, 476, 481-483, 492, 497, 500, 503, 508, 514, 515, 523, 533, 539, 557, 564
Mandala, 75
Mantras, 503
marital relationships, 351
Martin and Elder, 289
masked grief, 287
materialism, 69, 73
Maya, 74, 497, 498
McGoldrick, 289
medical, 1, 2, 20-23, 28, 29, 73, 79, 86, 94, 101, 117, 119, 121, 123-128, 130-136, 138-140, 141-144, 156, 173, 174, 179, 181-187, 192-195, 199, 202, 214, 215, 217-219, 221, 222, 224, 225, 227, 229, 234, 236, 247, 251, 253, 257, 259, 268, 282, 291, 305, 315, 317, 335, 352, 366, 367, 377, 389, 396, 401, 406-409, 427, 430, 432, 436-438, 457, 464-469, 480, 529, 560-562, 567
medical education, 1, 124, 126, 128, 131, 134-136, 138-140, 194, 195
medical technology, 21, 22, 259, 366, 367, 430, 467
medicine, 1, 3, 21, 22, 28, 29, 31, 72, 75, 78, 79, 124-128, 131-133, 135-141, 142, 184, 187, 189, 193-195, 211-213, 224, 235, 282, 310, 360, 388, 417, 423-425, 428, 431, 436, 437, 469, 547

memento mori, 160, 501
memory, 35, 46, 48, 58, 59, 145, 189, 244, 248, 264-267, 289, 302, 304, 312, 313, 352, 382, 396, 398, 435, 479, 502, 559
Menninger, 513, 515, 523
mental, 75, 134, 176, 205, 220, 231, 232, 234, 244, 245, 247, 255, 278, 282, 286, 300, 302, 306, 310, 313, 316, 328, 354, 385, 401, 405, 410, 413, 415, 416, 418, 464, 496, 497, 499, 500, 504, 525, 530, 536, 537, 540, 548, 565, 567, 568
Messiah, 63, 487
Milton, 59
mimetic, 35, 40
modules, 3
Moksa, 497, 498, 500, 506
moral, 1, 22, 39, 73, 75, 87, 110, 142, 143, 145, 146, 148, 149, 154, 155, 159, 160, 222, 228, 423-425, 427-430, 432-434, 437-440, 442, 446, 452, 453, 455, 457, 459, 462, 463, 470, 473, 491, 499, 528, 536
Morgan, 1, 6, 11, 123, 140, 273, 306, 385-389, 400, 401, 475, 479, 495, 549
Mount, 14, 25, 93, 100, 123, 138, 152, 437
mourning, 26, 31, 45, 46, 67, 68, 73, 241, 246, 251, 258, 264, 265, 269, 270, 272, 275, 277, 280, 282, 285, 287-291, 302, 303, 305, 307, 311, 312, 315, 316, 319, 322, 370, 373, 381, 386, 388, 389, 392, 393, 398-400, 403, 411, 412, 416, 418, 514, 523
movies, 35, 36, 41, 43, 117, 404
Mujo, 506
multidimensional, 140, 181, 185, 306, 350, 353, 519, 523, 525
Mushin, 507
music, 15, 24, 34, 37, 61-64, 65, 136, 188, 221, 302, 379, 398, 477, 565
mutilation, 366
mythology of suicide, 527, 528
myths, 528, 529

natural, 1, 22, 33, 40, 47, 55, 68, 73, 75, 77, 86, 88, 123, 134, 158, 191, 197, 256, 263, 264, 289, 295, 299, 300,

[natural]
  302, 343, 361, 367, 379, 391, 408, 415, 431, 450, 451, 467, 469, 470, 476, 487, 503, 565
negative press, 519
neurotransmitters, 521, 556
Nietzsche, 490
Nirguna Brahman, 498
Nirvana, 500-504, 506, 508, 509
non-White, 411, 417
nonfunctionality, 364, 366, 367
normative, 347, 559
North American, 2, 3, 13, 19, 24, 26, 31, 35, 36, 256-261, 265, 267, 269, 271, 310, 516, 522
numbness, 245, 279, 328, 330, 397, 541
nurse, 12, 98, 118, 130, 138, 182, 198-202, 216-219, 221, 223, 235, 264, 544, 547
nursing care, 188, 197-199, 201, 208, 217, 219, 221, 225

old age, 25, 51, 52, 112, 139, 348, 365, 366, 444, 481, 551, 553, 556, 558, 559, 565, 567
Ortega y Gasset, 11, 29, 480, 483
outcome, 126, 193, 214, 231-233, 235, 294, 298, 306, 315, 320, 343, 388, 525, 536

pain, 12, 24, 29, 43, 46, 51, 67, 120-122, 126, 134, 143, 179, 181, 183-186, 188, 190, 194, 195, 199, 207, 210, 214, 216, 220, 222, 223, 225-228, 230-232, 235, 236, 244, 263, 264, 272, 285, 289, 290, 294, 304, 305, 312, 316, 328, 329, 332, 334, 342, 349, 366, 367, 369-371, 381-384, 394, 397, 399, 415, 428-431, 435, 442, 458, 460, 462-466, 468, 497, 498, 501, 507, 516-519, 522, 527-529, 531, 533, 539, 541, 542, 556, 563, 565, 566
palliative care, 4, 123, 127, 134, 136, 167, 171-173, 175, 179, 181-187, 189, 191, 192, 194, 195, 197-199, 201-212, 214, 215, 217-225,

[palliative care]
  227-229, 234-236, 269, 294, 387, 434, 439, 459, 465, 466
pangs of grief, 244
paramedical, 127, 218
parent, 2, 3, 30, 39, 55, 60, 61, 65, 69, 96, 111, 170, 174, 186, 188, 242, 243, 264, 273, 275, 276, 279, 280, 332, 347-356, 359-361, 365, 367, 368, 370-373, 375-378, 380, 381, 383-387, 393-396, 400, 401, 403, 408, 417, 418, 516, 534, 539, 543, 545
  death of a parent, 348, 359, 376, 393
Parkes, 123, 235, 236, 241, 253, 281, 283, 286, 305, 385, 388, 400
Parmenides, 478, 483
passive euthanasia, 458, 467
patient, 12, 21, 23, 27-29, 31, 120-123, 127, 128, 130, 131, 133-135, 138, 141, 167, 168, 174-176, 178, 180-185, 191-194, 197-208, 210, 212, 216-219, 221, 224, 225, 227-236, 250, 306, 311, 312, 423-437, 446, 460, 463, 464, 466, 467, 469, 537, 546
peace, 55, 110, 186, 228, 233, 250, 315, 399, 480, 493, 501, 506, 507, 515, 517, 563, 564, 566
peer, 155, 211, 391-396, 399, 522
person, 1, 4, 11-16, 18, 19, 21, 23-25, 27, 31, 36, 39, 45, 48, 50, 55, 72, 73, 82-84, 88, 93, 110, 111, 114, 118-120, 137, 141, 145, 167-170, 173, 174, 176-179, 181-187, 189, 191-194, 198-204, 218, 220, 222, 226, 241-252, 261-263, 265-270, 275, 277, 278, 280, 285, 286, 288-299, 301, 302, 304-306, 310-314, 316, 319-321, 331, 335, 336, 344, 348-351, 360, 362, 363, 365, 369, 374, 377, 381-384, 389, 391-393, 396, 398, 399, 410, 413, 423, 425, 426, 428-435, 439, 441-447, 449-455, 457-466, 469, 470, 472, 473, 476-482, 485, 488, 489, 496, 497, 499, 500, 503-505, 515, 516, 521, 527-532, 534-536, 540, 544-546, 559, 561, 564, 565, 567

personality, 286, 287, 294, 297, 306, 336, 363, 367, 368, 416, 434, 497, 518, 521, 524
personhood, 185, 186, 190, 191, 414, 429, 430, 434
perturbation, 519, 527
pet, 55, 276, 278, 282, 287, 378, 403
philosophical, 4, 16, 27, 30, 59, 71, 72, 135, 182, 185, 352, 440, 441, 476, 477, 483, 501, 505, 528, 536
philosophy, 3, 14, 16, 30, 46, 50, 72, 73, 75, 135, 139, 182, 197, 263, 265, 272, 291, 436-438, 448, 449, 473, 476-478, 483, 496, 505, 508
philosophy of care, 197
physical, 14, 16, 18, 26, 27, 51, 54, 70, 73, 75, 81, 85-87, 114, 121, 124, 126, 128, 131, 133, 139, 155, 167, 174, 178, 181-185, 187, 194, 197, 198, 203-205, 215, 216, 218, 220-223, 226-228, 230, 232-234, 244, 247, 264-268, 287, 294, 310, 313, 316, 317, 320, 324, 328, 329, 339, 342, 344, 350, 352, 362, 365, 368, 377, 378, 392, 393, 397, 400, 409, 411, 413, 415, 417, 444, 448, 450, 451, 456-458, 460, 470, 476, 477, 479, 487, 490, 491, 493, 495, 497, 499, 504, 522, 523, 525, 527, 556-559, 565, 566
physical differences, 339
physiological theories, 521
physical problems, 362
physician, 12, 13, 22, 28, 121, 123, 124, 135, 139, 182, 186, 193, 195, 219, 234, 328, 424-427, 438, 451, 459, 465, 467, 561
Piaget, 363, 386
Pine, 2, 6, 30, 93, 273, 282
place of death, 84, 86, 224, 225, 230, 232, 233, 235, 259
Plato, 14, 17, 477-479, 483
play, 13, 41, 48, 52, 62, 70, 81, 144, 151, 170, 184, 205, 246, 251, 270, 287, 342, 361, 362, 366, 397, 399, 408, 413, 415, 418, 500, 556, 557
poetry, 41, 45, 47, 59, 136, 251, 508
policy, 80, 111-114, 139, 204, 210, 223, 224, 235, 270, 418, 466, 540, 548
positive regard, 297-299

postvention, 539-541, 543, 548
poverty, 20, 27, 68, 406, 407, 409, 413, 414, 416, 417, 559, 560
Prakriti, 498
Prana, 497
premature death, 409, 414
prevention, 3, 6, 124, 126, 133, 135, 139, 154, 210, 283, 389, 418, 471, 472, 517, 524, 528, 530, 537, 540, 548, 549
private good, 109, 110
profession, 23, 73, 126, 145, 183, 208-210, 259-261, 265, 296, 335, 342, 360
professionalism, 118, 120, 133, 198
protest, 142, 143, 289, 312, 313, 368, 393
psychache, 519, 527, 529, 537, 568
psychodynamics, 514, 515
psychological differences, 340
psychological equilibrium, 316
psychological space, 70
psychological theories, 514, 517
psychosocial, 3, 30, 182, 185, 187, 197, 203-205, 208-210, 235, 236, 278, 280, 282, 306, 363, 377, 387, 400, 516, 567
Puccini, 30, 62
Purdy, 47, 59

quality of death, 236
quality of life, 23, 31, 181, 183, 184, 186, 197, 200, 201, 204, 225, 228, 229, 232, 235, 266, 305, 354, 406, 430, 443

Raja Yoga, 500
Raphael, 170, 179, 249, 253, 275, 281, 282, 388, 392, 394, 395, 400
relationship, 15, 18, 19, 25, 28, 35, 62, 63, 65, 71, 77, 111, 112, 169, 176, 188, 193, 198-201, 205, 210, 232, 236, 242-244, 250, 256, 264-269, 271, 275-277, 280, 282, 286, 289, 295-297, 299, 303, 312, 314, 317, 322, 329, 335, 348, 351-354, 356, 359, 363, 374, 376, 378, 383, 384, 389, 391, 392, 395, 397, 400, 403, 412, 431, 432, 447, 461, 481, 487,

[relationship]
488, 502, 503, 516, 517, 525, 558, 560
reliability, 192, 316, 317
religion, 1, 3, 24, 27-29, 76, 83, 156, 215, 242, 257, 266, 280, 294, 373, 374, 385, 388, 399, 401, 405, 481, 483, 486, 501, 503, 508, 562, 566
religious faith, 242
reorganization, 170, 174, 314, 393
requiem mass, 63, 251
research, 4, 5, 72, 79, 80, 103, 121, 128, 140, 141, 171, 194, 201, 204, 210, 211, 219, 224, 227-229, 233, 234, 242, 253, 273, 275, 277, 278, 280, 281, 285, 287, 297, 306, 307, 317, 332, 335, 339, 347, 350-354, 364, 365, 371, 378, 386-389, 393, 394, 398, 399, 401, 404, 405, 412, 414-416, 418, 515, 523, 556, 566
resurrection, 142, 476, 480, 485-493, 494
reunion, 18, 46, 291, 314, 321, 355, 393
reward, 488, 489
rights, 14, 23, 25, 82, 112, 135, 208, 296, 405, 411, 424, 428-432, 434, 435, 438, 439, 441, 455, 459, 471
risk, 27, 31, 110, 130, 141, 143, 150, 152, 207, 213, 244, 247-249, 251, 252, 280, 296, 323, 324, 342, 367, 368, 380, 405-407, 409-415, 418, 430, 449, 455, 516, 525, 527, 530, 533, 535, 537, 540, 541, 543, 545, 555-560
ritual, 85, 142, 155, 251, 256, 257, 260, 262, 263, 267, 269, 271, 272, 302, 303, 318, 342, 345, 412, 503
roles, 13, 23, 27, 56, 119, 169, 170, 175, 177, 178, 182, 185, 186, 191, 204, 205, 208-212, 220, 246, 251, 275-277, 279, 289, 317, 322, 333, 341, 351, 361, 370-372, 376, 378, 379, 392, 399, 405, 415, 536, 548, 561
rules, 4, 8, 27, 35, 36, 82, 84, 169, 170, 176, 177, 233, 336, 440, 490

Sabi, 506, 507
sacredness, 446, 447, 449
sad, 53, 188, 191, 231, 331, 362, 434, 435, 500, 518
Saguna Brahman, 498
Saint Exupery, 59
saltatus mortis, 144, 145, 147
salvation, 18, 21, 73, 491-494
Samadhi, 500, 505
Samsara, 497, 499, 501, 504, 507
sanctity of life, 24, 443, 446, 449
Satori, 505-508
Saunders, 3, 123, 139, 167, 195, 202, 216, 222, 234, 235
searching, 102, 176, 245, 255, 301
self, 15, 17-19, 23, 24, 26, 28, 36, 40, 62, 64, 65, 69, 70, 75, 104, 124, 135, 146, 149, 155, 172, 174, 185, 186, 188, 190, 191, 203, 206, 209, 210, 220, 243-245, 249, 251, 252, 258, 260, 269, 279, 286, 290, 291, 293-295, 297, 298, 300-303, 311, 313, 316, 318, 322-324, 327, 330, 331, 334, 348, 350, 351, 353, 367, 372, 375, 380, 381, 386, 391, 392, 395, 400, 401, 404-406, 410-416, 424-426, 430-434, 436, 437, 444, 448-453, 456, 457, 465, 470, 473, 478, 480-482, 485, 486, 489, 491, 494, 496-501, 506-508, 515, 517, 519, 522, 523, 525, 526, 533, 536, 540, 547, 553, 556-559, 561, 565, 566
self-concept, 367, 375, 386, 395, 400, 401, 404, 405, 416, 557, 558
self-destructive, 279, 311, 392, 405, 412-414, 517, 522, 523, 540
self-esteem, 174, 252, 311, 313, 316, 323, 351, 353, 367, 410, 414, 525, 533, 565
sense of self, 185, 186, 191, 350, 414, 425
Seppuku, 507
sequels, 34, 35
sex, 36, 68, 107, 142, 147, 149-151, 154-156, 158, 159, 232, 391, 414, 477, 553
sexual, 36, 82, 147, 155, 160, 169, 242, 296, 317, 323, 328, 329, 391-393, 410, 532
Shakespeare, 59, 60, 481, 483
Shelley, 46, 59
Shirley, 48, 59
Shneidman, 517, 519, 520, 522-524, 527, 537, 564, 568

shock, 34, 41, 46, 175, 215, 250, 272, 311, 312, 328, 330, 370, 372, 376, 377, 395, 397
sibling, 2, 55, 56, 185, 276, 281, 302, 348, 359-361, 367, 371, 372, 374, 375, 377, 378, 381, 384-388, 393-396, 400, 401, 418
Sidpa Bardo, 504
signs of suicide, 525, 527, 531
social, 2-4, 17, 25, 26, 29-31, 35-37, 43, 48, 50, 69-72, 77, 78, 81, 86-88, 109-115, 117, 119-122, 124, 126, 127, 130-135, 137-140, 148, 158, 167, 168, 170, 172, 175, 176, 178-180, 182, 183, 185, 190, 203-212, 214-216, 218, 221, 222, 230, 233, 241, 242, 244, 246, 251, 256, 265, 267, 270, 278-283, 286, 287, 289, 292, 294, 295, 297, 298, 302, 303, 310, 311, 313, 315-319, 322-324, 328, 329, 331, 349, 353, 355, 362, 368, 373, 375, 391-394, 399, 400, 404, 405, 411-413, 417, 418, 427, 444, 493, 498, 505, 507, 515, 516, 520, 523, 525, 530, 545, 553, 559, 560, 567
social equilibrium, 317
social good, 110
social interest, 109, 110
social justice, 109, 110, 112, 113, 115
social organization, 117, 124, 126, 138, 140, 282
social skills, 391, 392
social support, 28, 176, 178, 179, 204, 205, 279, 280, 392
social work, 3, 127, 167, 180, 203, 204, 206-212, 418, 567
socially disenfranchised, 349
society, 1, 5, 15, 17, 24, 26, 31, 33, 36, 50, 67, 69-72, 75, 76, 77, 78, 80, 81, 85-88, 90, 94, 98, 99, 109-113, 115, 117, 119, 124, 126, 135, 137, 138, 143-145, 197, 201, 203, 216-218, 234, 245, 253, 259, 261-263, 265, 267, 272, 273, 276, 277, 306, 327, 329, 330, 337, 349, 360, 368, 373, 380, 386, 400, 404, 405, 409, 411-415, 428, 430, 433, 435, 437, 439-443, 447, 451, 472, 473, 481,

[society]
503, 515, 516, 523, 540, 542, 556, 562, 566, 567
socio-situational, 67
socioeconomic, 31, 405-407, 409
sociological conjectures, 515
sociologist-ethicist, 121-123
Socrates, 14, 476
soul, 17, 18, 21, 42, 46, 48, 50, 52, 58, 63, 73, 81, 124, 137, 150, 151, 154, 159, 160, 184, 313, 323, 367, 381, 477-483, 490, 496-501, 503
Speece, 364, 386
specialization, 22, 127, 256, 258, 261, 430
spirit, 46, 52, 73, 143, 251, 262, 265, 272, 286, 288, 289, 304, 333, 367, 381, 482, 485, 490, 492-494, 498, 501, 506, 508
spiritual, 16, 26, 55-57, 59, 73, 75, 134, 143, 160, 167, 182, 185, 189, 197, 203, 205, 221-223, 256, 266, 267, 288, 310, 315-317, 328, 329, 352, 393, 431, 448, 481-483, 492, 496, 498-500, 502-505, 507, 508, 566
spiritual equilibrium, 317
spiritualism, 69, 73, 75
St. Christopher's, 195, 216, 217, 227, 230, 234, 235
stereotypical, 255, 404
Stillion, 4, 6, 368, 387, 524, 551, 567, 568
stoic, 16
Strauss, 62, 65, 138, 235
stresses, 167, 169, 173, 174, 176, 177, 179, 185, 186, 209, 220, 282, 354, 364, 370, 378, 379, 465, 522, 523
substituted judgment, 429
sudden death, 16, 369, 376, 377, 430, 437, 472, 541
suffering, 24, 43, 50, 67, 73, 120-122, 181, 183, 185-188, 194, 195, 214-216, 220, 230, 251, 264, 268, 302, 303, 317, 329, 366, 367, 369, 371, 382, 384, 397, 410, 415, 428, 430, 431, 433, 435, 436, 452, 462, 476, 483, 495, 496, 498, 501, 542, 563, 566, 568
suffocation anxiety, 366
suicide, 3-6, 27, 33, 80, 195, 249, 251, 276, 279, 283, 302, 316, 319, 323, 324, 366, 367, 369, 372, 376-378,

588 / INDEX

[suicide]
380, 383, 389, 392, 393, 400, 405, 410, 412-414, 418, 427, 428, 431, 433, 438-442, 445, 447, 451-453, 458, 459-463, 465-467, 470-472, 473, 475, 507, 513-537, 539-549, 551, 553-557, 559-564, 566-568
suicide among the middle-aged, 522
suicide notes, 514, 522, 524, 562, 563, 568
suicide theories, 513
suicide trajectory, 555, 559
Sunyata, 502, 504, 507
support groups, 207, 271, 327, 331, 337, 382, 389, 396, 398, 401, 544, 545, 547
support service, 218
Supreme Court, 436-441, 442, 470
symptom control, 212, 220, 222, 223, 226, 231, 232
symptom management, 183, 185, 195, 199, 235
symbolism, 45, 54, 503, 508

tamed death, 15, 17
Tantras, 502
Taoism, 505
Tat Twam Asi, 500
Tathagata, 507, 508
team, 172, 175, 181-184, 186, 191, 194, 197-201, 203-205, 207-210, 216-220, 223, 228, 234, 286, 297, 342, 548
team support, 204, 209
technology, 21, 22, 26, 34, 37, 83, 133, 140, 197, 259, 261, 265, 366, 367, 430, 467
teenager, 387-389, 400, 401, 514, 517, 549
Tennyson, 59
terminal care, 30, 182, 202, 212, 213, 216, 219, 222, 227, 229, 233-236, 253, 378
terminal phase, 291
theology, 65, 446, 483, 485, 493
therapists, 71, 127, 220, 228, 286, 287, 294, 565
Tibetan Book of the Dead, 1, 21, 503, 508
Tolstoy, 59
traditions, 12, 13, 16, 24, 33, 256, 266, 373, 405, 495-497

training, 1-3, 114, 123, 126-128, 130, 136, 184, 187, 191, 193, 199, 208, 209, 212, 216, 219, 223-225, 229, 246, 259, 273, 287, 288, 330, 389, 396, 401, 440, 442, 540, 564
transfer of wealth, 88, 110, 111
transition, 1, 42, 112, 180, 182, 183, 242, 244, 246, 251, 262, 264, 267, 271, 310, 348, 355, 360, 399, 431, 547, 548
trauma, 41, 55, 248, 250, 251, 315, 317, 327, 388, 410-412, 418, 531
traumatic, 67, 72, 248-250, 260, 287, 292, 315, 316, 319, 377, 379, 388, 392, 410, 412, 418, 520, 527, 535, 544, 559
traumatic agent, 315, 316
Triumph of death, 144, 146, 159, 160
Trivarga, 498
Turiya, 496, 502

uncertainty, 171, 173, 177, 265, 366, 367, 372, 376, 430, 544
understanding of death, 13, 285, 352, 360-365, 367, 373, 382, 384, 503, 505
unit of care, 167, 183, 203, 250
universality, 65, 364, 367
Upanishads, 496-498, 501, 502, 505, 508

value, 14, 27, 28, 38, 70, 80, 95, 101, 109, 113, 142, 156, 168, 187, 189, 194, 200, 218, 224, 225, 246, 252, 268, 271, 272, 298, 310, 327, 343, 349, 354, 377, 383, 404, 411, 430, 438, 439, 441-452, 456, 469, 470, 473, 495, 506, 527, 565
Vasavartin, 506
vault, 83, 92, 95
Vidya, 499
violence, 5, 14, 15, 27, 35, 36, 39, 40, 48, 52, 82, 148, 149, 169, 264, 320, 321, 323, 324, 368, 372, 375, 379, 380, 383, 387, 405, 406, 409-414, 416-418, 456, 491, 492, 494, 495, 530, 546
vulnerability, 118, 120, 170, 248, 249, 296, 297, 351, 369, 379, 392, 408, 410, 435

Wabi, 506, 507
war, 11, 13, 14, 16, 19, 26, 31, 55, 85, 141, 142, 156, 157, 214, 246, 259, 315, 317, 321, 367, 368, 379, 380, 457, 515, 516, 551
wards, 117, 128, 130, 133, 136, 214, 219, 250
weakness, 71, 186, 220, 230, 232, 310, 313, 507, 515, 557
wealth, 77, 88, 109-113, 115
widow, 244-246, 302, 327-332, 351

Worden, 167, 169, 253, 281, 286, 288-290, 306, 367, 368, 373, 375, 376, 381-383, 385, 395-398, 401
worldview, 348

Yalom, 293, 306, 331, 335, 337
Yeats, 46, 59

Zen, 264, 505-509